The Formation and Significance of the
Christian Biblical Canon

The Formation and Significance of the Christian Biblical Canon

A Study in Text, Ritual and Interpretation

Tomas Bokedal

Bloomsbury Academic
An imprint of Bloomsbury Publishing Plc

B L O O M S B U R Y
LONDON • NEW DELHI • NEW YORK • SYDNEY

Bloomsbury Academic

An imprint of Bloomsbury Publishing Plc

50 Bedford Square
London
WC1B 3DP
UK

1385 Broadway
New York
NY 10018
USA

www.bloomsbury.com

BLOOMSBURY and the Diana logo are trademarks of Bloomsbury Publishing Plc

First published 2014
Paperback edition first published 2015

British Library Cataloguing-in-Publication Data
A catalogue record for this book is available from the British Library.

ISBN: HB: 978-0-56737-890-3
PB: 978-0-56766-371-9

Library of Congress Cataloging-in-Publication Data
Bokedal, Tomas
The Formation and Significance of the Christian Biblical Canon/Tomas Bokedal p.cm
Includes bibliographic references and index.
ISBN 978-0-567-37890-3
(hardcover)

Typeset by Fakenham Prepress Solutions, Fakenham, Norfolk NR21 8NN

To Dearest Anna

Contents

Preface

The present monograph is a revised version of my ThD thesis The Scriptures and the LORD: Formation and Significance of the Christian Biblical Canon. A Study in Text, Ritual and Interpretation (Lund University, 2005). In this work I study the emergence and the significance of the Christian biblical canon for the early as well as for the contemporary church. Throughout the discussion I present some major challenges to previous research on the biblical canon.

The issue of the church's canon can be made indefinitely vast. At the heart of this investigation are some central theological concerns. Others are left out, or have only surfaced, such as a comprehensive historical account, usually treated in manuals on the canon formation. In order to grasp the complex phenomenon of biblical canonicity, I have chosen to focus on four aspects, namely effective-historical, textual and material, performative, and ideational dimensions of the canon. The apostolic formula 'the Scriptures and the Lord' is defended as a good summary of the Christian canon, its formation and significance.

In short, I conclude that the canon was formed in a process, with its own particular intention, history, and direction. History and theology, past and present, are considered alongside one another throughout the study. By using a Gadamerian hermeneutics of tradition, I wish to draw the reader's attention to historical dimensions of the canon and its interpretive possibilities for our time. The notion of *Wirkungsgeschichte* (effective-history) as well as the interaction between text, community and reader are crucial to my argument. The canonical text as text, its interpretation and ritual contextualization are highlighted as unifying elements for the communities being addressed. An important outcome of the study is the appeal for the reintroduction – in one form or another – of the triadic system of the *nomina sacra* in contemporary Bibles.

I am indebted to a number of individuals and institutions for their support. University of Aberdeen awarded various travel grants between 2009 and

2012. Thanks are due to my colleagues Dr. Donald Wood and Dr. Jane Heath for feedback on parts of the text and to the anonymous reviewers of the first draft of the manuscript for helpful suggestions. I am also grateful to Dominic Mattos and Caitlin Flynn at Bloomsbury T&T Clark for accepting the book for publication and to Kim Storry at Fakenham Prepress for professional handling of the manuscript. Finally, I wish to thank Professor John Webster for his encouragement and for commenting on the manuscript.

This monograph is gratefully dedicated to my dear wife Anna.

Tomas Bokedal
Aberdeen, Scotland, April 2013

From the Preface to the 2005 Dissertation

I would like to thank several persons and institutions that have supported this project in different ways. First of all, I want to thank my *Doktor-Vater*, Professor Werner G. Jeanrond for his very generous, patient and caring supervision. I wish to express my deep gratitude to my supervisor for tirelessly seeking to teach me classic and modern theology for our time. Without his love of theology and expertise within the fields of systematic theology and hermeneutics my work would have turned out very differently.

I would also like to thank Professor Oskar Skarsaune, The Norwegian Lutheran School of Theology, who helped me in his capacity as external expert. I am most thankful for his warm and devout assistance during these years. Special thanks to Docent Rune Söderlund for accepting me as a doctoral student at Lund University and for suggesting, and introducing me to, the topic of my work. I also thank Dean Dr. Rune Imberg, The Lutheran School of Theology, Göteborg, for his constant encouragement and for giving me the opportunity to teach in various fields of theology. I am most grateful for his determined support and steadfastness.

Initial conversations with Professors Bengt Hägglund, Gösta Hallonsten, Samuel Rubenson and Peter Stuhlmacher were also important to me. I furthermore had some inspiring discussions on parts of my work with Professors Robert W. Jenson, Christoph Schwöbel and Francis Watson, as well as with Docent Arne Rasmusson and Rev. Axel W. Karlsson.

I am most grateful to Per Holmer for proofreading the whole manuscript, not forgetting our inspiring talks on theology and life. I wish to express my special gratitude to my wife Anna Bokedal for reading, discussing and editing the text. My sincere thanks also go to Marie Asking for her generous support, and to Docent Arne and Mrs. Nina Hjorth. My parents, Roger and Lilly Hansson, and parents-in-law, Rev. Torsten and Mrs. Margareta Bokedal, have wholeheartedly supported me and my family during these years. I regret that my mother, father- and mother-in-law were not able to see the completion of this study.

I owe thanks to the Royal Society of Letters at Lund for a full year's grant, and to Insamlingsstiftelsen Bo Giertz 90-årsfond as well as various funds at Lund University for travel scholarships. I am grateful to the Centre for Theology and Religious Studies, Lund University, for having granted me a two-year fellowship in support of my research, and to the Lutheran School of Theology, Göteborg.

My children: Johanna, Naomi, Benedikta, Elias and Josef, all at an early age learned to imitate their father, sitting silent in a row on the sofa, each with a book in their hands. I envy them their energetic concentration and wish them all the best for the future!

I dedicate this book to my wife Anna for endless support and care.

Tomas Bokedal
Göteborg, Sweden, August 2005

Introduction

1

The Question of the Biblical Canon

The Bible is present in the church as part of the continuous proclamation of the gospel.[1] Because it is encountered primarily as read in the Christian community, it is more than a collection of documents. So, the Bible is handed down to the contemporary reader and listener not as a series of texts or artefacts from the past, but as a theologically defined literary unit.

The Christian church has always read a two-testament Bible in this way, as a single,[2] largely self-signifying whole[3] – the Christian biblical canon of Sacred Scripture.

---

[1]   '[P]roclamation of the gospel' here refers to preaching of the gospel with regard to Christian faith, practice and reflection. Cf. Rom. 10.17; Farley and Hodgson, 'Scripture and Tradition', in *Christian Theology: An Introduction to Its Traditions and Tasks*, (eds) Hodgson and King (Philadelphia: Fortress, 1985), 61; and Jenson, *Systematic Theology*, vol. 1, *The Triune God* (New York: Oxford University Press, 1997), 11. See further, section 1.2.1. On the concept of church – besides the classic definition provided by the church's Scriptures set apart as canon, i.e. as address and criterion whereby the church, its faith and practice are to be largely recognized – see the following earlier, ecumenically concerned documents: 'The Augsburg Confession', in *The Creeds of Christendom*, vol. 3, ed. Ph. Schaff (New York: Harper & Brothers, 1877), Art. 7; Augustine, *City of God* (London: Penguin Books, 1972), I, 35; and, for a systematic elaboration, Jenson, *Systematic Theology*, vol. 2: *The Works of God* (New York and Oxford: Oxford University Press, 1999), 165–305.

[2]   In (post)modernity the biblical writings are still commonly published and referred to as a single volume. Nevertheless, the view of Scripture as canonical has generally become somewhat changed. Cf., e.g. Loughlin, 'The Basis and Authority of Doctrine', in *The Cambridge Companion to Christian Doctrine*, ed. Gunton (Cambridge: Cambridge University Press, 1997), 47: 'Traditionally, doctrine was founded upon scripture and piety; but that changes with the coming of nominalism. Now the scripture – the canonical texts of "old" and "new" testaments – is but one more singular text, the meaning of which is transparent and singular also.'

[3]   So, e.g. Origen in *Joa. Comm.* V, 6 (*Sources Chrétiennes* 120, 383f.); cited from Nardoni, 'Origen's Concept of Biblical Inspiration', *The Second Century* 4 (1984): 14: 'There is [in the OT] more than one book written about Christ, for it is written about him in the Pentateuch, in each of the Prophets, and in the Psalms; in one word, as the Savior himself says: "In all the Scriptures." To them all he refers when he says: "You search the Scriptures, because you think that in them you have eternal life; and it is they that bear witness to me. ..." Christ refers to them all, and not just to this or to that text. ... All the Scriptures are one book because all the teaching [λόγου] that has come to us about Christ is recapitulated in one single whole.' Cf. also Irenaeus, *Proof of the Apostolic Preaching* 52; and Clement of Alexandria, *Stromateis* VII, 16 (ANF 2:550–54 [551]): 'For we have, as the source of teaching, the Lord, both by the prophets, the Gospel, and the blessed apostles, "in divers manners and at sundry times," leading from the beginning of

However, are not these writings just a set of dispersed, sometimes offensive memories and literary expressions written down by religious individuals from very different historical and cultural backgrounds? Cannot these writings and their interpretations be construed in an endless number of ways by a number of very different interpretive communities?[4] What is it that makes exactly these writings so important?

It seems clear to me that the reading of these texts as canon, in one way or another, is a matter of great importance to every Christian community. It is also clear that the issue of the canon is multifaceted, although it can be put in a simple formula as well, as, for example, in Origen (ca. AD 185–254): 'All the Scriptures are one book [κεφαλίδα] because all the teaching [λόγον] that has come to us about Christ is recapitulated in one single whole.'[5] Here the reader needs to bear in mind that as canon, in this theological sense, the Scriptures cannot be read 'like any other book'.[6] Rather, as canonical, the biblical texts are

---

knowledge to the end.' See also various Catholic, Orthodox and Protestant confessional writings on scriptural authority; and David Kelsey's remark on the role of Scripture for theology (*Proving Doctrine: The Uses of Scripture in Modern Theology* [Harrisburg, PA: Trinity Press, 1999], 1): 'Virtually every contemporary Protestant theologian along the entire spectrum of opinion ... has acknowledged that any Christian theology worthy of the name "Christian" must, in *some* sense of the phrase, be done "in accord with scripture."'

[4]   On both these questions, see Jenson, *Systematic Theology*, vol. 1, 59. Cf. also, e.g. Thompson, *Writing the Wrongs: Women of the Old Testament among Biblical Commentators from Philo through the Reformation* (Oxford: Oxford University Press, 2001); and Jasper, *Readings in the Canon of Scripture: Written for our Learning* (London: Macmillan and New York: St. Martin's Press, 1995).

[5]   See n. 3 above. Cf. also Plantinga, 'Two (or More) Kinds of Scripture Scholarship', in *'Behind the Text': History and Biblical Interpretation*, 4, (eds) C. Bartholomew et al. (Grand Rapids: Paternoster & Zondervan, 2003), 25: 'Scripture is not so much a library of independent books as itself a book with many subdivisions but a central theme: the message of the gospel.' On the lack of appeal to Jesus and the general abstraction from Jesus to the Christ in the theology of Origen, see Gunton, *Father, Son & Holy Spirit: Toward a Fully Trinitarian Theology* (London: T&T Clark, 2003), 64 for further references.

[6]   In fact, as Hans-Georg Gadamer points out, all textual understanding presupposes a living relationship between the interpreter and the text. Hence, 'the question is whether all literature is not subject to conditions of understanding other than those formal general ones that have to be fulfilled in regard to every text', *TM*, 331. Cf. Josipovici (*The Book of God: A Response to the Bible* [New Haven: Yale University Press, 1988], 307), where the uniqueness of the Bible is equaled to that of a person. In contrast to this, the 'master principle' of historico-critical interpretation is that the Bible should be read 'like any other book', e.g. as presented to English speaking readers by Benjamin Jowett one and a half centuries ago (*On the Interpretation of Scripture, The Interpretation of Scripture and Other Essays* [London: Routledge, 1860]. 31). For a critical discussion on some of the problems here involved, see Vanhoozer, *First Theology: God, Scriptures & Hermeneutics* (Downers Grove, IL: InterVarsity and Apollos, 2002), 209. At the foundation of the normative function of the canon, which is dealt with throughout this study, lies the willingness (which is not to be equaled to the personal piety) of the scholar or reader to subject him- or herself to the context of faith. See Fernhout, *Canonical Texts: Bearers of Absolute Authority: Bible, Koran, Veda, Tipitaka: A Phenomenological Study* (Amsterdam: Rodopi, 1994), 203; and Childs, *The New Testament as Canon: An Introduction* (London: SCM, 1984), 38f.

held to be authoritative, divinely inspired writing,[7] present in the church as a sign[8] – i.e. they only present themselves to the one who is ready to accept them as such, who looks for him- or herself, and actually sees something there of this integral whole.[9] But also, as sign, the readings of these foundational texts, like all religious speech encountered in Christianity, represent aids to faith (in the broadest sense).[10]

The overall goal set for this investigation is to highlight the presiding theological question, 'What is the biblical canon? What does it mean that the Bible is functioning as canon for the church?'

In order to grasp the very complex notion of Christian Scripture and its canonization, bearing in mind the extensive scholarly work that has already been achieved in this area, the concept of canon focused in the following is analysed by means of four dimensions. These are:

a) an effective-historical and linguistic dimension;

b) a textual-material;

c) a ritual; and, providing frameworks of meaning,

d) an ideational dimension.

---

[7] Achtemeier, *Inspiration and Authority: Nature and Function of Christian Scripture* (Peabody, MA: Hendrickson, 1999), 104f. See further, nn. 11–13. Cf., however, Kelsey, *Proving Doctrine*, 16–31.

[8] I am here making use of Gadamer's definition, according to which 'sign' is defined as a form of counterconcept of the symbol (that, through which someone or something is known and recognized), Gadamer, *The Relevance of the Beautiful and Other Essays* (New York: Cambridge University Press, 1986), 152. The sign 'is not something that everyone has been able to see, not something to which one can refer, and yet, if it is taken as a sign, there is something incontestably certain about it. There is a saying of Heraclitus that illuminates this matter very well: "The Delphic god neither reveals nor conceals, but gives a sign." One needs only to understand what "giving a sign" means here. It is not something that takes the place of seeing, for what distinguishes it precisely from all reports or from its opposite, silence, is the fact that what is shown is only accessible to the one who looks for himself and actually sees something there.' See also Barth, *Church Dogmatics*, I/2 (Edinburg: T&T Clark, 1936–1962), 457f.

[9] Gadamer, *The Relevance of the Beautiful*, 152, n. 7. Preconditions for such seeing or other preconditions for accepting the biblical text(s) as canonical are not discussed here.

[10] Cf. ibid., 152, 149. The portrayal above of the canonical writings as representing 'aids of faith' comes close to the following broad description by Anthony Thiselton, *New Horizons in Hermeneutics: The Theory and Practice of Transforming Biblical Reading* (Grand Rapids: Zondervan, 1992), 17f: 'The biblical writings, it may be argued, embody an institutional framework of covenant in which commitments and effects become operative in acts of promise, acts of blessing, acts of forgiveness, acts of pronouncing judgement, acts of repentance, acts of worship, acts of authorization, acts of communion, and acts of love.' Cf. also in this regard the three main dynamics of faith discussed by David Ford, *Self and Salvation: Being Transformed* (Cambridge: Cambridge University Press, 1999), 5: 'worship and prayer; living and learning in community; and speech, action and suffering for justice, freedom, peace, goodness and truth.'

1.1 On 'canon'

In this opening section I shall briefly examine a theological understanding of the concept of canon, by relating it to the notions of contingency and inspiration.

The formation of the Christian biblical canon is at one and the same time a contingent act and a carefully designed literary work of art. It has taken place as a spontaneous process driven by contingent events. To this extent, 'canon' is a success word; it designates those books that the Christian assembly regards as authoritative, which together happen to lay the foundation for ecclesial life and teaching; and as such it happens to be the documents bound together in one book. Although on one level contingent, this act is not accidental. Instead, one finds in the major church traditions room for deliberate and conscious selection, preservation and interpretation closely tied up with the notion of inspiration (the canon as gift/a given[11]): the contingent act leading up to the formation of the canon conducted by the Spirit of God.[12]

---

[11] See Harnack, *Lehrbuch der Dogmengeschichte*, vol. 1 (Tübingen: J. C. B. Mohr [Paul Siebeck], 1909), 378, n. 4. Already Irenaeus, Tertullian and Clement of Alexandria treat the authoritative ecclesial collection of Scriptures as gift/a given. The givenness of the biblical canon is related to the character of the gospel message – the *scopus* of Christian Scripture – as gift and promise (which is binding in another way than Old Testament Law, which everyone has to obey). See in this regard, e.g. Rom. 1.1–17, Gal. 3, Heb. 1.1-2 and 1 Pet. 1.1-12. Cf. also Gadamer, *The Relevance of the Beautiful*, 148: 'It is the acceptance alone that gives binding validity to the promise, and not anything that we might perform in addition.' To Gadamer this appears to provide a good secular, structural analogy for the concept of faith. The gospel is freely proffered and only becomes good news for one who accepts it. On the relation between inspiration and canonicity, see Harnack, *Lehrbuch*, vol. 1, 379. For a different viewpoint, see Metzger, *The Canon of the New Testament: Its Origin, Development, and Significance* (Oxford: Clarendon, 1987), 254–7.

[12] Cf. 2 Tim. 3.16 with its emphasis on *all Scripture*, πᾶσα γραφὴ θεόπνευστος (*all* Scripture/all *Scripture* is inspired by God), which – due to this dual emphasis of all-inclusiveness and openness – may very well include not only the 'Old Testament', but (through anticipation) 'New Testament' writings as well, that is *all* Scripture/all *Scripture*. See further, e.g. Origen, *On First Principles (De Principiis)*, Preface, 8 (ANF 4: 241), written about AD 200: '[T]he Scriptures were written by the Spirit of God'; according to Origen, commenting on 2 Tim. 3.16, the apostolic writings are to be regarded as no less inspired than the Scriptures of the old covenant. Cf. Pannenberg, *Systematic Theology*, vol. 1 (Grand Rapids: Eerdmans, 1991), 217; and further Schleiermacher, *The Christian Faith* (Edinburgh: T&T Clark, 1999 [1830]), 602: '[T]he faithful preservation of the apostolic writings is the work of the Spirit of God acknowledging his own products.' See also Balla, *Challenges to Biblical Theology* (Leicester: InterVarsity, 2000), 23f.: 'Slight but nevertheless significant pieces of evidence suggest there were Jews at the time of Jesus who believed that in the final days new sacred writings would be revealed and added to the "canonical" OT. … Thus the apostles, who saw themselves as living in the end times, inaugurated by the coming of the Messiah, may have thought that they were writing sacred books that would become a "second canon".' For an elaboration of this thought, see Smith, 'When Did the Gospels Become Scripture?', *JBL* 119 (2000). Cf. also Deut. 29.29; and John 14.18-26. Regarding the wording above of 2 Tim. 3.16, this is the rendering (my emphasis), with minor variations, of NRSV, RSV, NIV, NJB and AV. For a different translation,

Furthermore, the notion of contingency in this connection is not a negative notion. God's contingent choices in the history of salvation are plentiful (e.g. YHWH's election of Israel and Mary), and consequently necessary from the viewpoint of divine supreme freedom. Therefore, the books bound together could have had a different composition. But the fact that they have been formed into a single volume is certainly not accidental.

In addition to other approaches, theology is needed to explain the process by which this took place.[13] This will be elaborated in the chapters to follow. The monumental scholarly contributions by Theodor Zahn, Adolf von Harnack, Karl Barth and Brevard Childs have helped setting this theological agenda.[14]

Accordingly, canonical Scripture may be described as a carefully designed, and yet spontaneous, literary creation in and for the church, providing textual and theological basis for ecclesial existence.

Since the eighteenth century we have been furnished with numerous isagogical and historical studies on the formation of the Old and the New Testament canon.[15] Throughout the latter part of the twentieth century, other scholarly disciplines have been drawn on as well, stressing new dimensions of the canon, such as biblical theological, doctrinal, effective-historical, socio-logical, codicological, textual, literary, ritual and semiotic.[16] This has led to a

see Stuhlmacher (*Biblische Theologie des Neuen Testaments: Band II: Von der Paulusschule bis zur Johannesoffenbarung Der Kanon und seine Auslegung*, 328), which does not, however, affect the point I am making here. For a general discussion on the problems of translating in this connection, see, e.g. Kelly, *The Pastoral Epistles*, 202–4.

[13] See esp. Childs, *The New Testament as Canon,* and idem, *Biblical Theology of the Old and New Testaments* (London: SCM, 1992).

[14] Within the exegetical and historical guilds, leading scholars such as C. A. Credner, B. F. Westcott, Theodor Zahn (who is probably the one single scholar who has done the most comprehensive work in this area), Robert M. Grant, Hans von Campenhausen, Ernst Käsemann, Roger T. Beckwith, Bruce M. Metzger, F. F. Bruce, Harry Y. Gamble, John Barton, David Trobisch, James A. Sanders and Lee McDonald, among others, may (also) be mentioned.

[15] For references, see, e.g. Sanders and McDonald, (eds), *The Canon Debate* (Peabody, MA: Hendrickson, 2002); McDonald, *The Biblical Canon: Its Origin, Transmission, and Authority* (Peabody, MA: Hendrickson, 2007); idem, *Forgotten Scriptures: The Selection and Rejection of Early Religious Writings* (Louisville: Alban Books, Westminster/John Knox, 2009); Bruce, *The Canon of Scripture* (Downers Grove, IL: InterVarsity, 1988); Beckwith, *The Old Testament Canon of the New Testament Church and its Background in Early Judaism* (Grand Rapids: Eerdmans, 1985); Sanders, 'Canon: Hebrew Bible', in *Anchor Bible Dictionary*, vol. 1 (1993), 837–52; Metzger, *The Canon of the New Testament*; Gamble, 'Canon: New Testament', in *Anchor Bible Dictionary*, vol. 1 (1993), 852–61.

[16] See, e.g. Childs, *The New Testament as Canon*; and idem, *Biblical Theology*; Bartholomew, Hahn, Parry, Seitz, and Wolters, (eds), *Canon and Biblical Interpretation*, vol. 7, The Scripture and Hermeneutics Series (Milton Keynes and Waynesboro, GA: Paternoster, 2006); Ohlig, *Die theologische Begründung des neutestamentlichen Kanons in der alten Kirche* (Düsseldorf: Patmos-Verlag, 1972); Bruns, *Hermeneutics Ancient and Modern* (New Haven and London: Yale University Press, 1992). For comparative-religious aspects of canon formation, see, e.g. Bultmann, 'The Problem

higher degree of critical awareness, but, at the same time, to a (post)modern destabilization of the very concept of canon. Despite extensive scholarly efforts, however, clarifying research regarding a more comprehensive view, combining various such dimensions of the canon and the theological connection to these other disciplines, is partly lacking (see further section 1.3).

1.2 The Scriptures and the Lord: Formation and significance of the Christian biblical canon

1.2.1 The central thesis of this study

The central thesis of this study is:

> Integral to the life of the church, in particular the ecclesial practice of proclamation and prayer, the formation and continuous usage of the Christian biblical canon is an act of literary preservation and actualization of the church's apostolic normative tradition – 'the Scriptures and the Lord', by which the church is and remains church, appealing to a variety of textual, ritual and doctrinal materials.

When defining biblical canonicity in this way, the Bible in its 'resting position' is of minor importance. This argument calls for a rather different view, defining these central ecclesial texts according to their primary ecclesial functioning.[17]

---

of Hermeneutics', in idem, *Essays: Philosophical and Theological* (New York: Macmillan, 1955); and Finkelberg and Stroumsa, *Homer, the Bible, and Beyond: Literary and Religious Canons in the Ancient World* (Leiden: Brill, 2003). On canon and ritual, see, e.g. Lathrop, *Holy Things: A Liturgical Theology* (Minneapolis: Fortress, 1993); and Wainwright, *Doxology: The Praise of God in Worship, Doctrine and Life* (London: Epworth, 1980, 1982). For a semiotic analysis of canon, see Aichele, *Sign, Text, Scripture: Semiotics and the Bible* (Sheffield: Sheffield Academic, 1997); and idem, *The Control of Biblical Meaning: Canon as Semiotic Mechanism* (Harrisburg, PA: Trinity Press, 2001). For a general overview of current canon research, see van der Kooij and van der Toorn, (eds), *Canonization and Decanonization* (Leiden: Brill, 1998); Sanders and McDonald, (eds), *The Canon Debate*; Auwers and Jonge, (eds), *The Biblical Canons* (Leuven: Leuven University Press, 2003); Barton and Wolter (eds), *Die Einheit der Schrift und die Vielfalt des Kanons/The Unity of Scripture and the Diversity of the Canon* (Berlin: Walter de Gruyter, 2003); and Thomassen, ed., *Canon and Canonicity: The Formation and Use of Scripture* (Copenhagen, Denmark: Museum Tusculanum Press, 2010).

[17] Cf. below, Ch. 7; and Childs, *The New Testament as Canon*, 14. The placing of writings and titles within the corpus of biblical books is here considered important for the ecclesial functioning, as are various other literary qualities of the Scriptures. A fully fledged ecclesiology would require a wider focus than that aimed at here, including issues of liturgy, practice, etc.

Two features make my thesis point beyond self-evident common sense, namely, on the one hand, *the stress laid on biblical canonicity's necessary contextualization as part of the life of the Christian church*, without which there can be no real talk of this canon; and, on the other hand, *the stress laid on the one event of canonization and canonical function*. This event contains both a process of coming into being, and the canon's perennial ecclesial usage. The identity of the canon here comes to the fore as an act of continuous preservation and actualization of the church's foundational literary tradition, for the sake of mediating continuity with apostolic Christianity, historic and contemporary.[18]

Accordingly, the emerging canon – from the Jewish Scripture of the first Christians to today's biblical canon with its sometimes negotiable, or even negotiated, textual arrangement, storyline, function, scope and *scopus*[19] – turns out to be more than a book and its edition, more than a rule of faith or a delimited collection of authoritative writings, along with major criteria such as apostolicity, catholicity and established usage. Together, however, these are significant dimensions of the canon, its formation and function. That is why the meaning of the canon as a textual whole, embracing these textual, ritual and doctrinal dimensions, is not something added to the texts as biblical texts,[20] i.e. an additional text.[21] Instead, the meaning is related to the way in which the texts in question, in their ecclesial context, are juxtaposed and

---

[18] On the function of prejudices in acknowledging authority (such as the Protestant and Catholic principles of apostolicity), see Gadamer, *TM*, 280. For a discussion on Gadamerian hermeneutics on the relation between past and present truth and knowledge of a phenomenon, cf. Carr, *Newman & Gadamer: Toward a Hermeneutics of Religious Knowledge* (Atlanta, GA: Scholars Press, 1996), 30–6 and 44.

[19] Cf. quotation below (section 1.2.4) from Barton, *The Spirit and the Letter: Studies in the Biblical Canon* (London: SPCK, 1997), 1.

[20] Cf. Jeanrond, 'Text/Textuality', in *Dictionary for Theological Interpretation of the Bible*, ed. Vanhoozer, (London: SPCK and Grand Rapids: Baker, 2005), 782: 'A "biblical text" may refer to a particular book of the Bible or parts thereof (such as the readings in church service or any other religious reading program); it may refer to the OT, the NT, the Apocrypha, or the entire Bible. In whatever extension a biblical text is heard or read, it is received as a *text*.'

[21] The notions of canon and biblical text here involve first of all the biblical writings as Scripture but also their ecclesial normative reading, intertextuality, arrangement and interpretation. As compared to, e.g. in Via (*What Is New Testament Theology?* [Minneapolis: Fortress, 2002], 25–9), the two categories 'textual' and 'extra-textual' are here differently distinguished. However, most importantly, as pointed out by Webster (*Holy Scripture*, 51): 'in its service of the divine Word, Holy Scripture cannot be made into part of the stock of traditional meanings which the church builds up over the course of time. Accordingly 'tradition' is best conceived of as *hearing* of the Word rather than a fresh act of *speaking*.'

intertextually connected with one another theologically[22] and by the church as community, through the apostolically defined and therefore church-constitutive acts of biblical reading.[23] In this process the hearer or reader of the 'Old Testament content' is commended, to a certain extent, by means of revisionary interpretation, to turn his or her attention away from the sensory occurrence, the visual historical element, and towards the prophetical, typological and figural meaning, centring in Messianism and the Christ-event.[24]

The function of these intra- and intertextual strategies of Bible reading is to interpret the textual parts successfully in light of the canon as textual whole, and the other way around, in an ongoing process. Canonicity as a property of Sacred Scripture, then, is the church's and the churches' own literary organization(s) and their normative theological, ethical and liturgical reading(s) of their Scriptures. That is to say, these various dimensions and communicative perspectives are part and parcel of this specific text as text, and without them there would be no such text.[25] They express the nature of

---

[22] As John Webster stresses ('The Dogmatic Location of the Canon', 28), the concept of canon requires careful dogmatic articulation: 'canon is a plausible notion only within the setting of a range of doctrinal material, each part of which is needed if distortions or misapprehensions are not to creep in.' Dogmatic portrayal of the canon further involves (ibid., 27) 'an account of the communicative character of the saving economy of the triune God', 'an account of the sanctification of texts in the complex processes of their history', 'careful theological specification of the church's act of canonization' and 'an account of the work of God in shaping the reader of the canon.'

[23] On the apostolicity of the church as closely related to the church's evocation through the Word, see Webster, *Holy Scripture*, 50–2. Cf. also W. A. Bienert in his summary of the significance of the concept of the apostle: 'The question of the *primitive Christian apostle concept* is closely connected with that of the origin of the Christian Church and the beginning of its offices and norms of faith'; citation from Balla, *Challenges to New Testament Theology: An Attempt to Justify the Enterprise* (Tübingen: Mohr Siebeck, 1997), 121. On the early history of the concept of apostolicity, see, e.g. Skarsaune, *Hvilket lys kaster NT's kanonhistorie over teologihistorien i det 1. århundre?*. On the ecclesially normative, the canon, as the apostolic, which is also historical, see Barth, *CD*, 1/1, 101. As for the necessary temporal quality of the normative classic text, and its being articulated historically, cf. also Gadamer, *TM*, 288.

[24] Cf. Auerbach, *Mimesis: The Representation of Reality in Western Literature* (Princeton, NJ: Princeton University Press, 1953), 48f.; cf. ibid., 16–18 and 73; Wilken, 'In novissimis diebus. Biblical Promises, Jewish Hopes and Early Christian Exegesis', *Journal of Early Christian Studies* 1 (1993): 19; in this regard see also Martin Luther's exegetical distinction between *sensus literalis historicus* and *sensus literalis propheticus*, Pedersen, *Luther som skriftfortolker: En studie i Luthers skriftsyn, hermeneutik og exegese*, vol. 1 (Copenhagen: 1959). See further Öberg, *Bibelsyn och bibeltolkning hos Martin Luther* (Skellefteå: Artos & Norma bokförlag, 2002), 348ff.; Vaticana, *Catechism of the Catholic Church* (London: Geoffrey Chapman, 1994), 34 §128, 251 §1094. As to the question of OT exegesis in the early church, see, e.g. Ellis, *The Old Testament in Early Christianity: Canon and Interpretation in the Light of Modern Research* (Grand Rapids: Baker Book House, 1991); Skarsaune, *The Development of Scriptural Interpretation in the Second and Third Centuries – except Clement and Origen*; and Young, *Biblical Exegesis and the Formation of Christian Culture*.

[25] That is not to say that there is no Christian Scripture, irrespective of the more elaborated intertextuality inherent in the Scriptures *as canon* focused here (cf., e.g. Rev. 1.3; 22.18f. and the use of γράφω in 1.19; 2.1 et passim). Cf. Jeanrond, 'Text/Textuality', 783–84: 'A reading perspective is

the Scriptures *as canon*, i.e. 1) as normative in various ways over against the church,[26] and 2) as an ecclesiastically and apostolically defined textual whole.[27] Textual meaning here is not a gap to be filled; rather, the concept of canon refers to the Christian Scriptures as a theologically normative intratextual matrix, involving first of all the contents, but, also the textual arrangement, scope and ecclesial function of the scriptural canon. And precisely as normative, that is, as a function of revelation, the canon cannot be merely a list or code.[28] More accurately, 'it is a specification of those instruments where the church may reliably expect to encounter God's communicative presence, God's self-attestation. It is normative because of what it presents or, better, indicates.'[29] Within the limits set for the present investigation, my aim is to elaborate on this specification.

---

adequate only when it corresponds to the text's own communicative perspectives and potential. If it does not, the text will be misread. The communicative potential of most biblical texts is theological: it reflects upon experiences of the creative and redemptive presence of God in Israel, the world, Jesus Christ, the church, and eternal life. Although all kinds of perspectives have been applied to read and examine biblical texts, no reading genre appears to be fully adequate that is not open to the texts' own particular theological potential. Depending on the function of a biblical text in particular religious contexts, additional strategies of reading will be added to this basic approach to the textuality of the text.' See also Jenson's similar argumentation, *Systematic Theology*, vol. 1, 59; and Jeanrond, 'Text: II Religionsphilosophisch/III. Fundamentaltheologisch', *Religion in Geschichte und Gegenwart*, 4th edn, vol. 8 (2005), 198.

[26] Cf. Gadamer, *TM*, 330f.

[27] Brevard Childs (*The New Testament as Canon*, 28) is only partly right when maintaining that the *skandalon* of the NT canon is that the testimony of Jesus Christ has received its normative shape through an interpretive process of the post-apostolic age. First of all, the canon as it receives its penultimate shape in the latter half of the second century is all the way through apostolically defined with its basis in the oral and written apostolic tradition. For an early dating of the NT canon, see Trobisch, *First Edition*; and Nicholas Wolterstorff (*Divine discourse: philosophical reflections on the claim that God speaks* [New York: Cambridge University Press, 1995]), who summarizes the early canonical process as follows: '[B]y around 200, the *practice* of treating certain books as belonging to a new sacred canon was everywhere accepted, as was, with just a few exceptions, the actual list'. Second, the canonical impulse comes from within the emerging (Old and) New Testament literature itself, as Childs tends to stress more than anything else. For him it is crucial that the church never claimed to have 'created' a scriptural canon, but rather, through a process of discernment, to have recognized certain writings as apostolic (*The New Testament as Canon*, 44). On the meaning of 'apostolic' and the various types of 'apostleship', see Wolterstorff, *Divine Discourse*, 288–96. Worth noticing here is the legitimate critique of von Campenhausen's view of the 'apostolic principle', ibid., 324.

[28] On the relation between the theme of revelation and the biblical witness, see, e.g. Pannenberg, *Systematic Theology*, vol. 1 (Grand Rapids: Eerdmans, 1991), 195: 'If the concept of revelation is said to be basic to the claim of the biblical God to be the one true God, this has to be true in the biblical testimonies as well.'

[29] Webster, 'The Dogmatic Location of the Canon', 30.

1.2.2 The Scriptures

Neither the history, nor the liturgy, textuality or theology involved in the unique 'creation' of the biblical canon can be understood apart from the church's continuous reference to Second Temple and Rabbinic Judaism, and their respective understanding, hope, use, interpretation, delimitation, preservation and actualization of the Scriptures. On a basic level, the emergence of the Christian scriptural canon is only 'secondary',[30] always indebted to the faith community of the 'First Testament' of the Law, the Prophets and the other writings (the Writings), and their 'primary' canonization.[31]

1.2.3 The Lord

Beginning in the first century AD, specifically Christian Scriptures appear to be exceptionally important, in various ways, for community life, indicating that a canonizing process is already at hand. This new process does not end up as something totally new in relation to the old Scriptures. Instead, it emerges as the *Scriptures*, the old as well as the new specific Christian Scriptures simultaneously, as by and large the same canon as that inherited from Judaism,[32] and yet different regarding scope, structure and function. Essentially, the emergence of the Christian canon is also something radically new, a new textual interpretive paradigm, originating in the authority of the 'Lord Jesus Christ', speaking, 'through an enfleshed and acted-out word'.[33] In Anthony Thiselton's phrasing, '[i]n Christ the truth of God is *spoken, embodied, and lived*'.[34] On a par with the Scriptures (αἱ γραφαί) as the primary and undisputed authority, therefore stands, side by side, the Lord (ὁ κύριος).

---

[30] So Finkelberg and Stroumsa, *Introduction: Before the Western Canon* (Leiden: Brill, 2003), 3f.: 'There is no arguing that the Christian canon, as it crystallizes between the second and the fourth centuries CE, represents, with the addition of the New Testament, a radical transformation of the Jewish Biblical canon.'

[31] See, e.g. Beckwith, *The Old Testament Canon*; and Barton, *The Spirit and the Letter*, 1.

[32] See n. 30 above.

[33] Thiselton, *New Horizons in Hermeneutics*, 69; on the question whether the authority of the words and deeds of Jesus as told by the New Testament derives from Jesus, the Messiah or from the early church's proclamation of the Messiah, see Balla, *Challenges to New Testament Theology: An Attempt to Justify the Enterprise*, 119–21. On Jesus as Lord, see Hurtado, *Lord Jesus Christ: Devotion to Jesus in Earliest Christianity* (Grand Rapids: Eerdmans, 2003).

[34] Thiselton, *New Horizons in Hermeneutics*, 68.

1.2.4 The Scriptures and the Lord

By the second century a debate had arisen among the Jewish and Christian communities on the issue, 'whose Scriptures?'[35] To whom did they and their interpreting belong? To the synagogue or to the Christian assembly? The church here felt the need to prove its rights to the Scriptures over against the Jewish community. The New Testament scholar Reidar Hvalvik remarks that this apologetical venture 'was a fight for the Church's own *raison d'être*'.[36] The recurrent polemic with various Gnostic and 'heterodox' movements over the Scriptures also involved this element. In this connection, by the turn of the century, Tertullian (ca. AD 160–220) gives voice to such an ecclesial apologetic strategy: 'we oppose to them [the adversaries] this step above all others, of not admitting them to any discussion of the Scriptures … it ought to be clearly seen to whom belongs the possession of the Scriptures'.[37] Possession of the books, accordingly, as Robert Wilken stresses, implied understanding – and also a right to interpret and comment on – their content[38] (a principle still to some extent at work, e.g. in Bible translating and editing).[39]

The church managed with both these parallel undertakings concurrently – possessing the books/taking the books into possession and thereby interpreting them; and vice versa, taking into possession through interpreting. The latter is exemplified by the new manuscript title 'Old Testament' (cf. Ch. 5), by the highlighting of the sacred figures of the faith contained in the Christian scriptures (the so called *nomina sacra*; see Ch. 3), and by the adoption of the codex as the new book format (Ch. 4). The Jewish Scriptures were being Christianized, and so, once again, textually sanctioned and received as canon.

---

[35] See Hvalvik, *The Struggle for Scripture and Covenant*; and Dunn, *The Partings of the Ways: Between Christianity and Judaism and their Significance for the Character of Christianity* (London: SCM, 1991).

[36] Hvalvik, *The Struggle for Scripture and Covenant*, 136.

[37] *De Praescr. Haer.* 15 (ANF 3:250).

[38] Wilken, 'The Jews and Christian Apologetics After Theodosius I Cunctos Populos'; cited from Hvalvik, *The Struggle for Scripture and Covenant*, 136. For a different view, see Taylor, *Anti-Judaism and Early Christian Identity: A Critique of the Scholarly Consensus* (Leiden, New York and Köln: Brill, 1995).

[39] I am here thinking especially of different faith communities' variations in preferred or prescribed canonical scope, biblical translation principles employed, and the character of biblical notes, headings and commentaries used – not only variations between Jewish and Christian, but also between different Christian Bible editions. Cf. Davies, *Whose Bible is it Anyway?* (Sheffield: Sheffield Academic, 1995).

As for the New Testament material in the nascent church, the remembered and transmitted words of Jesus were treasured and used, 'taking their place beside the Law and the Prophets and being regarded as of equal or superior authority to them'.[40] Two textual centres here emerge: *the Scriptures* and *the Lord*. Hermeneutically, these come to stand in a mutual critical relation to one another, with the latter, (the words and deeds of) the Lord, becoming, so to speak, the 'nucleus' of the new Christian canon.[41] Soon this teaching of the Lord Jesus is converted from an oral/aural textual form into various written/aural narrative compilations.[42] Documents of this kind underlie the canonical Gospels, and are referred to in the preface to the Third Gospel (Luke 1.1, 4).[43] As the apostolic interpretation of the significance of Jesus' person and work for the lives of the believers became fundamental for the primitive community, a new authoritative appeal was made also to 'the Lord and the apostles', to which the church referred 'in all matters of faith and practice.'[44] For Ignatius of Antioch and many early church leaders and theologians, the primary authority was the apostolic preaching – with its strong focus on the life, death and resurrection of Jesus[45] – which was fixed textually as the central part of the written canon, typically referred to as 'the Scriptures, the Lord and the apostles'. With this formula as its basis, primitive Christianity forms a closed literary fellowship by AD 70–120.[46]

- *Liturgically*, the earliest church's worship of Jesus of Nazareth as Lord and God gives rise to a new norm for Christian life and teaching, reaching a full expression in the formula 'the Scriptures and the LORD' (αἱ γραφαὶ

---

[40] Metzger, *The Canon of the New Testament*, 3.

[41] Cf. ibid. Cf. also Schröter, 'Jesus and the Canon': The Early Jesus Traditions in the Context of the Origins of the New Testament Canon, in *Performing the Gospel: Orality, Memory, and Mark*, (eds) Horsley, Draper and Foley (Minneapolis: Fortress, 2006), 108ff.

[42] See, e.g. McIver, *Memory, Jesus, and the Synoptic Gospels* (Atlanta, GA: Society of Biblical Literature, 2011); Byrskog and Kelber (eds), *Jesus in Memory: Traditions in Oral and Scribal Perspectives* (Waco, TX: Baylor University Press, 2009); and Gerhardsson, *The Reliability of the Gospel Tradition* (Peabody, MA: Hendrickson, 2001).

[43] Metzger, *The Canon of the New Testament*, 3.

[44] Ibid., 6.

[45] Ibid., 49.

[46] Cf. Theissen (*The New Testament: History, Literature, Religion* [London: T&T Clark, 2003], 171–4), who describes the New Testament as the result of a process in three phases. The first is 'a fellowship with oral communications.' 'In the second phase of the history of primitive Christian literature a *closed literary fellowship* formed within the communities. The period from around AD 70 to AD 120 is the heyday of primitive Christian literature ... The primitive Christianity which has newly come into being certainly forms a literary fellowship', ibid. 171f., 174.

καὶ ὁ $\overline{Kς}$;[47] cf, e.g. Paul's appeal to ὁ κύριος in 1 Cor. 9.14, 11.23-5, 1 Thess. 4.15; and Clem. *Strom.* VII, 16.95f., quoted in 2.5.2 below; cf. also Phil. 2.5-11; Tit. 2.13; John 20.28, Ignat. *Smyrn.* 1.1, 10.1).[48]

• *Textually*, the early Christian formulae 'the Scriptures and the LORD', 'the Scriptures and the Gospel' (cf., e.g. *2 Clem.* 2.4 and 8.5; *Did.* 11.3, 15.3), 'the Prophets, the Gospel and the Apostle' (cf. Iren. *Adv. Haer.* II, 27.2; III, 8.1), 'the Old and the New Testaments' (cf. Clem. *Strom.* II, 29.2), and corresponding titles of the emerging Christian canon bear witness to the proclamation of and about Jesus, now being fixed in writing, and, prior and parallel to that, partly being fixed also as oral text. This apostolically defined text comes to function in conjunction with the Scriptures as textual norm in regard to the church, with the Lord of the church as the One ever present to His community through these texts.[49] From the outset this written communication was deliberately inter- and intratextual – dependent on the Jewish Scriptures and earlier oral and written layers of the 'New Testament' material, and so canonical – with the function of

---

[47] For Lord (κύριος) as a *nomen sacrum*, see Ch. 3. For early Christian devotion to Jesus as related to Jewish monotheism, see Hurtado, *Lord Jesus Christ: Devotion to Jesus in Earliest Christianity.* See also Childs, *Biblical Theology: A Proposal* (Minneapolis: Fortress, 2002), 26f.: '[V]ery soon after the inception of the church a different attitude toward the Jewish scriptures arose within the church, which claimed a warrant in the traditions of Jesus' own use of scripture. The most fundamental material change was in assigning primary authority to Jesus Christ of whom scripture functioned as a witness'; cf. the fine analysis by Stuhlmacher, *Biblische Theologie des Neuen Testaments,* vol. 2, 281; and also Harnack, *The Origin of the New Testament,* 7f.: 'The earliest motive force [leading to the creation of the New Testament], one that had been at work from the beginning of the Apostolic Age, was the supreme reverence in which the words and teaching of Christ Jesus were held. ... He Himself had often introduced His message with the words "I am come" (i.e. to do something which had not yet been done), or, 'But I say unto you' (in opposition to something that had been hitherto said). This claim received its complete recognition among the disciples in the unswerving conviction that the words and directions of Jesus formed the supreme rule of life. Thus side by side with the writings of the Old Testament appeared the Word of "the Lord," and not only so, but in the formula αἱ γραφαὶ καὶ ὁ κύριος the two terms were not only of equal authority, but the second unwritten term received a stronger accent than the first that had literary form. We may therefore say that *in this formula we have the nucleus of the New Testament*.'

[48] For a brief treatment of the authority of 'the Lord', see Schröter, 'Jesus and the Canon: The Early Jesus Traditions in the Context of the Origins of the New Testament Canon', 108–10.

[49] The notion of oral text here signifies the stage of transmission of the Jesus tradition between the primarily oral/aural and written/aural. The citation above (Harnack, *The Origin of the New Testament,* 8) continues: 'But even in the Apostolic Age and among the Palestinian communities it [αἱ γραφαὶ καὶ ὁ κύριος] had become interchangeable with the formula αἱ γραφαὶ καὶ τὸ εὐαγγέλιον.' A characteristic of the primitive Christian literature arising and being redacted after AD 70 or thereabout, is the growing degree of independence of the texts from oral communication. The Gospels 'seek to be self-sufficient as depictions of the life and teaching of Jesus'. Luke-Acts, further, seeks to give a comprehensive description of earliest Christianity; similarly John, without suppressing other Jesus traditions, with its claim to be the authentic testimony to the truth sufficient for salvation (Theissen, *The New Testament: History, Literature, Religion,* 174).

preserving, improving on, correcting, fixing and actualizing the tradition, the oral as well as the written.[50]

- *Theologically*, as indicated by the first-century canonical system of the *nomina sacra* (see Ch. 3), the formation of the Christian canon does not start in the biblical text, nor in the faith community, 'but in the Lord of Israel, YHWH, when he reveals Himself in Jesus and is identified as the Lord of the Church.'[51] In this process, apostolicity, referring primarily to the divine commissioning and sending, is predicated of the new Scriptures.[52]

- *Historically*, with John Barton's words,

> THE FORMATION OF the Christian Bible is a story with neither beginning nor end. The first Christians already had a scripture, inherited from Judaism, whose origins time has concealed; while still today the edges of the biblical canon are blurred, with old disputes about the 'deuterocanonical' books asleep perhaps, but by no means dead. But no one would deny that there was a critical period for the canonization of the New Testament portion of this Bible. Its outer limits are marked by the life and teaching of Jesus, and the series of fourth- and fifth-century conciliar decisions which settled all but a few marginal uncertainties about the contents of the New Testament.[53]

From the scholarly as well as from the ecclesial viewpoint, the formation of the Christian Bible has indeed proved to be 'a story with neither beginning nor end.'[54] This observation, however, does not make the issue of the canonical shape, i.e. the delimitation of books to be included in the canon, less urgent;[55] on the contrary, the disagreements and uncertainties regarding exact

---

[50] Cf. Theissen, ibid., 171f., who maintains that the Christian literature which arose after AD 70 'deliberately or in fact had the function of correcting the tradition'. Various improvements on the tradition, of course, took place for some time, irrespective of Theissen's more specific isagogical argumentation: The Gospel of Matthew, James and the Deutero-Pauline letters correcting Paul, and the Gospel of John improving on and correcting 'the simpler synoptic Christianity', ibid., 172f.

[51] Jenson, *Systematic Theology*; cf. Barth, *CD*, II/2, 457.

[52] On the early history of the concept of apostolicity, see, e.g. Skarsaune, *Hvilket lys kaster NT's kanonhistorie over teologihistorien i det 1. århundre*; for a brief theological orientation, see Webster, *Holy Scripture*, 50ff.

[53] Barton, *The Spirit and the Letter*, 1.

[54] See also Zahn, *Den blivende betydning af den nytestamentlige kanon for Kirken* (Kristiania: Steen'ske bogtrykkeri og forlag [Th. Steen], 1899). Childs, *Biblical Theology: A Proposal*, 29: Due to variations among the large ecclesiastical traditions 'the exact nature of the Christian Bible both in respect to its scope and text remains undecided up to this day.'

[55] Cf. Zahn's remark somewhere, that it is because of the uncertainty regarding the shape of the canon that there is a history of the canon in the first place.

canonical scope among the communities help to focus repeatedly on this and other aspects of the canon.

The formation of the canon with its documented binding power on the community of faith,[56] therefore, is not primarily a matter of historical reconstruction, but, more significantly, a story with a binding power being preserved and handed down, which also involves the present situation. The constructive task of critically 'providing' a canon of Scriptures for the contemporary church[57] is necessarily rooted in this story. It is my opinion that the fact of Scripture and canon, both positively and negatively, has shaped Christian thinking continually, including present studies on the canon itself.[58] In other words, Christian theology always, directly or indirectly, relates to that which has been generally considered to be the primary norm of faith and practice: the canon with its effective-history.[59]

The emergence of the Christian Bible, as described here, could not have exerted a greater impact had the scope, essence or meaning of the canon been finally and once and for all defined; for instance, by way of a carefully prescribed canonical model for scriptural interpretation,[60] or a definite number of writings to be included. Quite to the contrary, the ongoing canon debate provides the possibility of reaching at even a better understanding of the canonical shape and function. This comes to the fore most clearly when

---

[56] Cf. below, n. 58.

[57] This is largely the task for the church as community in service of the church as association of persons. Cf. Jenson, *Systematic Theology*, vol. 1, 28. See section 1.2.1 for my understanding of the canonical process.

[58] If for no other reason, in Janowski's phrasing, 'the fact that without Sacred Scripture there would be no Christianity', Janowski, 'Der eine Gott der beiden Testamente' in *ZThK* 95 (1998): 1; on this also Barth, *CD*, II/2, 460: 'The Bible has always remained in the Church as the regular textual basis of proclamation. Biblical criticism and later biblical scholarship, which were now the main interest of theology, bore indirect, but for that reason all the more impressive, witness to its authority.' On a more basic level, the reason why the canon has attained such a pronounced role for Christian theology, according to Jenson, is the original and simple meaning of the canonical event (Jenson, *Systematic Theology*, vol. 1, 27f.): as the community became aware that the apostles were gone it collected and certified 'documentary relics of the apostolic message. The church did this because she is to bring the same message she brought while the apostles guided her.' Jenson adds that the belief that the gospel is still extant embraces the belief that the canon is adequate.

[59] In some church traditions sometimes along with other norms, such as a more broadly conceived tradition of the church, reason and the current situation. Cf., however, the classic phrasing in the sixth-century *Decretum Gelasianum* (cap. 350–4; Denzinger, *Enchiridion symbolorum definitionum et declarationum de rebus fidei et morum* [Freiburg im Breisgau: Herder, 1991], 162ff.): '*propheticae et evangelicae atque apostolicae scripturae, quibus ecclesia catholica per gratiam Dei fundata est*' (the prophetic, evangelical and apostolic Scriptures [is it], on which the catholic church by God's grace is founded).

[60] Cf. Jenson's comment (*Systematic Theology*, vol. 1, 33) on the scriptural test of a theologoumenon in terms of its success as a hermeneutical principle.

contrasted with studies where the scholarly discussion is put to an end from early on, or worse, from the beginning.[61]

The question raised with regard to the origins of the Christian biblical canon still largely focuses on the exact number of books to be included, e.g. as posed by John Barton: 'How and why did the Church come to accept as authoritative Scripture a New Testament containing no more and no less than twenty-seven books, and to place this alongside either the Hebrew or the Greek Scriptures, renamed the "Old Testament"?'[62] Even so, the *how* and the *why* should attract the reader's attention, because the canon is more than knowledge of the number of volumes or pages of a particular book or collection of books. As a property of Sacred Scripture the canon concept is often used interchangeably with 'Scripture'; but 'canon' is also employed to signify the Rule of Faith and an historically mandatory listing of the Scriptures. These three ecclesial denotations of 'canon' – *Scripture, Rule of Faith* and *mandatory listing of the Scriptures* – stand in continual and mutual communication. Through these and some other interacting dimensions (see 2.6), the church is capable of attaining anew an historically definite and authoritative collection of writings; a rule of faith and practice that is, at the same time, identified with this authoritative collection of Scriptures.[63] For this reason, in order to include ritual, textual, material, theological and other dimensions embraced by the church's concept of canon, it needs to be broadly categorized – on the one hand, as a primarily *intrinsic* category, 'largely synonymous with the religious authority of biblical traditions and texts *prior* to any official "closing" of the canon', and on the other hand, as an *extrinsic* category, denoting 'the *late extrinsic fixing* of the contents, order and text of the biblical books.'[64] As the evaluation of these two categories also varies over time, depending on historical and ecclesial

---

[61] As to the impossibility of an absolutely closed canon, see Barth, CD, II.2, 476; cf. idem, *Die Schrift und die Kirche*, Theologische Studien 22 (Zollikon – Zürich: Evangelischer Verlag, 1947), 8. From a different critical viewpoint, cf. Jenson, Systematic Theology, vol. 1, 28. See also, section 9.2, n. 17.

[62] Barton, *The Spirit and the Letter*, 2.

[63] This is already evident in the theology of Irenaeus (see Ch. 8), and from the time of Augustine onwards 'canon' is being used to designate the biblical writings themselves. See Ohme, *Kanon ekklesiastikos* (Berlin: Walter de Gruyter, 1998), 482.

[64] Chapman, 'How the Biblical Canon Began: Working Models and Open Questions', in *Homer, the Bible, and Beyond: Literary and Religious Canons in the Ancient World*, (eds) M. Finkelberg and G. Stroumsa (Leiden: Brill, 2003), 34f. As Chapman points out, the field of canonical research has been split into two groups with these respective emphases regarding the notion of canon. Brevard Childs is a representative of the first approach, emphasizing the intrinsic category, and Albert C. Sundberg of the latter, focusing on the extrinsic fixing of the canon.

context, they need to be continuously reappropriated as part of the church's theological self-reflection (which is to be distinguished, though not separated, from theological reflection based on the canon).[65]

1.2.5 Towards a semiotic definition of the biblical canon

The formation of the Christian Bible cannot be understood only as the emergence of an artefact, i.e. a physical object, taking the form of a text and a book. It can in equal measure be conceived as an arteact, that is, as an artefact – a text – determined by its reception, function and interpretation in the Christian community, but also by its reception as a literary classic and its evaluation by critical scholarship. So, to speak of 'a critical period'[66] for the canonizing of the Christian Scriptures, especially the New Testament portion, implies a critical period of origin for the Bible both as artefact and arteact. Studying the canonical process, consequently, relates not only to the physical appearance of the canon in the early church, but also to the early ecclesiastical use and interpretation in which the biblical text and reading emerged.[67] The canon in this regard is inseparable from the church in its constitutive historical manifestations.

Another largely neglected aspect of this canonical tradition is the authority immanent in the very process of handing it down to coming generations, as stressed by Hans-Georg Gadamer within a general hermeneutical framework:

> That which has been sanctioned by tradition and custom has an authority that is nameless, and our finite historical being is marked by the fact that the authority of what has been handed down to us – and not just what is clearly grounded – always has power over our attitudes and behaviour.[68]

We need to add that the particular tradition viewed here is not any ecclesial tradition or other, but the canon used to regulate the church's talk to and of its

---

[65] Cf. John Webster's remark, referred to above, n. 21.

[66] See quotation above, n. 53.

[67] Cf. Young (*Biblical Exegesis and the Formation of Christian Culture*, 299) on the seemingly homogenous models for the interpretation of Scripture in the early church. She writes: 'The most striking thing, in fact, is the consistent way in which the Bible was read in differing contexts. If commentaries were meant to deal with problems in the text and homilies to focus the more obvious features, still one has an overriding feeling of similarity in the kinds of senses discerned and the "reading strategies" adopted.' In other words, according to Young, it is possible to find a form of overarching reading strategy that seems to have been applied parallel and together with a number of other more specific typological and allegorical reading strategies. Cf. ibid., table, p. 213.

[68] Gadamer, *TM*, 280. See further ibid., Part Two.

God – perhaps 'the best' that was thought, said and preserved as ecclesial text from the Apostolic and Sub-Apostolic Age.[69]

With this in mind, a pattern that I would like to stress emerges, which corresponds to the concept of the Christian biblical canon as it was to be understood and defined from early on, at a critical moment of its history of formation. This pattern embraces four distinguishable – though never separated – elements or fields of signification inherent in the notion of canon.

As elaborated in section 1.3.3, these are: an element pertaining to linguistic and other tradition (Part One); a textual-material (Part Two); a performative element (Part Three); and an ideational element (Part Four). All are equally necessary to grasp the dynamic, multidimensional character of the Christian canon. This definition pertains to the canon as a form of sign language with material elements producing semiotic relations to that which is signified.[70]

The biblical canon, again, is not only an extrinsic isagogical problem, limiting itself to a discussion concerning the number of books in the right order included on the canonical list of Sacred Scriptures – a thesis maintained already by Friedrich Schleiermacher (1768–1834).[71] Nor is it exclusively an intrinsic question of a canon within the canon, a rule of faith setting the agenda for proper scriptural interpretation, as proposed by Gotthold Lessing (1729–81).[72]

In the following I shall seek to demonstrate that, as part of its canon formation, early Christianity forms a closed literary fellowship in the period AD 70–120, with an in-principle closed two-testament canon at hand circa AD 200. This is the outcome of an extended process, marked by continuity and a strong ecclesial consensus as to the scriptural core, structure and approximate literary scope.

As this canon does not arise suddenly, with Marcion or with Irenaeus in the second century, with Origen in the third or with Athanasius during the latter half of the fourth century, the twofold Christian Bible (OT and NT), emerging between AD 30 and 200, can be defined by the various linguistic, tradition-related, textual, material, ritual and doctrinal elements that help

---

[69] Cf. ibid., 337.
[70] See section 9.12.
[71] Schleiermacher, *The Christian Faith*, 603.
[72] Lessing, *Lessing's Theological Writings* (Stanford: Stanford University Press, 1956), 62f.

form it. Some of these, it seems, are spontaneously established, preceding the late(r) ecclesial concept(s) of canon, while others are the results of deliberate communal decision and action.[73] Further, these constitutive elements, which together make up the context of the emerging canon and the notion of a Christian Bible, have implications for today's understanding of the concept of canon. The question of what defines the biblical canon needs to be answered not only, or primarily, by reference to monolithic isagogical treatment, local church tradition or scholarly dating of the extrinsic fixing of the number and order of books. It demands sincere engagement theologically and historically with the various linguistic, textual, ritual and ideational dimensions that constitute and continually establish the Christian Scriptures as canon.

1.3 Purpose and method

As indicated, my own emphasis in this study, dealing with various dimensions of canon and canon formation, will be on text/textuality, ritual/liturgy, doctrine/theology, linguistic tradition, isagogics and effective-history – frequently using a Gadamerian hermeneutics of tradition combined with insights gained from semiotic studies. From the results following this analysis, I shall theologically evaluate some aspects of the canonical process, the literary and ritual character of canonical Scripture, as well as some views on the canon shaped by dogmatics.

1.3.1 The potential of Gadamer's hermeneutics for canon research

Throughout the study I will be referring in various ways to the German philosopher Hans-Georg Gadamer (1900–2002).

Although relating extensively also to other scholars, the numerous references and allusions to Gadamer do stand out. Yet, on the whole, my work largely relies on the efforts made by scholars more specifically devoted to the

---

[73] In this connection, cf. John Webster's critique (*Holy Scripture*, 63) of Jenson's conclusion (*Systematic Theology*, vol. 1, 27f.) that the canon of Scripture is a dogmatic decision of the church. To be sure, the emergence of the scriptural canon involves dogmatic considerations, and even conscious decisions; in addition to this, however, it also emerges as a spontaneous creation within the earliest church, deeply affecting dogma, liturgy and teaching office.

area of canon research. However, Gadamer's work within the field of herme-neutics, in my view, successfully elaborates many of the interpretive themes and problems central to a textual and theological analysis of the canon.[74]

In his magnum opus, *Wahrheit und Methode* (ET *Truth and Method*; below referred to as *WM* and *TM*), Gadamer treats of major issues involved in philo-sophical hermeneutics. At the heart of the work lies the question of truth as it emerges in the experience of art (*WM/TM,* Part I) and in the understanding within the human sciences (*WM/TM,* Part II). His ontological and herme-neutical turn to tradition and effective-history (*Wirkungsgeschichte*), to the subject matter (*Sache*) of texts and literature and to language has to do with the dynamic and conversational character of understanding in which also experience of meaning and of application is involved. As Gadamer sees it, this whole process of hermeneutic experience, of coming to understanding, has primarily a verbal character (*WM/TM,* Part III).

Of particular weight for the present study is Gadamer's analysis of the notion of texts and their interpretation, the hermeneutical circle, effective-history and the constant re-appropriation and re-interpretation thereby implicated.[75] Regarding my analysis below of ecclesial biblical interpretation and the notion of canon, the Gadamerian concepts of the classic, effective-history, *Urliteratur,* ritual embeddedness of emerging texts, text and interpreter, eminent text, textual whole and textual subject-matter receive special attention.

1.3.2 Scripture, theology and history: A Gadamerian hermeneutics of tradition

It belongs to the nature of the Christian tradition to be historical, and, consequently, to be in continual dialogue with its foundational sources and

---

[74] See, e.g. Dostal, 'Gadamer: The Man and His Work', in *The Cambridge Companion to Gadamer,* ed. Dostal (New York: Cambridge University Press, 2002), 1–35. For a critical evaluation of Gadamer's hermeneutics from a theological viewpoint, see Jeanrond, *Text and Interpretation as Categories of Theological Thinking* (Dublin: Gill and Macmillan, 1988); cf. also Jasper, *A Short Introduction to Hermeneutics* (Louisville, KY, Westminster and John Knox, 2004), 106ff.

[75] For discussions on major hermeneutical debates in which Gadamer took part, see, e.g. Warnke, *Gadamer: Hermeneutics, Tradition, and Reason* (Stanford: Stanford University Press, 1987); Dostal, ed., *The Cambridge Companion to Gadamer* (New York: Cambridge University Press, 2002); Grondin, *Hans-Georg Gadamer: A Biography* (trans. J. Weinsheimer; New Haven and London: Yale University Press, 2003); and Jeanrond, *Theological Hermeneutics: Development and Significance* (London: SCM, 1991, 1994), 64ff.

documents, becoming in this respect contemporaneous with the present ecclesial situation.[76] Understanding, here, is less to be thought of 'as a subjective act than as participating in an event of tradition, a process of transmission in which past and present are constantly mediated.'[77] In this connection it is no mere accident that the church has made communal memory last by means of writing – the writing of literature (in the broadest sense) – which means something very different from other forms of tradition, such as vestiges from past life, inscriptions and the like.[78] On this, Gadamer remarks:

> [I]t is true of everything that has come down to us by being written down that here a will to permanence has created the unique forms of continuance that we call literature. It does not present us with only a stock of memorials and signs. Rather, literature has acquired its own contemporaneity with every present. To understand it does not mean primarily to reason one's way back into the past, but to have a present involvement in what is said.[79]

The consciousness of the – still partially ongoing[80] – canonical process, leading up to and being integral to the 'final' literary form[81] and the continuous edition of the Christian Bible, points to the same hermeneutical fact.[82] That is, this

---

[76] Cf. Jenson's remark, as to the distinction between contextual and other contemporary theology, that all theology is 'contextual' (*Systematic Theology,* vol. 1, ix). See also Rudolf Bultmann, for whom critical and historical New Testament research is only preliminary (*Theology of the New Testament,* vol. 2 [London: SCM, 1955], 251). Thus, according to Bultmann, the reconstruction of early Christian history stands 'in the service of the interpretation of the New Testament writings under the presupposition that they have something to say to the present.' On the historicity of the Jesus-tradition, cf. Pannenberg, *An Introduction to Systematic Theology* (Edinburgh: T&T Clark, 1991), 5: 'The story of Jesus Christ has to be history, not in all its details, but in its core, if the Christian faith is to continue.' On the pastness of the present Jesus in the NT, see Smith, *The Fourth Gospel in Four Dimensions: Judaism and Jesus, the Gospels and Scripture* (Columbia, SC: University of South Carolina Press, 2008), 57ff.

[77] Gadamer, *Truth and Method* (New York: Continuum, 1989), 290. From a Christian theological viewpoint this dialogue and process of transmission is variously enabled by the Ever Present One, the Trinitarian God of history.

[78] Ibid., 391.

[79] Ibid. Cf. Thiselton, *New Horizons in Hermeneutics,* 266. Understanding the notion of canon, too, is a process, rather than a single event.

[80] See section 1.2.1.

[81] The 'final' literary form, which is not always absolutely stable, can be seen as the composition level giving the greatest promise, at a particular moment, of providing a normative control.

[82] That the diachronic and synchronic components involved in the canonical process (with its theological *telos*) are also a part of the biblical text in its 'final' ecclesial form means, among other things, that what speaks to us in Sacred Scripture does not first of all rest upon the art of writing, but 'upon the authority of the one who speaks to us in the Church', Gadamer, *The Relevance of the Beautiful,* 142 (cf. section 9.5.3, n. 63). See also Dunn, 'Levels of Canonical Authority', in *New Horizons in Biblical Theology,* 4 (1982), 13–60; idem, *The Living Word* (London: SCM, 1987); cf. Thiselton, *New Horizons in Hermeneutics,* 37; and Wall, 'The Significance of a Canonical Perspective of the Church's Scripture', in *The Canon Debate,* (eds) M. L. McDonald and J. Sanders (Peabody,

awareness necessarily has a present, effective-historical involvement through which the collection of these disparate writings is apprehended together – as a single whole, to which (namely, the Old and New Testaments) and out of which (namely, the Jewish Scriptures and the new covenant inaugurated by Jesus Christ) they have been formed.[83]

In this process, the relative closedness of the Hebrew Bible is partly opened up by a penultimate eschatological event, post-resurrection faith in Christ Jesus (Heb 1.1-3). So, a new communal understanding of the textual whole is perceived,[84] now consisting of two in principle closed,[85] mutually interacting textual entities, soon to be called the 'Old' and the 'New Testaments'.[86] The Jewish corpus of writings remains largely intact in this process of canonical change.[87] Thus, while acknowledging the integrity of the Jewish community,

---

MA: Hendridckson Publishers, 2002), 528–40. Generally, regarding the ancient texts of the Bible, knowledge of the particular historical and cultural situation in which the text was produced 'is indispensable for a sensitive reading of the final form', as pointed out by Noble, *The Canonical Approach: A Critical Reconstruction of the Hermeneutics of Brevard S. Childs* (Leiden: Brill, 1995) , 151. For further arguments as to the needed historical knowledge for a semantic understanding of the canonical text, see Sternberg, *The Poetics of Biblical Narrative: Ideological Literature and the Drama of Reading* (Bloomington: Indiana University Press, 1985), 7–23. For a lucid discussion on the necessary view of language, both as 'representational and wholly transparent', on the one hand, and 'a multi-layered matrix of effects generated by shifting community-attitudes and social conventions', on the other, see Thiselton, *New Horizons in Hermeneutics*, 20.

[83] For, as Karl Barth put it in his Göttingen lectures on dogmatics in 1924/25 (*The Göttingen Dogmatics: Instruction in the Christian Religion,* vol. 1 [Grand Rapids: Eerdmans, 1991], 16), 'holy scripture in the strict sense is the totality of the prophetic and apostolic witness and not a single text as such, not even the text that 'God is love' [1 John 4.8] or the like.' That is, the present scriptural involvement with what is said is always dealing with this textual totality.

[84] Cf., e.g. Wall, *The Significance of a Canonical Perspective of the Church's Scripture*, 536–8; Moberly, *The Bible, Theology, and Faith: A Study of Abraham and Jesus* (Cambridge: Cambridge University Press, 2000); and Wilken, 'In novissimis diebus. Biblical Promises, Jewish Hopes and Early Christian Exegesis'. Cf. also Aichele, *The Control of Biblical Meaning*, 31, who opts for talking of two Christian canons: 'The Christian double canon transforms the Jewish Scriptures into the first Christian canon, the Old Testament. The scriptures are rewritten, not physically but logocentrically.' In the end, however, within this 'logocentric' matrix, we are still dealing with a textual whole, i.e. the Christian canonical reading. See further ibid., 200.

[85] Cf. Kermode, 'The Argument about Canons', in *The Bible and the Narrative Traditiom*, ed. McConnell (New York: Oxford University Press, 1986), 78: 'The ecclesiastical canons are, allowing for a small measure of sectarian variation, fixed; and their fixity, however come by, is a matter of principle or doctrine.'

[86] In order for this textual process to take place, an already existing written tradition constituting a whole was thus needed. Otherwise the hermeneutical accent would have been primarily on ritual practice, rather than on text, and an already existing literary tradition now being expanded. So, the chapter in this volume on ritual (Ch. 7) is placed after the chapters on textuality (Chs 3–6). The textuality here in question is, however, also and at the same time ritually defined (Chs 6 and 7). Cf. Gadamer, *The Relevance of the Beautiful*, 145, on the gradual transition, in general, from ritual to the literary work. See also Tim Murphy, 'Elements of a semiotic Theory of Religion', *Method & Theory in the Study of Religion* 15 (2003): 49–50.

[87] Cf., however, Chs 3 and 4, in which the changed canonical order of OT books, Greek as the inspired language, the codex as the new book format and the introduction of the *nomina sacra* mark the

covenant and Scripture, the church, when relating to its Jewish roots, will profit from taking into account the ecclesial process of canonization as part of its reading the scriptural canon of – simultaneously – Jewish and Christian writings.[88] The Jewishness of the books of the Christian Bible can, so to speak, be enacted anew in new Christian readings of these entirely Jewish and entirely Christian texts.[89] The eschatological event of Jesus the Messiah is here closely tied up with the history-of-salvation-scheme as it is conceived in the early Christian usage of the Scriptures, e.g. as it is archetypically expressed in Luke, 'beginning with Moses and all the prophets' (Luke 24.27).[90]

To set it forth christologically is a hermeneutical starting point for the identification and usage of Christian Scripture. But the common scriptural Judaic heritage – something that is shared by Jews and Christians – also presents itself and is appropriated in this act of interpretation, as is the serious reading of the text as text. Reading canonically, a twofold biblical text appears with a typical intratextual to-and-fro movement between old and new Scriptures.[91] Such biblical reading, centring in the Christ-event and the inter-dependent scriptural texts, has been recently discussed by the New Testament scholar Francis Watson. In his elaboration of Pauline hermeneutics, he writes:

> Scripture is not a secondary confirmation of a Christ-event entire and complete in itself; for scripture is not external to the Christ-event but is constitutive of it,

---

Christian OT off against the Jewish Scriptures. See also Bokedal, 'Scripture in the Second Century', in *The Sacred Text: Excavating the Texts, Exploring the Interpretations, and Engaging the Theologies of the Christian Scriptures*, (eds) M. Bird and M. Pahl (Piscataway, NJ: Gorgias, 2010), 44, 57–60. Differently Stuhlmacher, *Biblische Theologie des Neuen Testaments: Band II*, 291–93.

[88] See, e.g. Jenson, *Systematic Theology*, vol. 1, 30, n. 23. Cf. also Wright, *God Who Acts: Biblical Theology as Recital* (London: SCM, 1952), 17: 'Surely, if the New Testament is not proclaimed as the fulfilment of the Old, if the Gospel as proclaimed by Jesus and by Paul is not the completion of the faith of Israel, then it must inevitably be a completion and fulfilment of something which we ourselves substitute – and that most certainly means a perversion of the Christian faith.'

[89] Arguably, by and large all the writings in the Christian Bible are written by Jews. Cf. Jenson, *Systematic Theology*, vol. 1, 30, n. 23.

[90] See further, e.g. Hays, 'Can the Gospels Teach Us How To Read the Old Testament', *Pro Ecclesia* 11 (2002); Hagner, *The Use of the Old and New Testaments in Clement of Rome* (Leiden: Brill, 1973); Skarsaune, *The Development of Scriptural Interpretation in the Second and Third Centuries – except Clement and Origen* (Göttingen: Vandenhoeck & Ruprecht, 1996); and Young, *Biblical Exegesis and the Formation of Christian Culture* (Cambridge: Cambridge University Press, 1997). On the scheme of salvation-history, see Farley and Hodgson, 'Scripture and Tradition', 64–7; Just, *The Ongoing Feast: Table Fellowship and Eschatology at Emmaus* (Pueblo, Collegeville, MN: Liturgical Press, 1993).

[91] Cf. Matthew 5.17-20; John 5.47; Romans 1.1-4. For some different approaches to scriptural intertextuality, see, for example, Hays, Alkier and Huizenga, (eds), *Reading the Bible Intertextually* (Waco, TX: Baylor University Press, 2009); Porter, ed., *Hearing the Old Testament in the New Testament* (Grand Rapids and Cambridge: Eerdmans, 2006); and Albl, *'And Scripture Cannot be Broken': The Form and Function of the Early Christian Testimonia Collections* (Leiden: Brill, 1999).

the matrix within which it takes shape and comes to be what it is. … Without scripture, there is no gospel; apart from the scriptural matrix, there is no Christ.[92]

The new textual whole, concentrating on the Christ-event and the Scriptures of the old and the new covenants, is being expressed within this hermeneutical field of scriptural movement – and so accounting for, among other things, the Christian prophecy-fulfilment interpretations, as well as the textual expansion of the Scriptures, for which the totality of the classic prophetic and apostolic literature sets the goal.[93]

Accordingly, as classical text,[94] the biblical canon is at this time in a process of 'textual expansion', being defined as self-referential and largely self-interpreting, to the extent that it interprets itself.[95] This self-signification is due to the theological end towards which the transmission of the biblical text material is directed, taking place during the period of an expansion.[96]

In other words, there are intra- and intertextual 'theological forces' at work in the way these mutually interdependent texts are constructed, categorized

---

[92] Watson, *Paul and the Hermeneutics of Faith* (London: T&T Clark International, 2004), 16f. Cf. Ibid. 17: 'It is scripture that shapes the contours of the Christ-event, and to discern how it does so is to uncover the true meaning of scripture itself.' Cf. also Watson ('The Bible', in *The Cambridge Companion to Karl Barth*, ed. J. Webster [Cambridge: Cambridge University Press, 2000], 67) on Barthian scriptural hermeneutics. For a different accentuation, cf. Holmgren, *The Old Testament and the Significance of Jesus: Embracing Change – Maintaining Christian Identity: The Emerging Center in Biblical Scholarship* (Grand Rapids: Eerdmans, 1999), 54: 'Clearly, the New Testament writers did not first consult the Old Testament and then form their opinion about Jesus. On the contrary, they moved from Jesus to the Old Testament scripture. Viewed in the light of Christ, certain texts took on new meaning which gave early Christians fuller insight into this figure in whom they experienced the presence of God.' Cf. also ibid., 30; and Childs, *Biblical Theology*, 381–2.

[93] Cf. n. 83 above. See also von Harnack's presentation of 'forerunners and rivals' of the New Testament. It could well have happened, as he argues, that the church, apart from several other alternatives, had chosen as its Bible 'an expanded and corrected Old Testament' (Harnack, *The Origin of the New Testament and the Most Important Consequences of the New Creation* [London: Williams & Norgate, 1925], 169–83). Cf. also Cullmann, 'The Plurality of the Gospels as a Theological Problem in Antiquity: A Study in the History of Dogma', in Cullmann, *The Early Church* (London: SCM, 1956).

[94] See section 2.4.

[95] Gadamer, *WM*, 273-4/*TM*, 289. Cf. n. 98. Webster (*Holy Scripture: A Dogmatic Sketch* [Cambridge: Cambridge University Press, 2003], 93) argues that '[a]t one level, talk of Scripture as "self-interpreting" or "perspicuous" is a protest against the authority of interpretative traditions or élites. In part, therefore, the point of such talk is to defend the priority of 'original' reading over reading which is merely customary or derivative'. Cf. also Thiselton, *New Horizons in Hermeneutics*, 38–42, 495–9, on the concepts of biblical intra- and intertextuality, inner-biblical exegesis and re-contextualization.

[96] Childs, *Biblical Theology*, 70, 104–6, 216–17, 262–5, 534–7. On systems of self-signification, see George Aichele, *Sign, Text, Scripture: Semiotics and the Bible*; and Tim Murphy, 'Elements of a semiotic Theory of Religion'.

and received as classical canonical Scripture.[97] As Gadamer remarks: 'the classical is what preserves itself, *because* it interprets itself'.[98] That is to say, the classic text is not only self-signifying, but also self-explanatory. As far as the text of the biblical canon goes, today, as well as in the past, the church's interpretive task is to expand the unity of the understood meaning 'centrifugally', letting the harmony of all the details with the whole form the criterion of 'correct understanding'.[99]

As the Christian movement emerges as a sect within Early Judaism, a new envisagement, grounded in the event of Christ, is born with regard to textual details as well as to the notion of a scriptural whole. Here text and (normative) ecclesial interpretation mutually depend on one another.[100] The conditions of thought imposed on the text do not primarily come from an outward agent.[101] Rather, it is a question of an inward canonical shaping of the biblical text in order for it to function as a regulative within the church and towards ecclesial practice and teaching.[102] The biblical accounts attain, implicitly and explicitly, the function of a constitutive ecclesial text. In this way the novel conception of a new covenant in and with Jesus soon receives its classic oral and written textual form. It becomes canon for the church. In Francis Watson's wording: '"Classic" or "canonical" status means that a work is borne along into a future of indefinite duration by a communally-authoritative tradition which has found in the work a claim to normative significance'.[103] That is to say, when applied to the Christian biblical writings, the sense of the whole, towards which the 'centrifugal' hermeneutic movement is directed, is reached, not least, by the strong eschatological centring in a textual midpoint: the coming of the Kingdom of God in and with Jesus Christ, as this relates to the 'divine' covenants, the old and the new.[104]

---

[97] Childs, *Biblical Theology*, 71. For a different view, see Bultmann, *Theology of the New Testament*, vol. 2, 127–42.

[98] Gadamer, *WM*, 273-4/*TM*, 289: 'Klassisch aber ist, wie Hegel sagt: "das sich selbst Bedeutende und damit auch sich selber Deutende". – Das heißt aber letzten Endes: Klassisch ist, was sich bewahrt, *weil* es sich selber bedeutet und sich selber deutet.'

[99] Gadamer describes the process of coming to understanding in these terms, *TM*, 291.

[100] Cf. section 6.4, esp. section 6.4.4.

[101] Cf. the discussion by Vanhoozer, *First Theology*, 210.

[102] Cf. the systemic character of the canon discussed in section 2.3.

[103] Watson, *Text and Truth: Redefining Biblical Theology* (Edinburgh: T&T Clark and Grand Rapids: Eerdmans, 1998), 49.

[104] According to Karl Barth, Scripture is the witness of God's revelation in Jesus Christ. In the Old Testament this witness takes the form of expectation, in the New of recollection, *CD*, I/2, 481–83.

In this connection, Gadamer's emphasis – that *understanding* (here, as always) is to be thought of not so much as a subjective act, but rather as a participation in an event of tradition – is useful:

> A person who does not admit that he is dominated by prejudices will fail to see what manifests itself by their light. It is like the relation between I and Thou. A person who reflects himself out of the mutuality of such a relation changes this relationship and destroys its moral bond. *A person who reflects himself out of a living relationship to tradition destroys the true meaning of this tradition in exactly the same way.*[105]

Understanding biblical canonicity is not possible for a person who seeks to reflect him- or herself out of a potentially vivid relationship to the tradition pertaining to the canon. Rather, seeking to remain in this (prejudiced) relation is a precondition for understanding the mutuality between the effective-history of the biblical canon and its emergence within mainstream Christianity, as we encounter today in its various manifestations. In this mutuality, however, it is clear that the understood intratextual meaning of the canon 'is concretized and fully realized only in interpretation', but, at the same time, 'the interpretive activity considers itself wholly bound by the meaning of the text.'[106]

Moreover, as scriptural hermeneutics presupposes a relationship to the content of the Bible, we may ask with Gadamer, 'what kind of "presupposition" this is'.[107] Is the assumption that one is moved by the question of God, in the end, far more specific than we would expect? In responding to this question, Gadamer draws our attention to an old hermeneutical debate, that between

---

Wolfhart Pannenberg and Jürgen Moltmann, among others, emphasize the proleptical coming of the eschatological end-event in and with the Resurrected One as a centrepiece of biblically grounded theology. See Pannenberg, *Revelation as History* (New York: Macmillan, 1968); and Moltmann, *The Theology of Hope* (London: SCM, 1967). On Pannenberg's and Moltmann's different emphases, see Kelsey, *Proving Doctrine*, 53–5, n. 84.

[105] Gadamer, *TM*, 360. Gadamer asserts that 'to be in a conversation means to be beyond oneself, to think with the other and to come back to oneself as if to another.' Gadamer, *Gadamer in Conversation: Reflections and Commentary* (New Haven: Yale University Press, 2001), 13.

[106] Gadamer, *TM*, 332. In other words, in the dialectic relation between text and reader, there is still an interpretation that 'the texts, of themselves, call for.' Ibid., 336. Cf. also ibid., 398, where Gadamer discusses interpretation as something already potentially contained within the understanding process.

[107] Ibid., 331. The two alternatives elaborated on by Gadamer are, on the one hand, that this presupposition is 'something that is given with human life itself', or, on the other, that it is 'first from God – i.e. from faith – that human existence experiences itself as being affected by the question of God'.

Jews and Christians on the Bible: Which is the right interpretation of the Old Testament,

> the Jewish one or the Christian one in light of the New Testament? Or are both legitimate interpretations – i.e. do they have something in common, and is this what is really being understood by the interpreter? The Jew who understands the text of the Old Testament in a different way than the Christian shares with him the presupposition that he too is concerned with the question of God. At the same time, he will hold that a Christian theologian misunderstands the Old Testament if he takes its truths as qualified by the New Testament. Hence the presupposition that one is moved by the question of God already involves a claim to knowledge concerning the true God and his revelation. Even unbelief is defined in terms of the faith that is demanded of one.[108]

Nevertheless, although the question of God (*die Gottesfrage*) is presupposed in the interpretations made throughout this study, the analysis of the emergence of the Old and New Testaments as canon for the church is, of course, marked by the present author's preference, interpretation and involvement with tradition.[109] As Gadamer puts it: 'The theme and object of research are actually constituted by the motivation of the inquiry.'[110]

The canonical process takes place as a part of the Christian community's institutionalized (public and private[111]) reading of the Bible – the books that become the Book through this reading. To read it from this communal perspective is to be implicated in a textual event of which also the canonical process is a part.[112] In other words, how the Jewish Scriptures and the

---

[108] Ibid., 331f.

[109] Such involvement in interpretation is emphasized, e.g. by Rudolf Bultmann in his discussion of the role of pre-understanding in hermeneutics. An interpretation, he writes, is 'governed always by a prior understanding of the subject. ... The formulation of a question, and an interpretation, is possible at all only on the basis of such a prior understanding.' Bultmann, 'The Problem of Hermeneutics', 239; cited from Shin, 'Some Light from Origen: Scripture as Sacrament', *Worship* 73 (1999): 404. Cf. Gadamer, *TM*, 331f.

[110] Gadamer, *TM*, 284. The quote continues: 'Hence historical research is carried along by the historical movement of life itself and cannot be understood teleologically in terms of the object into which it is inquiring. Such an "object in itself" clearly does not exist at all.'

[111] See sections 7.7.4 and 7.7.5.

[112] This thought has similarities with Brevard Childs's and James Sanders's canonical approach (Fernhout, *Canonical Texts*, 202–5), where 'interpretation is a matter of interaction between text and reader. As far as this is concerned, a remarkable parallel exists between current interpretation and the coming into existence of the text in the early Christian community, for the text itself is also the result of interaction – between the community and an earlier text', ibid. 204. See further Childs, *Introduction to the Old Testament as Scripture* (London: SCM, 1979); Sanders, *Canon and Community: A Guide to Canonical Criticism* (Philadelphia: Fortress, 1984); and Watson (*Paul and the Hermeneutics of Faith*, 4, n. 1), who points to the contribution of Brevard Childs as having

inauguration of the new covenant by Jesus become the Christian biblical canon of Old and New Testaments is part, on a foundational interpretive level, of any Christian reading representing the hermeneutical back-and-forth movement between the Jewish Scriptures and the new Christian textual tradition (with its dependency on the Scriptures), necessary for the specific ecclesial conception of the textual whole.

Another aspect of Gadamer's reflections on biblical hermeneutics relates to this, namely his understanding of canonical Scripture as constitutive for ecclesial existence, i.e. of having 'an absolute priority over the doctrine of those who interpret it'.[113] For this reason, he maintains, 'the gospel acquires no new content in being preached'.[114] Does this have to do with some kind of *de facto* or *de iure* function of the canon to which the church and the interpreter are bound?[115] A similar line of thought is found in Karl Barth's discussion of the canon early in his *Church Dogmatics*, where he states, categorically, that 'the Bible constitutes itself the Canon. It is the Canon because it imposed itself upon the Church as such, and continually does so. ... the Bible is the Canon just because it is so. It is so by imposing itself as such.'[116] It might be that Gadamer here is somehow influenced by Barth's and (neo)conservative Protestantism's view on Scripture.[117] In one sense he even seems to move a step beyond Barth's theology of Scripture, namely in holding that 'Scripture is the word of God'[118] and that such an idea in relation to Scripture, as indicated above, also has direct implications for the fore-understanding of the question of God.

---

shown 'how the "canonical form" of a text mediates between its circumstances of origin and its later usage.'

[113] Gadamer, *TM*, 331.

[114] Ibid., 330.

[115] The categories *de facto* and *de iure* are here used straightforwardly, i.e. *de iure* refers to an explicit ecclesial (and so juridically binding) normative doctrine of the Scriptures as canon, while *de facto* pertains to what the canon's authority means practically speaking – in David Kelsey's own words: 'in your practice of doing theology regardless of what your doctrine of scripture may say about scripture's authority de jure', Kelsey, *Proving Doctrine*, xiii.

[116] Barth, *CD*, I/1, 107. The citation continues: 'And if we can only register this event (as such) as the reality in which the Church is the Church, nevertheless, when this is done, it is not impossible afterwards, exegetically, to state in what this self-imposing consists and how far it sets a limit to the wisdom of our dialogue with ourselves.' Cf. Hofius, *Das apostolische Christuszeugnis und das Alte Testament. Thesen zur Biblischen Theologie* (Paderborn: UTB für Wissenschaft, 1995), 196.

[117] Cf. his positive evaluation in Gadamer, *TM*, 521: 'In his great work *Church Dogmatics*, Karl Barth contributes to the hermeneutical problem explicitly nowhere and indirectly everywhere.'

[118] Gadamer, *TM*, 331. On Barth's elaboration on the relationship between revelation, i.e. the Word of God, and the Bible, see, e.g. Barth, *CD*, I/1, 113.

1.3.3 A semiotic approach to canon formation

In the following, the hermeneutics of tradition outlined above will be complemented with some insights gained from the semiotic study of culture (cf. section 1.2.5), in order to identify not only the various traditions, signs, dimensions or functions involved in dealing with the emergent concept of canon, but also their various and often complex relations. As an intra- and intertextual system of signs and meanings, the canon must be understood from the viewpoint of the high-context setting of the Christian community in which it arose and continues to function – naturally involving profound theological dimensions. As already pointed out, this does not mean that the Bible is made into a mere historical object, ascribing to it dead meaning. Quite the contrary, canonical Scripture is there, if it is there, precisely to inspire the very same community in which it originated. Part of the reason why this high-context setting should draw our attention today is the relative absence of historical distance between the apostolic community of interpretation, in which these writings arose, and the communities that now need to interpret them. Robert Jenson's claim in this regard is significant: 'there is *no* historical distance between the community in which the Bible appeared and the church that now seeks to understand the Bible, because these are the same community.'[119] Admittedly, to a major degree this is one of the reasons the canonical text, defined for and by the apostolic and sub-apostolic community, has bearing upon today's community. *Its* (core) canon has been, and has been meant to be, the canon of the Christian community ever since. Therefore, on

---

[119] Jenson, *Systematic Theology*, vol. 2, 297f.; and idem, 'The Religious Power of Scripture', *Scottish Journal of Theology*, 52 (1999): 97–9; cf. in this regard Vincent of Lerin's well-known dictum of what is catholic (geographically and temporally): *quod ubique, quod semper, quod ab omnibus creditum est*. Gadamer's category of *Horizontverschmelzung* is here crucial for a deeper understanding of the continuous act of identification of the apostolic community in history and of today; cf. also Bauckham, 'For Whom Were Gospels Written?', in ed. Bauckham, *The Gospels for All Christians: Rethinking the Gospel Audiences* (Grand Rapids: Eerdmans, 1998), 46f.: Bauckham's argument that the Gospels initially were written not for a specific Christian audience, but for a general Christian audience 'smooths the hermeneutical path from the way the Gospels addressed their first readers – an open category of readers/hearers in any late-first-century Christian church to which the Gospel might circulate – to the way the Gospels have been read ever since.' See also Childs, *The New Testament as Canon*, 23; Barth, *The Epistle to the Romans* (New York: Oxford University Press, 1968 [1933]), Preface to the Second Edition, 7; and the comment, here quoted out of context, by Robert Morgan (in *Biblical Interpretation*, (eds) Morgan and Barton [New York: Oxford University Press, 1988], 178): 'Biblical scholars clarify what the Bible meant for its original authors, not (if that is different) what it might mean for anyone today'. On the historical distance necessary for the practice of biblical criticism in this connection, see Jenson, *Systematic Theology*, vol. 2, 281.

the basis of this identification, although the danger of historicization must be avoided,[120] there is a sense in which consideration of the past is crucial for the present community. A part of this past is the search for the historical roots of the Scriptures as canon, and, accompanying it, the 'classic' narrative pattern of biblical interpretation; as the theologian George Lindbeck tellingly remarks, 'because an understanding of the historic role of this way of interpreting and using Scripture is the best argument for present need and possibility.'[121]

The complexity of a cultural phenomenon, such as the Christian canon, however, can be understood more thoroughly if it is also seen from the semiotic point of view.[122] This does not mean that the phenomenon of the canon is reduced to signs and their signification.[123] Rather, its web of signification and meaning focused by the semiotic analysis is a way of reaching towards that which cannot be finally defined, such as the multidimensional character of the canon. In Part One, I point out several dimensions to that effect, which will be further elaborated in Parts One, Two and Three.

Another aspect tied to semiotics, and especially to the semiotics of culture, as remarked by the anthropologist Clifford Geertz,[124] is that it requires of the investigator to ask questions concerning the most self-evident, commonsensical patterns and structures for those at home in the culture being studied, in this case the Christian community with particular focus on the sign system, the unitary language or 'grammar' of its Scriptures *as canon*.

Systematic questioning can make communal patterns emerge which at first glance may seem unfamiliar to those most at home in the community. Therefore, semiotic analysis can be called a 'decoding' of the day-to-day codes used by a community, or a 'recoding' of them into a metalanguage that is useful for understanding, although not altogether natural to everyday language.[125]

The fourfold structure of the present study has been inspired by the semiotic approach to cultural studies advanced by Jens Loenhoff and Robert

---

[120] On (post)modern 'naturalization' and historization of the scriptural canon, see Webster, 'The Dogmatic Location of the Canon', *Neue Zeitschrift für systematische Theologie und Religionsphilosophie* 43 (2001): 17–43.

[121] Lindbeck, *Scripture, Consensus, and Community* (Grand Rapids: Eerdmans, 1989), 75f. Cf. also Gadamer, *TM*, 284, cited above, n. 110.

[122] Eco, *A Theory of Semiotics* (Bloomington: Indiana University Press, 1976), 27.

[123] Cf. ibid.

[124] Geertz, *The Interpretation of Cultures* (New York: Basic Books, 1973), 5.

[125] Schreiter, *Constructing Local Theologies* (Maryknoll, NY: Orbis Books, 1985), 56.

Schreiter.[126] Loenhoff and Schreiter have used the three categories ideational, performantial (performative) and material.

I shall make use of these in analysing the ecclesiastical concept of canon. This approach, I hope to show, makes the rather complex notion of canon come to the fore more easily, as compared to studies where a more narrow perspective is aimed at, e.g. when central theological, ritual or material dimensions of canon (formation) are left out.

To Loenhoff's and Schreiter's three categories I have added yet another two: text and tradition. My working definition of the Christian scriptural canon, then, reads as follows:

A) The canon is *sanctioned by tradition* – it pertains to linguistic and other tradition(s), and to something durative by establishing a nameless authority and authoritative tradition over time. (Part One, Ch. 2).

B) The canon is *material* – an artefact embracing symbolizations that become a source of identity; and *textual* – a meaningful and structured whole, the meaning of which transcends the sum of its individual words and sentences. (Part Two, Chs 3–6).

C) The canon is *performative* – it involves rituals that bind the members of the church together to provide them with a participatory way of embodying and enacting their histories and values. (Part Three, Ch. 7).

D) The canon is *ideational* – by providing systems or frameworks of meaning which serve both to interpret the world (theological perspectives), and to provide guidance for living in the world. This dimension of canon embodies beliefs, values, attitudes, and rules for behaviour. (Part Four, Chs 8 and 9).

The central thesis of the present study, as outlined in section 1.2.1, is formulated against the background of this semiotic working definition (One–Four) and the initial question of the biblical canon treated in this introductory chapter.[127]

---

[126] Loenhoff, *Interkulturelle Verständigung Zum Problem grenzüberschreitender Kommunikation* (Leske and Budrich: Oplade, 1992), 144; the reference is taken from Schreiter, *The New Catholicity: Theology between the Global and the Local* (Maryknoll, NY: Orbis Books, 1997), 29, 79ff.; cf. idem, *Constructing Local Theologies*.

[127] This understanding of 'canon' is largely in agreement with Brevard Childs's definition (Childs, *The New Testament as Canon*, 26; cf. nn. 54 and 55) in which 'canon' refers to the process of theological interpretation by a religious community that left its mark on a literary text which did not continue to evolve and which became the normative interpretation of the words and events to which it bore witness for those identifying with that community; cf. Neusner and Chilton, *Revelation: The*

1.4 The structure of the present investigation

Following the introductory presentation above, Part One deals with linguistic and tradition-related aspects of the canon. More specifically, following the Introduction, Chapter 2 provides a general hermeneutical framework for the present study discussing the concept of effective-history (*Wirkungsgeschichte*) and the hermeneutical circle, as these relate to the notion of canon. In the latter part of Chapter 2, I apply the semiotic approach described above and discuss various dimensions (or signifiers) of canon involved in the formation and perennial function of the Christian Bible.

Part Two treats textual and material aspects of the canon. A twofold emphasis is made in Chapter 3, by presenting the canonical system of the *nomina sacra* as being both textually and theologically significant. In the subsequent chapter, Chapter 4, another innovation for preserving the church's Scripture enters my discussion, namely the codex. From very early on in the Christian communities the codex appears to be replacing the traditional book format, the scroll. With this new format for their Scriptures, both a material and a textual side of canonicity come to the fore. By changing book format and adopting the *nomina sacra* practice, the early church with its old and new Scriptures becomes textually and textually–materially distinguished vis-à-vis both the synagogue and the pagan literary world.

Chapter 5 deals with yet another aspect of textuality, that of the dialectic between the oral and the written modes of textual transmission. A more detailed analysis of textuality related to our topic is provided in Chapter 6.

Having dealt with the notion of canon primarily as text and material entity, the book goes on in Part Three to treat another significant dimension, namely

Torah and the Bible (Valley Forge, PA: Trinity Press, 1995), 14. Cf. also Barth, *CD*, I/1, 107, cited here in n. 59; and Jenson, *Systematic Theology*, vol. 2, 274, cited in Ch. 2, n. 15. On text/textuality, see Jeanrond, *Text and Interpretation*; Trobisch, *The First Edition of the New Testament* (Oxford: Oxford University Press, 2000). On ritual, see Zahn, *Geschichte des Neutestamentlichen Kanons*, vol. 1 (Erlangen: Verlag von Andreas Deichert, 1888); Gamble, 'The Canon of the New Testament', in *The New Testament and Its Modern Interpreters*, (eds) Epp and MacRae (Philadelphia, PA: Fortress, and Atlanta, GA: Scholars Press, 1989). Cf. the comment by Stuhlmacher (*Wie treibt man Biblische Theologie?* [Neukirchen-Vluyn: Neukirchener, 1995], 66): 'Schon in der ersten Hälfte des 2. Jh.s n.Chr. gehören also die γραφαὶ ἅγιαι, die Evangelien und die Paulusbriefe, zu den Schriften, die in den frühchristlichen Gemeindeversammlungen regelmäßig verlesen werden. Oder anders ausgedrückt: Die genannten alt- und neutestamentlichen Schriften genießen kanonische Geltung.' On doctrinal features, see Webster, *Holy Scripture*; Barth, *CD*, I/1, 101; 1/2, § 19; Aland, *The Problem of the New Testament Canon* (London: Mowbray, 1962); and Childs, *Biblical Theology*.

the interaction of canon with ritual. Chapter 7 looks at some ritual dimensions involving scriptural use. It is argued that the textuality of the scriptural canon cannot be properly understood without also taking ritual and liturgical practices into account.

In Part Four, ideational aspects are focused. Chapter 8 elaborates on the canonical narrative structure and theology expressed through the Rule of Faith as an integral part of my canon definition. The Rule is crucial, when seeking to grasp not only the earliest use and signification, but also the continuous ecclesial function, of the notion of the canon. The canonical scope, formula and process are discussed, using Irenaeus's second-century perspective to highlight these perennial issues.

In Chapter 9, classic criteria of scriptural canonicity are treated. Of these, apostolicity is suggested as the principal criterion; it is, however, noted that the act of handing on the gospel by means of writing is significant in itself, irrespective of the criteria discussion. Interestingly, and of significance for the Christian canon formation, there are some indications that the first and last books of the New Testament present themselves as 'Scripture'. Chapter 9, titled 'The Logic of the Christian Canon', draws some further conclusions from previous chapters with bearing on the criteria question, the integrity of the canon and the canon's function as authoritative instrument. The hermeneutics of tradition involved when relating the canon of the early church with the present community is explored.

Finally, Chapter 10 contains a summary of the book with some concluding remarks.

Part One

Linguistic and Tradition-Related Aspects of the Canon

2

The Concept of Canon

When in the fourth century the word 'canon' and its cognates came to denote the Christian normativity and literary scope of the Scriptures, its previous use in the church, together with its general Hellenistic meaning, formed part of its new connotation. This concept, so significant within Hellenistic philosophy, science and art, injected new potential meanings to the Christian Scriptures and their function as regulative documents for the communities. To this extent, 'canon' and 'Scripture' were not always synonymous. Canonicity (pertaining to the canon of the Old and New Testament Scriptures) came to be understood as a property of Sacred Scripture, designating primarily its 'apostolically defined' scope, but also its *scopus* (the central point of view), intratextuality, narrativity and normativity for the faith community. Here, in the broad sense, the canon criterion par préférance is that of apostolicity.

This chapter details some of the different meanings of the concept 'canon', analyses how they have been applied to the Bible, and introduces the claim that the scriptural canon and its formation can be understood as a whole only if the hermeneutical dimension of effective-history (*Wirkungsgeschichte*) is taken into account. That is to say, any interpreter, in order to understand at all, must be part of the historical continuum that he or she shares with the phenomenon being studied. Just so, the concept of the canon can be taken seriously only when the canonical form and function of a biblical text is understood to mediate between its circumstances of origin and its later usage.[1] In this sense, the vibrant ecclesial notion of canon predates the application of the term 'canon' to the two-testament Bible. With this terminology, the Bible is extrinsically delimited, regarding scope, on the one hand, and regulative

---

[1] Cf. Watson, *Paul and the Hermeneutics of Faith* (London: T&T Clark, 2004), 4, n. 1.

for church practice, liturgy and teaching, on the other. Likewise, this property of Scripture – that of being in principle a closed biblical text and narrative *as normative towards the community* – is older than the ecclesial use of the word 'canon' employed to signify it. None the less, a clue to understanding this lies in the *signified's* linguistic mediation and function as bearer of tradition. To grasp the emergent concept of canon and its ecclesiastical usage, we begin by investigating the mutual interaction between the word and the concept, mediated to contemporary Christian communities through language and tradition.

2.1 The ecclesial reality of the canon

The question of the biblical canon is a question of the possibility of understanding the Bible as an authoritative textual and theological whole: an explicitly delimited and fixed whole in terms of which one may understand its constituent parts.[2] The Scriptures of the church, with their rich web of inter- and intratextual meaning, have traditionally been considered to form such a unified whole; but with the rise of historical criticism in the eighteenth century, the traditional ecclesial view of the scriptural canon came into question.[3]

This tension between historic-critical biblical interpretation and the ecclesial reality of the canon results from two different modes of thinking: on the one hand, a reasoning shaped (or prejudiced) by the Christian tradition;[4] on the other hand, one marked by historical criticism. The modern question of the canon and its justification is a question of critical thought, largely raised in the wake of the Enlightenment.

Furthermore, it is a question that presupposes consciousness of the canon as an already existing reality within the faith community. Implicitly or explicitly, contemporary biblical and Bible-related scholarship therefore has to reckon

---

[2]   That is, the parts are understood in light of the whole and vice versa.

[3]   On the necessity of free Bible exegesis 'for the sake of a free Bible', see Barth, *CD*, I/1, 106.

[4]   Against the modern Enlightenment's radical 'prejudice against prejudices' and its maxim 'we can know better', with which it chose to approach tradition, the German Enlightenment, in Gadamer's wording, recognized the 'true' prejudices of the Christian religion. 'Since the human intellect is too weak to manage without prejudices, it is at least fortunate to have been educated with true prejudices'. Gadamer, *Truth and Method* (New York: Continuum, 1989), 272f.

with the canon as a historically given.[5] The canon viewed from this perspective can be perceived as an irreversible, though not altogether unalterable, ecclesial construction and reading of the biblical writings. 'Canonical' or 'classical' status here means that it cannot be explained wholly by reference to its circumstances of origin or any other single scheme of interpretation.[6]

The problem with the critical historical approach, therefore, is its neglect of the effective-historical movement from the past into the present – a movement that draws critical attention to the work being studied in the first place.[7] As the Norwegian patristic scholar Oskar Skarsaune has pointed out, the discussions on the biblical canon '*presuppose* a canon which is already there'.[8] When the canonical process has come to an end and reached its 'fulfilment', only then can the conversation regarding the exact scope of the writings in the margins begin.[9] At that moment of development, an awareness of a whole – of unity

---

[5] Cf. Robert Jenson's critical remark in this regard, *Systematic Theology,* vol. 1: *The Triune God* (New York: Oxford University Press, 1997), 59. Jenson's attempt at bridging ecclesial and historic-critical readings is thought-provoking (ibid., 174f.). Cf. also the volume edited by Birger Olsson (*Kristna tolkningar av Gamla Testamentet* [Stockholm: Verbum, 1997]), a collection of essays, mainly by Swedish scholars, discussing Christian interpretations of the Old Testament from a wide variety of perspectives and concerns. In common for all of them, however, is the weight variously ascribed to these writings. They are not just past history, not even when seen from an historical viewpoint. Even for an ecclesial canonical reading – i.e. when viewing this disparate collection of writings from a Christian horizon, as a whole, and as the regular textual basis of proclamation – this indirect witness to the 'authority' of these Scriptures seems to be most important; see also Cristina Grenholm, *The Old Testament, Christianity and Pluralism*, Beiträge zur Geschichte der biblischen Exegese 33 (Tübingen: Mohr Siebeck, 1996).
[6] According to David Tracy ('Writing', in *Critical Terms for Religious Studies*, ed. M. C. Taylor, [Chicago: University of Chicago Press, 1998]), there is reason to distinguish between the two categories of canon and classic. In the present work I am using the concept of classic as a dimension of canon (see section 2.6).
[7] So Watson, *Text and Truth: Redefining Biblical Theology* (Edinburgh: T&T Clark, and Grand Rapids: Eerdmans, 1998), 49; and Gadamer, *TM*, 287: 'The classical is something that resists historical criticism because its historical dominion, the binding power of the validity that is preserved and handed down, precedes all historical reflection and continues in it.' Cf. Jeanrond, *Text and Interpretation as Categories of Theological Thinking* (Dublin: Gill and Macmillan, 1988), 13
[8] Skarsaune, *Loven, Profetene og Skriftene: Jødedommens Bible: kanon og tekst* (Oslo: Verbum, 1984), 170; and idem, *Kodeks og kanon: om brug og avgrensning av de gammeltestamentlige skrifter i oldkirken* (Oslo: Verbum, 1994), 241.
[9] On the formation of the New Testament books into a canon, see Chs 4 and 7. See also Stuhlmacher (*How To Do Biblical Theology*, Princeton Theological Monograph Series, 38 [Eugene, OR: Pickwick Publications, 1995], 53–71), who discusses a Christian core canon consisting of an Old Testament and some 20 New Testament writings which were practically never disputed in the early church. Cf. also Barton, *The Spirit and the Letter: Studies in the Biblical Canon* (London: SPCK, 1997), 20: 'The statistics of citation in the second century provide little evidence for disputes about 'the canon'. Everyone used much the same Scriptures as the essential core, and controversies, such as there were, concentrated on the edges of what would later be the canon: on questions such as whether particular books were to be rejected altogether or allowed a subordinate place, whether there were one, two, or three genuine Johannine epistles, or whether Hebrews was really Pauline and hence *as* authoritative as the letters that certainly were.'

in diversity within this particular historical process – is not only sensed but acted upon by means of ardent discussions on canonical function and scope. In fact, what characterizes such attempts of delimitation also always includes knowledge of what is on both sides of it.[10]

2.2 Viewing the canonical process as an integral whole

Within a Christian setting, when focusing attention on the emerging New Testament, the idea of a canon or canonical tradition that is already present can be perceived. In addition to the various canonical functions of the Jesus logia in Paul and the Synoptics, of the Gospel of Mark in Matthew's Gospel, and of the Pauline tradition in 1-2 Peter, the canon of Israel's Scriptures here provides a sheer *given*, the canon *as Scripture* which is there, and so sets the agenda for the new, larger and modified canon – the result of a 'secondary' canonization of Scripture. The fact that this process is best described and appropriated as set in relation to the 'primary' Jewish canon provides not only the necessary continuity between the two main parts of the new scriptural corpus, but also their respective relations, primary in relation to what is secondary, an old process in relation to a new, and vice versa. That is, the particular relationship, from a Christian vantage point, can be understood as primary and secondary, old and new, first and second only in a most specific sense; the Scriptures of Early Judaism here make up the canonical prototype (cf. Josephus, *Against Apion* 1.37–43). What is historically primary is, from another – i.e. a christological – vantage point, theologically secondary, and the other way around. The movement between these two textual corpora makes up, not only a motive force for the canonical process, but also the 'glue' or 'energy', enabling the specific inter- and intratextual play that helps constitute the Old and the New Testaments as a textual whole. In line with the term 'the Lord' (ὁ κύριος) within this intertextual matrix – representing a binitarian interpretation of the Godhead[11] – likewise 'the Scriptures' becomes a means of denoting the Jewish Scriptures and the new Christian Scriptures as a coherent

---

[10] Cf. Gadamer, *TM*, 343.
[11] See Ch. 3; cf. Hurtado, *One God, One Lord: Early Christian Devotion and Ancient Jewish Monotheism* (Edinburgh: T&T Clark, 1998).

whole. The identities of the two categories 'Lord' and 'Scripture' are the same as before – that is, their Jewishness is preserved. However, at the same time they undergo a metamorphosis, turning out to be something different. Without this sameness in difference – in various other respects as well – the emerging Christian community cannot be understood as fundamentally part of a Jewish identity or belonging.[12]

Regarding the specifically Christian literary writings that became the New Testament, therefore, in their relation to this whole – to the Old Testament and to one another – it was the event of Jesus understood against the backdrop of Early Jewish understanding of Scripture that gave rise to the apostolic teaching of the Name, alongside the new scriptural intratextuality and narrative potential. This, in turn, motivated or even necessitated their inclusion into the scriptural canon.[13] A narrative general interpretation, initiated within the apostolic circle, was itself the principle of their gathering, and thus also of the transmutation of the old Scriptures into something new: an enlarged and in principle closed literary corpus.[14] In Robert Jenson's phrasing: 'The church's continuing practice of proclamation and prayer, and the collection of Scripture as it was gradually shaped, were simply versions in two media of the same story.'[15] Two phases in the canon development illustrating this activity (of collecting authoritative texts and Jesus traditions within the Christian community) arguably occurred in the mid- to late first and the early second centuries, with the initial steps taken towards a Pauline letter corpus,[16] and with the notion of 'Gospel' conceived of as a written text,

---

[12] Within their liturgical framing these early Christian concepts, such as 'Lord' and 'Scripture', could not be properly understood without consideration of their Jewish background (cf. Ch. 7). As the theologian and Judaica scholar Roger Beckwith points out ('The Jewish Background to Christian Worship', in *The Study of Liturgy*, (eds) C. Jones et al. [London: SPCK, rev. edn. 1992], 68.): 'in their practice, Jesus and his first followers conformed to a large extent to Jewish customs. When, therefore, the question is asked against what background Christian worship arose, the only answer that can be given is Jewish worship.'

[13] Cf. Jenson, *Systematic Theology*, vol. 1, where name and narrative are treated as a unity. On the Name, see further Chs 3 and 8.

[14] Cf. Jenson, *Systematic Theology*, vol. 1, 30; and idem, *Systematic Theology*, vol. 2: *The Works of God* (New York: Oxford University Press, 1999), 274. Cf. also Stuhlmacher, *How To Do Biblical Theology*, 54: In light of Heb 1.1-2 and in order for the whole of God's revelation in His Son to be heard, Stuhlmacher comments: 'The saving word of God is only fully heard when the γραφαὶ ἅγιαι are understood in the light of the appearance of Jesus Christ and read together with the witness of the apostles.'

[15] Jenson, *Systematic Theology*, vol. 2, 274. Cf. my argument above on the expansion and canonical interpreting of the Scriptures as part of one and the same hermeneutical act.

[16] For an updated discussion, see Porter, 'Paul and the Process of Canonization', in *Exploring the Origins of the Bible*, (eds) Evans and Tov (Grand Rapids: Baker, 2008), 173–202. As part of his

arguably already in Matthew (24.14 and 26.13) and in the *Didache* (8.2; 11.3; 15.3–4f.).[17]

As this emerging collection of scriptures has been traditionally analysed, various dogmatic, historical and literary models have been applied to explain the growth of the New Testament material into diverse forms of unified wholes.[18] However, these attempts at understanding the canonical process have often been lacking in coherence. To begin with, they have not accounted for the relevance of the process for 'the actual shaping of the New Testament literature itself'.[19] As Brevard Childs kept emphasizing from the 1970s on, canonization is something inherent in the shaping on all levels of the biblical literature. Furthermore, due to the historico-critical methods that have been commonly used, one can see a fundamental lack of awareness in the exchange of prejudices when switching from that of the ecclesial dogmatic tradition to the prejudice of reason as set by the standards of the Enlightenment.[20] Rather, one finds too much emphasis on general historical analysis. Consequently, the specific history and concern for whose attestation the church assembled this collection in the first place – the Incarnation and Resurrection of Christ – is largely neglected.[21]

Speaking with Gadamer, the potential authority claimed for the Christian tradition through this corpus of biblical writings comes to expression by the sheer fact that what is written down is not altogether easy to realize as something that can be untrue:

> The written word has the tangible quality of something that can be demonstrated and is like a proof. It requires a special critical effort to free oneself from

---

conclusion on p. 202 Porter writes: 'there is reasonable evidence to see the origin of the Pauline corpus during the latter part of Paul's life or sometime after his death, almost assuredly instigated by Paul and/or a close follower or followers, and close examination of the early manuscripts with Paul's letters and of related documents seems to support this hypothesis.'

[17] So Stanton, *Jesus and Gospel* (Cambridge: Cambridge University Press, 2004), 52–9; cf. Kelhoffer, 'How Soon a Book' Revisited: ΕΥΑΓΓΕΛΙΟΝ as a Reference to "Gospel" Materials in the First Half of the Second Century', *ZNW* 95 (2004): 1–34. For a brief discussion of *Barn.* 4.14, see Bokedal, 'Scripture in the Second Century', in *The Sacred Text: Excavating the Texts, Exploring the Interpretations, and Engaging the Theologies of the Christian Scriptures*, (eds) M. Bird and M. Pahl (Piscataway, NJ: Gorgias, 2010), 49.

[18] Childs, *The New Testament as Canon: An Introduction* (London: SCM, 1984), 5–15.

[19] Ibid., 9f.

[20] See Gadamer, *TM*, esp. 271–85. Cf. also idem, *Philosophical Hermeneutics* (Berkeley: University of California Press, 1976), 29: 'Only a naive and unreflective historicism in hermeneutics would see the historical-hermeneutical sciences as something absolutely new that would do away with the power of "tradition"'.

[21] Jenson, *Systematic Theology*, vol. 1, 59.

the prejudice in favor of what is written down and to distinguish here also, no
less than in the case of oral assertions, between opinion and truth.[22]

That the written word in some early Christian circles was appropriated as
written in an eminent sense, most noteworthy in the *Corpus Johanneum* (1
John 2, Rev. 1.3, 11, 19; 2.1; 21.5),[23] underscores its quality as true within the
range of meaning set by the (local) Christian tradition. This implies, in various
ways, that the canonical process – here coming to expression through the act
of gradually putting into writing and editing to the same effect – is an indispensable part of the biblical literature understood as a whole. That is to say,
canonization is neither simply a question of discretely adding newly written
and specifically Christian texts, i.e. texts understood as beforehand being
isolated from the Scriptures, to an already existing corpus of Scriptures;[24] nor
is it a question of simply reconstructing the original canon development. In
fact, it is not possible to harbour such a view of an objective whole, excluding
the horizon of the present situation. When the question of the canonizing
process is raised, an ecclesially affected view of the process as a whole needs
to be taken into account. As Hegel, in Gadamer's phrasing, understands the
historical task: 'the essential nature of the historical spirit consists not in the
restoration of the past but in *thoughtful mediation with contemporary life.*'[25]
To this extent, a hermeneutics that regarded understanding as only reconstructing the original would be no more than handing on dead meaning.[26]
Rather, 'canon consciousness' as the *telos* and thereby the driving force and
outcome of the process is to be found all through the different stages of
transmission. That is to say, canon is primarily a historically effected 'ecclesial

---

[22] Gadamer, *TM*, 272.

[23] See further, e.g. Smith, 'When Did the Gospels Become Scripture?', *JBL* 119 (2000): 3–20.

[24] Cf. ibid. The OT as Scripture was presupposed when Matthew was being written down. None
the less, as Smith argues, this Gospel was itself presented as Scripture from the very moment of
writing it down. In this way Matthew and other apostolic texts come into existence from within the
Christian biblical narrative tradition, being part of a canonical process.

[25] Gadamer, *TM*, 168f. Also, as Hegel indicates, in order to be in a position to perceive an historical
phenomenon, an appropriate perspective is needed.

[26] Ibid., 167 (where Gadamer discusses the experience of art); that is, understanding is more than
reconstructing the original. Cf. ibid., 296, where the understanding of texts is described as both
a productive and reproductive activitiy. Focused above are hermeneutical and effective-historical
concerns; for the place of traditional historical-critical scholarship in biblical studies, see, e.g.
Barton, *Reading the Old Testament: Method in Biblical Study* (London: Darton, Longman and Todd,
1996); and Hagner and Young, 'The Historical-Critical Method and the Gospel of Matthew', in
Methods for Matthew, ed. M. A. Powell, Methods in Biblical Interpretation (Cambridge: Cambridge
University Press, 2009), 11–43.

consciousness' of the transmitted prophetic and apostolic texts as address and criterion.[27]

In the present chapter I assume the task of providing two kinds of historical analyses: On the one hand, a reconstruction of some aspects of the early ecclesiastical concept of canon pertaining to the development of the new corpus of Sacred Scriptures; and, on the other hand, a reconstruction as part of a hermeneutics of tradition that not only aims at the restoration of something past, but mediates with the contemporary ecclesial situation for which the canon is of concern. Both these aims take their point of departure in the biblical text as part of a living ecclesial tradition, focusing on the unity of the content of the scriptural transmission.[28] In this way, Childs's primary concern, that of seeing the canonical process as an inherent part of the biblical material itself, and Gadamer's analysis of the necessary hermeneutical dimension of historical research, are both taken into account.[29] In Gadamer's wording: 'The true historical object is not an object at all, but the unity of the one and the other, a relationship that constitutes both the reality of history and the reality of historical understanding.'[30] When applied to the scriptural canon, two scholarly focal points come to the fore: 1) the possibility for the biblical material itself to provide a principal context for, and to further, the canonical process[31] and, 2) the possibility for such a process-marked tradition to function, for every new situation, as literature with a unique effective-history. These focal points find support, although from another perspective, in Gerd Theissen's *A Theory of Primitive Christian Religion*, as he elaborates on the systemic, self-organizing character of religious sign languages.

---

[27] As with other forms of understanding, understanding the canon '*is to be thought of less as a subjective act than as participating in an event of tradition*, a process of transmission in which past and present are constantly mediated', Gadamer, *WM*, 295; *TM*, 290 (italics original).

[28] Gadamer, *TM*, 179. As Gadamer points out elsewhere, texts always express a whole: 'Meaningless strokes that seem strange and incomprehensible prove suddenly intelligible in every detail when they can be interpreted as writing – so much so that even the arbitrariness of a corrupt text can be corrected if the context as a whole is understood.' Ibid., 390. Gadamer's view on writing here significantly differs from that of postmodern deconstructionist theorists, such as Jacques Derrida.

[29] As for the time needed for the understanding of the canon emerging out of a canonical process, i.e. the canonical development understood as a whole, cf. Schleiermacher (*Werke*, I, part 7, 33; cited from Gadamer, *TM*, 192): 'nothing that needs interpretation can be understood at once.'

[30] Gadamer, *TM*, 299.

[31] Cf. Stuhlmacher, *How To Do Bilical Theology*, 61: 'Today, there is even agreement among Protestant and Catholic theologians over the statement that the churches did not simply create the Bible themselves, but that the biblical revelation was the motivating force of the canonical process.'

Generally speaking, a system, Theissen maintains,[32] has the ability *to organize itself* from its own centre. Moreover, it has the ability to distinguish itself from its environment – i.e. to differentiate between *reference to itself* and *reference to outsiders*. In the present investigation, the notion of canon and the canonical process with its distinguished effective-history may be described as such a system. It has the predilection *to organize itself* from its own centre and *to demarcate itself* from its environment.[33] Beside the doctrinal remark that the Spirit of God guides the formation of the church's canon,[34] this presumed systemic character is the very foundation of there being a coherent and unifying process of canonization in the first place, rooted in what we may refer to as the apostolic system-organizing code 'the Scriptures and the Lord'.

2.3 A process of organic continuity

At a closer look, we may notice a rather self-evident rationale behind the formation of the Christian Bible. It emerges as an integral part of the process of fixation and structuring of the Jesus-tradition ('the Lord'); and as the transmission of the apostolic tradition (including the Jewish Scriptures) to the dispersed faith communities.[35] As such it is an event of preservation and

---

[32] Theissen, *A Theory of Primitive Christian Religion* (London: SCM, 1999), 5.

[33] Ernst Käsemann's 'no' to the question posed in his famous lecture, 'Is the New Testament Canon the Foundation for Church Unity?', diverges from the view presented here (Käsemann, 'The Canon of the New Testament and the Unity of the Church', in idem, *Essays on New Testament Themes* [London: SCM, 1968]).

[34] Cf. Pannenberg, *Systematic Theology*, vol. 1 (Grand Rapids: Eerdmans, 1991), 31f.

[35] This process of formation spans from the earliest oral to the redactional and later stages of tradition transmission. See Schneemelcher, 'Bibel III: Die Entstehung des Kanons des Neuen Testaments und der christlichen Bibel', in *TRE*, vol. 6 (Berlin and New York: Walter de Gruyter, 1980). On the relation between prejudices in favour of a person, on the one hand, and a content, on the other, see Gadamer, *TM*, 280. See also Bauckham (*For Whom Were Gospels Written?*, in *The Gospels for All Christians: Rethinking the Gospel Audiences*, ed. R. Bauckham [Grand Rapids: Eerdmans, 1998], 9–48), who comments on geographical aspects of the early Christian transmission of the gospel tradition by means of writing. He argues that '[t]he obvious function of writing was its capacity to communicate widely with readers unable to be present at its author's oral teaching'. He then concludes in a note that '[t]he evidence suggests that in early Christianity this function of writing (communication across space) was more important than the ability of writing to give permanence (communication over time)'. None the less, the other dimension of writing, communication over time, is an immediate extention of the former (communication across space). For some New Testament texts, e.g. the Johannine writings, Luke, and the late letters of the *Corpus Paulinum*, the temporal motive even appears to be primary or, at least, equally important. In these writings it seems difficult to make any sharp distinction between the two dimensions. In either case, and of interest for the present study, they are both ingredients in the emerging concept and criterion of catholicity (see Ch. 9).

actualization of traditions of first- and early second-century Christianity. This supports an early beginning of the Christian canon.[36] As Wilhelm Schneemelcher points out, the core of the notion of the New Testament canon grew out of 'internal ecclesiastical motives', such as the fixation of the authentic and true tradition (*Festlegung der echten und wahren Tradition*).[37] However, it is also the case, as B. F. Westcott, Adolf von Harnack and Schneemelcher himself underscore, that the canon formation is an intrinsic part of 'the entire church and doctrine-historical development'.[38] Nevertheless, these two entities – the church's canon, on the one hand, and church history and church dogmatics, on the other – though never separated, can and must be distinguished, due to the canon's basic function of address and criterion, for the church to persist.[39]

This is in line with von Harnack's statement nearly a century ago, that we have the nucleus of the emerging New Testament in the formula 'the Scriptures and the Lord' (αἱ γραφαὶ καὶ ὁ κύριος). Already in the Apostolic Age this was interchangeable with the formula 'the Scriptures and the Gospel' (αἱ γραφαὶ καὶ τὸ εὐαγγέλιον).[40] Von Harnack here suggests a dynamic view of the canon formation as a process, around which the present study evolves.[41]

---

[36] Cf. Balla, *Challenges to New Testament Theology: An Attempt to Justify the Enterprise* (Tübingen: Mohr Siebeck, 1997), 98.

[37] Schneemelcher, 'Bibel III: Die Entstehung des Kanons des Neuen Testaments und der christlichen Bibel', 46.

[38] Ibid., 23: 'die gesamte kirchen- und dogmengeschichtliche Entwicklung'; cf. Balla, *Challenges to New Testament Theology: An Attempt to Justify the Enterprise*, 96; Westcott, *A General Survey of the History of the Canon of the New Testament* (London and New York: Macmillan, 1896): 'It cannot be too often repeated, that the history of the formation of the whole Canon involves little less than the history of the building of the Catholic Church', 1–15. However, cf. John Webster in Ch. 1, n. 21.

[39] See, e.g. Barth, *CD*, I/1, 99–111. Cf. Joseph Ratzinger's and Wolfhart Pannenberg's remarks in this respect; Ratzinger, *Das zweite Vatikanische Konzil*, II, (eds) Brechter et al. (Freiburg: Herder, 1968), 520; and Pannenberg, *Systematic Theology*, vol. 1, 31. See also *Dei Verbum* 21, in *Concilio Vaticano II*, B. A. C. (Madrid: La Editorial Catolica, 3rd edn, 1966), 176.

[40] Harnack, *The Origin of the New Testament and the Most Important Consequences of the New Creation* (London: Williams & Norgate, 1925). See further Ch. 1. Cf. in this regard also Marxen, *Introduction to the New Testament* (Philadelphia: Fortress, 1968), 282f.: 'The real Canon is prior to the New Testament ... It is impossible, therefore, to describe the New Testament as it stands at present as the Canon, for in the strict sense only the apostolic testimony to Jesus as the Divine revelation can be described as canonical. On the other hand, however, this Canon can only be arrived at via the New Testament.' Such a genetic-historical perspective does not have to exclude an approach to the New Testament on the textual or redactional level, as hinted at in the above citation.

[41] However, many scholars following Zahn (*Geschichte des Neutestamentlichen Kanons*, vol. 1 [Erlangen: Verlag von Andreas Deichert, 1888], 83), Campenhausen (*The Formation of the Christian Bible* [Philadelphia: Fortress, 1972]) or Sundberg ('Towards a Revised History of the New Testament Canon', *Studia Evangelica* 3 [Berlin: Akademie-Verlag, 1968]), are not inclined to accept

A canonizing process emerging out of a nucleus accords well also with Theissen's argument regarding the systemic character of religious sign languages (cf. section 2.2). In treating the Bible canon as such a language, the formula(s) laid out by von Harnack embodying the inner motive force of the canonical process expresses the two discussed systemic characteristics: the ability 1) *to organize itself* from its own centre (not unlike the function of the genetic code of a cell),[42] and 2) to distinguish itself from its environment – i.e. to differentiate between *reference to itself* and *reference to outsiders*.[43] To this extent the canon's primary function as criterion, and as address to the church, depends on the eventual success of this process.

Harnack's formula, then, is not only a short form for the canonical process, it largely explains it. In retrospect, therefore, 'the Scriptures and the Lord' can be viewed as the formulation of a program, the canonization of normative textual tradition drawing up lines of organic continuity within this particular historical process. As for the formation of the New Testament part of the emerging canon, the two intertwined traditions here focused, the role of the *Scriptures* and of the *Lord*, lay the pattern of continuity for the process as a whole. The continuity of such traditions is stressed by Brevard Childs, who argues that

> the issue of canon turns on the authoritative role played by particular traditions for a community of faith and practices. Canon consciousness thus arose at the inception of the Christian church and lies deep within the New Testament literature itself. There is an organic continuity in the historical process of the development of an established canon of sacred writings from the earliest stages of the New Testament to the final canonical stabilization of its scope.[44]

Adolf von Harnack, too, comes close to the view of the New Testament canon development as a teleological process, traceable from particularly important theological traditions:

> A simple 'collection' of writings need not be final; rather it can even more or less purposely be left open, especially if it serves ends (such as public reading) which

---

as meaningful either Harnack's dogmatic-linguistic twist of the problem (critiqued by Zahn and Sundberg) or Harnack's early date for the beginning of the canonization of the New Testament.

[42] Cf. Childs's use of the expression 'organic continuity' in the citation below.

[43] Cf. the canonical formula, Ch. 8.

[44] Childs, *The New Testament as Canon*, 21. The quote coninues: 'That the continuity was hammered out in continuous conflict is also true.'

do not forbid enrichment from the stores of the present. And yet a collection of fundamental documents has already *the tendency to become final*, and certainly a collection of fundamental documents of a *Covenant* carries in itself the idea of complete finality. It is also certain that a compilation of writings is always in danger of disintegration if it is not in some way limited, in *idea* at least. A hundred years ago Novalis advanced the very reasonable question: 'Who declared the Bible (the Canon of the New Testament) to be closed?' Our answer to the question is: The idea, firmly held, that the new books were fundamental documents *of the Second Covenant* which God had established through Jesus Christ, was the intellectual originator of the 'closed' *instrumentum novum*.[45]

Von Harnack here draws our attention to a central aspect of the New Testament canon formation.[46] For one thing, to the extent that strong theological forces, such as that of the new covenant notion (as set in relation to the symbolic universe of another, older one), come to function teleologically, a collection of fundamental documents of such a covenant appears to carry in itself 'the idea of complete finality'. Further, the theological potential inherent in the grand themes of Covenant (Testament), Lord and Scripture do seem to function as 'intellectual originators' of the act of preserving these particular traditions by means of a bipartite Bible. This act has hermeneutical implications, not only for the early church in its interpretation of Scripture, but also for the present ecclesiastical situation. The ecclesial categories of Lord, Covenant and Scripture, inherent in the notion of canon, cannot be understood in isolation, but are continuously interpreted in light of one another. The communicative perspective of the latter – that is, of Scripture – embraces the two former categories through the hermeneutical-editorial function of the (supra-)textual marker K̄C̄, 'Lord', and the other *nomina sacra* (see Ch. 3 below), and through the rubrics 'Old' and 'New Testament' applied to the entire collection of Christian Scriptures from the late second century on.[47]

To the extent that our emphasis of organic continuity in the process of canon formation can be described as various acts of preservation, including

---

[45] Harnack, *The Origin of the New Testament*, 33f.; see also Zahn, *Grundriss der Geschichte des Neutestamentlichen Kanons: Eine Ergänzung zu der Einleitung in das Neue Testament* (Leipzig: A. Deichert'sche Verlagsbuchh. Nachf. [Georg Böhme], 1901), 11: 'Die Vorstellung einer *abgeschlossenen Sammlung von Offenbarungsurkunden* ist früher durch παλαιά und καινή διαθήκη ausgedrückt worden, und die Zugehörigkeit zu dieser seit Origenes durch ἐνδιάθηκος.'

[46] Cf. Müller, 'The Hidden Context: Some Observations to the Concept of the New Covenant in the New Testament' (Oslo, Copenhagen, Stockholm and Boston: Scandinavian University Press, 1995).

[47] See Chs 3 and 4.

self-preservation, a similar approach may be taken towards another related theme: the notion of the classic.

2.4 Canon and the concept of the classic

Some years ago the literary critic Northrop Frye offered a vivid definition of the term 'classic', identifying it as primarily 'a work that refuses to go away, that remains confronting us until we do something about it, which means also doing something about ourselves'.[48] In this way, Frye maintains, the canon of Scripture eventually comes to function as *the* literary classic, not only for the church in the narrower sense, but also for the wider Christian community, as the Great Code of (Western) Christian culture.[49] This understanding of the church's canon implies an historical and a normative aspect, both of which ask for contextualization in the present situation. Precisely as classic, then, the canon has the potential of surviving the contingencies of history, as well as historical reflection. In Gadamer's phrasing: '[t]he classical is something that resists historical criticism because its historical dominion, the binding power of the validity that is preserved and handed down, precedes all historical reflection and continues in it.'[50] Inasmuch as it functions as classic for the present, Gadamer puts forth the classical as a 'truly historical category, precisely because it is more than a concept of a period or of a historical style.'[51] His presentation of the general category of the classical thereby applies straightforwardly to an important aspect of the ecclesial process of scriptural canonization:

> It does not refer to a quality that we ascribe to particular historical phenomena but to a notable mode of being historical: the historical process of preservation (Bewahrung) that, through constantly proving itself (Bewährung), allows something true (ein Wahres) to come into being.[52]

The biblical canon *as classic* is repeatedly defined by its historical roots, and by constantly confronting us in the present. This means that the canon is

---

[48] Frye, 'The Double Mirror', *Bulletin of the American Academy of Arts and Sciences* 35 (1981): 32–41.
[49] See Young, *Biblical Exegesis and the Formation of Christian Culture* (Cambridge: Cambridge University Press, 1997).
[50] Gadamer, *TM*, 287.
[51] Ibid.
[52] Ibid.

there as a profoundly historical category for the present – a unity of past and present constituting 'both the reality of history and the reality of historical understanding.'[53] Ultimately the canon and its formation is always also a matter of reception.

The element of reception is, in fact, already embraced in these discussions. The question is whether it is even possible to envision the birth of the canon or its appropriation at a particular moment or location. It rather appears as a process extended in time and space, in one sense prolonged also beyond the critical period and the places of formation of the early Christian centuries. Canonization, then, is both the justification and the outcome of established usage of certain scriptures, continuously received as Scripture. There can be no Old and New Testament for the contemporary situation without this continuous history of canon reception.

The specific reason for the reception of something classical, such as the emerging scriptural canon, is 'a consciousness of something enduring, of significance that cannot be lost and that is independent of all the circumstances of time – a kind of timeless present that is contemporaneous with every other present.'[54] In that spirit, as classical Scripture, the early church received the Law and the Prophets, the Holy Writ of the synagogue and the Temple, by quoting and using it as Christian Scripture – very much, *mutatis mutandis*, along the lines of Second Temple and Rabbinic Judaism.[55] In the parallel process of separation from the synagogue and the continuous usage of the Jewish Scriptures, a Christian 'recanonization' appears to have taken place, in the sense of a rereading and a reorganization of the Scriptures. The Jewish Torah-oriented pattern of interpretation was (gradually) exchanged for a new centring, on the one hand, in the interpretive midpoint of a Christian 'proof-from-prophecy' pattern,[56] and, on the other, in the gospel narrative.

Two features are to be noted. First, even though the Jewish canon *as shape*

---

[53] See n. 30 above.

[54] Gadamer, *TM*, 299.

[55] See, e.g. Childs, *Introduction to the Old Testament as Scripture* (London: SCM, 1979), 659–71; Hvalvik, *The Struggle for Scripture and Covenant: the purpose of the epistle of Barnabas and Jewish-Christian competition in the second century* (Tübingen: Mohr Siebeck, 1996).

[56] That is, the early Christian foreshadowing-fulfilment pattern of biblical reading. As for the second- and third-century church, in addition to the dominating 'proof from prophecy' tradition, Skarsaune mentions the *paraenetic homily* and 'Biblical Antiquities' as two alternative Christian genres dealing with Old Testament interpretation ('Scriptural Interpretation in the Second and Third Centuries', 376).

remained largely intact for the early church, this canon *as function* changed.[57] Second, a Christian experience of 'timeless present' of these Scriptures prepared the ground for the turn in canonical function.

In the course of time, as the Christian communities more definitely parted from the synagogues, a new subtle development of the biblical canon took place in some church regions as apocryphal writings, sometimes with Christian glosses, were increasingly being used (cf. section 8.3.5). At the same time a restrictive tendency – partly as a counter reaction with regard to these writings – could be observed in Jewish as well as in Christian communities.

In line with these early restrictions, the hypothesis stemming from the eighteenth and nineteenth centuries of the existence of a larger Alexandrian canon inherited by the early church has proved inaccurate.[58] Already Philo of Alexandria (ca. 20 BC–AD 50), throughout his extensive literary production, bears witness to a use of Scripture corresponding to the Palestinian custom. He never cites the apocryphal writings as Scripture, and in that regard he seems to be in agreement with Josephus on the canonical shape.[59] Similarly, Ben Sira, the authors of the Maccabees, Hillel, Shammai and all the first-century Tannaim never cite or include the apocryphal writings among the Scriptures.[60] Christians largely seem to have followed this Jewish practice from the outset; but, gradually, the use of a broader selection of Scriptures can be observed in some early writers such as Clement of Alexandria.[61] As will be

---

[57] Cf. Childs, *Introduction to the Old Testament as Scripture*, 659–71. See also Ch. 1.

[58] Hengel and Deines, 'Die Septuaginta als "christliche Schriftensammlung" und das Problem ihres Kanons', in *Verbindliches Zeugnis*, vol. 1: *Kanon – Schrift – Tradition*, (eds) W. Pannenberg and T. Schneider (Freiburg im Breisgau: Herder and Göttingen: Vandenhoeck & Ruprecht, 1992), 35f.; Sundberg, *The Old Testament of the Early Church* (Cambridge: Harvard University Press, 1964); Beckwith, *The Old Testament Canon of the New Testament Church and its Background in Early Judaism* (Grand Rapids: Eerdmans, 1985), 382–6; and McDonald, *The Biblical Canon: Its Origin, Transmission, and Authority* (Peabody, MA: Hendrickson, 2007), 100–3.

[59] See ibid.; Mason, 'Josephus and His Twenty-Two Book Canon', in *The Canon Debate*, (eds) L. M. McDonald and J. A. Sanders (Peabody, MA: Hendrickson, 2002), 110–27; and Ellis, *The Old Testament in Early Christianity: Canon and Interpretation in the Light of Modern Research* (Grand Rapids: Baker Book House, 1991), 8f.

[60] So Childs (*Biblical Theology of the Old and New Testaments* [London: SCM, 1992], 60), in agreement with Sid Leiman, Roger Beckwith, Earle Ellis and others (*pace* Martin Hengel, Hartmut Gese and Peter Stuhlmacher). Childs draws the conclusion that 'at least within the circles of rabbinic Judaism a concept of an established Hebrew canon with a relatively fixed scope of writings and an increasingly stabilized authoritative text had emerged by the first century BC.' Cf. also Cross, *From Epic to Canon: History and Literature in Ancient Israel* (Baltimore and London: Johns Hopkins University Press), 219–29.

[61] See Hengel and Deines, *Die Septuaginta als 'christliche Schriftensammlung' und das Problem ihres Kanons*; Osborn, *Clement of Alexandria* (Cambridge: Cambridge University Press, 2005), 76.

demonstrated below (Chs 4 and 8), the church, despite this development, largely adhered to the narrower canonical scope as defined by Pharisaic and Rabbinic Judaism (see section 8.5.3).[62]

In the reception of canon and of classics generally, the time element of a particular tradition as well as the inherent qualities, such as style and content, are to be noticed. The concept of the classical combines both an historical and a normative side.[63] As developed by Gadamer, Ricoeur, Tracy, Jeanrond and others, the category of the classic is a category of reception.[64] This feature needs to be emphasized, also regarding the canon *as classic*. Otherwise, the risk of historicizing is always there. The Swedish theologian Henry Cöster has made a distinction between a 'history of accumulation' and a 'history of reception', which may be useful in order to underline not only the passivity but the element of activity inherent in all reception. He also points out that, 'as soon as it has become passed history, it is no longer a question of reception, but rather a result of a specific need and reaction of a particular historical situation.'[65]

For the majority church the formation and usage of the biblical canon is not so much a 'history of accumulation', but a matter of reception, which centres in a continuous assessment, appropriation and theological reading of the biblical texts.[66] In fact, '[w]orks which become classics are accorded authority by the community, but do so because they seem to have an authority of their own.'[67] The historical dimension remains, but in the context of a living community it will constantly be reassessed and conquered anew.[68]

---

[62] Cf. Cross (*From Epic to Canon: History and Literature in Ancient Israel* [Baltimore and London: Johns Hopkins University Press, 1998], 219–29), to whom Hillel and Josephus are central witnesses for his reconstruction of the stabilization of the Canon of the Hebrew Bible.

[63] Gadamer, *TM*, 286f.

[64] Jeanrond, *Text and Interpretation*, 140.

[65] Cöster, *Kyrkans historia och historiens kyrka* (Stockholm/Stehag: Symposion, 1989), 28; my translation.

[66] On theological reading, see Morgan and Barton, *Biblical Interpretation* (New York: Oxford University Press, 1988), 274: 'The main conclusion, or rather thesis, of this book is that anyone who uses the Bible as scripture engages (whether knowingly or not) in theological interpretation.' See also Jeanrond, *Text and Interpretation*, 124–27. Cf. Gadamer, *TM*, 287, n. 50.

[67] Young, *Virtuoso Theology: The Bible and Interpretation* (Cleveland, OH: The Pilgrim Press, 1993), 32.

[68] Cf. the hermeneutic maxim – in Hans Robert Jauss's words – 'daß eine Vorgeschichte erst aus der Nachgeschichte einer eingetretenen Wende voll erkennbar werden kann' (Jauss, *Die Theorie der Rezeption – Rückschau auf ihre unerkannte Vorgeschichte* [Konstanz: Universitätsverlag Konstanz GMBH, 1987)], 6). See also the citation from Gregory the Great (Moralia in Iob XX, I, 1; quoted from Jauss, *Die Theorie der Rezeption*, 10): *Scriptura sacra ... aliquo modo cum legentibus crescit* [Holy Scripture grows in some way with the ones who read]. Though Gadamer similarly argues

2.5 Canon: Term and concept

It is now time to draw our attention to the etymology of the term 'canon' with bearing on its ecclesiastical usage. When the word 'canon' was opted for by the early church to designate its Rule of Faith, its ethical code, its Scriptures and their literary scope, the meanings of these constitutive elements for the community of faith were placed within a partly new semantic field. The word 'canon' had its roots in Hellenistic ground. When referring to the Rule of Faith (or the *kerygma*), various aspects of Christian ethics, or the body of biblical writings, the term 'canon' was applied not so much in a new, specifically Christian sense, but according to the conventional, somewhat heterogeneous use of the word in Antiquity. In this section I analyse the Christian concept of canon in relation to this Hellenistic background. I then differentiate between various uses of the concept as applied to the biblical writings.

2.5.1 General meaning of 'canon'

Before elaborating on the early Christian use of the word 'canon', it will be helpful to mention some of its general Greek and Latin connotations. The Greek word κανών is derived from the loan word κάνη, κάννα, based on a Semitic botanic term meaning *reed*. In Hebrew this word is rendered קָנֶה, which from early on attained also the meaning *measuring reed* (cf. Ezekiel 40.3-8; 42.16-19). By further extension, it even came to designate, for example, the *beam of a balance* (Isaiah 46.6).[69]

When the word was transferred to the Greek linguistic context, the basic meaning of κανών became *straight rod*, *bar*, from which were derived several usages of the word with the meaning *straightness*. This was a purely formal denotation, which seemed to exclude reference to material aspects.[70] It was the *straightness*, *to keep a thing straight* that was signified. In Antiquity the

---

along these lines, see, however, *TM*, 331, on his description of the absolute character of Christian Scripture as word of God; cited in section 1.3.2.

[69] Oppel, Κανών *Zur Bedeutungsgeschichte des Wortes und seiner lateinischen Entsprechungen (regula-norma)* (Leipzig: Dieterich'sche Verlagsbuchhandlung, 1937); Zahn, *Grundriss der Geschichte des Neutestamentlichen Kanons*, 1–4; Beyer, 'Kanon', in *Theologisches Wörterbuch zum Neuen Testament*, vol. 3 (Stuttgart: 1937); 600–6; Theron, *Evidence of Tradition* (Grand Rapids: Baker Book House, 1957), 21f.

[70] Oppel, Κανών, 5, 8.

word came to refer to things characterized by straightness, or devices that kept other things straight, such as the level and the plumbline, utilized by carpenters or masons to determine the right direction of material used for building. To the straightness that gave the direction another aspect soon was added, that of *measure*. As for the κανών, the ruddled line used for carpentry, both aspects, that of straightness and that of measure, were relevant. On Latin ground, this was the case also for a tool used by the scribe, namely the ruler, which was called *regula*, the Latin rendering of 'canon'.[71]

From these two basic meanings of the word, *straightness* and *measure*, three areas of figurative senses of 'canon' emerged. In the schema developed by H. Oppel in his extensive study of the term from 1937 these areas are: A) 'Canon' as a catchword for *exactitude* and *precision* (ἀκρίβεια); B) 'Canon' as expression for the Hellenistic notion of *imitation* or *representation* (μίμησις); and C), 'Canon' in connection with the notion of *limit* or *boundary* (ὅρος).

2.5.2 Uses of the word 'canon' in the early church

The church in its various usage of the word drew on the basic sense, *measure*, as well as the three areas of meaning listed above, 'canon' as ἀκρίβεια, μί μησις and ὅρος. The common signification of κανών in the early ecclesial context, accordingly, came to be 1) *measure*; 2) *prototype* or *model*; 3) *norm, rule* or *standard*; 4) *limit* or *boundary*; 5) *tool of exactitude* or *criterion*; 6) *prototype of proportionality and symmetry*; and 7) *table providing a standard*. The meanings attached to the word were, to a varying degree, related to one another. Consequently, two or more of these seven connotations could be drawn on. Still, we are not dealing with a polysemic term, but rather with aspects of meanings of one and the same word, all of which stand in an *etymological* connection to the basic Greek meaning *straight rod, straightness* and *measure*.[72]

Philo and Clement of Alexandria used the word in the second sense within the area of ethics, applying it to the exemplary person, such as Moses, who became a model, a canon, of right behaviour to be imitated. In the field of arts

---

[71] Cf. Metzger, *The Canon of the New Testament: Its Origin, Development, and Significance* (Oxford: Clarendon Press, 1987), 289.
[72] See, e.g. the citation from Aristotle below.

the prototype to be copied likewise was called a 'canon'. 'Canon' in the third sense, as *norm*, *rule* or *standard*, could refer to the religious law, the *nomos*.[73] In this sense, and of particular interest for the present study, Clement of Alexandria also referred to the *Gospel* as canon.[74] When turning to the fourth sense, 'canon' as *limit* or *boundary*, Aristotle provides a fine illustration of the connection between the primary Greek meaning and the figurative meaning of the word by a parable:

> As the workman makes use of the plummet and the level (κανών) in order to investigate even closer that which seems already straight and smooth, in such a way even the politician needs to be in possession of boundaries (ὅρος) by which he can judge what is right, good and beneficial.[75]

In this passage canon is used as a form of ethical concept demanding boundaries (the figurative meaning C, above). The precision by which the workman is said to carry out his work, however, leads us to the figurative meaning A, namely that of ἀκρίβεια, i.e. *exactitude* and *precision* as practised by the good craftsman. Under this category the epistemological concept 'criterion' (κριτήριον) is to be placed as well. This concept acquired the same meaning as 'canon'. The two words were interchangeable in the philosophical terminology of the third and second centuries BC. Similar to the way in which Irenaeus later on speaks of the canon of truth (*regula veritatis*), the Stoics and Epicureans used the concept 'criterion of truth' as a spiritual tool, a spiritual measuring instrument, used for judgement regarding all that can be designated true or false.[76] Another aspect of canon as ἀκρίβεια is found in late Platonic and early Aristotelian ethics, where κανών and ὅρος are terms used to construct an exact ethical science. The ethical ideas were to be defined in order to distinguish the ethical good from the bad, 'for a person must not only be in possession of an undefined feeling for what is good and bad, but it is indeed a matter of clearly knowing the two opposites in their distinctiveness.'[77]

From the examples so far, we have attained references of 'canon' to 1) *a*

---

[73] Oppel, Κανών, 59f., referring to Philo, *De Leg. Spec.* III, 164; and to Clement, *Strom.* I, 167.

[74] Oppel, Κανών, referring to Clement, *Strom.* IV, 15.

[75] *Iambl. Protr.* X.; cited from Oppel, Κανών, 28.

[76] Striker, 'κριτήριον τῆς ἀληθείας', *NAWG.PH* 2 (1974), 53f.; Ohme, *Kanon ekklesiastikos* (Berlin: Walter de Gruyter, 1998), 24.

[77] Oppel, Κανών, 23: 'denn der Mensch soll nicht nur ein unbestimmtes Gefühl für Gutes und Schlechtes besitzen, sondern es gilt in aller Schärfe die Gegensätze zu erkennen'.

measure; 2) *a prototype* or *model*; 3) *a norm, rule* or *standard*; 4) *a limit* or *boundary* and 5) *a tool of exactitude* or *a criterion of truth*. In addition to these five senses, yet another two, as anticipated above, are relevant for the understanding of, for example, Irenaeus' use of the expression 'Rule of Truth' (κανὼν τῆς ἀληθείας) when referring to *the body of regulative Christian teaching*.[78]

Reference to the etymological development of the word, from signifying the craftsman's level to denoting the instrument of the musical theoretician, the κανὼν ἁρμονικός, is due not only to the straight form of the musical instrument, but also to the exactitude by which the mathematically skilled musician (the Pythagorean or 'Canonician', ὁ κανωνικός) carried out his/her work. In this connection 'canon' as *a tool of exactitude and precision* (ἀ κρίβεια) had yet another meaning, namely *measure or model of proportion* (*Verhältnismaßstab*). This meaning of the word is also found in the work Κανών by Polyclet, unfortunately extant only in two short fragments, where he deals with various kinds of proportionality, e.g. the right proportions of numbers and the proportions of the human body. By applying aesthetical criteria, it was thought that the beauty of the human body depended on the right proportions between the different members to one another.[79] H. Oppel writes that

> no fixed schema, as in the Egyptian art, should control the presentation of the human body, but a system freer from laws, being signified as *symmetria* in Greek aesthetics. The *maestro*, thus, could find no more suitable signification than *canon*, i.e. *rule of right proportions*, for the writing in which the results of these calculations of proportions were put down.[80]

In a similar fashion the musical theoretician needed a canon. In this case, however, 'canon' was not a written record but the designation of his/her stringed instrument, by which musical harmony was attained. This was accomplished by correctly relating the tones into well-sounding melodies, harmonies or symphonic orchestrations. As mentioned above, canons in the

---

[78] See Hägglund, 'Die Bedeutung der "regula fidei" als Grundlage theologischer Aussagen', *Studia Theologica* 12 (1958): 1–44. See further Ch. 8.
[79] Oppel, Κανών, 14f.
[80] Ibid.

sense of *prototypes for artistic creation* were similarly used in painting and sculpturing.

When 'canon' referred to various kinds of tables, other figurative senses of the word were important as well. The listing of certain profound information in tables (canons) – such as the basic astronomical data in tables needed for astronomical calculations, or the chronological tables made up of historians providing fixed points for historical calculation and narration – means that these tables were not just catalogues, but rather *tables providing some kind of standard.*[81] When applied to the canon lists of the biblical writings, it is not just the table *qua* table that constitutes the canon. Rather, the canon-table as a 'pointer' to what is enlisted provides the standard, the canon of Sacred Scriptures. This, in turn, determines what is to be included in the canon list.[82]

To summarize, these latter two senses – of weight for the early Patristic use of the word – denote 'canon' as 6) a *prototype of proportionality and symmetry*, and 7) a *table providing a standard.*

As the word 'canon' often attained the meaning *rule* or *norm of what was to count as the characteristics of Christian belief and morals*, it soon took on the function as catchword in the Christian literature (late second century onwards). Similar functions were also given the word elsewhere. On the whole, in the Hellenistic context 'canon' came to be used as an overarching concept, expressing *notions of normativity, measure, regulation*, or, even, *the characteristics of entire fields of artistry, grammar, ethics or science* often attaining the form of a book, a written record.[83]

Below follow some quotations illustrating how the notion of canon, drawing on the general Hellenistic meaning, was used within the church:

---

[81] Ibid., 66–8: The commonly suggested idea that 'canon' came to depict simply a list or catalogue with no kind of material denotation can hardly be maintained when applied to the canon of biblical writings. The examples given by Oppel of a purely formal use of *canon* as applied to tables are not convincing. They all seem to provide some kind of standard. Cf., however, Oppel's words, ibid., 6: 'Dazu tritt etwa seit der Kaiserzeit die Bedeutung *Tabelle*. Das ist die sichtbar gemachte Regel'. See also ibid., 27 and 67.

[82] This explains the mutual relation between the Greek Christian use of 'canon' *as a table of biblical books providing the standard* and the Latin Christian use of 'canon' designating *the biblical books themselves as providing the standard*. In other words, when looking at the effective-history of the concept, especially in the West, it is not easy to separate these two dimensions of canon from one another. Cf. Zahn, *Die bleibende Bedeutung des neutestamentlichen Kanons für die Kirche: Vortrag auf der lutherischen Pastoralkonferenz zu Leipzig am 2. Juni 1898 gehalten* (Leipzig: U. Deichert'sche Verlagsbuchh. Nachf. [Georg Böhme], 1898), 4. See also Metzger (*The Canon of the New Testament*, 293) for a similar argument.

[83] See Oppel, Κανών.

1) Canon *as measure*

We, however, will not boast beyond limits, but will keep within the field (μέ
τρον τοῦ κανόνος) that God has assigned to us, to reach out even as far as you.

(2 Cor. 10.13)[84]

2) Canon *as prototype or model*

In like manner he also who retains unchangeable in his heart the rule of the
truth (τὸν κανόνα τῆς ἀληθείας) which he received by means of baptism, will
doubtless recognise the names, the expressions, and the parables taken from the
Scriptures, but will by no means acknowledge the blasphemous use which these
men [the Valentinians] make of them. For, though he will acknowledge the
gems, he will certainly not receive the fox instead of the likeness of the king. But
when he has restored every one of the expressions quoted to its proper position,
and has fitted it to the body of the truth, he will lay bare, and prove to be without
any foundation, the figment of these heretics.

(Irenaeus, *Adv. Haer.* I, 9.4)[85]

3) Canon *as norm, rule or standard*

But to apply expressions which are not clear or evident to interpretations of the
parables, such as every one discovers for himself as inclination leads him, [is
absurd.] For in this way no one will possess the rule of truth (*regula veritatis*);
but in accordance with the number of persons who explain the parables will
be found the various systems of truth, in mutual opposition to each other,
and setting forth antagonistic doctrines, like the questions current among the
Gentile philosophers.

(Irenaeus, *Adv. Haer.* II, 27.1)[86]

4) Canon *as limit or boundary*

Let each of you, brothers, give thanks to God with your own group, maintaining
a good conscience, not overstepping the designated rule of his ministry (μὴ
παρεκβαίνων τὸν ὡρισμένον τῆς λειτουργίας αὐτοῦ κανόνα), but acting
with reverence.

(*1 Clem.* 41.1)[87]

---

[84] NRSV. For various interpretations of 2 Cor. 10.13-16, see Ohme, *Kanon ekklesiastikos*, 40–4.
[85] ANF 1:330. Cf. Oppel, Κανών, 40–50; Ohme, *Kanon ekklesiastikos*, 26.
[86] ANF 1:398.
[87] Holmes, *The Apostolic Fathers: Greek Texts with English Translations* (Grand Rapids: Baker, 3rd edn,
2007), 98f. Cf. Oppel, Κανών, 69.

5) Canon *as tool of exactitude and criterion*

[S]o also are we bound in no way to transgress the canon of the Church (κανὼν ἐκκλησιαστικός). And especially do we keep our profession in the most important points, while they [the heretics] traverse it. ... And as, while there is one royal highway, there are many others, some leading to a precipice, some to a rushing river or to a deep sea, no one will shrink from travelling by reason of the diversity, but will make use of the safe, and royal, and frequented way; so, though some say this, some that, concerning the truth, we must not abandon it; but must seek out the most accurate knowledge respecting it. ... we ought also to discover the sequence of the truth. ... There being demonstration, then, it is necessary to condescend to questions, and to ascertain by the way of demonstration by the Scriptures themselves how the heresies failed, and how in the truth alone and in the ancient Church is both the exactest knowledge, and the truly best set of principles ...

But those who are ready to toil in the most excellent pursuits, will not desist from the search after truth, till they get the demonstration from the Scriptures themselves. ... For those who make the greatest attempts must fail in things of the highest importance; unless, receiving from the truth itself the rule of the truth (κανὼν τῆς ἀληθείας), they cleave to the truth. But such people, in consequence of falling away from the right path, err in most individual points; as you might expect from not having the faculty for judging of what is true and false, strictly trained to select what is essential. For if they had, they would have obeyed the Scriptures ...

For in the Lord we have the first principle of our teaching (ἀρχὴ τῆς διδασκαλίας), both by the prophets, the Gospel, and the blessed apostles, 'in divers manners and at sundry times,' leading from the beginning of knowledge to the end. But if one should suppose that the first principle required something else, then it could no longer truly be preserved as a first principle.

He, then, who of himself believes the Scripture and voice of the Lord, which by the Lord acts to the benefiting of men, is rightly [regarded] faithful. Certainly we use it as a criterion (κριτήριον) in the discovery of things. What is subjected to criticism is not believed till it is so subjected; so that what needs criticism cannot be a first principle. Therefore, as is reasonable, grasping by faith the indemonstrable first principle, and receiving in abundance, from the first principle itself, demonstrations in reference to the first principle, we are by the voice of the Lord trained up to the knowledge of the truth. ...

Since also, in what pertains to life, craftsmen are superior to ordinary people, and model what is beyond common notions; so, consequently, we also, giving a complete exhibition of the Scriptures from the Scriptures themselves, from faith persuade by demonstration.

And if those also who follow heresies venture to avail themselves of the prophetic Scripture; in the first place they will not make use of all the Scriptures, and then they will not quote them entire, nor as the body and texture of prophecy prescribe. But, selecting ambiguous expressions, they wrest them to their own opinions, gathering a few expressions here and there; not looking to the sense, but making use of the mere words. For in almost all the quotations they make, you will find that they attend to the names alone, while they alter the meanings; neither knowing, as they affirm, nor using the quotations they adduce, according to their true nature.

But the truth is not found by changing the meanings (for so people subvert all true teaching), but in the consideration of what perfectly belongs to and becomes the Sovereign God, and in establishing each one of the points demonstrated in the Scriptures again from similar passages of the Scriptures themselves.

(Clement of Alexandria, *Strom.* VII, 15–16)[88]

6) Canon *as a prototype of proportionality, symmetry and harmony*

You may take music in another way, as the ecclesiastical symphony at once of the law and the prophets, and the apostles along with the Gospel … the ecclesiastical rule (καυὼν ἐκκλησιαστικός) is the concord and harmony of the law and the prophets in the covenant delivered at the coming of the Lord.

(Clement of Alexandria, *Strom.* VI, 11 and VI, 15)[89]

7) Canon *as a table providing a standard*

'Forasmuch as some have taken in hand,' to reduce into order for themselves the books termed apocryphal, and to mix them up with the divinely inspired Scripture, concerning which we have been fully persuaded, as they who from the beginning were eyewitnesses and ministers of the Word, delivered to the fathers; it seemed good to me also, having been urged thereto by true brethren, and having learned from the beginning, to set before you the books included in the Canon, and handed down, and accredited as Divine; to the end that any one who has fallen into error may condemn those who have led him astray; and that he who has continued steadfast in purity may again rejoice, having these things brought to his remembrance.

---

[88] ANF 2:549–51; modified. See Ohme (*Kanon ekklesiastikos*, 149–55) for a summary account of Clement's varied use of the term 'canon'.
[89] ANF 2:500, 509. Cf. also Irenaeus, *Adv. Haer.* I, 8.1-10.1.

There are, then, of the Old Testament, twenty-two books in number; for, as I have heard, it is handed down that this is the number of the letters among the Hebrews; their respective order and names being as follows. The first is Genesis, then Exodus …

Again it is not tedious to speak of the [books] of the New Testament. These are, the four Gospels … Acts of the Apostles and Epistles (called Catholic), seven. In addition, there are fourteen Epistles of Paul. And … the Revelation of John.

These are fountains of salvation, that they who thirst may be satisfied with the living words they contain. In these alone is proclaimed the doctrine of godliness. Let no one add to these, neither let him take anything from these. For concerning these the Lord put to shame the Sadducees, and said, 'Ye do err, not knowing the Scriptures.' And He reproved the Jews, saying, 'Search the Scriptures, for these are they that testify of Me.'

But for greater exactness I add this also, writing of necessity; that there are other books besides these not indeed included in the Canon, but appointed by the Fathers to be read by those who newly join us, and who wish for instruction in the word of godliness. The Wisdom of Solomon, and the Wisdom of Sirach, and Esther, and Judith, and Tobit, and that which is called the Teaching of the Apostles, and the Shepherd. But the former, my brethren, are included in the Canon, the latter being [merely] read; nor is there in any place a mention of apocryphal writings. But they are an invention of heretics, who write them when they choose, bestowing upon them their approbation, and assigning to them a date, that so, using them as ancient writings, they may find occasion to lead astray the simple.

(Athanasius, *Thirty-Ninth Festal Epistle*)[90]

---

[90] NPNF 2.4:552, modified; Cf. Bruce, *The Canon of Scripture*. (Downers Grove, IL: InterVarsity, 1988), 78f., 208f.. In the *Thirty-Ninth Festal Letter*, the so called canon of Athanasius, The *Shepherd* of Hermas is said not to be among the canonical writings (μὴ ὂν ἐκ τοῦ κανόνος), i.e. among the number of writings canonized or listed in the canon, the table containing the exact number of books to be counted among the Holy Scriptures of the Old (22 [=38] books) and the New (27 books) Testaments.

2.6 Dimensions of the concept of canon as applied to the biblical writings

With the above overview in mind, in this section I shall suggest another set of categories useful for the systematic elaboration of the Christian notion of canon.

Some decades ago, Hans Lietzmann stated that the history of the canon is 'one of the most complicated aspects of the study of church history'.[91] It was in his time, and still is, well known that the historical process of canonization is complex, containing an unexhaustive variety of aspects. Is the question of the canon then more, or perhaps less, than a question? As indicated above, John Barton even considers it to be a *Scheinfrage* that 'bundles together so many questions that apparently conflicting "solutions" of it seldom in reality share any common ground on which to meet and clash'.[92] Despite the complexity, I intend to elaborate on this question by analysing some of the terminology pertaining to the canon.

As a first step I suggest some distinctions between various dimensions or signifiers of canon, as related to the formation and function of the Christian Bible. The most important, and the semantically broadest, of these signifiers, as I choose to use them here, is canon *as Scripture* (in boldface below), designating the *Sacred Scriptures* the way that the New Testament and the subsequent church tend to use the word (cf. 2 Pet. 3.16; 2 Tim. 3.15f.; Amphilochius of Iconium, *Iambi ad Seleucum*).[93] In the following list, then, the ten signifiers are viewed as various properties of Scripture (canon *as Scripture*):

Canon as   **Scripture**
regional list of Old and New Testament writings
the book(s) of the Bible
Rule of Faith

---

[91] H. Lietzmann, 'Wie wurden die Bücher des Neuen Testaments Heilige Schrift?' in *Kleine Schriften*, vol. 2, ed. H. Lietzmann (TU 68; Berlin: Akademie, 1958), 15–98, at 3; cited from Gamble, 'The New Testament Canon: Recent Research and the Status Quaestionis', in *The Canon Debate*, (eds) J. A. Sanders and L. M. McDonald (Peabody, MA: Hendrickson, 2002), 267.

[92] Barton, *The Spirit and the Letter*, 2.

[93] In the poem *Iambi ad Seleucum*, written ca. AD 380, bishop Amphilocius of Iconium remarks at the close of an enumeration of the books of the Old and New Testaments: 'This is perhaps the most reliable canon of the divinely inspired Scriptures'; see Metzger, *The Canon of the New Testament*, 292.

> *scriptural intertext*
> *scriptural metatext*
> *the Old and New Testaments*
> *the prophetic and apostolic Scriptures*
> *collection of authoritative writings*
> *divine lection of Scripture*
> *classic collection of literature*

When using the word 'canon' in biblical studies, scholars most often take it as referring to a normative list enumerating the exact scope of the biblical writings (canon *as regional list of Old and New Testament writings*). This is the usage of the word κανών and its derivatives κανονικός and κανονίζειν in the second half of the fourth century made by Athanasius and Amphilocius of Iconium (who is the first to use the noun κανών in this connection). Further, the word is also taken to denote the biblical books themselves or the Bible *as book* (canon *as the book(s) of the Bible*) the way Augustine used it.[94] Two centuries earlier, around AD 200, the term 'canon' had often been used to refer to the *Rule of Faith* or the *Ecclesiastical Canon* (canon *as Rule of Faith*).[95] From the latter part of the second century, in writers like Irenaeus and Clement of Alexandria, the biblical writings stood in a close dialectical relationship to this ecclesiastical canon.[96] The Scriptures (canon *as Scripture*), therefore, came to play a central role in defining the second- and third-century concept of canon (the canon *as Rule of Faith*). The mutual relation between Scripture and canon *as Rule of Faith* also gave room for the opposite move, where canon *as Rule of Faith* helped define the canonical function and scope of the Scriptures (canon *as Scripture*). The two concepts were thus sometimes interchangeable.

On another interpretive level, canon *as Rule of Faith* is closely connected with canon *as scriptural intertext*, signifying the inter- and intratextual theological substructure of the New Testament writings. This comes to expression through engaging particular texts (the proof-texts utilized) along with the pattern for intertextual use and interpretation of the Jewish Scriptures in the new apostolic writings.[97] The cross-references between

---

[94] Ohme, *Kanon ekklesiastikos*, 482.
[95] On the synonymity of the Rule of Faith and the Ecclesiastical Canon, see Hägglund, *Die Bedeutung der 'regula fidei' als Grundlage theologischer Aussagen*; and Ohme, *Kanon ekklesiastikos*.
[96] See Bokedal, 'The Rule of Faith'.
[97] Cf., e.g. Porter, ed., *Hearing the Old Testament in the New Testament* (Grand Rapids and Cambridge: Eerdmans, 2006).

the variously interdependent New Testament writings are also part of this dimension of canonicity. Canon *as Rule of Faith* as an overarching theological reading of the Scriptures further relates to canon *as scriptural metatext*, that is, as a function of canon as a way of seeking to end the endless demand of interpretation borne out of the texts as writing; in the wording of George Aichele, canon is here understood as a way of 'completing the uncompleteable story'.[98] Canon *as scriptural metatext* is the attempt of the church

> to clarify the text's meaning and to achieve narrative completeness through a form of intertextual commentary. The canon defines a metatext, comprised of all the texts on the authorized list, and the interplay between these texts on the authorized list, and the interplay between these texts enables this larger metatext in effect to comment upon itself.[99]

The emerging canon *as scriptural metatext* and *Rule of Faith* – in addition to the above partly oral, partly written textual and theological dimensions – also involves various linguistic, tradition-related, ritual and ideational components (cf. Ch. 1).

The mutuality of these dimensions of canon from early on led to a series of reflections on and formulations of what was to be regarded canonical and normative for the church, in the process of which these Scriptures themselves came to be regarded as canonical in a more definitive and final sense. However, at this early date the term 'canon' was not frequently[100] used to designate the authoritative listing of Old and New Testament writings, as understood from the mid-fourth century on (canon *as regional list*).[101] A term with a similar function being employed already by Origen (*Philocalia* 3) and Eusebius (*Hist. Eccl.* III, 3.1) was ἐνδιάθηκος (meaning 'contained in the covenant'), as opposed to 'apocryphal'.[102]

---

[98] Aichele, *Sign, Text, Scripture: Semiotics and the Bible* (Sheffield: Sheffield Academic, 1997), 127.

[99] Ibid., 128.

[100] The manner in which Clement, Origen and Eusebius use the term may be exceptions to this rule. See McDonald, *The Formation of the Christian Biblical Canon* (Peabody, MA: Hendrickson, 1995), 16. The fourfold Gospel is referred to as the canon/the canon of the church, by Clement as well as by Origen (Clem. *Strom.* IV, 15; *Hist. Eccl.* VI, 25.3). Such usage may have inspired the later fourth- and fifth-century employment of the term as applied to all the Scriptures.

[101] Cf. McDonald (*Formation*, 2), who gives some possible examples of earlier usage of 'canon' denotating the scriptural canon.

[102] Cf. Metzger, *The Canon of the New Testament*, 292.

According to Theodor Zahn, the bulk of the New Testament writings, which were designated 'canon' in the fourth century, existed as a collection of apostolic literature as early as the late first or early second century. By the word 'canon' he understood the collection of authoritative apostolic writings used for divine lection in corporate worship (canon *as collection of authoritative writings* and canon *as divine lection of Scripture*). Adolf von Harnack, on the contrary, could not accept this definition. In his view the authoritative collection of apostolic writings only became canonical when the individual writings were clearly regarded as *Scripture* on a par with the Jewish Scriptures (canon *as Scripture*) in the latter part of the second century.[103] As I will argue (in Chs 7 and 9), due largely, but not exclusively, to their function in corporate worship, the new Christian writings attained partial or even full scriptural status earlier than von Harnack assumed. In any case, from early on, most, or all, New Testament writings stood in a close relation to the principal signifier, canon *as Scripture*.[104]

As the concept of canon *as list* arose in the Eastern Church towards the middle of the fourth century, it was soon taken over by Latin Christianity, however, with a shift in meaning taking place. As indicated above, canon *as list* quickly attained an extended, or transferred, meaning. Now, the biblical books themselves received Latin titles such as *canon*, *libri canonici*, *canon scripturarum*, *scripturae canonicae*, *litterae canonicae*, and were said to have *canonica auctoritas*.[105] A new meaning of the word arose, namely 'canon' as representing, not a list of authoritative books, but the biblical books themselves (canon *as the book(s) of the Bible*).

Yet another three dimensions of canon may be added, namely 'canon' as signifying the *Old* and *New Testaments* (canon *as the Old and New Testaments*), which became a common way of designating the two parts of the Christian Bible from the late second and early third century on. These titles, used by the redactors and editors of the Christian Bible,[106] implied a

---

[103] For a fuller analysis, see Gamble, 'The New Testament Canon: Recent Research and the Status Quaestionis'.

[104] Cf. the references made to the 'entire Scriptures' in Irenaeus (*universae scripturae*; *Adv. Haer.* II, 27.2), and the entire New Testament/Instrument in Tertullian (*integrum instrumentum*; *De Praescr.* 38).

[105] For references, see Ohme, *Kanon ekklesiastikos*, 478.

[106] On this, see Trobisch, *Die Endredaktion des Neuen Testaments: Eine Untersuchung zur Entstehung der christlichen Bibel* (Freiburg, Switzerland: Universitätsverlag Freiburg and Göttingen: Vandenhoeck

form of materialization or textualization of the new covenant between God and God's people.[107] The differences between the authoritative collection of New Testament writings of these early editions (canon *as the Old and the New Testaments*) as compared to the canon of the New Testament as defined in the latter half of the fourth century (canon *as regional list of Old and New Testament writings*) should not be exaggerated, as Eusebius' and Origen's notion of ἐνδιάθηκος (from διαθήκη; cf. *Hist. Eccl.* III, 3.1) indicates. This is in line not only with Zahn's evaluation, a century ago,[108] but also with David Trobisch's research on NT manuscripts, reaching the conclusion that the 'canonical archetype' of the third- and fourth-century Bible codices, as well as other extant Greek Bible manuscripts, goes back on a single second-century archetype, the *editio princeps*, containing the 27 books of the New Testament (see section 4.6).[109]

Further, the concept of canon *as the prophetic and apostolic Scriptures* designates the Bible as the prophetic and the apostolic writings. This label for the Scriptures was common from early on. The Lutheran reformers of the *Formula of Concord* in the 1570s similarly made use of it, as they had not been able to agree among themselves on the exact canonical delimitation.[110] The designation leaves room for 'objectivity' as well as openness regarding the exact scope of the biblical writings. Canon *as the prophetic and apostolic Scriptures* refers to those writings that are apostolic (in the broad sense) and prophetic, even if it may not be possible to agree on exactly which these writings are. Corresponding to this designation, of course, is the so-called canon criterion of apostolicity. After all, the criterion par préférance for a writing to count as Scripture, or canonical Scripture, was that of apostolicity, not only in the early

---

& Ruprecht, 1996); ET: Trobisch, *The First Edition of the New Testament* (Oxford: Oxford University Press, 2000).

[107] *Pace* von Campenhausen, *The Formation of the Christian Bible*, 267.

[108] See Zahn, *Grundriss der Geschichte des Neutestamentlichen Kanons.*

[109] Trobisch, *First Edition*; cf. David C. Parker's review of Trobisch's book in *JTS* 53 (2002): 298–305. For a more critical evaluation, see Holmes, 'Text and Transmission in the Second Century', in *The Reliability of the New Testament: Bart D. Ehrman & Daniel B. Wallace in Dialogue*, ed. Stewart (Minneapolis: Fortress, 2011), 62–5.

[110] 'The Formula of Concord', in *The Creeds of Christendom, with a History and Critical Notes*, vol. 3, ed. P. Schaff (New York: Harper & Brothers, 1877 [1576]), 93–180.

church, but later on as well. Other canon criteria[111] pertaining to the New Testament usually go back on this first principle of canonicity.[112]

Canon *as classic collection of literature*, finally, designates the status that the biblical writings have attained as tradition-sanctioned classical literature in Christianity.

In the discussions throughout the nineteenth and twentieth centuries, several proposals as to what should be understood by the canon concept have been made. A common Protestant view has been to regard the canon of Scripture as synonymous with the Bible (canon *as the book(s) of the Bible*). For Catholics and for many Reformed churches the concept of canon *as list of Old and New Testament writings* has been emphasized against other aspects of canonicity. As already mentioned, canon *as the prophetic and apostolic Scriptures* has been stressed by Lutheran churches which adhere to the *Formula of Concord*. Modern scholarship, on the other hand, has introduced yet other preferences and distinctions. Some scholars have opted for a clear distinction between Scripture, i.e. canon *as Scripture*, and 'canon proper', i.e. canon *as list* (Sundberg, Barr). Others have made an equally clear distinction between canon *as Rule of Faith* and canon *as list* (Lessing, Baur and Zahn), and, by focusing on canon *as list* when discussing the canon formation, many scholars have chosen to leave out other aspects.

A different approach as compared to more traditional research has recently been suggested by a group of scholars, such as Eldon Jay Epp and David Trobisch,[113] who have chosen to work less with the Patristic material; they have instead directed their attention towards analysing the New Testament manuscript tradition. As already mentioned, according to Trobisch the formation of the NT canon could be explained simply as the edition of a book some time during the second century. The aspect emphasized here pertains to canon as the first Christian edition of the 'Old' and the 'New Testaments', i.e.

---

[111] See, e.g. McDonald, *Formation*, 228; and idem, 'Indentifying Scripture and Canon in the Early Church: The Criteria Question', in *The Canon Debate*, (eds) McDonald and Sanders (Peabody, MA: Hendrickson, 2002), where he treats the criteria of apostolicity, orthodoxy, antiquity, inspiration and usage.

[112] See Skarsaune, 'Hvilket lys kaster NT's kanonhistorie over teologihistorien i det 1. århundre?', *Religio* 25 (1986): 63–83.

[113] Epp, 'Issues in the Interrelation of New Testament Textual Criticism and Canon', 485–515; Trobisch, *First Edition*.

canon *as the book(s) of the Bible* and canon *as the Old and the New Testaments*. All in all, various emphases as to what should count as canon and canonization continue to see the light of day.

Also other distinctions than the ones I have suggested above have been launched in order to better grasp the composite notion of canon. James A. Sanders,[114] John Goldingay[115] and G. T. Sheppard have each contributed, with yet other categories.[116] Making a distinction between canon *as function* and canon *as shape,* Sanders writes:

> The function of a written canon has antecedents in the very process by which the concept arose, that is, in the function of authoritative traditions when there was as yet no written literature deemed canonical in the sense of *norma normata,* or shape.[117]

Goldingay, on the other hand, distinguishes between 'Scripture as canon' and 'the canon of scripture', and Sheppard/Sanders between 'canon 1' (an authoritative oral or written word) and 'canon 2' (the books of the Bible being fixed and stabilized).[118]

I take these categories to be attempts at emphasizing that the notion of biblical canonicity embraces several components that need to be highlighted, if significant dimensions of the first- to fourth-century process of canonization, as well as the continuous ecclesial canon reception, are not to be left out.

2.7 Canonizing scripture as an ecclesial process

From the second half of the first to the early third century, a heterogeneous process of canonization took place as the Christian Scriptures

---

[114] Sanders, 'Canon: Hebrew Bible'.

[115] Goldingay, *Models for Scripture* (Grand Rapids: Eerdmans, 1994), 102.

[116] McDonald, *Formation,* 20, 40, 92, 106–8 and 295.

[117] Sanders, 'Canon: Hebrew Bible', 847; cf. Bruce Metzger (*The Canon of the New Testament,* 283), who distinguishes an active and a passive sense of the word κανών. The former refers to those books that serve to mark out the norm for Christian faith and life, while the latter passive sense refers to the list of books that have been marked out as normative by the church. To describe these two meanings of the word κανών Metzger uses the two Latin tags, *norma normans* ('the rule that prescribes'), and *norma normata,* ('the rule that is prescribed', i.e. by the church). According to these two senses of the word, Metzger argues, the New Testament can be described either as a 'collection of authoritative books', or as 'an authoritative collection of books'.

[118] For references, see McDonald, *Biblical Canon,* 55–8.

gradually emerged as regulative writings for the communities of faith. This process involved elements of 1) composition, 2) circulation, 3) redaction, 4) collection, 5) selection and 6) final textual and literary shaping.[119] The recognition of aspects of the biblical material as canonical, that is, as normative and regulative, could basically occur at any of these stages.[120] Behind this scheme of canonization lies, of course, also various theological, interpretive and socio-cultural motives. Brevard Childs in his *Biblical Theology of the Old and New Testaments* thus argues that the canonical formation of the biblical material involves 'a profoundly hermeneutical activity on the part of the tradents'.[121] As discussed above, this hermeneutical activity can be said to be teleological in the sense that the overall pattern – the process of canonization – appears to have a theological end. It is this theological end, as an inherent quality in the process, which makes it meaningful to talk of canonization in the first place. Understood in this way, canonization aims at representing the theological, hermeneutical and socio-cultural forces involved in the composition, reception and transmission of the biblical material, whereby these traditions maintain 'a normative function for subsequent generations of believers within a community of faith'.[122] Using Childs's model, canonization (and canon) therefore can be best described as a form of cipher to encompass the various factors involved in the formation of the biblical literature as Scripture and canon.

In line with this type of definition, I also choose to focus attention on canonization as governed by theological forces, and canonization understood as a process, in order 'to demonstrate that the concept of canon was not a late, ecclesiastical ordering which was basically foreign to the material itself, but that canon-consciousness lay deep within the formation of the literature.'[123] One aim, then, is to focus on and describe this canonical process as it occurred in the first and second centuries. Here a remark needs to be made to

---

[119] The first five stages have been suggested by H. E. Ryle and R. Beckwith. A. C. Sundberg has proposed yet other stages: Rise to the status of scripture, the conscious grouping of such literature into closed collections, for example, the four Gospels and the epistles of Paul, and the formation of a closed list of authoritative literature. See Beckwith, *The Old Testament Canon*, 66; and McDonald, *Formation*, 17.

[120] For the five first elements/stages, see Beckwith, *The Old Testament Canon*, 66.

[121] Childs, *Biblical Theology of the Old and New Testaments*, 70.

[122] Ibid.

[123] Ibid., 70f.

legitimate the presumed continuity between the process up to the beginning of the second century, described by Childs, James A. Sanders and others, and that taking place from the latter part of that century. As I have sought to demonstrate, there are reasons for talking of a unified process of canonization stretching beyond the time when the bulk of the New Testament formed in the period preceding AD 150. One feature that connects, let's say, Irenaeus' contributions to the canonical process, ca. AD 180–200, and earlier phases, seems to be the common semiotic system embodied in the sociolinguistic community of the church, from which he draws his biblical traditions and canons of interpretation.[124]

Now, before proceeding further, I shall briefly mention some criticism launched by James Barr towards such an understanding of canonization, that is, as a process characterized by continuity. In his book *Holy Scripture* Barr sets out to criticize the canonical approach introduced by Childs and his followers. In his own alternative reconstruction of the canon formation, Barr presupposes a sharp distinction between Scripture and canon. A point of departure for his thinking is a presumed dichotomy between biblical times and the succeeding patristic period to which scriptural canonizing is thought to belong:

> Canonization was done under a faith structure very different from that of the biblical community. For Christianity this means in effect a sharing of authority between scripture and the patristic period. I think that this, rather than the novel fashions of canonical criticism, is the real alternative to the lines that modern biblical scholarship has followed.[125]

The problem with the category of 'canon', when compared to that of 'Scripture', according to Barr, is that 'it implies a clear distinction between scripture and non-scripture, inspired and non-inspired, divine and human, authoritative and non-authoritative, which very probably was not there.'[126] However, in contrast to Barr, the conventional usage of the two concepts shows what Lee Martin McDonald describes as a 'considerable overlap' between 'scripture'

---

[124] For this way of presenting Irenaeus, see Young (*Virtuoso Theology: The Bible and Interpretation*, 58), who uses thoughts developed by Hans Frei. Cf. Clement of Alexandria, *Strom.* VII, 15: 'it is only in the true and the ancient Church that there is the most exact knowledge and the really best school of thought.' Trans. F. J. A. Hort and J. B. Mayor, Greek and Roman Philosophy, vol. 9, ed. L. Tarán (New York and London: Garland Publishing, 1987). Also quoted above in section 2.5.2.

[125] Barr, *Holy Scripture: Canon, Authority, Criticism* (Oxford: Clarendon Press, 1983), 66.

[126] Ibid., 57.

and 'canon'.[127] As suggested above, the canonization of Scripture is best understood as a multidimensional process in several stages, in which the latter are dependent on the preceding ones. On the other hand, when a sharp distinction between Scripture and canon is suggested, the concept of canon tends to become separated from the historical process of canon formation. 'Canon' is then – as in Barr and A. C. Sundberg – used exclusively to signify a closed collection of scriptural texts, while 'Scripture' is meant to be a more open and fluid category.[128] Interestingly, Michael Holmes has recently argued for a similar distinction between 'scripture' (i.e. religiously authoritative writings) and 'canon' (defined as a 'list' or 'catalogue' of writings considered to be scripture) as that used by Sundberg:

> When the two terms are distinguished in this way, it is clear that 'canon' presumes the existence of 'scripture', but 'scripture' does not require a 'canon'. There can be scripture without a canon, but no canon without scripture – no 'list' or 'catalogue', because there would be nothing to put on the list. Canonicity is a matter of listmaking, not scriptural status.[129]

As already indicated, several objections to such a distinction can be made. First, the argument may seem somewhat weak ('there can be ... no canon without scripture ... Canonicity is a matter of listmaking, not scriptural status'). The concept of canon is not without connection with the earlier history of formation of the biblical literature, that is, with the canonical process prior to the fourth century, when the notion of the canon *as list* was introduced. Indeed, this prior textual history is the rationale for the drawing up of subsequent canon-lists, that is, canon *as Scripture* still provides the basis for the multidimensional notion of biblical canonicity (see section 2.6). Second, on Latin as well as on Greek ground this new concept of canon does not signify *any* catalogue or list; it is the canon (Lat. *canon*) of the canonical Scriptures (*canonicae scripturae*),[130] which could mean either that the canon list only enumerates those books that may already be called 'canonical', or

---

[127] McDonald, *Formation*, 13: The notion of canon is here defined as a 'fixed standard or collection of writings that defines the faith and identity of a particular religious community'. In this sense, McDonald maintains, all scripture is canon.

[128] Scalise, *From Scripture to Theology: A Canonical Journey into Hermeneutics* (Downers Grove, IL: InterVarsity, 1996), 45

[129] Holmes, 'The Biblical Canon', in *The Oxford Handbook of Early Christian Studies*, (eds) S. Ashbrook Harvey and D. G. Hunter (Oxford: Oxford University Press, 2008), 406f.

[130] Theron, *Evidence of Tradition*, 126: The Canon of the Synod of Carthage (AD 397).

that these books are labelled 'canonical' because they are now enlisted. In the Canon of the Synod of Carthage from AD 397, there seems to be a dialectical relation between the 'Divine Scriptures', also called the 'canonical Scriptures', and the list – labelled 'canon' – containing these writings. Here, the Scriptures themselves are called 'canonical', irrespective of (or parallel with) their formal listing on a particular canon list. According to Zahn, this transferred meaning of 'canon', depicting the Bible itself, arises only some years after these canon lists have been drawn up on Syrian and Latin ground, where the authoritative character of the Scriptures (canon *as Scripture*; i.e. the rule that prescribes, *norma normans*) seems to have merged with the notion of canon list (canon *as list*; i.e. the rule that is to some extent prescribed, *norma normata*) to form a new hybrid, the canon *as the book(s) of the Bible*.[131]

Such conceptual intermingling, however, had already occurred in the canon lists of the fourth century, e.g. in the Canon of the Synod of Carthage (AD 397), where Canon 47 reads:

> And so it seemed good that nothing should be read in the Church under name of the Divine Scriptures except the canonical writings. The canonical writings, then are these: …[132]

Further, in Canons 59 and 60 of the Synod of Laodicea (ca. AD 360), we read:

> [It is decreed] that private psalms should not be read in the Church, neither uncanonized books, but only the canonical [books] of the New and Old Testament. … The books which should be read: …[133]

And in the *Canon of Mommsen* (ca. AD 360):

> [So] our fathers approved that these books are canonical (*hos libros esse canonicos*) and that the men of old have said this: The content of the New Testament, then, is: …[134]

In other words, only truly New and Old Testament Scriptures (canon *as the Old and New Testaments*) may be defined as canon, one consequence of which is 'the treatment of "scripture" and "canon" as nearly synonymous terms'.[135]

---

[131] Cf. Zahn, *Grundriss der Geschichte des Neutestamentlichen Kanons*, 8. For the *norma normans/ norma normata* distinction, see n. 117.

[132] Theron, *Evidence of Tradition*, 127.

[133] Ibid., 125. On problems regarding dating, see Metzger, *The Canon of the New Testament*, 210, 312.

[134] Ibid., 121.

[135] Holmes, 'The Biblical Canon', 406.

Nevertheless, as Holmes points out, 'canon' and 'scripture', still are not quite synonymous. As the broad historical notion of 'biblical canonicity' outlined in section 2.6 indicates, an additional dimension of canonicity is added with the introduction of the new ecclesial notion of canon *as list*. For one, by comparing variations in existing local and regional New Testament manuscripts, the new notion of an agreed list of accepted books to be included takes the concept in a universalizing direction. From now on, one of the effects of the scriptural canon catalogue becomes its function as a standard list for the books to be included when producing NT manuscripts for a geographically wider area of dissemination.

Again, however, we need to remind ourselves of the tradition and history behind the emergence of canon *as list*. The formation of the concept as such had long since been prepared for within the Greek and Latin languages (see above).[136] Not least the *Canon of Mommsen* (see above) seems to problematize the common view among scholars that 'canon', applied to the Bible, ought to refer only to a list or catalogue. However, as observed already by Zahn, the Latin church did not use the concept in the same sense as did the Greek. Taken at face value, the attribution 'canonical' instead seems to have referred to the books themselves and not to the list as such. In fact, the reference to the 'men of old', the *seniores*, as a source of information, implies that the canon listed relies on earlier tradition. The very reason for cataloguing the contents (*indiculum*) of the New (and Old) Testament is that there has been some disagreement as to exactly what should be contained in the New Testament. That is not to say, though, that the local or regional demarcation of this content is in any way independent of already existing NT editions or collections of NT writings. According to Zahn, such decisions and delimitations had been made long ago in the church(es), for example when second-century editions of the New Testament were made, or when the collection of New Testament writings were titled 'the New Testament' (ἡ καινὴ διαθήκη):

The idea of *a closed collection of revelatory documents (Offenbarungsurkunden)*

---

[136] Cf. Gadamer, *The Beginning of Philosophy*, translated by Rod Coltman (New York: Continuum, 1998), 34.

is earlier expressed by (παλαιά and καινὴ) διαθήκη, and the belonging to these, since Origen's time, by ἐνδιάθηκος.[137]

The word 'encovenanted' or 'testament-ed' (ἐνδιάθηκος; cf. Euseb. *Hist. Eccl.* III, 3.1) thus is the third century equivalent to 'canonical', and the term 'Old Testament', signifying a delimited collection of Scriptures (22 books), is employed probably already towards the end of the second century by Melito of Sardis (Euseb. *Hist. Eccl.* IV, 26.12-14). Some years later the title 'New Testament' is used by Clement of Alexandria (*Strom.* I, 5) and Tertullian (*Adv. Marc.* IV, 1) to designate the book(s) of the New Testament. The number of covenant Scriptures contained in different editions of the Christian Bible in principle seems to have been delimited, even if local and regional variations existed as to their exact scope. These variations, however, did not disappear with the introduction of canon lists in the fourth century. Rather, the variations arguably affected the regional needs and requests for such lists, which, in their turn, affected the overall canonical process in the faith communities.

In his book *Holy Scripture* James Barr analyses the relation between Scripture and canon. He defines the word 'canon' as meaning 'simply "list", i.e. the list of books that counted as holy scripture'.[138] Later on he adds: '[t]he canon tells one, after the decisions have been made, what the decision was; but it is not an important or even a useful factor at the time when the decision has still to be made'.[139] If I understand him correctly, Barr seems to be saying that what counted as Scripture was a decision made in the fourth century, despite the fact that the category of Scripture, applied to the New Testament writings, by then had been in use for some two centuries. The conceptual problem lying behind this confusion is found in the very formulation used in the fourth-century canons (canon *as regional list*). The wording 'the canon of the Old and New Testaments' or 'the canon of Scriptures' aimed at depicting or pointing out a standard, a canon, of what was already regarded as the *Divine Scriptures* (cf. Athanasius, 2.5.2). Only such Scriptures, i.e. sacred Scriptures, could be included among the normative writings catalogued in the normative list. The process leading up to the designation 'canon' (canon *as regional list*

---

[137] Zahn, *Grundriss der Geschichte des Neutestamentlichen Kanons*, 11; my translation.
[138] Barr, *Holy Scripture: Canon, Authority, Criticism*, 49.
[139] Ibid., 59f.

of Old and New Testament writings) embraces also other aspects, including as well, of course, the basic concept of canon *as Scripture* (cf. section 2.6). Moreover, an obvious reason for a broader concept of canon than Barr's and Sundberg's is the variation as to the number of biblical books included in the regional canon lists of the fourth and fifth centuries. As Zahn and others have stressed, agreement regarding the canonical scope is not even reached in the sixth and seventh centuries. Within this larger historical framework, the various fourth- and late second-/early third-century editions of the Bible, with regard to canonical scope, looked very much alike. Regional variations of the late second century had not been eliminated two centuries later. Therefore, the labels 'the Old and New Testaments' of the early third and 'the canon of the Old and New Testaments' of the late fourth century seem, by and large, to have had the same, or similar, denotation.

To conclude the above, the canonical lists of the fourth and fifth centuries are part of an ongoing canonical process. However, what was called the 'canonical Scriptures' (canon *as regional list* and canon *as the book(s) of the Bible*) in the fourth century largely overlapped with the second-century denotation 'the holy Scriptures' (canon *as Scripture*) and 'the Old and New Testaments' (canon *as the Old and New Testaments*). The same canon criteria, applied to determine the scope of the early part-Bible editions labelled 'the New Testament' in the late second/early third centuries,[140] were arguably used to determine what in the fourth century was named 'the canon of the New Testament'.[141] That the concepts of the New Testament canon of the third and fourth centuries are comparable with one another is further confirmed by the various scope of the NT among the regional churches even in the fourth century. A similar conclusion had already been drawn by Origen and Eusebius by classifying the New Testament Scriptures as either 'undisputed' or 'disputed' (ὁμολογού μενα; ἀντιλεγόμενα).[142] And variations in canonical scope among the church provinces still differed for some centuries yet. Seen from a wider ecclesial perspective, the effective history of the empirical investigation carried out by Origen in this matter did not take a drastically new turn with the inauguration

---

[140] Cf. Trobisch, *Endredaktion*.

[141] For details as to when and how the Hellenistic concept of canon came to be associated with the biblical writings, see above.

[142] Cf. *Hist. Eccl.* III, 25. For terminology used by Origen, see Metzger, *The Canon of the New Testament*, 141.

of the mid-fourth-century concept of canon (canon *as regional list of Old and New Testament writings*). Origen's studies were relevant for the question of the canon, even if he was unfamiliar with the fourth-century ecclesial notion of canon (canon *as list*). At face value, therefore, Barr's conclusion seems to be in agreement with, e.g. Zahn's judgement regarding the original meaning of the fourth-century concept, canon *as regional list, catalogue* or *table*.[143] However, Barr draws further hermeneutical and theological conclusions from his strict terminological analysis, claiming that: 'Scripture is essential, but canon is not. Canon is a derivative, a secondary or tertiary, concept, of great interest but not of the highest theological importance'.[144] And further: 'canons are not particularly hermeneutical in their character. One of the deepest assumptions of modern canonical criticism is that canons give hermeneutical guidance and are intended to do so. This, however, is not their function.'[145] Against this evaluation, I have argued that canon is to be understood as a property of Scripture. As argued above, this is also indicated terminologically: 'canon' as meaning *table, list* or *catalogue* in fact presupposes the normative, i.e. canonical, character of what is enumerated on the canon list. Again, according to the definition above (section 2.5.2), the seventh meaning of 'canon', *table providing a standard*, is not any table, but one that provides a standard. The standard laid forth in the ecclesial fourth-century canons is *the canon of the Old and New Testaments*, or *the canon of the Divine Scriptures*.

Charles Scalise similarly criticizes a distinction between Scripture and canon, introduced to separate the two concepts:

> Childs's definition of *canon* is particularly in tension with the work of scholars (e.g. Albert Sundberg) who want to make a sharp distinction between *Scripture* and *canon*. Such a sharp distinction separates the concept of canon from the long historical process of the formation of Scripture. According to this opposing view, *canon* should be used only to refer to a 'closed collection' of scriptural texts. *Scripture* is seen as a more open and fluid category, while *canon* points to an authoritative fixed list of books. Canon is thus set apart from the historical

---

[143] Ibid., 293: So Zahn and Souter. Westcott and Beyer think that the meaning 'rule' (i.e. 'standard' or 'norm') and not 'list' was the first intended meaning of the word κανών, 'it was the material content of the books that prompted believers to regard them as the "rule" of faith and life'.
[144] Barr, *Holy Scripture: Canon, Authority, Criticism*, 63.
[145] Ibid., 67.

process of the origin and development of Scripture. Instead, canon is restricted to the final boundary-setting process Childs calls canonization.[146]

Adolf von Harnack's view on the canonization of the NT canon likewise stresses the continuity between the emergence of the concept of a biblical canon (which he places around the year AD 200) and its 'pre-history': '[I]t was because Christian writings were in public actually treated like the Old Testament, without being simply included in the body of the old Canon, that the idea of a second sacred collection could be realised'. As discussed above, he considers the logic, or code, behind the New Testament canon formation to be found in the formulas αἱ γραφαὶ καὶ ὁ κύριος and αἱ γραφαὶ καὶ τὸ εὐ αγγέλιον. That is to say, the Christ-event and the proclamation of the gospel in the church anticipate the later canonical development into a bipartite Christian Scripture canon.[147] Von Harnack here derives an ongoing canonical *Wirkungsgeschichte* from earlier layers of the Christian tradition. 'Canon' is thus used as a broader category than, e.g. in Sundberg and Barr.

2.8 Conclusion

In order to understand the concept of canon as applied to the biblical writings, it is important to take into consideration its composite character, derived from its various ecclesial usage – but also from its treatment by church leaders, theologians and biblical scholars. Because of the organic continuity seen in the process of canon formation, on the one hand, and the self-organizing character of the canon – its function as a basic sign language in the ecclesial setting – on the other, we are apt to regard the process leading up to an in principle closed canon as a unified whole, having the ability to organize itself from its own centre. Or, from a different vantage point, the self-organizing of this canon only occurs when biblical texts are treated as a literary unity.

As I have underscored in this chapter, the category of *Wirkungsgeschichte* is most crucial, by underlining that the canon can only be very poorly under-stood, when made into an object; if objectified or historicized. None the less,

---

[146] Scalise, *From Scripture to Theology: A Canonical Journey into Hermeneutics*, 45.
[147] Harnack, *The Origin of the New Testament*, 7f., 26; cf. also Metzger, *The Canon of the New Testament*, 3.

as a true historical object, the canon is to be seen as the unity of the one and the other, a relationship that constitutes both the reality of history and the reality of historical understanding. In fact, the term 'canon' as a designation for the body of biblical literature seems to have been suggested by the history of its meaning within the church. Some central aspects of this history have been outlined in the present chapter together with a brief account of the word's general Hellenistic background and usage. Against this backdrop, I have sought to describe the canonizing process as an integral whole by focusing various dimensions of the notion of canon useful for a systematic treatment. These include canon *as Scripture, as regional list of Old and New Testament writings, as book(s) of the Bible, as Rule of Faith, as scriptural intertext, as scriptural metatext, as the Old and New Testaments, as the prophetic and apostolic Scriptures, as collection of authoritative writings, as divine lection of Scriptures,* and *as classic collection of literature.*

The dynamics of the ecclesial use of the concept of canon can be seen as well in the early meanings attached to the word 'canon', e.g. canon 1) *as measure,* 2) *as prototype* or *model,* 3) *as norm, rule* or *standard,* 4) *as limit* or *boundary,* 5) *as tool of exactitude* and *criterion,* 6) *as a prototype of proportionality, symmetry and harmony,* and 7) *as a table* or *list providing a standard.*

Even if canon *as a list* is stressed amongst biblical scholars, as exemplified by some recent research, such cataloguing or listing, too, is arguably linked to other, less specified meanings (e.g. canon *as rule* or *standard*). A broader notion of canon is also indicated by the use of the word in some fourth-century canon lists. In this connection the more narrow definition of 'canon' *signifying a list,* used by James Barr and A. C. Sundberg, is criticized, as is their sharp distinction between 'scripture' and 'canon'.

In this chapter we also note the creative uses made of the canon concept by Irenaeus (canon *as a prototype* and *model*), inspired by Hellenistic artistry, and by Clement of Alexandria (canon *as tool of exactitude* and *criterion*). Balancing the interpretation of the two Testaments that together make up Christian Scripture is important for these writers: The Canon of Faith/Truth (Irenaeus) and the Ecclesiastical Canon (Clement) teach the church 'to read the Old Testament as the promise of the Gospel and the Gospel as the fulfilment of that promise.'[148]

---

[148] See Edwards, *Catholicity and Heresy in the Early Church* (Farnham: Ashgate, 2009), 40.

Part Two

Material and Textual Aspects of the Canon

3

The *nomina sacra*: Highlighting the Sacred Figures of the Text

Practically all dimensions of canonicity discussed in the previous chapter owe some of their functioning to the specific textuality of the emerging Christian Bible.[1] A central feature of this textuality comes to expression by consistently highlighting a series of keywords throughout the Christian manuscript tradition, most notably the Greek names for *God, Lord, Jesus, Christ*, and for the most part also *Spirit*.

Although almost forgotten in modern times, until the fifteenth century this strictly limited selection of Christian keywords – the so called *nomina sacra* – was graphically marked off by contraction, suspension or a combination of both in basically all Greek and Latin Christian biblical manuscripts. Since 1907, when the classicist Ludwig Traube published his monumental study on this scribal phenomenon,[2] these special abbreviations have been extensively studied. The question has also been raised whether their original function could somehow be set in connection with the canonization of the Christian Bible. In this chapter I shall try to answer this question affirmatively, by arguing that the introduction of the system of *nomina sacra* into the biblical texts – immediately indicating a Christian context for these writings – was a decisive step in the early stages of the canonical process. The *nomina sacra* attained this function by marking out a centre – focusing on the Greek names for *God, Jesus* and *Spirit* – within the Christian Scriptures, a textually, devotionally and theologically determined *Mitte der Schrift*.[3] And, as far

---

[1] On text and textuality, see Chs 3–6, esp. Ch. 6.

[2] Traube, *Nomina sacra: Versuch einer Geschichte der christlichen Kürzung* (München: C. H. Beck'sche Verlagsbuchhandlung, 1907).

[3] On the notion *Mitte der Schrift*, see Stuhlmacher (*Wie treibt man Biblische Theologie?* [Neukirchen-Vluyn: Neukirchener, 1995], 68–76) for further references.

as the extant manuscript evidence takes us, writings that did not contain these markers were not part of the Christian Scriptures. Furthermore, the system added an unmistakable Christian stamp to the texts containing them, especially as the scribal pattern for using the demarcations became relatively standardized and recognizable throughout the text corpora forming the New Testament.[4] Most significantly, this scribal practice embraced both what came to be labelled the 'Old' and the 'New Testament' writings – and thus textually–editorially placing old (the OT) and new (the NT) Christian Scripture on a par from early on.

3.1 General usage of *nomina sacra* in the biblical manuscripts

An excerpt from the Chester Beatty papyri – P[46] (Chester Beatty II) – appears in a somewhat different form than we are used to from modern editions of the Greek biblical text. It consistently highlights these specially abbreviated names, central for Christian faith – since the time of Traube usually labelled *nomina sacra*:

οιδα τ[ε οτι ερχομενος προς υμας εν πληρωματι] ευλογιας Χ͞ρ͞υ ελευσομαι παρακαλω δε υμας δια του Κ͞υ ημων Ι͞η͞υ Χ͞ρ͞υ και δια της αγαπης του Π͞ν͞ς συναγωνισασθαι μοι εν ταις προσευχαις υπερ εμου προς τον Θ͞ν (Rom 15.29-30).[5]

In fact, before the art of printing, nearly all Christian Greek biblical manuscripts contain this system of abbreviation with a stroke over the contracted or

---

[4] For some critical comments on the standardization of the early system of *nomina sacra*, see Kim Haines-Eitzen, *Guardians of Letters: Literacy, Power, and the Transmitters of Early Christian Literature* (Oxford: Oxford, 2000), 92–4. Haines-Eitzen is partly right in emphasizing that some of the scribal variations, inconsistencies and idiosyncracies in the way *nomina sacra* were written, found among our earliest manuscripts, point 'toward a mode of transmission in which standardization and uniformity was not in existence' (93). However, the basic four or five *nomina sacra* abbreviations are present everywhere and contain only minor variations (e.g. Ι͞η, Ι͞η͞ς, Ι͞ς, and in P[66] Ι͞η͞υ͞ς, for forms for *Jesus*). That we are dealing here with an easily recognizable scribal *system* of demarcating these words even in the earliest period is not in doubt, however – and to that extent the scribal standardization is very early. No extant manuscripts demonstrate the developing *nomina sacra* convention prior to the standard practice of regularly marking off the four names God, Lord, Jesus and Christ.

[5] P[46] (Chester Beatty II and P. Mich. Inv. 6238; ca. AD 200); cf. Aland, *The Text of the New Testament: An Introduction to the Critical Editions and to the Theory and Practice of Modern Textual Criticism* (Grand Rapids: Eerdmans, 1989), 88.

suspended forms.[6] The abbreviated names above, and at most some 10 other words, are apparently for reverential reasons ('highlighting the sacred figures of the Christian faith')[7] given special treatment in writing. Due to a 'certain broad phenomenological similarity between the *nomina sacra* and Jewish reverential treatment of the divine name', this scribal practice has commonly been associated with the special treatment accorded the divine name(s) in Early and Rabbinical Judaism.[8] In one way or another, the immediate background, as well as parallel, to the above five *nomina sacra* (or at least the earliest four; see section 3.2) – $\overline{Ku}$, $\overline{Iηu}$, $\overline{Xρu}$ (Κυριου Ιησου Χριστου), $\overline{Πνς}$ (Πνευματος) and $\overline{Θν}$ (Θεον) – thus seems to be the reverential treatment associated with the Tetragrammaton, יהוה, in the Jewish Scriptures (see section 3.4).

In terms of significance, we may also point to the immediate textual association between the words marked off in this way: the Greek words for *Lord* and *God* being graphically associated with *Jesus* and *Christ*,[9] and the other way around. In any case, the emergence of what are probably the four earliest *nomina sacra* – the characteristic abbreviations of *Jesus*, *Christ*, *Lord* and *God* – seems to be closely linked to early devotional practices and chris-

---

[6]   The abbreviations occur in the form of contractions, suspensions, or combinations of both. The system of *nomina sacra* is also kept more or less intact in the Latin, Coptic, Slavonic and Armenian versions of the Christian biblical writings. Two major works that treat the *nomina sacra* in the Greek biblical manuscripts are Traube, *Nomina sacra*, and Paap, *Nomina sacra in the Greek Papyri of the First Five Centuries A.D.: The Sources and Some Deductions* (Leiden: Brill, 1959). Paap's investigation has more recently been supplemented by Jose O'Callaghan, *Nomina Sacra in Papyrus Graecis Saeculi III Neotestamentariis* (Rome: Biblical Institute Press, 1970). Cf. also O'Callaghan, '"Nominum sacrorum" elenchus in Graecis Novi Testamenti papyris a saeculo IV usque ad VIII', *Studia Papyrologica* 10 (1971): 99–122. For treatment of the *nomina sacra* in the Septuagint, see Bedodi, 'I "nomina sacra" nei papiri greci veterotestamentari precristiani', *Studia Papyrologica* 13 (1974): 89–103; Jankowski, 'I 'nomina sacra' nei papiri dei LXX (secoli II e III d. C.)', *Studia Papyrologica* 16 (1977): 81–116. Cf. also Parker, *Codex Bezae: An Early Christian Manuscript and Its Text* (Cambridge: Cambridge University Press, 1992), 97–106; and Kenyon, 'Nomina Sacra in the Chester Beatty Papyri', *Aegyptus* (1933): 5–10.

[7]   Heath, 'Nomina Sacra and Sacra Memoria Before the Monastic Age', *JTS* 61, no. 2 (2010): 536. Tuckett's suggestion ('"Nomina Sacra": Yes and No?', in *The Biblical Canons*, (eds) J.-M. Auwers and H. J. de Jonge [Leuven: Leuven University Press, 2003, 431–58]) that *nomina sacra* may have been introduced as reading aids in the Christian manuscripts has been criticized by Hurtado (*Artifacts*, 122–34) and Heath, 'Nomina Sacra and Sacra Memoria Before the Monastic Age', 518–23. See further section 3.4.1.

[8]   Hurtado, *Artifacts*, 106. For a different view, see Tuckett, '"Nomina Sacra": Yes and No?'.

[9]   On Paul's use of Χριστος, cf. Hurtado, *Lord Jesus Christ*, 99–100: 'On the one hand, in Paul's letters the term 'Christ' has clearly become so closely associated with Jesus that it functions almost like an alternate name for him … On the other hand, the varying position of the term in the fuller expressions is one of several indications that for Paul and others who used these terms, *Christos* had not simply been reduced to a name (e.g. Jesus' cognomen) but instead retained something of its function as a title [cf., e.g. Rom. 9.3, 5].'

tological reflection in the faith communities (see below). However, to many scribes, already by the early fourth century, the *nomina sacra* practice very much seems to have become a convention.

From a hermeneutical viewpoint, it may be helpful to think of the initial use of these four or five early *nomina sacra* as an implicit dialogue between two practices happening on the written page: a new Christian scribal treatment of the divine/sacred name(s), on the one hand, and early Jesus devotion, on the other. The dialogical components then would consist of: on the one hand, finding a *Christian* identity in *Jewish* scribal treatment of the divine Name – association of the name of *Jesus* and *Christ* with reverential treatment of *God* and *Lord* (the two standard christological titles in, e.g. Ignatius of Antioch); and, on the other hand, modifying *Jewish* reverential traditions associated with the one God by associating them with other sacred names from the *Christian* religious sphere.

Having in mind the scribal demarcation of these names – the textual association of Θεος and Κυριος with Ιησους, Χριστος and Πνευμα – as well as the common reading of the Tetragrammaton as 'LORD' in the Old Testament of current English Bibles, a possible modern rendering of Rom. 15.29-30 (cited above) that takes into account the presence of *nomina sacra* (highlighted in both Greek Old and New Testament manuscripts) could look as follows: [10]

> … and I know that when I come to you I shall come in the fullness of the blessing of CHRIST. I appeal to you, brethren, by our LORD JESUS CHRIST and by the love of the SPIRIT, to strive together with me in your prayers to GOD on my behalf …

No doubt, a particular emphasis is here (cf. the Greek text above) provided for the five words in capitals, the potential significance of which seems to affect the biblical text as a whole.

The relatively consistent Christian usage of the *nomina sacra* from the first to the fifteenth centuries[11] meant that the Jewish practice of giving only

---

[10] On *nomina sacra* in early OT manuscripts, see, e.g. Hengel, *The Four Gospels and the One Gospel of Jesus Christ* (London: SCM, 2000), 280, n. 480.

[11] From the sixteenth century on, printed editions of the Bible began to replace the manuscripts. Many printed versions preserved some of the features characteristic of the *nomina sacra,* e.g. the Luther Bible of 1534, where Lord is rendered by *HERR/HErr*, God by *GOtt* and Jesus by *JEsus*. In the Swedish Bible edition of 1703, the Bible of Charles XII, the Tetragrammaton is similarly rendered

the Tetragrammaton, *YHWH*,[12] special graphic treatment in the biblical texts, from early on was modified by the church.[13] To the extent that this *nomina sacra* practice had significance – which has recently been disputed by Christopher Tuckett (see below) – a key issue involved seems to have been the scribal intention to textually link the name of *God* with that of *Jesus*, or to give textual expression to a devotional pattern in which Jesus features beside God. The later additions of some short forms to the list of *nomina sacra*, such as *Father* (Π̄η̄ρ̄) and *Son* (Ῡϲ̄), seem to have been similarly motivated.[14]

In Pauline language, the new unique way 'the God of Abraham, Isaac and Jacob' is spoken of in the Christian life-setting is as the 'God and Father of our Lord Jesus Christ' (Rom. 15.6; 2 Cor. 1.3; 11.31; Eph. 1.3).[15] As it was associated with such language, describing the Christian God, the logic behind the early *nomina sacra* convention may be theologically–devotionally, rather than christologically–devotionally, motivated: God cannot be spoken of or honoured except by means of reference to Jesus (cf. Phil. 2.9-11; John 5.23).[16] As Hurtado recently put it: 'Early Christians thought God demanded Jesus worship.'[17] In other words, if we assume a close connection between Jesus devotion and the *nomina sacra* practice, the primary question behind the introduction of the *nomina sacra* into the early NT writings might not have been whether or not Jesus was thought to be divine, but how the community

---

by *HERren* and Jesus by *JEsus*. The editors of the King James Bible, on the other hand, have chosen to treat only the Tetragrammaton, rendered like LORD, in the Old Testament as a *nomen sacrum*.

[12] For other Hebrew names of God treated like the Tetragrammaton, see Howard, 'The Tetragram and the New Testament', *JBL* 96 (1977): 63–83.

[13] The Christian scribal practice of using *nomina sacra* seems to be in agreement with the earliest christology, which, as Richard Bauckham argues, 'was already the highest Christology'. Jesus was from the earliest post-Easter beginnings of christology onwards included, 'precisely and unambiguously, within the unique identity of the one God of Israel'; and this was done by including Jesus in 'the unique, defining characteristics by which Jewish monotheism identified God as unique.' Bauckham, *God Crucified: Monotheism and Christology in the New Testament* (Carlisle: Paternoster, 1998), vii–viii. Cf. also Newman, *The Jewish Roots of Christological Monotheism: Papers from the St. Andrews Conference on the Historical Origins of the Worship of Jesus* (Leiden: Brill, 1999).

[14] Arguably including also *man/human being*. However, both *son* and *man/human being* as *nomina sacra* tend to have a broader denotation than *Jesus*.

[15] Cf. Hurtado, *God in New Testament Theology* (Nashville: Abingdon, 2010), 37–8.

[16] Hurtado (*God in New Testament Theology*, 44) underlines that this Christian devotional pattern 'is not "ditheism," the worship of two gods, but a new kind of monotheistic devotional practice in which "God" is worshiped typically with reference to Jesus, and Jesus is reverenced in obedience to "God" and to the glory of this God.' Cf. also Schrage, *Unterwegs zur Einheit und Einzigkeit Gottes: Zum 'Monotheismus' des Paulus und seiner alttestamentlich-frühjüdischen Tradition*, Biblisch-theologische Studien 48 (Neukirchen–Vluyn: Neukirchener, 2002), 135–86.

[17] Oral response by Hurtado at the *Day in Honour of Professor Larry W. Hurtado* arranged by the Centre for the Study of Christian Origins in Edinburgh on 7 October 2011.

was to speak meaningfully about (the one) God who had revealed himself in and through Jesus Christ. In any case, the core group of *nomina sacra* introduced are very likely directly related to first-century Christian God-talk and devotional practices.

3.2 Frequency of *nomina sacra* in the earliest manuscripts

Since Traube's palaeographic work on the *nomina sacra*, some rather detailed discussion as to the origin, development and meaning of the contractions adopted by Christian scribes can be noted. What Traube named *nomina sacra* are a strictly limited number of words in Christian sources written in special abbreviated forms, apparently indicating their intrinsic or contextual religious or sacred character. And, as argued by some scholars, the earliest four contracted words – *God*, *Lord*, *Jesus* and *Christ* – may, perhaps more accurately, be called *nomina divina* (Shuyler Brown) or *nomina dei* (Christian von Stavelot).[18]

Although abbreviations were generally used by Hellenistic and Jewish scribes in the first and second centuries AD,[19] the system of *nomina sacra*, embracing up to 15 words (mainly nouns), most probably originated within the Christian scribal practice for reasons other than the saving of time and space.[20] To judge from our second- and third-century Bible manuscripts,[21]

---

[18] Traube, *Nomina sacra*, 6, 17f., 33: Traube introduced the Latin designation *nomina sacra*. Earlier terminology that influenced Traube's is: E. M. Thompson's expression *sacred and liturgical contractions*, H. Omont's designation *mots consacrés* and Christian von Stavelot's label *nomina dei*. Following Shuyler Brown ('Concerning the Origin of the *Nomina Sacra*', *Studia Papyrologica* (1970): 7–19), the designation *nomina divina* is in some regards an even better term than *nomina sacra*. I choose, however, to stick to the conventional designation initiated by Traube. My reason for this is twofold: First, there seems to be relative agreement nowadays regarding the use of the term *nomina sacra*, and I find no compelling reason to deviate from this consensus. Second, this designation is better suited for the group of 15 abbreviations taken as a whole.

[19] Nachmanson, 'Die schriftliche Kontraktion auf den griechischen Inschriften', *Eranos* 10 (1910): 101–41; Rudberg, *Neutestamentlicher Text und Nomina sacra* (Uppsala: A.-B. Akademiska Bokhandeln, 1915); Driver, 'Abbreviations in the Massoretic Text', *Textus* 1 (1960): 112–31; McNamee, 'Abbreviations in Greek Literary Papyri and Ostraca', *Bulletin of the American Society of Papyrologists*, Supplements 3 (1981).

[20] Paap, *Nomina sacra in the Greek Papyri of the First Five Centuries A.D.*, 2: Paap lists four peculiar characteristics of the *nomina sacra* that set them apart from the ordinary manner of abbreviation: 1) There is always a horizontal stroke over the whole of the contraction or suspension. 2) The number of the *nomina sacra* is strictly limited. 3) The beginning and end of the contractions are regulated by certain rules. Finally, 4) saving of space and time is not the reason why the abbreviated forms are used. To this list can be added the christological and trinitarian reverential dimension of the *nomina sacra* paralleling the Jewish reverence of the Name.

[21] See Roberts and Skeat, *The Birth of the Codex* (London: Oxford University Press, 1983); Turner,

it quickly found universal acceptance among the regional churches. Hence, all our extant Greek and Latin manuscripts[22] of the Old and New Testaments contain the *nomina sacra*, papyri as well as manuscripts, uncial as well as minuscule manuscripts, Old Testament Scriptures as well as gospels, acts, letters, apocalypses, but also apologetic and other literary writings produced within the Christian religious sphere.[23] Interestingly, however, the scribal practice was more consistently carried out in OT and NT texts and other Christian literary writings than in Christian 'documentary' texts, such as letters.[24]

Usually included are the following 15 words (or 17, if the words for *cross* and *crucify*, on the one hand, and *Spirit* and *spiritual*, on the other, are treated separately). The approximate frequency of these *nomina sacra* forms in 74 early NT manuscripts are shown below (roughly second- to early fourth-century, up to and including P[123]):[25]

1. The primary group (99%–100% *nomina sacra* forms in the singular):

Frequency	Greek	English	Nominative	Genitive
100%	Θεος	GOD	$\overline{\Theta\varsigma}$	$\overline{\Theta\upsilon}$
100%	Χριστος	CHRIST	$\overline{X\rho}$, $\overline{X\rho\varsigma}$, $\overline{X\varsigma}$	$\overline{X\upsilon}$
100%	Ιησους	JESUS	$\overline{I\eta}$, $\overline{I\eta\varsigma}$, $\overline{I\varsigma}$	$\overline{I\upsilon}$
99%	Κυριος	LORD	$\overline{K\varsigma}$	$\overline{K\upsilon}$

2. The secondary group (89%–95% *nomina sacra* forms)

95%	σταυρος	CROSS	$\overline{\sigma\tau\varsigma}$, $\overline{\sigma\tau\rho\varsigma}$	$\overline{\sigma\tau\upsilon}$
89%	Πνευμα	SPIRIT	$\overline{\Pi\nu\alpha}$	$\overline{\Pi\nu\varsigma}$

The Typology of the Early Codex (Philadelphia: University of Pennsylvania Press, 1977); and Haelst, *Catalogue des papyrus littéraires juifs et chrétiens* (Paris: Publications de la Sorbonne, 1976).

[22] Coptic, Armenian and Slavonic manuscripts could be added as well.

[23] See Aland, *Repertorium der Griechischen Christlichen Papyri*, I-2 (Berlin and New York: Walter de Gruyter, 1976); However literary writings, as for example Irenaeus' *Adversus Haereses*, were often published as scrolls, the regular book format. See, e.g. Roberts and Skeat, *The Birth of the Codex*.

[24] Hurtado, *Artifacts*, 98.

[25] For details on the frequency of *nomina sacra* in 74 early NT manuscripts (based on the November 2009 Accordance version of P. W. Comfort and D. P. Barrett (eds), *The Text of the Earliest New Testament Greek Manuscripts* [Corrected and enlarged, Accordance electronic ed.; Wheaton: Tyndale House Publishers, 2001]), see my 'Notes on the *Nomina Sacra* and Biblical Interpretation', in *Beyond Biblical Theologies*, (eds) H. Assel, S. Beyerle and C. Böttrich (WUNT 295; Tübingen: Mohr Siebeck, 2012), 263–95.

3. The tertiary group (23%–62% *nomina sacra* forms)

62%	σταυροω	CRUCIFY	Verb forms	
53%	Πατηρ	FATHER	$\overline{\Pi\eta\rho}$	$\overline{\Pi\rho\varsigma}$
45%	ανθρωπος	HUMAN BEING	$\overline{\alpha\nu\circ\varsigma}$	$\overline{\alpha\nu\circ\upsilon}$
44%	Ιερουσαλημ	JERUSALEM	$\overline{I\lambda\eta\mu}$	
36%	Yιος	SON	$\overline{Y\varsigma}$	$\overline{Y\upsilon}$
24%	Ισραηλ	ISRAEL	$\overline{I\eta\lambda}$	
23%	πνευματικος	SPIRITUAL	Adjectival forms	

4. The quaternary group (0%–5% *nomina sacra* forms)

5%	ουρανος	HEAVEN	$\overline{\circ\upsilon\nu\circ\varsigma}$	$\overline{\circ\upsilon\nu\circ\upsilon}$
3%	μητηρ	MOTHER	$\overline{\mu\eta\rho}$	$\overline{\mu\rho\varsigma}$
0%	Δαυιδ	DAVID	$\overline{\Delta\alpha\delta}$	
0%	σωτηρ	SAVIOUR	$\overline{\sigma\eta\rho}$	$\overline{\sigma\rho\varsigma}$

The suprascript line above the contraction had the function of drawing the reader's attention – a warning that the word could not be pronounced as written (due to the strange letter sequence). And, as we will see below, originally it might also have had the function of classifying the word as a numerical sign (cf. *Barn.* 9.7-9). Based on the frequency of the *nomina sacra* forms listed above, in the following I shall focus attention first of all on the primary group (ca. 100 per cent *nomina sacra* forms), but also on the secondary (ca. 90 per cent *nomina sacra* forms) and tertiary (ca. 25–60 per cent *nomina sacra* forms) groups.

The frequency of *nomina sacra* in the two fourth-century codices Vaticanus and Sinaiticus serve as good illustrations of the significance of the scribal practice, at least as far as consistency goes: in the NT portion of Vaticanus the core group of four words (Θεος, Κυριος, Ιησους, Χριστος) are abbreviated in almost every case, whereas Πνευμα is written as a *nomen sacrum* in only 3 per cent of the occurrences of the noun.[26] In Codex Sinaiticus (OT and NT), on the other hand, the core group consists of five words (Θεος, Κυριος, Ιησους, Χριστος, Πνευμα), all of which are almost exclusively written as *nomina sacra*. Here Πνευμα is abbreviated in 99 per cent of the occurrences of the word and the other four names in 98–100 per cent.[27] The NT of Vaticanus,

---

[26] Ibid., 277.

[27] Jongkind, *Scribal Habits of Codex Sinaiticus* (Piscataway, NJ: Gorgias, 2007), 67–8; and Bokedal, 'Notes on the *Nomina Sacra* and Biblical Interpretation', 277f.

on the other hand, seems to demonstrate what is probably a conservative use of contractions, limiting the words treated in this way to four. Nevertheless, in this regard Vaticanus turns out to be an exception when compared to other extant manuscripts. The palaeographer C. H. Turner, therefore, could say in 1924 that of all our Greek manuscripts one hand of Vaticanus provides the only exception to the universal practice of abbreviating Πνευμα as a *nomen sacrum*.[28] So, in line with the overall impression we get from the manuscript tradition, we may describe these textual markers as triadic (a core group of five *nomina sacra* as found in most Christian Greek OT and NT manuscripts), or dyadic (a core group of four *nomina sacra*, as found in the NT portion of Vaticanus).

Most importantly when seeking to establish links between the *nomina sacra* convention and the early Christian canon formation, we should note the tendency to variously limit the number of *nomina sacra* in some early manuscripts: four or five (P[13]; the NT portion of Codex Vaticanus; the Latin text of Codex Bezae), eight (P[45]; Codex Bezae), nine (P[46]; P[66]), 11 (P[75]), 13 (Codex Washingtonianus), or some 15 Christian keywords in the more developed fourth- and fifth-century system (Codex Sinaiticus, Codex Alexandrinus).[29]

3.3 *Nomina sacra* and canonization

The four earliest *nomina sacra* – the abbreviated forms of *Jesus, Christ, Lord* and *God* – most probably originated in a Jewish Christian milieu, no later than the late first or early second century. Due to the consistent treatment of Ιησους, Χριστος, Κυριος and Θεος as *nomina sacra* (next to perfect consistency in the earliest Christian NT manuscripts) and Πνευμα (next to perfect consistency, e.g. in Codex Sinaiticus; ca. 90 per cent consistency in the

---

[28] Turner, 'The *Nomina Sacra* in Early Latin Christian MSS', *Studi e Testi* 40 (1924): 66–9. See also Bokedal, 'Notes on the *Nomina Sacra* and Biblical Interpretation', 272–79: Πνευμα is abbreviated as a *nomen sacrum* in 83 per cent of the occurrences of the noun in the Latin and 84% in the Greek text of Codex Bezae; in Codex Washingtonianus the frequency is 91 per cent (with the nine occurrences of the word written in full being non-sacred uses of Πνευμα); and in the 74 second- to fourth-century NT manuscripts up to and including P[123] referred to above, Πνευμα is abbreviated in 89 per cent of the occurrences of the word. In Codex Vaticanus, as mentione above, the corresponding figure is 3 per cent.

[29] See further my 'Notes on the *Nomina Sacra* and Biblical Interpretation'.

second- to fourth-century NT manuscripts), the divine name as it relates to the name of Jesus receives continuous readerly attention. The major effects, which I would like to emphasize here, of the introduction of these scribal demarcations into the Christian writings with an impact on the canonical process, were:

1. To graphically identify the sacred Tetragrammaton (in Greek rendered as Θεος and Κυριος) with the Greek names for *Jesus* and *Christ* (section 3.4), thereby textually indicating an already existing binitarian pattern of devotion in the faith communities and the typical manner in which Christians spoke of the one God. (In Hurtado's wording, and within the broader theological context of the NT, 'we can say that in the view attested in the NT, "God" is so closely linked with Jesus and Jesus so closely linked with "God" that one cannot adequately identify the one without reference to the other.');[30]

2. To modify the identity of the Scriptures as Scriptures over against the synagogue, making them specifically Christian, and/or vice versa, making the Scriptures specifically Christian, thereby modifying the identity of the Scriptures as Scriptures vis-à-vis the synagogue (section 3.5);[31]

3. To editorially indicate a unity of the Scriptures and a Christian narrative and theological[32] focus (sections 3.4, 3.5, 3.6 and 3.8);

---

[30] Hurtado, *God in New Testament Theology*, 43.

[31] In a Jewish context, the Torah made up the centre and ground of the biblical writings. With the introduction of the *nomina sacra* this was arguably exchanged for a Christian narrative reading. The Scriptures from now on received a new identity as clearly Christian Scriptures, lacking the most characteristic Jewish scriptural marker, the Tetragrammaton. See also Barton, *The Spirit and the Letter: Studies in the Biblical Canon* (London: SPCK, 1997), 108–21: In the Mishnah, in the tractate Yadaim 3.5, it is stated that 'all holy scriptures (*kitbe ha-qôdesh*, "writing of holiness") make the hands unclean'. If treated outside the sphere of the Temple or of Synagogue worship the Scriptures are thought to make the hands unclean. The technical term for 'Scriptures' is here 'Writings of holiness' (*kitbe ha-qôdesh*). Barton contends that it is the very occurrence of the sacred Tetragrammaton (or other names for God) that makes a writing holy with the result of defiling the hands of anyone handling it outside the context of the sacral. Thus, 'writings of holiness' perhaps means not 'holy scriptures' but 'writings containing the Name'. If this is correct, the Christian writings could not be regarded as Scripture because of their lack of the Name, or at least the Name in its proper form, correctly rendered according to the strict regulations connected with the writing of the Name (see further, section 3.5, n. 120). From this, or against a similar Jewish background, the introduction of the *nomina sacra* could arguably have meant an important stage in the process of canonization of the Christian Scriptures, the 'Old' as well as the newly written 'New Testament' portions.

[32] The particular character of this limited number of words pertains to the sacred (cf. the modern designation *nomina sacra*; cf. n. 18), especially the divine name and some central christological titles and sacred figures of early Christian faith.

4. To engraft, using the wording of C. H. Roberts, 'what might be regarded as the embryonic creed of the first Church'[33] onto the textuality of the Scriptures (sections 3.6 and 3.8). The *nomina sacra* word-group and the emerging vocabulary profile typical of the Rule/Canon of Faith here finds a common textual platform;[34] and

5. To juxtapose the new Christian writings used for worship, missionary preaching, argumentation and devotion to the Jewish Scriptures (section 3.7). Given these features and assumptions, the inauguration of the *nomina sacra* may be characterized as a key element in the early canonization of the Christian Bible. It could perhaps even be argued that it would be difficult to envisage a Christian scriptural canon formation without the *nomina sacra* practice preparing the ground for placing OT texts side by side with newly composed 'apostolic' writings. For early Christianity as for early Judaism, it seems to have been the case that a writing without a strong emphasis on the sacred name(s) could not make any strong claim towards scripturality (cf. note 31).

3.4 Origin and development of the *nomina sacra*

3.4.1 On the origin of the *nomina sacra*: Three major models

Since Traube's pioneering work a century ago, a handful of publications have appeared that treat the question of the origin of the *nomina sacra*.[35] According to Traube, the practice of writing the Tetragrammaton in a special reverential form had been transferred to the word Θεος by the

---

[33] Roberts, *Manuscript, Society and Belief in Early Christian Egypt* (Oxford: Oxford University Press, 1979), 46.

[34] See my 'The Rule of Faith: Tracing Its Origins', *Journal of Theological Interpretation* 7, no. 2 (forthcoming).

[35] Nachmanson, 'Die schriftliche Kontraktion auf den griechischen Inschriften'; Rudberg, *Neutestamentlicher Text und Nomina sacra*; Paap, *Nomina sacra in the Greek Papyri of the First Five Centuries A.D.*; Brown, 'Concerning the Origin of the *Nomina Sacra*'; Howard, 'The Tetragram and the New Testamen'; Roberts, *Manuscript, Society and Belief in Early Christian Egypt*; Treu, 'Die Bedeutung des Griechischen für die Juden im römischen Reich', *Kairos* 15 (1973): 123–44 (English translation by Adler and Kraft can be found online at http://eawc.evansville.edu/essays/nepage.htm (accessed 20 June 2013); Trobisch, *Die Endredaktion des Neuen Testaments: Eine Untersuchung zur Entstehung der christlichen Bibel* (Freiburg, Switzerland: Universitätsverlag Freiburg and Göttingen: Vandenhoeck & Ruprecht, 1996); Hurtado, 'The Origin of the *Nomina Sacra*: A Proposal', *JBL* 117 (1998): 655–73; idem, *Artifacts*, 99ff.

Greek-speaking Jews, through omission of the vowels, using the contracted form Θ͞ς. From this term the system of *nomina sacra* was developed, first by the Jews who began to use contracted forms of Κυριος, Πνευμα, Πατηρ, ουρανος, ανθρωπος, Δαυιδ, Ισραηλ and Ιερουσαλημ, and later by the Christians who added the contractions of Ιησους, Χριστος, Υιος, σωτηρ, σταυρος, and μητηρ.[36]

A. H. R. E. Paap, who in 1959 updated Traube's results,[37] basically took over this scheme of development. Paap, however, thought that the initial word Θεος was the only Jewish contribution. The rest of the terms had, in his view, been elaborated by the Christians.[38]

A decade later Schuyler Brown proposed the contraction of Κυριος as the initial *nomen sacrum* introduced, not by the Jews, but by the church. As this term for the early Christians referred both to the God of Israel and to Jesus Christ, the practice of reverential contraction was soon extended 'in one direction to Θεος and in the other direction to Ιησους and Χριστος.'[39]

Still another suggestion as to the original term was made by Kurt Treu and George Howard, who argued that Κυριος as well as Θεος were the original contractions, according to Treu introduced by the Jews and in Howard's view by the Christians as substitutions for the Tetragrammaton. More recently Robert Kraft has argued along the lines of Treu, favouring a Jewish origin for the earliest contraction of Κυριος.[40]

Despite the relative strength of these options, I shall here follow the suggestion made by C. H. Roberts and Larry Hurtado, who both opt for a Christian origin of the system, and the abbreviation of Ιησους as the first *nomen sacrum*.[41] Hurtado argues as follows (points 1–6):[42]

---

[36] Traube, *Nomina sacra*, 27–44.
[37] Paap, *Nomina sacra in the Greek Papyri of the First Five Centuries A.D.: The Sources and Some Deductions.*
[38] Ibid., 119–27.
[39] Brown, 'Concerning the Origin of the Nomina Sacra', 18.
[40] Treu, 'Die Bedeutung des Griechischen für die Juden im römischen Reich'; English translation by Adler and Kraft can be found online at http://eawc.evansville.edu/essays/nepage.htm (accessed 20 June 2013). Howard, 'The Tetragram and the New Testament'. Cf. Hurtado, 'The Origin of the *Nomina Sacra*', 665. Kraft, 'The 'Textual Mechanics' of Early Jewish LXX/OG Papyri and Fragments', in *The Bible as Book: The Transmission of the Greek Text*, (eds) S. McKendrick and O. O'Sullivan (London: British Library, 2003), 51–72. Cf. Hurtado, *Artifacts*, 107f.
[41] Roberts, *Manuscript, Society and Belief in Early Christian Egypt*, 35–48; Hurtado, 'The Origin of the *Nomina Sacra*', 665–71.
[42] Hurtado, 'The Origin of the *Nomina Sacra*', 664–71.

1. The provenance of the manuscript evidence points to a Christian origin reflecting the Jewish reverence for the Name.[43]

2. The early variation in the spellings of some of the *nomina sacra* (contraction, suspension and combinations of both) suggests a Christian origin, rather than an already developed Jewish practice.

3. The early occurrence of both the contracted form, $\overline{I\varsigma}$, and the suspended form, $\overline{I\eta}$, of Ιησους, over against the more regularly rendered forms of the other three[44] of the earliest *nomina sacra*, supports Ιησους as the initial term.

4. The only one of the earliest attested *nomina sacra* commented on in the Patristic material is the suspended form of Ιησους, $\overline{I\eta}$.[45] Pre-Constantinian mosaics and graffiti also support 'Jesus' as the primary *nomen sacrum*.[46]

5. $\overline{I\eta}$ is proposed as the first *nomen sacrum*, which is consistent with the religious significance associated with Jesus' name, and its ritual use in the early church.[47]

6. In *Barn.* 9.7-8 and Clem. *Strom.* VI, 11, the *nomen sacrum* $\overline{I\eta}$, which here represents the number 18, is associated with a Jewish Christian reflection on the number 318 (see section 3.4.2), which provides an explanation of the peculiar suprascript line normally associated with the *nomina sacra*.

The existence of this type of *linea superscripta,* placed squarely over the abbreviated word, may otherwise be difficult to explain. It does not look like the overbar used for ordinary abbreviations placed at the end of the word. The suprascript line attached to the *nomina sacra*, on the other hand, looks like the

---

[43] Cf. Roberts, *Manuscript, Society and Belief in Early Christian Egypt*, 34.

[44] In particular Κυριος and Θεος. As regards Χριστος, one of the earliest four *nomina sacra*, which is not as regularly rendered, further discussion is needed. See below.

[45] *Barn.* 9.7-8. For Clement of Alexandria the attribution of 18 as the numerical value of $\overline{I\eta}$ seems to be regarded as an old and perhaps no longer current tradition (*Strom.* VI, 11; ANF 2:499): 'As then in astronomy we have Abraham as an instance, so also in arithmetic we have the same Abraham. "For, hearing that Lot was taken captive, and having numbered his own servants, born in his house, 318 (ΤΙΗ)," he defeats a very great number of the enemy. They say, then, that the character representing 300 is, as to shape, the type of the Lord's sign, and that the *Iota* and the *Eta* indicate the Saviour's name; that it was indicated, accordingly, that Abraham's domestics were in salvation, who having fled to the Sign and the Name became lords of the captives, and of the very many unbelieving nations that followed them. Now the number 300 is, 3 by 100. Ten is allowed to be the perfect number. And 8 is the first cube, which is equality in all the dimensions – length, breadth, depth.'

[46] Wicker, 'Pre-Constantinian *Nomina Sacra* in a Mosaic and Church Graffiti', *Southwestern Journal of Theology* 52, no. 1 (2009): 68. I am grateful to Benjamin Laird for drawing my attention to this article.

[47] Hurtado, 'The Origin of the *Nomina Sacra*', 670; Hurtado, *One God, One Lord: Early Christian Devotion and Ancient Jewish Monotheism* (Edinburgh: T&T Clark, 1998).

strokes used above letters that served as number signs. Hurtado concludes his argumentation by suggesting $\overline{\text{Iη}}$ (=18) as an early Jewish Christian play with gematria, numerically equivalent with the Hebrew word for life, ‏חי‎ (=18; ‏ח‎=8; ‏י‎=10). Having given examples of gematria associations across the Hebrew and the Greek alphabets, Hurtado even hints at a connection between $\overline{\text{Iη}}$ and John 20:30, where the words 'have life in his name' are put forth as a possible allusion to the proposed gematria (cf. also section 3.4.5).[48]

A quite different view on the origin and significance of the scribal practice as compared to the ones discussed above is attained by C. M. Tuckett. In an essay titled "Nomina Sacra': Yes and No?' he sets out to underline some incongruities in recent research on the *nomina sacra*. Criticizing David Trobisch's account of the New Testament canon formation,[49] for example, he argues that the system of the *nomina sacra* 'does *not* appear to be a feature which distinguishes Christian *Scripture*.'[50] Though he notes some inconsistencies in previous scholarship on origin and Christian identity tied to these abbreviations, he does not convincingly offer any real alternative historical account to that of Traube, Roberts and Hurtado. As Hurtado and Heath have argued (see note 7), his suggestion that these short forms primarily functioned as reading aids seems unlikely. Furthermore, the theological and textual issues at stake, with which I am here concerned, are only addressed in passing, with a rather questionable conclusion: 'They may be "nomina" – yes (or at least in part and perhaps in origin); but "sacra" – no!'[51]

To sum up, three major models accounting for the origins and significance of the *nomina sacra* convention are still in play: 1) the *nomina sacra* are of Jewish origin and they mean something (Treu and Kraft);[52] 2) the *nomina*

---

[48] Hurtado, 'The Origin of the *Nomina Sacra*', 664–71. Cf. also McHugh, 'In Him was Life' (Tübingen: Mohr Siebeck, 1989), 123: 'It is a commonplace to say that where the Synoptic Gospels speak of the kingdom, the Fourth Gospel, with the sole exception of John 3.3, 5, speaks instead about life.' For caution on the use of the notion of gematria, see Hvalvik, 'Barnabas 9.7-9 and the Author's Supposed Use of Gematria', *NTS* 33 (1987): 276–82; and Heath, '*Nomina Sacra* and Sacra Memoria Before the Monastic Age', 539, n. 67.

[49] On Trobisch, see below.

[50] Tuckett, '"Nomina Sacra": Yes and No?', 443.

[51] Ibid., 458.

[52] The theory of a possible Jewish origin of the *nomina sacra* was first suggested by Ludwig Traube and has recently been argued by James R. Edwards for the occurrence of Θεος written as a *nomen sacrum* in the Sardis Synagogue, *JBL* 128, no. 4 (2009): 813–21. For a wider discussion on the possible Jewish origin of the practice, see Treu, 'Die Bedeutung des Griechischen für die Juden im römischen Reich', *Kairos* 15 (1973); English translation by Adler and Kraft can be found online at http://eawc.evansville.edu/essays/nepage.htm (accessed 23 March 2013).

sacra are of Christian origin and they have no meaning (Tuckett); and 3) the *nomina sacra* are of Christian origin and they mean something (Roberts, Hurtado).[53]

3.4.2 The Tetragrammaton and the *nomina sacra*

Now, if we stick to Roberts's and Hurtado's model on origins, assuming that Ιησους was the first Christian *nomen sacrum*, presumably soon followed by Χριστος, a next step in the development of the scribal practice would then be the inclusion of Κυριος and Θεος. The change that took place with the latter two being added may not have been obvious to the contemporary church, given the reverential practice already associated with the name of Jesus.[54] However, looked at from a Second Temple or Rabbinic Judaism perspective, the decisive step from a single *nomen sacrum* (Ιησους; Ιη, Ιης, Ις) to the graphic association of *Jesus* and *Christ* with *Lord* and *God* (Ις, Χς, Κς and Θς) seems to have been crucial (if this is the way the scribal practice developed). From the moment Κυριος and Θεος were graphically treated just like the initial *nomen sacrum*, Ιησους – which was arguably soon followed by Χριστος – and at the same time attained the function as transcriptions of the Tetragrammaton in the Christian writings, a shift in the status of these short forms arguably took place. Graphically they now were to parallel the very source of sacredness in the Jewish Scriptures, the ineffable *nomen divinum, Shem hameforash,*[55] *YHWH.*[56] In Hurtado's phrasing:

---

[53] I owe the formulation behind this simple structuring of the various players to a recent conversation with Professor Larry Hurtado.

[54] See Hurtado, *One God, One Lord,* for references.

[55] According to the Mishnah tractate *Yoma,* the Name was uttered only once each year by the High Priest during the liturgy of Yom Kippur (Laato, *Monotheism, the Trinity and Mysticism: A Semiotic Approach to Jewish-Christian Encounter* (Frankfurt am Main: Peter Lang, 1999), 55). What S. Cohon says about the role played by the other names of God in Jewish theology is of interest for my treatment of the *nomina sacra* (cf. esp. section 3.8): 'All the names of God represent the efforts of men to make His being real to themselves, and to express the prevailing ideas of His nature and actions, i.e. His attributes' (Cohon, *Jewish Theology* (Assen: Royal van Gorcum, Prakke & Prakke, 1971), 213. Cited from Laato, *Monotheism, the Trinity and Mysticism,* 55.)

[56] See, e.g. the Septuagint rendering of the prohibition in Lev. 24.16, where death is invoked on one who 'pronounces the name of the Lord', whereas the Hebrew text only forbids 'blaspheming the name of Yahweh', *Migne* CVI 1278 (as referenced by Traube); Christian von Stavelot in the ninth century used the term *nomina dei* to designate those of the Christian abbreviations that referred to the divine name or persons. The earliest abbreviations seem to have included only this category, while a somewhat later development in the late first or early second century also included the words 'Cross', 'Israel', 'Jerusalem' and 'Heaven' (Traube, *Nomina sacra,* 6). As already mentioned, Schuyler Brown ('Concerning the Origin of the *Nomina Sacra*') prefers the term *nomina divina* to designate

[I]t seems likely that Jewish reverence for the divine name, and particularly the Jewish practice of marking off the divine name reverentially in written forms, probably provides us with the key element in the religious background that early Christians adapted in accordance with their own religious convictions and expressed in the *nomina sacra.*[57]

The collective role of the four earliest contracted forms seems to have been to function as Christian representations of the divine name(s), being associated with, or being substitutes/abbreviations for, *YHWH, God* and *Lord,* in the Scriptures, and in the new Christian writings. According to the new christo-logical scheme, the names *Jesus, Christ, Lord* and *God* were thus graphically and textually placed on an equal level. Two features of the development of the *nomina sacra* confirm such a rendering.

First, the psychological impulse to the origin of the system[58] most likely derives from the Jewish practice of treating the divine name, the Tetragrammaton, with the utmost awe according to well defined rules, including also scribal and various ritual and creedal practices.[59] Two of the four earliest *nomina sacra* – Θ̅ς̅ and Κ̅ς̅ – are special abbreviations for *God,* Θεος, and *Lord,* Κυριος, respectively, and used as Greek transcriptions of *YHWH.*[60] Furthermore, *Jesus* and *Christ* were analogously contracted in the same way as *Lord* and *God.*

This is surprising, not so much because of the parallel graphic treatment of *Lord* and *Jesus,* but because of the potential interpretation that seems to be suggested to the reader, of a connection between the names *Jesus* and *YHWH.* This connection is by graphic analogy also established between the other

---

the earliest phase of the system of special Christian abbreviation; Hurtado similarly thinks that the (four) earliest words are more correctly designated *nomina divina,* 'The Origin of the *Nomina Sacra*'.

[57] Ibid., 662–3. See also idem, *Artifacts,* 104–06.

[58] It is proper to talk of a system of *nomina sacra* as soon as the four earliest *nomina sacra,* the abbre-viations of *Jesus, Christ, Lord* and *God,* all are treated alike, as a group of *nomina sacra.* This stage of development is to be distinguished from the earliest phases of the phenomenon, when the first *nomen sacrum,* arguably the suspension of Jesus, began to be commonly used.

[59] The divine Name should not, for example, be pronounced aloud; Barton (The Spirit and the Letter, 108–23). On scribal practices related to the Name, cf. ibid., 119–20. For creedal functions, see sections 3.4.3 and 3.6.2. A handy overview of some different positions on the pronunciation of the Name is found in De Troyer, 'The Pronunciation of the Names of God', in Gott Nennen, (eds) Dalferth and Stoellger, Religion in Philosophy and Theology 35 (Tübingen: Mohr Siebeck, 2008).

[60] Metzger, *Manuscripts of the Greek Bible: An Introduction to Greek Palaeography* (New York and Oxford: Oxford University Press, 1981), 35; Howard, 'The Tetragram and the New Testament': In commenting on Psalm 2.2, Origen tells that among Greeks Adonai is pronounced κύριος (Sel. in Psalmos, Ps. 2.2 Migne PG, xii, col. 1104A), as referred by Howard.

nomina sacra and the Tetragrammaton through the Greek renderings Θεος (Θ̅ς̅) and Κυριος (Κ̅ς̅). Most importantly, as the *nomina sacra* practice as a whole seems to be best accounted for by reference to the Jewish reverence for the divine name and the special scribal treatment of the Tetragrammaton, the basic motivation for the practice may have been fundamentally theological rather than christological or creedal (cf. section 3.1).

Even though the first *nomen sacrum* most likely was the suspended form for *Jesus* (Ι̅η̅), the new scribal practice will soon imply associations to the Tetragrammaton, at the latest when *nomina sacra* are systematically introduced into Christian Septuagint manuscripts.[61] This event does not only form a part of the sanctioning of an official 'Old Testament' translation in Greek. It also marks a crucial step in the canonization process of the Christian Scriptures.

Septuagint and emerging New Testament texts are here treated alike, where some special features of the 'New Testament' texts appear to be transferred back on to the 'Old Testament' (cf., e.g. *Barn.* 9.7-9).[62]

Second, these four, five, eight, nine, 11, or, in their developed Byzantine form, approximately 15 contracted names in the biblical manuscripts (cf. section 3.1 above) also stand out as sacred contractions for another reason. The abbreviated forms occur typically only when used in a sacral sense. Although not always consistently carried out, this is especially the case for

---

[61] A new awareness regarding the necessity of an edition of a specifically Christian Bible consisting of the Septuagint and a New Testament part is instigated towards the middle of the second century beginning with Justin and continuing with Irenaeus and Tertullian among others, for whom the Septuagint text as well as the delimitation of the New Testament portion of the one Bible are being focused. The formation of the 'New Testament' may here be described as a process in three phases. Using the schema of Gerd Theiseen, the first phase can be viewed as a *'fellowship with oral communication'* (*The New Testament: History, Literature, Religion* [London: T&T Clark, 2003]). Second, from around AD 60 or 70 to AD 120 a *'closed literary fellowship formed within the communities'* (ibid.). From about 120 some problems regarding diverse and even 'heterodox' handling of the Scriptures arose within the communities (*Epistle of Barnabas*, Marcion, Christian Gnostics). In the third phase, between AD 145 and AD 200 (which – as in the case with the previous two phases – cannot be demarcated from the previous one) various attempts at closing the Christian literary canon are made, such as the formation and publication of an early 'canonical archetype' (Trobisch) and other similar regional and/or catholic editions of the 'New Testament'. The new notions of a literary 'Old Testament' as well as a 'New Testament' are the primary outcome of this process. Parallel with this development Christianity 'becomes a *literary fellowship which is opening up*.' This leads to the production of various apocryphal writings, apologetic writings addressed to the outside world, and Gnostic literature (Theissen, *The New Testament*).

[62] On canonization in two directions, from 'Old Testament' to 'New Testament' and vice versa, see section 3.7. Cf. also Barton, *The Spirit and the Letter*, 122f. For a brief overview of *nomina sacra* in early Old Testament manuscripts, see, e.g. Hengel, *The Four Gospels and the One Gospel of Jesus Christ*, 280, n. 480.

the word Θεος.[63] A clear distinction is made by scribes between *God* or *Lord* as sacred names (written as *nomina sacra*) and these words as profane words in the plural (*gods* and *lords*, written in full). Almost all 50 or so Greek manuscripts containing 1 Cor. 8.4-6 included by Reuben Swanson in his *New Testament Greek Manuscripts* make this distinction.[64]

Again, the initial aim of the *nomina sacra*, it seems, is 'to express religious reverence, to set apart these words visually in the way they are written.'[65] If we allow ourselves to speculate a bit, we may ask whether this scribal practice may have been a parallel exegetical development to that of the gospel tradition focusing on the Greek text of Psalm 110. As creative exegesis of the Scriptures was 'the principal medium in which early Christians developed even the most novel aspects of their thought', Psalm 110.1 (and other texts brought into exegetical relationship with it such as Psalm 8.6 and Daniel 7.13-14) becomes the key text to indicate Jesus' participation in the unique divine sovereignty,[66] including God's cosmic rule over all things.[67]

Further, in passages such as Heb. 1.4 and Phil. 2.9, where the exalted Jesus appears to be given the divine Name, as the Exalted One,[68] the *nomina sacra* practice as a whole may give some graphical support to a high-christological reading (cf. above, 3.4.2).[69]

---

[63] See, e.g. Tuckett, "Nomina Sacra': Yes and No?'. A good illustration of the consistency of the usage of *nomina sacra* forms only in a sacred context is the way Θεος in the plural regularly is written in full; it is found eight times in the plural in the New Testament of Sinaiticus and Vaticanus (always with a non-sacral meaning; John 10.34, 35; 1 Cor. 8.5 [twice], Gal. 4.8, Acts 7.40, 14.11 and 19.26). The distinction between reference to the one God and the gods is here underlined. See n. 64 below.

[64] Swanson, ed., *New Testament Greek Manuscripts: Variant Readings Arranged in Horizontal Lines Against Codex Vaticanus. 1 Corinthians* (Wheaton, IL: Tyndale House Publishers, and Pasadena, CA: William Carey International University Press, 2003), 113f.

[65] Hurtado, 'The Origin of the *Nomina Sacra*', 659; ibid. 658: 'These abbreviated words are distinctive in form, subject matter, and function from other scribal phenomena, so much so that it is widely (but not universally) accepted that the presence of any of them in a manuscript is itself a good indication of its Christian provenance.'

[66] Bauckham, *God Crucified*, 29.

[67] Bauckham, *Jesus and the God of Israel: 'God Crucified' and Other Studies on the New Testament's Christology of Divine Identity* (Colorado Springs, CO: Paternoster, 2008), 173.

[68] So Bauckham, *God Crucified*, 29–34, esp. 34.

[69] The particular *nomina sacra* in these passages are: SON in Heb 1.2; JESUS CHRIST in Phil 2.5, 10.

3.4.3 The earliest creedal formulations and the *nomina sacra*[70]

In his learned, however much neglected, study *Der Katechismus der Urchristenheit*, Adolf Seeberg pointed out already a century ago the abundance of creedal elements present in the writings that were to form the New Testament.[71] In accordance with second- and third-century ecclesial mainstream belief, he argued that what was later called the 'Rule of Faith' was ultimately traceable to the apostolic age, or, in the words of Irenaeus, to 'the Apostles and their disciples' (*Adv. Haer.* III, 4.1). In 1950, part of Seeberg's research was furthered by J. N. D. Kelly in his investigation of early Christian creeds, with a second and a third revised edition appearing in 1960 and 1972.[72] Likewise, Ferdinand Hahn and Bengt Hägglund have taken up and elaborated on Seeberg's pioneering work.[73] For my present purpose it will suffice to provide a few examples of christological creedal patterns found in the NT material.

Already the early one-clause christologies will give us clues for linking them to the emerging system of the *nomina sacra*. Kelly provides some illustrative examples from the New Testament,[74] the most popular of which seems to have been 'Jesus is Lord' ($\overline{K\varsigma}\,\overline{I\varsigma}$; e.g. Rom. 10.9, Phil. 2.11). Another succinct formula is 'Jesus is the Christ' (Mark 8.29 and 1 John 2.22); furthermore, 'Jesus is the Son of God' (1 John 4.15). In addition to these brief formulas we find in the New Testament numerous christological kerygmas attaching the name of Jesus to 'selected incidents in the redemptive story' (Rom. 1.3f.; 1 Cor. 15.3; Phil. 2.6-11; 1 Pet. 3.18ff. etc.).[75] Typical stereotyped binitarian formulas occur as well, such as 'the God and Father of our Lord Jesus Christ' (τον $\overline{\Theta v}$ και $\overline{\Pi\rho\alpha}$ του $\overline{Ku}$ ημων $\overline{Iu}$ $\overline{Xu}$; Rom. 15.6, Eph. 1.3 etc.), embracing,

---

[70] The argument in this section is more fully developed in Bokedal, 'The Rule of Faith'.
[71] Seeberg, *Der Katechismus der Urchristenheit* (Leipzig: A. Deichert'sche Verlagsbuchhandlung Nachf. [Georg Böhme], 1903).
[72] Kelly, *Early Christian Creeds* (New York: Longman Publishing, 1972).
[73] Bengt Hägglund has made use of A. Seeberg in some articles elaborating on his study from 1958 (Hägglund, 'Die Bedeutung der 'regula fidei' als Grundlage theologischer Aussagen', *Studia Theologica* 12 [1958]: 1–44). See now also idem, *Sanningens regel: Regula Veritatis: Trosregeln och den kristna traditionens struktur* (Skellefteå: Artos & Norma bokförlag, 2003), for further references. Ferdinand Hahn wrote an introduction to Seeberg's work for the 1966 edition published in *Theologische Bücherei* 26, München 1966.
[74] The examples are taken from Kelly, *Early Christian Creeds*, 13ff. Commenting on a draft of this chapter, Dr Timo Laato reassured me of the likely connection of the *nomina sacra* with the earliest one-clause christologies.
[75] Kelly, *Early Christian Creeds*, 18.

we may note, four (Codex Vaticanus, with 'Father' written in full) or five (Codex Sinaiticus) *nomina sacra*. The early sources also evidence an emerging triadic (or Trinitarian) kerygmatic pattern (2 Cor. 13.14; Matt. 28.19). From this, Kelly draws some important conclusions: 'The binitarian schema, it is evident, was deeply impressed upon the thought of primitive Christianity; so, it would appear, was the Trinitarian.'[76] And further, '[o]ur conclusion must be that one-membered, two-membered and three-membered confessions flourished side by side in the apostolic Church as parallel and mutually independent formulations of the one kerygma; and this is a datum of prime importance.'[77] No doubt, these kerygmatic formulations, based on revelatory events, experiences,[78] early devotional patterns and theological reflection, laid the foundation for the developing and variously expressed kerygma, with its threefold form of invocation, doxology and narrative.[79] In the course of this process, Name and narrative become integral parts of the one gospel (1 Cor. 15.1ff.).[80]

3.4.4 Dating, location, manuscript types

As to the origin of the use of *nomina sacra*, Hurtado estimates that '[a]llowing even minimal time for the practice to gain sufficient recognition and standardization would require an origin no later than the first century.'[81] Roberts and Skeat arrive at a similar conclusion. Roberts somewhat speculatively even suggests a more precise dating as well as location, opting for a pre-70 date in Jerusalem or Antioch.[82] As for the emergence of the system of *nomina sacra*, the association of the practice with the Jewish treatment of the divine Name, the selection of words included such as 'Christ' and 'Jerusalem', and the

---

[76] Ibid., 22.
[77] Ibid., 24.
[78] See Hurtado, 'Religious Experience and Religious Innovation in the New Testament', *JR* 80 (2000): 183–205; and ibid. *Lord Jesus Christ*, 70–4.
[79] See further, Ch. 8, esp. sections 8.2 and 8.4; see also sections 5.2 and 5.3.
[80] See sections 3.6.2 and 3.8.
[81] Hurtado, 'The Origin of the *Nomina Sacra*', 660. Peter Balla remarks that the *nomina sacra* point to the likelihood of recensions of the New Testament aiming at a standardized text for Christian worship; his dating of the *nomina sacra* in the second, and not later than the third century, however, can only be maintained for the development and expansion of a system of sacred abbreviations that had been introduced and partly standardized at the latest towards the end of the first century (Balla, 'Evidence for an Early Christian Canon (Second and Third Century)', in *The Canon Debate*, (eds) J. A. Sanders and L. M. McDonald [Peabody, MA: Hendrickson, 2002], 376).
[82] Roberts, *Manuscript, Society and Belief in Early Christian Egypt*.

'strong sense of connection of the OT and Jewish traditions' all point in the direction of 'a time prior to 70 CE when we commonly suppose the influence of Christian Jews was greater than in later decades.'[83] The Jewish Christian isopsephy in *Barn.* 9, and possibly also in John 20.30 (see sections 3.4.1 and 3.4.6), similarly signals a first-century origin.

For the establishment and sanction of the basic features of the practice, therefore, no later church authorities seem to have been needed. *Nomina sacra*, therefore, may have been employed by Christian scribes by the time the Fourth Gospel was written, and probably even earlier.[84]

As I have argued elsewhere, there are some indications that Ignatius of Antioch may point to knowledge of *nomina sacra* in his epistles; and if the *Epistle of Barnabas* can be 'assigned, with fair probability, to the very end of the first century', as William Horbury suggests, we have a first-century example of a probable reference to the *nomina sacra* practice (*Barn.* 9.7-9; see section 3.4.6).[85]

The seemingly universal occurrence of *nomina sacra* in the earliest extant Christian documentary and literary manuscripts also points us towards a first-century origin. Hurtado lists three such early categories of texts: 1) Christian biblical manuscripts; 2) non-canonical religious texts (e.g. the Egerton Gospel fragment); and 3) 'orthodox' and 'unorthodox' Christian writings (e.g. the Coptic Gospel of Thomas, Acts of Peter, Acts of John). 'All this', he maintains, 'indicates a remarkable instance of standardization that contrasts with the wide diversity we have come to associate with the earliest centuries of Christianity.'[86] The fact that Gnostic texts draw from the same Christian 'orthodox' list of *nomina sacra* adds further testimony to an early date for their introduction.[87]

---

[83] Hurtado, 'The Origin of the *Nomina Sacra*', 672.

[84] This thesis would combine in an interesting way with T. C. Skeat's rather speculative hypothesis of the introduction of the codex format as a result of the publication of the Fourth Gospel, Skeat, 'The Origin of the Christian Codex', *Zeitschrift für Papyrologie und Epigraphik* 102 (1994): 263–8. Cf. also n. 48, above, on the phrase 'life in his name' as used in the Fourth Gospel. See also section 3.4.6.

[85] See Heath, '*Nomina Sacra* and Sacra Memoria Before the Monastic Age'; and Bokedal, 'Notes on the *Nomina Sacra* and Biblical Interpretation'. On dating, see Horbury, *Jews and Christians: In Contact and Controversy* (Edinburgh: T&T Clark, 1998), 131–3.

[86] Hurtado, 'The Origin of the *Nomina Sacra*', 658.

[87] Ibid., 672.

3.4.5 Ἰησους, the staurogram and the christogram

In addition to possible allusions in the New Testament to Ἰησους as a form of gematria (John 20.30), further indications of such allusions are found in some Patristic sources, e.g. in the christological exposition of Deut. 28.66. As part of the oldest christological testimonies, this verse was homogeneously expounded by early Church Fathers.[88] In Book Five of *Adversus Haereses*, Irenaeus writes:

> He came to His own in a visible manner, and was made flesh, and hung upon the tree, that He might sum up all things in Himself. 'And His own peculiar people did not receive Him,' as Moses declared this very thing among the people: 'And thy life shall be hanging before thine eyes, and thou wilt not believe thy life' [Dtn. 28:66 LXX]. Those therefore who did not receive Him did not receive life. (*Adv. Haer.* V, 18.3)[89]

In Tertullian's *Adversus Iudaeos* (ch. 11), where Deut. 28.66 is also cited, 'thy life'[90] similarly refers to Jesus, which recalls the proposed tentative numerical connection above between the *nomen sacrum* Ἰη (=18) and the Hebrew word for life, חי (=18). The context here is the mystery of the Hebrew sign 'Taw' (Ezekiel 9.4ff.). In his traditional Christian exposition, Tertullian combines the Old Testament meaning of 'Taw'[91] with the symbol of the cross:

> Now the mystery of this 'sign'[92] was in various ways predicted; (a 'sign') in which the foundation of life was forelaid for mankind; (a 'sign') in which the Jews were not to believe: just as Moses beforetime kept on announcing … and thy life shall hang on the tree [*in ligno*] before thine eyes; and thou shalt not trust thy life. (*Adv. Iud.* 11)[93]

As has been convincingly shown by Erich Dinkler,[94] the early church integrated the Hebrew symbol 'Taw' (ת) into the graphics of two other early *nomina*

---

[88] E.g. Irenaeus, Cyprian, Melito, Hippolytus, Lactantius, Novatian, Tertullian, Clement, Origen and others. Cf. Prigent, *Justin et l'Ancien Testament* (Paris: Librairie Lecoffre, 1964), 177f., 189–94 and 346; Reijners, *The Terminology of the Holy Cross in Early Christian Literature: As Based upon Old Testament Typology* (Nijmegen–Utrecht: Dekker & Van de Vegt, 1965), 146–62; see also Skarsaune, *The Proof from Prophecy: A Study in Justin Martyr's Proof-Text Tradition: Text-Type, Provenance, Theological Profile* (Leiden: Brill, 1987), 437.

[89] ANF 1:547.

[90] Cf. Col. 3.4; John 1.4, 14.6.

[91] See Dinkler, *Signum Crucis* (Tübingen: Mohr Siebeck, 1967), 1–54, esp. 15–21.

[92] The Septuagint rendering of 'Taw' is σημεῖον.

[93] ANF 3:168.

[94] Dinkler, *Signum Crucis*; Dinkler-von Schubert, 'CTAYROC: Vom "Wort vom Kreuz" (1 Kor 1,18) zum Kreuz-Symbol', in *Byzantine East, Latin West: Art-Historical Studies in Honor of Kurt*

sacra, namely contractions of σταυρος and Χριστος, both of which came to be represented by the same symbol, the staurogram/christogram.[95] However, 'Taw', whose meaning was 'sign' as well as 'cross sign', could be graphically rendered both as 'x' and as '+'.[96] This partly explains why the graphic analogy between the Hebrew 'Taw' and the Greek letters 'Chi' (Χ) and 'Tau' (Τ) was combined by the early Christians with the *nomina sacra* forms of σταυρος and Χριστος. These two *nomina sacra* were graphically connected also by the staurogram/christogram.

Further confirmation of the letter 'T' as symbolizing the cross is given by Lucian[97] and Tertullian.[98] In the latter writer, Ezekiel 9.4-6 ('put a mark on the foreheads of those who sigh and groan over all the abominations …') is connected with the cross. This exposition of the cross is also found on Jewish ground.[99] Accordingly, as Dinkler has argued, the 'Taw' as cross in the Jewish setting is either a sign of protection (*Schutzzeichen*) or a sign of belonging to YHWH for those who obey him (*Eigentumszeichen Jahwes für die ihm Gehorsamen*).[100] Such Jewish usage also explains the occurrence of the sign of the cross found on Jewish graves from the first century AD.

To conclude my argument, there are reasons to accept Ιησους (Ιη) as the initial *nomen sacrum*. However, as the early Christian exposition of the Scriptures developed, the symbol of the cross, combined with the Taw-sign, came to be influential together with the *nomen sacrum* Χριστος. An argument for including Χριστος among the two or three earliest *nomina sacra* would be the same as that listed above (sections 3.4.1 and 3.4.2): On the one hand, the early occurrence in the manuscripts of the contracted form of Χριστος, Χς, and on the other, a few occasions of the suspended form, Χρ, as well as the combined form, Χρς, against the more regularly contracted forms of Κυριος, Κς, and Θεος, Θς, give support to Χριστος as an earlier *nomen sacrum* than these latter terms. This is also confirmed by Latin sources, e.g. Codex Bezae,

Weitzmann, (eds) C. Moss and K. Kiefer (Princeton: Department of Art and Archaeology, Princeton University, 1995).

[95] See Black, *The Chi-Rho Sign – Christogram and/or Staurogram?* (Paternoster, 1970).

[96] Dinkler, *Signum Crucis*, 16.

[97] *Iudicio Vocalium* 12; for reference see Dinkler, *Signum Crucis*.

[98] *Adv. Marc.* III, 22.5-7; *Adv. Iud.* 11; Reijners, *The Terminology of the Holy Cross in Early Christian Literature: As Based upon Old Testament Typology*, 146–62.

[99] Dinkler, 'Zur Geschichte des Kreuzsymbols', and idem, 'Kreuzzeichen und Kreuz – Tav, Chi und Stauros', in idem, *Signum Crucis*, 1–54.

[100] Dinkler, 'Kreuzzeichen und Kreuz – Tav, Chi und Stauros', in idem, *Signum Crucis*, 32.

where the suspension $\overline{XR}$ is the normal form beside the combined form $\overline{XRS}$.[101]

3.4.6 'Cross' and 'crucify' as *nomina sacra*

The oldest explicit testimony to the use of *nomina sacra* that we know of is found in the epistle of *Barnabas*, written around AD 70–135.[102] In *Barn.* 9.7-9 the author presents an allegorical reading of the circumcision of Abraham's household by elaborating on the number 318 – in the source rendered by the Greek letters ΤΙΗ, which is instanced also in some other contemporary Christian manuscripts.[103] This seems to indicate that the author of *Barnabas* had a Christian copy before him of Gen. 14.14:[104]

> For Abraham, the first to perform circumcision, was looking ahead in the Spirit to Jesus when he circumcised. For he received the firm teachings of the three letters [λαβὼν τριῶν γραμμάτων δόγματα]. For it says, 'Abraham circumcised eighteen and three hundred men from his household.' What knowledge, then, was given to him? Notice that first he mentions the eighteen and then, after a pause, the three hundred. The number eighteen [in Greek] consists of an Iota [Ι], 10, and an Eta [Η], 8. There you have Jesus. And because the cross was about to have grace in the letter Tau [Τ] [ὅτι δὲ ὁ σταυρὸς ἐν τῷ ταῦ ἤμελλεν ἔχειν τὴν χάριν], he next gives the three hundred, Tau. And so he shows the name Jesus by the first two letters, and the cross by the other. For the one who has placed the implanted gift of his covenant in us knew these things. No one has learned a more reliable lesson from me. But I know that you are worthy.[105]

Here, the *nomen sacrum* for *Jesus*, represented by ΙΗ (=18), meets for the first time in our sources together with the symbol of the cross, the Greek letter Τ (=300). The specific meaning of the three letters may already be known by the readers. It is associated with certain 'firm teachings' (δόγματα). The symbol

---

[101] Cf. Traube, *Nomina sacra*, 152ff., where both Ιησους and Χριστος are treated as irregularly rendered; and Parker, *Codex Bezae*. See further Bokedal, 'Notes on the *Nomina Sacra* and Biblical Interpretation'.

[102] Hvalvik (*The Struggle for Scripture and Covenant: the purpose of the epistle of Barnabas and Jewish–Christian competition in the second century* [Tübingen: Mohr Siebeck, 1996], 23) dates Barnabas to AD 130–2, whereas William Horbury (*Jews and Christians*, 133) prefers a late first-century date. Since the dating of *Barnabas* is still much of an open question, what can be regarded as certain for its composition is a date between AD 70 and the end of the second century (ibid., 17).

[103] For references, see Hurtado, Artifacts, 146f.

[104] For references to extant OT manuscripts, see Hurtado, *The Earliest Christian Artifacts: Manuscripts and Christian Origins* (Grand Rapids and Cambridge: Eerdmans, 2006), 146f.

[105] *Barn.* 9.7-9; trans. Ehrman, *The Apostolic Fathers*, vol. 2, 45–7.

of the cross is said to express grace – a theme further developed in *Barn.* 11 and 12, in connection with the Christian baptism and typological interpretation of the serpent raised by Moses in the desert.

Extant Christian OT manuscripts that contain the short form ΤΙΗ for the Greek number 318, referred to by *Barnabas,* include the fourth-century Chester Beatty Papyrus IV and most probably also the early second- to third-century P. Yale 1.[106] That the symbolic interpretation of the number 318 was well known in Christian circles is further confirmed by Clement of Alexandria in his reading of Gen 14.14. However, for him such isopsephy seems to be more of a tradition than part of his own immediate exegesis (however, cf. note 45). Clement comments: 'For it is said [φασιν] that the character for 300 is by its shape a symbol [τύπος] of the cross of the Lord [τὸ κυριακὸν σημεῖον]'.[107]

3.5 Provenance, possession and interpretation of the Scriptures

The presence of any of the *nomina sacra* in a manuscript is itself a good indication of its Christian provenance. The selection and combination of these four to 15 names in effect immediately indicate a Christian context.[108] As textual markers they are distinctive 'in form, subject matter, and function from other scribal phenomena'.[109] The Christian texts containing them are thereby set apart from the Scriptures of the synagogue as well as from other writings. Thus, as characteristic identity markers, the *nomina sacra* arguably conveyed to the lector or teacher something like a textual code.[110]

---

[106] See Hurtado, *The Earliest Christian Artifacts,* 146f.; for P. Yale 1, see Dinkler, 'Papyrus Yalensis 1 als ältest bekannter christlicher Genesistext: Zur Frühgeschichte des Kreuz-Symbols', in *Im Zeichen des Kreuzes: Aufsätze von Erich Dinkler,* (eds) O. Merk and M. Wolter (Berlin and New York: Walter de Gruyter, 1992), 341–5.

[107] *Strom.* VI, 11. Quoted in n. 45 above.

[108] Cf. Schubert, 'Editing a Papyrus', in *The Oxford Handbook of Papyrology,* ed. Roger Bagnall (Oxford: Oxford University Press, 2009), 200.

[109] Hurtado, 'The Origin of the *Nomina Sacra*', 658.

[110] *Barn.* 9.7-9 is our earliest indication of a connection between the graphics of the *nomina sacra* and their interpretation. In addition to being openly explained to the faith community, as in *Barn.* 9 and Clem. *Strom.* VI, 11, the information transmitted by the system of *nomina sacra* was probably also addressed to the professional reader and expositor of the text. Perhaps the parallel is too far-fetched, but, to me, there seems to be some similarity between the textual code transmitted by the *nomina sacra* and the 'surplus' of information addressed to the instrumentalist sometimes contained in a musical score. During the Baroque era this type of communication between the composer and the

Originally, such an implied code of sacred name/word combinations probably pertained also to the liturgical practice of the earliest communities.[111] Theologically, these 'sacred and liturgical contractions', as E. M. Thompson labelled them, were initially shaped in a binitarian format, which was soon developed into a triadic schema. GOD, JESUS and SPIRIT, here 'amount to a kind of summary of the Rule of Faith, and indicate that these texts were read within the contours of a developing creedal confession.'[112]

In his reconstruction of Jewish–Christian interrelations of the early decades of the second century, Reidar Hvalvik elaborates the theory that Jews and Christians were engaged in a contest for the possession of the Scriptures.[113] In this struggle for Scripture – which took place within the broader process of 'the parting of the ways'[114] – the question 'whose books?' turns out to be central beside the issue of Scripture interpretation. As part of the polemics between church and synagogue, which reached a climax at the time of the second Jewish revolt, it could even be said that 'possession of the books implied understanding of their content'.[115]

The introduction of the *nomina sacra* in the biblical manuscripts occurred at a time when Christians were adopting a distinctive identity as a *tertium genus* against both Judaism and the pagan world.[116] The issue of Christian distinctiveness could very well have been involved as the early *nomina sacra* – reflecting the binitarian structure of Christian devotion – were introduced into the Scriptures. As regards the second-

---

musician was elegantly developed, e.g. in the full scores of J. S. Bach. A resemblance between the *nomina sacra* and these scores may be seen in the allusions to or symbolizations of the Christian cross in the manuscripts, and in the musical notes, respectively. None of these symbolizations were intended to sound as the text were read or the scores performed; they were rather meant as a piece of information/symbolization of a theoretical, spiritual or decorative kind, that could shape the interpretation on a higher level. Both in regard to the *nomina sacra* and these typical Baroque scores a similar relation between provenance and interpretation may suggest itself.

[111] See Hurtado, 'Christ-Devotion in the First Two Centuries: Reflections and a Proposal', *Toronto Journal of Theology* 12 (1996); and idem, *One God, One Lord*.

[112] Barton, Review of the 2005 ThD edition of the present book, *JTS* 58:2 (2007): 620.

[113] Hvalvik, *The Struggle for Scripture and Covenant*.

[114] The process was intensified between the fall of Jerusalem, AD 70, and the second Jewish revolt, AD 132–5. See Dunn, *The Partings of the Ways: Between Christianity and Judaism and their Significance for the Character of Christianity* (London: SCM, 1991); Lieu, "The Parting of the Ways': Theological Construct or Historical Reality', *JSNT* 56 (1994): 101–19; cf. also Taylor, *Anti-Judaism and Early Christian Identity: A Critique of the Scholarly Consensus* (Leiden, New York and Köln: Brill, 1995).

[115] Wilken, 'The Jews and Christian Apologetics After Theodosius I Cunctos Populos', *HTR* 73 (1980): 468; cited from Hvalvik, *The Struggle for Scripture and Covenant*, 136.

[116] Cf. Stanton, 'The Fourfold Gospel', *New Testament Studies* 43 (1997): 339: Stanton's claim concerns the codex format, but it appears to be even more applicable to the system of *nomina sacra*.

century situation, Hvalvik's thesis that Jewish–Christian competition implied a mutually exclusivizing identity of the Scriptures also accords with this assumption. To the author of the *Epistle of Barnabas*, to Justin in his *Dialogue with Trypho* as well as to Tertullian in *Prescription Against Heretics*,[117] the issue 'whose Scriptures?' was of utmost importance.[118] In this connection the *nomina sacra* could very well have contributed to a distinct Christian textual identity of the Scriptures in relation to the synagogue.[119] This hypothesis finds further support in some recent discussions on the close correlation between the concept of Scripture and the divine Name in Judaism during this period. John Barton, in his book *The Spirit and the Letter*, relates to this discussion:

> Perhaps a definition of a canonical text for Judaism in our period would be: a text in which it is legitimate to write the Tetragrammaton. Otto Betz argues along exactly these lines that the Qumran Temple Scroll was regarded by the community as 'canonical': it contains the Tetragrammaton (in square script). This is an entirely *physical* idea of the nature of a sacred book, and one which students of the canon may not have been sufficiently sensitive to.
>
> In the Middle Ages the idea that the divine Name or names were what gave the Bible its sanctity was more or less taken for granted within the Jewish mystical tradition.[120]

If the presence of *nomina sacra* in an 'Old Testament' manuscript clearly sets it apart as of Christian provenance, it may also be of interest to mention the special Rabbinic rulings for destroying heretical scriptures. If we keep to the widely held supposition that it was the existence of the Tetragrammaton in a writing that made it a candidate for storage in a genizah, the usage by the Christians of writings containing the Name became problematic. As these were considered to be inaccurate writings, they could not, of course, be used by Jews who happened to come across Christian scriptural (OT) writings. However, since they contained the Name, nor could they be destroyed

---

[117] *Praescr. Haer.* 15 (ANF 3:250): In his debate with the Gnostics, Tertullian says that 'it ought to be clearly seen to whom belongs the possession of the Scriptures'.

[118] Hvalvik, *The Struggle for Scripture and Covenant*, particularly 134–6, 203f.

[119] Cf. Hurtado, 'The Origin of the *Nomina Sacra*', 658: 'These abbreviated words are distinctive in form, subject matter, and function from other scribal phenomena, so much so that it is widely (but not universally ...) accepted that the presence of any of them in a manuscript is itself a good indication of its Christian provenance.'

[120] Barton, *The Spirit and the Letter*, 118–20.

according to the normal procedure. In these cases particular rulings for handling heretical writings were applied.

In the Christian Scriptures the Name was sometimes transcribed as ΠΙΠΙ (pipi), or rendered in some other way, possibly also in Hebrew script.[121] However, by far the most common rendering was usage of the two *nomina sacra* K̅C̅ (Κυριος) and Θ̅C̅ (Θεος). Is this the typical Christian practice to which the Rabbis refer when prescribing particular rulings on the legitimacy of destroying heretical (especially Christian) scriptures 'with their names'?[122] If this is the case, then the question arises if 'their names' refers not only to the Tetragrammaton when used in Christian Scriptures, but also to the early *nomina sacra*.[123] Barton, who is sceptical as to this possibility, comments:

> It should be noted that Christian books, though they used *nomina sacra* for many holy words, which being contractions would not in Jewish eyes constitute 'names', sometimes transcribed the Tetragrammaton itself in Hebrew characters.[124]

Nevertheless, there is reason to consider the possibility that indeed the *nomina sacra* are referred to when the Rabbis talk of 'their names' in the plural. If the Tetragrammaton or some Christian transcription of the divine name is meant, we should expect the use of the singular 'their name', which, of course, would appear rather strange, given that the divine name in that case would be identical with the name of YHWH, or an alternative rendering of the Name. In other words, 'their names' could very well refer not only to 'heretical' transcriptions of the Tetragrammaton but also to the ecclesiastical Greek contractions of *Lord, God, Jesus, Christ, Father, Son* and *Spirit*.

We have reasons to believe that from early on Christian scribes took over many of the Jewish scribal practices (cf. section 3.4.4 above).[125] The church's change of attitude towards the divine name, therefore, was arguably to some degree a conscious modification of the Jewish convention of meticulously regulating the reverence, pronunciation and writing of the Name.[126] The

---

[121] See citation below, n. 124; Barton, *The Spirit and the Letter*, 186, n. 22.

[122] *Shabbat* 116a, *t. Shabbat* 13:5, *t. Yadaim* 2:13; referred to by Barton, *The Spirit and the Letter*, 118.

[123] Included among the *nomina sacra* of the early second century were the Greek words for *God, Lord, Jesus, Christ* and *Spirit*.

[124] Barton, *The Spirit and the Letter*, 186, n. 22.

[125] Roberts, *Manuscript, Society and Belief in Early Christian Egypt*; Barton, *The Spirit and the Letter*.

[126] Barton, *The Spirit and the Letter*, 108–21; Roberts, *Manuscript, Society and Belief in Early Christian Egypt*, 28–33.

abandonment of the older theory embraced by Traube and Paap, according to which the system of *nomina sacra* is of Jewish origin, is here presupposed. In the last decades, a *Christian* rather than a *Jewish* origin of the system has been forcefully argued by George Howard, C. H. Roberts, Hurtado and others. Roberts, in 1979, writes:

> Perhaps the most conclusive evidence is that of the Greek inscriptions from Palestine covering the period from Qumran to Bar Kokhba; there are 184 instances of κύριος in a sacral sense and 109 of Θεός and in not one is either word contracted. For the formal origin of *nomina sacra* we must look elsewhere.[127]

The place to look for the Christian origin, development and emerging standardization of the *nomina sacra* practice, hence, is the first- and second-century church. Here the Scriptures used for worship were not yet terminologically divided into Old and New Testament (at least not before Melito of Sardis, ca. AD 175); nor were the new Christian Gospel writings commonly named 'Scripture', γραφή, alongside the Old Testament writings. The new writings needed to be used parallel to and together with the old Scriptures for yet some decades before they could themselves be generally labelled γραφή towards the mid-second century.[128] In this process, the introduction of the *nomina sacra* into the manuscripts seems to have mattered more than has been previously recognized. Roberts's view of the *nomina sacra* as forming 'what might be regarded as the embryonic creed of the first Church', engraved into the texts, certainly underlines their significance.[129] Barton approvingly comments:

> Clearly in a sense the *nomina sacra* are related to the meaning of the texts, in that they are words with a special significance for Christians: Roberts remarks that they almost form a little creed – Jesus, Christ, Lord, and God could be treated as a quick guide to the essence of Christian faith.[130]

---

[127] Roberts, *Manuscript, Society and Belief in Early Christian Egypt*, 34. Similarly Howard, 'The Tetragram and the New Testament', 65f. Similarly Hurtado, *Artifacts*, 105. For alternative views, see De Troyer, 'The Pronunciation of the Names of God', 143–72

[128] For the development of the category of 'Scripture' as applied to the Gospels, see Chs 4, 5 and 9.

[129] Roberts, *Manuscript, Society and Belief in Early Christian Egypt*, 46.

[130] Barton, *The Spirit and the Letter*, 122: However, Barton immediately adds: 'But the convention of writing them contracted is a purely graphic convention and does not affect the meaning of the texts so written. It does, however, mark them out as Christian manuscripts; and the fact that Christian scribes applied the same convention in writing Old Testament texts is one clear indication that they had begun to treat Old and New Testament books as sacred texts in much the same sense – transferring special features of the New Testament back on to the Old.'

The system of *nomina sacra* marks the text with regard to provenance, subject matter and function.[131] By this fusion of creedal-like elements and the biblical text, a distinct Christian sacred text was established for the faith communities. On the textual-graphic as well as the liturgical-theological level the *nomina sacra,* therefore, ought to be considered when discussing the texture of the Greek biblical text.[132] From the discussion above – on the supposed correlation between the concept of Scripture and the Tetragrammaton[133] – we may even consider the possibility that without the adoption of *nomina sacra* into the Christian scriptures, these writings could not have attained the status of Scripture, eventually placing them on a par with the Jewish Scriptures. The passage cited above from the *Epistle of Barnabas*, which comments on the 318 (ΤΙΗ=318) circumcised servants, is our earliest testimony to an emphasis on the role of *nomina sacra* for scriptural identity:

> He [Abraham] signifies, therefore, Jesus by two letters, and the cross by one, He knows this, who has put within us the engrafted gift of His doctrine. No one has been admitted by me to a more excellent piece of knowledge than this.[134]

We have here an early indication of the supposed correlation between the graphics of the Christian text and its theological interpretation. The fact that *nomina sacra* from early on are 'lifted out' of the biblical texts to be used in Christian graffiti and inscriptions, or in Christian art, particularly on icons, provides further indication of their status as sacral names in the texts.[135]

3.6 Distinct textual markers

3.6.1 Graphics

In several ways the *nomina sacra* attained the function of distinct textual markers.

To begin with, on the graphic level, the following elements can be noted:

---

[131] Hurtado, 'The Origin of the *Nomina Sacra*', 658 (cited above).

[132] The place to elaborate on theological aspects implied by the scribal *nomina sacra* convention is first and foremost the liturgical, devotional and theological settings of the church, for which the Scriptures are crucial.

[133] See the citation from Barton, *The Spirit and the Letter*, 118–20.

[134] *Barn.* 9.8-9 (ANF 1:142f.); cf. Ehrman's translation above, 3.4.6.

[135] See further below.

1) the *linea superscripta*; 2) the free space that is left around the abbreviation, interrupting the normal *scriptio continua*;[136] 3) the contraction, which in the Hellenistic setting was only rarely used for the purpose of abbreviation; 4) the strictly limited number of words included among the Greek *nomina sacra*; and 5) the beautifully ornamented *nomina sacra* in some Christian manuscripts, such as the Codex Purpureus Petropolitanus (N). In this manuscript Πατηρ, Υιος and Πνευμα – the three central divine names of the Nicene (and the Apostolic) Creed – are written in gold, and the rest of the *nomina sacra* in silver letters.[137] The Book of Kells, in which the magnified *nomen sacrum* for Χριστος, X̄ρ̄, is most elegantly designed, is another example of the particular emphasis ascribed to the names in the *nomina sacra* word-group.[138]

3.6.2 Theological context: The *nomina sacra* and the Rule of Faith

Getting behind the graphics, we recall two major contextual features that ought to be considered when analyzing the system of *nomina sacra*:

1. The connection between the (variously rendered) Tetragrammaton and the *nomina sacra*.[139] On this C. H. Roberts writes: '[T]he ineffability of the name of God, expressed when the Law was read in Hebrew by replacing the vowels proper to it by those of Adonai ("Lord"), is directly or indirectly the psychological origin of the *nomina sacra*' (cf. sections 3.1 and 3.4.2).[140]

2. The parallel between the *nomina sacra*, central terms embraced by the early Christian kerygma/creed, and early Christian scriptural interpretation (cf. section 3.4.3). In early kerygmatic formulations such as 'Jesus is Lord' (K̄ς̄ Ῑς̄), or the five words that give the acronym ΙΧΘΥΣ

---

[136] See Roberts, *Manuscript, Society and Belief in Early Christian Egypt*.

[137] The practice of marking out the divine name in gold is found also among Jewish scribes in the first centuries AD; cf. Howard, 'The Tetragram and the New Testament'.

[138] See O'Reilly, 'Gospel Harmony and the Names of Christ: Insular Images of a Patristic Theme', in *The Bible as Book: The Manuscript Tradition*, (eds) J. L. Sharpe III and K. van Kampen (London: The British Library & Oak Knoll Press in association with The Scriptorium: Center for Christian Antiquities, 1998).

[139] On variations in the rendering of the Tetragrammaton, see Howard, 'The Tetragram and the New Testament'; Williams, 'The Tetragrammaton-Jahweh, Name or Surrogate?', *ZAW* 54 (1936): 262–9; Brinktrine, 'Der Gottesname 'AIA' bei Theodoret von Cyrus', *Biblica* 30 (1949): 520–23; Barton, *The Spirit and the Letter*, 120; cf. also Driver, 'Abbreviations in the Massoretic Text'.

[140] Roberts, *Manuscript, Society and Belief in Early Christian Egypt*, 28f. For a more cautious phrasing, see Hurtado, *Artifacts*, 106.

– Ιησους Χριστος Θεου Υιος Σωτηρ – all words are *nomina sacra*.
Furthermore, in the more comprehensive formulations expressed by the
Rule of Faith and the emergent Trinitarian creeds with their articles of
faith, the words marked off as *nomina sacra* seem to provide the central
terms by a) marking out the two or three articles of faith (in boldface in
the quote below), b) by elaborating on these articles, and c) by focusing
– within a Christian monotheistic setting – on the divine Name(s), GOD,
JESUS and SPIRIT. Our oldest Christian catechesis, *Proof of the Apostolic
Preaching* (6) – put down in writing by Irenaeus ca. AD 200 – provides a
fine illustration (underlined are eight *nomina sacra* commonly employed
at the time of Irenaeus, who himself seems to have made use *nomina
sacra* in his writings; cf. section 3.2):[141]

> And this is the drawing-up of our faith, the foundation of the building, and
> the consolidation of a way of life. God, the Father, uncreated, beyond grasp,
> invisible, one God the maker of all; this is **the first** and foremost **article**
> [Armenian *glux* corresponding to Greek κεφαλή, κεφάλαιον] of our faith. But
> **the second article** is the Word of God, the Son of God, Christ Jesus our Lord,
> who was shown forth by the prophets according to the design of their prophecy
> and according to the manner in which the Father disposed; and through Him
> were made all things whatsoever. He also, *in the end of times*, for the recapitu-
> lation of all things, is become a man among men, visible and tangible, in order
> to abolish death and bring to light life, and bring about the communion of God
> and man. And **the third article** is the Holy Spirit [cf. *Epid.* 3: 'the Holy Spirit of
> God'], through whom the prophets prophesied and the patriarchs were taught
> about God and the just were led in the path of justice, and who *in the end of
> times* has been poured forth in a new manner upon humanity over all the earth
> renewing man to God. (Iren. *Epid.* 6)[142]

More generally, terms from the *nomina sacra* word-group involved in similar
formulaic renderings of the christological kerygma and/or the Rule of Faith
(as found in the author of *1 Clement*, Ignatius, Justin, Irenaeus, Tertullian,
Clement of Alexandria and others) include:

---

[141] For a fuller treatment of the relation between *regula fidei* and *nomina sacra*, see Bokedal, 'The Rule of Faith'.

[142] Irenaeus, *Proof of the Apostoloc Preaching [Epideixis]*, translated and annotated by J. P. Smith, Ancient Christian Writers, no. 16 (New York: Newman Press, 1952), 51 (boldface and underlinings not in the original). The number of *nomina sacra* in some NT manuscripts demarcated by scribes around the time when Irenaeus writes is eight to 11, as testified to by P⁴⁵ (eight), P⁴⁶ and P⁶⁶ (nine), and P⁷⁵ (11).

The First Article of Faith: Θεος, Κυριος, Πατηρ

The Second Article of Faith: Ιησους, Χριστος, Κυριος, Υιος, ανθρωπος,
Πνευμα, μητηρ, Δαυιδ, σταυρος/σταυροω, σωτηρ, ουρανος, Θεος, Πατηρ

The Third Article of Faith: Πνευμα, Θεος (Ισραηλ, Ιερουσαλημ)

Of these, Δαυιδ appears as an element in early creedal formulations in the New Testament, as well as in the Apostolic Fathers (cf. section 3.2 above).[143] In Justin Martyr, Ισραηλ and Ιερουσαλημ are also central concepts.[144] The *nomen sacrum* for σωτηρ appears somewhat later in the manuscripts, as does μητηρ (third century on; see section 3.2), which is contained in the Athanasian Creed of the late fifth or early sixth century.

As regards the phrasing ο υιος του ανθρωπου, it may have had some early connection with the *nomina sacra* convention, but this is difficult to prove.[145] As seen in the quote from *Epideixis* 6 above, ανθρωπος is part of the early church's language when addressing the theme of incarnation. Πνευμα seems to have been added to the list from the late first or early second century, and was not part of the core group of the earliest four names. This is supported by the lack of this *nomen sacrum* in several early Latin (and Greek) manuscripts (see also the figures in section 3.2).[146] As to the occurrence of creedal statements in this period, it can also be noted that two-clause and three-clause confessions are found side by side.[147]

Given this parallelism between the *nomina sacra* and the Rule-of-Faith pattern, it is worth repeating Roberts's judgement[148] that the *nomina sacra*

---

[143] Kelly, *Early Christian Creeds*, e.g. 17ff, 68f.; Skarsaune, 'The Development of Scriptural Interpretation in the Second and Third Centuries – except Clement and Origen', in *Hebrew Bible/Old Testament: The History of Its Interpretation*, ed. M. Sæbø (Göttingen: Vandenhoeck & Ruprecht, 1996), 379f.; Seeberg, *Der Katechismus der Urchristenheit*, esp. 73f. and 137f.

[144] As for testimonies on the church (*Testimonies de ecclesia*), see Skarsaune, 'The Development of Scriptural Interpretation in the Second and Third Centuries – except Clement and Origen', 401–4; cf. also *Const. Apost.* VII, 36.2, where the expression ἀληθινὸς Ἰσραήλ occurs.

[145] See Jongkind, *Scribal Habits*, 71–2.

[146] Cf. Parker, *Codex Bezae*, 97–106: A somewhat heterogeneous use of the *nomina sacra* can be seen in some early manuscripts. The investigation of Codex Bezae by D. C. Parker, e.g. shows some layers of development in the Gospel writings of the practice. In the Latin version of the book of Luke, the development of the contraction of *Spirit* is only half complete, while the four earliest *nomina sacra* are more or less fully developed. This indicates that the old Latin original behind the book of Luke, in Codex Bezae, goes back to a date when the *nomina sacra* had been introduced but were still developing.

[147] Kelly, *Early Christian Creeds*, 24ff.

[148] *Pace* Tuckett and others, who do not ascribe the contractions any significance. Cf. also Barton, *The Spirit and the Letter*, 122: 'the convention of writing them [the *nomina sacra*] contracted is a purely graphic convention and does not affect the meaning of the texts so written. It does, however, mark them out as Christian manuscripts'.

may be regarded as 'the embryonic creed of the first Church'.[149] Indeed, the addition of, e.g. Πνευμα, Πατηρ and Υιος (arguably in that order; see again the figures in section 3.2) to the earliest core group of four words (cf. section 3.4), gives further support to Roberts's assumption. The addition of these words, then, roughly appears to parallel the development of the emerging Rule-of-Faith pattern, as found in *1 Clement*, Ignatius, Justin, Irenaeus, Tertullian and others.[150] In fact, these three terms, *Father*, *Son* and *Spirit* (preceded by the early *nomina sacra* word-groups *God*, *Jesus* and *Spirit*; and *Jesus* and *cross*) constitute the basis around which the Rule of Faith developed. The varying number of *nomina sacra* found in some early manuscripts containing Matt 28.19 (εις το ονομα του Πατρος και του Υιου και του αγιου Πνευματος) are illustrative: Codex Vaticanus here has none of the words marked as *nomina sacra*, whereas Codex Bezae has one *nomen sacrum* (*Spirit*), Codex Sinaiticus and Codex Washingtonianus two (*Father* and *Spirit*) and Codex Alexandrinus and the Majority Text – probably influenced by the practice of baptizing in the Triune Name – three (*Father*, *Son* and *Spirit*).

Besides the suitable designation 'embryonic creed', we could also speak of the *nomina sacra* as an important link bridging the potential structural, theological and narrative gap between the Scriptures and the second-century oral kerygma, the developing *regula fidei*. We have already seen possible connections between the second-century *nomina sacra* and the Rule of Faith in Irenaeus. The close relationship between the church's *regula fidei* and the Scriptures will be further discussed below (see sections 3.8 and 5.3, and Ch. 8).

3.6.3 The wider devotional context

The *nomina sacra* are found not only in a scriptural and liturgical context but in the wider devotional setting as well, including inscriptions on houses, graves, ossuaries, churches, amulets, coins; and reproductions on frescoes, mosaics and icons.[151] As James Wicker points out,

---

[149] Roberts, *Manuscript, Society and Belief in Early Christian Egypt*, 46. Cf. section 3.3.
[150] Cf. Skarsaune, 'The Development of Scriptural Interpretation in the Second and Third Centuries – except Clement and Origen'; and Bokedal, 'The Rule of Faith'.
[151] For a fine summary, see Wicker, 'Pre-Constantinian *Nomina Sacra*', 52–72.

the use of *nomina sacra* in a pre-Constantinian Christian mosaic and graffiti helps to show the use of *nomina sacra* at least by the third century AD may have been common among literate Christians – not just Christian scribes. Trained mosaicists used them, pilgrims etched them as graffiti in the House of St. Peter in Capernaum, and either clergy or members of the congregation etched them on the wall of the Dura-Europos *domus ecclesiae*.[152]

It is worth noticing that, very likely, in the case of such inscriptions and reproductions '[e]ven an illiterate person could see the unusual feature of the overbar with the few letters of *nomina sacra*'.[153]

Regarding the interplay between the biblical text and early Bible illustrations, Kurt Weitzmann and others have argued that from early on in the history of Christian book production the biblical text was read in light of illustrations of various kinds, and the other way around.[154] This is perhaps most clearly seen when studying the place of origin of much Christian art, which, according to Weitzmann, appears to be the Bible manuscripts themselves.[155] Text and textual illustration in the early Christian setting seem to make up a single 'textual' unit. As Christian art develops from the second century on, the *nomina sacra* become a common denominator between the biblical text and various Christian artworks. In this connection, we can note the early use of the staurogram, which is probably the earliest representation of a Christian visual culture: the pictographic representation in P[66] and P[75], and other early papyri, of the crucified Jesus.[156]

3.7 Canonization in two directions: From new to old, from old to new

A traditional understanding of Scripture canonization seems to imply that the sacred status ascribed to the Jewish Scriptures by the synagogue and the early church was conveyed to the new Christian writings. The 'New

---

[152] Ibid., 71.
[153] Ibid.
[154] Weitzmann, *Illustrations in Roll and Codex* (Princeton, NJ: Princeton University Press, 1970); idem, *Age of Spirituality: Late Antique and Early Christian Art, Third to Seventh Century* (New York: The Metropolitan Museum of Art, published in association with Princeton University Press, 1979).
[155] Weitzmann, *Illustrations in Roll and Codex.*
[156] See Hurtado, *Artefacts*, 135–54; and Dinkler, *Signum Crucis.*

Testament' writings were thus gradually given the same type of reverence as those of the 'Old Testament'. The process whereby this took place is generally held to be complex. However, there are reasons to suspect that the *nomina sacra* within the early Christian high-christological context[157] constitute an important link in this process. Depending on the way in which we conceive the emergence and development of the *nomina sacra*, various alternatives of how to envision the New Testament canon formation offer themselves. If the Christian system of contractions can be shown to be derived from the reverential contraction (and suspension) of Ἰησοῦς, 'the most important *nomen sacrum* of all',[158] there are good reasons to think that the system was first elaborated for the earliest 'New Testament' material and perhaps also for so called Christian Testimonies containing 'Old Testament' texts intertwined with Jesus traditions.[159]

By the time the *nomina sacra* for *Lord* and *God* were introduced, the emerging system of sacred short forms arguably began to be equally used for the 'Old Testament' and the 'New Testament' material.[160] If so, there was arguably a mutual influence of the two types of texts or text corpora on one another: the 'New Testament' material on the 'Old Testament', and, vice versa, the *nomina sacra* used in the 'Old Testament' (substituting the Tetragram) on the 'New Testament' texts. As regards their function, we may then even expect that 'scriptural' (or 'crypto-scriptural') status was attributed to the emerging New Testament at an early date, even prior to the time when the included literature more generally were referred to as 'Scripture'.[161] Examples of such early attribution are found in 2 Pet. 3.16, Rev. 1.4 and *Barn.* 4.14 and *2 Clem.*

---

[157] Cf. sections 3.1 and 3.4.2.

[158] Barton, *The Spirit and the Letter*, 123.

[159] See section 4.2.

[160] Alternatively, *nomina sacra* for *Lord* and *God* had already been introduced on Jewish ground, or at least the reading *Kyrios* for YHWH, cf. Pietersma, 'Kyrios or Tetragram: A Renewed Quest for the Original LXX', in *De Septuaginta: Studies in honour of John William Wevers on his sixty-fifth birthday*, (eds) A. Pietersma and C. Cox, (Mississauga, ON: Benben Publishers, 1984); in this case, the *nomen sacrum* for *Jesus* was juxtaposed with these earlier Jewish renderings of the Name. See further section 3.4.

[161] This is in line with McDonald's observation in this regard: 'The fact that early Christian scribes contracted special words from both the Old Testament and the New Testament suggests that they viewed both collections as sacred in the same sense.' (McDonald, 'Identifying Scripture and Canon in the Early Church: The Criteria Question', in *The Canon Debate*, (eds) J. A. Sanders and L. M. McDonald [Peabody, MA: Hendrickson, 2002], 421); see also Barton, *The Spirit and the Letter*, 122f. (cf. n. 126 above).

2.4.[162] Perhaps the 'paradox' pointed to by Stuhlhofer here finds a partial explanation:

> We see here a paradox. The early Church cited the Old Testament as 'Scripture', but to begin with tended to possess it only in a fragmentary form. The New Testament, on the other hand, was widely available and was used much more heavily, but it was not yet cited as 'Scripture'.[163]

Out of the statistical investigation of Scripture citation presented by Stuhlhofer, Barton concludes:

> The central importance of most of the writings that would come to form the New Testament is already established in the early second century, by the time of the Apostolic Fathers, and all but a very few Old Testament books (such as Isaiah or the Psalms) already play second fiddle to the Christians' own writings. Indeed, it is not until the third century that citations begin to level out as between the two Testaments. All the indications are that the New Testament became almost instantly more important than the Old for the nascent Church[.][164]

Part of the role that the Jewish Scriptures had during the Apostolic Age was carried over to the 'New Testament' writings. Unexpectedly, the *nomina sacra*, as I have argued, seem to have played a role very early in this process, which partially explains how there could be such vivid reciprocity between the two collections of writings in the first place.

3.8 The *nomina sacra* as a narrative and theological centre in the Scriptures

In our discussion above (section 3.6.2) we noticed some structural relationship between the *nomina sacra* and the Rule-of-Faith pattern. The Rule of Faith tended to develop around the following two (i and ii) or three (i, ii and iii) groups of *nomina sacra*: i) Θεος, Κυριος, Πατηρ; ii) Κυριος, Ιησους,

---

[162] W.-D. Köhler (*Die Rezeption des Matthäusevangeliums in der Zeit vor Irenäus* [WUNT 2/22; Tübingen: Mohr Siebeck, 1987)]) argues that dependence on Matthew is quite possible for *Barn.* 4.14; 5.8f and 7.9b. Metzger (*The Canon of the New Testament: Its Origin, Development, and Significance* [Oxford: Clarendon, 1987], 57) does not convince to the contrary.

[163] Stuhlhofer, *Der Gebrauch der Bibel von Jesus bis Euseb: Eine statistische Untersuchung zur Kanonsgeschichte* (Wuppertal: Brockhaus, 1988), 68.

[164] Barton, *The Spirit and the Letter*, 64f.

Χριστος, Υιος; and iii) Πνευμα. Given the essential role this typical creedal structure – binitarian and/or triadic/Trinitarian – had within the emerging Christian faith, it seems inappropriate not to take the suggested relationship between *regula fidei* and *nomina sacra* into serious consideration. The *nomina sacra* appear to have attained a textual-hermeneutical and theological function as part of the Christian Scriptures. Given this, it seems reasonable to conclude that the addition of the three *nomina sacra* Πατηρ, Υιος and Πνευμα[165] – included already in P[46] and P[66] (both ca. AD 200) – were directly or indirectly related to the second-century development of the *regula fidei*. We have previously seen that the Rule of Faith was structured around these three names.

The gradual and sometimes ambivalent development, from a primarily two-clause to a mainly three-clause creedal formulation, is also to be sought here.[166] That the historical development of the three-clause formulas arguably goes from baptismal confession over *nomina sacra* to *regula fidei* does not contradict the theological interest in mutually relating the Rule of Faith and the *nomina sacra*, and in making them interdependent on one another. The Rule of Faith, which we will discuss in Chapters 5 and 8, has the crucial function of establishing a *Mitte der Schrift* and a textual biblical whole, as well as providing a fundamental framework for the canon formation process. This further legitimizes the close connection between the two. The five rules for scriptural interpretation proposed by Robert Jenson (see section 6.7) as well as my argumentation below of the Bible as pointer to the *regula fidei*, and vice versa (sections 8.3.6 and 8.4), also have bearing on the postulated close – and, perhaps even necessary – connection between the *nomina sacra* and the Rule of Faith. As to their narrative and dogmatic imperatives, the following statement by Jenson seems to apply equally well to the – narratively, liturgically and theologically defined – Rule of Faith as to the second- and third-century system of *nomina sacra*:[167]

---

[165] These additions were most probably inspired by the baptismal ritual (cf. Matt. 28.19); see Balla, *Challenges to New Testament Theology: An Attempt to Justify the Enterprise* (Tübingen: Mohr Siebeck, 1997), 361f.

[166] See, e.g. Kelly, *Early Christian Creeds*, 24–6. I note here Kelly's legitimate criticism of a stereotypical development (ibid, 24): 'one-membered, two-membered and three-membered confessions flourished side by side in the apostolic Church as parallel and mutually independent formulations of the one kerygma; and this is a datum of prime importance.' See also Bokedal, 'The Rule of Faith'.

[167] See further, sections 7.2, 8.2 and 8.4.

the phrase 'Father, Son, and Holy Spirit' is simultaneously a very compressed telling of the total narrative by which Scripture identifies God and a personal name for the God so specified; in it, name and narrative description not only appear together, as at the beginning of the Ten Commandments, but are identical. ... The church is the community and a Christian is someone who, when the identity of God is important, names him 'Father, Son, and Holy Spirit.' Those who do not or will not belong to some other community.[168]

3.9 Conclusion

The *nomina sacra* established a relationship between the biblical text and some central Christian key words. This relationship has the following implications:

1. The divine Name, rendered by the Greek words for *Lord* and *God*, is marked out as the centre in the biblical text, in close connection with the words *Jesus* and *Christ* (textually indicating an already existing binitarian pattern of devotion), and very soon also *Spirit* and *cross* (first/second century).

2. Additional words were added to the earliest list of *nomina sacra* (first to third century), such as *Father, Son, man/human being, Israel* and *Jerusalem*. These 11 early *nomina sacra* (all present in P[75]) appear to connect the scribal practice to devotional patterns associated with the early Christian confession and creedal development. Editorially, the presence of *nomina sacra* indicates a unity of the Scriptures and a particular Christian narrative and theological focus, engrafting 'what might be regarded as the embryonic creed of the first Church' (Roberts) onto the textuality of the Scriptures. Various confessional/creedal structures (binitarian, Jesus and the cross; triadic/trinitarian, Rule of Faith) may readily be associated with the *nomina sacra* demarcations. The *nomina sacra* practice is an instance of editorial continuity shared by various early Bible versions that goes back to the very origins of Christian Scripture.

3. As *nomina sacra* are present in basically all Christian Greek biblical

---

[168] Jenson, *Systematic Theology*, vol. 1: *The Triune God* (New York: Oxford University Press, 1997), 46.

manuscripts, their seemingly universal reception by the early faith
communities strongly suggests a doctrine of the unity of the Christian
Scriptures, placing the emergent NT writings side by side with the
Scriptures of Judaism (the OT). The Christian Scriptures contain the
nomina sacra, which are being introduced also into the Jewish Scriptures,
and both OT and NT writings are used together for the divine lection
as part of the worship services. In this way – and of further significance
for the canon formation – the Christian identity of the Scriptures as
Scriptures vis-à-vis the synagogue is emphasized. Now, if the above
analysis is correct, and if we make use of an essential component from
von Harnack's canon definition, we need to date a central aspect of
the NT canon formation to around AD 100 (rather than ca. AD 200, as
suggested by von Harnack), when the Christians' own writings in this way
are put on a par with the Jewish Scriptures (cf. section 7.3). Justin Martyr
in Rome testifies to an already established tradition in this regard, with
the Gospel being read publicly alongside the Prophets (see section 7.7.4).

The editorial graphic, textual, narrative and theological pattern
provided by the *nomina sacra*, accordingly, suggests that these markers
are key elements in the early canonization of the Christian Bible. The
nomina sacra appear to have prepared the way for placing OT texts on a
par with the new 'apostolic' (NT) writings; and it seems rather difficult
to envisage a Christian scriptural canon formation without them. As for
early Judaism, so also for early Christianity which embraced the *nomina
sacra* practice: it appears to have been the case that a writing without a
strong emphasis on the sacred name(s) could not make any strong claim
to scripturality; and we seem to have a few very early such claims for the
new Christian scriptures (2 Pet. 3.16; Rev. 1.4; *Barn.* 4.14, *2 Clem.* 2.4; cf.
section 9.6).

4. The next to universal presence of *nomina sacra* in Christian Greek,
   Latin, Coptic, Armenian and Slavonic Bible manuscripts, from the first
   to the fifteenth centuries AD, suggests a reintroduction – in one form or
   another – in modern Bible editions of this characteristic textual identity
   marker (which at present is visible, more or less, only within the sphere of
   Christian inscriptions and Christian art, primarily on icons).

   Even today the *nomina sacra* could have the important ecclesiastical textual, liturgical and theological function of underlining the biblical books as a unified collection of writings that come to expression in the two concepts 'Bible' and 'Scripture'. A suggestion for their outer appearance in modern Bibles was presented above (section 3.1):

> … and I know that when I come to you I shall come in the fullness of the blessing of CHRIST. I appeal to you, brethren, by our LORD JESUS CHRIST and by the love of the SPIRIT, to strive together with me in your prayers to GOD on my behalf … (Rom. 15.29-30)

This way of marking out the Christian Names, 'the sacred figures of the Christian faith' (Heath), would highlight the textual and theological unity of the Scriptures, as was done in the manuscripts up to the sixteenth century (and often later). The reason why modern editors of Christian Bibles have followed the Jewish convention of graphically marking out only the Tetragrammaton – usually rendered 'LORD' – in the biblical text (only the OT), seems to be due more to oblivion regarding the original function of the *nomina sacra* in the Christian biblical writings, than to a deliberate preference to a primarily Jewish rather than a Christian textual marker, representing the Name.

In modern literary or scholarly editions of the biblical texts, where a more 'neutral' or non-denominational version is aimed at, a possibility to avoid the preference to either Jewish or Christian scribal practices would be not to textually mark off any of the discussed sacred names at all, including also the Tetragrammaton. Nevertheless, from an ecclesial point of view, such a change may weaken the identity of the Bible as canon for the church.

4

The Bible Codex: A Material Symbol of Christian Textuality

Having discussed the distinctive textual markers provided by the system of *nomina sacra*, I shall now look at another peculiar feature pertaining not only to the textuality of Christian Scripture, but also to its materiality. From early on the church seems to have largely abandoned the standard Jewish book format of the scroll, choosing a new physical form for their scriptures – the codex. This appearance of new material in canonical Scripture has been interpreted by some scholars as a physical conquest of the old Scriptures by the church, whereas others discuss the discrepancies in this regard between Judaism and the emerging Christian movement in less dramatic terms. In the present chapter I shall focus attention on this novelty vis-à-vis Christianity's Jewish origins and its implications for the formation of a specifically Christian canon. How, if at all, did the codex, or leaf-form of book, adopted by first- and second-century Christianity affect the formation of the Christian Bible?

4.1 The church's strong preference for the codex over the roll

According to contemporary literary conventions, the scroll was the standard format for book publication up to the fourth century AD. Following Larry Hurtado's 2006 statistics, based largely on the Leuven Database of Ancient Books,[1] about 98 per cent of the non-Christian literary texts of the first

---

[1] Hurtado, *The Earliest Christian Artifacts* (Grand Rapids and Cambridge: Eerdmans, 2006), 44–9. The Leuven Database accessed November 2005.

century were written on rolls.[2] The corresponding figure for the total number of texts from the second century is 94[3] per cent.[4] Referring to William Johnson's 2004 study, Hurtado comments, 'the roll was overwhelmingly preferred in the general culture for literary texts for several centuries, only slowly losing ground to the codex significantly after the fourth century CE'.[5] This general pattern of strong preference for the roll was also embraced by Jewish groups, such as the Qumran community, the Zealots struggling on Massada, and the allies of Bar Kokhba. Consequently, basically all Jewish Septuagint manuscripts have come down as rolls.[6]

Against this unanimous pagan and Jewish background, the early church's strong preference for the codex seems odd. Earlier statistics provided by Roberts and Skeat in 1983 revealed that, of the extant Christian Bible manuscripts from the three (or four) first centuries, not a single one was found in the form of a normal roll, written on the recto.[7] We may have expected to see these figures overturned with Hurtado's recent study, *The Earliest Christian Artifacts*, referred to above. Again, however, despite the fact that the number of texts included by Hurtado is larger, the result for the second-century situation comes close to that of Roberts and Skeat. Of the 45 Christian manuscripts from the second century, six (or possibly seven) are written on an unused roll and 29 on codices. It is to be noted, though, as Hurtado remarks, that rolls appear to have been used by Christians especially for theological treatises, such as Irenaeus' *Against Heresies* (*Adv. Haer.*), and for edifying texts, such as the *Shepherd* of Hermas.[8] In other words, in contrast to pagan and Jewish texts, Christian biblical manuscripts still seem to have

---

[2]   Items listed as either rolls or codices are counted, omitting those tagged by the database as 'sheets' and 'fragments'; 77.5 per cent, if the items listed as 'sheets' and 'fragments' are also included.

[3]   94 per cent when items listed as either rolls or codices are counted, omitting those tagged by the database as 'sheets' and 'fragments'; 73.8 per cent if 'sheets' and 'fragments' are included.

[4]   Total: 2,276 second-century items. To some, the roll may have been the only acceptable book form to the extent that there were doubts whether the codex belonged at all to the literary book genre. This is indicated by the jurist Ulpian, ca. AD 215, as he is trying to settle the question whether codices should be counted among the books listed in a testament. Cf. also Harris, *Ancient Literacy* (Cambridge, MA and London: Harvard University Press, 1989), 294f.

[5]   Hurtado, 'Early Christian Manuscripts as Artifacts', in *Jewish and Christian Scripture as Artifact and Canon*, (eds) C. A. Evans and H. D. Zacharias, Studies in Scripture in Early Judaism and Christianity 13 (London and New York: T&T Clark, 2009), 73; Johnson, *Bookrolls and Scribes in Oxhyrhynchus* (Toronto: University of Toronto Press, 2004).

[6]   Cf. Skarsaune, 'Den første kristne bibel: Et blad av kodeksens historie', in *Det levende Ordet: Festskrift til professor dr. theol Age Holter*, ed. I. Asheim (Oslo, 1989), 29f.

[7]   Roberts and Skeat, *The Birth of the Codex* (London: Oxford University Press, 1983), 38–44.

[8]   Hurtado, *The Earliest Christian Artifacts* (Grand Rapids and Cambridge: Eerdmans, 2006), 56.

been almost exclusively published in the codex format. For the second- and third-century situation, Hurtado can therefore conclude that 'so far as biblical texts are concerned … there is no New Testament text copied on an unused roll among second- or third-century Christian manuscripts.'[9] The surprisingly unambiguous figures for the early NT manuscripts from Roberts' and Skeat's 1983 study can thus still be sustained for the first three centuries. We may conclude that by the second century, if not earlier, the codex had replaced the scroll as the standard scriptural format in Christian circles.

When compared to other literary writings of the period, the great majority of which are rolls, the contrast is conspicuous, and the question readily poses itself: Why did earliest Christianity (as far as we can judge from the extant manuscript evidence), contrary to its parent religion and to contemporary literary practice, prefer the codex format over the roll for biblical texts? Why is it that this preference is so overwhelming in the early stages of Christian usage of the codex? Although our answers to these questions necessarily are going to be somewhat tentative, it still seems to be a legitimate task to reflect on the potential bearing of the novel Christian book format on the emergent Christian Bible canon. On one level, and to some readers, Bible codex and Bible canon, or delimited part-volumes of the canon, may even be equivalent, or overlapping notions, coming to visual expression in the great ancient and medieval Bible manuscripts, such as P[46], our earliest extant Pauline letter corpus (ca. AD 200), P[45], our earliest extant Four-Gospel codex (early third century AD; including also Acts), and Codex Sinaiticus, our earliest complete NT and whole-Bible codex (ca. AD 350). All along, within the Christian setting, this non-standard book form – the codex – seems to be tightly associated with Christian Scripture.

4.2 Has the codex form influenced the canon formation?

A recurring question in canonical research, raised by Theodor Zahn, Hans von Campenhausen, C. H. Roberts, T. C. Skeat, Robert Kraft, Harry Gamble, Eldon Jay Epp, Graham Stanton and others, is whether there might have

---

[9] P. Oxy. 1228 (P[22]) is here taken to be an opisthograph. Hurtado, *The Earliest Christian Artifacts*, 58.

been a connection between the choice of format for the Scriptures and the formation of the Christian canon, the eventual outcome of which indeed looked rather different from the Jewish Bible? In 1983, the possibility of such a connection was answered in the negative by Roberts and Skeat. However, not only Skeat changed his mind in this regard; others have followed, and new evidence suggesting further positive or negative connections between codex and canon needs highlighting.

As a preview, I shall present in brief some of the central issues involved in our question. The Christian use of the codex for the Scriptures is both remarkably early and extensive; this fact naturally evokes the question of why the normal scriptural scroll format (cf. Luke 4.17) was so rapidly and apparently unanimously exchanged by the early church, when commencing its own book production.

The codex appears to have had a direct implication on canonical Scripture when second-century Christian OT texts are copied in the new format, thereby abandoning the standard scriptural format of the roll. Such clear connection between codex and Scripture taking place very early in the production of Christian texts finds a similarly forceful connection in the fourth century, with the production of mega-codices containing the whole Bible. It is one of the arguments in the present book, however, that, as far as concerns the New Testament writings, the part-volumes (in codex form) making up the NT books – such as the Gospels and the Pauline Letters – seem to be as important for the notion of an NT canon, as is the NT as a 27-book corpus, or the Bible as a 65- (Athanasius; cf. section 2.5.2 above for his 49-/65-book canon) or 66-book corpus. In other words, here the New Testament is not so much a collection of individual writings but rather the inclusion of some two to four codices or part-volumes (typically Gospels, the Pauline letters, the Praxapostolos and Revelation) under the rubric 'New Testament'. The earliest part-collections most probably emerged prior to the formation of the larger corpus of writings titled 'the New Testament'. Scholars are still challenged by the question when this happened.

Irenaeus' emphasis around AD 180 on a delimited Four-Gospel canon can be visually related to some early Christian Four-Gospel codices, such as P[45] (early third century) or perhaps already P[64+67+4] (ca. AD 200) and possibly

P[75] (ca. AD 200), as argued by Skeat.[10] Once the Four-Gospel canon has become the established ecclesial standard, this is also reflected in the Greek NT manuscripts containing only the four Gospels (some 2,000 extant). Whether or not the codex format as such can be shown to have had a direct impact on the formation of the Four-Gospel canon (Skeat, Elliott) or the Pauline corpus (Gamble, Richards) is not the main point here, but, rather, whether there is a demonstrable mutuality between the church's strong preference for a fourfold Gospel and the technology of Gospel production in the church.[11] We can safely conclude that this is the case, and that both ideational (Irenaeus' argument regarding the fourfold Gospel, *Adv. Haer.* III, 11.8) and material-textual dimensions (production of Four-Gospel codices) have bearing on the canonical process.

4.2.1 A view on codex and canon

Before commenting on some different themes pertaining to codex and canon (see section 4.2.2) and outlining some various scholarly positions (section 4.3), I shall briefly outline my own view on the relation between Christian use of the codex format for the Scriptures and the canonical process:

1. Although several scholars assume or hypothesize that the Gospels and even the Pauline letters were written on scrolls (Kraft, Epp, Van Haelst, Hamel),[12] it might very well be the case that the Gospels were originally published in codex format (Hengel, Gamble, Roberts, Skeat). Reasons for that could have been: a) early notes containing Jesus logia and traditions were preserved as some form of codex (Riesner, Hengel); b) the codex form employed by the early Christians may have indicated that the first versions of the Gospels or Proto-gospels were not regarded as finalized literature, but left one foot still in the oral culture of early

---

[10] Skeat, 'The Oldest Manuscript of the Four Gospels?', *NTS* 43 (1997): 1–34

[11] On dating in this connection, see Hurtado, 'The New Testament in the Second Century: Text, Collections, Canon', in *Transmission and Reception: New Testament Text-Critical and Exegetical Studies,* (eds) J. W. Childers and D. C. Parker (Piscataway, NJ: Gorgias, 2006), 19–24; and Stanton, 'The Fourfold Gospel', *NTS* 43 (1997): 317–46.

[12] Haelst, 'Les origines du codex', 35; Hamel, *The Book. A History of the Bible* (London: Phaidon Press, 2001), 47.

Christianity; c) early Pauline letter collections may have circulated in codex form, inspiring subsequent Christian literary production in that format (Gamble, Richards); d) early Christian testimony collections, and subsequently other Christian literature, may have been disseminated as codices (Gamble, Kraft, Skarsaune). That is, basically all authoritative Christian literature (especially OT texts, Gospels and apostolic letters) might have been published in codex format. I tend to think that Hengel is more or less right in his analysis of the earliest Christianity, when he claims that in the beginning is not the roll, but 'the still relatively thin codex of a single writing'.[13]

2. A probable first-century dating for the early Christian use of the codex is implied in the following interesting quote,[14] again from Hengel:

> The revolutionary introduction of the codex and the *nomina sacra* cannot possibly be the result of a later 'redaction' of the four Gospels or other New Testament writings, as the numerous earliest LXX manuscripts from the first/second century in practice already similarly also contain this special form throughout. ... In my view it could already derive from the separation between church and synagogue, which goes back in Antioch and Rome to the 40s.[15]

3. The codex form is significant for understanding the formation of the biblical canon, as it emerged during the first two to four Christian centuries. From our rather limited extant manuscripts from this period, the following stages may be distinguished:

A. From early on, and for various reasons, Christian writings, especially OT Scriptures (including testimony collections/sources),[16] Pauline

---

[13] Hengel, *Die vier Evangelien und das eine Evangelium von Jesus Christus* (WUNT 224; Tübingen: Mohr Siebeck, 2008), 91. For comments on the size of early as compared to later Christian codices, see Epp, 'Codex and Literacy in Early Christianity and at Oxyrhynchus: Issues Raised by Harry Y. Gamble's *Books and Readers in the Early Church*', *Critical Review of Books in Religion* 11 (1998): 19–20; and Turner, *The Typology of the Early Codex* (Philadelphia: University of Pennsylvania Press, 1977), 14–25.

[14] Cf. ibid., 200.

[15] Hengel, *The Four Gospels and the One Gospel of Jesus Christ: An Investigation of the Collection and Origin of the Canonical Gospels* (London: SCM, 2000), 118–19.

[16] See Albl, 'And Scripture Cannot be Broken': The Form and Function of the Early Christian *Testimonia* Collections (Leiden: Brill, 1999); and Skarsaune, *The Proof from Prophecy: A Study in Justin Martyr's Proof-Text Tradition: Text-Type, Provenance, Theological Profile* (Leiden: Brill, 1987); idem, 'From Books to Testimonies: Remarks on the Transmission of the Old Testament in the Early Church', *Immanuel* 24/25 (1990): 207–19.

letters and Gospels, seem to have circulated in codex form. These codices may have contained only a single book, along the lines of some later second- to fourth-century manuscripts.[17]

B. Between AD 100 and AD 250, and in some cases possibly earlier, NT texts were being grouped together.[18] Certain typical combinations stand out, such as the four Gospels and the Pauline letters.

C. The groupings of NT texts become more standardized, including the ordering of the writings within the part-collections,[19] as indicated by second- to fourth-century manuscripts and by church teachers such as Irenaeus, Origen and Athanasius.

D. From the fourth century on, whole-Bible codices and whole-NT codices are being produced; these mega-books, however, never become the sole or dominating format in the Greek manuscript tradition (Epp, building on the Alands, lists 59 Greek manuscripts containing the entire NT and another 149 containing all books except Revelation).[20]

4. Since a few scholars recently have dated the likely emergence of the fourfold Gospel to the early second century (Kelhoffer, Heckel, Hill, Stanton and Hurtado),[21] and the formation of a Pauline letter corpus by many is placed in the first century,[22] there are reasons to take into account the potential of the new book format (that probably was used for these alleged collections, or for the individual writings included) for the early canonical process. It is worth noting that ideational arguments for a delimited Four-Gospel canon – surfacing in Irenaeus,[23] and to some degree also in Clement of Alexandria, the Muratorian Fragment and

---

[17] As for 20 extant manuscripts containing Pauline letters 'plausibly dated before 350 CE', Royse ('The Early Text of Paul (and Hebrews)', in *The Early Text of the New Testament*, (eds) Charles E. Hill and Michael J. Kruger [Oxford: Oxford University Press, 2012], 200) comments: 'of our twenty manuscripts it seems reasonable to think that four are manuscripts of the corpus: P^{13}, P^{30}, P^{46}, and P^{92}. Of course, there is nothing to exclude that all twenty once contained the corpus.'

[18] See Hurtado, 'The New Testament in the Second Century: Text, Collections, Canon'.

[19] This has been emphasized especially by David Trobisch.

[20] Epp, 'Issues in the Interrelation of New Testament Textual Criticism and Canon', in *The Canon Debate*, (eds) L. M. McDonald and J. A. Sanders (Peabody, MA: Hendrickson, 2002), 486–87. For early Christian OT manuscripts, see Hurtado, *The Earliest Christian Artifacts*, 210–17.

[21] For references, see Hurtado, 'The New Testament in the Second Century', 20.

[22] For an overview, see Porter, 'When and How was the Pauline Canon Compiled? An Assessment of Theories', in *The Pauline Canon*, ed. S. E. Porter (Leiden: Brill, 2004), 95–127.

[23] E.g. *Adv. Haer.* III, 11.8.

perhaps also in Serapion of Antioch – are later.[24] Hurtado is therefore right in emphasizing that the formation of a 'New Testament' in the second century is, in a sense, 'a collection of prior collections'.[25] To judge from the manuscript tradition, the codex form arguably had a natural role in this process, frequently containing either the four Gospels, the Pauline Letters, or Acts + Catholic Epistles + Pauline Letters. Combinations like Gospels and Pauline Letters are rare (five minuscules).[26] And, given this surprisingly early, extensive and organized utilization of the codex form in Christian circles, two further areas appear to be significant for assessing the relation between codex and canon: the questions of identity and textuality. J. Keith Elliott touches on one significant aspect of both of these, as reviewed by Epp: 'we have no manuscripts in which "apocryphal" gospels were bound with any one or more of the "canonical" four, and … the codex possessed an automatic limiting or "canon" factor, for (unlike a roll) it demands advance planning, especially if it consists of a single quire.'[27]

4.2.2 Codex and canon: Themes and questions

In what follows I shall offer some further comments on recent research on the codex format (section 4.3). I will also discuss potential implications of the early Christian use of codex and *nomina sacra* for church organization (section 4.4), the possible use of the codex also as a notebook format for the Jesus logia (section 4.5), canonization understood as the edition of a book (section 4.6), and the role of the codex for early 'mini-closures' (Gospels and Pauline letters) of the emerging New Testament (section 4.7). First, however, I shall briefly elaborate on the Christian adoption of the codex by outlining some themes of relevance for the question of the relation, if any, between the codex form and the canon formation process:

---

[24] See Hill, 'The Four Gospel Canon in the Second Century', paper presented at the SBL, San Francisco, SBL Consultation on the Cross, Resurrection, and Diversity in Earliest Christianity (2011). Available online at http://austingrad.edu/images/SBL/Four%20Gospel%20Canon%20.pdf (accessed 9 February 2012).

[25] Hurtado, 'The New Testament in the Second Century'.

[26] See Epp, 'Issues in the Interrelation of New Testament Textual Criticism and Canon', 487. Cf. Ch. 9, n. 106.

[27] Ibid., 511; Elliott, 'Manuscripts, the Codex and the Canon', *JSNT* 63 (1996): 110 and 107.

Remarkably early

To some scholars it seems reasonable to assume that 'in the beginning was the scroll' for the emerging Christian movement engaging with its Scriptures.[28] However, for various reasons, and from very early on, the papyrus (and later the parchment) codex was the material and form chosen for preserving the (oral/aural and written/aural) gospel tradition – the Gospels as well as the Pauline and other letters – in writing. It is noteworthy that our earliest OT and NT manuscript evidence (Ralphs 962 and 2082; and P[52]) already testify to the Christian use of the codex.[29]

As referred to above, already in 1981 Martin Hengel pointed out that the specifically Christian texts probably were written on codices from the beginning.[30] If this was the case, the codex was simply the book format used – and perhaps deliberately chosen – by the earliest church, for letters as well as for the written gospel tradition, in line with our second- and third-century manuscript evidence. The reasons for this usage, according to Hengel, were that the leaf-book was i) easier to handle than the scroll, ii) cheaper to produce (ca. 26 per cent, according to Skeat) and iii) more convenient to carry for missionary purposes. For such practical reasons, Hengel maintains, the letters of Paul were already published in codex form, possibly in analogy with longer letters or records in antiquity, e.g. the reports of Caesar to the Senate as testified to by Suetonius.[31] If Hengel is correct, the publications of both the Pauline letters and the Gospels, as well as Christian LXX texts, are involved in the first and early second centuries when the codex format defines the Christian book standard. Beside such practical considerations, Hengel – rightly in my opinion – also emphasizes the Christian identity aspect vis-à-vis the synagogue (see further section 4.3), and the probable preservation of notes in codex form containing the earliest Jesus logia and Jesus traditions (section 4.5).[32] Practical

---

[28] Kraft, 'The Codex and Canon Consciousness', 229.

[29] For dating, see Hurtado's list of Christian literary texts in manuscripts, *The Earliest Christian Artifacts*, 209–29.

[30] Hengel, *Die Evangelienüberschriften*, 41.

[31] *Vit. Caes.* I, 56.6, referred to by Hengel, *Die Evangelienüberschriften*, 41f.

[32] Hengel, *Die vier Evangelien und das eine Evangelium von Jesus Christus*, 202–3, n. 588. For early note-taking of the Jesus tradition, see Riesner, *Jesus als Lehrer*, 491–98; and Gerhardsson, *The Reliability of the Gospel Tradition*, xix, 66–77, esp. 71, n. 25. Riesner compares Hellenistic didactic practices to those associated with the Christian Διδάσκαλος. He argues that these pre-Christian practices of teaching and transmission, where writing also was used, were adopted by the Rabbis as well as by the Christian movement.

motives[33] as well as reasons of identity, and of continuity with the earliest Jesus tradition, thus could lay behind the early standardization of the new Christian book format.

Grouping into collections

The early Christian tendency of grouping writings into collections can also be seen in some of the earliest codices. Thus, the earliest extant Pauline letter is only preserved together with (the) other letters in the corpus, including the Letter to the Hebrews (P[46]). However, in this regard our evidence is ambiguous, since a large portion of our earliest extant NT texts have come down as manuscripts containing only a single text.[34]

Textuality and editorial characteristics

Along with the characteristic Christian *nomina sacra* convention (see Ch. 3) and other editorial features, the codex form had implications for the textuality of the Scriptures (see Ch. 6; and section 4.4).

An ecclesial standard

In this process, which I prefer to describe in four stages (see section 4.2.1, point 3), the new Scriptures in codex form became an ecclesiastical standard influencing as well the Christian 'adoption' of the Jewish Scriptures. The patristic scholar Frances Young has described this process as an act of partial 'decanonization', that is, the abandonment of the scroll – used for the Jewish Scriptures – the only and proper scriptural format.[35]

Abandonment of the scroll

The fact that the church quickly abandoned the scroll may need some kind of

---

[33] Practical considerations for the Christian adoption of the codex are emphasized by Van Haelst, 'Les origines du codex', 35. However, according to Roberts and Skeat (*The Birth of the Codex*, 45–53) the '"practical" advantages of the codex (more economical, compact, able to bring together a number of writings in one manuscript, convenient to use, easy to reference) do not bear up well under scrutiny'; see also Gamble, *Books and Readers in the Early Church*, 54–6; and Hurtado, 'The Earliest Evidence of an Emerging Christian Material and Visual Culture', 273.

[34] See ibid.; Gamble, *Books and Readers*, 67. Cf. also the comment by James Royse in this regard (n. 17 above).

[35] Young, *Biblical Exegesis and the Formation of Christian Culture* (Cambridge: Cambridge University Press, 1997), 13.

extraordinary explanation, plausibly pertaining to elements involved in the canonization process (see sections 4.4 and 4.5).

Scriptural delimitation indicated by the codex

To some extent the codex seems to have indicated its own scriptural delimitation.[36] It can therefore be said to complement the functions of canon lists (e.g. as provided by Origen and Eusebius)[37] and the Scriptures previously laid up in the Temple.[38] As Christian codices commonly contain the four Gospels and the Pauline letters, these correspond to the listing and delimitation of Gospels and Pauline epistles in extant canon lists.

Scriptures marked out as Christian Scriptures

The specific identity of the church as a *tertium genus* can be said to be emphasized also by means of the codex, among other features, used for the Christian Scriptures: to physically mark out the Scriptures as *Christian* Scriptures vis-à-vis the synagogue (see section 4.3).

The Old and New Testament placed on a par, and in a particular mutual relation to one another

As part of this process, the Old and the New Testaments could more easily be put side by side. Before not too long, the writings of the two main parts of the Christian Scriptures were carefully distinguished, although not separated, by the use of the terms 'Old Testament' and 'New Testament'. This editorial distinction could easily be made in the large fourth- and fifth-century codices. In this process, it seems to me that the adoption of the codex format for the Scriptures was an integral part of the canonical process, which to some degree helped initiate a new Christian conception of the Jewish Scripture. That is, the Torah did not occur in its proper

---

[36] See, e.g. Elliott's argument ('Manuscripts, the Codex and the Canon', *JSNT* 63 (1996): 107 and 110), referred to below (also n. 27 above), for the relation between the delimited fourfold Gospel and the codex.

[37] Already Josephus' 22-book canon in *Against Apion* 1.37-43 is an early example of a form of listing even if he does not mention all the individual books included. See Mason, 'Josephus and His Twenty-Two Book Canon', in *The Canon Debate*, (eds) L. M. McDonald and J. A. Sanders (Peabody, MA: Hendrickson, 2002), 110–27.

[38] See, e.g. Beckwith, *The Old Testament Canon of the New Testament Church and its Background in Early Judaism* (Grand Rapids: Eerdmans, 1985).

format, i.e. as scroll, and was not primarily read as Torah any longer, but as oracle.[39]

The historical emergence of the Bible codex

Historically,

a. The codex may very well have been considered a proper textual medium for the oral Jesus tradition;

b. The exceptional authority of the Jesus tradition became manifest not least when set in relation to the Torah (cf. section 4.5);

c. The early Christian texts, letters, Gospel material, and also most probably the so called testimony collections, here could be categorized as attaining a status in between the oral and the literary text. There may have been a development from the notebook towards the literary text. As Stanton puts it: 'with hindsight, the use of codices for more permanent writings than ephemeral notes was a very natural development'.[40] As such 'in between texts', they also seem to have been rather closely bound up with the early context in which the texts were used, as distinct from a standard literary text being more detached from its context of origin and early usage (cf. section 6.1).

d. Because codices were more portable than rolls, often being made rather small as well as compact with a protecting cover, they were arguably the superior format for Christian missionaries, messengers and travellers. Eric Turner in his *Typology of the Early Codex* also pointed out that these early codices were handy and modest in size, no more than about seven inches (18 centimetres) wide.[41] As the preferred literary format for both Jews and pagans was the roll, this preferred use of the codex among Christians may as well have been associated with a counter-cultural stance, which arguably would not be much of a problem anyway for these early Christians. Also, if the codex form could be associated with some type of low-culture mark, as suggested by Skarsaune and Horsley (contra Harris), that also could have been in line with the early Christian profile.

---

[39] Cf. Gal. 3.13; Luke 24; Skarsaune, *The Proof from Prophecy: A Study in Justin Martyr's Proof-Text Tradition: Text-Type, Provenance, Theological Profile* (Leiden: Brill, 1987).

[40] Stanton, *Jesus and Gospel*, 181.

[41] Turner, *The Typology of the Early Codex*.

e. Directly associated with the changes in textual form was a new type of textuality. Revelatory speech here appeared in a new format. More importantly, the missionary agenda related to this speech was physically built into the form of book used. The physical appearance of the Christian biblical writings in this way carries with it a missionary component, helping to define the new type of textuality: writings suitable for carrying, composed for missionary activity. Such advantages were pointed out also by the late first-century Roman author Martial, who commends parchment codices because of their convenience for travellers and because of the space the format saves in the library as compared to rolls.[42]

f. Connected with this textual aspect, however, comes another related one, that of providing the means of searching the Scriptures. With the new book format there followed a type of text that was no longer continuous like the roll, but fragmented. The 'page' of the codex arguably encouraged piecemeal reading and the comparing of different parts of the textual corpus or corpora with one another, in particular Jewish prophecies and their fulfilment in the Jesus event, the gospel and the church. Some of the writings, such as Matthew's Gospel, scriptural excerpts and testimony collections/sources, already encouraged such reading. Scriptural excerpts and testimonia may have been grouped thematically, as Skarsaune convincingly argues.[43] Perhaps Paul is referring to something like this in 2 Tim. 4.13, when he mentions the parchments left at Troas.

g. The last stages – Stages C and D (in section 4.2.1, point 3) in this characterization of the function of the codex for biblical canonization – probably start already in Irenaeus with his notable eagerness to include all authentic writings among the Scriptures (arguably existing in codex form; initial groupings of NT writings in part-collections, such as P[45] and P[46], stem from this period), while excluding others (see section 8.3).

---

[42] See Roberts and Skeat, *The Birth of the Codex*, 24ff.; and n. 72 below.

[43] Skarsaune, 'The Development of Scriptural Interpretation in the Second and Third Centuries – except Clement and Origen', in *Hebrew Bible/Old Testament: The History of Its Interpretation*, vol. 1, ed. M. Sæbø (Göttingen: Vandenhoeck & Ruprecht, 1996), 373–442. Some scholars, such as Albl and Skarsaune, have argued in favour of the testimony hypothesis developed by Rendel Harris and others. Parallel with the 4Q-testimonia found at Qumran, earliest Christianity seems to have made use of such collections of testimonies, anthologies of texts extracted from the Jewish Scriptures and compiled as proof texts for Christian claims. By comparing Justin's *Apology* with the *Dialogue*, Skarsaune has argued in a series of studies that Justin Martyr made use of such testimony sources.

In Origen such reflection is further developed and is soon to be seen in various NT canon lists, of which the Muratorian canon is probably the earliest example. Possibly the inclusion of disputed writings in various Bible codices also belongs here, such as Codex Sinaiticus, ending with the *Shepherd* and the *Epistle of Barnabas* after the NT writings. It is here worth noting the potential of the codex having the included writings in a particular order. The *Shepherd* and *Barnabas*, e.g. may be understood as an appendix after the, more or less, undisputed NT writings in Codex Sinaiticus. The notion of correct order between the writings influenced the manuscript tradition. Thus, as David Trobisch argues,[44] the early canonical Greek New Testament comes down to us in the sequence Gospels (in canonical order), Acts + Catholic Epistles, Paul and Revelation. However, as already mentioned, there are plenty of variations. Within the part-volumes, the arrangement of the Gospels occurs in 12 various sequences, and there are at least seven for the Catholic Epistles.[45] For the Paulines, we note the placing of Hebrews early (after Romans in P[46]) or late in the collection, which may be significant in terms of the epistle's canonical status.[46]

Also, the statistics of the number of Greek NT manuscripts preserved indicate various preferences. In an essay published in 2002, Eldon Jay Epp mentions 2,361 manuscripts that contain the Gospels, 792 containing Paul, 662 with Acts and Catholic Epistles, and 287 containing the Revelation of John.[47]

The whole Greek New Testament is preserved only in three majuscules (Sinaiticus, Alexandrinus and Codex Ephraimi Rescriptus), and 56 minuscules, while, in Epp's count, 149 Greek manuscripts have the entire collection, except the Revelation.[48] The production of these large-scale codices seems particularly significant during this stage of the process (fourth century onwards).

---

[44] Trobisch, *First Edition.*

[45] Schmidt, 'The Greek New Testament as a Codex', in *The Canon Debate*, (eds) L. M. McDonald and J. A. Sanders (Peabody, MA: Hendrickson, 2002), 469–84.

[46] See Laird, 'Early Titles of the Letters of the Pauline Corpus' (paper presented at the annual Graduate Conference for Biblical and Early Christian Studies. St Andrews, Scotland, 8 June 2012).

[47] Epp, 'Issues in the Interrelation of New Testament Textual Criticism and Canon', 485–515.

[48] Ibid., 487.

Also, reviewing the reception history, a quick look at the whole manuscript tradition already leaves one in no doubt which books have been considered as canonical in the various parts of the church and at different times, namely the 27 writings that today make up our New Testament.

The visual dimension

Visually, 'the codex came to be identified as the earthly vessel of the Word' and consequently is represented so in Christian art. Our earliest extant representations of the codex book are Christian bibles. It soon was 'variously depicted closed in the hands of the Pantocrator in the vault of a basilica or open before an evangelist busily copying the text.'[49] The codex also in this respect attained the position as a sacred artefact, a physical means and symbol of the Word of God.

A straightforward connection between codex and canon

Gamble argues 'that only the codex format would allow for the collection of the Pauline Letters in one volume, because an eighty-foot roll would be required to contain them, which is twice the maximum length and three times the normal length of Greek rolls.'[50] Similar arguments have been made with respect to the Four-Gospel codex (see section 4.3).

4.3 Further comments on recent research

In the last few decades, various theories have been proposed to account for the consistent Christian preference for the codex format. In 1945 Peter Katz argued that the adoption of the codex by early Christianity took place for theological reasons, in order for the church to theologically distance itself from the synagogue.[51] This hypothesis has been further developed more

---

[49] Sharpe III, 'Some Representations of the Book and Book-Making, from the Earliest Codex Forms to Jost Amman', in *The Bible as Book: The Manuscript Tradition*, (eds) Sharpe III and van Kampen (London: The British Library & Oak Knoll Press in association with The Scripturium: Center for Christian Antiquities, 1998), 197.

[50] Gamble, *Books and Readers in the Early Church*.

[51] Katz, 'The Early Christians' Use of Codices Instead of Rolls', *JTS* 46 (1945): 63–5; Skarsaune, *Den første kristne bibel: Et blad av kodeksens historie*, 30.

recently by Irven Resnick, who emphasizes the possible function attained by the new book format of marking out a distance by the earliest Christians to the binding power of the Law.[52]

A decade after Katz's 1945 article, Roberts pointed out that the Jewish convention of writing regarding the oral Torah was a direct parallel to the handling of the Jesus tradition in the church.[53] Roberts's work was further elaborated in 1983 by Roberts and Skeat in their important study *The Birth of the Codex*, in which a first-century, or even a pre-AD 70 Antiochene or Jerusalem origin of the codex was suggested.

In the 1980s Martin Hengel and Joseph van Haelst, instead of the Jesus tradition – as proposed by Roberts and Skeat – set forth economical and practical reasons as the major driving force behind the choice of the new book format.[54] Still another theory, presented by Oskar Skarsaune and G. H. R. Horsley,[55] sought to explain the anomaly with reference to certain popular or low-culture marks among the Christian communities, as distinct from the corresponding practice found within the literary classes, to which the leaders of contemporary Judaism belonged.[56]

In the 1990s a more radically flavoured hypothesis was suggested by Skeat, who, in order to explain 'the extraordinary predilection of the early Christians for the codex form of book', abandoned his earlier position from 1983.[57] Instead, he now argued that the codex was actively chosen as the new book format around AD 100, when the Fourth Gospel was published, simply in order to be able to contain the whole text of all four Gospels. In his opinion

[52] Resnick, 'The Codex in Early Jewish and Christian Communities', *The Journal of Religious History* 17 (1992): 1–17.

[53] Roberts, 'The Codex', *Proceedings of the British Academy* 40 (1954): 169–204; Sirat, 'Le livre hébreu dans les premiers siècles de notre ère: le témoignage des textes', in *Les débuts du codex*, ed. Alain Blanchard (Turnhout: Brepols, 1989), 115–24. I am here using the concept of 'oral Torah' in the traditional sense. See esp. Gerhardsson, *Memory and Manuscript: Oral Tradition and Written Transmission in Rabbinic Judaism and Early Christianity* (Lund and Copenhagen: C. W. K. Gleerup and Ejnar Munksgaard, 1961). For a critical discussion of the concept, see, e.g. Sanders, *Jewish Law from Jesus to the Mishnah* (London: SCM, and Philadelphia: Trinity Press International, 1990), 97–130.

[54] Hengel, *Die Evangelienüberschriften: vorgetragen am 18. Oktober 1981* (Heidelberg: Carl Winter Universitätsverlag, 1984); and van Haelst, 'Les origines du codex'.

[55] Skarsaune, *Kodeks og kanon: om brug og avgrensning av de gammeltestamentlige skrifter i oldkirken* (Oslo: Verbum, 1994); Horsley, 'Classical Manuscripts in Australia and New Zealand and the Early History of the Codex', *Anthichton: Journal of the Australian Society for Classical Studies* 27 (1995): 60–85.

[56] Skarsaune, 'Den første kristne bibel: Et blad av kodeksens historie'. For general criticism of this view, see Harris, *Ancient Literacy*, 294f.

[57] Skeat, 'The Origin of the Christian Codex', *Zeitschrift für Papyrologie und Epigraphik* 102 (1994): 263.

the Gospels from the outset circulated in the form of a Four-Gospel codex, and were thereby safeguarded from either addition or subtraction. By arguing that P[64], P[67] and P[4] come from the same codex, which was almost certainly a Four-Gospel codex dating from the late second century, Skeat suggested P[64-67+4] as our oldest manuscript of the four Gospels.[58] He also proposed P[75] as being part of another very early Four-Gospel codex. Hence, in his view the use of the codex affected the canonization of the fourfold Gospel. 'Only a codex – and not a roll – could hold the four gospels.'[59]

Along the lines of William Harris, Joseph van Haelst and E. J. Epp, Graham Stanton in 2004 lightly criticized Roberts's and Skeat's 'big bang' theories accounting for the early Christian choice of the codex for their Scriptures.[60] In Stanton's view, 'once Christian scribes began to use the codex, their precocious devotion to the new format was sustained by a variety of pragmatic factors, some of which will have been more influential than others at particular times and in particular locations'.[61]

A slightly different emphasis on the potential bearing of the codex on the canonical process has been offered by Harry Gamble, who makes a case for the earliest Pauline corpus adopting the codex form.[62] This format was then used also a little later when the Gospels were published. In this way the codex form became the standard biblical format. Robert Kraft, on the other hand, argues that the significance of the codex for the canon is clearly seen first in the fourth century with the production of whole bibles as one single multi-quire codex. Yet another approach towards our topic, referred to above, is offered by David Trobisch and Eldon Jay Epp, who both pay attention to the significance of the ordering of the NT books within a codex for questions relating to the NT canon.[63]

---

[58] Skeat, 'The Oldest Manuscript of the Four Gospels?', *NTS* 43 (1997): 1–34.

[59] Epp, 'The Codex and Literacy in Early Christianity', 17. Cf. also Hurtado, *The Earliest Christian Artifacts*, 35-38; for a critical treatment of Skeat, see Head, 'Is P[4], P[64] and P[67] the Oldest Manuscript of the Four Gospels? A Response to T. C. Skeat', *NTS* 51 (2005): 450–57.

[60] Stanton shares this criticism with William Harris, Joseph van Haelst ('Les Origines du Codex', 12--35) and Epp ('The Codex and Literacy', 15–37); Stanton, *Jesus and Gospel* (Cambridge: Cambridge University Press, 2004), 165–91.

[61] Stanton, *Jesus and Gospel*, 171.

[62] Gamble, *Books and Readers in the Early Church*, 58ff.; for a different theory similarly focusing on the role of the codex for the emergence of the Pauline corpus, see Richards, *Paul and First-Century Letter Writing: Secretaries, Composition and Collection* (Downers Grove, IL: InterVarsity, 2004), 218–23.

[63] Kraft, 'The Codex and Canon Consciousness', in *The Canon Debate*, (eds) L. M. McDonald and J. A. Sanders (Peabody, MA: Hendrickson, 2002), 229–33; Epp, 'Issues in the Interrelation of New Testament Textual Criticism and Canon', 485–515; Trobisch, *First Edition*.

None of these hypotheses, however, has been unanimously agreed upon, although they all potentially contribute to a more comprehensive understanding of the canonical process and the historical development of the new biblical book format.

To some extent the scholarly discussion regarding book form – scroll or codex – has come to focus on various datings of the early Christian manuscripts. Contrary to Roberts's and Skeat's traditional dating of the manuscripts that are thought to be prior to the fourth century, the late Eric Turner proposed a redating of these documents, placing them roughly 50 years later in almost every case.[64] Van Haelst adopts the results from Turner and so is in a position to criticize the stand taken by Roberts and Skeat. Contrary to these two scholars, van Haelst further opts for practical reasons to account for the Christian preference for the codex. If the dating by Turner and van Haelst proved to be the more accurate, we still, however, have Christian papyrus codices from the early to mid-/late second century, such as P[52] (P. Ryl. 457) and P[90] (P. Oxy. 3523),[65] which nevertheless indicates an extremely early adoption of the new book format in the church. Irrespective of exact details of dating, however, is not the almost complete lack of the use of rolls by the early Christians for their Scriptures in need of some kind of extraordinary explanation, such as the ones referred to above by Katz, Resnick, Roberts, Skeat and Gamble?

In terms of the new format's effect on the canon formation, it appears to be the case that the effective-historical impact of the codex form within the larger time frame is as important as the historical cause-and-effect explanation applied to a particular moment and a particular location.

---

[64] Birdsall, 'Review of Les débuts du codex. Edited by Alain Blanchard, 1989', *JTS* 41 (1990); Roberts and Skeat, *The Birth of the Codex*; Turner, *The Typology of the Early Codex* (Philadelphia: University of Pennsylvania Press, 1977); Blanchard, *Les débuts du codex* (Turnhout: Brepols, 1989). See also Epp, 'The Codex and Literacy', 16. For general difficulties dating manuscripts, see Barker, 'The Dating of New Testament Papyri', *NTT* 57 (2011): 571–82.

[65] Haelst, 'Les origines du codex', 35; Birdsall, 'Review of Les débuts du codex'.

4.4 Codex, *nomina sacra* and the early church organization

As we have seen, practically all biblical manuscripts of Christian provenance are codices.[66] In the first century AD, at the time when the Christian mission reached out in the Roman Empire, the literary form of the codex, which was soon to be counted as an ecclesiastical standard,[67] was discussed on Latin ground as a new book format.[68] Sometime in the first (or early second) century, the new leaf-book, well suited for missionary activity,[69] was generally introduced in the churches. As in the case with the *nomina sacra*, the codex used for the Christian Scriptures appears to have been next to universally accepted by the faith communities well by the second century. Together, the introduction of the system of *nomina sacra* and the adoption of the papyrus codex may serve as sound proof of a two programmes standardization, having an impact on the organization of the earliest church. Contra Kurt and Barbara Aland,[70] Epp argues:

> What these practices do suggest … is that the churches in this earliest period, at least in the East, were perhaps not as loosely organized as has been assumed,

---

[66] Roberts and Skeat (*The Birth of the Codex*, 1) define the codex 'as a collection of sheets of any material, folded double and fastened together at the back or spine, and usually protected by covers.' See also Hurtado, 'The Earliest Evidence of an Emerging Christian Material and Visual Culture: The Codex, the Nomina Sacra and the Staurogram', in *Text and Artifact in the Religions of Mediterranean Antiquity*, (eds) Wilson and Desjardins (Waterloo, Ontario: Wilfrid Laurier University Press, 2000); and Hurtado, *The Earliest Christian Artifacts*.

[67] Resnick, 'The Codex in Early Jewish and Christian Communities', 12: 'By the time the Church had become a largely gentile community – that is, by about the middle of the second century – Christianity had disavowed the use of the roll for biblical literature.'; Eusebius, *Vita Constantini*, IV, 36 (referred to by Resnick): In AD 331 the new book standard is sanctioned by a letter written by the Emperor Constantine to Eusebius, after the great loss of bibles in the Diocletianic and other persecutions, where he orders 50 parchment Bibles for his new foundations in Constantinople.

[68] Roberts and Skeat, *The Birth of the Codex*, 24ff.: Martial (ca. AD 85) tells of authors whose works were available *in membranis* or in *pugillaribus membranis*. He commends these parchment codices because of their convenience for travellers and because of the space it saves in the library compared to the roll. The new book format is also mentioned by Paersius (ca. AD 55–60) and by Quintillian (ca. AD 90); cf. Gamble, *Books and Readers in the Early Church: a History of Early Christian Texts* (New Haven: Yale University Press, 1995), 52: Among the 18 non-Christian manuscripts containing literary works that are in codex form from the second century, the earliest one, P. Oxy. 30, called *De bellis Macedonicis*, which is the only Latin text of the 18, has been dated to the beginning of the second century. According to Eric Turner (*The Typology of the Early Codex*, 38), this codex 'does not seem to be an experimental type of book, and its mere existence is evidence that this book form had a prehistory.'

[69] See the comments by Martial in the note above.

[70] Aland, *The Text of the New Testament: An Introduction to the Critical Editions and to the Theory and Practice of Modern Textual Criticism* (Grand Rapids: Eerdmans, 1989), 55f., 59.

and, therefore, they also were not as isolated from one another as has been affirmed.[71]

This thought was put forth already in 1969 by Skeat, who then, for the first time, suggested a connection between the introduction of the *nomina sacra* and the adoption of the codex:

> The significant fact is that the introduction of the *nomina sacra* seems to parallel very closely the adoption of the papyrus codex; and it is remarkable that those developments should have taken place at almost the same time as the great outburst of activity among Jewish scholars which led to the standardisation of the Hebrew Bible. It is no less remarkable that they seem to indicate a degree of organisation, of conscious planning, and uniformity of practice among the Christian communities which we have hitherto had little reason to suspect, and which throw a new light on the early history of the Church.[72]

What is particularly worth noting for our present purpose is the general rather uniform arrangement and design of the Christian Scriptures, paralleling the energetic scribal activity in the synagogue with the Jewish Scriptures.[73] In several respects, the canonical process in the church appears to parallel such scribal activity in the synagogue, depending heavily – positively and negatively – on the notion of a canon of Sacred Scriptures (cf. Josephus, *Against Apion* I, 37–43) as these functioned in the Jewish community.

On one level, it seems to be difficult to explain the universal, unanimous and early usage of the new, somewhat odd book format, in particular so when used for the Jewish Scriptures. As Frances Young (in line with Roberts) points out: 'it would be unthinkable that the "scriptures" be inscribed on anything but rolls. ... It is therefore something of a shock to discover that Christians

---

[71] Epp, The Significance of the Papyri for Determining the Nature of the New Testament Text in the Second Century: A Dynamic View of Textual Transmission (Grand Rapids: Eerdmans, 1993), 288. Cf. also Haines-Eitzen (Guardians of Letters: Literacy, Power, and the Transmitters of Early Christian Literature (Oxford: Oxford, 2000), 91–6); cf. n. 72 below.

[72] Skeat, 'Early Christian Book-Production: Papyri and Manuscripts', in *The Cambridge History of the Bible*, vol. 2, *The West from the Fathers to the Reformation*, ed. G. W. H. Lampe (Cambridge, Cambridge University Press, 1969), 72f.; cited in Roberts and Skeat, *The Birth of the Codex*, 57. Cf. Haines-Eitzen (*Guardians of Letters*, 94–5), who stresses 'a network of scribes who communicated with each other' to explain the 'spread' of the *nomina sacra*, and the 'private transmission of early Christian literature' as well as inter-communal organizational efforts to account for the uniform use of the codex among Christian communities: 'Skeat, quite rightly, proposes that the organizational effort would have taken place *between communities*, and we should avoid the notion that "conscious planning" took place at some kind of inceptive stage'. Cf. also Ch. 3, n. 4, for comments on her view on the emergent *nomina sacra* convention.

[73] This Jewish scribal activity included revisions of the Greek Bible.

were producing copies of the Torah and Psalms in papyrus codices as early as the middle of the second century [and probably earlier still; author's comment] – sacred books in notebook format!'[74] On a fundamental level, the idea of Scripture, both materially and textually, was different in the Christian community as compared to the synagogue. In terms of organization, we can notice with Skeat and Kim Heines-Eitzen (see note 72) that in order to account for the uniformity amongst the faith communities in their use of codex form and *nomina sacra* (cf. Ch. 3, note 4) we should allow for some form of very early intercommunal organizational effort.

4.5 The codex: A notebook on Jesus logia?

As the geographical place of origin of both the *nomina sacra* and the Christian codex, Roberts and Skeat have suggested Antioch[75] and Jerusalem, or a combination of these two early ecclesiastical centres. This hypothesis is based on an earlier theory developed by Roberts,[76] which assumes that the Gospels were already published in codex form in the first century. The reason for the choice of the codex, as their argument goes, was not primarily economical or practical, which has been maintained by some scholars,[77] but rather the ready-at-hand analogy between the transmission

---

[74] Young, *Biblical Exegesis and the Formation of Christian Culture*, 13. Roberts, *Books in the Graeco-Roman World and in the New Testament*, 61: 'the transference of the Law from its sacrosanct form to a format of no antiquity and little regard … must have seemed to the Jew an act of sacrilege,' citation from Young, *Biblical Exegesis and the Formation of Christian Culture*, 13.

[75] Ibid., 60: 'Once the Jewish War began, the dominating position of Antioch as the metropolis of Christianity in the Greek-speaking world would have been unchallenged, and any development of the tablet into the codex is most likely to have taken place here, thus laying the foundation of the city as a centre of Biblical scholarship.' Given the end of the first or beginning of the second century as the *terminus ante quem* for the adoption of the codex, the proposed Antiochene hypothesis, although somewhat tentative, needs to be seriously considered.

[76] Roberts, 'The Codex', in *Proceedings of the British Academy* 40 (1954): 187–9: According to this hypothesis the suggestion is that the Gospel of Mark emerged in Rome, in the form of a parchment codex. It was later carried over to Alexandria where it was copied and spread as papyrus codices, thereby establishing a powerful example for Christian practice; See also Roberts, 'Books in the Graeco-Roman World and in the New Testament', in *The Cambridge History of the Bible*, vol. 1 (Cambridge: Cambridge University Press, 1970); Roberts and Skeat, *The Birth of the Codex*, 54–8.

[77] So Hengel, *Die Evangelienüberschriften: vorgetragen am 18. Oktober 1981* (Heidelberg: Carl Winter Universitätsverlag, 1984), 41 (but cf. section 4.2.2, for a somewhat revised opinion); and van Haelst, 'Les origines du codex', 28f. However, cf. p. 35, where van Haelst refrains from relating to the analysis made by Roberts and Skeat (*The Birth of the Codex*, 45–53), in which they seek to demonstrate the inadequacy of practical considerations to explain the Christian adoption of the codex. See also Gamble, *Books and Readers in the Early Church*, 54–6.

of the sayings of Jesus and the preservation of the oral Torah.[78] The transmission of oral tradition within these two Jewish contexts required a handling other than that of the written Torah.[79] The oral tradition emerging from Jesus, accordingly, could only be written down as notes for private usage, with very little legal authority in analogy with contemporary rabbinic conventions. However, van Haelst and Gamble are probably right in some of their criticism of this theory;[80] but it is still not unreasonable to hypothesize that parts of the Jesus-tradition was preserved from early on by some form of note-taking. The leaf-book, or codex, was a common Jewish as well as Hellenistic[81] form for such notes, or ὑπομνήματα,[82] which in the Jewish Palestinian setting helped to uphold the oral didactic tradition.[83] Because of the ancient injunction prohibiting the publication in writing of the oral Torah,[84] the sayings that were transmitted orally[85] by the Rabbis could only be written down 'in epistles, in private rolls and, above all, on πίνακες, codices (or single tablets which could subsequently be bound in a codex).'[86] To this distinction between authorized published editions and private notebooks, parallels are also found in the differentiation between the Hellenistic concepts ἐκδόσεις (authorized publications) and the ὑπομνήματα (notes).[87] Tied to the above, it is interesting to note Justin's desig-

---

[78] For a discussion on 'oral Torah', see Sanders, *Jewish Law from Jesus to the Mishnah*; and Gerhardsson, *The Reliability of the Gospel Tradition* (Peabody, MA: Hendrickson, 2001), 9ff., esp. 12.

[79] Lieberman, *Hellenism in Jewish Palestine: Studies in the Literary Transmission Beliefs and Manners of Palestine in the I Century B.C.E.–IV Century C.E.* (New York: The Jewish Theological Seminary of America, 1950).

[80] Van Haelst, 'Les origines du codex', 31–2; Gamble, *Books and Readers*, 57–8.

[81] Riesner, *Jesus als Lehrer: Eine Untersuchung zum Ursprung der Evangelien-Überlieferung* (Tübingen: Mohr Siebeck), 1988), 491–4; Kennedy, *A History of Rhetoric II: The Art of Rhetoric in the Roman World 300– B.C.-A.D. 300* (New York: Princeton, 1972), 58f., 277; Kennedy, *Classical and Christian Source Criticism* (San Antonio, 1978), 131.

[82] Kennedy, *A History of Rhetoric II*, 85, 110, 287f.; Kennedy, *Classical and Christian Source Criticism*, 136f.

[83] Riesner, *Jesus als Lehrer*, 87.

[84] The rabbinic prohibition against writing down the oral Law is for the first time explicitly stated by R. Juda b. Nachmani (ca. AD 250): 'You shall not deliver/transmit sayings (transmitted) in writing orally; you shall not deliver/transmit sayings (transmitted) orally in writing.' (b Git. 60b; b Tem. 14b). Cited from Gerhardsson, *Memory and Manuscript*, 159. Birger Gerhardsson comments that this practice seems to 'be established before the beginning of the Christian era'. Cf. also Riesner, *Jesus als Lehrer*, 493.

[85] That is, before the later publications of the *Mishna*.

[86] Lieberman, *Hellenism in Jewish Palestine*, 204, 84ff. Cf. also Hurtado, *The Earliest Evidence of an Emerging Christian Material and Visual Culture*, 272f.

[87] Gerhardsson, *Memory and Manuscript*, 159, 163; on the distinction between ἐκδόσεις and written ὑπομνήματα, see Roberts, *The Codex 1954*, 169ff.; when this distinction between public books and notebooks was at times neglected, e.g. when disciples of a great master, like Quintilian (*Inst.*

nation of the Gospels as ἀπομνημονεύματα (notes of memorization) and Tertullian's reference to the Gospels as *commentarii*, the Latin rendering of ὑπομνήματα (notes; Tert. *De Ieiunio* 10.3). Saul Lieberman's argument, when applied to the apostolic transmission of the sayings tradition, proceeds as follows:

> Now the Jewish disciples of Jesus, in accordance with the general rabbinic practice, wrote the sayings which their master pronounced *not* in form of a book to be published, but as notes in their *pinaces*, codices, in their note-books (or in private small rolls). They did this because otherwise they would have transgressed the law. In line with the foregoing we would naturally expect the *logia* of Jesus to be originally copied in codices.[88]

Roberts and Skeat have based their argument on Lieberman's philological analysis[89] of פנקס, πίναξ, *pinax*, with the meaning 'writing-tablet'. These *pinaces*, or tablets, were of three different kinds – 1) with waxed boards, 2) with polished surfaces (e.g. the ivory tablets of the Romans) or 3) named *apiporin* (of wood and/or possibly papyrus, the material that the Christians from early on chose for their codices; however, the μεμβράναι mentioned in 2 Tim. 4.13 are likely parchment notebooks/codices).[90] These were all commonly used as notebooks, ὑπομνήματα. Using the suggested analogy between the transmission of the *logia* of the gospel tradition, and the preservation of the oral Law, Roberts and Skeat argue: 'If the first work to be written on a papyrus codex was a Gospel, it is easy to understand that the codex rapidly became the sole format for the Christian Scriptures, given the authority that a Gospel would carry.'[91] In fact, if this was a 'necessary' development, this necessity may arguably have been built into the early canon development. The authority ascribed to the Gospel in codex form may be

---

I, praef. 7-8) issued an edition (ἐκδόσεις) of their notes, 'the result sometime was that the teacher felt compelled to publish his work in order to correct the errors and blunders in the edition of his pupils', Lieberman, *Hellenism in Jewish Palestine*, 87.

88 Ibid., 205.

89 Lieberman, however, draws on the analysis made by Roberts.

90 Hurtado, *The Earliest Evidence of an Emerging Christian Material and Visual Culture*, 272; Gamble, *Books and Readers in the Early Church*, 64–5; Lieberman, *Hellenism in Jewish Palestine*, 203f., with further references; and Roberts and Skeat, *The Birth of the Codex*, 59; *pace* Sirat ('Le livre hébreu dans les premiers siècles de notre ère', 120), who regards it as very unlikely that *apiporin* could mean 'papyrus codex'. Cf. also Richards (*Paul and First-Century Letter Writing*, 218, 223), who argues that one of the 'parchments' (or notebooks) Timothy is asked to bring (2 Tim. 4.13) most likely contained copies of Paul's letters.

91 Roberts and Skeat, *The Birth of the Codex*, 60.

what motivated the early Christian production of the Jewish Scriptures in the new literary format.

4.6 Canonization as the edition of a book

An important aspect of biblical canonization is the edition of the New Testament, or parts of the New Testament, as a literary corpus. As discussed above, there are some indications of a connection between the adoption of the codex and the formation of the four Gospels. If the Gospels soon were copied and received, not in the form of scrolls or as four separate codices, but as one book, as in P[45],[92] there could very well be some correlation between the outer form and the strict limitation of the number of authoritative Gospels that occur towards the end of the second century in the writings of Irenaeus, Clement of Alexandria and in the Muratorian fragment.[93] However, this explanation of the emergence of the Four-Gospel canon was dismissed by Hans von Campenhausen in 1968. Instead, he regarded the unity of the fourfold Gospel as a theological phenomenon that had nothing to do with 'book production'.[94] By contrast, J. Keith Elliott has reminded us of the potential inherent in the new book format by making the interesting point that 'no extant codices up to the third century exceed three hundred pages, indicating that this early codex format "helped to limit the number of Gospels to these four and no more"'.[95]

A more comprehensive model, treating the theme of canon and book production, has been suggested by David Trobisch. In his *Habilitationsschrift*, *Die Endredaktion des Neuen Testaments*, Trobisch sets out to analyse the

---

[92] P[45] contains the four Gospels and Acts.
[93] Cf. n. 24 above. On the dating of the Muratorian fragment, see Verheyden, 'The Canon Muratori: A Matter of Dispute', in *The Biblical Canons*, (eds) Auwers and de Jonge, Bibliotheca Ephemeridum Theologicarum Lovaniensium (Leuven: Leuven University Press, 2003), 491; Stanton, 'The Fourfold Gospel', *NTS* 43 (1997); Schnelle, *Einleitung in das Neue Testament* (Göttingen: Vandenhoeck und Ruprecht, 1996); Barton, *The Spirit and the Letter: Studies in the Biblical Canon* (London: SPCK, 1997); Metzger, *The Canon of the New Testament: Its Origin, Development, and Significance* (Oxford: Clarendon, 1987). For a later dating, see Hahneman, *The Muratorian Fragment and the Development of the Canon* (Oxford: Clarendon, 1992); McDonald, *The Formation of the Christian Biblical Canon* (Peabody, MA: Hendrickson, 1995).
[94] Campenhausen, *The Formation of the Christian Bible* (Philadelphia: Fortress, 1972), 174.
[95] 'Manuscripts, the Codex and the Canon', *JSNT* 63 (1996): 107. Cited from Epp, 'Interrelation of NT Textual Criticism and Canon', 511. Cf. also Hill, *Who Chose the Gospels?*, 116.

earliest editions of the entire New Testament by investigating the extant Greek New Testament manuscripts. He reaches the conclusion that the formation of the New Testament canon should not be understood as a process extending over several centuries. Instead, he maintains, 'the history of the New Testament is the history of a book; a book that was published by a concrete publisher or publishing circle [*Herausgeberkreis*] at a concrete place and at a particular time.'[96] In his English summary he further concludes:

> The New Testament is a publication of the second century and not the result of a gradual growth process extending over several centuries. The titles, the number of writings, and their arrangement were determined from the very beginning and represent one single archetype. The argument is based on the textual critical evidence and on the observation that the New Testament displays features of a uniform final redaction.[97]

According to Trobisch, the striking uniformity of the arrangement and order of the books in the manuscripts can only be explained as the result of an early canonical archetype, a published manuscript that he calls the 'Canonical Edition' (*Die Kanonische Ausgabe*).[98] Because of the broad influence of this archetype on a majority of later editions of the Christian Bible, he argues, it deserves the attribute 'canonical'.

Throughout Trobisch's analysis the codex format is presupposed. The book titles, the order of the biblical books and other editorial features of the literary archetype gave the codex a catalysing, if not an indispensable, function as this 'canonical edition' was received and spread in the Christian communities. None the less, Trobisch adds a crucial restriction: 'In the second century, for the time being, also the Canonical Edition is only one Christian literary work among many. It has powerful competitors.'[99] In either case, however, in the 'canonical' as well as in other editions of the collections of New Testament books, the codex seems to have been involved.

Though I can follow Trobisch's main argument, I have one reservation. It seems to me that his dismissal of a 'canonical process' is unnecessary for his overall argument (as the above quote might indicate). Nevertheless, his

---

[96] Trobisch, *Die Endredaktion des Neuen Testaments*, 11.
[97] Ibid., 185.
[98] Ibid., 5.
[99] Ibid., 68.

central argument for a probable 'publication' of a second-century archetypal New Testament, containing perhaps 27 – or at least some 20 to 27 – books (27, according to Trobisch), will be used in the following.[100] The publication of such a 'Canonical Edition', in my opinion, could be considered as part of – as well as a major outcome of – the canonical process focused in the present study.

4.7 Mini-closures of the canon

As we have already seen, several attempts have been made to link the formation of the canon to the codex form as the new Christian book format. Although the codex enabled the collection of several books into one, scholars have doubted that it had any major role in the closure of the Christian Scriptures.[101] The early use of the codex form does not appear to have particularly stimulated large-sized editions of the Bible in which, e.g. all of the NT is included in a single codex. Still in the Middle Ages part-collections, rather than a single volume containing all NT writings, are more common. Of the 2,646 minuscule manuscripts listed by Kurt Aland in his *Kurzgefasste Liste der griechischen Handschriften des Neuen Testaments,*[102] less than 10 per cent contain the NT complete.[103] Out of these, 136 (149 in Epp's updated list, see section 4.2.1) contain the NT without the Apocalypse, while only 59 contain the full 27-book edition.

Traces of the history of reception of the Apocalypse can, of course, be read out of these extant codices, as can other information of interest for the history of the canon. The function of the codex form as an organizing device of the NT material is here of special importance for the relation between canon and codex. Although the codex format most probably did not primarily help forming the 22- (Peshitta, the canon of John Chrysostom),[104]

---

[100] See D. C. Parker's review of the English translation of Trobisch's book, in *JTS* 53:1 (2002) 298–305.
[101] So Roberts and Skeat, *The Birth of the Codex*, 62–6.
[102] Aland, *Kurzgefasste Liste der griechischen Handschriften des Neuen Testaments*, vol. 1: Gesamtübersicht (Berlin: Walter de Gruyter, 1963).
[103] This is only one aspect of the NT writings understood as a textual whole. Other dimensions, as well, such as ritual, doctrinal etc., often treat the NT and/or the Bible as a whole.
[104] The Peshitta and the canon of John Chrysostom (ca. AD 347–407), e.g. embraced 22 New Testament writings. Cf. Metzger, *The Canon of the New Testament*, 214f.; 2 Peter, 2 and 3 John, Jude and Revelation are not included.

26- (Eastern Church) or 27-book (Eastern and Western Church) corpora as single volumes, it seems to have contributed by delimiting and closing the major three or four part-collections making up the New Testament. That is, in particular the fourfold Gospel, and the *Corpus Paulinum*, but also the so-called Praxapostolos (Acts and the Catholic Letters) and the Apocalypse (cf. section 4.2).[105] In scholarly discussion on the canon this organization of the NT material, in three or four closed collections/codices, has been largely neglected. When, for example, the distinction between 'canon 1' and 'canon 2' is made,[106] or 'canon *as function*' and 'canon *as shape*',[107] it would be most helpful to consider the organization of the NT material in part-volumes. Using this terminology, with regard to the *Corpus Paulinum* and the fourfold Gospel, 'canon 2'/'canon *as shape*' may be at hand as early as ca. AD 60–140 and 100–180, respectively.[108]

From the above analysis, we can conclude that due attention should be given to the formation of the three or four individual sub-units that constitute the New Testament. That is, the NT canon debate should not focus only, or primarily, on the final 27-book collection, but also on the central question whether a writing may or may not be included in one of these units (with particular attention given to the specific form of book title expected for each part-collection). As an essential aspect of the canon formation, it seems historically accurate to discuss the Four-Gospel codex, the *Corpus Paulinum*, the Praxapostolos and the Book of Revelation one at a time.[109] Using such a method, one could well argue for the canonization (and closing) of the

---

[105] Note the common ancient canonical sequence of Acts and the Catholic Letters, followed by the *Corpus Paulinum* (so Vaticanus and Alexandrinus; not, however, Sinaiticus). See further Trobisch, *First Edition*, 24–5, 103. See also section 4.2.1, under 4; and 4.2.2, under 9.

[106] McDonald, *Formation*.

[107] Sanders, 'Canon: Hebrew Bible' in *Anchor Bible Dictionary*, vol. 1, ed. D. N. Freedman (New York: Doubleday, 1992), 837–52.

[108] See Murphy-O'Connor, *Paul the Letter-Writer: His World, His Options, His Skills* (Collegeville, MN: A Michael Glazier Book, The Liturgical Press, 1995); Porter, 'Paul and the Process of Canonization', in *Exploring the Origins of the Bible*, (eds) Craig A. Evans and Emanuel Tov (Grand Rapids: Baker, 2008), 173–202; Stanton, 'The Fourfold Gospel'; Hurtado, 'The New Testament in the Second Century: Text, Collections, Canon', 19–24. Cf. also J. K. Elliott's comment in n. 109 below.

[109] Cf. Elliott, 'The Early Text of the Catholic Epistles', in *The Early Text of the New Testament*, (eds) Charles E. Hill and Michael J. Kruger (Oxford: Oxford University Press, 2012), 207: 'The fourfold Gospels seem to have emerged and to have been accepted as authoritative early and certainly before the New Testament canon was eventually agreed upon and fixed. The Pauline Corpus also seems to have been established relatively early'. For some valuable comments on the Catholic Epistles' and Acts' more complex history of reception into the NT canon, see ibid, 206–7. For a discussion of the book titles of the NT writings, see Trobisch, *First Edition*, 38–43; and Laird, 'Early Titles of the Letters of the Pauline Corpus'.

Four-Gospel canon before the time of Irenaeus (or even before the time of Justin, as suggested by some scholars).[110] As for the Pauline corpus, one 10-letter and/or one 13- or 14-letter corpus were probably circulating among the Christian communities from the early second century.[111] So the formation of the Pauline letter collection arguably took place, at the latest, around the turn of the second century (ca. AD 80–120), or perhaps even earlier.[112] This is why the 13- or 14-letter corpus (including the letters addressed primarily to the presbyters) seems to be, more or less, closed by the late second century, but probably considerably earlier. In 2 Pet. 3.15f. and in Irenaeus, the Pauline writings are already put on a par with the 'Old Testament' writings; and Tertullian complains that Marcion has excluded the Pastoral Epistles from his emended Pauline 10-letter corpus (cf. sections 5.6.3 and 5.6.4).

When proceeding to the Apocalypse, discussions regarding its scriptural/canonical status do not seem to have occurred prior to around the early third century,[113] when the so-called Alogoi, the Roman presbyter Gaius and Dionysius of Alexandria began criticizing its canonicity.[114]

Thus, when discussing the New Testament canon *as a list*,[115] there may be reasons to focus primarily on the more disputed collection of writings commonly named the Praxapostolos.[116] As for so-called NT Apocrypha, J. Keith Elliott has pointed out that there are no extant manuscripts in which apocryphal Gospels were bound together with any of the canonical four (cf. citation, note 27); and regarding other texts of interest in this connection, such as the *Epistle of Barnabas* and the *Shepherd* of Hermas, we note that they did not belong to any particular collection of writings, as did the majority of the Scriptures that were to form the New Testament. In this function, the three

---

[110] Cf. Hurtado, 'The New Testament in the Second Century: Text, Collections, Canon'; and Stanton, 'The Fourfold Gospel'.

[111] Cf. Schmid, *Marcion und sein Apostolos*. Cf. also Trobisch, *Die Entstehung der Paulusbriefsammlung: Studien zu den Anfängen christlicher Publizistik* (Göttingen: Vandenhoeck & Ruprecht, 1989). Our earliest Pauline letter collection, P⁴⁶ (ca. AD 200), contains the Letter to the Hebrews after Romans.

[112] Murphy-O'Connor, *Paul the Letter-Writer: His World, His Options, His Skills* (Collegeville, MN: Michael Glazier, The Liturgical Press, 1995); and Zahn, *Geschichte des Neutestamentlichen Kanons*, vol. 1 (Erlangen: Verlag von Andreas Deichert, 1888). Cf. Porter, 'Paul and the Process of Canonization', 173–202.

[113] However, cf. Irenaeus. *Adv. Haer.* III, 11.9.

[114] See Zahn, *Die bleibende Bedeutung des neutestamentlichen Kanons für die Kirche* (Leipzig: U. Dichert'sche Verlagsbuchh. Nachf., 1898), 8–9; and Metzger, *The Canon of the New Testament*, 104f.; 150, 205.

[115] For various dimensions of canon, see Ch. 2.

[116] See Trobisch, *First Edition*. Cf. section 9.8.1.

or four codices/part-collections making up our present New Testament seem to have had a stabilizing function on the canonizing process. Writings that, in the long run, were not frequently included in one of these three or four part-collections, never made it into the canon. Again, in Hurtado's words: the formation of a 'New Testament' in the second century, in a sense, 'is a collection of prior collections'.

4.8 Conclusion

In various ways the Christian choice of the codex as the scriptural format seems to be connected with the biblical canon formation. Practical motives, such as missionary purposes and easier handling, probably played a role, beside reasons related to Christian identity, in the church's choice of the codex for its Scriptures. It appears to be significant that there is still 'no extant New Testament text copied on an unused roll among second- or third-century Christian manuscripts' (Hurtado).

From early on, Gospels and letters were collected in codices. P[45] (Gospels and Acts) and P[46] (Pauline Epistles, including Hebrews) are examples of such editorial activity from the late second/early third century. A more complex formation process can be demonstrated for what was later to constitute the Catholic Epistles, the Petrine and Johannine letter corpora, which, together with Acts, James and Jude, eventually were to form the so called Praxapostolos.

A case for the codex format's early role at the formation of the NT canon has been stressed by David Trobisch, who has argued that an archetypal Canonical Edition of the New Testament was published in the second century. This edition, he maintains, consisted of four part-volumes in codex format, with the books arranged in 'canonical' order. Later NT editions largely followed the editorial features of this First Edition of the Greek New Testament. As emphasized by Trobisch, throughout the Greek NT manuscript tradition we can note some characteristic editorial features with respect to book order, grouping and number of writings within the codices. I use parts of Trobisch's model as a further indication of the significance of the new book format for the canonical process.

The codex seems to have had a direct implication for canonical Scripture when second-century Christian OT texts are copied in the new format, thereby abandoning the standard Jewish (and pagan) scriptural format of the roll. Consequently, there is a clear interplay between the codex format and Christian Scripture, which takes place very early in the preparation of Christian texts – not least with regard to OT writings. With the production of (second- and) third-century Four-Gospel codices and the fourth-century mega-codices containing the whole Bible, this interplay is further elaborated.

There are also other areas where the codex appears to have had a role as part of the canonical process:

1. The early New Testament canon is best described as a collection of prior collections of writings (in codex form), rather than a collection of 27 or so individual writings. In the case of the fourfold Gospel and the Pauline letters, delimited collections probably circulated already in the second century.
2. As J. Keith Elliott points out, we have no manuscripts where 'apocryphal' Gospels have been bound together with any of the 'canonical' four Gospels; he further recounts that the codex automatically delimited the canon since, unlike a roll, the codex required advance planning, especially if it contained a single quire.
3. We also note another interesting observation by Elliott, namely that no extant codices up to the third century exceed 300 pages, indicating that this early codex format 'helped to limit the number of Gospels to these four and no more'.
4. As for the Pauline epistles, Gamble has argued that the technology of the codex could have played a role in the collecting of the letters into a corpus: 'only the codex format would allow for the collection of the Pauline letters in one volume, because an eighty-foot roll would be required to contain them, which is twice the maximum length and three times the normal length of Greek rolls.'

However, whether or not the codex format as such can be shown to have had a direct impact on the formation of the Four-Gospel canon (Skeat, Elliott) or the Pauline corpus (Gamble, Richards) is not the main emphasis here. Equally important is whether there is a demonstrable mutuality between the church's strong preference for a fourfold Gospel and the technology of Gospel production in the church. We can safely conclude that this is the case, and that both ideational (Irenaeus' argument for a delimited Four-Gospel canon) and material-textual dimensions (production of the Four-Gospel codex and the Pauline Corpus) have bearing on the canonical process.

Also – taking into account the reception history reflected in our extant codices containing Greek NT texts – a quick look at the manuscript tradition as a whole already leaves one in no doubt what books have been considered as canonical in the various parts of the church and at different times, namely the 27 writings that today make up our New Testament.

On icons, frescoes or mosaics, the codex is often portrayed in the hands of the Lord Jesus, as a symbol, we may argue, of textual stability. The Scriptures and the Lord go together. The symbol consisting of the Scriptures and the Lord is one piece (cf. Ch. 10). In John Sharpe's wording: 'Whether in frescoes, mosaics, or manuscripts, the codex for Christians is a symbol of their faith in that it represents the Word made flesh.'

Oral and Written Text: Two Media of the Christian Canon

The previous chapter argued that the codex format functions as both an oral and a written textual medium for the early Christians. The more fundamental question now arises, that of the relationship between the two textual forms of mediation. When seeking to understand the transmission of the apostolic gospel tradition in the first and second centuries, the dialectics between oral and written text turn out to be crucial.[1] In this chapter I will investigate how the interplay of these two textual media affects the early Christian notion of canon.

5.1 Background

The adoption of the codex format by the church, as argued above, may have been related to orality-oriented means of communication.[2] The preference for the codex as the proper book format for the gospel tradition may be taken to indicate the existence of a significant oral dimension of the earliest Christianity. As the Form Critical School in its way stressed this dimension by categorizing early Christianity as a fundamentally non-literary phenomenon,

---

[1] For the early Christian culture, in which both orality and literacy are significant for handing on the gospel, the aurally transmitted tradition is equally important. That is to say, in the ecclesial setting, the oral tradition is always oral/aural, and the written tradition often written/aural.

[2] Lieberman, *Hellenism in Jewish Palestine: Studies in the Literary Transmission Beliefs and Manners of Palestine in the I Century B.C.E.-IV Century C.E.* (New York: The Jewish Theological Seminary of America, 1950), 205–6; Barton, *The Spirit and the Letter: Studies in the Biblical Canon* (London: SPCK, 1997), 88–91; 100ff. On the development of the codex in this connection from notebook to book, see Gamble, *Books and Readers in the Early Church: a History of Early Christian Texts* (New Haven: Yale University, 1995), 70; and Ch. 4.

the written Gospels came to be treated one-sidedly as the natural outworkings of oral tradition. In Rudolf Bultmann's opinion, Christian tradition 'primarily existed only orally, and gained its written form only gradually due to the necessities of life.'[3] A thorough critique of this position has been provided by Harry Gamble.[4] Despite the occurrence of obvious oral elements of the Jesus tradition and in the composition of written Gospels, Gamble argues that Christianity prior to AD 70 none the less cannot be described as an exclusively oral culture, since it emerged out of the 'matrix of a broadly literate Judaism'. Although it did not at first produce much literature itself, early Christianity still 'was never without a literary dimension'.[5]

With redaction criticism, a shift of interest came about as the emphasis was laid on the Gospel text in its final redacted form. The perspective of the individual author was now focused. While form criticism – for which obvious literary features in the Gospel writings could be neglected – treated them a priori as *Kleinlitteratur*, redaction criticism upheld a sharper distinction between the oral and the written modes of ecclesial transmission of tradition.[6] The period of transition from orality to literacy in the church was sometimes even thought to lead to a divided history of reception regarding the gospel tradition, where the oral and the written elements were to be treated apart. Werner Kelber has emphasized such a line of demarcation between a pre-literate and a literate Christian culture by stressing the difference in the way they transmit and preserve information.[7] The idea of such a dichotomy has been rightly criticized, e.g. by Birger Gerhardsson, who has stressed that both at the time at which, and after, the Gospels were written down, the gospel largely remained orally transmitted. Samuel Byrskog has further elaborated

---

[3] *Religion in Geschichte und Gegenwart (RGG)*, vol. 3, 2nd edn (1929), 1681; citation from Gamble, *Books and Readers in the Early Church*, 14.

[4] Ibid., 10ff.

[5] Ibid., 29f. For further critique of Bultmann in this regard, see, e.g. Gerhardsson, *Memory and Manuscript: Oral Tradition and Written Transmission in Rabbinic Judaism and Early Christianity* (Lund and Copenhagen: C. W. K. Gleerup and Ejnar Munksgaard, 1961); and idem, *The Reliability of the Gospel Tradition* (Peabody, MA: Hendrickson, 2001).

[6] Cf. Gamble, *Books and Readers in the Early Church*, 19.

[7] Kelber, *The Oral and the Written Gospel: The Hermeneutics of Speaking and Writing in the Synoptic Tradition, Mark, Paul, and Q* (Bloomington and Indianapolis: Indiana University, 1983, New Introduction 1997). In his 1997 New Introduction to the book (p. xxi), Kelber partly distances himself from the notion of a 'Great Divide' between orality and literacy that his critics has 'projected between oral tradition and Markan textuality'; 'the attentive reader will observe that my under-standing of tradition and gospel is more nuanced than the label of the Great Divide gives it credit for.'

this line of thought and used terms such as 're-oralization'[8] and 'oral text'.[9] By contrast, for Kelber, as Gerhardsson puts it, 'the written Gospel is a direct counter-move against the oral tradition ... the evangelist who writes wants to dethrone the authorities of the existing gospel proclamation.'[10] Gamble also sides with this criticism, arguing that the emergence of early Christian texts 'cannot be taken to mark a sea change in Christian attitudes toward written materials', but is rather to be understood as part of a (textual) tradition already very familiar to the written word. Moreover, 'a strong distinction between the oral and the written modes is anachronistic to the extent that it presupposes both the modern notion of the fixity of a text and modern habits of reading.'[11]

None the less, taking into account a wide variety of works on orality and literacy during the past 50 years – including studies by Gerhardsson, Kelber, Ong, Bailey, Riesner, Dunn and Baum – it is worth noting, as Richard Beaton does, some commonalities between these writers when compared with the early form critics.[12] The latter typically tended to see the Jesus tradition as composed of a series of edited layers of new retellings.[13] Against this, Dunn stresses that a tradition is performed, not edited, in oral transmission, which provides elements of both stability and variability, 'stability of subject and theme, of key details or core exchanges, variability in the supporting details and the particular emphases to be drawn out.'[14] We can also note that Bultmann's tendency to dichotomize the sayings material and the narrative

---

[8] Byrskog, *Jesus the Only Teacher: Didactic Authority and Transmission in Ancient Israel, Ancient Judaism and the Matthean Community* (Stockholm: Almqvist & Wiksell International, 1994), 341–49; ibid. 339: 'Orality is empathetic and participatory rather than objectively distanced. In a setting fostering a keen interest in the teaching, the life and the status of Jesus, the teacher, we expect factors preventing the Jesus tradition from its total literization to be inherent in the transmission process. These factors come to the surface in the existence of special oral traditions and in the re-oralization of the written traditions.'

[9] Ibid., 164: The term 'oral text' is used with regard to the communication of ancient texts, e.g. the traditing of written or oral texts in the prophetic setting of the Old Testament, where orality is the dominating mode of transmission as even the written texts often were committed to memory.

[10] Gerhardsson, 'Oral Tradition (New Testament)', in Coggins and Houlden, *A Dictionary of Biblical Interpretation* (London: 1990), 500; citation from Barton, *The Spirit and the Letter*, 104. Cf., however, n. 7 above. For thorough criticism of Kelber's thesis, see Halversen, 'Oral and Written Gospel: A Critique of Werner Kelber', *NTS* 40 (1994): 180–95. Cf. Kelber, *The Oral and the Written Gospel*, xxv: 'I interpret Mark's polemic against the disciples, family, and prophets as an estrangement from the standard-bearers of oral tradition.'

[11] Gamble, *Books and Readers in the Early Church*, 29f.

[12] Beaton, 'How Matthew writes', in *The Written Gospel*, (eds) M. Bockmuehl and D. A. Hagner (Cambridge: Cambridge University, 2005), 116–34.

[13] Cf. Dunn, *Jesus Remembered*, Christianity in the Making 1 (Grand Rapids: Eerdmans, 2003), 248.

[14] Ibid. 249. For criticism of Dunn's model, see, e.g. Gerhardsson, 'The Secret of the Transmission of the Unwritten Jesus Tradition', *NTS* 51, no. 1 (2005): 1–18, esp. 7ff.

material at a pre-Synoptic stage is part of his method.[15] Such an approach may seem remote from the viewpoint of a more informed consideration of ancient orality and communication. On the overall textual fixation by writing down the synoptic tradition, Beaton thoughtfully remarks that 'the gospel authors inherited a more stable core of oral tradition than is often assumed; discrepancies could be attributed to regional diversity.'[16]

Using Gerhardsson's terminology, three helpful categories may be used to roughly classify the main scholarly descriptions of the largely pre-literate oral traditioning of the gospel: a) as an informal uncontrolled tradition (Bultmann); b) as an informal controlled tradition (Kelber); and c) as a formal controlled tradition (Gerhardsson, Riesner).[17] The eyewitness tradents (as Dunn admits) are also of importance for evaluating the early gospel transmission. Scholars who have recently drawn attention to this neglected dimension include Byrskog and Bauckham.[18] Another potentially crucial component noted by Riesner, Ellis, Millard and Stanton is the not unlikely possibility of some form of early note-taking as an integral part of the traditioning process (see further Ch. 4).[19]

When we move on to the second century, the dividing line between oral and written gospel is still rather fluid. This is so, despite the fact that the two modes of transmission must be differently characterized, compared to the period preceding the publication of the canonical Gospels. In his book *Beyond the Written Word* W. A. Graham presents a theory that accords well with the patristic sources of the period in which the gradual reception of the

---

[15] So Byrskog in his finely balanced discussion of Bultmann's *The History of the Synoptic Tradition*, *JBL* 122 (2003): 549–55 (esp. p. 553); here it is also pointed out (554) that 'what is essentially problematic is precisely that his method does not work as a tool of historical inquiry. Wherever Bultmann speaks of tendencies, we meet irregularities.'

[16] Beaton, 'How Matthew writes', in *The Written Gospel*, (eds) Bockmuehl and Hagner (Cambridge: Cambridge University Press, 2005), 119. Cf. also Riesner's argumentation in this regard, 'Jesus as Preacher and Teacher', in *Jesus and the Oral Gospel Tradition*, ed. Wansbrough (London and New York: T&T Clark, 1991), 185–210, esp. 207f..

[17] Gerhardsson, 'The Secret of the Transmission of the Unwritten Jesus Tradition', 5.

[18] Byrskog, *Story as History – History as Story: The Gospel Tradition in the Context of Ancient Oral History* (WUNT 123; Tübingen: Mohr Siebeck, 2000); Bauckham, *Jesus and the Eyewitnesses: The Gospels as Eyewitness Testimony* (Grand Rapids: Eerdmans, 2006).

[19] Riesner, *Jesus als Lehrer: Eine Untersuchung zum Ursprung der Evangelien-Überlieferung* (Tübingen: Mohr Siebeck, 3rd edn, 1988); idem, 'Jesus as Preacher and Teacher'; Millard, *Reading and Writing in the Time of Jesus* (BS 69; Sheffield: Sheffield Academic, 2000), 223–9; Ellis, *Christ and the Future in New Testament History* (NovTSup 97; Leiden: Brill, 2000), 3–19. Cf. Dunn, *Jesus Remembered*, 243. Stanton, *Jesus and Gospel* (Cambridge: Cambridge University Press), 186–91.

gospel tradition can be studied.[20] Graham's investigation deals with literate societies 'such as those where Islam is dominant, and where a written text is all-pervasive, yet that text is encountered by most people in an oral form.'[21] When applied to the church, Graham correctly underlines the 'orality' of Scripture also in contexts where literacy is widespread, for instance where the written Gospels are read out aloud at worship, intensely studied and to varying degrees memorized by catechumens and devout community members.

5.2 Oral and written: Two parallel modes of structuring the Gospel

The relation between oral and written described above resonates with what we find also in Justin Martyr. In Justin we are dealing with a secondary or tertiary growth of the oral gospel tradition.[22] As Eric Osborn points out, '[b]etween the original oral synoptic tradition and Justin's oral tradition stand the written gospels. Oral tradition in Justin is largely the transmission in unwritten form of what had been written in the synoptic gospels.'[23] In other words, as late as ca. AD 150–60 the oral character of the gospel traditioning was still very much alive in the church, parallel to the written Gospel. C. H. Cosgrove, in an article on Justin Martyr, makes an apt portrayal of the interplay between the oral mode of gospel transmission and the emerging canonization of the New Testament, by which the Gospel as written text gradually became the dominating medium of transmission:

> Narratives and sayings material even in Justin's day represented separate streams of oral tradition, and these strands of Gospel material continued to have a life of their own separate from their joint literary incorporation into written Gospels. Consequently, it is possible, even natural, for the second-century church of

---

[20] Graham, *Beyond the Written Word: Oral Aspects of Scripture in the History of Religion* (Cambridge: Cambridge University Press, 1987).

[21] Barton, *The Spirit and the Letter*, 91.

[22] Osborn, *Justin Martyr* (Tübingen: Mohr Siebeck, 1973), 132.

[23] Ibid. A complicating factor as we try to relate the way orality and literacy interacted in Justin is his use of various written sources in addition to the Synoptic/canonical Gospels. As Michael Holmes ('Text and Transmission in the Second Century', in *The Reliability of the New Testament: Bart D. Ehrman & Daniel B. Wallace in Dialogue*, ed. Stewart [Minneapolis: Fortress, 2011], 74) points out, 'Because Justin used a wide range of sources, we cannot simply assume that a reading that parallels Matthew, for example, or Luke or Mark is from that gospel.'

Justin's time to think of the logia of Jesus or the events of his life quite apart from the evangelical literature and to conceive of the Gospels as mere guardians of such tradition. The 'orthodox' Gospel literature represents not so much right interpretation, though this is not entirely absent, as correct circumscription and preservation. It is Marcion who most accentuates the redactional issue, and to this extent he is the first *Tendenzkritiker* … This forces the issue of authority … This meant that the authority of the Jesus tradition no longer stood on its own as dynamic and self-attesting … The Gospels are now viewed not only as living guardians of the sacred tradition but as literary *guarantors* of the tradition. This is the decisive move, and one which Justin apparently resists. The words of Jesus (for him) need no secondary props, for they possess intrinsic authority.[24]

For Justin the logia of Jesus and the events of his life are handled quite apart from the written Gospels.[25] But still, the written sources which Justin designates (the 'so called') εὐαγγέλιον or εὐαγγέλια[26] at the same time obtain a crucial role in his argumentation.[27] What we have here is a critical encounter between oral and written *euangelion*, which, as we shall see, eventually will set its mark on the redaction of the Christian Bible. In the latter half of the second century, when the Christian Scriptures took a more definite form while being disseminated in the faith communities,[28] the interplay of orality and literacy provides a key to our understanding of the emergent concept of canon. Just how central the gospel *as oral gospel* was, is emphasized by Gerhardsson:

> In the hermeneutical debate today, there are reasons for thinking once more about the early church Fathers' theme … that the gospel is a spoken word (*viva vox*). The double point of departure is that books surely are permitted and important … but that the gospel was from the beginning a markedly oral word,

---

[24] Cosgrove, 'Justin Martyr and the Emerging Christian Canon: Observations on the Purpose and Destination of the Dialogue with Trypho', *Vigiliae Christianae* 36 (1982): 226; cited from Barton, *The Spirit and the Letter*, 81f. This tendency, that the real authority lies in the Jesus logia, can still be sensed in Irenaeus a generation later. See also Ch. 8.

[25] *Pace* Koester, 'From the Kerygma-Gospel to Written Gospels', *NTS* 35 (1989): 380: 'Justin adopts Marcion's concept of a written gospel and distances himself from the oral tradition. He agrees with Marcion: the 'Gospel' of the church must be a written document.'

[26] Justin, *Dial.* 10.2 (Markovich, ed., Berlin and New York, de Gruyter, 1994): 'ἃ γέγραπται ἐν τῷ λεγομένῳ εὐαγγελίῳ'; *1 Apol.* 66.3: 'ἃ καλεῖται εὐαγγέλια'.

[27] Koester, 'From the Kerygma-Gospel to Written Gospels', 377.

[28] As to the hypothesis of the publication of a Canonical Archetype of the New Testament around the mid-second century, see Trobisch, *Die Endredaktion des Neuen Testaments: Eine Untersuchung zur Entstehung der christlichen Bibel* (Freiburg: Universitätsverlag Freiburg Schweiz and Göttingen: Vandenhoeck & Ruprecht, 1996), ET: *The First Edition of the New Testament* (Oxford: Oxford University Press, 2000). See Holmes, 'Text and Transmission in the Second Century', 62–5, for a critical assessment of Trobisch's thesis. For a more appreciative reading, see D. C. Parker's review in *JTS* 53, no. 1 (2002): 298–305.

which should be written 'in the heart' of the listeners. ... To achieve this aim, it was vital that the message was living, flexible speech.[29]

The other side of the coin, however, is the emergence of the New Testament as a scriptural corpus on a par with the Law and the Prophets. The juxtaposition of the two forms of the gospel, the oral and the written, placed side by side in the discourse and life of the Christian community, resulted in two different structures, one oral and one written–redactional. In this connection John Barton has made the following crucial point:

> The 'New Testament canon' of the early Church was thus organized rather differently in people's minds from the way it was organized on paper. So far as we know, there has never been a physical New Testament consisting of (a) Jesus' sayings, (b) accounts of Jesus' actions, and (c) the teachings of the apostles: one would have to reshuffle the material in the Christian books to produce such a New Testament. But from very early times the New Testament was *perceived* as consisting of these elements, and that is the shape the Christian 'oral law', as we might call it, had in people's minds. I do not think that traditional studies of 'canonization' have seen how difficult this makes it to answer 'yes or no' questions about the status of our written New Testament texts in the first two centuries.[30]

The existence of these two parallel modes of structuring the gospel is further exemplified in the early church writers, most noteworthy in Irenaeus, where the written Gospel and the orally transmitted Rule of Faith are juxtaposed.[31]

Although nascent Christianity formed what we could call a literary fellowship in the period AD 70–120,[32] this did not mean that the faith community had left the oral tradition behind. As has been widely recognized by recent scholarship, the introduction and use of written forms of communication in the ancient world did not exclude interaction between oral and written mediation. On the contrary, the opposite can be observed even where the literary form is the dominant paradigm, as within the Judaeo-Christian tradition.

---

[29] Gerhardsson, 'Oral Tradition (New Testament)', 500; cited from Barton, *The Spirit and the Letter*, 104f. Cf. also Gregory and Tuckett (eds), *The Reception of the New Testament in the Apostolic Fathers* (Oxford: Oxford University Press, 2005).

[30] Barton, *The Spirit and the Letter*, 104f.

[31] See section 5.3.

[32] So Theissen, *The New Testament: History, Literature, Religion* (London: T&T Clark, 2003), 171–4.

In the second-century Christian setting, a dialectical interaction between these two modes of communication can be seen. As in contemporary Judaism with its written as well as oral form of Torah,[33] the Christians likewise repeatedly read and interpreted the Jewish Scriptures in light of the orally transmitted Christian tradition. The awareness of such a twofold tradition in oral and written form is exemplified by Papias, as testified by Eusebius, around AD 110 (or one or two decades later):

> And I shall not hesitate to append to the interpretations all that I ever learnt well from the presbyters and remember well … I inquired into the words of the presbyters, what Andrew or Peter or Philip or Thomas or James or John or Matthew, or any other of the Lord's disciples, had said … For I did not suppose that information from books would help me so much as the word of a living and surviving voice. (*Hist. Eccl.* III, 39.2-4)[34]

As Helmut Koester has pointed out, the traditions about Jesus in written form at this time did not carry 'any greater authority than that which was transmitted orally. The written Gospels's authority is assured by the same technical terms which had been established for the oral tradition.'[35] The gospel tradition was transmitted in two ways, with textual authority ascribed to both its oral and its written forms. We should here notice the change of view among scholars on the evaluation of Papias in this regard. Accordingly it seems as if Papias' words of the 'living and surviving voice' early in the second century are not so much about preference for oral tradition, but instead 'reflect the *literary* conventions of his time, in which one sought authority for one's *written* reports through claiming that they rested on authentic witnesses.'[36] For our present purposes, we may note the double emphasis on oral and written gospel.

In the ancient world, oral and written cultures existed side by side.[37] The interaction between these two cultural spheres was sensed also in the second-

---

[33] On the concept of oral Torah within early Judaism, see section 4.5.

[34] LCL 153:290–93; cf. Munck, 'Presbyters and Disciples of the Lord in Papias', *HTR* 52 (1959): 223–43. According to Munch 'antiquity' and 'authority' are the basic meaning of 'presbyter', a term that in his view needs to be defined rather vaguely.

[35] Koester, *Ancient Christian Gospels: Their History and Development* (London: SCM and Philadelphia: Trinity Press International, 1990), 33.

[36] Hurtado, 'The New Testament in the Second Century: Text, Collections and Canon', in *Transmission and Reception: New Testament Text-Critical and Exegetical Studies*, (eds) J. W. Childers and D. C. Parker (Piscataway, NJ: Gorgias, 2006), 26.

[37] See Achtemeier, 'Omne Verbum Sonat: The New Testament and the Oral Environment of Late Western Antiquity', *JBL* 109 (1990): 3–27.

century church. It soon became a crucial factor in the canon formation, in the composition and redaction of the individual Gospels and other writings and their collection in Gospel and Apostle, especially when the oral elements of the Christian tradition gradually were being replaced by the more solid 'New Testament' text. This development has commonly been described as a necessary consequence of the increasing temporal distance from the apostolic age.[38] It is interesting to note that, despite the more fluid forms of oral transmission – or, often more likely, the oral *usage* of texts which were already available in written form[39] – the scribal preservation of the written text appears to have been surprisingly stable. That is, 'existing documents appear to have been utilized as sources for new documents rather than revised and then circulated under the same name.'[40]

Even when shortcomings in the oral transmission of tradition were observed, the process of canonization seems to have proceeded. With time the various uses of the biblical writings became standardized, e.g. in worship and in the catechetical instruction. One result of this development was the nimbus of exigency and sanctity ascribed to the new Christian Scriptures, placing them on a par with the 'Old Testament' writings.[41]

Despite this development, we also need to stress the oral element of the twofold transmission, having in mind that in practice the interaction between the oral and the written form was,[42] and still is, common. As Finnegan reckons, 'the idea that the use of writing *automatically* deals a death blow to oral literary forms has nothing to support it.'[43] In what follows, we shall focus attention on an aspect of our question as it becomes more broadly defined a generation after Justin's time in the writings of Irenaeus.

---

[38] See Ch. 6, and section 9.5.3.

[39] Barton, *The Spirit and the Letter*, 92. Barton's observation of the similarity between early patristic loose quotations from the Old Testament with the equally loose quotations from the New is helpful in this regard.

[40] Holmes, 'Text and Transmission', 75; see also Wasserman, 'The Early Text of Matthew', in *The Early Text of the New Testament*, (eds) C. E. Hill and M. J. Kruger (Oxford: Oxford University Press, 2012), 106–07.

[41] See Ch. 7.

[42] Cf. Warren, 'The Transmission of the Remembered Jesus: Insights from Textual Criticism', in *Memories of Jesus: A Critical Appraisal of James D. G. Dunn's Jesus Remembered*, (eds) Robert B. Stewart and Gary R. Habermas (Nashville, TN: B&H Publishing Group, 2010), 159–72.

[43] Finnegan, *Oral Poetry: Its Nature, Significance and Social Context* (Cambridge: Cambridge University Press), 60; cited from Achtemeier, 'Omne Verbum Sonat: The New Testament and the Oral Environment of Late Western Antiquity', 5, n. 8.

5.3 Oral and written tradition: The twofold norm in the writings of Irenaeus

In Irenaeus, Tertullian and Clement of Alexandria, to whom the written record is clearly receiving canonical status (see section 8.3) the oral dimension of the transmission process still is indispensable for the interpretation of the tradition as a textual whole. That is to say, there is no canon without addressing this form of view to the whole. Moreover, the fact that the dogmatically and historically defined criterion of apostolicity[44] determines the nature of the canon has implications for the *Wirkungsgeschichte* of the concept of canon.

At a period of transition when the written form of tradition for various reasons becomes the more dominating, we would still expect some tensions within the process of transmission.

In Irenaeus, nevertheless, a marked continuity between the oral and the written forms of the Christian tradition can be observed.[45] He seems to be aware of some differences between the two modes, but most often he falls back into an accustomed way of handling the 'twofold' tradition as an integral whole. So, no clear distinction can always be determined between these two textual forms in his writings towards the end of the second century.[46]

None the less, two elements in particular work as catalysts in the gradual development towards the predilection for the written record: on the one hand, the increasing distance in time from the apostolic period; and, on the other, the emergence of apostasy and of nonconventional, 'heretical' methods for interpreting the Christian tradition.[47] Irenaeus becomes an exponent of both elements; he senses the temporal distance between himself and the apostles,

---

[44] The criterion of apostlicity is also transmitted both orally and literally.

[45] Cf. Blanchard, *Aux sources du canon, le témoignage d'Irénée* (Paris: Les Éditions du Cerf, 1993), 323; Osborn, *Irenaeus of Lyons*, 181.

[46] This is still the case in Tertullian and Clement a couple of decades later.

[47] Concerning the teachings of Marcion and the Gnostics Irenaeus says that they entered the scene too late, that is after the apostles. In *Adv. Haer.* III, 4.3 (ANF 1:417) he writes: 'But all these broke out into their apostasy much later, even during the intermediate period [or: in the middle of the times] of the Church'. *Pace* Blum (*Tradition und Sukzession: Studien zum Normbegriff des Apostolischen von Paulus bis Irenäus* (Berlin and Hamburg: Lutherisches Verlagshaus, 1963), 166f.), who (due to the apostolic character of the church) wrongly claims that there is no dividing line in Irenaeus between apostolic times and the time of the church. Blum's standpoint is here determined by his understanding of the concept of apostolicity, which shall not only be understood in terms of *Heilsgeschichte* but also in categories of pneumatology, i.e. as something *aktuell-pneumatisch*; cf. also Unnik, '῾Η καινὴ διαθήκη – a Problem in the early History of the Canon', *Sparsa Collect: The Collected Essays of W. C. van Unnik*, vol. 1 (Leiden: Brill, 1961), 157–71.

and he proves to be the bishop *par excellence* of his day, setting out to defend Christian faith against heresy.

In an often-cited passage, highlighting a smooth transfer between the oral and the written gospel,[48] found at the beginning of the Third Book of *Adversus Haereses*, the bishop of Lyons writes:

> For we have known the 'economy' for our salvation (*dispositionem salutis nostrae*) only through those through whom the gospel came to us; and what they then first preached they later, by God's will, transmitted to us in the scriptures so that would be the foundation and pillar of our faith. (*Adv. Haer.* III, 1.1)[49]

The term 'gospel' is here, as almost everywhere in Irenaeus, used in the singular, and works as a designation of the oral as well as the written proclamation.[50] In his outline of the gospel, Irenaeus continues in the same paragraph with a short presentation of the four evangelists and their written versions of the gospel. He then concludes: 'These have all declared to us that there is one God, Creator of heaven and earth, announced by the law and the prophets; and one Christ, the Son of God' (*Adv. Haer.* III, 1.2).[51] What he seems to be saying is that the Rule of Faith (or Rule of Truth)[52] – providing a form of summary of the essentials of Christian faith – is closely related, or equivalent, to the kerygma laid forth in the written Gospel.[53]

Throughout his presentation Irenaeus continues to square these two entities, the Scriptures and the Rule, both of which are considered to be

---

[48] For a negative view as to such a continuity between oral and written mediation, as now also between written and electronic communication of the biblical texts, see, e.g. Aichele, *The Control of Biblical Meaning: Canon as Semiotic Mechanism* (Harrisburg, PA: Trinity Press International, 2001), 55ff., 218ff.

[49] *Irenaeus of Lyons*, trans. Robert Grant (London and New York: Routledge, 1997), 123f., modified.

[50] See the references in Stanton, 'The Fourfold Gospel', *NTS* 43 (1997): 319, n. 6: 'Benoit notes that in Book III, 'Gospel' is used in the singular 41 times, 12 times for a particular Gospel, only 6 times in the plural.' Yves-Marie Blanchard counts 75 occurrences of 'Gospel' in Book III, only five of which are in the plural. Hoh, *Die Lehre des hl. Irenäus über das Neue Testament* (Münster i. W.: Verlag der Aschendorffschen Verlagsbuchhandlung, 1919), 5: The term *euangelion* in Irenaeus, according to J. Hoh, is used in a threefold way: 1) *euangelion* = teaching, the content of the gospel, e.g. *Adv. Haer.* III, 1.1; 2) *euangelion* = Scripture (as a whole or in four books), e.g. *Adv. Haer.* II, 22.3 and IV, 34.1; and 3) *euangelion* = new covenant, new *Heils-* and *Lebensordnung*, *Adv. Haer.* V, 22.1 and V, 9.4.

[51] ANF 1:414.

[52] The Latin expression behind the English phrase Rule of Faith, or alternatively Rule of Truth, used in *Adv. Haer.* is *regula veritatis*. See Ohme, *Kanon ekklesiastikos* (Berlin: Walter de Gruyter, 1998), 63. Cf. also Hägglund ('Die Bedeutung der 'regula fidei' als Grundlage theologischer Aussagen', *Studia Theologica* 12 (1958): 5), who emphasizes that it is Truth itself that is being the rule or norm (epexegetical genitive).

[53] Passages in Irenaeus explicitly referring to the Rule of Truth/Faith include: *Adv. Haer.* I, 9.4; I, 22.1; II, 27.1; III, 2.1; III, 11.1; III, 12.6; III, 15.1; IV, 35.4; *Proof* 3.

authentic expressions of the apostolic tradition. As indicated in *Adv. Haer.* III, 1.1, The Rule of Faith is often very closely related to the Gospels and the Scriptures, and vice versa (see further, Ch. 8). Nevertheless, in the Third Book of *Adversus Haereses*, where he sets out to 'adduce proofs from the Scriptures' (Preface), we can sometimes sense some tension between this written record and the oral tradition. As we observed in Papias, there was from early on a consciousness of the written account *qua* written. However, these written records were to a large extent understood as an integrated part of the larger communal tradition. The situation can be similarly described some decades later. Thus, Irenaeus is a bit surprised by the way his Gnostic adversaries handle these records:

> When, however, they are confuted from the Scriptures, they turn round and accuse these same Scriptures, as if they were not correct, nor of authority, and [assert] that they are ambiguous, and that the truth cannot be extracted from them by those who are ignorant of tradition. For [they allege] that the truth was not delivered by means of written documents (*per litteras traditam*), but *viva voce.* (*Adv. Haer.* III, 2.1)[54]

Irenaeus' first intent is to demonstrate the Christian position from the Scriptures, but his adversaries are not willing to follow him on this point. From their perspective he is not in possession of the right hermeneutical key, the esoteric tradition of Valentinus, Marcion, Cerinthus or Basilides. The old preference for, or emphasis on, the living voice – in a different context hinted at already by Papias – is here carried to the extreme: The essential tradition of the 'heretics' is not *per litteras* but has been handed down to certain men *per vivam vocem*. Consequently, when the argumentation based on written documents no longer works and the adversaries draw on esoteric teaching, Irenaeus concludes that his opponents, in preaching themselves, have depraved the Rule of Faith (*Adv. Haer.* III, 2.1). Hence, 'these men do now consent neither to Scripture nor to tradition' (III, 2.2).[55]

Another illuminating passage, in which the oral and the written modes of tradition are actually distinguished, speaks about the preservation of the

---

[54] ANF 1:415.
[55] Cf. Osborn, *Irenaeus of Lyons* (Cambridge: Cambridge University Press, 2001), 172.

oral tradition among the 'barbarian peoples', who cannot read the Scriptures. Positing the imaginary case in which the apostles had not left us the Scriptures, Irenaeus elaborates his interesting argument:

> If some question of minor importance should arise, would it not be best to turn to the most ancient churches, those in which the apostles lived, to receive from them the exact teaching on the question involved? And then, if the apostles had not left us the scriptures, would it not be best to follow the sequence of the tradition which they transmitted to those to whom they entrusted the churches? Many barbarian peoples who believe in Christ assent to this sequence, and possess salvation, written without paper or ink by the Spirit in their hearts, diligently observe the ancient tradition. They believe in one God, maker of heaven and earth and everything in them, and in Christ Jesus the Son of God.' (*Adv. Haer.* III, 4.1-2)[56]

If, according to Irenaeus, the apostles had not left us the Scriptures, it would be best to follow the sequence of the tradition, that is, as here portrayed, the Rule of Faith/Truth. Again, we are able to trace a dialectical relationship within the tradition handed down both in written and in oral form. In Book Four of *Adversus Haereses* Irenaeus makes this dialectics explicit. To the one who 'diligently read the Scriptures in company with those who are presbyters in the Church, among whom is the apostolic tradition, to him every word shall also be consistent' (*Adv. Haer.* IV, 32.1).[57] Hence, in his view, the Scriptures should be read in light of the Rule of Faith – preserved by the churchly office – which summarizes and embraces the defining characteristics of the apostolic tradition, or, as he prefers to say, 'truth itself'.[58]

Is Irenaeus here making use of two canons, the Scriptures and the Rule of Faith, placing them side by side? I believe not. Rather, he is again working with what is better described as a twofold norm. Karlmann Beyschlag similarly suggests: 'Rule of Truth and twofold Scripture, thus, are not two different norms, but, in the end, only two sides of one and the same norm, that is, the transmitted Christian truth itself'.[59]

---

[56] *Irenaeus of Lyons*, transl. Robert Grant, 127.

[57] ANF 1:506.

[58] See also *Proof of the Apostolic Preaching*, 98. For a discussion whether the *regula veritatis* should be understood as an objective or epexegetical genitive, see Ohme, *Kanon Ekklesiastikos*, 66-67. Cf. n. 52 above.

[59] Beyschlag, *Grundriß der Dogmengeschichte*, vol. 1 (Darmstadt: Wissenschaftliche Buchgesellschaft, 1982), 169f.

Conversely, G. Blum has tried to problematize this harmonizing tendency in Irenaeus, where the contents as well as the form of text and oral teaching are deliberately juxtaposed and amalgamated:

> Although here two different forms of apostolic tradition are being distinguished, still no reflection is found on the relationship between apostolic tradition as a whole and scriptural Gospels. The apostolic tradition and the apostolic scriptural account are an unproblematic unity. Also when the turning-into-writing of the apostolic teaching in this connection is heavily emphasized, it still remains the case that the primary concept of the personal authority of the apostles and the apostolicity of the kerygma are the superior authority vis-à-vis the Scriptures. The Scriptures cannot claim any independence against their apostolic origins. However as the scriptural codification – and as the most comprehensive form of expression – of the tradition, they make up a principle of historical continuity with, and a well-suited means for a detailed demonstration of, the apostolic truth.[60]

Blum's way of problematizing the two forms of transmission – the oral and the written – is helpful as it touches on one of the most important aspects of the category of canon (*as Rule of Faith* and *as Scripture*), namely its historicity. Blum emphasizes that the Scriptures cannot claim any independence against their apostolic origin. Orality and literacy here belong together. The question of the Christian canon cannot be adequately dealt with without solid reference to the oral culture in which it arose. The high degree of amalgamation of the orally transmitted Rule of Faith and the canonical corpus of prophetic and apostolic writings[61] is by Irenaeus aimed at, it seems, precisely to provide a historically grounded understanding of Scripture as normative.[62] For our understanding of the canonical process, we can here note the close relation between the *regula fidei*, the already received canonical writings, and the disputed, or not yet generally received, Scriptures. In Karl-Heinz Ohlig's phrasing:

> Thus, the Rule of Faith is not an independent principle and *norma normans* beside Scripture, and the criterion of orthodoxy not a measuring stick coming from the outside, but these are nothing else than the usage of that which one

---

[60] Blum, *Tradition und Sukzession*, 180; my trans.

[61] 'Apostolic' is here used in the second-century sense, i.e. the term is both dogmatically and historically defined. See further, section 9.11.

[62] On the balancing between historical and historically effected consciousness, see Chs 1 and 2.

already recognized through the appropriated Scriptures, as applied to what was still disputed.[63]

A few years ago this conclusion was reached also by Paul Achtemeier, Joel Green and Marianne Meye Thompson. They argue that before the limits of the authoritative writings were determined, a criterion was already in operation by which the early Christians could differentiate writings to be accorded normative status from those that were not, regardless of a writing's claims to authorship. This criterion was the Rule of Faith. Surprisingly, during a major portion of the period of canon formation, the Rule of Faith had no absolutely fixed formulation. Nor was there a major expression of that Rule of Faith apart from the writings that eventually were included in the canon. Therefore, to some degree the selected books themselves provide their own criterion for selection: 'those books themselves contained the criterion the community applied in their selection'.[64] This, of course, is partly a circular line of thought; yet, however, Achtemeier, Green and Meye Thompson can still conclude: 'that is how – as nearly as we can determine it – the canon was formed'.[65] Their argument brings to mind an understanding of canonical Scripture as self-referential and self-organizing, as outlined in this study (see sections 2.2 and 2.3; and Chs 1 and 9).

To the above accounts of the Rule, however, we need to add that the Rule is not identical with either Scripture or the apostolic tradition, but, as Heinz Ohme underlines, in its functional meaning – but not with regard to its contents – the Rule may be said to precede both Scripture and tradition.[66] In Ohme's phrasing: 'with regard to contents, it embraces all that belongs to truth (*omnia quae sint ueritatis*) and that which in the fullest sense is brought together in the church from the apostles (*plenissime* [*Adv. Haer.*] III 4,1)'.[67] In other words, signifying this fullness the Rule is not to be submitted to any other criterion (see further, Ch. 8).

---

[63] Ohlig, *Die theologische Begründung des neutestamentlichen Kanons in der alten Kirche* (Düsseldorf: Patmos-Verlag, 1972), 174.

[64] Achtemeier, Green and Meye Thompson, *The New Testament: Its Literature and Theology* (Grand Rapids and Cambridge: Eerdmans, 2001), 607. Cf. also the quote by Ohlig above.

[65] Achtemeier, Green and Meye Thompson, *The New Testament: Its Literature and Theology*, 607. Cf. below, n. 81.

[66] Ohme, *Kanon ekklesiastikos*, 69–70.

[67] Ibid., 70.

5.4 New covenant and New Testament

From the introductory remarks on the interplay of oral and written communication, we would a priori be inclined towards a rather indistinct use of the two Christian concepts *euangelion* and *new covenant* as literary designations for books or book sections of the Christian Bible. In fact, this appears to be the case regarding the late second-century use of these concepts. In order to explain their adoption as designations for book collections, as we take the oral–written scheme into consideration, two alternatives suggest themselves.

On the one hand, if the dividing line between oral and written communication was thought of as relatively impermeable – which is less probable – when these titles of the new biblical book sections were introduced during the first half of the second century (εὐαγγέλιον)[68] and ca. AD 170–90 (ἡ καινὴ διαθήκη),[69] it seems plausible to interpret the editorial choice of these titles as a deliberate attempt to closely link the oral tradition with the newly edited books. On the other hand, if the oral and written communication of the gospel was thought more of as two aspects of the gospel material – which seems much more likely – the preference for these two literary titles still appears to indicate an emphasis on the written medium, as the primary source, comprising that which had traditionally been an orally transmitted gospel and covenant.[70]

To label the new Scriptures the 'New Testament', and at the same time place them on a par with the Jewish Scriptures, may have sounded rather odd to a third-century theologian such as Origen, who occasionally speaks of the two parts of the Bible as 'the so called Old and New Testament'.[71] To some extent these titles make Christianity appear as a religion of the book, though a book

---

[68] I am here following the proposed dating of the fourfold Gospel made by Stanton ('The Fourfold Gospel') and others; see further, section 4.2.1 under 4.

[69] See, e.g. Zahn, *Geschichte des Neutestamentlichen Kanons,* vol. 1 (Erlangen: Verlag von Andreas Deichert, 1888), 103–5; Trobisch, *Endredaktion*, 68–70.

[70] Cf. 2 Cor 3:6, where Paul says that God has made him a servant of the new covenant; see also Müller, *The Hidden Context: Some Observations to the Concept of the New Covenant in the New Testament* (Oslo, Copenhagen, Stockholm and Boston: Scandinavian University Press, 1995), 653: '[I]n my opinion, probably no other Old Testament conception has had such a conclusive impact on New Testament theology as this preaching of God concluding a new covenant with his people in the last days.'

[71] *Joa. Com.* V, 4; *De Orat.*, 22; referred to by Zahn, *Geschichte des Neutestamentlichen Kanons*, vol. 1, 103.

with significant oral dimensions. These Scripture collections, labelled the 'Old Testament' and 'New Testament', represent God's covenants with his people. More precisely, being canonical, these Scriptures are now understood to be the covenantal books, or even the covenants themselves, as the new titles may suggest (cf. section 2.6).

Here another question needs to be mentioned in passing, namely whether the label 'New Testament' seeks to relate the new writings to the Pauline teaching of the covenant, 2 Cor. 3.6 (as interpreted in 3.3-11)[72] and 1 Cor. 11.25. In an article on the new covenant, Mogens Müller makes the following comment: 'It was no idle label when the addition which the Church later on added to its Bible was named τὰ τῆς καινῆς διαθήκης βιβλία'.[73] Another type of connection or continuity between the new title and the canonical process is further stressed by Theodor Zahn:

> Now, as the name 'New Testament' unambiguously expressed and doubtlessly presupposed the full equality between the apostolic Scriptures and the Old Testament, not only in function, but also in the church's perception, we may say that one can only talk of a 'New Testament' with full historical right where the attribute 'sacredness' has been awarded to the therein unified writings. Thereby, however, we have already said that with some historical right one can also talk about a New Testament with respect to the time during which the name 'New Testament' was not common.[74]

When the terms 'New Testament' and, later on, 'canon' are introduced to designate the collection of apostolic writings, in Zahn's view the canonical process has reached a high point. That he describes the new designation 'New Testament' as a spontaneous 'symptom' of the canonical process, and 'as little revolutionizing (*ebensowenig epochemachend*) … as the appearance of the concepts "canon" and "canonical"',[75] is not in opposition to my argument above. On the contrary, just as Origen may have sensed the oddity of using the label 'New Testament', καινὴ διαθήκη – a concept that already had a more or less precise meaning – as a title for a collection of writings, a similar sense of

---

[72] On the relationship between the old and the new covenant, see Müller, *The Hidden Context: Some Observations to the Concept of the New Covenant in the New Testament*, 656.

[73] Ibid.

[74] Zahn, *Einige Bemerkungen zu Adolf Harnack's Prüfung der Geschichte des neutestamentlichen Kanons (Erster Band. Erste Hälfte.)* (Erlangen and Leipzig: A. Deichert'sche Verlagshandlung Nachf. [Georg Böhme], 1889), 16–18.

[75] Ibid.

anomaly certainly came about when the new writings were put on a par with the collection of old sacred Scriptures during the first and second century. However, Zahn can still take his point of departure in the canonical process as a spontaneous development of natural growth. Nevertheless, in the wake of this process something radically new emerges: the new covenant becoming Scripture. This whole process comes to expression through the new terms introduced to designate the new sacred texts, such as the late second-century title 'New Testament', the first- and second-century designation 'Gospel', and the fourth-century label 'canon'.

5.5 Attempts at separating the Rule of Faith from the canonical Gospels

Among modern Gospel interpreters, Walter Schmithals stands out through his claim that the written Gospels did not play any major role in the Christian community for several decades. In his opinion the canonization of the Gospels has to be regarded as a late second-century occurrence, extending into the third and fourth centuries. The Gospels, generally, were not really publicly known until after the canon was formed. From this, Schmithals draws the conclusion that the Gospels did not influence the earliest theological development in the church.[76]

If most of the canonical Gospels were written towards the end of the first century, the period under discussion would be the first decades of the second century. During this period, Schmithals's argument goes, the Gospels, on the whole, did not exert any major theological influence. Schmithals adopts the classical view of G. E. Lessing, according to whom the Rule of Faith is 'the rock, onto which the church of Christ was built, and not the Scripture'. Not only the first Christians, but the Christians of the first four centuries, have used this *regula* as ecclesiastical norm.[77] We notice how Schmithals lets this kerygmatic regulation of Christian faith set the theological agenda also for the Gospel writers. None of the Evangelists aspired to write a foundational or

---

[76] Schmithals, *Die Bedeutung der Evangelien in der Theologiegeschichte bis zur Kanonbildung* (Leuven: Leuven University Press, 1992), 129.

[77] Ibid., 154f.

comprehensive expression of the gospel. Rather, 'each of them considered the "rock" of the *regula fidei* to be permanent'.[78] Schmithals concludes his argument by ascribing the later authority of the Gospels to the canonical process, while the early *regula*, the Rule of Faith, which, according to Schmithals, was connected to the baptismal teaching, must be understood in isolation from the New Testament writings.[79] Here he agrees with Lessing, who maintains that '[d]uring the first four centuries, the Christian religion was never demonstrated from the NT Scriptures, but became at most only casually explained and confirmed'.[80] On this point Schmithals's view is very different from the argument put forth in the present work. First of all, the Gospels and the Rule of Faith were intimately connected. There never was 'a major expression of that rule of faith apart from the writings that eventually were included in the canon'.[81] Second, in contrast to Schmithals's suggestion, the Gospels – in oral and written form – clearly exerted a major influence during the early period, as shown, e.g. by Édouard Massaux (with Arthur Bellinzoni) in his important study *The Influence of the Gospel of Saint Matthew on Christian Literature before Saint Irenaeus*.[82] We also note that in Justin Martyr by the mid-second century, the *lectio continua* Gospel reading has already been part of Christian worship services for some time (see Ch. 7).

5.6 Marcion and the question of canon

The interaction between oral and written modes of gospel tradition is fundamental also when studying Marcion's role for the canon formation. When the oral as well as the written dimensions of the transmission of tradition are emphasized, some old questions pertaining to the canon need to be raised

---

[78] Ibid., 155, my transl.; cf. also Strecker, *Schriftlichkeit oder Mündlichkeit der synoptischen Tradition? Anmerkungen zur Formgeschichtlichen Problematik* (Leuven: Leuven University Press, 1992), 161.

[79] A similar position is embraced by Koester, *Ancient Christian Gospels*, 29: 'There is no justification whatsoever to speak of Mark's writing as an attempt to transform the oral "gospel" (= the Christian proclamation) into a literary document. There is indeed no evidence that the writers of the 2nd century who first used the term "gospel" as a reference to a written source had any awareness of the kerygma-character of this literature.'

[80] Schmithals, *Die Bedeutung der Evangelien in der Theologiegeschichte bis zur Kanonbildung*, 155.

[81] Achtemeier, Green and Meye Thompson, *The New Testament: Its Literature and Theology*, 607.

[82] Massaux, *The Influence of the Gospel of Saint Matthew on Christian Literature Before Saint Irenaeus* (Macon, GA: Mercer University Press and Leuven: Peeters, 1990–3).

anew: Was Marcion the creator of the catholic New Testament? Should the second-century canon of Marcion be compared to the biblical canon of the fourth- and fifth-century church? In the sections below, I shall analyse the scriptural canon of Marcion in regard to these and some related issues.

5.6.1 Was Marcion the creator of the catholic New Testament?

The significance of Marcion for the formation of the scriptural canon has been emphasized ever since Adolf von Harnack attributed to him the role as anticipator and creator of the catholic New Testament:[83] 'The catholic NT beat the Marcionite Bible; but this NT is an anti-Marcionite creation on a Marcionite basis.'[84]

Hans von Campenhausen adhered to this line of thought and ascribed the key role in the emergence of the Christian Bible to Marcion, who, in his view, had created the idea and reality of a Christian Bible. Campenhausen thus argues that the church, having rejected Marcion's work, did not precede him in terms of canon development, but, formally seen, followed his example.[85]

Contrary to this view, many scholars preferred to ascribe to Marcion a more modest role as catalyst for the formation of a specifically Christian bible. But the question still remained: In what way, if at all, did Marcion influence the church's decision in the second century to accept a fourfold Gospel and a two-part Bible?

In his book *The Spirit and the Letter* John Barton takes a rather unconventional stand in this regard:

> Marcion's innovation does not lie in his creation of a New Testament. The movement that would lead inexorably towards one was already well under way before him; while the theory that would make it part of a 'Christian Bible' – the same sort of thing as the Old Testament – had not yet arrived; and, when it did, it owed nothing to him.[86]

---

[83] This is also the view of, e.g. Westcott, *A General Survey of the History of the Canon of the New Testament* (London and New York: Macmillan, 1896), 318.

[84] Harnack, *Marcion: Das Evangelium vom fremden Gott: Eine Monographie zur Geschichte der Grundlegung der katholischen Kirche* (Leipzig: J. C. Hinrichs'sche Buchhandlung, 1921), 357; my trans.

[85] Campenhausen, *Die Entstehung der christlichen Bibel* (Tübingen: Mohr Siebeck, 2003), 174; ET, 148.

[86] Barton, *The Spirit and the Letter*, 45. See also Barton, 'Marcion Revisited', in *The Canon Debate*, (eds) L. M. McDonald and J. A. Sanders (Peabody, MA: Hendrickson, 2002); cf. Barton's concluding remarks: 'Marcion, we may conclude, was important for two reasons. He rejected the Old Testament

Barton is right in emphasizing that the development of the Christian Bible was considerably more gradual – formed by natural growth/reception – than was earlier presumed by Harnack and Campenhausen.[87]

5.6.2 Tertullian's *Adversus Marcionem* and Marcion's *Antitheses*

Of the disputes in which the second-century church was involved, the conflict with Marcion was the most severe. Marcion, who according to a somewhat uncertain tradition was a ship-owner from Pontos and the son of a bishop, came to Rome in AD 137.[88] Soon he publicly declared his new teaching to the gathered presbytery of Rome. Hoping to win their approval, this, instead, resulted in his immediate excommunication. The event marks the rise of a new faith community, the Marcionite church.

Tertullian, Celsus, Epiphanius, Cyrillus of Jerusalem and others soon bear witness to the striking similarity between the two communities, the Marcionite and the catholic. Marcion took over his mother church's baptism and communion praxis, the church order with bishops and presbyters, as well as a great deal of its liturgy, including the order for divine service. So the breach with the catholic church seems to have been primarily grounded on theology.

In his First Book of *Adversus Marcionem*, Tertullian writes that 'Marcion's special and principal work is the separation of the law and the gospel' (19.4).[89]

---

as the document of an alien religion; and he taught that Jesus had come to save humankind from the control of the evil Creator to whom the Old Testament witnesses. … In short, Marcion was not a major influence on the formation of the New Testament; he was simply a Marcionite.' See also Bovon, 'The Canonical Structure of Gospel and Apostle', in *The Canon Debate*, (eds) L. M. McDonald and J. A. Sanders, (Peabody, MA: Hendrickson, 2002).

[87]   Barton, *The Spirit and the Letter*, 37.

[88]   Grant, *Heresy and Criticism: The Search for Authenticity in Early Christian Literature* (Louisville, KY: Westminster and John Knox, 1993), 33. For a later dating to AD 138 or 139, see Knox, *Marcion and the New Testament: An Essay in the Early History of the Canon* (Chicago: University of Chicago Press, 1942), 5; Harnack, *Marcion: Das Evangelium vom fremden Gott: Eine Monographie zur Geschichte der Grundlegung der katholischen Kirche* (Darmstadt: Wissenschaftliche Buchgesellschaft, 2nd edn, 1924), 21ff.; Wilson, *Marcion: A Study of a Second Century Heretic* (London: Clarke, 1933), 50ff; for different dating, see Hoffmann, *Marcion: On the Restitution of Christianity* (Chico, CA: AARAS, 1984), 44–7. According to older research, AD 144, but this dating seems to be contradicted by a statement made by Justin around AD 150 (*Apol.* 26), that Marcion was alive 'even until now'. By this time the Marcionite churches were spread all over the Roman empire. This supports the thesis that Marcion as church leader ought to have been active at least ten to twenty years prior to AD 150, Clabeaux, 'Marcion', in *Anchor Bible Dictionary*, vol. 4, ed. D. N. Freedman (New York: Doubleday, 1992); Hoffmann, *Marcion: On the Restitution of Christianity*, 44–7.

[89]   *Separatio legis et euangelii proprium et principale opus est Marcionis* (ANF 3:285).

These words contain a theological as well as a material dimension, by referring to the biblical books and the scriptural teaching of the church. At the outset of Marcion's critically reconstructed Gospel, his anti-Judaistic programme is already sensed. Far distant from the Jewish arena, his Gospel – according to Tertullian – begins *in medias res*, something like this: 'In the fifteenth year of the principate of Tiberius he came down to Capernaum. They were astonished at his teaching, *which was against the law and the prophets*' (Luke 3.1a; 4.31, 32; 3.1b-4.30 omitted; Marcion added the words italicized).[90] When referring to Marcion's Gospel, Irenaeus seems to confirm such an opening: 'Jesus came into Judaea from that Father who is above the world-creating god. He was manifest in the form of a man, in the times of Pontius Pilate the governor, the procurator of Tiberius Caesar. He destroyed the prophets and the law and all the works of that god who made the world.'[91]

A brief look at the outline of *Adversus Marcionem* underscores the anti-Judaistic programme of Marcion's *Antitheses*. In the First Book, where Tertullian treats the attributes of God, Marcion is accused of having created a new god. In the Second Book, Tertullian seeks to prove that the Creator is both the good and the just God. Even Book Three frequently treats basic themes in Tertullian's anti-Marcionite argumentation, e.g. that Christ is the son of the Creator, whose advent has been foretold by the prophets. Not until the last two books are the specific questions pertaining to the text and shape of the Scriptures addressed, focusing on the Gospel of Luke (Book Four) and the Pauline letters (Book Five).

In his analysis of the *Antitheses*, Tertullian concludes: 'Marcion's *Antitheses*, or contradictory propositions … aim at committing the gospel to a variance with the law, in order that from the diversity of the two documents (*utriusque instrumenti*) which contain them, they may contend for a diversity of gods also' (*Adv. Marc.* I, 19.4).[92] In addition to the two books (*instrumenta*) of

---

[90] Grant, *Heresy and Criticism*, 38; *Adv. Marc.* IV, 7.7. Cf. also *Adv. Marc.* IV, 42.1. Marcion's addition is directed against the Jewish teaching as codified in the Scriptures. In his view Jewish interpolations are further to be found in the new apostolic writings received by the church. The words about the law and the prophets seem to reflect Matt. 5.17. See also Harnack, *Marcion: das Evangelium vom fremden Gott; eine Monographie zur Geschichte der Grundlegung der katholischen Kirche. Neue Studien zu Marcion. Adolf von Harnack* (Darmstadt: Wissenschaftliche Buchgesellschaft, 2nd edn, 1924), 249*–254*.

[91] *Adv. Haer.* I, 27.2; cited from Grant, *Heresy and Criticism*, 38.

[92] ANF 3:285. This is repeated in *Adv. Marc.* IV, 1.1; cf. also IV, 6.1.

the Old and New Testaments, Tertullian in this connection refers to a third writing (*instrumentum*) of the highest documentary rank, namely Marcion's own *Antitheses*. Tertullian apparently regarded it as the sovereign book, or means (*summo instrumento*),[93] for the Marcionite teaching.[94] While among the Marcionites this work is held in high regard, it is selected by Tertullian as the main focus in his attack on Marcion: 'Proof out of [the *Antitheses*] is enough for me' (*Ex his mihi probatio sufficit*).[95] E. C. Blackman similarly maintains that the *Antitheses* served as something much more than an introduction to Marcion's system of belief: '[I]t was an exposition of Marcion's whole system – his systematic as well as his biblical theology – the *summum instrumentum* for the Marcionite Church.'[96]

A striking detail, it may seem, is that Marcion did not make any prophetic or other claims.[97] Instead, he wrote the *Antitheses*, which is now only fragmentarily known,[98] as a form of hermeneutical manual to his Gospel. Several times Tertullian gives summaries of the *Antitheses*, on which he seems to build his outline in the Fourth and Fifth Books of *Adversus Marcionem*.[99]

> To encourage a belief *of this Gospel* he has actually devised for it a sort of dower, in a work composed of contrary statements set in opposition, thence entitled *Antitheses,* and compiled with a view to such a severance of the law from the gospel as should divide the Deity into two, nay, diverse, gods – one for each Instrument, or Testament as it is more usual to call it. (*Adv. Marc.* IV, 1)[100]
>
> For it is certain that the whole aim at which he has strenuously laboured even in the drawing up of his *Antitheses,* centres at this, that he may establish a diversity between the Old and the New Testaments, so that his own Christ may be separate from the Creator, as belonging to this rival god, *and* as alien from the law and the prophets. (*Adv. Marc.* IV, 6)[101]

---

[93] R. Braun in *Sources Chrétiennes* gives the translation 'le livre souverain'.

[94] For criticism of the Marcionite belief as mainly practically oriented, see Taylor, *Anti-Judaism and Early Christian Identity: A Critique of the Scholarly Consensus* (Leiden, New York and Köln: Brill, 1995).

[95] *Adv. Marc.* IV, 4.

[96] Blackman, *Marcion and his Influence* (London: SPCK, 1948), 50.

[97] However, cf. Knox, *Marcion and the New Testament*, 13.

[98] For a reconstruction, see Harnack, *Marcion: Das Evangelium vom fremden Gott,* 74ff.

[99] Blackman, *Marcion and his Influence*, 50.

[100] ANF 3:345.

[101] ANF 3:351.

Regarding the function of the Rule of Faith in Irenaeus and Tertullian, in particular its function for the exposition of the Scriptures, we can discern some parallels between it and that of Marcion's introductory commentary. The Rule and the *Antitheses*, in their respective contexts, both attain a prime function for Scripture reading and interpretation: The *Antitheses* by establishing 'a diversity between the Old and the New Testaments' and the Rule of Faith by teaching the church 'to read the Old Testament as the promise of the Gospel and the Gospel as the fulfilment of that promise'.[102]

5.6.3 On the relation of the Rule of Faith and the Scriptures

The Marcionite church did not think of itself as a mutilator of the Rule of Faith, as the catholic church maintained. To the contrary, Marcion was said to have restored the Rule to its original formulation after it had been previously 'adulterated' (*Adv. Marc.* I, 20.1; 4.20). The Marcionite Rule (*regula*) is here referred to as the basic structure of Marcionite faith, the basis on which Marcion is in a position to emend the text of his Gospel and Apostle.[103] The means by which this Rule was officially expressed was naturally the *Antitheses*. In the discussions with his adversaries, Tertullian frequently returns to the relation between the Rule and the Scriptures. In *De Praescriptione* this theme is laid out in some detail:

> [The heretics] actually treat of the Scriptures and recommend (their opinions) out of the Scriptures! To be sure they do. From what other source could they derive arguments concerning the things of the faith, except from the records of the faith? … we oppose to them this step above all others, of not admitting them to any discussion of the Scriptures … It is indeed a necessary consequence that they should go so far as to say that adulterations of the Scriptures, and false expositions thereof, are rather introduced by ourselves, inasmuch as they, no less than we maintain that truth is on their side. Our appeal, therefore, must not be made to the Scriptures … 'With whom lies that very faith to which the Scriptures belong. From what and through whom, and when, and to whom, has been handed down that rule, by which mean become Christians?' For wherever it shall be manifest that the true Christian rule and faith shall be, *there* will

---

[102] Cf. Edwards, *Catholicity and Heresy in the Early Church* (Farnham: Ashgate, 2009), 40.
[103] See, e.g. *Adv. Marc.* I, 1.7, where Tertullian describes the characteristic Marcionite doctrines as the rule of his adversaries.

likewise be the true Scriptures and expositions thereof, and all the Christian traditions. (*De Praes.* 14, 19)[104]

In Book Four of *Adversus Marcionem* Tertullian is more elaborate as to the content of the Rule:

> Of the apostles ... John and Matthew first instil faith into us; whilst of apostolic men, Luke and Mark renew it afterwards. These all start with the same principles (*isdem regulis*) of the faith, so far as relates to the one only God the Creator and His Christ, how that He was born of the Virgin, and came to fulfil the law and the prophets. Never mind if there does occur some variation in the order of their narratives, provided that there be agreement in the essential matter of the faith, in which there is disagreement with Marcion. (*Adv. Marc.* IV, 2.2)[105]

When emphasized, these four points of the catholic Rule of Faith – 1) God as Creator, 2) the Christ as the Son of the Creator, 3) the Son as incarnated, 4) who came to fulfil the law and the prophets – can all be described as anti-Marcionite. Ulrich Schmid's careful investigation of the Pauline texts used by Marcion provides some additional details to Tertullian's analysis.

According to Schmid, the longer continuous passages which were excluded by Marcion from the Pauline letter corpus contain the following themes: 1) Abraham as father of all believers; 2) 'Israel' and its promises as a positive point of reference for the Christian church; and 3) the mediation of Christ in creation. Further, although not as unequivocally testified, the following two themes may be included as well: 4) Texts announcing judgement by works (Rom. 2.3-11); and 5) passages relating to the 'flesh of Christ' (Eph. 2.14; Col. 1.22).[106]

Opposing the 'Roman' church, the Marcionite community did not aim at corrupting the Rule of Faith, but rather at restoring it to its original formulation.[107] The medium through which the Marcionite *regula* came to the fore was the frequently used *Antitheses*, the *summum instrumentum*. The two different canons (*regulae*), the *Antitheses* and the catholic, orally transmitted, Rule of Faith (including literature built on the catholic *regula*), show several

---

[104] ANF 3:250–51.
[105] ANF 3:347.
[106] Schmid, *Marcion und sein Apostolos: Rekonstruktion und historische Einordnung der marcionitischen Paulusbriefausgabe* (Berlin and New York: Walter de Gruyter, 1995), 282.
[107] Tertullian, *Adv. Marc.* IV, 20.

similarities on the functional level. They both provide guidelines for the relation between the Jewish and the Christian Scriptures and for the relation between the Creator God and Christ.

Attempts have been made to demonstrate direct anti-Marcionite formulations in the Old Roman Creed, although no direct evidence for this has as yet been presented.[108] A. McGiffert formulates a possible connection as follows: 'All Marcion's views which were offensive to the church are ruled out by the Old Roman Symbol – how account for this except by the hypothesis that the Symbol is specifically anti-Marcionite?'[109]

From this discussion on early creedal formulation – though it partly contradicts some more recent scholarship[110] – the intense conflict with the Marcionites still has a role to play in the use and understanding of the Rule of Faith, to which Tertullian provides some witness. However, even if this correspondence between the Old Roman Creed and Marcionite theology cannot be ascertained, E. C. Blackman still draws the reasonable conclusion that

> in the last decades of the second century certain articles of the Creed were reiterated with new emphasis against the Pontic heresiarch. This applies particularly to the first article. ... Christians were to believe that the God who created the universe is the same being as the Father of the Saviour, Jesus Christ. Christianity was not to become exclusively a religion of redemption. Redemption was to be linked up with creation as the concern of the same God – and not of the same God only, but of the same saviour.[111]

The Rule of Faith – which from at least AD 180 onwards was taken to be generally known in the church[112] – was tied to the catechetical teaching, and was well known by the teachers appointed by the bishop to teach the catechumens. As W. C. van Unnik persuasively has argued, there are clear

---

[108] On the relation between the Old Roman Creed and the Rule of Faith, see Kelly, *Early Christian Creeds* (New York: Longman, 3rd rev. edn, 1972), 40–52. Cf. also Liuwe H. Westra, *The Apostles' Creed: Origin, History, and Some Early Commentaries* (Turnhout: Brepols, 2002), 56–60 and 37–43.

[109] McGiffert, *The Apostles' Creed. Its Origin, its Purpose, and its Historical Interpretation. A Lecture, with Critical Notes* (Edinburgh: 1902), 173; cited from Blackman, *Marcion and his Influence*, 93.

[110] Cf. Kelly, *Early Christian Creeds* (New York: Longman Publishing, 1972); Hägglund, 'Die Bedeutung der "regula fidei" als Grundlage theologischer Aussagen'; and Skarsaune, *Troens ord: De tre oldkirkelige bekjennelsene* (Oslo: Luther Forlag, 1997).

[111] Blackman, *Marcion and his Influence*, 95f.

[112] For the early development of the *regula*, see Kelly, *Early Christian Creeds*; Ohme, *Kanon ekklesiastikos*; and Bokedal, 'The Rule of Faith: Tracing Its Origins', *Journal of Theological Interpretation* 7, no. 2 (forthcoming).

parallels between Clement of Alexandria's now unfortunately lost writing, *Canon Ecclesiasticus*, against the Judaists, and the *Didascalia Apostolorum*, both of which seem to depict the bishop as the responsible expositor of the theological correspondence between the Old and the New Testaments.[113] In chapter four of the *Didascalia Apostolorum*, which occupies itself with the tasks of the bishop, we read: 'And let him compare the Law and the Prophets with the Gospel, so that the sayings of the Law and the Prophets may be in accord with the Gospel.'[114] The *Ecclesiastical Canon* is by van Unnik thus defined as the 'typological correspondence between OT and NT', which is in line with the specified definition given by Clement of Alexandria in *Strom.* VI, 15 (see below).[115] Clement's more general definition of the Rule of Faith (the Ecclesiastical Canon) is interesting in this connection. It is described by H. W. Beyer as follows:

> This ecclesiastical canon embraces the baptismal confession, formulated as a *regula veritatis* (Iren. I 9.4), as well as the current church teaching in its entirety (Cl. Al. *Strom.* VII 15, 90, 2), but also the accurate completion of the ecclesiastical acts. To the third century, accordingly, the Rule of Faith is the *canon* of the church, long before the Sacred Scripture was designated by this word.[116]

The decisive aspect of the church's canon in the second and early third centuries is not primarily tied to a fixed collection of writings, i.e. to a formal principle, neither in the Marcionite nor in the catholic communities. Rather, the decisive element is the exposition of the Scriptures (see further, Ch. 8), which in Marcion's Bible edition can be seen also from his excisions and interpolations, or, as Marcion himself preferred to view it, adjustments of the corrupt text. To Marcion's Gospel and Apostle is added the introductory commentary, the *Antitheses*, i.e. the manual guaranteeing the proper exposition of his 'apostolic' writings.

Once more, it is worth underlining that the emergence of the scriptural canon cannot be understood in isolation from its interpretation. In addition

[113] Unnik, 'Notes on the Nature of Clemens Alexandrinus' Canon Ecclesiasticus', in *Sparsa Collecta: The Collected Essays of W. C. van Unnik*, vol. 3 (Leiden: Brill, 1961), 40–9.
[114] Connolly, R. H. *Didascalia Apostolorum, the Syriac Version translated and accompanied by the Verona Latin Fragments* (Oxford: Oxford University Press, 1929), 34; cited from Unnik, 'Notes on the Nature of Clemens Alexandrinus' Canon Ecclesiasticus', 47.
[115] Cf. Mogens Müller, section 5.4, above.
[116] Beyer, 'Kanon', in *Theologisches Wörterbuch zum Neuen Testament*, ed. G. Kittel (Stuttgart, 1937). My parentheses.

to 1) an authoritative collection of books, and 2) an authorized text, the concrete understanding of the canon also contains 3) an authorized interpretation. Such interpretation provides certain guidelines for understanding the mutual relation between various canonical dimensions (canon *as Rule of Faith*, canon *as intertext* and canon *as metatext*; cf. section 2.6). The canonical hermeneutics involved here pertains not least to the relation between the old Jewish and the new Christian Scriptures.[117] Furthermore, the element of interpretation is not only connected to the formation of canonical Scripture. It occupies also other roles. This is clear from another, more specified definition of the Ecclesiastical Canon (the Rule of Faith) presented by Clement of Alexandria. According to Clement's account, especially when read together with the similar formulation in *Didascalia Apostolorum* (see quotation above), we notice that the bishop may have been responsible for the mediation of the Rule to the catechumens:

> If 'all things were made by Him, and without Him was not anything made that was made,' consequently also prophecy and the law were by Him, and were spoken by Him in parables. 'But all things are right,' says the Scripture, 'before those who understand,' that is, those who receive and observe, according to the Ecclesiastical Canon, the exposition of the Scriptures explained by Him; and the Ecclesiastical Canon is the concord and harmony of the law and the prophets in the covenant delivered at the coming of the Lord. (κανὼν δὲ ἐκκλησιαστικὸς ἡ συνῳδία καὶ συμφωνία νόμου τε καὶ προφητῶν τῇ κατὰ τὴν τοῦ κυρί ου παρουσίαν παραδιδομένῃ διαθήκῃ).[118]

In the second century this Ecclesiastical Canon had an anti-heretical interpretive function.[119] The immediate purpose of comparing Marcion's *Antitheses* with this canon (κανών) is to show: 1) the impact of the *Antitheses* in Tertullian's and Clement's time, which in Tertullian results in the prominence given to the Rule of Faith as a direct response to the *Antitheses*; and 2) that the emphasis of the ecclesial anti-Marcionite response is found in theology and exegesis, not, it seems, in defining a scriptural canon. There seems to be little focusing on the more narrowly defined question of canon, the canon *as shape* or *as list*.

---

[117] Cf. Blackman, *Marcion and his Influence*, 35.
[118] *Strom.* VI, 15.
[119] Nevertheless, this canon, it seems, is not primarily drawn up against the 'heretics'. See further, Ch. 8.

Set in relation to the canonization of the catholic Scriptures, three other aspects of Marcion's canon call for consideration:

1. The next to canonical function that Marcion's *Antitheses* received beside his *Euangelion* and *Apostolos*. On this von Harnack remarks:

> It is interesting that Marcion also added to his collection a work of his own as a canonical book – a work which he called *Antitheses,* showing the *discordance* between the Old Testament and the Gospel. ... his book seemed to him so important that he formally canonised it for his Church.[120]

2. A wider *de facto* canon in the Marcionite church, including not only Luke and ten Pauline epistles, but also parts of Matthew, Mark and John.[121]
3. A continued textual revision of this scriptural canon carried out by Marcion's disciples. On this E. C. Blackman comments:

> Marcion's work as a Biblical critic was carried on by his disciples. Seeing that he himself claimed no special inspiration for his alterations of the text he could hardly expect others to feel themselves unworthy of this task. Indeed, it is probable that he laid express commands upon his followers to continue his efforts to free the text of the Gospel and the Apostle from all corruptions. To these scholars are probably to be ascribed ... the admission of the Pastoral Epistles to the Marcionite canon.[122]

In addition to these remarks, scholars have also for other reasons opposed the old thesis of Marcion as the creator of the New Testament canon.[123] Some of these will be briefly discussed in the following.

---

[120] Harnack, *The Origin of the New Testament and the Most Important Consequences of the New Creation* (London: Williams & Norgate, 1925), 30; cf. Jülicher, *Einleitung in das Neue Testament* (Tübingen: Mohr Siebeck, 1931), 480: 'In a larger work, Ἀντιθέσεις, Marcion has presented and defined his viewpoint over against the church; however, when his followers later took up these *Antitheses* beside Gospel and Apostle in their canon, that very much took place against the intention of the Master.'

[121] Blackman, *Marcion and his Influence*, 48f.

[122] Ibid., 48.

[123] See Lindemann, *Der Apostel Paulus im 2. Jahrhundert* (Leuven: Leuven University Press, 1989); Schnelle, *Einleitung in das Neue Testament* (Göttingen: Vandenhoeck und Ruprecht, 1996); Metzger, *The Canon of the New Testament: Its Origin, Development, and Significance* (Oxford: Clarendon Press, 1987).

5.6.4 Objections to the Marcionite canon hypothesis

Several objections have been raised to von Harnack's classical formulation of Marcion's role in the emergence of the Christian Bible. Recently John Barton has revisited Marcion's function in this regard and offered a more nuanced reconstruction. In Barton's judgement Marcion cannot be held to be either anticipator or creator of the catholic Bible. In marked opposition to Harnack, Barton underlines that '[t]he New Testament is not an "anti-Marcionite creation on a Marcionite basis"; it is the result of the church's allowing Scripture to form by natural (and untidy) growth, rather than by the kind of consistent and rational criticism of which Marcion was an exponent.'[124] The view that Marcion, by rejecting the Old Testament, had to fill the gap with a New Testament, namely his own Gospel and Apostle, according to Barton and others, clearly needs revision.

First of all, Marcion did not just reject the Old Testament Scriptures, but repudiated what the church called 'apostolic tradition' on a much broader scale. Not only the Old Testament was thought to contain revelation from the Creator God, according to Marcion, but parts of the oral and written gospel tradition as well, as transmitted by the church. Wilhelm Schneemelcher here makes the sensible note that the question, whether Marcion wanted to replace the 'Scriptures' of the church, i.e. the 'Old Testament', with his 'New Testament', must be denied. The question at stake was much broader. Although the rejection of the 'Old Testament' was a central part of Marcion's teaching, its dismissal would naturally also bring about a radical transformation of the oral and written tradition, which until then had been living within the church.[125]

Von Campenhausen made a similar point a couple of years earlier, maintaining that it is inappropriate to regard the formation of Marcion's NT as just a substitute for the existing OT Scriptures, on the supposition that a church without Scripture is unthinkable.[126] And, as already indicated, the question of a scriptural canon is not at all the primary issue in the Marcionite conflict. Instead, it is the Christian theological identity and the doctrinal tradition as a whole – not least in its relation to the Jewish heritage – that is

---

[124] Barton, *The Spirit and the Letter*, 48.
[125] Schneemelcher, *Bibel III: Die Entstehung des Kanons des Neuen Testaments und der christlichen Bibel* (Berlin, New York: Walter de Gruyter, 1980), 37.
[126] Campenhausen, *The Formation of the Christian Bible* (Philadelphia: Fortress, 1972), 152, n. 15.

at stake. In this connection von Campenhausen points out that, according to Marcion, the Christian message and preaching had to be rejected, since even the earliest disciples had misunderstood Jesus' words and consequently adulterated them with Jewish interpretations.[127]

In Marcion's view, not only the 'New Testament' Scriptures, but the whole of the Christian tradition had been corrupted and therefore could not be trusted any longer. We may note that historical reconstructions which seek to accentuate the scriptural canon in a narrow sense, in this situation when the totality of Christian identity was at stake, tend to miss the broader issue at stake. The anti-Marcionite reaction concentrated on what was more important under these circumstances, namely fundamental theological issues such as the question of God, ecclesial theology and tradition, continuity with the Jewish prophets and the apostolic origin.

It is here worth noting some further remarks listed by Wilhelm Schneemelcher:[128] 1) prior to Marcion, the Old Testament was sacred Scripture for the church; 2) the Pauline corpus, consisting of ten letters, was found by Marcion as used in the church before he 'cleansed' it;[129] 3) the Jesus tradition as recorded in the Gospels, such as the Gospel of Luke used by Marcion, was already regarded as normative in the church; and, 4) Marcion's 'New Testament' did not possess any sacredness.

Another interesting point to be made is the fact that Justin, Irenaeus and Tertullian in their polemics against Marcion primarily concentrate on his rejection and handling of the 'Old Testament'. The 'New Testament' is focused upon only secondarily. The New Testament, as argued above, formed by 'natural growth' rather than by sudden criticism of Jewish elements of the Christian Scriptures inspired by Marcion. The authority of the old Scriptures, moreover, belonged to another category than that of the new apostolic writings. These simply could not replace the OT.[130] We may also ask whether the new writings at that early date really would count as sacred books in

---

[127] Ibid., 151f.

[128] Schneemelcher, *Bibel III: Die Entstehung des Kanons des Neuen Testaments und der christlichen Bibel.*

[129] So also Schmid, Trobisch and Murphy-O'Connor. Cf. Barton's more cautious view (*The Spirit and the Letter*, 41): 'There may have been a Pauline corpus before Marcion, though this is speculative.'

[130] Cf. Stuhlhofer, *Der Gebrauch der Bibel von Jesus bis Euseb: Eine statistische Untersuchung zur Kanonsgeschichte* (Wuppertal: R. Brockhaus Verlag, 1988), 74: 'in Marcion fell … a portion of the books that were recognized in the church away – it was no exchange: NT instead of OT.'

precisely the same way as the OT did (however, cf. Chs 3, 4 and 7, and section 9.6). Here we need more than one perspective in order to understand what appears to be a very complex process, leaving room for personal, communal and geographical variations.[131]

Barton's analysis of the difference in authority between the two book collections is worth noting: 'the words of the Old Testament are assumed to be spoken by God because they are in the sacred books; the words of Jesus or Paul are authoritative because of who spoke them,'[132] and these words were known from tradition. People knew, independently of the written Gospel, what the gospel message was. Now, as Barton points out, '[o]n the basis of that tradition [Marcion] is in a position to emend the Gospel(s) and render them more accurate.'[133] Marcion's way of critically handling the 'apostolic' texts may support the observation that the OT Scriptures initially were placed in a different category than that of the NT writings. This is further confirmed by the continued revision of both biblical text and canon by the disciples of Marcion, who, as part of their scriptural revisions, soon accepted the Pastoral Epistles and parts of the four catholic Gospels into their Bible.[134]

From these considerations, it seems to me that a different biblical canon was actively elaborated or created within the Marcionite church, whereas the early phase of reception of NT writings in the catholic church was characterized by passivity, as Franz Stuhlhofer has argued. The active and reflective phases of the canon formation took place only secondarily.[135]

Nevertheless, concerning its function, 'scriptural' (or 'crypto-scriptural') status can be shown to have been attributed to the emerging New Testament before it was cited as Scripture. This is observed by Stuhlhofer, who concludes from his statistical investigations on the early usage of the emergent NT texts:

---

[131] The time factor in this regard has rightly been underlined by M. Haran ('Problems of the Canonization of Scripture', in *The Canon and Masorah of the Hebrew Bible. An Introductory Reader*, ed. S. L. Leiman [New York: KTAV, 1974], 225:): '... an attitude of holiness ... can come to the fore only after a considerable period of time has elapsed. ... a process of sanctification and canonization ... whose main instrument was time.'

[132] Barton, *The Spirit and the Letter*, 44.

[133] Ibid., 45.

[134] Blackman, *Marcion and his Influence*, 48f.

[135] Stuhlhofer, *Der Gebrauch der Bibel von Jesus bis Euseb*, 69–80. I basically agree with Stuhlhofer in this regard. However, I do not think that his description is quite correct with respect to some of the early Christian leaders, who probably actively and consciously affected the canonical process in various ways, some of which are treated in this study (e.g. Ch. 3, and section 9.6).

We see here a paradox. The early Church cited the Old Testament as 'Scripture', but to begin with tended to possess it only in a fragmentary form. The New Testament, on the other hand, was widely available and was used much more heavily, but it was not yet cited as 'Scripture'.[136]

Commenting on Stuhlhofer's figures on early Christian Scripture citations, Barton writes:

> All the indications are that the New Testament became almost instantly more important than the Old for the nascent Church, and that this introduced a disequilibrium which – if Marcion had had his way – could easily have led to a considered demotion of the Old Testament.[137]

To sum up my discussion on Marcion and the emerging Christian Bible canon:

- There already existed a core NT consisting of 'Gospel and Apostle' before the breach between Marcionites and catholics.[138]
- The text and the shape of the scriptural canon of the Marcionite Church seems to have been continually revised.
- As a critique of Harnack's position, the objections discussed above are not new. Already in 1942 J. Knox remarks:

> The denial that Marcion had the first Christian Scripture takes two forms. In one of these forms the term 'Scripture' is the object of attack, and in the other, the term 'first'. One denies that Marcion's canon had for him and his churches the value of Scripture; the other denies that it was the first collection of Christian writings to have such value.[139]

Of these two forms of critique, I have focused primarily on the second. Concerning the first form of criticism addressing the scriptural status of Marcion's collection of writings, it is worth noting the complex relation between the scriptural status of the OT, on the one hand, and that of the

---

[136] Stuhlhofer, *Der Gebrauch der Bibel von Jesus bis Euseb,* 68. Also cited above.

[137] Barton, *The Spirit and the Letter,* 64f.

[138] Stuhlhofer, *Der Gebrauch der Bibel von Jesus bis Euseb,* 112f.: The structure 'Gospel and Apostle' of the emerging NT can be seen already in the Apostolic fathers, where the Gospel of Matthew and the Pauline letters make up about three-fifths of all NT citations/allusions according to Stuhlhofer's count.

[139] Knox, *Marcion and the New Testament: An Essay in the Early History of the Canon* (Chicago: The University of Chicago Press, 1942).

newly composed Gospel and Apostle together with Marcion's newly authored *Antitheses*, on the other. We already concluded that his *Antitheses* seems to have had something of the same function for the Marcionite community as the Rule of Faith had for the church.

The *Antitheses* constituted a primary and new theological contribution. What was particularly new was Marcion's dogmatic exposition, rather than his shaping of a new corpus or Scriptures. It was the programme of the *Antitheses* that led to 1) the rejection of the Jewish Scriptures, long since 'adopted' by the church; 2) the formation of a two-part canon, most certainly made up of a revised Luke and 10 letters of Paul[140] (an alternative to the Gospel and Apostle in the catholic church); and 3) the textual criticism applied by Marcion to his new canon. It was out of the ideas presented in his *Antitheses* that Marcion's theological method was extrapolated.

The question, then, whether Marcion directly influenced the emergence of the second-century New Testament must be answered in the negative. This evaluation finds support also when performative (cf. Ch. 7) and certain material aspects (cf. Chs 3 and 4) of canonicity are considered. In Christian worship, all Scriptures, the old as well as the new, seem to have been treated alike from early on. Theodor Zahn's assessment also points in this direction:

> The matter here at stake – a collection of Scriptures that we call the *New Testament* disseminated in all parts of the church, a *de facto* distinction between these from other scriptures, and a powerful influence of this collection on ecclesial life – must be older than the solid imprint of these honorary titles and dogmatic conceptions, both deriving from the above listed matter of facts.[141]

In other words, the collection of NT writings predated the label 'New Testament', as well as some additional dogmatic attributes associated with these texts. Consequently, several dimensions of canonicity – material, textual, ritual and theological (see Chs 3, 4, 6, 7, 8, 9) – were at hand in the faith communities prior to, and independent of, Marcion.

Nevertheless, there were other aspects directly influenced by the intense and prolonged polemic between Marcion and the catholic church. The issue of textual criticism, for example, was actualized anew. Justin, in his *Dialogue*,

---

[140] See, e.g. Barton, *The Spirit and the Letter*, 171, n. 23.
[141] Zahn, *Geschichte des Neutestamentlichen Kanons*, vol. 1, 84.

already seems to have contributed to a new ecclesial awareness of referring to the right textual variant, i.e. the sanctioned text of the Septuagint.

With Irenaeus and Tertullian this awareness of the biblical text was renewed and further elaborated, as a part of their theological method.[142] Now, in the discussions with Marcion, textual issues – this time pertaining to the New Testament – are being actualized in a new way. This aspect of biblical textuality are important when trying to identify the Christian canon. What is at stake is neither primarily the category of 'collection', which Zahn emphasized, nor the category of 'New Testament' or 'Scripture', as set forth by Harnack. In his disputes with the Marcionites, Tertullian instead gives a key to a broader agenda when handling the Scriptures' authenticity and status in the second- and early third-century church:

> Now this heresy of yours does not receive certain Scriptures; and whichever of them it does receive, it perverts by means of additions and diminutions, for the accomplishment of its own purpose; and such as it does receive, it receives not in their entirety; but even when it does receive any up to a certain point as entire, it nevertheless perverts even these by the contrivance of diverse interpretations. Truth is just as much opposed by an adulteration of its meaning as it is by a corruption of its text (*stilus*). (*De Praes.* 17)[143]

Certain Scriptures, such as the Pastorals and the Gospel of Matthew, were not initially received at all by the Marcionites. And those that were received, like the Pauline writings and Luke, were emended. The implication of the redactional work was a different theological usage compared to that of the catholics with their scriptural Rule. In the catholic camp this Rule was reinforced by the new structuring of the biblical books, making them into a two-part canon of 'Old Testament' and 'New Testament'. The sensed newness, and perhaps the somewhat odd choice of terminology, may be reflected in Origen's mention of the two scriptural parts as 'the *so called* Old and New Testament'.

In my opinion, this and other central redactional modifications of the biblical texts would not have taken place were it not for the severe theological

---

[142] See Skarsaune, *The Proof from Prophecy: A Study in Justin Martyr's Proof-Text Tradition: Text-Type, Provenance, Theological Profile* (Leiden: Brill, 1987); and idem, 'The Development of Scriptural Interpretation in the Second and Third Centuries – except Clement and Origen', in *Hebrew Bible/ Old Testament: The History of Its Interpretation*, vol. 1, ed. M. Sæbø (Göttingen: Vandenhoeck & Ruprecht, 1996).
[143] ANF 3:251.

debate with Marcion, the Jews and the Gnostics. Although the discussions with Marcion are the most important in the second-century context, the apologetical and theological agenda provided by the church to meet unorthodox thinking had been prepared for earlier, at the end of the first and beginning of the second centuries. This earlier period was often characterized by fierce opposition with the synagogue. Indeed, the theological agenda provided in *Adversus Marcionem* is probably best understood as an inversion of the traditional anti-Jewish argumentation, as put forth, e.g. in another of Tertullian's major works, his *Adversus Ioudaios*.[144]

Even if it is not correct to maintain what John Knox wrote in 1942, that 'the structural principle of Marcion's canon became the organizing idea of the catholic New Testament',[145] the need to structure the church's own canon by deliberately using quite other methods than those of Marcion was borne. A need to deeply focus and reflect on the relation between the old and the new covenants had seen the day. The following three examples may serve as illustrations: 1) Clement of Alexandria's definition of the Ecclesiastical Canon as the right balancing of the two testaments to one another; 2) the two new book titles, the 'Old Testament' and the 'New Testament', introduced into Christian manuscripts; and 3) the task defined in *Didascalia Apostolorum* for the bishop to be responsible for the right exposition of the Scriptures in regard to the relation between the two covenants.

We may possibly conclude from this that Harnack's and Campenhausen's old argument could even be reversed. The emergence of a written Marcionite Gospel and Apostle, with their dependence on the particular oral tradition of the Marcionite Church, could very well have as its prime source of inspiration the intense scribal activity of the sub-apostolic community, i.e. the edition of apostolic writings and the transition from oral to written gospel tradition in the undivided church.

---

[144] See Skarsaune, 'The Development of Scriptural Interpretation in the Second and Third Centuries', 429–34.

[145] Knox, *Marcion and the New Testament*, 31.

5.7 Conclusion

In this chapter we have seen that there is a continuous interaction between the oral and written modes of Christian tradition. A number of second-century figures (Papias, Marcion [for a brief summary, see section 5.6.4], Justin, Irenaeus, Clement) testify to the great significance of the oral–written dynamics. The orality of the gospel tradition – focusing on the Lord, His words and deeds – lived on in the midst of scriptural tradition, as a way of providing an alternative textual structuring, parallel to the written account.

It is in this process that the evaluation of the scriptural tradition can be observed, along lines similar to those found in Early and Rabbinic Judaism. The notion of sacred text becomes important for Christian identity. In this regard, the church was to follow its mother religion, becoming all the more a people of the sacred text. Still, however, it did not dismiss the oral dimensions (and phases) of the gospel transmission.

For today's understanding of the church's canon, in my opinion, the reader would benefit from taking into account this oral textual dimension, being preserved parallel to, and as a part of, the written text. Terms such as 'Gospel', 'Old and New Testament', and 'Ecclesiastical Canon/Rule of Faith', embracing obvious oral as well as written dimensions, still make this connection explicit, as does, in various ways, the ecclesial handling of the Scriptures in worship. Irrespective of the medium – oral or written (and now also electronic) – the church has known its own specific textual tradition all along.

The theological question lurking behind the modern problem of orality–literacy, when applied to the emerging canon, is not so much whether there was any continuity between the two media handing on the Christian gospel and textual tradition. Rather, the question of greater interest is how to study, 'construct', or even understand the notion of living biblical textuality, which refuses to turn the texts of the Bible into something that they are not.

Using an analogy from the natural sciences, a parallel to the type of investigation on biblical textuality I am pursuing here would be a biological study *in vivo*, rather than that *in vitro* (cf. section 7.1). The ecclesial text, construed as canon for the church, cannot really be understood at all outside its perennial contextualization as part of the church's life, in and for which the mediations of orality as well as literacy have, and have had, a part to play.

6

The Canon as Text

I have now treated three specific features of biblical textuality: the *nomina sacra* as triadic textual markers, the (closed) codex as the biblical book format, and the vivid interdependence of oral and written textual tradition.

In this chapter I turn to the broader notion of textuality applied to the biblical writings. In the following the notion of textuality will refer to qualities pertaining to textual being, to the characteristics of texts seen as texts.

At the heart of the modern canon debate lies the question concerning the nature of the canonical text. This issue of textuality is profoundly hermeneutical, involving intricate relations between authors and authorship, communities and the church universal, meanings and the classical interpretive agendas, texts and text reception as well as the situations in which the individual readers, communities, clergy or scholars find themselves. The deconstructionist critique of so called logocentric discourse also makes us aware of critical inquiry concerning the very textuality of texts.[1] With the French philosopher Jacques Derrida we may ask whether a text at all can be regarded as 'a finished corpus of writing, some content enclosed in a book'.[2]

---

[1] As to the complaint directed against Gadamer's philosophical hermeneutics in *Truth and Method* (applications of which are used in the present study) as being one of the last great formulations of logocentric discourse, Gadamer comments briefly in a late interview: 'I would ask those who raise this objection to please undertake a serious reading of my book. After that I would seek to begin a conversation with them [Gadamer repeatedly sought to initiate such conversation with the founder of deconstructionism, Jacques Derrida, who always (even when the two met) avoided such dialogue; my remark]. No, I believe I have learned from Heidegger [both Gadamer and Derrida are renowned students of and commentators on the philosophy of Heidegger; my remark] that philosophy does not happen in the form of propositions and judgements. For this reason I would characterize the general direction of my own efforts as follows: Do not think against language but with language', Gadamer, *Gadamer in Conversation: Reflections and Commentary* (New Haven: Yale University Press, 2001), 68.

[2] Derrida, *Deconstruction and Criticism* (London: Routledge and Kegan Paul, 1979), 84; citation from Thiselton, *New Horizons in Hermeneutics: The Theory and Practice of Transforming Biblical Reading* (Grand Rapids: Zondervan, 1992), 57.

It seems that the reader is here confronted with two options: open text versus closed book.[3] As Anthony Thiselton reminds us, precisely this, the issue concerning the nature of texts, has turned out to be 'the most radical question of all in hermeneutics.'[4] A theological hermeneutic focusing on canon and canonization depends not plainly on authorial intention or the needs of the modern reading community, but also, more fundamentally, on the understanding and interpretation of the canonical text as text.

In this chapter, therefore, I shall investigate the canon as text and the manner in which the emerging biblical canon attains, for the church, various textual properties: In which way does the canon become an eminent, or even *the* eminent text, the principal manifestation of Christian textuality? How is this textuality to be grasped? In what manner is it to be understood as a uniquely fabricated text, and how is it to be equalled to other texts?

6.1 Canon as a textual whole

With what right can we talk of the canon as a unity, or the multifarious textual process of canon formation as a unified process? What is the glue that holds the writings and cover of the book(s) called the Bible in place? This question was raised already in Chapters 2 to 5. Here I shall treat it from a text-hermeneutical point of view. Is the Bible an anthology, with God, Israel and a possible history of salvation as the major storyline? Are the Christian Scriptures really a book with a book cover and textual parts in the ordinary sense? Do we need to open up for a different and more specific concept of textuality when dealing with the Bible as a book, also including other dimensions than just letters, words and plain contents?

At face value it could seem as if the event of canonizing the Scriptures, and receiving them as canon for the church, was primarily an act of defining the precise number of writings to be included in the one canonical book, or enumerated on the one canonical list. However, variations in the canonical lists

---

[3]   See further, e.g. Vanhoozer, *Is There a Meaning in This Text? The Bible, the Reader, and the Morality of Literary Knowledge* (Grand Rapids: Zondervan, 1998). Cf. also Watson, ed., *The Open Text* (London: SCM, 1993).
[4]   Thiselton, *New Horizons in Hermeneutics*, 49.

can be seen from early on. Furthermore, as pointed out above, many aspects of canonicity need to be dealt with quite apart from such lists or catalogues. Instead, essential dimensions of the problem of the canon ultimately appear to be questions of textuality. More specifically, their focal point is the Bible's final textual form and *telos* (cf. section 1.3.2, note 81). The search for such a final textual shape among first- and second-century Christian scribes and leaders meant that the relative textual fluidity and much of the redaction work with the Bible came to a halt.[5]

One reason why the final text here ought to be in focus, although by no means exclusively, is the fact that only then, when the text is intended as text and written down as literature in the narrow sense – what Gadamer calls an 'eminent text' – is it really freed from the original situation in which it came into being. In Gadamer's view, the 'eminent text' does not resemble the written notes we make when, for example, we wish to preserve a written record of the lecture, or when we write a letter instead of communicating orally. In both these cases the written form refers back to the original speech, as a reminder of our own thought.[6]

I am here using the expression 'eminent text' of the textual state towards which the emerging 'New Testament' Scriptures are gradually moving, from the time of their being fixed in writing until the parallel oral gospel tradition attains a secondary role in transmitting the gospel.

Although being eminent texts in this sense, the New Testament writings, to some degree, none the less still refer back to the original historical situation.[7] The gospel codified in writing is, as Justin Martyr points out, the remembrances/memoirs (τὰ ἀπομνημονεύματα).[8] But, at the same time, from the early to mid-second century on, they are also received as literary Gospel

---

[5] See further Kermode, 'The Argument about Canons', in *The Bible and the Narrative Tradition*, ed. F. McConnell (New York: Oxford University Press, 1986); and Holmes, 'Text and Transmission in the Second Century', in *The Reliability of the New Testament: Bart D. Ehrman & Daniel B. Wallace in Dialogue*, ed. Robert B. Stewart (Minneapolis: Fortress, 2011), 61–79.

[6] Gadamer, *The Relevance of the Beautiful and Other Essays* (New York: Cambridge University Press, 1986), 142. On Gadamer's use of the notion of eminent text, see Lawrence, 'Gadamer, the Hermeneutic Revolution, and Theology', in *The Cambridge Companion to Gadamer*, ed. R. J. Dostal (New York: Cambridge University Press, 2002), 191.

[7] As for the Gospels, see, e.g. Hengel, 'Eye-witness memory and the writing of the Gospels', in *The Written Gospel*, (eds) M. Bockmuehl and D. A. Hagner (Cambridge: Cambridge University Press, 2005), 70–3; and Lemcio, *The Past of Jesus in the Gospels* (SNTS MS 68; Cambridge: Cambridge University Press, 1991).

[8] Regarding 'the memoirs' and 'the gospel' as referring to both oral and literary aspects, see Ch. 5.

writings – as the Gospel(s).[9] They attain the paired function of being both notes, i.e. aids of memory, unified in the continuity of memory, and literature with canonical validity. In their capacity as notes they are elaborated and established as historical records; being eminent texts they are exactly that, texts (cf. Ch. 7, nn. 35 and 39). So, we point to them as something that 'stands written', turning into a self-signifying textual unity alongside the Scriptures of Judaism.[10]

None the less, from a critical historical, literary or theological point of view, we may question such an approach towards the biblical text. Is it altogether commendatory to view the Bible as a totality, when its individual textual parts may be deconstructed by the critic into fragments and isolated pericopes that do not easily, necessarily or even naturally harmonize? But how, on the other hand, could the church from early on say of these writings, 'That's the total! That is the whole out of which we attain our ecclesial identity, evaluating the details, fragments and incongruities of the Christian discourse'?[11]

Although insights gained from general hermeneutics should be encouraged for a better understanding of biblical textuality, it is still a fact to be agreed upon that the Bible, like any other text, must also be interpreted on its own terms. The way all understanding presupposes a living relationship between the interpreter and the text, his or her previous connection with the topic that is dealt with, so 'scriptural hermeneutics presupposes a relationship to the content of the Bible'.[12] Gadamer gives some clues to this dual way of interpreting, namely by pointing to the effective-historical component, which (for the well-schooled interpreter) does not exclude, beforehand, various multiple ways of understanding. These include, e.g. historical-critical, literary, or various premodern, modern or postmodern hermeneutical renderings – and, most importantly, the specific hermeneutical sensitivity that must be repeatedly sought for understanding each individual text. What is particularly important here is the grasp of the *scopus*, the principal intention, the central

---

[9]   For the dating of the fourfold Gospel to the early second century, see Hurtado, 'The New Testament in the Second Century: Text, Collections, Canon', in *Transmission and Reception: New Testament Text-Critical and Exegetical Studies*, (eds) J. W. Childers and D. C. Parker (Piscataway, NJ: Gorgias, 2006), 3–27.

[10]   Cf. Gadamer, *The Relevance of the Beautiful and Other Essays*, 142.

[11]   See, e.g. Ch. 1, n. 2.

[12]   So Gadamer, *TM*, 331.

point of view, when trying to understand a text appropriately, the grasp of the *scopus* that 'forms the basis for the endless nuancing work involved in understanding'.[13]

6.2 Text and reader: 'Objectivity' and authentic subjectivity

The argumentation above might sound as if we were moving primarily towards the 'textual side', and not within the reader's own time-horizon. However, the understanding taking place already includes a mediation of both horizons, that of the text, which is always profiled against that of the interpreter. The reader's 'projecting of the historical horizon that is profiled against the horizon of the present is ... both annulled and taken up into a higher form ... in understanding, which signifies the gaining of a new historical horizon'.[14] In this process, understanding is not something that occurs at the end of the inquiring into a text, but stands at the beginning, governing the whole process of questioning. On the 'textual side', this may also imply a cautiously positive evaluation of historical diachronic methods as well as synchronic, and other perspectives, in the textual analysis.[15]

Accordingly, there is never such a thing as a purely objective text or reader. The text is always also interpreted. As regards eminent texts, in particular, 'reading is exposition', according to Gadamer, 'and exposition is nothing but the articulated conclusion of the reading'.[16] Likewise, there never is an

---

[13] Idem, *Gadamer in Conversation: Reflections and Commentary*, 52.

[14] Ibid., 48. Gadamer here uses the German term *aufgehoben*.

[15] Gadamer, 'Zur Problematik des Selbstverständnisses: Ein hermeneutischer Beitrag zur Frage der "Entmythologisierung"', *Gesammelte Werke*, vol. 2 (Tübingen: Mohr Siebeck, 1993 [1983]), 122. In Gadamer's view, the genetic question, which aims at explaining the transmitted meaning out of the historic situation, will arise only when the immediate knowledge of what is said in the text is unclear, unattainable or irrational. The historical questioning can be illegitimately applied when 'the truth of what is said' is what is looked for. However, the historical dimension of *Wirkungsgeschichte*, of which the implications of historical-critical and other methodology are also a part, is always present in interpretation. Furthermore, there may be space left for more than one perspective in understanding, which is always the case anyway. That is to say, communication always occurs at different levels. What Gadamer correctly wants to underline is the priority in textual communication to that which is actually said, that is, what is manifest in the text *qua* text. This allows for historical-critical thinking, also when dealing with literature. Nevertheless, the text that is understood historically, in which the past is seen from a historical standpoint – which is not always equivalent with applying historical-critical methods in textual analysis – 'is forced to abandon its claim to be saying something true' (*TM*, 303).

[16] Idem, 'Der "eminente" Text und seine Wahrheit', in *Gesammelte Werke*, vol. 8 (Tübingen: Mohr

objective horizon of the text that can be objectively attained. On the contrary, the horizon of the text is always annulled and taken up by the present reader into a higher form of the new historical horizon, occasioned by the process of interpretation.

The hermeneutical situation of the contemporary reader, who seeks to understand the texts of the Bible as canonical, is not distantiation, but to stand between strangeness and familiarity, between the mere objectivity of what has been handed down to him or her and the fact of his/her belonging to this heritage.[17] This is well phrased by the New Testament scholar Ben Meyer who asserts that somehow the way to 'objectivity' is through 'authentic subjectivity', for which 'objectivity' depends on the subject's effort to perform his or her task well.[18]

However, as Gadamer warns, there is always the risk that we seek to transpose ourselves into the historical situation in order to reconstruct it. What really happens then is that we give up 'the claim to find in the past any truth that is valid and intelligible for ourselves.'[19] Furthermore, when the otherness of the other is handled in this way, making him or her the object of objective knowledge, this also involves the fundamental suspension of his/her claim to truth.

Instead, our appeal in meeting with the past, through texts, should be that the hermeneutically trained consciousness be sensitive to the alterity of the text.[20] The way between the Scylla of objectivity and the Charybdis of subjectivity ought to be described in a dynamic manner, where the otherness of the text becomes the focal point against one's fore-meanings and prejudices in the process of understanding. 'The important thing is to be aware of one's own bias, so that the text can present itself in all its otherness and thus assert its own truth against one's own fore-meanings.'[21] And, to be sure, inappropriate fore-meanings are plentiful.

Understanding turns out to be a risky undertaking, in which present

---

Siebeck, 1986), 289: 'Lesen ist Auslegen, und Auslegen ist nichts als der artikulierte Vollzug des Lesens.'

[17] Idem, *Gadamer in Conversation: Reflections and Commentary*, 47.

[18] Meyer, *Reality and Illusion in New Testament Scholarship*, 4.

[19] Gadamer, *TM*, 303.

[20] Ibid., 269.

[21] Ibid. Cf. also above, on the emergence of a new historic horizon when past and present are fused in the appropriation of texts.

anticipatory projections are constantly questioned, confirmed and changed in meeting with the text. The interpreter here has a primary responsibility towards the text – often similar in nature to that of meeting another person – to inform him- or herself about the otherness of the text. So, it is quite right for the interpreter not to approach the text directly or too quickly, relying only on the fore-meaning already available to him/her, but rather explicitly 'to examine the legitimacy – i.e. the origin and validity – of the fore-meanings' dwelling within him or her.[22] Indeed, if this does not take place, Gadamer asks, 'what characterizes the arbitrariness of inappropriate fore-meanings if not that they come to nothing in being worked out?'[23] Not unexpectedly, it must be the other way around with the act of real understanding, namely, that appropriate projections, anticipatory in nature, are being confirmed by 'the things themselves', that is, by what the text says, in the constant task of understanding. Still, however, the primary 'objectivity' here is the confirmation of 'a fore-meaning in its being worked out'.[24]

6.3 The text: A woven texture that holds together

Having said this about texts and their continuing mediation with contemporary readers, let us now inquire into the character of the text as text.

What is a text? On the way to an answer I shall use Werner Jeanrond's analysis presented in *Text and Interpretation* and *Theological Hermeneutics*.[25] To begin with, commonly a text is understood to be a meaningful whole, a structured whole – containing words and/or sentences – the meaning of which transcends the sum of its words or sentences.[26] In his analysis of the concept of text Jeanrond makes the following remarks as to the connections of sentences (and words) normally achieved by a text: First, we expect texts to be

---

[22] Gadamer, *TM*, 267. Cf. in this connection the parallel – though perhaps somewhat farfetched – between Gadamer's appeal to the changing of one's fore-meanings in order to understand the otherness of the other (including that presented by texts) and Kierkegaard's so called Copernican revolution.

[23] Ibid.

[24] Cf. Ibid.

[25] Jeanrond, *Text and Interpretation as Categories of Theological Thinking* (Dublin: Gill and Macmillan, 1988); and idem, *Theological Hermeneutics: Development and Significances* (London: SCM, 1991, 1994).

[26] Jeanrond, *Theological Hermeneutics*, 84.

characterized by thematic [or semantic] progression; that is, we expect that a text pursues 'one theme or a couple of related themes'.[27] Second, we anticipate texts to convey this thematic unity 'through grammatical [or syntactical] devices, such as pronominal substitution.'[28] Third, we acknowledge written texts as texts also because of the simple fact that 'a flow of black ink on paper comes to a halt, or that the book which we read has no more pages.'[29] These levels of organization are simultaneously found in the text, the level of meaning, of grammar and of printing (alternatively, handwriting, or oral text). As Jeanrond points out, most crucial when focusing on textuality is the fact that the meaning of the printed sentence 'is ultimately characterised by its reference within the wider system of meaning and reference, namely that of the *TEXT*.'[30]

These three levels of textual organization – that of meaning, of grammar and of printing – are found not only in the various biblical texts and pericopes, but arguably also throughout the biblical text viewed as a whole, and can therefore be applied to the issues pertaining to the canon.[31] The following questions will serve as examples:

- As to the thematic progression, we may ask to what degree it is the case that the heterogeneous biblical text still expresses a whole for contemporary readers? I choose to approach this question in various ways throughout this book. Given that the story of the gospel makes up the narrative centre of the biblical text, the redactional textual division within the Christian canon in Old and New Testament, in Gospel and Apostle, and so forth, relates to a textual concept of the Bible as a whole. Furthermore, the Rule of Faith is often mentioned not only by the early Church Fathers and the Reformers, but also by

---

[27] Ibid.

[28] Ibid.

[29] Ibid. Today, this statement may be in need of some revision. I can also perceive as a type of text that which I never experience the end of, such as seemingly never-ending rolling messages on Text TV or large scrolling datafiles on my laptop or iPad. This, however, is 'text' in another sense than I treat here.

[30] Ibid., 85; Jeanrond here distinguishes between 'meaning', 'reference' and 'sense'. A sentence in the text thus functions within the communicative structure of that text, while the reference of the entire text is directed towards some kind of extra-textual reality in the world of the reader. 'This reference of the text to at least one aspect of the reader's world we called the 'sense' of the text. Hence, we can say that the reference of a text is its sense, whereas a sentence refers always to the textual whole.' (Ibid.).

[31] Cf. Jeanrond, *Text and Interpretation*.

more recent interpreters as providing an inner structuring function, or a basic narrative framework, vis-à-vis the Scriptures (see further, Ch. 8).[32]

- On the level of grammar, concerning the divine name and its pronominal substitution, we may further ask what the system of *nomina sacra* – being part of the earliest Christian Scriptures – implies for the thematic and syntactical understanding of the text. As I have argued above, the *nomina sacra* help to integrate the collection of biblical writings into a coherent thematic and grammatical whole. They achieve this by centring on the Name and by highlighting a triadic structure of the biblical narrative/ material. In some measure these editorial markers may perhaps also relativize the stress laid on multiple authorship of the Scriptures, and, as a *signum* of the church's scriptural identity, may indicate to the community a divine genre, message and origin (the notion of inspiration) of these texts read *as Scripture*.

- As to the level of printing, we may also query the variations in the ordering of the biblical books and whether these variations have any biblical theological implications, e.g. when placing the Wisdom literature rather than the Late Prophets immediately before the Gospels in the canon lists or large Bible codices (Codex Sinaiticus, Codex Alexandrinus; Rufinus).[33] Moreover, what changes of textuality take place, i) when churches/theologians in principle exclude (or distinguish) Apocrypha/ Deuterocanonical books from the Old Testament canon (Melito of Sardis, Origen, Cyril of Jerusalem, Jerome), ii) when including Apocrypha/ Deuterocanonical books among the Old Testament writings (Codex Vaticanus, Codex Sinaiticus; Augustine), and iii) when placing Old Testament Apocrypha in between the text corpora of the two Testaments (Luther)?

---

[32] Martin Chemnitz, one of the leading Lutheran theologians of the Post-Reformation Period, e.g. talks of the inner structuring function of the *regula fidei* as the *character fidei* or the *forma doctrinae*. See further Hägglund, *Chemnitz – Gerhard – Arndt – Rudbeckius: Aufsätze zum Studium der altlutherischen Theologie*, Texte und Studien zum Protestantismus des 16. bis 18. Jahrhunderts (TSP), vol. 1 (Waltrop: Verlag Hartmut Spenner, 2003), 55ff. See also Bokedal, 'The Rule of Faith: Tracing Its Origins', *Journal of Theological Interpretation* 7, no. 2 (forthcoming).

[33] Cf. the various early OT lists in McDonald, *The Biblical Canon: Its Origin, Transmission, and Authority* (Peabody, MA: Hendrickson, 2007), 439–44.

Additional related questions that could be asked easily line up: What is implied in the exclusion of the Apocalypse – which is often placed at the concluding end of the biblical narrative – as was common until modern times in many Eastern churches? Should we not assume that the original canonical ordering of the books of the New Testament closed with the Revelation to John? When considering the 26-book NT of many Eastern churches, are we here dealing with the same full biblical text as in the West? Does the narrative structure provided by the Rule of Faith, centring on the first and second coming of the Christ, make a good enough substitute when some of the written text is lacking? As I shall elaborate below, the concept of textual *sameness in difference* may help the reader on the way towards clarity on some of these matters.

Central New Testament writings such as Matthew and John were arguably intended not only as texts, but as literature, even biblical literature (cf. sections 9.6 and 9.7). Unlike the early stages of the process of gospel transmission, as literature they do not any longer belong to the textual genre of notes or occasional writings. The interpretation of the latter relate back, first of all, to the speaker/author. Gadamer chooses to explain it in the following manner: '[w]hen I read the notes that someone has made, it is the speaker rather than the text that is, as it were, to be brought to speak again.'[34] However, regarding the literary text in the more narrow sense – the eminent text, to which biblical writings also may be counted – we note that it is intended to be precisely what it is, namely text, 'so that we point to it as something that "stands written"'.[35] This means that it does not primarily refer back to the original speech or speech situation, but is intended to stand on its own, referring primarily to its own literary presentation as a meaningful whole. This characterizes the genuine text, which, as Gadamer stresses, is exactly what the word literally says, 'a woven texture that holds together.' This is what was intended, and this is what remains written. Thus it 'stands written', as a literary work of art held together by this woven texture: the work itself as woven texture that holds together, and so presents itself as a literary work to everyone being addressed.

---

[34] Gadamer, *The Relevance of the Beautiful and Other Essays*, 142.
[35] Ibid.

Gadamer furthers this thought by mentioning the independence of such a text – holding together as a whole with textual parts – in relation to its origin as well as its future contexts of reception: It 'holds together in such a way that it "stands" in its own right and no longer refers back to an original, more authentic saying, nor points beyond itself to a more authentic experience of reality.'[36] This, of course, does not mean that textual interpretation and reception, on the part of the reader, is unimportant. As all understanding also implies interpretation (not, however, the other way around), the reader's horizon always has to be taken into account. Still, however, the text 'stands in its own right'. As a point of fact, when reading takes place, it is, in the first place, the *text* that is being understood; and this text can be autonomous in different ways. However – and most important for the present investigation – the biblical texts are not unambiguously autonomous when understood as scriptural or canonical writings. As for the biblical writings, Gadamer instead tends to treat these texts as partly supported by 'ecclesiastical practices'. Another way of saying the same thing, which I have preferred here, is to describe central aspects of the ecclesial reading, handling and understanding of these texts, when seen as canonical, as a fully justified way of discussing the textuality of these texts. In a particular sense the ecclesiastical practices are rather inherent in these texts' quality of being canonical texts, along the lines many readers still relate to these writings.[37] After all, in some segments of spoken and read English, 'scripture' is still often immediately understood to mean the Bible:[38] the Bible in its traditional theological function addressing the church (and, indirectly, the world), and that Bible as a whole.

One way of talking of the Bible as canon, thus, is as 'woven biblical texture that holds together'. Throughout the present study, my aim is to be attentive to various aspects of canonicity in this sense. In Chapter 2, the concept of canon and its effective-history pointed to the canon as a whole, indicated already by the rich meaning inherent in the word 'canon' used to designate it. In the subsequent chapter, the *nomina sacra* as textual markers found throughout the Greek Old and New Testaments were highlighted; it was argued that both

---

[36] Ibid.
[37] Cf., however, Webster's important distinction above (Ch. 1, n. 21), stressing that 'tradition' here is best conceived of 'as *hearing* of the Word'.
[38] Ibid., 140.

the biblical text as a whole and the textual parts are dependent on this system made up of some five to 15 Christian keywords, the core of which are JESUS and the divine Name. Chapter 4 described the codex form as part of the physical 'glue' that keeps the texts making up the canon in place, and so being part of the texture that helps group the writings into characteristic OT and NT part-collections – thus holding them together. The chapter on oral and written textuality, furthermore, helped to widen the issue of text by embracing certain oral features as part of the notion of the canonical whole. Likewise, the next two parts of the study will treat a few additional dimensions that are useful in establishing this sense of biblical wholeness: the ritual embeddedness (Ch. 7) and various ideational characteristics of the canon (Chs 8 and 9). First, however, I shall continue the discussion on textuality outlined for the present chapter.

6.4 The whole and the parts

6.4.1 The text as greater totality

For a basic definition of the concept of canon as textual whole, I want to make use of some insights from the field of linguistics, where the text seen as a whole is often emphasized and considered to stand in a particular relation to its parts, that is, to the sentences that make up the text. In fact, as soon as we are dealing with a text we anticipate a textual meaning, some kind of totality.

Hans-Werner Eroms describes this procedure: '[T]his greater totality, the text, which we presuppose, *forces* the ordering of the sentences into the text. This is evidenced by the fact that we always try to construe as a text, configurations which contain several sentences.'[39] Werner Jeanrond develops this thought. In *Text and Interpretation* he applies text-linguistic insights to the biblical material. Regarding the Book of Proverbs, for example, he points out that we acknowledge this writing as a large, coherent whole and not just as a series of single texts, and that is for at least two reasons:

(i) We approach all biblical 'books' with the expectation of contextuality, and (ii) this expectation in regard to the *Book of Proverbs* is strengthened by the fact that

---

[39] Cited from Jeanrond, *Text and Interpretation*, 81.

these texts are exteriorly printed together and interiorly deal with a thematically unified area.[40]

From this, Jeanrond concludes that the Book of Proverbs as a biblical book fulfils, structurally and thematically, our expectation of coherence. This is not at all self-evident, however, if the theological context and the literary synchronic approach are abandoned for a minute. In the case of the Book of Proverbs the individual sayings would not constitute a coherent text at all were it not for the biblical collection of writings to which they were once added, or for the literary redactional decisions made by Second Temple Judaism.[41] The canonical reading implied tends to take the final stage of text redaction as its point of departure (cf. section 1.3.2, note 81). Thus, yet another reason for viewing the text as an integral whole can be added, namely the specific contextuality of the canonical corpus as Sacred Scripture, into which the text is being incorporated.[42]

Nevertheless, even when the canonical text as a coherent whole is made the principal context of interpretation, problems of text identity remain; questions such as 'whose text?', 'precisely what text?', 'what general context of interpretation – e.g. a primarily academic, theological, spiritual, ecclesial and/or literary setting?', and 'what reflections on the text's *Wirkungsgeschichte* are to be preferred?' In current discussion on the status of biblical theology such queries are often brought to the table. In his 2000 edition of *Beyond New Testament Theology*, Heikki Räisänen, following William Wrede, opts for the rejection of the category of canon altogether in the historical study of the Bible,[43] because 'canon is a dogmatic concept'.[44]

---

[40] Ibid., 82.

[41] See, e.g. Zenger, *Einleitung in das Alte Testament*, Studienbücher Theologie, vol. 1,1 (Stuttgart: Kohlhammer, 6th edn, 2006).

[42] For a critical assessment as to this possibility, cf. Wesley Kort's negative evaluation of the aptitude for today's Bible readers to view the text in line with such 'precritical' modes of interpretation: 'At one time people knew what it meant to read a text as scripture, but we no longer do, because this way of reading has, since the late medieval and reformation periods, been dislocated and obscured. This dislocation has been so thorough that it is difficult today to know how to raise the prospect of reading a text as scripture, to regain a sense of what such a practice would be like, why it should be engaged, and what difference it would make'. Kort, *'Take, Read': Scripture, Textuality, and Cultural Practice* (Pennsylvania: The Pennsylvania State University Press, 1996), 1. The use of Gadamer's hermeneutical concepts of horizon, effective-history and sameness in difference may be helpful in further analyzing this problem as posed by Kort.

[43] Cf. in this regard my suggestion above (Ch. 1) of the understanding of the canonical validity of Sacred Scripture as a sign.

[44] Räisänen, *Beyond New Testament Theology: A Story and a Programme* (London: SCM, 2nd edn, 2000), 21.

We have reason here to be hesitant about Räisänen's historicizing approach. After all, as much as the predicate 'canonical' was lacking for the early New Testament writings, so was the attribution 'New Testament'.[45] If we set out to argue in this manner, we will find it problematic to agree on criteria to be applied for deciding what should count as a New Testament writing, or, by extension, as New Testament theology or exegesis. Of course, by engaging in biblical studies we always run the risk of letting the text become 'a prisoner of its own reception'.[46] None the less, the textual character of the canon has already incorporated an element of reception into the text itself; in that regard we are 'imprisoned' from the outset. Brevard Childs makes this inherent canonical dimension clear: 'the concept of canon was not a late, ecclesiastical ordering which was basically foreign to the [biblical] material itself, but ... canon-consciousness', he maintains, 'lay deep within the formation of the literature.'[47] In fact, the emergent concept of canon is largely an awareness of the establishment and development of Christian biblical textuality – i.e. that the writings are held, and hold, together. A more fragmentary, and indeed problematic, view of the formation of the canonical text can be seen in James Barr, who claims that canonization was pursued under a faith structure that was very different from that of the biblical community.[48] In Barr, too, as in Wrede and Räisänen, to whom traditional historical-critical methodology is crucial, canonization is understood to be a theological and political act carried out in the fourth century. Hence, to them this 'act' is done in isolation from other textual properties of the canonical process.[49]

A particular problem with the historical, or historicizing, approach surfaces when scholars as their topic of study choose written tradition as 'a fragment of a past world'.[50] Here Gadamer has made us aware that written tradition already has 'raised itself beyond this into the sphere of the meaning that it

---

[45] On the modern awareness of this incongruity, see the discussion on New Testament theology in Balla, *Challenges to New Testament Theology: An Attempt to Justify the Enterprise* (Tübingen: Mohr Siebeck, 1997).

[46] Davies, *Whose Bible is it Anyway?* (Sheffield: Sheffield Academic Press, 1995), 13.

[47] Childs, *Biblical Theology of the Old and New Testaments* (London: SCM, 1992), 70.

[48] Barr, *Holy Scripture: Canon, Authority, Criticism* (Oxford: Clarendon Press, 1983), 66. Cf. full quote above, section 2.7, n. 125.

[49] Cf. Stuhlmacher, *Wie treibt man Biblische Theologie?* (Neukirchen-Vluyn: Neukirchener, 1995), 64; English trans. (Pickwick, 1995), 57: 'Traces of this new canonical process can be seen as early as the middle of the first century.'

[50] Gadamer, *TM*, 390.

expresses'. Since the concept of canon exemplifies precisely this – that the writings included form a literary unit, being normative also in regard to the present community – it is true that this text as a classic always expresses a whole, the *scopus* and scope of the Bible as canon. In other words, it is of little relevance to the issue of canon formation to emphasize, as do Wrede, Barr and Räisänen, the difference in faith structure between the biblical and the later community. This is so, because it is not this canonized collection of writings, 'as a piece of the past, that is the bearer of tradition but the continuity of memory. Through it tradition becomes part of our own world, and thus what it communicates can be stated immediately'.[51] The way the Scripture principle of the Reformation Period was intended to function is a good illustration of this.[52] By contrast, Barr's attempt at deconstructing this particular literary tradition misses this point of canonical functioning, i.e. the elements of textual preservation and actualization. To him the scriptural canon is defined in some other way.[53]

6.4.2 The canon and the hermeneutical circle

Through Schleiermacher, Heidegger and Gadamer we know that the structure of all understanding is that of the dialogue between the whole and the parts, often called the hermeneutical circle. This is not a *circulus vitiosus*, as it is not here applied on a methodological level but is only describing the structure of what always occurs when understanding takes place. Gadamer recalls this hermeneutical circle also when describing how the Bible has been commonly expounded:

> The literal meaning of Scripture, however, is not univocally intelligible in every place and at every moment. For the whole of Scripture guides the under-standing of individual passages: and again this whole can be reached only through the cumulative understanding of individual passages. This circular relationship between the whole and the parts is not new. It was already known to classical rhetoric, which compares perfect speech with the organic body, with the relationship between head and limbs. Luther and his successors transferred

---

[51] Ibid.
[52] This principle is found as well among early church teachers, arguably already in Clement of Alexandria. Cf. Mathison, *The Shape of Sola Scriptura* (Moscow, ID: Canon Press, 2001), 19–48.
[53] See section 2.7.

this image, familiar from classical rhetoric, to the process of understanding; and they developed the universal principle of textual interpretation that all the details of a text were to be understood from the contextus and from the scopus, the unified sense at which the whole aims.[54]

This is not the place to make a sharp distinction between *Mitte der Schrift* and Scripture as a whole, as, e.g. Krister Stendahl attempts,[55] for the simple reason that in understanding – as Gadamer maintains – the whole aims at exactly this: the *scopus*, the unified sense. This hermeneutical insight was underlined already by Wilhelm Dilthey when speaking of 'structure' and of the 'centering in a mid-point,' which enables the understanding of the whole.[56]

The attempt at centring in such a mid-point by the early church teachers, as they discussed the Rule of Faith, is crucial for understanding the theological dimensions of the canonical process. Stendahl remarks that the question of canon tends towards great variations depending on whether one accentuates 'mid-point' or 'wholeness'. This may be true on a more superficial level and when applied to certain modern discussions, e.g. that between some conservative Reformed and some Lutheran churches.[57] However, Stendahl's distinction does not quite hold its ground. It is not generally the case that the question of canon becomes less interesting for those who stress 'mid-point', while, by contrast, the canon turns out to be theologically significant to those who emphasize 'wholeness'. The question of 'mid-point' as encountered in the various discussions on the *Mitte der Schrift* (the centre of Scripture) is usually distinguished from the question of canonical shape. However, as in the case of Luther, the 'mid-point' may very well affect the view one takes on the latter. Luther's rejection of four 'New Testament' writings was based on his view of the scriptural whole, which in turn derived from his understanding of a theological 'mid-point'.[58] Similarly, some Reformed theologians' stress laid on the canonical shape and the whole of Scripture, i.e. a written canon containing a well defined number of books, should not in principle exclude their explicit or implicit interest in finding a scriptural centre. The prejudice as to what is to count as the whole, which Stendahl here helps us detect, however, is of interest

---

[54] Gadamer, *TM*, 175.
[55] Stendahl, *Meningar* (Älvsjö: Verbum, 1986), 78.
[56] Gadamer, *TM*, 291.
[57] Stendahl, *Meningar*, 78.
[58] Cf. Morgan and Barton, *Biblical Interpretation* (New York: Oxford University Press, 1988), 112.

since it leads towards a fuller understanding of the hermeneutics involved. The question of canonical shape and the theological (and other) forces involved in the canonical process are part of a greater totality, namely the necessity of getting at the whole when seeking to grasp the notion of canon.

6.4.3 Expressing the whole

The early Christian vision of a textual whole was a reason for forming, re-forming and preserving the scriptural canon. In the earliest church, as stressed above, this totality was expressed in relation to the already existing Jewish Scripture, with formulas such as 'the Scriptures and the Lord'. In this formula we may even say that we have the nucleus of the New Testament (see section 2.3), despite the fact that the term 'Lord' at this early date designated a more or less unwritten tradition.[59] It is encountered already in the Apostolic Age, where the formula had been interchangeable with 'the Scriptures and the Gospel'. Somewhat later, in 2 *Clement*, we find the expression 'the Books and the Apostles' (14.2). Soon, in the late second or early third century, e.g. in Clement of Alexandria and Tertullian, the titles 'Old Testament' and 'New Testament' were used to the same, or similar, effect. The fact that one can detect parallel Jewish usages of similar formulas, such as 'the Law and the Prophets', indicates that they are different ways of appealing to a greater totality, the scriptural whole. The particulars of the biblical writings were meant to be grasped with this scriptural whole in mind. Especially the formula 'Old and New Testament', making use of the Greek term διαθήκη (covenant; testament), emphasizes this greater totality as something that both points to and goes beyond the written testimony.

We are here dealing with a dual textuality – oral and written – in this early Christian setting, as indicated by the choice of terminology: the *Lord*, the *Gospel*, the *Apostles* and the *New Testament*. These terms all originate in an oral milieu and cannot – not even after they came to designate collections of biblical writings – completely free themselves from their original and continuing ecclesial denotation. The terminology here serves to preserve the connection between the oral and the literary modes of the Christian canon.

---

[59] Cf. the notion of oral text, Ch. 5; and section 1.2.

From the forming of the 'First Testament' we recognize a similar and, in fact, parallel terminology, namely, the *Torah* and the *Prophets*. The *Torah* and the *Gospel*, too, cannot easily be understood exclusively as written text; they are also 'living tradition', orally transmitted and partly independent of written communal discourse, as long as the Jewish and Christian interpretive communities persist.[60] Furthermore, it would be odd for the church to treat the *Prophets* or the *Apostles* as mere writings without the closest possible connection to their present function, and their historical setting, made up of the collective of charismatic leaders chosen as ecclesial warrants of the texts bearing their names.[61]

These texts are held to be authoritative by the faith community, not least because of the prophetic and apostolic sanction believed to legitimize them as scriptural.[62] Admittedly, the form of textuality implied here is not easily grasped. Worth noting is that the textual whole is never isolated from the community of readers or from its *Wirkungsgeschichte*. We could also add the historical setting in which the texts came into being, even if this is not required for a successful act of strict textual interpretation. However, even the historical dimension, which has always been (implicitly or explicitly) present in the church, should be accounted for if we wish to find a well-balanced understanding of the notion of canon. In this connection we can recall Gadamer's analysis of the fusion of reason (historical research) and tradition:

> At the beginning of all historical hermeneutics, then, *the abstract antithesis between tradition and historical research, between history and the knowledge of it, must be discarded*. The effect (Wirkung) of a living tradition and the effect of historical study must constitute a unity of effect, the analysis of which would reveal only a texture of reciprocal effects. Hence we would do well not to regard historical consciousness as something radically new – as it seems at first – but as a new element in what has always constituted the human relation to the past. In other words, we have to recognize the element of tradition in historical research and inquire into its hermeneutic productivity.[63]

---

[60] See Graham, *Beyond the Written Word: Oral Aspects of Scripture in the History of Religion* (Cambridge: Cambridge University Press, 1987).

[61] On the biblical writings as *Urliteratur*, see section 9.5.3.

[62] As to apostolicity as a principal criterion of canonicity, see Skarsaune, 'Hvilket lys kaster NT's kanonhistorie over teologihistorien i det 1. århundre?', *Religio* 25 (1986): 63–83.

[63] Gadamer, *TM*, 282f.

By combining theological, literary and historical dimensions, the particular textuality, intertextuality, intratextuality and metatextuality character of the church's canon may be seen as dependent on such integration of historical research and tradition.[64] A multidimensional approach like this has several implications, for example, when seeking to grasp the notion of the 'apostolic'. In line with first-, second- and third-century reflection, the 'apostolic' needs to be understood equally as a theological, literary and historical concept. Brevard Childs's impression – pondering the apostolic status claimed for Mark and Luke – that 'the later expositions of the criteria of canonicity were, in large part, after-the-fact explanations ... evoked by continued use of certain books' therefore needs to be reconsidered.[65] The early church was well aware of the inherent complexity when dealing with the notion of apostolicity.[66] Childs recognizes another significant ingredient for the formation of (the corpora of) new apostolic writings. He suggests that the sense of the whole out of which the Christian canon was formed was immediately dependent on the prototype that the Jewish canon had set. Childs writes: 'the presence of an Old Testament canon of normative writings ... ultimately established a pattern by which the varying qualities of writings within the church were measured.'[67] New writings were from early on[68] attributed 'the same divine status ... as obtained for the sacred scriptures of the Old.'[69] As I have indicated above, the importance for the church of the Jewish conception of Scripture, and the Jewish notion of a whole projected onto the Scriptures as word of God, become the starting point for the Christian continuous anticipation of such a whole as the *telos* of the Bible's canonizing.

---

[64] Cf. Childs, *The New Testament as Canon: An Introduction* (London: SCM, 1984), 38f.

[65] Childs, *The New Testament as Canon*, 32.

[66] Cf. Blum, *Tradition und Sukzession: Studien zum Normbegriff des Apostolischen von Paulus bis Irenäus* (Berlin and Hamburg: Lutherisches Verlagshaus, 1963); Skarsaune, *Hvilket lys kaster NT's kanonhistorie over teologihistorien i det 1. århunde?*.

[67] Childs, *The New Testament as Canon*, 31.

[68] On this, see esp. Stuhlhofer, *Der Gebrauch der Bibel von Jesus bis Euseb: Eine statistische Untersuchung zur Kanonsgeschichte* (Wuppertal: Brockhaus, 1988).

[69] Childs, *The New Testament as Canon*, 31.

6.4.4 Gradually reaching the textual whole

Guided by the same principle – that the whole can be reached only through the cumulative understanding of its individual parts – it is still possible to attain a revised understanding of the whole when looking at the question of the canon. Developed in the early church, the concept of canon necessarily was formed only gradually. This cannot be stressed enough. A sudden emergence of a new Christian conception of the scriptural total, with its hermeneutic oscillation between the parts and the structural whole, is hardly possible to envisage; even less so a concept of a static and fixed whole.[70]

Both Clement of Alexandria and Augustine seem to be aware of this, when discussing the church's exegesis of the Old Testament in its relation to the New. They both advocate a dynamic view of canonical exegesis, Clement by referring to the exegetical tradition regulating the balance between the two text corpora, coming to expression through the Rule of Faith/the Ecclesiastical Canon (see Ch. 8), and Augustine by referring to the Rule of Faith beside the principle of *caritas*. Both Clement and Augustine understood canon as reaching for the scriptural whole. In this connection they did not primarily focus on the exact shape or the exegetical details of the biblical text.

For Augustine, to whom the delimitation of the number of canonical books is still of some importance in his discussions with Jerome, the inclusion of the Apocrypha into the Old Testament did not notably challenge the concept of the canonical whole from which the exegesis of the individual writings was carried out.[71] The same could arguably be said of Origen, who, according to Eusebius, excludes the Apocrypha from the Scriptures, but at the same time frequently makes use of these writings. Hans von Campenhausen comments on such exterior discrepancies in the composition of the canon – between the Christians as well as between Jews and Christians – that they were 'never taken very seriously'.[72]

From early on, the concept of the textual whole as applied to the Scriptures

---

[70] However, cf. Metzger, *The Canon of the New Testament*, 275 (quoted in section 9.9); see also sections 1.1, 9.2 and 9.4.

[71] As to the great significance of the LXX translation legend of the *Letter of Aristeas* for Augustine in his discussion with Jerome, see Hengel, *The Septuagint as Christian Scripture: Its Prehistory and the Problem of Its Canon* (London and New York: T&T Clark, 2002), 51–4.

[72] Campenhausen, *The Formation of the Christian Bible* (Philadelphia: Fortress, 1972), 65.

was conceptualized in a variety of ways. This was also the situation when the number of canonical writings in various church regions tended to vary somewhat. The fact that these most valued and frequently used writings became part of the scriptural collection that were to be universally privileged meant that the preconception of catholicity was an integral part of the concept of canon. The notion of canon was here developed as part of the interpretive interaction between the category of catholicity, alongside other canon criteria, and the 'canonical' writings themselves.

'Canonical' was understood as that which was regarded as catholic, i.e. universally accepted among the communities. This becomes clear when focusing on the inductive, rather non-dogmatic, method employed by Origen and Eusebius, when deciding which writings are and which are not to be counted as canonical (ἐνδιάθηκος, 'encovenanted', 'testament-ed'; *Hist. Eccl.* III, 3.1). Those mentioned by Eusebius as used and accepted by practically all communities are labelled *homologoumena* – all in all 22 books (including Revelation, 'if it seems desirable'), and those disputed, or accepted only by a scarce majority, *antilegomena* (James, Jude, 2 Peter, 2 and 3 John); in addition Eusebius lists writings that are 'not genuine' (*notha*) such as the *Acts of Paul, the Shepherd* of Hermas, the *Apocalypse of Peter*, the *Epistle of Barnabas*, and the *Didache* (*Hist. Eccl.* III, 25.3-4). To this Eusebian model with its appeal to usage in the communities (in effect a form of majority or universality model), Augustine, in his analysis, adds the recommendation to turn to the churches of greater authority for knowledge regarding the biblical canon (*De Doct. Chr.* II, 12).

In addition to catholicity, other canon criteria are introduced, such as established usage and orthodoxy. In the end the overall picture tends to be rather complex. For a while rival canon projects emerge side by side until, eventually, it becomes more clear here what the unity of meaning may be; in this process of understanding, interpretation must begin with fore-conceptions being replaced by more suitable ones, in order to attain a 'final' textual shape of the church's canon. The constant process of new projection here makes up the movement of understanding the canon as a unified, as well as a unifying text – that which holds together – of the church universal (cf. section 9.5.2, note 60).[73] The concept of catholicity, associated with the canon, thus represents a

[73] Cf. Gadamer, *TM*, 267.

dimension of canonicity that 'holds together' both the inner and outer frame, the text as text and that text as unifying texture of the catholic community.[74]

With regard to the new Scriptures, a preconception of catholicity as well as orthodoxy, apostolicity and established usage was part of the ancient church's prejudice towards these writings, when seen as a literary unity. The writings united as Scripture, and the new text thereby formed, could then present itself in all its otherness, vis-à-vis this prejudice, and so assert its truth against the church's own fore-meanings on various matters. When interpreting the Scriptures, this implied a movement between the parts and the whole, so that the conception of the whole also had to be modified in order to reach understanding – i.e. harmonizing the parts and the whole.

Ecclesial understanding of the biblical message is not a matter of securing the community against the tradition that speaks out of the text. Rather, ecclesial understanding excludes everything that could hinder the church from understanding the text in terms of the subject matter. So, for the sake of continuity with historic apostolic tradition, to the extent that the church's listening to its own scriptural tradition fails, or if it prefers not to listen, it may be the 'tyranny of hidden prejudices' that makes it deaf to what speaks to it in tradition.[75] Even though the scriptural address may seem partly, or largely, irrelevant to current ecclesial concerns, it still ought to be considered as address, including also earlier generations of believers who in this way communicate to future Christian communities, asking to join them, by handing on the gospel message in textual form: a scriptural whole, and scriptural parts.

Martin Luther, too, was acting within a similar text-hermeneutical scheme, endeavouring to exclude four New Testament writings from the canon just because of prejudice towards the canonical whole.[76] Regarding his view on the Book of Revelation, Luther here joined Zwingli and other Reformers. Admittedly, Origen, Eusebius and the early Lutheran Scholastics were justified in making a distinction between the so called *antilegomena* and *homologoumena*, mainly because of the historical and textual canon principle of catholicity.

---

[74] See further below, ch. 9.
[75] Gadamer, *TM*, 269f.
[76] Cf. Morgan and Barton, *Biblical Interpretation*, 112.

We may here visualize the notion of the whole as something expanding in circles. When the principle of catholicity – as pointed out by the theologian Bengt Hägglund[77] – was often understood as a principle of orthodoxy and vice versa,[78] the criteria of canonicity were again reassessed in terms of an understanding of the greater totality. There is, in other words, a dynamic relationship amid the various canon criteria, and among these criteria and the canonical text. In this connection Gadamer has something to say of the interim character of the text, treating it in the act of understanding as 'a mere intermediate product [Zwischenprodukt], a phase in the event of understanding that, as such, certainly includes a certain amount of abstraction, namely, the isolation and reification that is involved in this very phase.'[79]

The reason why Gadamer chooses to view the text in this dynamic, interimistic, preliminary, and, indeed, transient manner, is that he has in mind not the grammatical and/or linguistic level, turning the text into an 'end-product', but rather the text as a hermeneutical concept. In other words, his focus is on the text and the textual content (*Sache*), text and interpretation, seen as inseparable entities in a most profound sense. In order to reach understanding of the formation and interpretation of the canonical text as canon, there are reasons to let the linguistics here have a secondary role, and to allow the textual understanding of what is said (content) to be the main focus. Again, being closely intertwined, text and interpretation cannot really be conceived apart:

> The closeness with which text and interpretation are interwoven is especially clear whenever the tradition of a text is not always pre-given as a basis for an interpretation. Indeed, it is often interpretation that leads to a critical restoration of the text. If one were able to clarify this inner relationship of interpretation and text, one would be able to realize a considerable gain methodologically.
>
> The methodological gain that accrues from our view of language is that 'text' must be understood as a hermeneutical concept. This means that the text will not be approached from the perspective of grammar and linguistics, divorced from any content that it might have. That is to say, it is not going to be viewed

---

[77] Hägglund, *Katholizität und Bekenntnis* (Hamburg: Verlag Herbert Renner GmbH & Co. KG, 1976).
[78] Cf., e.g. the way it is expressed in Vincent of Lerins; cf. above, Ch. 1, n. 119.
[79] Gadamer, *Text und Interpretation, Gesammelte Werke*, vol. 2 (Tübingen: Mohr Siebeck, 1993 [1983]), 341 (Eng. trans. Richard E. Palmer, *The Gadamer Reader: A Bouquet of the Later Writings*, Evanston, IL: Northwestern University Press, 2007).

as an end product whose production is the object of an analysis whose intent is to explain the mechanism that allows language as such to function.[80]

The very close relationship between text and interpretation, as posed here, is also indirectly addressed right at the outset of the second part of *Truth and Method*, where Gadamer quotes the Luther wording: *Qui non intelligit res, non potest ex verbis sensum elicere* [Whoever does not understand the subject matter, cannot elicit the sense from the words].[81]

6.5 Preservation of a textual tradition

In the introductory chapter I discussed the canon formation of the early church as something partially ongoing, as an act of both preserving and actualizing apostolic tradition. There we presupposed the assumption that canonization cannot be understood only as something past. It is rather to be thought of as something partially still taking place in the church. This has to do with the character of tradition in general and sacred texts in particular, such as the biblical texts being transmitted in the church with a distinctive communal narrative and meta-narrative framework.[82] Such texts are appropriated, interpreted and received anew in every new generation. According to Gerald Bruns,

> [a] text, after all, is canonical not in virtue of being final and correct and part of an official library but because it becomes *binding* on a group of people. The whole point of canonization is to underwrite the authority of a text, not merely with respect to its origin as against competitors in the field – this, technically, would simply be a question of authenticity – but with respect to the present and future in which it will reign or govern as a binding text.[83]

Gadamer also portrays such continuous reappropriation of textual tradition, and tradition in general, by using the notion of preservation. He does not perceive this as passively being caught by, or uncritically appropriating, a

---

[80] Ibid.
[81] Gadamer, *TM*, 171.
[82] Cf. Frei, *The 'Literal Reading' of Biblical Narrative in the Christian Tradition: Does It Stretch or Will It Break?* (New York: Oxford University Press, 1986), 72f.
[83] Bruns, *Hermeneutics Ancient and Modern* (New Haven and London: Yale University Press, 1992), 65f.

tradition.[84] Even less such a retrieval of canonical tradition is a question of authority in the sense of power, the way Bruns, in company with Michel Foucault and others, would have it.[85] By contrast, part of Gadamer's description of the characteristics of tradition – textual and non-textual – instead runs as follows:

> [I]n tradition there is always an element of freedom and of history itself. Even the most genuine and pure tradition does not persist because of the inertia of what once existed. It needs to be affirmed, embraced, cultivated. It is, essentially, preservation, and it is active in all historical change. But preservation is an act of reason, though an inconspicuous one. For this reason, only innovation and planning appear to be the result of reason. But this is an illusion. Even where life changes violently, as in ages of revolution, far more of the old is preserved in the supposed transformation of everything than anyone knows, and it combines with the new to create a new value. At any rate, preservation is as much a freely chosen action as are revolution and renewal.[86]

This also has implications for the act of ecclesial Scripture canonizing, which does not persist only because of 'the inertia of what once existed'. It therefore needs to be affirmed, embraced and cultivated. Competitors and alternative accounts to canonical Scripture are plentiful, and the list of late-modern decanonizing agendas can be made long. In the midst of this, the Bible *as canon* is one of the church's perennial concerns. As such, it, too, can be described in terms of preservation as an act of reason – even if an inconspicuous one – being active in all historical change.

---

[84] On the critical task and the historical, systematic and hermeneutical character of Christian selfunderstanding, cf. Pannenberg (Pannenberg, *Systematic Theology*, vol. 1 (Grand Rapids: Eerdmans, 1991), x–xi), who writes: 'For one thing, Christian doctrine is from first to last a historical construct. Its content rests on the historical revelation of God in the historical figure of Jesus Christ and on the precise evaluation, by historical interpretation alone, of the testimony that early Christian proclamation gives to this figure. The terminology, which has evolved since apostolic times in attempts to formulate the universal scope of the divine action in the person and history of Jesus, cannot be understood apart from its place within the history of these attempts. … As regards the truth claims raised in the investigation and presentation of Christian doctrine, historical and systematic reflection must continually permeate one another.' Closely tied to this, the canon is the testimony, the primary witness, that the early Christian proclamation gives to the historical figure of Jesus Christ. Or in the wording of Robert Jenson ('The Religious Power of Scripture', *Scottish Journal of Theology* 52 (1999): 90): 'the gospel is a narrative, and this book is that telling of the narrative from which all others draw, quite apart from any need for their correction by it.'

[85] Cf. Bruns, *Hermeneutics Ancient and Modern*, 65f.

[86] Gadamer, *TM*, 281f.

6.6 Scriptural unity and diversity

In Chapter 2 I discussed an aspect of Scripture's self-organizing capacity. Assent to a similar view on the Scriptures has been made ecumenically in the important volume *Kanon–Heilige Schrift–Tradition*, edited by Wolfhart Pannenberg and Theodor Schneider. A consensus is there reached, maintaining that the churches are not the creators of the biblical canon(s). On the contrary, the biblical witness itself is held to be the driving force behind the canonical process. From this Peter Stuhlmacher concludes: 'The Sacred Scriptures of Old and New Testaments, that emerged from this process, must therefore keep having priority over all church teaching.'[87]

This is a traditionalist stand in line with not only certain ecumenically oriented Roman Catholic theology, but also with much traditional Anglican, Lutheran and Reformed thinking, as classically expressed, e.g. by Jean Calvin:

> For by his Word, God rendered faith unambiguous forever, a faith that should be superior to all opinion. Finally, in order that truth might abide forever in the world with a continuing succession of teaching and survive through all ages, the same oracles he had given to the patriarchs it was his pleasure to have recorded, as it were, on public tablets.[88]

Here the scriptural canon as a form of 'icon' (see Ch. 8) – 'heading for this once and for all revealed mystery' – is making a strong claim on the church,[89] the reception of which in the end also functions as 'a measure of *ecclesiastical acceptability*'.[90]

Nevertheless, a quite different feature surfaces in the midst of this claimed unity and continuity of scriptural revelation, namely that of diversity. Although it is a fact that a majority of Christian churches accept, more or less, the same canon, it is still the case that they differ in a multitude of ways, as far as textual interpretation goes. As A. van de Beek well recognizes, it is difficult to overestimate this function of the canon.[91]

---

[87] Stuhlmacher, *Wie treibt man Biblische Theologie?*, 68; my trans.; Pannenberg and Schneider, *Verbindliches Zeugnis 1: Kanon – Schrift – Tradition* (Freiburg im Breisgau: Herder and Göttingen: Vandenhoeck & Ruprecht, 1992), 371–97.

[88] Calvin, *Institutes of the Christian Religion* (Philadelphia: The Westminster Press, 1960 [1559]), 71.

[89] Cf. in this regard Childs, *Old Testament Theology in a Canonical Context* (Philadelphia: Fortress, 1985), 22f.

[90] Beek, *Being Convinced: On the Foundations of the Christian Canon* (Leiden: Brill, 1998), 331.

[91] Ibid.

Since Ernst Käsemann's famous questioning of the unity as the most significant quality of the New Testament canon,[92] diversity has been a principal
attribute when evaluating the potential integrity of the New Testament. Gerd
Theissen, for example, thinks of the formation of the canon as a confession
of plurality: 'The canon preserves (and limits) the plurality of primitive
Christianity which had come about.'[93]

Treating the canonical process, it would be inadequate to stop with the
strive towards unity without also taking into account the obvious diversity
involved. A critical example would be the well-known comment by Clement
of Alexandria on the interpretation of the Bible as a whole: 'The Canon of
the Church is the concord and harmony of the Law and Prophets and the
Testament delivered at the coming of the Lord.'[94] Through this reference to
the Canon of the Church (the Rule of Faith) Clement here expresses what is at
the heart of Christian canonical reading: unity in diversity. We may here recall
again the quote from Origen in the opening section (Ch. 1): 'All the Scriptures
are one book', since the teaching that has been handed on to us about Christ is
'recapitulated in one single whole'.

In this connection I would like briefly to consider Jacques Derrida's
assessment in the opening section of his *Of Grammatology*, regarding 'the
book' as opposed to 'writing'. In his view the book symbolizes the 'idol of
determinacy', the illusion that texts have fixed meanings. As already pointed
out, it is precisely as text, as a larger text unit, that the book is something
more than the total sum of its words and sentences. The book is a structured whole with thematic coherence – an ideological 'glue',[95] if you will
– and in this respect closed. This fixation of the totality, marked out by a
beginning and an end, is symbolically visualized by the book's binding.[96]
Derrida writes:

> The idea of the book is the idea of a totality, finite or infinite, of the
> signifier. ... The idea of the book, which always refers to a natural totality,
> is profoundly alien to the sense of writing. It is the encyclopedic protection

---

[92] Käsemann, 'The Canon of the New Testament and the Unity of the Church', in *Essays on New
Testament Themes* (London: SCM, 1968).
[93] Theissen, *A Theory of Primitive Christian Religion* (London: SCM, 1999), 261.
[94] *Strom.* VI, 15.125.3.
[95] Vanhoozer, *Is There a Meaning in This Text?*, 104.
[96] Ibid.

of theology and of logocentrism against the disruption of writing ... against difference in general.[97]

On this, Kevin Vanhoozer comments: 'Because the idea of the book suggests totality, Derrida finds it inherently theological. Books stabilize, control, and close down the play of meaning.'[98] At issue here is a central feature actualized by deconstructionism, the fluid character of meaning inherent in all writing. No doubt this is a challenge for the church and the very nature of the canonical book to which it is bound. It seems to me that a way of positively affecting the discourse on the church's book in this regard is by showing an increased awareness of the things at stake, and by addressing the new formulations of the problems pertaining to biblical textuality. And not to forget, when dealing with biblical text and writing, that we need to keep in mind what always comes with it: a subject matter and its interpretation. That is to say, the question of 'open writing' or 'closed book', addressed by Derrida, is always also a matter of textual meaning, or the meaning of poststructuralist postponing of such a meaning.[99]

6.7 Scripture as a whole: Text, reader and community

What does the textual totality consist of? If we keep to a sharp hermeneutical distinction between the oral and written modes of language, as suggested by some hermeneuts, we may end up in a dilemma when seeking to claim any kind of autonomy for the text as distinguished from the reader. This, of course, is especially the case where the written text is deprived both of authorial intent and of any inherent textual meaning. By extension, the notion of canon may become heavily contextualized, constantly reassessed by the actual situation without due consideration given to the text as memory of the past. However, as I have argued above, the text is a hermeneutical concept in which text and interpretation are held together. This affects our basic understanding of what a text is with 'its constantly widening possibilities of significance and

---

[97] Derrida, *Of Grammatology* (Baltimore and London: Johns Hopkins University Press, 1976), 18; cited from Vanhoozer, *Is There a Meaning in This Text?*, 104.

[98] Ibid.

[99] For theological treatments of text and meaning, see, e.g. Jeanrond, *Theological Hermeneutics*, 78–119; Watson, *Text, Church, and World* (Edinburgh: T&T Clark, 1994), 15–153; and Vanhoozer, *Is There a Meaning in This Text?*, 37–195.

resonance, extended by the different people receiving it.'[100] The act of reading and application therefore needs to be taken into proper account when seeking to ascribe meaning to the biblical (or other) texts. Only in the process of understanding is the 'dead trace' of textual meaning 'transformed back into living meaning'.[101]

However, when applied to the canonical text, is this not a breach with 'precritical' and modern conceptions of biblical textuality? Yes and no. A few years ago, Robert Jenson made an interesting analysis of classic Christian hermeneutics. In his model, the Christian community is needed as the relatively stable context within which the text can be contextualized. This classical model of Bible reading is laid forth by Jenson in his urge for a reappraisal of an Irenaean biblical hermeneutics for the present community. In order to contravene various Gnostic and neo-Gnostic exegetical moves he commends five rules for canonical interpretation providing textual and hermeneutic stability. Noteworthy is his emphasis on today's church as standing in a particular and direct textual continuity with the church of the New Testament.[102]

Jenson's five rules of the canonical drama, in short, are:

Rule 1: Scripture is a whole.

Rule 2: Scripture *is* a whole because and only because it is one long *narrative*.

Rule 3: To be able to *follow* the single story and grasp Scripture as a whole, we need to know the story's general plot and *dramatis personae*, much as playgoers enduring a long, complex, and mystery-laden play need the catalogue of the drama with its list of characters and synopsis of the plot. Scripture is *not* in *that* sense self-explanatory, that anyone simply coming across the unfamiliar book and reading through it is likely to find in it what God intends to be found. It is not because Scripture is obscure that we need this prior knowledge, but more precisely because Scripture is very clear about what kind of book it is (cf. here the concept of Scripture's *autopistia*).

---

[100] Gadamer, *TM*, 462.
[101] Ibid., 164; an interesting parallel to our topic is Gadamer's example of the museum artwork (ibid., 167): 'Even a painting taken from the museum and replaced in a church or building restored to its original condition are not what they once were – they become simply tourist attractions. Similarly, a hermeneutics that regarded understanding as reconstructing the original would be no more than handing on a dead meaning.'
[102] Cf. Ch. 1, n. 62.

Rule 4: It is the *church* (see Ch. 1, note 1) that knows the plot and *dramatis personae* of the scriptural narrative, since the church is one continuous community with the story's actors and narrators, as well as with its tradents, authors and assemblers. In other words, the church is itself an integral part of the plot and, by inference, of the *dramatis personae* of this plot.

Rule 5: The church's antecedent knowledge of Scripture's plot and *dramatis personae*, without which she could not read the Bible as a whole, is contained in what Irenaeus calls the 'Rule of Faith', the canon that the church propounds and teaches to her members regarding how to think and talk as Christians. When Irenaeus stated this Rule, it came out as something much on the lines of the Apostles' Creed.[103]

In a wider semiotic framework, the issue here at stake can be more generally posed as a question of textuality, where the interdependence of writing and oral (or vocal) utterance, kept alive within a relatively stable community of readers, is stated anew. According to various deconstructionist schemes, 'writing' implies the absence of the author, being an open text with potential for multiple interpretations and the postponing of meaning. With a deconstructionist interpretive agenda, which radically problematizes the notion of (pre)modern textual meaning, the textuality of a text, such as that of the biblical canon, commends a renewed emphasis on the type of textual matrix as that portrayed by Jenson. This ecclesial hermeneutical model embraces a 'self-awareness' of the church, preserving and actualizing its essential message. In the Christian community this takes place in both an oral and a written form,[104] and as part of a theological programme in which systematic theology as such does not primarily ask what the apostles and prophets said, but what must be said 'on the basis of the apostles and prophets'.[105]

The two particular areas, according to Anthony Thiselton, in which semiotics has its distinctive importance are illustrative of the problem of textuality with which I am concerned here. The first area deals with 'the nature and status of the *codes* through which texts communicate

---

[103] Jenson, 'Hermeneutics and the Life of the Church', in *Reclaiming the Bible for the Church*, (eds) Jenson and Braaten (Grand Rapids: Eerdmans, 1995), 96–8.

[104] See Ch. 5. For a treatment of the theme of oral and written tradition in early Post-Reformation thought, see Torbjörn Johansson's dissertation on the reception of Augustine in the theology of Martin Chemnitz, Johansson, *Reformationens huvudfrågor och arvet från Augustinus: En studie i Martin Chemnitz' Augustinusreception* (Göteborg: Församlingsförlaget, 1999), 38–101.

[105] Barth, *Church Dogmatics*, I/1 (Edinburgh: T&T Clark, 1936-62), 16.

meanings.' The second concerns 'those forms of *non-verbal social behaviour* which, through the presupposition of a code, become signifying messages.'[106]

From this can be inferred that the textual character of our 'object', the canon, is immediately dependent on the various cultural and linguistic codes through and by which the notion of canon can at all communicate any particular meaning. Some of these codes are treated in this study, such as the various physical, ritual and ideational elements that help not only to contextualize the canonical text, but also *to fabricate the textuality and lattice that the church identifies as its canon*. When treated as a unified whole, the canon of the Old and New Testaments is a most particular book (of books), comparable in this regard also to other book genres, such as the lawbook or even the fairytale collection, whose respective textualities cannot be grasped without a similar assessment of pragmatics.

The self-organizing aptitude of religion – and by analogy of canon formation – discussed above (sections 2.2 and 2.3) is backed up by another capability, that of delimiting itself from its surroundings, i.e. to be in a position to differ between self-reference and reference to external entities.[107] In this regard Adolf von Harnack's remark pertaining to the closing of the canon is worth repeating: 'a collection of fundamental documents has already *the tendency to become final*, and certainly a collection of fundamental documents of a *Covenant* carries in itself the idea of complete finality.'[108]

The finality of the text, which according to von Harnack finds expression in the title given the new collection of writings, lies already in its character as 'fundamental document'. Here the canon represents the closure of 'a collection of fundamental documents' with its highly profiled theological end. As such it becomes the textual expression of the contemporaneity of apostolic and sub-apostolic tradition with every ecclesial present. In this way – being in principle a closed corpus of writings – the direction of the canon is towards the future.

---

[106] Thiselton, *New Horizons in Hermeneutics*, 80.

[107] Theissen, *A Theory of Primitive Christian Religion*, 6.

[108] Harnack, *The Origin of the New Testament and the Most Important Consequences of the New Creation* (London: Williams & Norgate, 1925), 33f.; see also Zahn, *Grundriss der Geschichte des Neutestamentlichen Kanons: Eine Ergänzung zu der Einleitung in das Neue Testament* (Leipzig: A. Deichert'sche Verlagsbuchh. Nachf. [Georg Böhme], 1901), 11.

None the less, the closedness of these foundational documents implies openness to the textual tradition thereby mediated. The heart of the canon's significance lies in its central message, and in the fact that its core, by and large, was generally accepted by the churches from the outset of the Christian movement, as John Goldingay rightly emphasizes: 'the core of the Second Testament, the Four Gospels and the Pauline letters, is a matter of no controversy.'[109] The reality that finds expression in the concept of the New Testament found a textual basis in the 22 (or 21; cf. Euseb. *Hist. Eccl.* III, 3.4) writings that were (next to) undisputed in the Western (which included the Apocalypse) and the Eastern churches (which included Hebrews). From the turn of the fifth century onwards this became more or less true for all the 27 New Testament writings, which from early on had been received in the East and, through the accomplishments of Athanasius, now also in the West.[110]

However, accounts of the formation of the Christian Bible often begin with an assertion of the Old Testament canon. As Hans von Campenhausen writes: 'The Christian Bible is not a completely new formation. Through its "*Old Testament*" it is linked with Judaism.'[111] Von Campenhausen hastens to add, though, that for Christians the Old Testament is 'no longer a canonical book in the same sense as it once was for the Jews'. From the beginning of the Jesus movement onwards the old Scriptures are related to Christ, who is now, on the basis of Scripture, revered as the Lord of the church.[112] The transformation of the biblical text in the early church from Torah to Christian canon consisting of an Old and a New Testament part was a complex hermeneutical enterprise involving, as well as theological, linguistic, historical, ritual and material dimensions, also a textual side.

Joseph Margolis, in his general study on textuality, has concluded that the interpretation taking place as the interpreter confronts texts is an activity that produces 'not commentaries, but the texts themselves'.[113] Although his

[109] Goldingay, *Models for Scripture* (Grand Rapids and Carlisle: Eerdmans, 1994), 182.

[110] For a detailed analysis, see Zahn, *Athanasius und der Bibelkanon* (Erlangen and Leipzig: A. Deichert'sche Verlagsbuchhandlung Nachf. [Georg Böhme], 1901).

[111] Campenhausen, *The Formation of the Christian Bible*, 1. Cf. Barton, *The Spirit and the Letter: Studies in the Biblical Canon* (London: SPCK, 1997), 1.

[112] Campenhausen, *The Formation of the Christian Bible*, 1. See also Jeanrond, *Theological Hermeneutics*, 18f.

[113] Margolis, *Interpretation Radical but Not Unruly: The New Puzzle of the Arts and History* (Berkeley: University of California Press, 1995); cited from Vanhoozer, *Is There a Meaning in This Text?*, 18. On the postmodern discussion on the nature of texts Anthony Thiselton (*New Horizons in*

approach strongly favours the role of the reader in the shaping of textuality, it is useful when seeking to reconstruct the formation of the biblical text. To discover Jesus Christ in the Hebrew Scriptures according to the interpretive agenda set by NT accounts such as Luke 24.27 and Romans 1.1-3, or by post-apostolic writers such as Ignatius of Antioch, or the author of the *Epistle of Barnabas*, is from a textual point of view to let 'the-whole-Christ-event'[114] interpret the text; i.e. letting the most decisive textual component determine the text as a whole. Such handling of the biblical text was more or less unanimous in the apostolic and sub-apostolic churches. With a view to its historical implication, this characteristic feature of biblical textuality is stressed by Robert Wilken:

> Early Christian interpreters did not impose an evanescent superstructure on the text without root in history or experience. Most Christian exegetes repudiated a literal or historical reading of the prophets, not because they preferred allegory or anagogy to history, but because they were attentive to a new set of historical events. If Jesus of Nazareth was the Messiah, as the Scriptures taught, the prophecies about the Messianic age had already been fulfilled, and it was the task of biblical interpreters to discover what the scriptural promises meant in light of this new fact. Paradoxically, in the language of early Christian exegesis, the spiritual sense *was* the historical sense.[115]

The classic, and at the same time paradoxical, formulation of the matter – Christ and the biblical texts – is elegantly posed by Ignatius of Antioch around AD 107/8:

> But I urge you to do nothing in a contentious way, but in accordance with the teaching of Christ. For I heard some saying: 'If I do not find it in the ancient records [= the Jewish Scriptures], I do not believe in the Gospel.' And when I said to them, 'It is written,' they replied to me, 'That is just the question.' But for me, Jesus Christ is the ancient records; the sacred ancient records are his cross

Hermeneutics, 15) comments: '[C]ontroversies have arisen about the very nature of texts. Such questions are implied by reader-response theories, which see readers as co-authors of texts. Texts are neither complete nor fully "given" until the community of readers creates for them a particular working currency. In post-modernism and in theories of deconstructionism texts assume the form of shifting textures. Their shape and function undergo constant transposition as new intertextual contexts and reading-contexts re-define their meaning-matrices and their effects'.

[114] This phrase was formulated by Leander Keck, as cited from Minear, *The Bible and the Historian: Breaking the Silence About God in Biblical Studies* (Nashville: Abingdon, 2002), 87.

[115] Wilken, 'In novissimis diebus. Biblical Promises, Jewish Hopes and Early Christian Exegesis', *Journal of Early Christian Studies* 1 (1993): 19.

and death, and his resurrection, and the faith that comes through him – by which things I long to be made righteous by your prayer.[116]

Regarding those who tended to let the Old Testament documents be primary in relation to the faith in Christ, the biblical scholar Mogens Müller comments: 'Ignatius maintains the prior claim of this faith (which was not a new body of writings)'.[117] However, as a concluding remark in his Septuagint study, Müller formulates the point in question in a slightly different manner:

> What is preached in the Old Testament as being in the future, as seen through the eyes of the New Testament authors, has already happened. Therefore, what was perceived as the central issue of Scripture has shifted considerably. Substance pertaining to the old covenant has been reduced to being a salvation-historical digression. What was a collection of scriptures centred on the Law, in the New Testament biblical theology becomes a promise of what has already become reality in the New Testament congregations; that is, it is considered under a prophetical perspective. To put it differently, time has become a decisive factor in interpretation.[118]

The textuality of the Scriptures addressed here is so thoroughly changed that it may be described as a new construct through the act of Christian reading, based on the Jesus-event.[119] This shift seems to me necessary to prepare room

---

[116] Ignat. *Phil.* 8.2. Translation by Bart Ehrman (modified), *The Apostolic Fathers*, The Loeb Classical Library 24, 1.291–2 (Cambridge, MA: Harvard University Press, 2003). Cf. my comments on *Phil.* 8.2 in Bokedal, 'Scripture in the Second Century', in *The Sacred Text: Excavating the Texts, Exploring the Interpretations, and Engaging the Theologies of the Christian Scriptures*, (eds) M. Bird and M. Pahl (Piscataway, NJ: Gorgias, 2010), 52f.

[117] Müller, *The First Bible of the Church: A Plea for the Septuagint* (Sheffield: Sheffield Academic, 1996), 140.

[118] Ibid., 144.

[119] This way of treating the texts was intimately linked to the apostolic authority. As this authority was specifically connected to the formation of a new canon, it became the primary criterion of canonicity, as such criteria were being used by the church authorities from Ignatius onwards, to legitimize the new form of the biblical text. Together with the revelatory events themselves this criterion was understood to be part of the textuality of the biblical documents. See further Skarsaune, 'Hvilket lys kaster NT's kanonhistorie over teologihistorien i det 1. århundre?'. Cf also Young, *Biblical Exegesis and the Formation of Christian Culture*, esp. p. 299, where a form of summary remark is made of the hermeneutics of Bible reading in the early church: 'The most striking thing, in fact, is the consistent way in which the Bible was read in differing context. If commentaries were meant to deal with problems in the text and homilies to focus the more obvious features, still one has an overriding feeling of similarity in the kinds of senses discerned and the "reading strategies" adopted'. For a more comprehensive analysis, see also Hagner, *The Use of the Old and New Testaments in Clement of Rome* (Leiden: Brill, 1973); Hvalvik, *The Struggle for Scripture and Covenant: the purpose of the epistle of Barnabas and Jewish–Christian competition in the second century* (Tübingen: Mohr Siebeck, 1996); and Skarsaune, *The Proof from Prophecy: A Study in Justin Martyr's Proof-Text Tradition: Text-Type, Provenance, Theological Profile* (Leiden: Brill, 1987).

for the new collection of writings soon to be added to the old Scriptures.[120] Both text and interpretation are changed in this process of textual transformation.

The introduction of the system of *nomina sacra* in the Jewish Scriptures, or in so-called testimony sources, containing Christian excerpts of the Scriptures (see Ch. 4), are illustrations of this construction of new text. As a form of Christian textual insignia, the *nomina sacra* highlight a new narrative and meta-narrative structure of the biblical writings (see Ch. 3). The reading and interpretation is here mirrored in the text *qua* text. The act of Christian devotional reading is anticipated in the text itself, and vice versa; that is, a textual and interpretive focus is marked out by these contractions associated with the Name. Consequently, the text cannot easily be treated like any other text, but is best interpreted in line with the indicated textual and theological agenda.[121] In this way non-Christian readings of the text become more difficult. Historically, however, reading strategies closely related to the Christian tradition, like various Gnostic interpretations, have been possible renderings; Gnostic and other readings with alternative christological textual agendas. The supratext made up of the *nomina sacra*, in its turn, is intimately connected to the Christian texture in a broader sense, the theology implicit in the system of the *nomina sacra*, and the various ritual usage of the biblical texts.

Nevertheless, in the reciprocal interaction always occurring between text and reader, the text 'is a somewhat weaker partner which, for instance, is unable to defend itself against violations of its integrity by ideological readers.'[122] From a typically Jewish viewpoint the Christian formation of biblical texts and attribution of textual meaning have been regarded as ideological from the very start. From another perspective, this change of textuality and reading can be viewed, more amply, as a natural consequence due to the historical appearance of the church within Israel. Robert Jenson comments in this connection on the problem of scriptural belonging:

> [T]he canon of Israel's Scripture is for the church a sheer *given*. As the apostles are an underivable condition of the existence of the church, so Israel's book is an underivable condition for the existence of the apostolate. It is perhaps not

---

[120] Cf. Irenaeus' phrasing in *Adv. Haer.* IV, 26.1 (ANF 1:496): 'For every prophecy, before its fulfillment, is to men [full of] enigmas and ambiguities. But when the time has arrived, and the prediction has come to pass, then the prophecies have a clear and certain exposition.'

[121] See Chs 1–5.

[122] Jeanrond, *Theological Hermeneutics*, 7.

strictly correct even to say that the church 'received' Israel's Scripture, since this Scripture was antecedently constitutive for the apostles' relation to their Lord and so for the existence of the church.[123]

The Scriptures came to stand as an underivable condition for the church in a dialectical relation to that same church. When the church – creatively seeking Christ in its prophetical texts – increasingly became more rooted in regard to its scriptural foundations, it simultaneously affected the texts as texts. In this process, text and communal reading came to mutually affect one another, even to the extent of editorial changes of the old Scriptures.[124] As a result, a new, specifically ecclesial text emerged, which was not identical to the Jewish writings.

This whole enterprise resulted in a restructuring, a reorganizing and eventually a natural growth of the church's Scriptures. In this process the probable usage of testimony collections, the codex as new book format, the salvation-historical outline and narrative framework provided by the Rule of Faith, the system of the *nomina sacra*, the rich intertextual exchange between the old and the new scriptural text corpora, as well as the time factor helped in the formation of the new canon.

Hence, the Scriptures shared between synagogue and church from early on came to have largely different canonical functions. As a corpus of Sacred Scripture they were partly read and interpreted out of two mutually exclusivating concerns. This difference in canonical conception soon gave rise to mutual suspicion towards one another. Influential Christians maintained that the Scriptures were theirs and that the Jewish leaders had misunderstood them, and the other way around.[125] The Scriptures of the 'Old Testament' were frequently used *as a Christian book*, as a christological proof-text. The prophecy-fulfilment scheme out of which it was read and interpreted differed from Jewish understandings of Scripture. The Christian view of the events, narratives and figures presented in the Scriptures varied to such an extent from that of the synagogue that a different understanding of canon soon emerged.

---

[123] Jenson, *Systematic Theology*, vol. 1: *The Triune God* (New York: Oxford University Press, 1997), 30. See also Theissen, *A Theory of Primitive Christian Religion*, 261; and Jenson, *Systematic Theology*, vol. 1, 30, n. 23.

[124] In some measure this textual interplay still takes place in Christian communities.

[125] See, e.g. Hvalvik, *The Struggle for Scripture and Covenant*.

This ecclesial understanding did not only embrace a new notion of the body of Scriptures shared with the Jews, but the shape of this canon was eventually enlarged and complemented with specifically Christian Scriptures. At face value, such a formal addition of new writings to the old Scriptures may seem strange, bearing in mind the rigorous notion of Holy Writ developed within early Judaism and continued within the church.

By examining the underlying stimuli for this new idea of canon, the pattern of a new Christian understanding can be elucidated. In order to grasp the textual shaping and reshaping at stake, a broad contextualization of the canon within the life and teaching of the community is necessary. Ritual and ideational elements are involved, as well as a novel conception of the Christian Bible as *Urliteratur* (cf. section 9.5.3).

6.8 Conclusion

What is a text? Is there a particular textuality tied up with biblical canonicity? And is the concept of text useful for analysing the canon?

Taking into account the results from Chapters 2 to 5 on some specific features of biblical textuality, this chapter, though far from being comprehensive, focuses on a broader notion of textuality. The following issues are treated:

When we discuss biblical canonicity, we must be attentive to the issue of the textual whole. Despite recurring attempts at deconstructing this particular text, it still constitutes a reality in the church, society and academy alike.

The disparate collections of writings forming the Bible are held together in a multitude of ways, not least by some very strong textual bonds. In this study, several past and present questions on the canon, derived from this 'bonding activity', arise. In the present chapter I have particularly focused on the character of the biblical texts as texts. In their capacity as canonical and classical writings, these texts stand on their own. That is to say, their main objective is not to refer back to the original speech or speech situation, but to make up a meaningful whole precisely as texts. Although segments of this written body of teaching, narrative and communication pertain as well to the original speech situation, having the character of notes or momentary accounts, the text as it now stands has attained status as literature. However, as shown in Chapter 5, even in its capacity as oral account, especially in its relation to the early orally transmitted gospel, it has textual character. That is, it largely belongs to the category of 'oral text'.

What is a text? As a meaningful and unified whole, with a beginning and an end, a text expresses thematic unity through grammar and semantic progression. Literary texts, such as the biblical accounts, are intended precisely as texts. This means that we point to them as something that 'stands written'. A 'text' in this sense means what the word literally says: 'a woven texture that holds together'. In this way, the text largely provides its own context of interpretation. With respect to the material dimension of the biblical writings as texts, they are held together by their book cover or binding which acts as a form of textual 'glue'. Furthermore, several other elements have similar functions, such as the narrative and thematic progression, cross-references, traditions, rituals, theologies and so forth, all variously tied to this scriptural corpus of writings that help constitute the text as text. This means that the biblical text can easily refer to its own literary presentation as a meaningful whole. Even the canonical process, through which the text and its normative interpretations come into existence, should be considered in this regard. The parts of the biblical account viewed as canon can be understood in light of this process, which expresses the textual whole.

I have argued that the grasp of the *scopus* – the principal intention, the central point of view – is crucial when trying to understand the biblical text. By assuming structure and meaning as well as the centring in a midpoint, the grasp of the *scopus* forms the basis for the endless fine tuning involved in understanding. The *scopus*, i.e. the subject matter being anticipated, together with the textual whole, 'forces' the ordering of the sentences into the text. Therefore the *scopus*, with regard to the Scriptures in their service as canon for the church, needs to be embraced in order to make a sensible interpretation of the biblical account, seen as a whole. This is a matter of harmonizing the whole and the parts, the scriptural midpoint and Scripture's circumscription. That is to say, the canonical shape is related to the *scopus* and vice versa.

Apart from the texts themselves, communities and readers are, of course, involved in the process of textual understanding. Typical readers are formed by their respective interpretive communities and approach individual books or passages of the Bible with the expectation of contextuality and coherence. They anticipate and expect that these are exteriorly printed together and interiorly deal with a thematically unified area. Here, the horizon of the text *qua* text constitutes a primary choice of context, and not that of history or some other context of interpretation, where the text as text is placed in the background.

When dealing with texts, however, the horizon of the text is always profiled against that of its readers. For this reason, there is never such a thing as a purely objective text or reader. None the less, in the process of understanding, the textual meaning should be sought, letting the otherness of the text become the focal point against the readers' own fore-meanings and prejudices. In this encounter, it is most important to become aware of one's own bias, so that the text can present itself in all its otherness, and so assert its own truth against one's own fore-meanings. The interpreter may even be said to have a primary responsibility towards the text in this respect, and to the text's otherness. So, appropriate projections and anticipations, on the part of the reader, may be confirmed by what the text says, in the constant task of understanding.

Contrary to popular view, written tradition, in the above sense, is never a fragment of a past world. In the act of reception, it has raised itself beyond past history into the sphere of the meaning that it expresses. This aspect of written tradition is, of course, involved also in the textual transmission taking place through the canonizing process, in the understanding of the biblical texts addressing the Christian community. Again, in contrast to appropriate attempts at understanding texts (e.g. as pertaining to the canon formation process) the arbitrariness of applying inappropriate fore-meanings comes to nothing in being worked out. With this in mind when considering the ecclesial canonizing of Scripture, we can say that the (emergent) canon does not persist only because of the 'inertia' of what once existed, but it needs to be affirmed, embraced and cultivated by present communities and readers alike. Thus, in the midst of the great variety of interpretive communities being addressed, canonization – and canonical reading – still to some degree takes place centuries after the close of the Apostolic Age.[126]

---

[126] Cf. Ch. 2, n. 31.

As textual understanding presumes a living relationship between the interpreter and the text, scriptural hermeneutics also presupposes a relationship to the content of the Bible. Five rules of such hermeneutics engaging both text and community are set forth (by Jenson): 1) Scripture is a whole; 2) Scripture is a whole only because it is one long narrative; 3) To be able to follow the single story and grasp Scripture whole, the interpreter needs to know the story's general plot and *dramatis personae*; 4) It is the church that knows this plot and *dramatis personae* of the scriptural narrative, since the church is one continuous community with the story's actors and narrators; and 5) The church's antecedent knowledge of Scripture's plot and *dramatis personae,* enabling a reading of the Bible as a whole, is contained in the Rule of Faith – the canon that the church propounds and teaches to her members regarding how to think and talk as Christians.

To conclude, the texts of the biblical canon are viewed as a theologically defined literary unit.

Part Three

Performative Aspects of the Canon

7

Canon and Ritual Interaction

In Part Two I first analysed some specific characteristics of biblical textuality and then proceeded to a general treatment of textuality, as applied to the canon. I will now focus on another closely related feature, namely the specific genre of the biblical writings as ritual communal texts, by and large covered by the notion of Scripture. Being expressed through the emergence of this specific textual and ritual genre are ever new experiences of the Scriptures as Scriptures. Ritual practice of the Christian Scriptures was a primary reason why further writings could be added to eventually form the New Testament. Such usage involved both redactional alterations in already accepted writings and the addition of new books. So, a development in the concept of canon took place in the first and second centuries due to ceremonial and other ritual usage, not only regarding the New Testament but also with reference to the Old.[1] In this chapter I shall address ritual elements that were and still are partaking when apprehending the canon. If the canon is largely to be understood within a liturgical context, how will that affect the understanding and experience of the textuality of the canon? To what extent can the canonical text be said to be disintegrated, incomplete or even deconstructed if isolated from its place of origin – Scripture's home – the worship of the Christian assembly?

---

[1] Beckwith, *The Old Testament Canon of the New Testament Church and its Background in Early Judaism* (Grand Rapids: Eerdmans, 1985), 71; Hengel and Deines, *Die Septuaginta als 'christliche Schriftensammlung' und das Problem ihres Kanons* (Freiburg im Breisgau: Herder and Göttingen: Vandenhoeck & Ruprecht, 1992).

7.1 New experiences of the Scriptures as Scriptures

There are several reasons why the category of experience is crucial for understanding what took place from earliest times in Christian congregations.[2] Experience was central for the hermeneutical and ritual changes that were to take place before and parallel with the gospel tradition being written down, and so – by the continuous ecclesial act of scriptural interpretation – making the presence of the church's past of unique revelatory experience into living meaning.[3] The gospel tradition came to represent a new communal identity with regard to the church's Jewish heritage. As Larry Hurtado has given much emphasis lately, 'revelatory religious experiences were significant factors in generating perhaps the most distinctive religious innovation characteristic of early Christianity: the cultic veneration of Jesus.'[4] In fact, the emergence of the new, specifically Christian Scriptures constitutes an integral part of this cultic innovation. In addition to this, when trying to understand today the authoritative collection of writings held as canonical, such experiences, along with their cultic setting(s), stand out as pivotal. These are still revelatory experiences, made by the church, closely related to this collection of scriptural witnesses, and, in the end, as with every communal experience, also by the individual.[5] Thus, the much cited statement by William Wrede, in which he classifies the canon as a dogmatic concept, confirms, in its own way, this experiential dimension of scriptural canonicity.

Wrede holds that anyone who treats early Christian writings as canonical in historical work places him- or herself under the authority of the early church.[6] This view of the concept's authoritative impact, however, even if not entirely wrong, does not get to the heart of regular canonical functioning as experienced in the churches. The biblical texts as a classic literary unit, with its rich web of communal textual meaning, carry an authority and

---

[2] See, e.g. Johnson, *Religious Experience in Earliest Christianity: A Missing Dimension in New Testament Studies* (Minneapolis: Fortress, 1998); and Hurtado, 'Religious Experience and Religious Innovation in the New Testament', *JR* 80 (2000): 183–205.

[3] Cf. Gadamer, *TM*, 164.

[4] Hurtado, 'Religious Experience and Religious Innovation in the New Testament', 184.

[5] Gadamer, *TM*, 351. Cf. Ch. 1, n. 8, on the canon as sign.

[6] Wrede, 'The Tasks and Methods of 'New Testament Theology'', in *The Nature of New Testament Theology. The Contribution of William Wrede and Adolf Schlatter*, ed. R. Morgan (SBT Second Series 25; London: 1973 [1897]), 68–116. Cf. Räisänen, *Beyond New Testament Theology: a Story and a Programme* (London, Philadelphia: SCM and Trinity Press, 2nd edn, 2000 [1990]), 21.

integrity that effective-historically come as part of their continual reception by contemporary liturgical and scholarly communities. This is at the same time an ongoing ecclesial experience of the same texts as canonical; that is to say, as textually and ritually belonging together as the authoritative collection of classic communal writings they prove themselves to be.

None the less, what Wrede – indirectly – in fact discusses is a new experience associated with these writings, turning them into a new object, clearly distinguished from the canon as it is experienced, transmitted and revered by mainstream Christianity. Instead, he chooses to study the biblical writings outside their ecclesial textual, liturgical and theological setting. A new modern academic experience – instead of the Christian cultic – is connected to these writings. On one level this is comparable to that taking place in the early church when the Jewish Scriptures turn Christian, and becoming, in an expanded and modified form, experienced and received as canon for the church. In both these widely different instances – for Wrede in his treatment of the Christian biblical canon, and in the case of the early church's modification of the old scriptural canon – we notice that the experiences made are initially experiences of negation.[7] Something is not what it was supposed to be, and so experienced anew, re-categorized, 'decanonized' and 'recanonized', in order to fit into the new context of appropriating these texts. As Gadamer points out: 'In view of the experience that we have of another object, both things change – our knowledge and its object. We know better now, and that means that the object itself "does not pass the test." The new object contains the truth about the old one.'[8] This is true – on the part of the church – especially of the Scriptures of the Christian new covenant in their connection to the Scriptures of Judaism. It is also true of the New Testament in its relation to the Old Testament. In fact, every new experience of the Scriptures, in its own way, not only makes their reception, but also what is received, into something novel for the one experiencing. In short, the Scriptures acquire ever new meaning also for the faith community, as experienced not least through ritual mediation.

---

[7] Cf., e.g. how the Christian Scriptures 'with their names' were ritually problematic from the viewpoint of the synagogue, Barton, *The Spirit and the Letter: Studies in the Biblical Canon* (London: SPCK, 1997), 118.

[8] Gadamer, *TM*, 354.

The biblical canon, although in principle closed within itself, is still functioning as if it was open toward the experience of the reader/listener, in whom it achieves its whole significance.[9] None the less, when a radical breach with the church's ritual and dogmatic tradition presents itself, as in the critical programme of historical objectivism outlined by Wrede, it can be explained by a similar hermeneutic process. The difference, however, is a clear discontinuity with the church's liturgical contextualization (broadly understood) – that is, a crucial part of the over-arching frame of reference by which the religious uses of biblical language become intelligible in the first place.[10] In Gadamer's phrasing: 'No one will be able to suppose that for religious truth the performance of the ritual is inessential.'[11] Rather, like the functions of material (such as ink and paper/papyrus) and ideational canonical dimensions, ritual is part of the coming-into-existence of the work of the canon itself: its being continuously used in corporate worship. Because 'it is in the performance and only in it – as we see most clearly in the case of music – that we encounter the work itself, as the divine is encountered in the religious rite.'[12] The bulk of the canon as an ecclesiastical work not only originated in, but also was arguably designed for, the continuing weekly and daily performance of the divine reading,[13] and thereby ritually and otherwise interpenetrating communal activity as a whole. Without such performance – which is certainly part of Scripture's essential being – the canon is not really encountered at all. To this extent Wrede and his modern followers are correct in their judgement on the canon in historical work.

7.2 Where text and ritual meet

Now, there are also other ways of being historical without losing either the textual or the ritual communal dimensions in sight. As shown in Part Two, due to the reverence accorded the divine name in the Christian assembly,

---

[9] Cf. ibid., 109.
[10] Cf. Thiselton, *Language Liturgy and Meaning* (Bramcote Nottingham: Grove Books, 1986), 4.
[11] Gadamer, *TM*, 116.
[12] Ibid.
[13] Regarding the Gospels, see, e.g. Hengel, *The Four Gospels and the One Gospel of Jesus Christ* (London: SCM, 2000), 116.

the textual markers made up by the *nomina sacra* were introduced into the biblical writings. The convention of demarcating the *nomina sacra* by means of contraction with a suprascript line indicates their high devotional status in the communities, from the time of their inauguration into the manuscripts in the first (or possibly early second) century AD. As indicated in Chapter 3, the *nomina sacra* here refer back to their origin as expressions of Christ-devotion, typically in dyadic–binitarian and triadic–trinitarian form. As signs,[14] however, they also point forward towards this same communal present and future devotional setting. So, the way these carefully selected names are written, the most important of which are JESUS, CHRIST, LORD, GOD, and SPIRIT (beside the likewise early-appearing CROSS), is *not* 'a purely graphic convention', which 'does not affect the meaning of the texts so written', as John Barton contends.[15] Considering the fact that some words are clearly marked off in the text, that these words obviously are most carefully selected, and that this most specific scribal practice had already become universal in Christian manuscripts by the second century, Barton's statement is hard to defend. Furthermore, as the *nomina sacra* from early on acquire a much wider ritual application, becoming an integral part of Christian art, architectonics and liturgy (e.g. liturgical objects),[16] such appearances both indirectly and directly give these markers in the Bible manuscripts a unique ritual role within the symbolic world of the Christian community.

As the *nomina sacra* are important for the understanding of the Christian Scripture as Scripture, the sacred names here indicated – together with the scriptural text as a whole – reach out even beyond the cultic sphere of the more narrowly defined assembly. In Gadamer's wording:

> Now, the Sacred Scripture does not meet as an arbitrary collection of sayings – passing on a mythical tradition or an artistic epic – but as the Scripture that 'stands written'. As such it belongs in the sphere of worship, that is, Scripture is itself part of the cultural reality, which has set its marks on the whole of our cultural tradition.[17]

---

[14] Cf. n. 5 above.

[15] Barton, *The Spirit and the Letter*, 122. Cf., however, Barton's positive review of the 2005 ThD edition of this present book, *JTS* 58, no. 2 (2007): 619–22.

[16] See, e.g. Weitzmann, *Age of Spirituality: Late Antique and Early Christian Art, Third to Seventh Century* (New York: The Metropolitan Museum of Art, published in association with Princeton University Press, 1979); and section 3.6.3.

[17] Gadamer, *Gesammelte Werke* 8, 178f. My trans.

The crucial turning point for this ritual paradigm as seen in relation to Jewish worship is, of course, the event of Jesus and the Christ-devotion of the nascent church. Ritually as well as textually, the *nomina sacra* set the Scriptures apart as Christian Scriptures; and further,

> the fact that Christian scribes applied the same convention in writing Old Testament texts is one clear indication that they had begun to treat Old and New Testament books as sacred texts in much the same sense – transferring special features of the New Testament back on to the Old. This is a further example of how 'canonization' could work in the reverse direction from that usually expected.[18]

Here text and ritual meet in a multidimensional way, with the old Scriptures essentially affecting the new, specifically Christian writings, and the other way around. The holiness of the Jewish Scriptures is textually and thereby liturgically affecting the new Christian Scriptures (as the two text corpora are similarly and complementarily used in worship).[19] And vice versa, special features of the 'New Testament' (and the Christian 'OT') texts are 'read back' onto the Law and the Prophets – most noteworthy, the Greek scribal *nomina sacra* practice – causing textual modifications in the emerging standard text of the Christian Greek 'Old Testament'. From a Jewish viewpoint, this amounts to a ritual alteration as well, directly affecting the more specific reverence of the Hebrew Tetragrammaton. For both Jews and Christians, certain physical features of the text were used to express its sacredness. For Christians this is indicated by the presence on the page of *nomina sacra*. Barton, referring to John Muddiman, interestingly suggests that 'the Christians who devised the system of *nomina sacra* were engaged in the task of "reinvent[ing] the sacred institutions of Judaism" – providing a Christian equivalent for the Name in Judaism.'[20] He further argues that it would be characteristic that the equivalent is a kind of inversion, so that sanctity is marked by contracting a word. For Jews, instead, it is registered by the care with which the whole word is copied.[21]

As part of the process of canonization, these and other redactional (or scribal/editorial) innovations are, most probably, also liturgically motivated.

---

[18] Barton, *The Spirit and the Letter*, 122f.
[19] Worship here includes divine lection, liturgy and homily.
[20] Barton, *The Spirit and the Letter*, 123.
[21] Ibid.

As Theodor Zahn puts it: 'What was later named "canonical", was originally called "read in corporate worship".[22] That is, the new Scriptures were put on a par with the Jewish Scriptures in a most particular way: They were read, or otherwise used, beside the 'OT' Scriptures on a regular basis in Christian worship. The primary *locus* of the Scriptures, including the emerging new Scriptures, therefore, was and is corporate worship. When seriously considering this ritual embeddedness of the canon, it is not clearly the case any longer that 'the books that came to be the Bible did not start off as books of the Bible'.[23] On the contrary, I would argue, in corporate worship it is precisely, or at least as a rule, the biblical books that are read out aloud as part of the common scriptural reading. The four Gospels were, it seems, even primarily composed for liturgical reading.[24] So, even if they are not books of the Bible in the strict sense, they have functionally already attained the most typical scriptural characteristics: to be recited in the Liturgy of the Word,[25] and to 'stand written', gradually turning into a self-signifying textual unity alongside the Scriptures of Judaism (see sections 6.1 and 6.3). Thus, the books that came to be the Bible started off, at least in part, as books with a unique status.

7.3 The genre of liturgical texts

As underlined in the previous chapter, the expectation of the reader in the mind of the writer helps create the genre of the text.[26] In the case of the biblical writings, they embrace the expectations implicit in these texts, added to and integrated into the canon – namely the expectations created by and associated with Holy Scripture. Both the readers and the liturgical framing within the faith community in effect help establish this genre of Scripture.

---

[22] Zahn, *Einige Bemerkungen zu Adolf Harnack's Prüfung der Geschichte des neutestamentlichen Kanons*, I/1 (Erlangen and Leipzig: A. Deichert'sche Verlagshandlung Nachf. [Georg Böhme] 1889), 14. My trans.

[23] Ulrich, 'The Notion and Definition of Canon', in *The Canon Debate*, (eds) L. M. McDonald and J. A. Sanders (Peabody, MA: Hendrickson, 2002), 35.

[24] Cf. Hengel, *The Four Gospels and the One Gospel of Jesus Christ*, 116.

[25] Cf. Lathrop (*Holy Things: A Liturgical Theology* [Minneapolis: Fortress, 1993], 10), who points to the liturgy as the place of origin for the Bible as a single book. Cf. sections 7.5 and 7.6.

[26] See, e.g. Watson, ed., *The Open Text* (London: SCM, 1993); Murphy, 'Elements of a Semiotic Theory of Religion', *Method & Theory in the Study of Religion* 15 (2003).

In an article written in 2000, Martin Stringer argues for an expanded view of textuality and the 'world of the text', as outlined by Paul Ricoeur. According to Stringer, as the practice of 'reading' is central to Ricoeur's understanding of the text, the interpretation that takes place when biblical texts are read in liturgy affects the basic comprehension of what should be meant by the 'world of the text'. This 'world' is definitely affected by the liturgical context. To this extent liturgical texts are not 'designed to be read as books, they are designed to be performed'.[27] Stringer states that it is by interacting with the 'world' of the liturgical text, as it is gradually revealed within the liturgical performance, that the self-understanding of the participant of the liturgy is transformed within the rite.[28] By postulating this modified understanding of textuality, the Bible, when performed in corporate worship, is to be understood as something rather different from what we normally understand by the concept of book or the textuality of a book. Instead we are dealing with a form of textuality that is 'gradually revealed within the liturgical performance'. As the liturgy is continuously repeated and often designed for an annual calendrical cycle, the concept of textuality is 'gradually revealed' also within a yet larger liturgical frame. Nevertheless, as I shall argue below (section 7.7.9), yet another dimension comes with such a gradually revealed notion of textuality. Within the scope of a one-year or a three-year cycle, Stringer's point is fully relevant. However, on a wider timescale the whole cycle will already have been completed and is thus repeated over and over again. Hence, the textual whole along with its expectations will be known already by a majority of the listeners. Moreover, the textual whole, at least as far as the basics of Christian faith and narrative go, is already known by the baptized adult portion of the community. In view of these observations we are faced with a most specific form of biblical textuality within this ecclesial liturgical setting.

---

[27] Stringer, 'Text, Context and Performance: Hermeneutics and the Study of Worship', *Scottish Journal of Theology* 52 (2000): 370.

[28] Ibid.

7.4 Scripture and liturgical worship

The liturgical theologian Geoffrey Wainwright compares the Bible as an actual book to some kind of sacrament of the word of God, in its resting position and, even more, in its liturgical use. Making use of scholastic categories, the printed and bound Bible is the *sacramentum tantum*, the external sign, like the bread and wine at the eucharist; the substantial or ideational content of the Bible is the *sacramentum et res*, the thing as signified, like the eucharistic body and blood of Christ. The *res sacramenti*, 'the purpose or fruit', Wainwright comments, 'is in both cases the communion of the Church with the God who gives himself to us in Christ.'[29]

This vision of the Bible might seem odd to a late-modern eye, much due to the sharp dividing line drawn by Modernism between a liturgical and an historical scholarly understanding of the biblical text. The Bible as book, however, cannot easily be compared with any other book or book genre, precisely because of its rootedness in the particular liturgy of the Christian community. To the extent that this rootedness is overlooked – which, of course, may be appropriate in some instances – other ways of viewing the Bible, e.g. *as literature* or *as an object of comparative religion*, suggest themselves more easily.

Concerning the deeply rooted liturgical dimensions of the Scriptures, it is the task of theology and critical scholarship to interpret the church's 'more or less raw experience of its use of the Scriptures in the liturgy.'[30] But, as Wainwright rightly emphasizes, the other direction is equally important. The church's experience of its writings in the liturgy should set one of the perspectives from which the Scriptures are considered by the biblical scholar as he or she seeks their meaning, and by the systematic theologian attempting to build the scriptural component into his/her thinking.[31] At first, this perspective seems to present only one set of interpretations – that of the church – but it is in fact broader than that. From a reception-historical point of view, the ecclesiastical understanding of the Scriptures

---

[29] Wainwright, *Doxology: The Praise of God in Worship, Doctrine and Life* (London: Epworth, 1980, 1982), 149f.
[30] Ibid., 150
[31] Ibid.

must always somehow be taken into account, irrespective of how the Bible has been received in various religious, societal or academic contexts. That such considerations are not only concerned with origin or with history is indicated by the continuous attendance of these writings in the church's liturgy, and even more so by 'the presence of the liturgy in the scriptures'.[32] Concerning the large bulk of the biblical writings, scholars have repeatedly pointed out their embeddedness in the cultic liturgies of the temple and/or the liturgical practices of the synagogue and the church.[33] On these texts' overall belonging – liturgically and otherwise – within the Jewish and Christian settings, Werner Jeanrond comments: 'the biblical texts stand firmly within the Jewish and Christian traditions of responding to God's call in human history. Every effort to isolate these texts from these concrete traditions will miss their true spiritual potential'.[34] Referring to David Tracy, Jeanrond remarks that

> we always see 'Scripture within tradition', because every biblical text points to its own context out of which it originally emerged.
>   The biblical texts are witnesses from within our traditions of responding to God's call in Israel and in Jesus Christ. For the reader they function as bridges between God's previous self-manifestations and his presence today.[35]

This very basic function, provided by the coming-into-being of the Christian Scriptures, is an implication of their continually being read, reflected on and commented on within the context of worship.[36] The common decontextualization within the academy of these writings with regard to their ritual embeddedness, therefore, needs to be reassessed from a theological and liturgical-theological viewpoint. A recent attempt at such reassessment has been made by Robert Jenson in his *Systematic Theology*, where he chooses to underscore the necessary interaction between the use and interpretation of the Scriptures, on the one hand, and the continuing communal tradition, on

---

[32] Ibid.
[33] Cf. ibid., 150–63.
[34] Jeanrond, *Call and Response: The Challenge of Christian Life* (Dublin: Gill & Macmillan, 1995), 128f.
[35] Ibid.
[36] Ibid., 129: In this way, Jeanrond maintains, 'they [the scriptures] provide us with a language through which we can relate to God. In this sense they are inexhaustible. They offer the Christian believer and the Christian community at the same time information, inspiration, examples, paradigms, challenge, companionship, admonition, comfort, and spiritual instruction. They are then the primary resource of all Christian renewal. Yet they are not the only resource.'

the other.[37] Due to their history of effects, the primary context for the majority of the canonical writings is still the ecclesiastical ritual context in which and out of which they have emerged, precisely *as canon* for the particular ritual setting of the Christian assembly. Without this ecclesiastical context the biblical text is devoid of textual aspects shared also by its authors/redactors and primary addressees/readers, i.e. in both cases (representatives of) the Christian community.

7.5 *Lex orandi, lex credendi*

The Latin tag *lex orandi, lex credendi* can be understood in two ways. The most common interpretation is the one that makes prayer a norm for belief. From a grammatical point of view, however, the opposite direction is also possible: the Rule of Faith being the norm for prayer: 'what must be believed governs what may and should be prayed'.[38] The critical mutuality of the rule of prayer and the rule of belief should, as Geoffrey Wainwright points out, not be underestimated. Not least when seeking to reconstruct the history of the canon, the critical interdependence of the two becomes crucial. The liturgical theologian Gordon Lathrop also underscores this mutuality, so important for a dynamic understanding of the concept of canon:

> Genuine authority in the Christian community is always grounded in the Bible, the authoritative witness to Christian faith that these voices are interpreting. But, again, the Bible most clearly … exhibits its authority in the gathering where it is read, sung, preached, and enacted. … the canon … is none other than the list of books for reading and preaching in the assembly, as that list is accepted in the catholic church. That we have a Bible and consider it authoritative may be interpreted as one primary example of the 'rule of

---

[37] As to the relevance of these writings for today's church, the continuous liturgy of the Christian assembly provides a crucial mediating function. See Jenson, *Systematic Theology*, vol. 2: *The Works of God* (New York, Oxford: Oxford University Press, 1999), 280: 'our present effort to understand a handed-down text cannot be hopeless, since it is merely the further appropriation of a continuing communal tradition within which we antecedently live. Past and present do not need to be bridged before understanding can begin, since they are always already mediated by the continuity of the community's language and discourse'. And further, ibid., 297f. (cf. citation, section 1.3.3).

[38] Wainwright, *Doxology*, 218.

prayer,' the practice and order of the Christian assembly, establishing the 'rule of believing.'[39]

When studying the canonical process of the New Testament writings, it is obvious that their regular usage established in corporate worship eventually affected their general communal reception as sacral writings. To some degree this development can also be understood as a process of sacralization.

7.6 Sacralizing the Christian Scriptures

As early as 1898, Henri Hubert and Marcel Mauss demonstrated how effectively ritual activities sacralize things, people or events. They inverted the contemporary scholarly agenda by tracing how religious phenomena and ideas derived from social activities.[40] Of course, also with regard to the early canonical process, various ways of understanding it are available, depending on what aspects of canonicity are considered to be fundamental. The dialogue between Theodor Zahn and Adolf von Harnack on the canon reflects this. In von Harnack's view, in order for a written text to be regarded canonical, it needs to be ascribed the attribution 'scriptural'. On the other hand, for Zahn, who holds this epithet to be merely a dogmatic label, calling a text 'scriptural' does not add anything essential to the basic fact that the writing in question is being read out aloud in corporate worship. However, it may be possible, in the end, to harmonize Zahn's and von Harnack's different perspectives on the origins of the Christian canon.[41] The following liturgical-theological observations by Gordon Lathrop seem to be rewarding in this regard:

---

[39] Lathrop, *Holy Things*, 9. Cf. Hengel, 'Eye-witness memory and the writing of the Gospels', in *The Written Gospel*, (eds) M. Bockmuehl and D. A. Hagner (Cambridge: Cambridge University Press, 2005), 92: '[T]he wishes, questions and impulses of the *hearers* (more than the readers) influenced the formation of the Gospels and their preceding tradition. Most Christians, who primarily came from the lower classes, were probably illiterate and were dependent upon hearing the report or reading in worship. The Gospels, at least Mark, Matthew and John, were written in the first place for worship. The hearers and – in the second place – the readers should place themselves in "the story of Jesus", should become "simultaneous" with it, should make his cause their own, although one always remained conscious of the uniqueness and singularity of Jesus and thus also of the historical distance.'

[40] Hubert and Mauss, *Sacrifice: Its Nature and Function* (Chicago: University Press of Chicago, 1981 [1898]); cf. Bell, *Ritual Theory, Ritual Practice* (New York and Oxford: Oxford University Press, 1992), 15.

[41] To some degree this is carried out in Barton, *The Spirit and the Letter*, 1ff.

[t]he fact that there is a single book called the Bible arises from the liturgy. …
That the texts are required to speak Christ in the assembly is, for the Christian,
the unity of the Bible. Diverse texts, different voices, are all brought to this single
task. The church hears four Gospels, and around them it hears many other
texts, and believes it encounters Christ in their midst. On any given Sunday, the
church usually hears more than one reading, the diverse words supplementing,
criticizing, breaking each other.[42]

Here something important pertaining to liturgy and christology is said about
how the Jewish and the Christian Scriptures come to constitute one single
scriptural entity. My thesis – which coincides with von Harnack's proposal – is
that we have the nucleus of the New Testament in the formula *the Scriptures
and the Lord* (see section 1.2.1), and that the Christian biblical canon as a
whole, to a large degree, may be perceived out of the liturgical components
implied in this formula.

Liturgy, e.g. teaches us that the full scriptural status attained by the 'New
Testament' writings did not occur all of a sudden, as von Harnack, despite his
above-mentioned thesis, seems to indicate.[43] Instead, 'Christ the Lord' is from
the outset of Christian worship understood to be present in the world of the
'Old Testament', and, all along, the real meaning of the Jewish Scriptures was
for the church a christological one.[44] As the Old Testament, by the earliest
Christian 'exegetes', is already believed to contain the gospel, it is virtually 'a
New Testament itself, once it is read through properly enlightened, that is,
Christian eyes.'[45] In the light of such observations, the formula *the Scriptures
and the Lord* appropriately takes into account dimensions of the canonizing
process that otherwise risk to be neglected. With this formula in view, we
can also more easily appreciate Theodor Zahn's assessment postulating the
existence of a collection of 'New Testament' writings already from the late
first/early second centuries on. In Zahn's view, the new collection was used as
part of the Liturgy of the Word alongside the christologically expounded 'Old
Testament'.

The unity of the Scriptures, the scriptural status, and, first and foremost, the
christological reading, were from the viewpoint of the divine lection, already,

---

[42] Lathrop, *Holy Things*, 175f.
[43] Harnack, *Lehrbuch der Dogmengeschichte*, vol. 1 (Tübingen: Mohr Siebeck, 1909).
[44] Cf Barton, *The Spirit and the Letter*, 75.
[45] Ibid., 76.

more or less, presupposed. The connection between dogma (cf. the dogmatic and ritual label 'scriptural') and liturgy (such as the established usage of Scripture), and the point where they both meet – namely in christological reading – once again confirms the close interaction between the emerging canon and corporate worship.

Few theologians have worked as thoroughly as Alexander Schmemann to highlight the stress laid on the organic connection between theology and liturgical experience by the Fathers of the Patristic Age. For them the liturgical tradition is the natural milieu for theology, 'its self-evident term of reference'. It is not an '*object* of theological inquiry and definition, but rather the living source and the ultimate criterion of all Christian thought'. Schmemann's theological motive is here in agreement with Irenaeus' famous *dictum*: 'Our opinion is in accordance with the Eucharist, and the Eucharist in turn establishes our opinion' (*Adv. Haer.* IV, 18.5).[46]

Nevertheless, when discussing the interaction between the canonical process and corporate worship, an additional remark may be made. The current view, that a writing, in order to become a candidate for canonicity, must have been read in worship, cannot be said to have been present in the early Christian communities. Not all portions of the Old Testament were normally read aloud in the assembly, and, similarly, in the case of the Book of Revelation, it did not attain the same status in worship as many other of the New Testament writings. This was particularly so in the East. Perhaps this might partly explain its ambivalent canonical status. However, there is nothing extraordinary within a Jewish or Christian context about having writings included in the canon which are not part of the public reading.[47] Karl-Heinz Ohlig is therefore overstating the case when he claims that: 'negatively it can be said, in any case, that Scriptures, found to be of no use in worship, were thereby excluded from the canon.'[48] Observations made by Roger Beckwith with reference to the Old Testament also confirm variation in this respect among the canonical Scriptures. Beckwith notes that 'the primary

---

[46] Fisch, *Liturgy and Tradition: Theological Reflections of Alexander Schmeemann* (Crestwood, New York: St Vladimir's Seminary Press, 1990), 12.

[47] See, e.g. Beckwith, *The Old Testament Canon*.

[48] Ohlig, *Die theologische Begründung des neutestamentlichen Kanons in der alten Kirche* (Düsseldorf: Patmos-Verlag, 1972), 297.

reason for laying up books in the Temple was not their liturgical usefulness but their sanctity'.[49]

7.7 The Jewish Scriptures as prototype

7.7.1 The Christian struggle for the Scriptures with the synagogue

In the first half of the second century the church and the synagogue became further engaged in a struggle that had started some decades earlier. This struggle largely came to focus on the right for Scripture and covenant. According to large portions of the church, the Scriptures as well as the covenant now belonged to them. The intolerance in the discussions, and the antagonism that followed, came to affect the sacral institutions of the church that had started to form. It is during this period that the Christians begin to refer to their own writings as 'Scripture'.

Because of this polarization between Jews and Christians, Jewish and Christian, around AD 140, Marcion is ripe for his project of totally separating the two (or more) covenants. In his view, the old Scriptures, used by the church, are about another God, the Creator God of the Jews. Instead, his *Gospel* and *Apostle*, a revised Gospel of Luke and 10 revised Pauline letters, together with his own work *Antitheses*, made up the textual basis for the new Marcionite church. Before the emergence of this particular antagonism between church and synagogue, Marcion's solution of separating the Scriptures and the divinities of the two covenants would have been incomprehensible. But now, because of the new awareness of the subtle relation between the Jewish and the specifically Christian Scriptures – including issues of disagreement on the interpretation of the notions of Israel, covenant and law – these tensions between the two communities were not so easily handled.

Of the early Christian writers, the author of the *Epistle of Barnabas* and Justin Martyr became involved in this antagonism. The position taken in *Barnabas* is that of denying the Jewish covenant altogether. Justin, on the other hand, represents the way the majority church was to proceed by its clear distinction between old and new. Arguably this soon resulted in a twofold

---

[49] Beckwith, *The Old Testament Canon*, 85.

Bible, consisting of an Old and a New Testament. This 'textualization' of the covenant/testament notion in the latter part of the second century – probably already in Melito of Sardis around AD 175 (Euseb. *Hist. Eccl.* IV, 26.12-14)[50] – can be explained as a natural outcome of the conflict with the synagogue over Scripture and covenant. To name the former part of the Christian Scriptures the 'Old Testament' and the latter the 'New Testament' was a distinct way of marking out the Christian assembly as the new and true faith community, with its own divine writings, against its mother religion. Here we approach the heart of the matter: In its search for a new and specific Christian identity, the church felt bound to relate, in multiform ways, to issues such as the Jewish covenant(s), Israel (cf. John 8, Rom. 9.11) and the Torah (cf. Matt. 5.17; Gal. 2.17–5.12).

As the problem of the canon was actualized from time to time, the church's ambivalence, due to its relation to its Jewish roots, was always there. The Christians ceaselessly felt bound to relate to its historical roots, in these ways, to its mother community, although some dominant Christian voices often denied, rather than assented to, these bonds of continuity with its Jewish past. The *Epistle of Barnabas*, Marcion, and later on Martin Luther, Adolf von Harnack and Rudolf Bultmann, are examples of a largely anti-Jewish inclination, in which Christian theologies were framed. As regards the second century, there are highlights of a sometimes very strong anti-Judaism, which – due to its manifold function – also helped to form the orthodox Christian tradition. With Marcion's denial of everything, or nearly everything, Jewish, the church was confronted with a new dilemma, the problem of finding a sound balance in relating to its Jewish heritage. The solutions, as formulated in the *Epistle of Barnabas* or by Marcion, were nothing but betrayals of deep and necessary Christian roots in the Jewish soil.

In fact, the emergence and sacralization of specifically Christian Scripture, such as the Gospel of Matthew, is, on a fundamental level, an outgrowth from these roots (cf. section 9.6). As has already been pointed out, the new canonical process was related to the notion of Scripture present within the

---

[50] Cf. Metzger, *The Canon of the New Testament: Its Origin, Development, and Significance* (Oxford: Clarendon, 1987), 123; and, Trobisch, *The First Edition of the New Testament* (Oxford: Oxford University Press, 2000), 44. *Pace* Campenhausen, *The Formation of the Christian Bible* (Philadelphia: Fortress, 1972), 265.

Jewish community. The canon *as text*, *as book*, *as holy*, *as rule* and *norm*, *as authoritative collection of writings*, *as a list of holy writings* or *as writings designed for divine lection* simply cannot be understood without relating it to the *Sitz im Leben* of the corresponding institutions of Early and Rabbinic Judaism. The introduction of the *nomina sacra* (Ch. 3), the choice of the codex format (Ch. 4), the labelling of the Scriptures as the *Prophets* and, later, the *Old Testament* (Ch. 5), the development of a prophecy-fulfilment scheme, the choice of the particular syntax of narrative Pentateuch Septuagint Greek, as the language of the Synoptic Gospels,[51] and the Septuagint as the inspired Scriptures,[52] are some of the components present in the construal of a specifically Christian canon, which, accordingly, stood in continuity to its Jewish equivalent, the Torah.

Various such strong connections to Second Temple and Rabbinic Judaism call for a close dialogue with Judaism even today, in relating to some central hermeneutical issues that mark out the distinctiveness of the Christian canon. Although Christianity is on its own, it always bears these institutional elements of, at the same time, Judaistic and 'anti-Judaistic' identity markers,[53] which call for continuous dialogue, interpretation, reassessment and elaboration.

---

[51] Walser, *The Greek of the Ancient Synagogue: An Investigation on the Greek of the Septuagint, Pseudepigrapha and the New Testament* (Stockholm: Almqvist & Wiksell International, 2001), 174–84.

[52] Hengel and Deines, *Die Septuaginta als 'christliche Schriftensammlung' und das Problem ihres Kanons*; Müller, *The First Bible of the Church: A Plea for the Septuagint* (Sheffield: Sheffield Academic Press, 1996).

[53] In the church's search for an identity of its own, certain 'anti-Jewish' features can be traced. To some extent an anti-Jewish consciousness and propaganda were felt necessary to the church's development from Jewish sect in the first century to a distinctive *tertium genus* around the middle of the second century. Miriam Taylor touches on this issue, catching the ambivalent mode that the church found itself in when choosing to relate to itself and others through its mother religion. In my view, however, she pushes her argument too far in the following quotes (Taylor, *Anti-Judaism and Early Christian Identity: A Critique of the Scholarly Consensus* [Leiden, New York and Köln: Brill, 1995] , 172, 171): 'The best weapon against Marcion's anti-Judaism, was the church's own brand of anti-Judaism … Marcion's challenge to the church's theological vision compelled the fathers to 'reaffirm' their own notion of an anti-Jewish God and of an anti-Jewish Christ.' Ibid., 171: 'Anti-Judaism played a role in the polemic against Marcion because it was intrinsic to the orthodox church's concepts of God, of Christ, and of the Scriptures, concepts which Marcion challenged directly. The use of the anti-Judaic tradition against Marcion provides confirmation not of a polemic directed at distinct groups, but of the theological foundation of anti-Judaism within the church. Anti-Judaism … was central to Christian self-affirmation not just in an incidental way, but in that it gave coherence and consistency to the theological construct that defined the church as the new Israel. Marcion's view of Christianity challenged and undermined this theological construct directly, and it forced the Christian writers to reaffirm their vision of the creator God, of Jesus as long prophesied Messiah, and of the Scriptures as holy and authoritative.'

7.7.2 Copying the Jewish service of worship

The first Christian congregations were normally, or ideally, a part of the synagogue, and often became only gradually detached from their original Jewish life-setting. Of particular interest to this study is the question to what degree the Jewish liturgy affected Christian worship. Although much is still unclear, striking resemblances between Jewish and Christian corporate worship are likely due to influences that the former exerted on the latter during the first century.[54] In Acts 19.8f. we find an example of a local church, which after its separation from the synagogue stood in close relation to its mother assembly in various ways, and hence probably identified itself as a synagogue.[55]

The scholarly views, however, balance between those who consider an essential continuity from Judaism to Christianity, and those whose emphasis is a radical breach with Jewish practice.[56] In consideration of the scarce material from the first and early second centuries, and the identity of the church as the heir of Judaism, it is still hard not to recognize the seemingly strong bonds of continuity between the Jewish liturgical praxis and the early Christian service of worship (cf., however, section 7.7.4). All, or most, early missionaries were, after all, Jewish-Christians, and they did not intend to leave all their Jewish identity behind. On the contrary, they considered themselves heirs of Judaism in several respects. In addition to this, the Christian movement arose within the matrix of Judaism, where the synagogue provided the context of regular worship. It therefore appears reasonable to describe the Christian house churches as a new class of synagogues, as James (2.2), the author of the *Shepherd* of Hermas (Mandate 11.14), and perhaps Luke, from their different viewpoints, seem to imply.[57]

Of course, there is the possibility to maintain with Walter Bauer that the Scriptures were not used liturgically in the Gentile Pauline communities, where the Jewish influence was thought to be insignificant. Yet, even though those letters by Paul which were addressed to Gentile Christians (Philippians,

---

[54] Beckwith, 'The Jewish Background to Christian Worship', *The Study of Liturgy*, (eds) Cheslyn Jones et al (London: SPCK, rev. edn. 1992), 69.

[55] Ibid., 71.

[56] Bradshaw, *The Search for the Origins of Christian Worship: Sources and Methods for the Study of Early Liturgy* (New York: Oxford University Press, 2002), 33.

[57] See Brox, *Kirchengeschichte des Altertums* (Düsseldorf: Patmos Verlag, 1992), 12f., 110f.

1 Thessalonians, Philemon) lack Paul's otherwise frequent appeal to Scripture, the scepticism of Bauer as to scriptural usage is, as Gamble remarks, drawn entirely from silence.[58] And as Martin Hengel points out,

> [d]idactic writings like Romans, Hebrews and I Clement, but also Barnabas and II Clement, presuppose a regular reading of the LXX in worship; otherwise the recipients would not have been able to understand at all these letters which argued using 'scripture'. Had the writings of the Old Testament been unimportant for early Christian worship, it would not have been possible to use them so intensively in arguments. The same is true of catechetical instruction. Presumably those writings which play an important role in quotations or allusions in the New Testament were also predominantly used in worship. They include the Pentateuch, above all Genesis, Exodus and Deuteronomy; the Psalms, as probably the most important early Christian text; and the Prophets, here primarily Isaiah, but also the others.[59]

That is why the lection of the Jewish Scriptures most probably was taken over by the entire early Christian world.[60] Moreover, for Paul, the great Gentile missionary, the scriptural canon was 'the grand textual matrix'[61] within which the apostle's understanding of the gospel took place, as clearly underlined by Gamble:

> There is scarcely a basic element of Christian teaching that Paul does not refer to scripture. ... The frequency, variety, and subtlety of Paul's recourse to scripture presumes not only that the communities he addressed acknowledged the authority of Jewish scripture, but also that they were sufficiently familiar with it to understand and appreciate his appeals to it ... indeed, 'whatever was written in former days was written for our instruction, so that by steadfastness and the encouragement of the scripture we might have hope' (Rom. 15.4).[62]

---

[58] Gamble, *Books and Readers in the Early Church: a History of Early Christian Texts* (New Haven: Yale University Press, 1995), 212; Harnack, 'Das Alte Testament in den paulinischen Briefen und in den Paulinischen Gemeinden', *SBA* (Phil.-hist. Kl.) (1928), 124–41.

[59] Hengel, *The Four Gospels and the One Gospel of Jesus Christ,* 117. A slightly different account of the earliest Christian use of Scripture is provided by Peter Stuhlmacher, *Wie treibt man Biblische Theologie?* (Neukirchen–Vluyn: Neukirchener, 1995), 61. See also Sundberg, *The Old Testament of the Early Church* (Cambridge: Harvard University Press, 1964); Ellis, T*he Old Testament in Early Christianity: Canon and Interpretation in the Light of Modern Research* (Grand Rapids: Baker, 1991); and Beckwith, *The Old Testament Canon.*

[60] Cf. Collins, *The Birth of the New Testament* (New York: Crossroad, 1993), 105.

[61] Hays, *Echoes of Scripture in the Letters of Paul* (New Haven and London: Yale University Press, 1989), 122.

[62] Gamble, B*ooks and Readers in the Early Church,* 213.

As Gamble concludes, the place in which these communities have been instructed – to be able to experience any encouragement of Scripture – is certainly the service of worship. The thesis that the Scriptures would not have been commonly used in the Gentile-Christian communities of Thessalonica or Philippi becomes improbable also in view of the relatively well-developed system of communications between individual provincial churches (cf. section 4.4).[63] Moreover, the frequent appeal to the Septuagint in Paul's first letter to the partly Gentile-Christian community of Corinth points in the same direction.[64] It is also worth noticing the role of the Jerusalem congregation, which from early on became a significant prototype for the common form of life and worship in other churches.[65] In line with this, Peter Lampe and others have confirmed the extensive Jewish influence on the earliest Christian communities in Rome.[66]

7.7.3 Reference to the Septuagint as canonical text

A typical example of an increased awareness of 'canonical' readings is the eagerness with which Justin fought for what he considered to be the authentic Septuagint reading of Isaiah 7.14. He quotes the Septuagint version ἰδοὺ ἡ παρθένος ἐν γαστρὶ λήψεται (behold the virgin will give birth) several times in his *Dialogue with Trypho*, thereby opposing the competing Jewish rendering ἡ νεανίς (the young woman). Countering the Ebionitic teaching and that of Trypho – Justin's Jewish dialogue partner – on the Messiah being an ἄνθρωπος ἐξ ἀνθρώπου (a man come from man), the Son of David, Justin sets out to 'demonstrate' the virgin birth by his insistence on the Septuagint reading ἡ παρθένος over against the competing ἡ νεανίς.

---

[63] Cf. 1 Thess. 1.8; 1 Cor. 11.16; see also Roberts and Skeat, *The Birth of the Codex* (London: Oxford University Press, 1983), 53, 61; Gamble, *Books and Readers in the Early Church*, 85.

[64] Becker, *Paul and His Churches* (Louisville, KY: Westminster and John Knox, 1993), 161.

[65] See Stuhlmacher, *Biblische Theologie des Neuen Testaments, Band 1 Grundlegung: Von Jesus zu Paulus*; Stuhlmacher seeks a link between the early Christian communities in the dispersion and the house churches of Jerusalem, which, apart from the gatherings in the temple, became the usual organized form of worship (cf. Acts 12.12-17). From early on the Jerusalem congregation became a significant prototype for the common form of life and worship in other churches.

[66] Lampe, *Die stadtrömischen Christen in den ersten beiden Jahrhunderten: Untersuchungen zur Sozialgeschichte* (Tübingen: Mohr Siebeck, 1989); see also Moule, *The Birth of the New Testament* (London: Adam & Charles Black, 1966), 11–32.

In his discussion in the *Dialogue*, he further presupposes a Jewish-Christian consensus regarding the authority of the Septuagint translation of the Seventy. Justin seems to be the first church leader who repeatedly, and with emphasis, points to this legend – apparently independent of the presentation in the *Letter of Aristeas* – which is later, in Irenaeus, more fully elaborated. Justin maintains that the authentic Greek translation is found in the Christian version of the text. As a consequence he accuses the Jews of having interpolated and even removed certain passages from the biblical text. The *Dialogue* (71-3), on Trypho's request, presents four examples of such excisions, by which the Messianic prophesies, in Justin's view, have been undercut. The last of these four examples treats Psalm 95.10 where he accuses the Jews of having cut out ἀπὸ τοῦ ξύλου (from the tree) after the phrasing ὁ κύριος ἐβασί λευσεν (the Lord reigned). However, Justin seems unaware of the fact that here, as elsewhere, it is a matter of Christian interpolations in his own text (i.e. probably some kind of testimony source; cf. Ch. 4). Even so, the Christian manuscripts of the Old Testament text, handed on by Christian scribes, are by Justin regarded as normative, containing the sanctioned text of the church. That his insistence regarding this and other passages from his own 'OT' text is best understood and interpreted within a liturgical frame has been pointed out by Eric Osborn. In his 1973 study on Justin Martyr, Osborn writes:

> Justin's insistence that the Jews have deleted the words from Psalm 95,10 shows how early the interpolation was established. The method of its introduction could only be through midrash to liturgy and then to text. Justin claims that the Jews do not follow the Septuagint but that he does. The additional words (e.g. ἀπὸ τοῦ ξύλου) would be used in midrashic exegesis. The exposition of the text passes into liturgical use. As liturgy is the chief way in which scripture is propagated, the liturgical form becomes the authoritative form. It is significant that each of the above interpolations is found in a citation from a psalm.[67]

We here detect a key pattern for the ritual dimension of the canonical process. The midrashic exposition of the Scriptures, exemplified in Osborn's analysis, was at the time being made within some authoritative circles of first- (or in some instances early second-) century Christianity, and was probably codified also in Christian OT testimony sources as well as in the emergent NT

---

[67] Osborn, *Justin Martyr* (Tübingen: Mohr Siebeck, 1973), 111f.

writings.[68] As such authoritative Christian exposition of the Old Testament text is taken into liturgical use, it soon becomes normative, even against the Septuagint text, which was still used by the synagogue. Though mistaken, Justin even considers his own OT texts, or testimony sources, to contain the authentic Septuagint rendering.[69]

7.7.4 Scripture reading on the Lord's Day: Outline of the early history

A great deal can be said about the differences between the Jewish Sabbath and the Christian Sunday – the Lord's Day.[70] In short, the alteration Sabbath–Sunday was an extended process in large areas of the church beginning already in the Apostolic Period.[71] It naturally contributed to a new organization of the public reading of Scripture. Many of the first Christians celebrated both the Sabbath and the Sunday, which gave continuity, and a context, to this reorganization.[72] To enable the transformation to Sunday as the primary

---

[68] See, e.g. Albl, *'And Scripture Cannot be Broken': The Form and Function of the Early Christian Testimonia Collections* (Leiden: Brill, 1999); and Skarsaune, 'The Development of Scriptural Interpretation in the Second and Third Centuries – except Clement and Origen', in *Hebrew Bible/ Old Testament: The History of Its Interpretation*, vol. 1, ed. M. Sæbø (Göttingen: Vandenhoeck & Ruprecht, 1996), 373–442.

[69] Ibid.; cf. Ch. 4.

[70] In Greek, the Sunday from the fourth century on was later named 'the Day of Resurrection' ά ναστάσιμος ἡμέρα and later analogously 'the Resurrection' in, for example, the Russian language (*wosskressenije*). The New Testament and Post-Apostolic designation of the day is commonly 'the Lord's day' (κυριακὴ ἡμέρα; cf. Rev. 1.10). For further reading on the theme Sabbath–Sunday, see for example Carson, ed., *From Sabbath to Lord's Day: A Biblical, Historical and Theological Investigation* (Grand Rapids: Zondervan, 1982); Talley, *The Origins of the Liturgical Year* (New York, Pueblo, Collegeville, MN: The Liturgical Press, 1986; 2nd emended edn, 1991); and Beckwith, *Calendar and Chronology, Jewish and Christian: Biblical, Intertestamental and Patristic Studies*, (Leiden: Brill, 1996); Rordorf, *Sabbat und Sonntag in der Alten Kirche: Geschichte des Ruhe- und Gottesdiensttages im ältesten Christentum*, Traditio Christiana 2 (Zürich: Zwingli-Verlag, 1972).

[71] It is worth noticing that the Christian Sunday celebration was generally not understood as a replacement for the Jewish Sabbath, but as a special Christian day of worship; this view arose already during the first century before the mission to the gentiles and before the church's organizational differentiation vis-à-vis the synagogue. See further Bauckham, 'The Lord's Day', in *From Sabbath to Lord's Day*, ed. D. A. Carson, 221–50. For a minority of Christians the ongoing major exchange with contemporary Judaism remained more or less intact. Several of the Church Fathers tell of Christians who celebrate the Sabbath together with the Jews. So, for example, John Chrysostom (AD 347–407): 'Many among us keep the Sabbaths' with the Jews, he says in a homily (Hom. on Gal. 1.7). Cited from Wilken, *John Chrysostom and the Jews: Rhetoric and Reality in the Late 4th Century* (Berkeley and Los Angeles: University of California Press, 1983), 73ff., citation from p. 75.

[72] For a discussion on Gentile–Christians' keeping of the Sabbath, see Bauckham, 'Sabbath and Sunday in the Post-Apostolic Church', in *From Sabbath to Lord's Day: A Biblical, Historical and Theological Investigation*, ed. D. A. Carson (Grand Rapids: Zondervan, 1982), 251–98.

Christian day of worship and lection, several components collaborated – all having their roots in the experience of the risen Lord. The strongest manifestation of this experience occurred in the primitive church, where Jesus from early on became a principal focus of worship, being directly associated with God. This christological monotheism,[73] the integrating of Christ in the Divinity, has been described as a 'mutation' or modification of Early Jewish monotheism,[74] which, according to some recent scholarship, occurred not only rapidly but 'explosion-like' among the earliest Christians.[75] The church leaders, which presumably were all Jews at this early date, must have been well aware that this, viewed from without, could look like apostasy – breaking of the First Commandment.[76] Yet they turn directly to Christ and establish their gatherings and readings with the divine Christ-presence as the evident point of reference. Doxologies, prayers, hymns and confessions directed to Christ are all part of this development.[77] Johannes Weiss, German biblical scholar at the turn of the twentieth century, has called this emerging devotion to Christ the most important stage of all for the rise of the Christian movement.[78] Along these lines, the Judaica scholar Lee Levine writes that, liturgically, the earliest church was 'responding to the divinity of Jesus, his passion, and his resurrection, with all the theological ramifications associated with these events as expounded by Paul and others.'[79] This implies, among other things, that the Rabbinic liturgy has not affected the Christian liturgy to the extent suggested by earlier scholarship. So, the major source of inspiration for the communities'

---

[73] See Bauckham (*God Crucified: Monotheism and Christology in the New Testament* [Carlisle: Paternoster, 1998], 25–42) for the usage of this designation.

[74] Hurtado, *One God, One Lord: Early Christian Devotion and Ancient Jewish Monotheism* (Edinburgh: T&T Clark, 2nd rev. edn, 1998 [1988]).

[75] See Hurtado, *Lord Jesus Christ: Devotion to Jesus in Earliest Christianity* (Grand Rapids: Eerdmans, 2003), 2: 'At the beginning there was not a 'quite rapid development,' but an 'explosion.', cited from Hengel and Schwemer, *Paul between Damascus and Antioch: The Unknown Years* (Louisville: Westminster and John Knox, 1997), 283f.

[76] Cf. the first Word of the Decalogue: 'you shall have no other gods before me' (Exod. 20.3; Deut. 5.7); for a critical discussion of Early Jewish and Christian monotheism, see Hurtado, *One God, One Lord: Early Christian Devotion and Ancient Jewish Monotheism*.

[77] Hurtado, *At the Origins of Christian Worship: The Context and Character of Earliest Christian Devotion* (Grand Rapids: Eerdmans, 1999). For a wider discussion, see Newman et al. (eds), *The Jewish Roots of Christological Monotheism: Papers from the St. Andrews Conference on the Historical Origin of the Worship of Jesus* (Leiden: Brill, 1999).

[78] Weiss, *Das Urchristentum* (Göttingen: Vandenhoeck & Ruprecht, 1917); Hurtado, 'Christ-Devotion in the First Two Centuries: Reflections and a Proposal', *Toronto Journal of Theology* 12 (1996): 17–33.

[79] Levine, *The Ancient Synagogue: The First Thousand Years* (New Haven: Yale University Press, 2000), 528f.

development of liturgical worship and reading is, not the destruction of the Temple in AD 70, as for the synagogue, but Jesus' passion, death and resurrection one generation earlier.[80]

The centrality of early Christian Sunday worship is seen already by the threefold combination of official prayer (carried out *daily* in the Temple), Scripture reading with exposition (taking place *every Sabbath* in the synagogue) and celebration of the eucharist (corresponding to the *annual* Jewish celebration of the Passover),[81] which are soon to be unified in the church's Sunday service – the new centre of all Christian worship. Behind this liturgical development in relation to contemporary Judaism lies a pivotal event, by the Christians associated with the first day of the week,[82] namely the Resurrection and the disciples' encountering the Risen One, which also, on several occasions, appears to have taken place on the first day (cf. John 20).[83]

Following the Resurrection, we have already highlighted that the earliest Christian experiences seem to have resulted in an 'explosive' development of the Jesus cult, especially during the first four to five years of the Christian movement.[84] Extant evidence from the second century further confirms the central Death–Resurrection motif[85] behind the introduction of weekly Sunday worship, but also behind the choice of Sunday as the principal day of Passover celebration.[86] In addition to the author of the *Epistle of Barnabas* (15.9) and Justin (*1 Apol.* 67.7), Ignatius of Antioch, too, touches on the issue in his Letter to the Magnesians (9.1):

---

[80] Ibid.

[81] See Skarsaune, *In the Shadow of the Temple: Jewish Influences on Early Christianity* (Downers Grove, IL: InterVarsity, 2002), 378f. For further argumentation for this interpretation of the eucharist, see ibid., 399–422.

[82] As for the meaning of the Christian designations 'the Lord's Day' and 'the Eighth Day', see Bauckham, 'The Lord's Day'; and idem, 'Sabbath and Sunday in the Post-Apostolic Church'.

[83] The above discussion is based on Skarsaune, *In the Shadow of the Temple*, 378f. That the Evangelists, who at other occasions do not mark what day a particular event takes place (except for when it concerns the Sabbath Day), accentuate the day of the Resurrection, the first day of the week, is an indication that this day has become significant for the earliest church as its principal day of worship. Cf. 1 Cor. 16.2 and Acts 20.7.

[84] See, e.g. Hengel, *Between Jesus and Paul: Studies in the Earliest History of Christianity* (Eugene, OR: Wipf and Stock, 2003 [1983]), 30–47.

[85] Cf. n. 92 below.

[86] The choice of Sunday as the principal day of the Christian Passover appears to have caused more disagreement among Christians as compared to the earlier Sabbath–Sunday discussion. In the second-century dispute on the Passover the two main positions consisted of, on the one hand, the so called Quartodecimans, who adhered to the Jewish calendar for the time of the Passover, and, on the other, those who came to be the dominant group, opting for the celebration of Easter Day on the following Sunday.

If then they who walked in ancient customs came to a new hope, no longer living for the Sabbath, but for the Lord's Day, on which also our life sprang up through Him and His death ... and by this mystery we received faith.[87]

Against this background we can perceive a double point of departure for the emergence of the Christian liturgy and its Scripture reading: on the one hand, in the traditions associated with the Jerusalem Temple[88] and the synagogue,[89] and on the other, with the first Christians' new forms of worship focusing on the event of Jesus. The close relation to the synagogue and the Temple is evident already in some New Testament texts. Jesus, as well as Paul and the other apostles, participate in the synagogue gatherings. The early community's meetings initially take place at the Temple, where the Christians gather for prayer and teaching (Acts 2.46, 3.1, 5.42). In addition to this, however, they meet in homes (κατ᾽ οἶκον) well suited for such assemblies (Acts 2.42, 46).[90]

Being central to these Scripture readings, the faith in Christ and the emerging christology stands out, not only in texts such as Luke 24.25–7 and the openings of John, Romans and Hebrews, but throughout the New and the christologically interpreted Old Testament. To Ignatius of Antioch, Christ is held to be the very goal of all Scripture reading, including that from the 'charters [the Old Testament]': 'to me the charters are Jesus Christ, the inviolable charter [Scripture] is his cross and death and resurrection, and the faith which is through him' (*Phil.* 8.2).[91] Once again, the Resurrection is the ultimate focus. Ignatius underlines that the Sunday Scripture reading 'is' and points to 'his resurrection, and the faith which is through him.'[92]

That the worship order on Sundays by and large paralleled that of the Jewish Sabbath assembly seems clear, not least when comparing the arrangement of the Scripture readings. As some recent scholarship has sought to establish,

---

[87] Translation, Kirsopp Lake, *The Apostolic Fathers*, The Loeb Classical Library (London: William Heinemann, 1945).

[88] As to the difficulty of distinguishing the effects of the Temple liturgy on later Rabbinic and Christian worship, see Bradshaw, *The Search for the Origins of Christian Worship*.

[89] Cf. Beckwith, 'The Jewish Background', 68: 'in their practice, Jesus and his first followers conformed to a large extent to Jewish customs. When, therefore, the question is asked against what background Christian worship arose, the only answer that can be given is Jewish worship.'

[90] Cf. Jungmann, *The Early Liturgy: To the Time of Gregory the Great* (Notre Dame, IN: University of Notre Dame Press, 1959), 13.

[91] Translation, Kirsopp Lake, *The Apostolic Fathers*.

[92] For Cross/Crucifixion, Death and Resurrection presupposing one another, see Jenson, *Systematic Theology,* vol. 1, 179–206.

the principal goal – or according to some scholars even the sole purpose – with the synagogue gathering on the Sabbath was the common reading from and exposition of the Scriptures.[93] The reading appears to have consisted of two parts, first the main lesson from the Torah, either in a one-year-cycle (Babylon) or in a three to three and a half-year-cycle (land of Israel), and then the lesson from the prophets (*Haftarah*).[94] The Christians' service on Sunday morning, to celebrate Christ's resurrection at daybreak, as attested in Pliny the Younger, ca. AD 112 (*Epistle* 10.96), seems to be such a gathering for Scripture reading and prayer with a framing that reminds of contemporary synagogue practice.[95] The meal, i.e. the eucharist, was celebrated later the same day, commonly towards the evening, after completion of a day's work.[96] From the middle of the second century there is evidence from the Roman community that the two Sunday gatherings,[97] in the morning and later during the day, have been fused into a common liturgical form with both Scripture reading and the celebration of the eucharist.[98] Justin Martyr is the first Christian writer to portray such a gathering (ca. AD 150). He relates the following in his *Apology*:

---

[93] P. van der Horst, 'Was the Synagogue a Place of Sabbath Worship before 70 CE?', *Jews, Christians, and Polytheists in the Ancient Synagogue: Cultural Interaction during the Greco-Roman Period*, ed. Steven Fine (London: Routledge, 1999), 18–43.

[94] For references, see Levine, *The Ancient Synagogue: The First Thousand Years* (New Haven and London: Yale University Press, 2000), 151–5.

[95] See Skarsaune, *In the Shadow of the Temple*, 381–5. In Pliny's account the hymns, too, are characteristic as an important part of corporate worship. For a striking argument for the probable parallel occurrence of prayer (and some kind of worship) in the synagogue, see Beckwith, 'The Jewish Background', 71. For an alternative interpretation of corporate worship as witnessed by Pliny, see Tripp, 'The Letter of Pliny', in *The Study of Liturgy*, (eds) Cheslyn Jones et al. (London: SPCK, 1992), 80f.

[96] See Skarsaune's argumentation, *In the Shadow of the Temple*, 381ff. During the Pre-Constantinian Period, Sunday was a normal working day. This, of course, is another reason for not too easily interpreting Sunday as a Christian Sabbath. See further Bauckham ('Sabbath and Sunday in the Post–Apostolic Church', 280–4), for argumentation against the view that the Christians from early on sought to abstain from work on Sunday.

[97] Also in the synagogue at this period two gatherings often took place, one in the morning and one in the afternoon. See further Bradshaw, *The Search for the Origins of Christian Worship*.

[98] 'Eucharist' is the common designation for the breaking of bread/holy communion at this period. Hence, it seems to have been celebrated in the evening, in connection with the main meal of the day, in analogy with Jesus' last meal together with his disciples. The thesis put forth by Oscar Cullmann, that all services of the Word from the outset were linked to the celebration of the eucharist, thus does not find support in the sources; however, there is a discussion whether the early eucharist was celebrated on the evening of Saturday or Sunday; corporate worship focusing on teaching, on the other hand, seems to have taken place in the morning gatherings (cf. Apg 5.21 and 2.1f.). That a distinction between the Liturgy of the Word and the eucharist is made in some congregations as late as ca. AD 200, seems to be indicated by Tertullian, *De Cult. Fem.*, 2.11. Cf. in this regard also Josef A. Jungmann, *The Early Liturgy*, 43. For further literature, see Bradshaw, *Daily Prayer in the Early Church: A Study of the Origin and Early Development of the Divine Office* (London: SPCK, 1981), 41, nn. 88 and 89, and above, n. 15.

[O]n the day called Sunday all [believers] who live in cities or in the country gather together at one place, and the memoirs of the Apostles or the writings of the Prophets are read, as long as time permits; then, when the reader has ceased, the president of the assembly in a speech admonishes and invites all to imitate such examples of virtue. Then we all rise together and pray, and … when our prayer is ended, bread and wine and water are brought, and the president likewise offers prayers and thanksgivings, to the best of his ability, and the people assent, saying 'Amen.' (*1 Apol.* 67)[99]

Here (and in the following section) the same basic order of worship is found that also was to be sanctioned later in the church's history.[100] By 'the Prophets' Justin most likely intended to mean the books of the Septuagint.[101] The 'memoirs of the Apostles', as Justin calls them, most probably refers to the Gospel reading.[102] It has traditionally been thought of as exclusively referring to the Gospels,[103] but other apostolic writings are not necessarily excluded.[104] The most interesting inference from the term 'memoirs', though, is the probable reference to the genre 'memoirs of a master of philosophy', like *The Memoirs of Socrates* by Xenophon. Furthermore, as Justin in his role of apologist sought to present Christianity, not just as a philosophy among others, but as *the* philosophy, the assimilation of the language to that of Greek philosophy and literature is no surprise.[105] By using such terminology, the Gospel read in worship and used for theological discourse is made a candidate for inclusion in one of the literary genres of Antiquity. The congregation, we notice, reads first from the Gospel[106] as long as time permits, so called *lectio continua* (the Gospels read in order, the reader picking up where the assembly left off the Sunday before), and then from the prophetical writings; exactly

---

[99] ANF 1:186, modified.

[100] See Skarsaune, *In the Shadow of the Temple*, 384f.

[101] See *Dial.* 71; Rordorf, *La Bible dans l'enseignement et la liturgie des premières communautés chrétiennes* (Paris: Beauchesne, 1984), 85.

[102] According to Graham N. Stanton, Justin had access to the four canonical Gospels. See his 'The Fourfold Gospel', *NTS* 43 (1997). Some scholars are open to the possibility that other New Testament writings could also have been embraced by the 'memoirs of the Apostles'.

[103] So Rordorf, 'La Bible dans l'enseignement et la liturgie des premières communautés chrétiennes', 85.

[104] Cf. Gamble (*Books and Readers in the Early Church*, 215), who refers to D. K. Rensberger, 'As the Apostle Teaches: The Development of the Use of Paul's Letters in Second-Century Christianity' (Ph.D. Diss., Yale University, 1981).

[105] Cf. Abramowski, 'Die 'Erinnerungen der Apostel' bei Justin', 346; Zahn, *Geschichte des Neutestamentlichen Kanons*, vol. 1 (Erlangen: Verlag von Andreas Deichert, 1888), 471.

[106] Justin uses the term 'gospel' in other passages, in both the singular and the plural.

as in the synagogue,[107] it seems, with the crucial difference, though, that the Torah lesson has given place to the Gospel reading.

In the synagogue setting, the Torah made up the primary text, but it also stood for the whole: the teaching, the Scriptures and their contents as a whole. Now, instead of the Torah, it turns out to be the Gospel which has, once and for all, acquired this place.[108]

7.7.5 The organizing of communal Scripture reading

The communal Scripture reading as presented by Justin Martyr is unique because of the placement of the Gospel as the first lesson, at least as an option,[109] before the Prophets. As far as I am aware this is our only historical documentation of such a grouping of the lessons.[110] The placing of the four canonical Gospels first in the New Testament, in analogy with the literary placement of the Pentateuch in the Old Testament, is arguably connected to this early practice that we meet in Justin. Soon, however, the Gospel acquired the place of the final lesson, as the culmination of the other Scripture readings.[111] In a few Bible manuscripts we can see traces of such a change; here, the New Testament letters have been placed before the Gospels, which is an indication that such a connection between liturgical worship and the ordering of the books in the Bible has existed.[112] The practice of *lectio continua*

---

[107] I here choose to interpret the two readings, *Gospel* and *Prophets*, as a direct parallel to the two readings in the synagogue from the Law and the Prophets. The text can also be translated 'the apostles' memoirs or the prophets' writings', which somewhat complicates such an interpretation. Cf. Skarsaune, *In the Shadow of the Temple*, 384f.

[108] Regarding the Eastern Orthodox tradition as a good representative of this hermeneutic of liturgical biblical usage, cf. Breck, *Scripture in Tradition: The Bible and its Interpretation in the Orthodox Church* (Crestwood, NY: St. Vladimir's Seminary Press, 2001), 15: 'The four Gospels remain constantly on the altar of our churches, bearing depictions of Christ crucified and resurrected. At the Matins service on the eve of Sundays and great feasts, following the reading of a resurrection Gospel, the book itself is brought to the center of the church and placed on a stand, where it is venerated by the faithful. If there is a 'canon within the canon' in Orthodoxy, it is precisely the book of the four Gospels, which contains both the witness of Jesus Christ and the witness to him.'

[109] Cf. n. 107 above.

[110] Jungmann, *Missarum Sollemnia: Eine Genetische Erklärung der römischen Messe*, vol. 1 (Wien: Verlag Herder, 2 Aufl., 1949, [1948]), 545.

[111] In a Syrian church handbook from the third century, *Kanones from Addai*, the following is said in regard to the Gospel reading: 'At the conclusion of all the scriptures let the Gospel be read, as the seal of all the scriptures; and let the people listen to it standing upon their feet, because it is the glad tidings of the salvation of all men.' W. Cureton, *Ancient Syrian Documents* (London, 1864), 27. Cited from Lamb, 'The Place of the Bible in the Liturgy', *The Cambridge History of the Bible*, vol. 1, (eds) P. R. Ackroyd and C. F. Evans (Cambridge: Cambridge University Press, 1970), 572.

[112] Zahn, *Geschichte des Neutestamentlichen Kanons*, vol. 2, 380f.

seems to have set traces in the redaction of the Bible manuscripts as well as in the early ecclesial lectionaries. A typical lectionary begins with readings from the Gospel of John during Easter. From the first Monday after Pentecost the lections are chosen from Matthew; from the twelfth week they are complemented with readings from Mark during weekdays. From the time around 14 September until Lent the lections are taken from Luke; between weeks 13 and 17 Luke is read parallel with the second half of Mark. This typical early ecclesiastical lectionary (a so called *synaxarion*) comes very close to being a *lectio continua*, however, with the interruption for the readings at special feast days.[113] The canonical Gospel order (Matthew, Mark, Luke, John), from the second- to fifth-century redaction of the biblical text, seems also to be reflected in the early lectionaries.[114] The order of the canonical Gospels is the same as that of the official lessons (or a permutation thereof), and vice versa – that is, this part of the Christian Bible is at times structured as a lectionary.[115]

The development of the divine lection in the West leads around the seventh century to a fixation of mainly two readings, first from the epistle and then from the Gospel. As to the development from the second century up to this fixation of two (or sometimes three) lessons more can be said. The recommendations from different church leaders vary, from two or three lessons in Augustine, to four in Tertullian (the Law, the Prophets, the Apostle and the Gospel). Yet more readings are commended by *The Apostolic Constitutions* (ca. AD 380): five lessons (VIII, 5.5; the Law, the Prophets, the Epistle, Acts and the Gospel), alternatively eight lessons (II, 57.5; the Law, the Historical Books,

---

[113] Metzger, 'Greek Lectionaries and a Critical Edition of the Greek New Testament', in *Die alten Übersetzungen des Neuen Testaments, die Kirchenväterzitate und Lektionare: der gegenwärtige Stand ihrer Erforschung und ihre Bedeutung für die griechische Textgeschichte; Arbeiten zur Neutestamentlichen Textforschung*, vol. 5, ed. K. Aland (Berlin: Walter de Gruyter, 1972), 480f.

[114] Matthew, Mark, Luke and John is the Gospel order found in Codex Vaticanus (followed by Codex Sinaiticus and Codex Alexandrinus) and in Irenaeus' *Adv. Haer.* III, 3.1 (followed by Codex Vaticanus, Codex Sinaiticus and Codex Alexandrinus) and in Irenaeus' *Adv. Haer.* III, 3.1 (followed also by Origen, Athanasius, Jerome, Augustine and others). For a possible second-century 'canonical archetype' which set the standard for later editions of the New Testament, see Trobisch, *The First Edition of the New Testament* (Oxford: Oxford University Press, 2000), 21–34.

[115] As outlined in Ch. 4, the Gospels were a clearly defined part of the New Testament (the four Gospels also frequently occurred as a separate codex). The entirety of the New Testament, 27 Scriptures, typically contains three to four such (more or less) delimited text collections. Out of the ca. 5,800 extant Greek NT manuscripts, only about 1 per cent (some 59 manuscripts) contain all four text corpora, i.e. 1) the Gospels, 2) Acts and the Catholic letters (*Praxapostolos*), 3) the Pauline letters, and 4) the Book of Revelation. For further reference see, e.g. Trobisch, *First Edition*, 103; Aland, *The Text of the New Testament* (Grand Rapids: Eerdmans, 1987; rev. edn, 1989). The remaining 99 per cent of the manuscripts consist of combinations of writings from one to three of the four text collections. For a somewhat more complex picture, cf. section 4.2.1 under point 4.

Job, the Books of Wisdom, the Prophets, Acts, the Epistle and the Gospel).[116] In the second century, however, we are still dealing with *lectio continua*, as in Justin (ca. AD 150), the weekly reading continuing where the assembly left off the Sunday before.

When the church gradually increased the number of feast days with special Gospel pericope readings, this continuous reading of the Gospel was often interrupted. As the Christian liturgical year attained greater importance, this probably took place to such an extent that the church instead moved on to pericope readings alone,[117] with a particular Gospel reading for each Sunday. Parallel to this development, the readings from the Prophets were repressed, and replaced by lessons from the rest of the New Testament literature. In the Western church, thus, the lessons were soon made up of two readings, from the Epistle and from the Gospel. However, in some areas of the Eastern church, the Old Testament reading(s) was kept, along with the (usually two) New Testament lessons.[118]

7.7.6 The Pauline corpus

Functional aspects, such as liturgical and other ecclesial usage, remain important as we turn to the *Corpus Paulinum*. When the author of Colossians asks his addressees to make arrangements so that his letter is read also in Laodicea, and that in turn the letter addressed to the Laodiceans is read in the Colossian community, such functional dimensions come to the fore.[119] Even if the context here would not intentionally be the public reading, which in a synagogual setting meet in Luke 4.16-30,[120] the request to interchange letters indicates some public character of these writings, perhaps also an already established practice of reciting them beside the Jewish Scriptures as part of the worship service, or the initiation of such a practice among the provincial churches.[121]

---

[116] Lamb, 'The Place of the Bible in the Liturgy', 570f.
[117] Exactly when this happened is a question of debate among scholars. It may have occurred from about the seventh century. See further Aland, *The Text of the New Testament*.
[118] Skarsaune, *In the Shadow of the Temple*, 385f.
[119] Col. 4.16.
[120] See also Matt. 13.54; Mark 1.21, 39; 3.1; Acts 9.20; 13.5; 13.14f.
[121] See Murphy-O'Connor, *Paul the Letter-Writer: His World, His Options, His Skills* (Collegeville, MN: Michael Glazier and Liturgical Press, 1995).

Gamble thinks that the reading of apostolic letters at an early date was a liturgical act only in the sense that it took place in a liturgical context, whereas the letters themselves were not liturgical or regarded as Scripture.[122] Nevertheless, already in the first century, the Pauline writings seem to have been used in ways similar to that of Scripture, as perhaps indicated by Paul himself in Romans or Galatians, or when commending his addressees to have the letter to the Thessalonians read to 'all the brothers' (1 Thess. 5.27). Even Gamble, however, favours the view that by the time Colossians was composed, the letters of Paul had probably begun to acquire 'a scriptural aspect'.[123]

In 2 Peter 3.15f. Paul's letters ('in all his letters') appear to count among the 'Scriptures', and from the point of view of the author of Revelation, public reading of new Scriptures is probably a relatively widespread custom, as he anticipates the reading of his own prophecy by a blessing upon 'the one who reads … and those who hear' (1.3).[124] Moreover, the study of Clement's First Letter to the Corinthians or the letters of Ignatius of Antioch seem to indicate that the writings of Paul were well known rather early. Further traces of Pauline influence confirm this: 1) in other (late) New Testament works, such as the Johannine corpus, Hebrews, 1 Peter and James; and 2) other early Christian writings, in particular 2 *Clements* and Polycarp (*Letter to the Philippians* and *Polycarp's Martyrdom*).[125] Kirsopp Lake maintains that the appreciation of Paul's writings evoked the desire to have as many letters as possible in the community. The various communities would then have requested copies from each other. In this way a number of local collections with differing content emerged. When these were compared, awareness of their circumscribed origin dictated a policy of addition for the sake of completeness rather than one of deletion for fear of forgery. 'Sometime in the second century it was recognized that all lists were identical in content even though diverse in order. At this point the Pauline canon closed.'[126]

---

[122] Gamble, *Books and Readers in the Early Church*, 206. For a different view, cf. Deines, 'Writing Scripture in the First Century', *European Journal of Theology* (forthcoming).

[123] Gamble, *Books and Readers in the Early Church*, 206.

[124] Ibid., 206, 322, n. 6.

[125] Murphy-O'Connor, *Paul the Letter-Writer*; and Lindemann, *Paulus im ältesten Christentum: Das Bild des Apostels und die Rezeption der paulinischen Theologie in der frühchristlichen Literatur bis Marcion, Beiträge zur Historischen Theologie* 58, ed. J. Wallman (Tübingen: Mohr Siebeck, 1979).

[126] Murphy-O'Connor, *Paul the Letter-Writer*, 115

Beside E. J. Goodspeed and J. Knox, who suggests that the Pauline collection was the work of the slave Onesimos soon after AD 85,[127] the somewhat speculative theory put forth by E. R. Richards is thought-provoking. He proposes that 'the first collection of Paul's letters were in codex form and arose from Paul's personal copies and *not* from collecting the letters from various recipients.'[128] Luke is suggested as the one responsible for the publication. Again, the codex format is thought to have played a role in the canon formation (see further, Ch. 4). However, the external manuscript evidence for a Pauline corpus circulating prior to the late second century is sparse.[129]

Again, focusing on the inner character of the letters, several of them are perhaps neither primarily occasional writings nor theological tractates, but rather, as Helmut Koester suggests, 'instruments of church policy'. The internal character of the apostolic writings, of course, also embodies their theological concerns.[130] However, as Koester views it, they also, from very early on, came to function along the oral communication in the organization of the communities,[131] thereby implying the congregational function and canonical status they increasingly were to obtain. The relatively early appearance of a growing Pauline letter corpus – with a 10- and 13-letter corpus in use perhaps around AD 100 – might point in this direction.[132]

---

[127] The hypothesis presupposes that the letters of Paul were forgotten, having achieved their immediate practical purpose, and, accordingly, were not used in the communities, neither liturgically nor theologically, between their reception and the publication of the Acts of the Apostles around AD 90.

[128] Murphy-O'Connor, *Paul the Letter-Writer*, 118; Richards, *The Secretary in the Letters of Paul*, WUNT 2/42. (Tübingen: Mohr Siebeck 1991).

[129] Gamble, 'The Canon of the New Testament', in *The New Testament and Its Modern Interpreters*, (eds) E. J. Epp and G. W. MacRae (Society of Biblical Literature, 1989), 207: 'The external evidence for the Pauline corpus prior to the late second century has remained difficult to define and to interpret (see Aland, 1979a). That Clement, Ignatius, Polycarp, and 2 Peter were acquainted with letters of Paul is beyond doubt, but it remains uncertain how many letters each knew and whether any of them had the letters in an actual "edition," in spite of claims that Ignatius (Rathke), Clement (Hagner), and Polycarp (Nielsen) knew a majority of Paul's letters and perhaps a full corpus. See Zahn, 1888–92, I/2:811–29). The alleged allusions do not support this (Lindemann: 201–16; Rensberger: 41–64; Schneemelcher, 1964). It is only with Marcion that we gain any detailed knowledge of an early edition of Paul's letters, but there is nothing to favor the surmise that he was 'the first systematic collector of the Pauline heritage' (Bauer, 221). Rather, it now appears that Marcion merely took over an existing edition and reworked it to his own purpose (Frede, 1969:295–96; Finnegan: 88; Dahl, 1978: 252–7; Clabeaux).'

[130] Thus Childs (*The New Testament as Canon: An Introduction* [London: SCM, 1984], 424), maintaining that the canonization of the Pauline letters cannot be explained primarily as a reaction to external threat, but that it is derived from intrinsic, theological concerns. Cf. idem, *The Church's Guide for Reading Paul: The Canonical Shaping of the Pauline Corpus* (Grand Rapids and Cambridge: Eerdmans, 2008), 3ff.; 19–21; 75–8.

[131] Koester, *Introduction to the New Testament*, vol. 2, 2–5

[132] Murphy-O'Connor, *Paul the Letter-Writer*, 126f.; Childs, *The Church's Guide for Reading Paul*, 75.

7.7.7 The New Testament: Three closed and one open collection of writings

As a liturgical collection of writings, the books of the New Testament cannot be understood in the same manner as texts are commonly viewed in historical scholarship. Although Friedrich Schleiermacher is right to remark that 'critical inquiry must ever anew test the individual writings of Scripture with a view to decide whether they rightly keep their place in the sacred collection,'[133] from a liturgical-theological point of view this statement does not give enough emphasis to the collection as a whole. The corpus of New Testament writings is not primarily to be understood as consisting of individual and separate books, but as books being part of a text (Ch. 6) and narrative (see further Chs 3, 5 and 8). Understood in this way, the individual writings are integrated within a narrative and meta-narrative framework, variously referred to as the gospel, the Christian biblical story, the kerygma, or the like. Again, the early emergence of the collection as a whole is not emphasized by Schleiermacher, and, accordingly, nor is the canonical status of an individual 'New Testament' writing:

> [A]lthough all the particular books in the collection belong to the Apostolic Age, the actual collection of them certainly does not; we cannot therefore have had handed down to us any strictly apostolic indication of what is canonical and normative.[134]

By contrast, when emphasizing the ecclesial collection as collection (made up of prior 'normative' collections), underlining its major constituent parts – three or four in the Old and New Testaments, respectively – or the public Scripture readings (cf. sections 7.7.5 and 7.7.8), a notion of canon or canonical status is already part of the scriptural interpretation. Such canonical reading is concerned not only with individual writings, but also with particular portions of Scripture, with the full text, and the divine lection. The individual texts are already being part of larger textual wholes (e.g. part-collections); and with the whole-biblical narrative as found in the 'prophetic' and 'apostolic' collections of Scriptures.

Schmid, *Marcion und sein Apostolos: Rekonstruktion und historische Einordnung der marcionitischen Paulusbriefausgabe* (Berlin and New York: Walter de Gruyter, 1995); cf. O'Connor, 'How the Text is Heard: The Biblical Theology of Brevard Childs', *Religious Studies Review* 21 (1995): 91–6.
[133] Schleiermacher, *The Christian Faith* (Edinburgh: T&T Clark, 1999 [1830]), 603.
[134] Ibid. 602.

It is essential for the apostolic and sub-apostolic corpus of writings, collected and designed for liturgical, catechetical and theological usage, not so much that its limits are apostolically sanctioned, but that there is, in the first place, such a thing as an 'apostolic' collection of writings. And, as we have seen (in Ch. 4), two or three of the four corpora making up the New Testament were regarded in principle as closed, and thus received as canon, by the mid-second century, or at least by the time of Irenaeus. As to the closing of the fourth collection, the so called *Praxapostolos* (Acts and the Catholic Letters),[135] we note that – if we except discussions on the canonical function of James – its exact delimitation has only rarely played a crucial role in the history of the church. Nevertheless, the old debate on some disputed NT writings still has a role to play (see section 9.8.1). It is here worth keeping in mind the various links between the Catholic Epistles and the early process of canonization that certainly included 1 John and 1 Peter, and the notion of in-principle closed part-collections.

In this connection, dating is of some significance, since by the early to mid-second century more or less closed collections of scriptural corpora seem to have appeared: the Jewish Scriptures made up of 22 books (so already in Josephus), the early Pauline corpus (arguably before Marcion) and the early fourfold Gospel (arguably before Justin Martyr).[136] If we add to this the view of 'scripture' conveyed by the Johannine corpus (cf. section 9.6), the late first and early second centuries seem to be perhaps the most crucial period for the formation of the idea of a new Christian Bible canon, designed for liturgical, catechetical and theological purposes.

---

[135] In the early third-century P⁴⁵, Acts is included together with the four Gospels. For different scholarly accounts of the Catholic Epistle Collection, see Metzger, *The Canon of the New Testament*; Trobisch, *First Edition*; and Nienhuis, *Not by Paul Alone: The Formation of the Catholic Epistle Collection and the Christian Canon* [Waco, TX: Baylor University Press, 2007]).

[136] For Josephus's 22-book canon, see section 2.4, n. 59; for the Pauline letter collection, see section 7.7.6. As to an early dating of the formation of the Pauline corpus and the fourfold Gospel, see, e.g. Porter, 'Paul and the Process of Canonization', in *Exploring the Origins of the Bible*, (eds) Evans and Tov (Grand Rapids: Baker, 2008), 173–202; and Hurtado, 'The New Testament in the Second Century: Text, Collections, Canon', in *Transmission and Reception: New Testament Text-Critical and Exegetical Studies*, (eds) J. W. Childers and D. C. Parker (Piscataway, NJ: Gorgias, 2006), 3–27.

7.7.8 The liturgical standardization of New Testament writings: The early Byzantine text

From the seventh century on, the most widespread Greek New Testament text was the so called Byzantine text, or Majority text.[137] Some 5,000 (i.e. ca. 90 per cent of a total of approximately 5,800) extant manuscripts belong to this text type, which came to be the text of choice among Greek copyists.[138] The Gospel text of the fifth-century Codex Alexandrinus is its earliest manuscript witness.

In the developing Byzantine text (fourth century onwards),[139] some typical characteristics can be observed that probably were meant to have the function of making the text more accessible for public reading at worship. This seems to be a reasonable assumption when we look at some of the textual variants that characterize this standard text.

First, the word ἀμήν has been added to the ending of the four Gospels, 13 Pauline letters, Hebrews, 1 and 2 Peter, 1 and 2 John, and Revelation in the Byzantine manuscripts. This may be of some interest also for the question of canon. To begin with, we notice that Acts, James and 3 John lack the redactional addition of ἀμήν in many of the Byzantine manuscripts. Does this mean that these books were not included in some Byzantine copies of the New Testament used for worship? Due to this lack of ἀμήν in James and 3 John, which, in terms of canonical status, were disputed books from the third century on, it may be argued that copyists of the Byzantine text did not include these writings as part of their New Testament used for divine lection.[140] The lack of a concluding ἀμήν in Acts might point in the same direction.

---

[137] Metzger and Ehrman, *The Text of the New Testament: Its Transmission, Corruption, and Restoration* (New York and Oxford: Oxford University Press, 4th edn, 2005), 280. For a brief historical background to the eventual dominance of NT manuscripts possessing 'a text of Byzantine character', see ibid., 220. For critical comments as to the unity of this text type, see Parker, *An Introduction to the New Testament Manuscripts and their Texts* (Cambridge: Cambridge University Press, 2008), 198-200.

[138] Metzger and Ehrman, *The Text of the New Testament*, 280.

[139] Ibid., 279: 'Recent studies of the Byzantine text have shown that it can be found in rudimentary form as early as the fourth century in such church writers as Basil the Great and Chrysostom but that its final form represents a slowly developing tradition, not one that sprang up immediately at one time and place. It was not, in other words, a textual recension created by a single person or community. It does appear, however, that the Byzantine editors formed their text by taking over elements of the earlier extant traditions, choosing variant readings from among those already available rather than creating new ones that fit their sense of an improved text.' For a possibly earlier dating of the Byzantine text, see ibid. 221f.

[140] Weitzmann, *Age of Spirituality*, 61, 164. As we will see below, none of the Catholic Epistles may have been included.

Second, when looking at the prescripts and subscripts of the Byzantine text, we observe the following phrasings:

Inscriptia (prescripts):

Matt:	Ευαγγελιον κατα Ματθαιον
Mark:	Ευαγγελιον κατα Μαρκον
Luke:	Ευαγγελιον κατα Λουκαν
John:	Ευαγγελιον κατα Ιωαννην

Subscriptia (subscripts):

Rom: Epistolh	προς Ρωμαιους εγραφη δια Φοιβες διακονου
1 Cor:	προς Κορινθιους α′ εγραφε απο Φιλιππων δια Στεφανα και Φορτουνατου και Αχαικου και Τιμοθεου
2 Cor:	προς Κορινθιους β′ εγραφε απο Φιλιππων δια Τιτου και Λουκα
Gal:	προς Γαλατας εγραφη απο Ρωμης
Eph:	προς Εφεσιους εγραφη απο Ρωμης δια Τυχικου
Phil:	προς Φιλιππησιους εγραφη απο Ρωμης δια Επαφροδιτου
Col:	προς Κολοσσαεις εγραφη απο Ρωμης δια Τυχικου και Ονησιμου
1 Thess:	προς Θεσσαλονικεις α′ εγραφη απο Αθηνων
2 Thess:	προς Θεσσαλονικεις β′ εγραφη απο Αθηνων
1 Tim:	προς Τιμοθεον α′ εγραφη απο Λαοδικειας ητις εστιν μητροπολις Φρυγιας της Πακατιανης
2 Tim:	προς Τιμοθεον β′ της Εφεσιων εκκλησιας επισκοπον πρωτον χειροτονηθεντα εγραφη απο Ρωμης οτε εκ δευτερου παρεστη Παυλος τω καισαρι Ρωμης Νερωνι
Tit:	προς Τιτον της Κρητων εκκλησιας πρωτον επισκοπον χειροτονηθεντα εγραφη απο Νικοπολεως της Μακεδονιας
Philem:	προς Φιλημονα εγραφη απο Ρωμης δια Ονησιμου οικετου
Heb:	προς Εβραιους εγραφη απο Ιταλιας δια Τιμοθεου[141]
Jas:	No *inscriptio* or *subscriptio*, according to NA[27]
1 Pet:	No *inscriptio* or *subscriptio*, according to NA[27]
2 Pet:	No *inscriptio* or *subscriptio*, according to NA[27]

---

[141] Worth noting in passing is the potential involvement of Paul's associates in the letter correspondence, as indicated in the Byzantine text tradition. Cf. Porter, 'Paul and the Process of Canonization'.

1 Joh:	No *inscriptio* or *subscriptio*, according to NA[27]
2 Joh:	No *inscriptio* or *subscriptio*, according to NA[27]
3 Joh:	No *inscriptio* or *subscriptio*, according to NA[27]
Jude:	No *inscriptio* or *subscriptio*, according to NA[27]

Inscriptio:

Rev: Ἀποκαλυψις Ἰωαννου του Θεολογου

From the above, we note that the Byzantine textual tradition contains a couple of peculiar editorial features of potential relevance for an aspect of the canon formation – redactional addition of ἀμήν, and the above prescripts/subscripts. The writings with these features, at least the former, appear to have been used for public reading. We may thus allow ourselves to speculate that the Byzantine New Testament canon, devised for corporate worship, may commonly have included (two or)[142] three major part-collections: the Gospels, the Pauline letter corpus and the Book of Revelation.

7.7.9 Reading and re-reading

Read these Scriptures over and over again! Perhaps this appeal is the most appropriate portrayal of the theological *locus de scriptura*. Is it perhaps even the primary doctrine of Scripture?[143]

The re-reading of the Scriptures was emphasized already in the synagogue's one- to three-year-cycles for the Sabbath lessons (cf. section 7.7.4). From the first century onwards, the main lesson on the Sabbath was also repeated in the afternoon assembly and further in the readings on Mondays and Thursdays. All in all, this makes three public re-readings of the weekly Torah lesson.[144] In a similar way many of the Church Fathers commend the assembly to read and meditate over the weekly Bible lesson at home. There are also examples of an announcement before the congregation of the coming week's section, to prepare for the next Sunday, as, for example, in Chrysostom (ca. AD 347–407).[145]

---

[142] Presumably two major part-collections for those Byzantine communities which did not include Revelation among the Scriptures.

[143] Cf. Jenson, 'The Religious Power of Scripture', *Scottish Journal of Theology* 52 (1999): 89–105

[144] Bradshaw, *Daily Prayer in the Early Church*, 19.

[145] Lamb, 'The Place of the Bible in the Liturgy', 575f.

Here, the textual whole is already anticipated by the full members of the community, that is, by everyone who has passed the training of the catechumenate and received baptism. This is an important aspect of these biblical readings and re-readings that deserves further reflection.

First of all, following in the steps of the Evangelist Luke (Luke 1.4), the continuous Gospel reading in the assembly always presumes the basic biblical teaching (e.g. narrative, kerygma, dogma and ethics) in which the catechumens have been already instructed. The Gospel narratives here presuppose faith in the basic christological formulas.[146]

Another point to make in this connection is the fact that the audience, in particular the full community members, already knew the course of later events in the story of Jesus. To exemplify, in regard to the traditions of Jesus' birth, the context for these traditions was provided by all the memories of the church, up to the time of each successive reading.[147]

Thus, the argumentation presented in section 7.3 about the effect of the liturgical year on biblical textuality needs to be somewhat modified. The whole gospel is already present in the minds of the community members. This contextualization of the gospel is already there – by oral transmission and memorization of the constantly repeated texts, narratives and associated doctrines – in every new reading of any portion of the gospel.[148] In short, the context of the biblical whole, here represented by the gospel, is already 'known' or presupposed. Thus, focusing on Jesus' birth, Minear writes:

> The Father ... was even now carrying out ... his program for the salvation of
> the world. Although the plan of this mystery was first disclosed in the death and
> exaltation of Jesus, the same invincible purpose had been at work secretly in all
> the preceding episodes. Since the heart of the mystery was the selfhumiliation
> of God's Son, the initial act of descent as narrated by Matthew and Luke carried
> within itself the whole plan of redemption, and should be understood as such
> (Phil. 2:5-11). Since each episode of humiliation concealed the whole eternal
> purpose, the eyes of faith discerned in each episode the major accents of that
> purpose: God's merciful invitation and stern judgment, the offense created by
> his Word, the creation of a new Adam and a new Israel, the powers of the new

---

[146] Cf. Minear, *The Bible and the Historian: Breaking the Silence About God in Biblical Studies* (Nashville: Abingdon, 2002), 91.

[147] Ibid., 91f.

[148] Ibid., 90–3.

age at work in those who seek that new age with all their heart, ... It is thus that the whole gospel furnished the central motifs in the tradition concerning Jesus' birth.[149]

As seen here, Minear makes a strong case for the whole gospel being heard in and with each new Gospel/Scripture reading before the community.

Now, recalling this section's initial statement of re-reading as the principal *locus de scriptura*, we may ask how these reflections on reading and hearing pertain to the canon. From my discussion above, it is clear that the many and diverse readings from various parts of the canon – taking place in the community – are marked by a view of Scripture and gospel as a well-defined whole. Being a property of Scripture, canon and canon consciousness express this sense of the whole by regulating the way the church reads and organizes its sacred writings as address and criterion. Thus, '[w]hen a text is actually read, it is not merely text but in one way or another is living address.'[150] So, the 'church *reads* Scripture, in expectation of faith.'[151] Robert Jenson here recalls a distinction proposed in old Protestantism, namely that the authority of Scripture is a 'double capacity: one to judge other writings and teachings ... another to bring about the assent of faith ...'[152] The latter sense – Scripture's authority happening in its being read before the community – is always a presupposition of the former. In helping to define this central aspect of canon-icity – Scripture's place in the church's ritual life – all kinds of issues addressing the topic of Scripture reading may be raised. Jenson notes some places where such reading may occur:

> Scripture is read in all services of the church, and its language and stories and sayings otherwise pervade them; Scripture is read in the devotions of Christian homes and religious communities, where it shapes the minds of sequential generations; Scripture is read by the pious quietly; and even a theologian checking a reference may be moved by it in unexpected fashion.[153]

The readings are part of the Scriptures in their function as canon for the church. When Scripture is thus read, the notion of canon is functioning as a

---

[149] Ibid., 92f.
[150] Jenson, 'The Religious Power of Scripture', 89.
[151] Ibid.
[152] Ibid. For reference, see ibid.; cited from Johannes Musaeus, *Introductio in theologiam* (1679), ii.iii.
[153] Jenson, 'The Religious Power of Scripture', 89.

Christian fore-meaning being worked out. Obviously there is a circular move here. The circle, however, is not a vicious one.

For practical purposes, the 'doctrine' and praxis of having the Scriptures read, according to Christian faith, serves as an imprint for the function of the Scriptures in the assembly; continuously read and re-read, not in a repetitive compulsive manner, but simply in the function as the church's primary means of grace.[154] The gospel – the oral and written, codified in book form – is offered to those who hear it, over and over again. In this way the texts of the Bible, from the earliest period, are privileged in the assembly. Their primary mark of signification, within the church's liturgical framing, is 'apostolic repetition' of the Gospel.[155] The Gospel is the Christian narrative, and these writings, which by definition are read and re-read in the midst of the community, are the proclamation of this narrative, from which all other ecclesial life proceeds.[156] That the orthodoxy of the early church, none the less – already in Irenaeus (ca. AD 125–202) and Clement of Alexandria (ca. AD 150–215) – formulates principles[157] to circumscribe Scripture's usage is a consequence of its acquired position as textual foundation for the church.[158]

7.8 Conclusion

Liturgical concerns were important from the beginning of the history of the New Testament canon. 'The Gospels, at least Mark, Matthew and John, were written in the first place for worship' (Hengel). In this chapter I have argued

---

[154] On the twofold form of the doctrine of Scripture's authority, see further Jenson, 'The Religious Power of Scripture'. See also Eriksson (*Auktoritet och nådemedel: Några huvuddrag i Martin Luthers bibelsyn* [Åbo: Studier utgivna av Institutionen för systematisk teologi vid Åbo akademi, nr 25, 1994]), who addresses questions in Martin Luther's thinking pertaining to Scripture's dual function as an authority and as a means of grace.

[155] Cf. Chrysostom's comment on the relation between the Scripture readings and the following homilia in church service: 'What need is there for a homily? All things that are in the divine scripture are clear and open.' (*Hom. on 2 Thess* 3.4, cited from Lamb, *The Cambridge History of the Bible*, vol. 1, (eds) P. R. Ackroyd and C. F. Evans (Cambridge: Cambridge University Press, 1970), 577. Cf. also the *Augsburg Confession*, art 7, ed. Ph. Schaff; Melanchthon, *Loci Communes*, (St. Louis, MO: Concordia Publishing House, 1992 [1543]), Locus 12, p. 131; Jean Calvin, *Institutes of the Christian Religion,* vol. 2, ed. J. T. McNeill (Philadelphia: Westminster, 1960 [1559]), 1041.

[156] Jenson, *Systematic Theology,* vol. 2, 273f.

[157] E.g. teaching on Scripture's inspiration, clarity, perfection and sufficiency (Iren. *Adv. Haer.* and Clem. *Strom.*).

[158] On the Bible as foundation for the church, cf. the classical formulation in the so called *Decretum Gelasianum*, above, Ch. 1, n. 59.

that the Christian Scriptures, set forth as canon, become dislocated and disintegrated when isolated from their place of origin – Scripture's home – the worship of the Christian community. This is not just a matter of preferred cultic setting but raises questions on a more fundamental level of interaction between text and interpreter, and their respective ritual embeddedness.

The canon may be critically taken apart, ritually as well as textually. In this connection particular attention is given to William Wrede's understanding of the New Testament canon. Different forms of experience with bearing on interpretation are tied to these texts, ecclesial cultic as well as scholarly historical.

The (never-ending) theme of textual particularity, addressed in earlier chapters, here surfaces again, now from the horizon of corporate worship. In fact, it is in the religious rite of public reading and homiletic exposition that the work itself is primarily encountered: Scripture in its key function as canon for the community of listeners and readers. Hermeneutically, the triadic system of the *nomina sacra* provides a focal point, where text and ritual can meet.

As a central part of worship, the Liturgy of the Word affects our understanding of Scripture seen as a liturgical text. In this sense the scriptural account is not designed to be read as 'any other book', but to be performed in the communities. Being a part of the daily, weekly and annual ritual performance, the textuality of canonical Scripture is only gradually revealed. On a broader scale, Scripture is always experienced within its own tradition, with the weekly corporate worship at its core. In this connection the mutuality between worship and teaching, the *lex orandi, lex credendi*, in the Christian tradition, may be understood as a sanction of such canonical reading by which the rules of faith naturally affect rules of prayer, and the other way around. To some extent, the sacralizing of Christian writings, received as Scriptures by the faith community, is an effect of such ritual practice. That is, the regular scriptural reading and functioning play a significant role for the shaping of the new canon.

In the latter part of the chapter, Jewish notions of Scripture and worship are shown to be central for the development of a particular Christian ritual identity, including the coming-into-existence of the canonical corpus of Scriptures. Yet, the event of Jesus the Messiah is pointed out as most crucial for developing a particular ecclesial Liturgy of the Word.

In the broad sense of the word, recurrent scriptural reading is central for a people of 'the book'. Ample acquaintance with Scripture introduces the assembly into the richness of the Christian literary tradition. This applies historically as well as to the present. Various cycles of organized readings of Scripture, often according to carefully designed lesson schemes, offer a particular construal of the ritually defined canonical text.

From early on the texts of the Bible have been privileged in the Christian assembly. Their primary mark of signification – within the church's liturgical framing – is the apostolic repetition of the gospel. The continuous communal Gospel reading typically presumes prior biblical teaching and acquaintance with the Christian biblical narrative. The so called *lectio continua*, practised during the early centuries, meant that large portions of Scripture, or even the entire biblical text, were read through and used by the assembly. Local variations, from two to eight lessons during Sunday worship, indicate wide differences amongst the faith communities.

As the church gradually came to celebrate more feast days with special Gospel pericope readings, the Christian liturgical year became increasingly important. In this situation pericope readings became more common. This marks a change in the close relationship between ecclesial lectionaries and Bibles at a time when the *lectio continua* was still widely used. Before not too long, only two readings remained in the Western church. Due to this ritual change, the Old Testament readings were repressed – and until quite recently the Old Testament was often hardly read at all in corporate worship. With the common decrease of lectionary readings (the often ambitious readings in convents exempted), both with regard to length and number of readings, a shift in the understanding of canon and its potential for community life appear to have taken place as well.

The textual arrangement of the writings within the biblical corpus and the lectionary selections and readings appears to affect the canonical structuring. So does these texts' overall function as part of the Christian liturgy. The number of lessons recommended for Sunday readings – two, four or eight – here makes a difference, as do the commended weekday readings for a community of faith.

Part Four

Ideational Aspects of the Canon

8

The Scriptures and the Rule of Faith: Story, Scope, *scopus*

Up to this point the theme of canonicity has been discussed as a twofold ecclesial function: on the one hand, as the textual and ritual organization of the Christian Scriptures, and on the other, as the theological formulation of the so called Rule of Faith (*regula fidei*), understood as the *scopus* of the Christian biblical narrative. That is, this Rule is held to be the central point of view, or the unified sense at which the whole aims, when the Scriptures are read by the church.[1]

From the first and second centuries on, the Rule of Faith was influential in the formation of Christian theology. Church teachers such as Irenaeus, Tertullian and Clement of Alexandria considered it to be the basic theology of the church. Its function was established by means of association between the *regula fidei*'s various kerygmatic formulations and the Christian Scriptures. Both *regula fidei* and Scripture could be referred to as the church's canon.

Linguistically and theologically, early Christianity established a specific relation between the two notions of Rule of Faith and Christian Scripture (Chs 2 and 5). The *nomina sacra* practice also testifies to the close connection between the two (Ch. 3). Oral dimensions, as well, indicate their interdependency and mutual interpretive agendas: the Scriptures in the *regula*, and the *regula* in the Scriptures (Ch. 5). In this way a dyadic–binitarian and triadic–trinitarian pattern, testified to by the Rule, becomes the basis for Christian faith and life. Textually and performantially, the necessary theological association of Christian Scripture and the Rule of Faith comes to

---

[1] Cf. Gadamer, TM, 175; and idem, Gadamer in Conversation: Reflections and Commentary, 52.

expression in the church's perennial concern for Scripture's unity (Chs 3, 6 and 7).

The early mutual dependency of Scripture and Rule of Faith seems to be paradigmatic for later ecclesial interpretation and translation of the Bible canon. As the formation of the Christian Bible takes place, the Rule offers a hermeneutical framework, within which this process can occur. My concern in the present chapter is to continue the discussion on this relationship between the Scriptures and the *regula fidei*, and the impact their symbiosis has had on the Bible, its formation and significance (cf. sections 2.5.2; 2.5.3; 2.6; 5.3; 5.5; 5.6.3). Irenaeus' second-century perspective will be used to highlight some perennial issues related to the church's canon.

8.1 Scripture and Rule of Faith: Two sides of one and the same norm

The Scriptures and the Rule of Faith have been described by the German theologian Karlmann Beyschlag as two sides of one and the same norm (*zwei Seiten einer Norm*).[2] Others have pointed to the fact that the Rule of Faith and the Scriptures always belonged together, that there never was any Rule without the Scriptures.[3] In particular, the significance of the *regula fidei* has been presented as the very framework within which the canonical process takes place, by referring to the totality of Christian faith.[4]

The reference to the *regula fidei* by Irenaeus and other early church teachers aims at providing a standard, a secure foundation, for Christian faith. The time had arrived for the church when such normalization of its faith was felt to be necessary. *Regula* in the meaning of criterion was here being employed in a way which was common in Antiquity, e.g. in Lucretius (ca. 97–55 BC),

---

[2] Beyschlag, *Grundriß der Dogmengeschichte*, vol. 1 (Darmstadt, 1982).

[3] So Kunze, *Glaubensregel, Heilige Schrift und Taufbekenntnis: Untersuchungen über die dogmatische Autorität, ihr Werden und ihre Geschichte, vornehmlich in der alten Kirche* (Leipzig: Dörffling & Franke, 1899).

[4] Aland, *Das Problem des neutestamentlichen Kanons* (Göttingen: Vandenhoeck & Ruprecht, 1970), 11; Childs, *Biblical Theology of the Old and New Testaments* (London: SCM, 1992), 31f., 67; Blowers, 'The *Regula Fidei* and the Narrative Character of Early Christian Faith', *Pro Ecclesia* 6 (1997), 199; Ohlig, *Die theologische Begründung des neutestamentlichen Kanons in der alten Kirche* (Düsseldorf: Patmos-Verlag, 1972), 174.

who uses the term to explain the weight of a canon for building.[5] Without a canon (*regula*), he says, there is no security (*De Rerum Natura* 4.505f.).[6]

The 'New Testament' writings are attaining normative status for the faith community through their church constitutive use alongside the Jewish Scriptures. This takes place primarily in the contexts of worship, mission and teaching, as part of the theological narrative and meta-narrative pattern, soon referred to as the ecclesial *regula* (κανών). Still, however, it may be tempting to propose a sudden formation of the New Testament canon, as the result of a defensive response to Marcion and the Gnostic movements. This is suggested by some leading twentieth-century scholars.[7] According to Hans von Campenhausen, Marcion functions as the catalyst for the church in a suddenly emerging canon formation. In his programmatic 1968 study on the canon formation (English edition in 1972) – which became the standard account for nearly a generation – von Campenhausen presents what he understands by canonization:

> To make my own position clear: by the beginnings of the canon I do not understand the emergence and dissemination, nor even the ecclesiastical use and influence of what were later the canonical writings. One can, in my view, speak of a 'canon' only where of set purpose such a document or group of documents is given a special, normative position, by virtue of which it takes its place alongside the existing Old Testament 'scriptures'. Nothing of this kind is to be observed before the middle of the second century; and the assertion that something of the sort must, nevertheless, already have begun and existed is neither provable nor probable. The fact that a work which later became a 'New Testament' book is occasionally echoed or utilised or alluded to is not 'canonisation'; indeed, taken for what it is and no more, it is not even a move in that direction.[8]

In my opinion, this is a rather narrowly defined view of Scripture canonization, draining the concept of canon of some of its effective-historical roots and potential.[9] As shown in the previous chapter, on performative aspects,

---

[5] See further, Ch. 2.

[6] Referenced in Osborn, 'Reason and the rule of faith in the second century AD', in *The Making of Orthodoxoy: Essays in Honour of Henry Chadwick*, ed. R. Williams (Cambridge: Cambridge University Press, 1989), 41.

[7] So Adolf von Harnack, John Knox and Hans von Campenhausen.

[8] Campenhausen, *The Formation of the Christian Bible* (Philadelphia: Fortress, 1972), 103.

[9] Cf. Chs 1 and 2.

already by the early to mid-second century, the bulk of the new Christian writings were practically equal in status with the Jewish Scriptures and often drawn on more frequently – though not yet typically referred to by the scriptural label.[10] Throughout the present study I seek to widen the understanding of canon formation as compared to that embraced by von Campenhausen and others.[11]

In this chapter, too, a broader, more inclusive understanding of canon will be endorsed, in which orally transmitted theological and narrative dimensions will be looked at. Canonization of the Christian Scriptures here takes place only as part of a larger unified process, beginning already in the New Testament.[12] The canonizing process itself even becomes a component of Christianity's more elaborate narrative; this includes, as well, telling the story of its Scriptures to itself and to Jews, to Greeks and to schismatics.

I shall start by treating the narrative framework provided by the Scriptures and the Rule of Faith.

8.2 The narrative form of the canon *as Rule of Faith* and *as Scripture*

In his exposition of the early Christian kerygma, the Patristic scholar Basil Studer distinguishes between three different kerygmatic forms. Alongside the invocation (*epiclesis*) and praise (*doxologia*) of God's name, the 'New Testament' kerygma also takes a narrative form (*narratio*).[13] Studer argues that, before AD 150, the extant Christian writings, because of their character as 'simple recollection of the divine acts of salvation[,]

---

[10] Cf. also Ch. 9.

[11] An alternative account of the Christian canon formation that does not embrace the canonical process is found in Trobisch, *The First Edition of the New Testament* (Oxford: Oxford University Press, 2000). He depicts the edition of what he calls the archetypal late second-century two-testament Bible as the earliest 'canon proper'. In his view, the canonical process is not extended over centuries, but is thought to be the editorial work preceding the 'publication' of the Christian Bible. In a somewhat similar vein, A. C. Sundberg (*Towards a Revised History of the New Testament Canon* [Berlin: Akademie-Verlag, 1968]), and others, have depicted the exact delimitation of the canonical scope in the late fourth-century canon lists as canonization proper. Earlier stages of this development are, at best, treated as 'pre-history' of the canon, to use Campenhausen's term.

[12] This point has been repeatedly emphasized by Brevard Childs.

[13] Studer, *Trinity and Incarnation: The Faith of the Early Church* (Edinburgh: T&T Clark, 1993), 22.

it is certainly not erroneous to label them as *narratio.*[14] These writings, especially the 'New Testament' Scriptures, refer in a particular way to *Jesus' saving deed* and the act of salvation which God has accomplished through Jesus Christ.

Moreover, from early on, a trinitarian pattern emerges in these texts. As discussed above, the phrase 'Father, Son, and Holy Spirit', in Robert Jenson's wording, is 'simultaneously a very compressed telling of the total narrative by which Scripture identifies God and a personal name for the God so specified; in it, name and narrative description not only appear together, as at the beginning of the Ten Commandments, but are identical.'[15] This reading of Name and narrative, as 'identical' entities, offers a hermeneutical key to understanding the juxtaposition of 'Scripture' and 'Lord' as basic components in the canon formation process (see section 1.2). As I have previously argued, the history of the Christian canon does not start off in the text of the Bible, nor in the community of faith, but in a revelatory event and experience. That is, in the Lord of Israel, being revealed in Jesus and identified as the Lord of the church.[16]

From the viewpoint of this Christian kerygmatic rendering, God is identified as 'whoever raised Jesus from the dead, having before raised Israel from Egypt.'[17] The biblical, 'Old Testament' narrative is continued in the life and words of Jesus, as witnessed in the early Christian preaching. Through this ecclesial construction, the Christian narrative understanding of the 'Old Testament' becomes part of a new text, and context, provided by Jesus and the early Christian assembly and documented in the 'New Testament' accounts. What was once spoken by the Law and the Prophets is set in immediate relation to the 'Son'. The old creeds of Israel are believed to be fulfilled in Christian ones, and the proper name of God is identified within a new narrative and meta-narrative framework.[18]

---

[14] Ibid.

[15] Jenson, *Systematic Theology*, vol. 1: *The Triune God* (New York: Oxford University Press, 1997), 46.

[16] Cf. section 1.2.4.

[17] Jenson, *Systematic Theology*, vol. 1, 63.

[18] Cf. ibid., 64: 'Since the biblical God can truly be identified by narrative, his hypostatic being, his self-identity, is constituted in *dramatic coherence*. The classic definition of this sort of coherence is provided by Aristotle, who noticed that a good story is one in which events occur 'unexpectedly but on account of each other', so that before each decisive event we cannot predict it, but afterwards see it was just what had to happen'; also Wilken, 'In novissimis diebus. Biblical Promises, Jewish Hopes and Early Christian Exegesis', *Journal of Early Christian Studies* 1 (1993): 1–19.

As the nature of the biblical narrative, due to its very narrativity, 'imposes a limit on theological comment',[19] and as theology is always important for Christian identity, the delicate task of balancing theology with the Christian story has to be sensitively worked out; story and confession/ dogma, narrative and meta-narrative in continuous dialogue. Related to this, the reader may recall the Christian kerygma taking a narrative form at the inception of Christian discourse, as indicated, e.g. by Tom Wright. He argues that the early Christians told and lived a form of Israel's story, reaching its climax in Jesus, which then issued in their spirit-given new life and task. This united them deeper than all diversity. In fact, Christian 'diversities were diverse ways of construing that basic point.'[20] Disputes among Christians, then,

> were carried on not so much by appeal to fixed principles, or to Jewish scripture conceived as a rag-bag of proof-texts, but precisely by fresh retellings of the story which highlighted the points at issue. Their strong centre, strong enough to be recognizable in works as diverse as those of Jude and Ignatius, James and Justin Martyr, was not a theory or a new ethic, not an abstract dogma or rote-learned teaching, but a particular story told and lived.[21]

The variously told, unifying narrative structure that Wright addresses here developed around a 'strong' dyadic-binitarian and triadic-trinitarian kerygma of the earliest church. A well-balanced analysis of a form of such a unifying kerygma of the New Testament was made a few years ago by Eugene Lemcio and Ben Meyer (see section 8.4). Their proposals fit well with the kerygmatic narrative structure found also in *1 Clement*, Ignatius and Justin Martyr – a structure being continuous with that provided by the *Rule of Faith*, used by the Anti-Gnostic Fathers.[22]

Other scholars, such as Robert Wall and Paul Blowers, have maintained a similar view. Wall writes: 'In my judgment the church's Rule of Faith is narrative in shape, trinitarian in substance, and relates the essential beliefs of

---

[19] Frei, *The Identity of Jesus Christ* (Philadelphia: Fortress, 1975), 125.
[20] Wright, *The New Testament and the People of God,* vol. 1 (Minneapolis: Fortress, 1992), 456.
[21] Ibid.
[22] See Skarsaune, 'The Development of Scriptural Interpretation in the Second and Third Centuries – except Clement and Origen', in *Hebrew Bible/Old Testament: The History of Its Interpretation*, vol. 1 (Göttingen: Vandenhoeck & Ruprecht, 1996), 373–442; cf. my argumentation, Ch. 5.

Christianity together by the grammar of christological monotheism.'[23] In like fashion, Blowers comments on Irenaeus' and Tertullian's uses of the *regula*:

> For Irenaeus and Tertullian alike it is imperative to identify the Canon of Truth or Rule of Faith as Scripture's own intrinsic story-line in order to avoid the Gnostics' double-talk, their propagating of one myth on the philosophical level while still trying, on another level, to communicate it with pieces of scriptural narrative. Thus when Irenaeus expounds the Rule of Faith for his friend Marcianus in his *Epideixis* (*Demonstration of the Apostolic Preaching*), he does it literally by retelling the biblical story and indicating the underlying nexus between its constitutive elements as though he were unfolding the sequences of a drama. The story of creation, paradise, and the fall presents a prelude.[24]

Blowers is right in his emphasis of the narrative connection between Scripture and *regula*. Yet, to be more precise, even if Irenaeus tends to understand the *regula* in this way (cf. *Epid.* 3ff.; *Adv. Haer.* III, 1.2), some caution is needed. In the strict sense the Rule is not identical to Scripture's own narrative or narratives, or even to a summary of the Scriptures.[25] However, already in the 1950s Bengt Hägglund pointed to structural–narratival similarities between the *regula fidei* and Christian Scripture. On Irenaeus' use of the Rule of Faith/ Truth, Hägglund concludes that the *regula* is not

> a summary of the teaching, but rather the events to which Sacred Scripture provides the authentic testimony: God's acts from creation until the foundation of the church through the apostles, as well as the acts of the future, belonging to the same history, the restoration of all creation, and the last judgment.[26]

The central revelatory acts of the Triune God are at the core of these renderings of the Christian Rule.

---

[23] Wall, 'Reading the Bible from within Our Traditions', in *Between Two Horizons: Spanning New Testament Studies and Systematic Theology*, (eds) J. B. Green and M. Turner (Grand Rapids: Eerdmans, 2000), 101.

[24] Blowers, 'The *Regula Fidei* and the Narrative Character of Early Christian Faith', 212.

[25] Cf. my discussion in Bokedal, 'The Rule of Faith: Tracing its Origins', *Journal of Theological Interpretation* 7, no. 2 (forthcoming). On the inner structuring function of the *regula fidei* as the *character fidei* or the *forma doctrinae*, see 6.3, n. 32 above.

[26] Hägglund, 'Die Bedeutung der 'regula fidei' als Grundlage theologischer Aussagen', *Studia Theologica* 12 (1958): 17; my trans. On the organic unity of the Rule of Faith and biblical teaching on right-eousness, see Gösta Hallonsten's discussion on the Joint Declaration, *Gemeinsame Erklärung zur Rechtfertigungslehre*, 'Kommentar – ett katolskt perspektiv' ... *att i allt bekänna Kristus* (Stockholm: Verbum, 2000), 115.

Using Irenaeus as an early representative and trendsetter for the interpretation of the canonical process, I will now further analyse his twofold understanding of the biblical canon as Scripture and Rule of Faith.

8.3 The canonical process in Irenaeus

8.3.1 Unity and harmony

If we were to single out one feature only as having the largest impact on the canonical process of the last quarter of the second century, it would most probably be the strive towards unity. Too much diversity created problems, as did in some instances even slight differences in practice or doctrine. At the outset of his career as a church leader, Irenaeus becomes involved as mediator in the affairs of the catholic church. Out of his experiences from Asia Minor, Lyons and Rome, he is able to handle, in a generous vein, questions of diversity that have arisen among the different church regions of his day. In the Quartodeciman struggle, where he takes on the role as diplomat promoting the unity of the church, he severely criticizes and admonishes Victor, the bishop of Rome,[27] who was about to break with the Quartodeciman churches of the East.

Although the expression *unitas ecclesiae*[28] is only rarely used in our Latin translation of Irenaeus' *Against Heresies*, and the term *una ecclesia* is not found at all, the notions of a unified church[29] and unity in all church doctrine are present all through the writing of Irenaeus. In opposition to his adversaries, the 'heretics', who in his view dissolve the most basic doctrines of the church – the *one* gospel and the *one* belief in *unum Deum, unum Christum, unum Spiritum*[30] – he presents the teaching of the church as a harmonious whole. Isidor Frank can thus depict the element of unity as the most important theme in the Irenaean theology: 'The leitmotif which controls the whole theological

---

[27] Eusebius, *Hist. Eccl.*, V, 24.
[28] *Adv. Haer.* IV, 26.1; V, 33.7.
[29] See esp. *Adv. Haer.* I, 10.1-3.
[30] Benoit, *Saint Irénée: Introduction a l'étude de sa théologie* (Paris: Presses universitaires de France, 1960), 204; ibid., 216: 'A la multiplicité, principe essentiel de l'hérésie, Irénée oppose donc sans se lasser, l'unité, principe essentiel et constitutif de l'Église. Car l'hérésie prône plusieurs dieux, plusieurs Christ, plusieurs évangiles, une multitude de traditions.'

thinking of Irenaeus is the idea of unity.' Moreover, the notion of unity is even described as 'the most important individual theological contribution by Irenaeus.'[31]

Unity as leitmotif becomes crucial also in relating the Old and New Testaments, and the different parts of Scripture, to one another. In *Adv. Haer.* IV, 27.2, where Irenaeus dwells on a discussion of obscure passages of Scripture, we read:

> [T]he entire Scriptures, the prophets, and the Gospels, can be clearly, unambiguously, and harmoniously understood by all, although all do not believe them.

The ideal reading of the Scriptures tends towards this type of harmonization. Again, in Frances Young's phrasing, 'The unity of the scriptures is recognised to have been a "dogma" among the Fathers.'[32] Irenaeus, being one of the first Christian theologians, is no exception. Every ambiguity is absorbed into a reading on a higher level that ultimately appears to promote the tradition of old,[33] of the *presbyteroi* of the church, who, by succession, have received the tradition from the apostles. Another passage further illuminates not only such intratextual harmonizing, but also a slightly different form of harmonization, namely that between the Old Testament writings and the Christ event. The 'enigmas' and 'fables' of the Scriptures, accordingly, are transmuted by the Christian reading and discovered *post eventum* to be a real treasure, 'brought to light by the cross of Christ':

> For every prophecy, before its fulfilment, is to men [full of] enigmas and ambiguities. But when the time has arrived, and the prediction has come to pass, then the prophecies have a clear and certain exposition. And for this reason, indeed, when at this present time the law is read to the Jews, it is like a fable; for they do not possess the explanation of all things pertaining to the advent of the Son of God, which took place in human nature; but when it is read by the Christians, it is a treasure, hid indeed in a field, but brought to light by the cross of Christ. (Iren. *Adv. Haer.* IV, 26.1)[34]

---

[31] Frank, *Der Sinn der Kanonbildung* (Freiburg: Herder, 1971), 190; my trans. Cf. Benoit, *Saint Irénée*, 203–19; and Kereszty, 'The Unity of the Church in the Theology of Irenaeus', *The Second Century* 4 (1984): 202–18.

[32] Young, *Biblical Exegesis and the Formation of Christian Culture* (Cambridge: Cambridge University Press, 1997), 7.

[33] It can be noted that for Irenaeus, as for Origen a few years later, every part of Scripture is significant, *Adv. Haer.* IV, 31.1.

[34] ANF 1:496.

When compared to earlier second-century exegesis, Irenaeus has obtained a new vision of text. On the one hand he is viewing the Scriptures out of a radical 'proof from prophecy' perspective (cf. *Adv. Haer.* IV, 33), where the New Testament Scriptures and events are the *demonstranda*, which need demonstration. However, in the new pluralistic setting, sensed from within the church since the break with Marcion, a new context for the interpretation of Scripture has emerged. The Old Testament text is no longer the *demonstrantes*, the axiomatic starting point for any theological argument.[35] On the contrary, now the Old Testament itself needs demonstration, something of which second- to fifth-generation Christians, like the author of the *Epistle of Barnabas* (ca. AD 70–135) and Justin (ca. AD 100–65), had been aware of in practice, however, not deliberately – as part of a hermeneutical agenda.

The hermeneutic 'turnround' that occurred with the influence on the church of the schools of Marcion and various Gnostic sects had to some extent already been anticipated. Therefore, the crises that appeared along with the 'heretic' movements in the church were from a hermeneutical point of view not as devastating as has occasionally been suggested.[36] The apologetic reaction of Irenaeus as a leading theologian is not so much to be characterized by a new biblical hermeneutics with no predecessor. Instead, the hermeneutical shift that takes place in his *Against Heresies* becomes crucial precisely as a part of the canonizing process of the biblical writings. The questions evoked by the 'heretics' called for a new approach to the Scriptures and the exegetical methods hitherto elaborated. A shift took place as the old proof-from-prophecy tradition to some extent was turned in the opposite direction. What Irenaeus sets out to do is to apply the old proofs from the Scriptures as something like a 'proof from fulfillment'. In Skarsaune's wording: 'The *harmony*, the *correspondence* between prophecy and fulfillment is still decisive, but for the opposite reason: it now proves that the Old Testament is the Bible of Jesus and the New Testament writers, that the prophets were true messengers of Christ, and that the God of the Old Testament is the Father of Jesus Christ' (cf. *Adv. Haer.* IV, 34).[37] However, perhaps the outcome of this

---

[35] Cf. Skarsaune, 'The Development of Scriptural Interpretation in the Second and Third Centuries – except Clement and Origen', 427.

[36] E.g. by Adolf von Harnack, John Knox et al.

[37] Skarsaune, 'The Development of Scriptural Interpretation in the Second and Third Centuries – except Clement and Origen', 427.

new contextualization of the scriptural proof was not so much an apology for the Old Testament as it was a sanction of the New Testament as Scripture, now that the NT texts were used in a similar manner and for a similar aim, as previously that of the Old Testament Scriptures. The process of canonization of the New Testament took place within, and as a part of, these two movements: the movement from old to new in the 'proof from prophecy' and that from new to old in the 'proof from fulfillment'.

Within the scope of this circular movement Irenaeus distances himself from the exclusive dependence on the Old Testament text by his vigorous usage of the New Testament in *Against Heresies*. This change of emphasis is better understood as the closing of a circle than as a deep hermeneutical crisis of the late second century. In *Against Heresies* Irenaeus is not primarily addressing the inner group of the church, but performing an apology for the tradition of the church within a new context. To some degree, one result of this was a new vision of the Scriptures. In the cases where this unified outlook of old and new as part of the Bible was already present, this understanding became standardized. The authorization of the New Testament texts as a necessary part of a unified collection of holy books has definitely taken place when the Jewish Scriptures, which had been received by all Christians, needed a carefully elaborated demonstration ('proof from fulfillment'). This could only be carried out by means of the new *corpora*, or part-collections,[38] of New Testament Scriptures, which had won next to universal credibility among the Christian communities, despite some variations in shape of these collections. Now, from this 'fulfillment' defence of the Old Testament it followed that the apostolic and sub-apostolic writings were confirmed in their normative role.

8.3.2 Continuity and contemporaneity

Irenaeus depicts his own traditionalist position as an ideal, i.e. to stand in continuity with the apostles, presbyters and bishops of old. This is generally considered to be in line with the mainstream Judaeo-Christian bias by the turn of the third century. In *Against Heresies* we read:

---

[38] The NT part-collections characteristically consisted of the Gospels, the *Praxapostolos*, the Pauline corpus and the Book of Revelation (see further, Ch. 4).

> Wherefore it is incumbent to obey the presbyters who are in the Church,
> – those who, as I have shown, possess the succession from the apostles;
> those who, together with the succession of the episcopate, have received
> the certain gift of truth, according to the good pleasure of the Father. (*Adv.*
> *Haer.* IV, 26.2)[39]

A parallel to the form of Christian traditionalism that we encounter in
Irenaeus – inherited from his background in Asia Minor – is found in post-70
Rabbinic Judaism. Lee Levine and Ben Bokser, e.g. show how the Rabbis
make use of elements of the tradition in order to emphasize continuity with
Jerusalem and the pre-70 past.[40] After Jerusalem's destruction, one particular
challenge was to legitimize a continuing celebration of Easter, since the basis
of some of the scriptural regulations had been withdrawn with the fall of the
Temple. In the meantime, a number of extra-biblical prescriptions had been
established as normative tradition. The solution that the Rabbis chose was to
present the practices of the Diaspora synagogues as old and well-established
traditions. They used the argument of tradition to be able to consistently
present and uphold their most important identity marker – the celebration of
the Jewish Easter – within a new setting.

This was their way of handling the problem of continuity, in a situation
where their own tradition had undergone radical change, while, at the same
time, the relation of Rabbinic Judaism towards its own past continued to be
largely traditionalistic.[41] Similarly, Irenaeus wishes to give the impression of
being contemporaneous with the ecclesial tradition of his predecessors, and,
in this endeavour too he largely succeeds.

8.3.3 Defining a canon of scriptures

Irenaeus' five-volume work *Against Heresies*, written between AD 180 and
185, is important for our understanding of the formation of the Christian
Bible. Although Irenaeus does not explicitly reflect on the canon *as list*, the so

---

[39] ANF 1:497.
[40] Bokser, *Pharisaic Judaism in Transition* (New York: Bloch Publishing, 1935); and Levine, *The Ancient Synagogue: The First Thousand Years* (New Haven and London: Yale University Press, 2000), 160ff.
[41] I owe the comments on the possible parallelism between the synagogue and the church to a conversation with Professor Oskar Skarsaune.

called 'canonical principle' – to neither add nor take anything away – found in Deuteronomy 4.2 and 12.32, is none the less there.

Regarding additions made to the Scriptures, he criticizes those who add unauthorized writings to the biblical books, like the Valentinians with their Gospel of Truth (*Adv. Haer.* III, 11.9), the disciples of Ptolemaeus who read what is unwritten (ἐξ ἄγραφον καὶ ἀναγινόσκοντες; *Adv. Haer.* I, 8.1), and the Marcosians[42] who use apocryphal and false (ἀποκρύφων καὶ νόθων) writings (*Adv. Haer.* I, 20.1).

Irenaeus further accuses Marcion of demolishing the fourfold form of the Gospel by only accepting the Gospel of Luke (*Adv. Haer.* III, 11.9; 12.12). The Ebionites who hold on to the Gospel of Matthew as the only Gospel and who do not accept the Pauline corpus (*Adv. Haer.* I, 26.2; III, 15.1) likewise are said to cut off writings from the canonical collection, as do those who reject the Gospel of John (*Adv. Haer.* III, 11.9), or the Acts of the Apostles (III, 14.3-4; 15.1).[43] Taken together, these examples certainly indicate the existence of a de facto canon available to the bishop of Lyons.

What Irenaeus really illustrates by his double concern – neither to add nor to take anything away from the Scriptures – is the canonical formula which was established not only within Judaism and the second-century church, but also more widely. Christoph Dohmen and Manfred Oeming, in their investigation of the canonical formula, give examples from the environment of Israel, the Hittite culture, Assyria, Babylonia, Phoenicia and classical Greece. They convincingly show the universal existence and character of this two-limbed formula,[44] which, indeed, is as straightforward as the books of Deuteronomy (4.2; 12.32) and Revelation (22.18f.) indicate.[45] In the wording of Dohmen and Oeming:

> The canonical formula consists of two parts: the prohibition against adding (*Erweiterungsverbot*), and the prohibition against abbreviating (*Kürzungsverbot*). The latter guarantees a minimum amount of text, below which we should

---

[42] The Marcosians were followers of Marcus, a second-century Gnostic leader and adherent of Valentinus in Asia Minor.

[43] Jaschke, 'Irenäus von Lyon', *TRE*, vol. 16 (1987), 258–68.

[44] Dohmen and Oeming, *Biblischer Kanon warum und wozu?* (Freiburg: Herder, 1992), 68. Brevard Childs is sceptical as to the central role of this formula in the canonical process of the OT. Dohmen and Oeming, however, use the formula to highlight what they call '[der] Übergang vom *kanonischen Prozeß* zur *Kanonisierung*'.

[45] Ibid., 68–89. Cf. also Eccles. 3.14; Jer. 26.2; Prov. 30.6; and Matt. 5.18.

not go. It is open towards explanatory, more precise or illustrative progress. However, that which was once known as religiously significant must not get lost. It all comes down to protecting against any loss of text, to guaranteeing already approved language, not to prohibiting any future expansion or addition.

The prohibition against adding text (*Erweiterungsverbot*), on the other hand, sets forth a maximum limit beyond which we cannot proceed. It thus makes an essentially larger claim than the prohibition against abbreviating, namely the claim to completeness, at the very least in view of that which is necessary. Addition is not only not necessary, it is harmful or hazardous and thus prohibited. The prohibition against adding still however allows for extracts, such as shorthand formulas (*Kurzformeln*) by means of handy summaries, or by highlighting key sentences. Its primary purpose is to end the process of progress. Substantially, nothing additional that is necessary can be given – essentially everything that is necessary is already said in a complete way.[46]

In *Against Heresies* (IV, 33.8) Irenaeus appears to make explicit reference to the formula, with its double function, and applies it to the Scriptures: 'Nothing is to be added, and nothing is to be taken away.' As seen above, Irenaeus makes frequent use of both parts of the formula. Concerning the *Erweiterungsverbot*, the prohibition against adding text, Dohmen and Oeming point out that this second half of the formula makes a considerably larger claim than the prohibition against abbreviating (*Kürzungsverbot*). As an implication and direct consequence of Irenaeus' Scripture-based argumentation, we repeatedly find the usage of what Dohmen and Oeming call 'extracts, such as shorthand formulas (*Kurzformeln*) by means of handy summaries, or by highlighting key sentences.' The crucial role of the Rule of Faith as a short formula – the sum content of apostolic faith as set down in Scripture and apostolic teaching – further illuminates this claim to completeness. According to Dohmen and Oeming, the *Kürzungsverbot* and the *Erweiterungsverbot* when taken together accomplish the act of canonization. The canonical process is brought to an end, while at the same time 'canonization proper' takes place by applying the canonical formula.[47]

Within Irenaeus' apologetic discourse in *Against Heresies* (III, 8.1), the prophets, the Lord and the apostles constitute a more or less closed collection of writings. Although these Scriptures – to which a specific biblical hermeneutics

---

[46] Dohmen and Oeming, *Biblischer Kanon warum und wozu?*, 69; my trans.
[47] Ibid., 68.

is applied[48] – are held to be perfect (*perfectae; Adv. Haer.* II, 28.2), Irenaeus nevertheless sets forth the *logia* of the Lord as the most eminent authority (*Adv. Haer.* I, pref. 1). He further establishes the *alētheia* – in *Adv. Haer.* III, 13.2 said to be God himself – as the source of all truth. In other passages, the domain of truth is denoted by the *regula veritatis* (*regula fidei*) and its equivalents. Another seemingly important feature ascribed to '*all* the Scriptures' is their character as inspired text (*Adv. Haer.* II, 28.3). The issue of inspiration as the qualification *par préférance* for a biblical writing, however, comes to the fore more specifically when discussing the translation of the Septuagint (*Adv. Haer.* III, 21.2).[49] Thus, when considering second-century canon reception, the question of inspiration is crucial (cf. Ch. 1, note 12; and section 2.5.2, note 90). Bruce Metzger's remark, that 'inspiration' should *not* be taken into account when discussing the issue of canonization, therefore needs reconsideration (cf. section 1.1).[50]

8.3.4 Comprehensiveness and indispensability

In the third book of *Against Heresies* Irenaeus presents an argument for the usage of the complete collection of Scriptures as he comments on the exclusion by his adversaries of certain books from the biblical canon:

> Now if any man set Luke aside, as one who did not know the truth, he will, [by so acting,] manifestly reject that Gospel of which he claims to be a disciple. For through him we have become acquainted with very many and important parts of the Gospel; for instance, the generation of John, the history of Zacharias, the coming of the angel to Mary, the exclamation of Elisabeth, the descent of the angels to the shepherds … There are also many other particulars to be found mentioned by Luke alone, which are made use of by both Marcion

[48] See, e.g. Brox, 'Die biblische Hermeneutik des Irenäus', *Zeitschrift für antikes Christentum* 2 (1998): 26–48; Young, *Virtuoso Theology: The Bible and Interpretation* (Cleveland, OH: The Pilgrim Press, 1993), 26–65; Jenson, *Hermeneutics and the Life of the Church* (Grand Rapids: Eerdmans, 1995), 96.

[49] See further Hengel and Deines, 'Die Septuaginta als 'christliche Schriftsammlung' und das Problem ihres Kanons', in *Verbindliches Zeugnis 1: Kanon – Schrift – Tradition*, (eds) W. Pannenberg and T. Schneider (Freiburg im Breisgau: Herder and Göttingen: Vandenhoeck & Ruprecht, 1992).

[50] Metzger, *The Canon of the New Testament: Its Origin, Development, and Significance* (Oxford: Clarendon, 1987), 254–7. Cf., e.g. Iren. *Adv. Haer.* II, 28.2: 'rectissime scientes quia scripturae quidem perfectae sunt, quippe a verbo Dei et spiritu eius dictae' (we must … correctly realize that the scriptures are perfect, since they were spoken by God's Word and his Spirit), citation from Brox, *Irenäus von Lyon: Adversus Haereses* (Freiburg: Herder, 1993). Trans. Robert Grant, *Irenaeus of Lyons* (London and New York: Routledge, 1997), 117.

and Valentinus. And besides all these, [he records] what [Christ] said to His disciples in the way, after the resurrection, and how they recognised Him in the breaking of bread. It follows then, as of course, that these men must either receive the rest of his narrative, or else reject these parts also. For no persons of common sense can permit them to receive some things recounted by Luke as being true, and to set others aside, as if he had not known the truth. And if indeed Marcion's followers reject these, they will then possess no Gospel. (*Adv. Haer.* III, 14.3-4)[51]

Irenaeus strongly recommends both those inside and those living on the margins of the Irenaean church to accept all Christian scriptural tradition – in this case, all that Luke has written down. The writings of Luke are thought to be indispensable for knowledge of the full gospel. The alternative, in his view, is to reject Lukan writings, both the Gospel and the Acts. As already mentioned, similar criticism as that towards Marcion is directed towards the Ebionites, who hold on to the Gospel of Matthew as their only Gospel, while rejecting the Pauline writings (*Adv. Haer.* I, 26.2; III, 15.1), and towards those who reject the Gospel of John (*Adv. Haer.* III, 11.9), or the Acts of the Apostles (14.3-4; 15.1). For a parallel, we can note that the (Irenaean) emphasis on the complete number of Scriptures is also found in Clement of Alexandria (*Strom.* VII, 16). By the late second century, the idea of comprehensiveness or completeness, characteristic also of the construction of the *regula fidei*, has become a significant element in the theological discussion. In an article on the biblical hermeneutics of Irenaeus, Norbert Brox thus can point to the bishop's inclination towards completeness as a first hermeneutical rule: 'The Bible is always to be used as a whole. Selection means abbreviation and loss of truth.'[52]

8.3.5 Writings included in the scriptural canon

Hans-Jochen Jaschke claims in an article on Irenaeus that 'practically the whole New Testament as well as the Old Testament belong to the "canon" of Irenaeus.'[53] With some modification, this comes close to what we find in the bishop's two extant writings.

---

[51] ANF 1:438f.
[52] Brox, 'Die biblische Hermeneutik des Irenäus': 'Die Bibel ist immer als Ganze zu benutzen. Auswahl bedeutet Verkürzung und Wahrheitsverlust'. My trans.
[53] Jaschke, 'Irenäus von Lyon', 261.

Regarding his Old Testament, Irenaeus tells the legend of the exact agreement and inspiration of the 70 individual translations of the Septuagint, which, he says, was recognized even by the gentiles (*Adv. Haer.* III, 21.1-3). The momentous role Irenaeus ascribes to the Septuagint is highlighted by the parallel he draws between this translation of the Hebrew Scriptures into Greek and the divine renewal of the Scriptures by Ezra, immediately after they had been annihilated during the Babylonian captivity. Similar to Justin, Irenaeus does not prioritize the Hebrew text. For him, Greek is the language of the one Bible.[54]

It is interesting to note that the existence of a particular Alexandrian Jewish canon has never been convincingly defended.[55] Nevertheless, the conscious choice of the Septuagint translation leads to certain additions, as compared to the 24 (or 22) books of the Hebrew Bible. For our purposes, it is worth noting the additions to Jeremiah (Baruch), cited twice by Irenaeus, and the Greek additions to Daniel, both of which were probably appended and accepted by the Greek-speaking Jews.[56] Roger Beckwith draws the conclusion with regard to the additions to Jeremiah (Baruch, Lamentations, and The Epistle of Jeremiah) that '[t]here is reason to think that, as in the case of Daniel, the Septuagint appendices had at least begun to be added in the Jewish period; and, as in the case of Daniel once more, this was presumably done for the same purposes of edification as motivated the midrashic expansions included in some books of the Septuagint within their text.'[57] These additions were regarded precisely as appendices (or as variations in textual form rather than various canonical scope),[58] which can be seen in the way they are cited.[59] As to the number of books included in the OT canon, the Church Fathers of the East adhere to the Jewish canon of 22 books (Justin, Melito, Origen, Cyril of Jerusalem, Athanasius, the Fathers of the Council of Laodicea, Gregorius of Nazians, Amphiloch of Iconium, Epiphanius of Salamis, Jerome, living in

---

[54] The labels 'Old Testament' and 'New Testament' for the two main parts of the Scriptures are presumably not known to Irenaeus when he writes his *Against Heresies*. Pace Trobisch, *First Edition*.

[55] See, e.g. McDonald, *The Biblical Canon*, 100–3.

[56] Beckwith, *The Old Testament Canon of the New Testament Church and its Background in Early Judaism* (Grand Rapids: Eerdmans, 1985), 341.

[57] Ibid.

[58] Skarsaune, 'Kodeks og kanon: om brug og avgrensning av de gammeltestamentlige skrifter i oldkirken', in *Text and Theology: Studies in Honour of Professor dr. theol. Magne Sæbø Presented on the Occasion of His 65th Birthday*, ed. A. Tångberg (Oslo: Verbum, 1994), 242.

[59] Beckwith, *The Old Testament Canon*, 339–42

the East, and others).[60] The one who breaks this chain of witnesses (to what seems to be a Jewish Rabbinic and Christian consensus) is Hilary of Poitiers in the fourth century, by making one small alteration in the old canon list of Origen. Whereas Origen explicitly excluded the two books of Maccabees,[61] Hilary instead adds the books of Tobit and Judith. Thereby he deliberately chooses to break with the general concern and consensus among the leading (Eastern) theologians of the early church – to stand in continuity with the synagogue on this particular issue.[62] In the wake of this new neglect of the Jewish background, Ambrose, who writes the first Christian commentary on an Apocryphal book (Tobit), and Augustine, with his strong argumentation against Jerome's learned remarks on the Apocrypha, brought a new agenda for the canon debate. This new agenda comes to the fore in several of the local synods held in the late fourth and the fifth centuries.

With this background and development in mind, we can place Irenaeus more or less in the Eastern tradition, in which OT Apocrypha – just as in the New Testament – are made use of but are not included among the Scriptures. Irenaeus alludes to 2 Macc. (7.28) once, which most certainly is a quote from *The Shepherd* of Hermas (26.1) in *Adv. Haer.* IV, 20.2, Sirach once and Wisdom four times. It is worth noting that, in Epiphanius, Sirach and Wisdom are included among the New Testament writings (*Pan.* 76.5).[63] Similarly, in the Muratorian fragment, Wisdom seems to be included in the New Testament list between the Pauline letters and the Book of Revelation. As the Old Testament part of the biblical writings was in principle closed, Apocryphal (or Deuterocanonical) books probably had to be placed elsewhere by those interested enough to reflect on the problem. The apparent fact that Apocryphal books were not generally included in the biblical canons of the early church is also hinted at by the manuscript evidence. In the phrasing of Beckwith, who

---

[60] Hennings, *Der Briefwechsel zwischen Augustinus und Hieronymus und ihr Streit um den Kanon des Alten Testaments und die Auslegung von Gal. 2,11-14* (Suppl. Vigiliae Christinae (Formerly Philosophia Patrum): Texts and Studies of Early Christian Life and Language, vol. XXI; Leiden: Brill, 1994), 146ff.

[61] Ibid.: this is the only explicit exclusion of books from the Old Testament canon made by Origen, who, despite his apparent insistence on the 22-book canon, had a very generous attitude towards those other books (apocrypha) from the Septuagint group that were used for worship.

[62] Hennings, *Der Briefwechsel zwischen Augustinus und Hieronymus und ihr Streit um den Kanon des Alten Testaments und die Auslegung von Gal. 2,11-14*, 184–6.

[63] See McDonald, *The Biblical Canon: Its Origin, Transmission, and Authority* (Peabody, MA: Hendrickson, 2007), 374–5.

refers to C. H. Roberts, 'up until the peace of the church in AD 313 the only books of the Apocrypha to occur are … Tobit, Ecclesiasticus and Wisdom.'[64] However, in light of recent manuscript finds, and Irenaeus' allusions to OT Apocrypha referred to above, we can add 2 Maccabees and perhaps Baruch to Beckwith's list of early Christian OT Apocrypha.[65]

As to the New Testament writings used by Irenaeus, Eusebius provides some helpful information (*Hist. Eccl.* V, 8.1-8). He first accounts for what Irenaeus says about the four Gospels (Matthew, Mark, Luke and John) and the Book of Revelation; further, that Irenaeus often quotes from 1 John and 1 Peter. He also observes that the bishop cites the *Shepherd* of Hermas as Scripture (*Adv. Haer.* IV, 20.2) and that he also quotes the book of Wisdom. As indicated by the Muratorian fragment, in some circles Wisdom may have counted among the books of the new covenant.

Although Eusebius is silent on the use of the *Corpus Paulinum* and Acts, these are to be added as well to the list of New Testament books available to, and used by, Irenaeus. All in all, the following writings were arguably included in Irenaeus' New Testament: the fourfold Gospel, Acts, 1–2 John, 1 Peter, 13 Pauline letters, and the Book of Revelation, that is some 22 books (cf. *Hist. Eccl.* V, 8.1-8 discussed above).[66] In the West,[67] towards the end of the second century, the scope of some regional NT canons seem to have included 21 or 22 books, with the probable addition of Wisdom and sometimes Ecclesiasticus, and the local inclusion of the *Shepherd* of Hermas, which seems to have been the most popular non-canonical writing among Christians before the fourth century.[68] In the East at this time[69] we see in some communities a larger

---

[64] Beckwith, *The Old Testament Canon*, 389; Roberts, *Manuscript, Society and Belief in Early Christian Egypt* (Oxford: Oxford University Press, 1979), 60f.

[65] See Hurtado, *Artifacts*, pp. 209–29; idem, 'Early Christian Manuscripts as Artifacts', in *Jewish and Christian Scripture as Artifact and Canon*, (eds) Craig A. Evans and H. Daniel Zacharias (Studies in Scripture in Early Judaism and Christianity 13; London and New York: T&T Clark, 2009), 67. On additions to Jeremiah and Daniel, see section 8.3.5.

[66] Cf. Schneemelcher ('General Introduction', in *New Testament Apocrypha*, vol. 1: *Gospels and Related Writings*, ed. W. Schneemelcher [Cambridge: James Clarke & Co. Ltd and Louisville: Westminster John Knox Press, 1991; 2nd edn], 26). The Letter of James may also be included.

[67] For an overview of the development of the NT canon in the West, see Metzger, *The Canon of the New Testament*, 143–64 and 229–47.

[68] See Osiek, *The Shepherd of Hermas* (Hermeneia; Minneapolis: Fortress, 1999), 1; and Hurtado, 'Early Christian Manuscripts as Artifacts', 69. However, we also note Jerome's testimony with regard to the *Shepherd*, that 'among the Latins it is almost unknown', even if it is 'read publicly in some churches of Greece' (*De vir. Ill.* 10; The Fathers of the Church 100:21).

[69] For an account of the canon history of the East, see, e.g. Metzger, *The Canon of the New Testament*, 113–41 and 209–28.

NT canon. According to David Trobisch, the canonical standard edition containing 27 books came to function as an archetype for the order and scope of a majority of the (extant) Greek manuscripts.[70] A gradual bridging of various regional scriptural canons, Eastern and Western, takes place from the third and fourth centuries on, giving rise to the catholic New Testament as received by the majority church. As for the attempts at closing the NT canon in the West, Bruce Metzger concludes: 'Twenty-seven books, no more, and no less, is … the watchword throughout the Latin Church.' Yet by the beginning of the fifth century the question of the canon is still not finally settled in all Christian communities.[71]

8.3.6 Difference in linguistic ground: The canon as *Rule of Faith* signifying the canon as *Scripture*

In his book *Symbolisme et interprétation* from 1978, the Franco-Bulgarian philosopher Tzvetan Todorov deals with direct and indirect meaning. Here the reader is informed that the twelfth-century Sanskrit poet Mammata (Kavyapraksa), in one of his comments on the distinctions to be made between the direct expression and the indirect suggestive force, talks of a difference in linguistic ground. By this is meant that what is expressed in speech or in writing comes forth by means of the words, while that which is said by suggestion, beneath the semantic level so to say, can be borne out of a sound, a phrase or a complete work.[72]

When Irenaeus elaborates on the Rule (Canon) of Faith, he uses the old and the new Scriptures in order to authenticate his argumentation. The complete work of *Adversus Haereses* turns out to be an example of how the Scriptures are used normatively and as ground for the orthodox position so exhaustively defended by Irenaeus. Even when, in company with other church leaders, he points to the Rule as the criterion of Christian faith, his writings none the less point to the Scriptures as the ultimate canon and criterion. An illustration of this is found in his *Epideixis*, where initially he introduces the Rule of Faith as the ecclesial norm. The whole work is then a long exposition of this Rule.

---

[70] Trobisch, *First Edition.*
[71] Metzger, *The Canon of the New Testament*, 238.
[72] Todorov, *Symbolik och tolkning*, trans. M. Rosengren (Stockholm/Stehag: Symposion, 1978).

However, what Irenaeus really appears to be doing is to use the Scriptures over and over, in order to elaborate on the Rule of Faith, thereby creating one of our earliest biblical-theological expositions. Behind the direct expression pertaining to the Rule of Faith lies hidden an indirect appeal to the repetitive usage of Scripture.[73] Again, this comes close to the *regula fidei* being viewed as the *scopus* of the Christian biblical text and narrative – the unified sense at which the whole aims.

8.4 The book as 'icon'

In Chapter 4 I discussed various aspects of the Bible as a book, in particular the faith community's choice of the codex format, in contrast to the traditional book form, the roll. One of the more radical suggestions laid forth in this connection is the hypothesis by T. C. Skeat where he seeks to explain anew[74] the formation of the fourfold Gospel. In his article 'The Origin of the Christian Codex'[75] he suggests that the motive for adopting the codex must have been 'infinitely more powerful than anything hitherto considered', such as the codex being *more* comprehensive, *more* convenient in use, *more* suited for ready reference, or *more* economical in comparison to the roll.[76] Skeat assumes that the Gospels initially circulated in the usual way, that is on papyrus rolls (however, cf. section 4.2.1). What induced the church 'so suddenly' and 'totally' to abandon rolls and substitute them, not only with codices, but with a single codex containing all four Gospels, Skeat propounds, was the publication of John.[77] Although this theory needs revision,[78] it is nevertheless of interest for at least two reasons. First, it directly opposes the statement made by Roberts and Skeat in 1983, that the adoption of the codex

---

[73] The same phenomenon can be detected in Tertullian, despite, or perhaps because of, his negative evaluation of the scriptural argument as basis for his discussion with heretics (*De Praescriptione* 18): 'Our appeal, therefore, must not be made to the Scriptures'; quoted also in section 5.6.3.

[74] See Ch. 4. Cf. also Roberts and Skeat, *The Birth of the Codex* (London: Oxford University Press, 1983), 54–61.

[75] Skeat, 'The Origin of the Christian Codex', *Zeitschrift für Papyrologie und Epigraphik* 102 (1994): 263–8.

[76] Ibid., 263.

[77] Ibid., 266.

[78] See Ch. 4; Hengel, *The Four Gospels and the One Gospel of Jesus Christ* (London: SCM, 2000), 119ff.

had no impact whatsoever on the formation of the canon.[79] Second, it draws attention to an obvious aspect inherent in the new book format. Its very cover marks out a textual beginning as well as an end, and it does so in a remarkably new way when compared to the scroll: Soon several volumes can be contained in a single volume. Our earliest unambiguous evidence of the four Gospels included in one codex is the early third-century P[45] (containing Gospels plus Acts). That is, we are dealing here not with four Gospels but one, the one Gospel in fourfold form.[80] The formation of the fourfold Gospel, according to Skeat, took place as a response to the somewhat uncontrolled production of new Gospels around the turn of the century, being a way of safeguarding the existing four Gospels from either addition or subtraction immediately after the publication of John.[81] Skeat concludes: 'The Four-Gospel Canon and the Four-Gospel Codex are thus inseparable.'[82] That there may be some truth to this claim – however, probably not as early as ca. AD 100, as Skeat proposes[83] – can perhaps be inferred from Irenaeus. Around AD 180, when he writes his *Adversus Haereses*, he appears to treat the four Gospels as canonical and, with regard to their order and delimitation, as contained in a codex.[84] In Irenaeus a whole theology is handed on and developed which can be easily associated with the physical codex of the fourfold Gospel. It has become Scripture, and, most typically, what is thought to be 'formal dogma' (the Gospel being fourfold) may in fact itself be 'highly material' (the Gospel appearing in codex form).[85] Similar to the intended transparency of an icon, the material Gospel codex seems to have been transparent, on the one hand, to the early 'theology of the four evangelists,[86] and, on the other, to previous oral gospel tradition

---

[79] Roberts and Skeat, *The Birth of the Codex..*

[80] See particularly Stanton, 'The Fourfold Gospel', *NTS* 43 (1997): 317–46. For various scholarly dating of the fourfold Gospel to the early second century, see Hurtado, 'The New Testament in the Second Century: Text, Collections, Canon', in *Transmission and Reception: New Testament Text-Critical and Exegetical Studies*, (eds) J. W. Childers and D. C. Parker (Piscataway, NJ: Gorgias, 2006), 19–24.

[81] Skeat, 'The Origin of the Christian Codex', 266.

[82] Ibid., 268.

[83] However, the formation of the fourfold Gospel has recently been dated to the early second century by a few scholars. See footnote above.

[84] See Blanchard, *Aux sources du canon, le témoignage d'Irénée* (Paris: Les Éditions du Cerf, 1993). The order of the canonical Gospels could differ, but not their number. Blanchard argues that Irenaeus made use of two Gospel codices with differing order.

[85] Cf. Barth, *Church Dogmatics*, vol. I/1 (Edinburgh: T&T Clark, 1936–62), 44, here quoted entirely out of context.

[86] Cf. Skeat's discussion on the old tradition of the four images associated with the four evangelists ('Irenaeus and the Four-Gospel Canon', *Novum Testamentum* 34 [1992]: 194–9).

(see section 4.5 and Ch. 5), and the Christ event behind the text to which the written Gospel points.

In order to highlight another 'icon-like' feature of Christian Scripture during these early years, I shall make use of the similarity of structure between the Rule of Faith and Christian Scripture in the minds of some early church teachers. To use the terminology of C. S. Pierce, the sign constituted by canonical Scripture as a whole functions as an icon in the sense that it is related to its object by similarity of structure.[87] This was true for the concept of canon as it was used interchangeably of the Rule of Faith, on the one hand, and of the Scriptures, on the other, in the second and third centuries. For Irenaeus as well as Tertullian it is imperative to identify the Rule of Faith as 'Scripture's own intrinsic story-line.'[88] Paul Blowers in an article on the *regula fidei* emphasizes the similar, or, from a Christian Rule-of-Faith-reading perspective, equal, narrative structure coming to the fore in the Rule and the Scriptures: 'Far from being imposed on Scripture from without, the *regula fidei* bears out the true dramatic narrative of Scripture within the church universal, which is its ever contemporary context' (cf., however, section 8.2).[89]

As mentioned above, the close relation, from early on, between the Rule of Faith and the Christian Scriptures has been described by Karlmann Beyschlag as 'two sides of one and the same norm'.[90] Similarly, Johannes Kunze comments on the chronological relation: there never was any Rule without the Scriptures.[91] And, as Kurt Aland, has indicated, the *regula fidei* was the framework within which the canonical process took place, by referring to the totality of Christian faith.[92]

---

[87] Peirce, *The Collected Papers of Charles Sanders Peirce* (Cambridge, MA: Harvard University Press, 1934–6), 249; Thiselton, *New Horizons in Hermeneutics: The Theory and Practice of Transforming Biblical Reading* (Grand Rapids: Zondervan, 1992), 86

[88] Blowers, 'The *Regula Fidei* and the Narrative Character of Early Christian Faith', 212.

[89] Ibid., 210. A similar approach to the relation between text and community is found in Robert Jenson (*Systematic Theology,* vol. 2: *The Works of God* [New York: Oxford University Press, 1999], 279. Cited also in Ch. 2): 'Whatever hermeneutical gaps may need to be dealt with in the course of the church's biblical exegesis, there is one that must not be posited or attempted to be dealt with: there is *no* historical distance between the community in which the Bible appeared and the church that now seeks to understand the Bible, because these are the same community.'

[90] Beyschlag, *Grundriß der Dogmengeschichte,* vol. 1 (Darmstadt, 1982).

[91] Kunze, *Glaubensregel, Heilige Schrift und Taufbekenntnis,* 100–27.

[92] Aland, *Das Problem des neutestamentlichen Kanons* (Göttingen: Vandenhoeck & Ruprecht, 1970), 11; Childs, *Biblical Theology of the Old and New Testaments* (London: SCM, 1992), 31f., 67; Blowers, 'The *Regula Fidei* and the Narrative Character of Early Christian Faith', *Pro Ecclesia* 6 (1997): 199; Ohlig, *Die theologische Begründung des neutestamentlichen Kanons in der alten Kirche* (Düsseldorf: Patmos-Verlag, 1972), 174.

As Aland points out, the structuring and collecting of the Scriptures that were to constitute the Christian Bible of the Old and New Testament were arguably carried out in this context of an already existing canon of the church, i.e. the Rule of Faith (κανὼν τῆς πίστεως). We can also see the similarity of structure between Scripture and Rule when we seek to characterize the *regula fidei*. Blowers uses the following description: 'The Rule of Faith served the primitive Christian hope of articulating and authenticating a world-encompassing story or metanarrative of creation, incarnation, redemption and consummation.'[93] The reason why Irenaeus is somewhat ambivalent in his usage of the expression 'Rule of Truth/Faith', with its twofold reference (cf. *Adv. Haer.* III, 1.2; and III, 15.1, where the *regula* refers to an individual book of the Bible),[94] seems to be what we may call the 'iconical function' – or better, the *scopus* – of the Scriptures: They are transparent to the central Christian metanarrative and story expressed by the *regula fidei*. However, in a reversed manner the Rule of Faith attained an equal function as 'icon', namely as transparent sign pointing towards and signifying the Scriptures as normative for communal life. In Chapter five, section 5.3, I treated this mutuality between the *regula fidei* and the Scriptures in some detail.

From the horizon of the early faith community, and as laid out by Irenaeus in our earliest catechetical treatise, *Epideixis*, the Rule and canonical Scripture cannot be understood apart. From their perspective, the textuality of canonical Scripture seems to be misconstrued if this unique oral, kerygmatic and narrative matrix of the first- and second-century church is not taken into account. This dialectics between Scripture and *regula* has its place even later in church history. On the hermeneutics of Augustine, for example, Werner Jeanrond comments:

> The rule of faith, i.e. the living tradition of the community of Christians, is the context for the responsible reading of the Scriptures. Thus, this tradition lives in a dialectical relationship with the process of reading itself: reading the Scriptures instructs the community, and the community which lives according to the Spirit of love, to which the Scriptures refer, provides the necessary perspective for responsible reading.[95]

---

[93] Blowers, 'The *Regula Fidei* and the Narrative Character of Early Christian Faith', 202.
[94] See Kunze, *Glaubensregel, Heilige Schrift und Taufbekenntnis*, 100–27; and Hägglund, 'Die Bedeutung der 'regula fidei' als Grundlage theologischer Aussagen', 13.
[95] Jeanrond, *Theological Hermeneutics: Development and Significance* (London: SCM, 1991, 1994), 25.

This critical mutuality between the Rule of Faith and the Scriptures is successively dissolved and deconstructed in post-Augustinian thinking, where a gradual disconnection between biblical interpretation and theological speculation takes place.[96] A renaissance in this regard, however, occurs most forcefully with the Reformation.

This is also the place to note some of the basic hermeneutics involved. As to the question of the reality coming to expression in the Christian story and metanarrative, a traditional understanding of Christian teaching cannot really follow a deconstructionist path, where there is nothing absolutely primary to be interpreted 'since fundamentally everything is already interpretation; every sign is ... but the interpretation of other signs'.[97] Instead, the signs and the narrative structure focus on God-talk, they converge into a single sign, namely the reality of God and the love of God. Umberto Eco's caution that '[t]here are somewhere criteria for limiting interpretation',[98] may here be useful. In fact, the picturing of the biblical text as 'icon' being transparent to the narrative and metanarrative structure of the *regula fidei* is meant to serve this purpose. Here the *regula* may function as a 'limit value' – to use a mathematical term – a limit, a canon set for scriptural interpretation, which is at the same time deeply integrated into the early Christian discourse. The decisive focus is the Triune God (indicated by *nomina sacra* and the triadic structuring of the Rule) and the central events in the Christian salvation-history.

In this connection Eric Osborn makes an interesting remark when discussing Tertullian's reflection on Paul's use of the term κανών/*regula* in Gal. 6.14-16 (*Adv. Marc.* IV, 5.1):

> For Paul there is no distinction between the gospel, the kerygma and the rule; it is concerned with the recital or proclamation of an event: Christ and him crucified. Verbal identity is impossible because words change, and inappropriate because truth is too big for words unless they too are seen as events.[99]

---

[96] Ibid., 26.

[97] Foucault, 'Nietzsche, Freud, Marx', *Cahiers de Royaumont philosophie* 6 (1967), 188; cited from *The Postmodern Bible*. The Bible and Culture Collective (New Haven: Yale University Press, 1995), 140.

[98] Eco, 'Interpretation and History', in *Interpretation and Overinterpretation*, ed. S. Collini (Cambridge: Cambridge University Press, 1992), 40.

[99] Osborn, 'Reason and the rule of faith in the second century AD', 47. A similar conclusion is also reached in Bengt Hägglund's analysis of the Rule in Irenaeus, Tertullian and Clement ('Die Bedeutung der "regula fidei" als Grundlage theologischer Aussagen').

Focusing on the kerygma as part of a New Testament ethics, a similar particularity and hermeneutical rootedness in history is underscored by Richard
Hays in his important monograph *The Moral Vision of the New Testament*.
He maintains that '[t]ruth is given to us in a particular person in a particular
time and place: Jesus of Nazareth.'[100] A related conclusion, as noticed above,
is reached also by Bengt Hägglund in his analyses of the Rule in Irenaeus,
Tertullian and Clement. In these writers the Rule of Truth is referring to
'the truth itself', that is, to 'the revelation of the history of salvation, evolving
through the Spirit of God' [*die Wahrheit selbst, d.h. auf die durch den Geist
Gottes geschehene Offenbarung der Heilsordnung*]. The Scripture, the Creed
and the tradition of the church are here seen as witnesses to this Rule, to truth
itself – the revelation of the history of salvation.[101]

Since the NT writings more than other texts are clearly related to the
salvation-historical centre around which the Rule of Faith evolves, the New
Testament, as well, may be construed around a similar kernel, like that
presupposed in the creedal development of the first and second centuries.[102]
By referring to two articles by Eugene Lemcio,[103] Ben Meyer offers some
concluding remarks along these lines, pointing to a unifying kerygma of
the New Testament. He thereby directly contests James Dunn's claim that
a unifying core kerygma in the New Testament is an abstraction.[104] Meyer
comments on the recurrent kerygmatic NT core:

---

[100] Cf. Hays, *The Moral Vision of the New Testament: A Contemporary Introduction to New Testament Ethics* (San Francisco: Harper Collins, 1996), 300.

[101] Hägglund, 'Die Bedeutung der "regula fidei" als Grundlage theologischer Aussagen', 17, 19.

[102] Meyer, *Reality and Illusion in New Testament Scholarship: A Primer in Critical Realist Hermeneutics* (Collegeville, MN: Michael Glazier, The Liturgical Press, 1994), 33ff.; Kelly, *Early Christian Creeds* (New York: Longman Publishing, 1972); Seeberg, *Der Katechismus der Urchristenheit* (Leipzig: A. Deichert'sche Verlagsbuchhandlung Nachf. [Georg Böhme], 1903). Kelly, in particular, emphasizes the kerygmatic and creedal continuity between the first century church and the nascent catholic church, Kelly, *Early Christian Creeds*, 7: 'the early Church was from the start a believing, confessing, preaching Church. Nothing could be more artificial or more improbable than the contrast so frequently drawn between the Church of the first century, with its pure religion of the Spirit and its almost complete absence of organization, and the nascent Catholic Church, with all its institutional appurtenances, of the late second century. Had the Christians of the apostolic age not conceived of themselves as possessing a body of distinctive, consciously held beliefs, they would scarcely have separated themselves from Judaism and undertaken an immense programme of missionary expansion. Everything goes to show that the infant communities looked upon themselves as the bearers of a unique story of redemption.'

[103] Lemcio, 'The Unifying Kerygma of the New Testament', *JSNT* 33 (1988): 3–17; Lemcio, 'The Unifying Kerygma of the New Testament (II)', *JSNT* 38 (1990): 3–11. Reprinted in *The Past of Jesus in the Gospels* (SNTS MS 68; Cambridge: Cambridge University Press, 1991), 115-31.

[104] For further critique of Dunn in this regard, see Childs, *The New Testament as Canon: An Introduction* (London: SCM, 1984), 29f.

This recurrent core is thematic, but not formulaic. It concerns

(1) God, who

(2) sent [=gospels]/raised [elsewhere]

(3) Jesus.

(4) A response (accepting, repenting, believing and the like)

(5) to God

(6) brings benefits (variously specified).

Formulas and non-formulaic texts are easily accomodated to this specifically *theological* (as distinct from strictly christological) schema.[105]

J. N. D. Kelly and others have demonstrated how various such early kerygmatic formularies have been handed on and elaborated throughout the first and second centuries.[106]

To conclude, the mutual relation between Scripture and the Rule of Faith can be described in the following way: The Rule of Faith as 'icon' is more than anything a signifier of the Scriptures, including the historical and narrative reality behind its formulations. The Scripture as 'icon' is more than anything transparent to the kerygmatic–narrative framework of the Rule of Faith.[107]

8.5 Conclusion

From the beginning of the Christian movement, kerygmatic summaries were used in a variety of ways. The first- and second-century emergence of the Rule of Faith (*regula fidei*; κανὼν τῆς πίστεως) is the compiled ecclesial outcome of the development of such summaries, evolving around the Triune Name and the theme of Christian salvation history.

In this chapter the theme of canonicity is discussed as a twofold ecclesial function: 1) as the textual arranging and reading of the Christian Scriptures; 2) as highlighted by the kerygmatic–narrative theological function of the Rule of Faith. In both Scripture and *regula fidei* it is argued that Name and

---

[105] Meyer, *Reality and Illusion in New Testament Scholarship: A Primer in Critical Realist Hermeneutics,* 39, paragraphing modified. Two classic studies on the subject that bridge the gap between the New Testament and the early Patristic era are Seeberg, *Der Katachismus der Urchristenheit*; and Kelly, *Early Christian Creeds*

[106] Ibid. Cf. Bokedal, 'The Rule of Faith: Tracing Its Origins'.

[107] See further, Chs 2, 5 and 6.

narrative are closely related. The core words of the *regula*, the three *nomina sacra* FATHER, SON and SPIRIT (cf. sections 3.4.3 and 3.6.2), can be viewed as a condensed telling of the total narrative through which canonical Scripture identifies God and the personal name for the God so specified. The Name embracing the narrative, the salvation-historical narrative centring on the Name.

At the core of this triadic–trinitarian (or dyadic–binitarian) Rule-of-Faith-pattern are some communally central revelatory acts testified to by the scriptural account. The parallel processes of scriptural canonization and the closely related narrative and metanarrative framework provided by the *regula fidei* are here presupposed in the theological interpretation of the ecclesial concept of canon. Together, Scripture and Rule of Faith may be said to constitute the texture making up the twofold corpus of canonical Scripture (OT and NT). In Irenaeus the Rule of Faith is viewed as the *scopus* of the scriptural narrative, the unified sense at which the whole aims. To him, and to other church teachers, Scripture and Rule make up two sides of the same norm. Irenaeus further addresses the issue of scriptural scope in this connection. A section is devoted to the writings included in Irenaeus' OT and NT (section 8.3.5).

There are various indications of a linguistic and effective-historical (Ch. 2), textual (Chs 3, 5 and 6) and theological (Ch. 8) connection between the Scriptures and the *regula fidei*. The three dimensions of the canon formation process studied in this chapter – story, scope and *scopus* – all have bearing on the central link between Scripture and Rule of Faith. The Scriptures (e.g. by means of the *nomina sacra*, and the scriptural account *qua* Scripture) relate to the *Rule*. The Rule (by its Scripture-based narrative and creedal components) relates to the basic theological and salvation-historical framework of the Christian scriptural account. Together the Scriptures *and* the *regula fidei* make up the Bible in its function as canon, addressing the church. Understood as two sides of the same norm, the early mutual dependency of Scripture and the Scripture-based Rule of Faith is paradigmatic for later ecclesiastical interpretation and translation of the Bible as canon.

9

The Logic of the Christian Canon: Authority, Integrity, Criterion

Is there a logic of the Christian canon? How do we know what is canon and what is not? Should parts of the canon be revoked? Some current popular agendas challenge the rationale of the canon, portraying it as something largely illegitimate. The success of these schemes commends serious thinking about the subject matter. In previous chapters we have seen several examples of the coherent relationship between various features of the canon. In this chapter, again, I shall address the issue of the logical coherence of the Christian canon: as an integrated whole, as authority and as criterion.

I find the Christian canon and its formation to be logical: the concept, the function, the structure, the interpretation, the history, the tradition, the texts, the collection. Being known as a hermeneutically complex subject, with which the church has long struggled, the canonization of the Christian Scriptures still turns out to be something reasonable, namely the act of preserving and actualizing the Scriptures, the authorized texts of the Christ-event and its apostolic interpretations.

Preservation, aptly understood, is an act of reason, 'though an inconspicuous one', Gadamer reminds us. This is also a concern of my overall thesis, to point at the preservation and actualization of the biblical material as a recurrent ecclesial act.[1] In the midst of this, however, our late-modern cultural situation poses some serious ideological, theological and hermeneutical challenges to this 'canonizing' and 'decanonizing' activity within the church.

The rationale of the canon is addressed throughout this study, and this particular chapter further outlines some of the logical coherence of the

---

[1] See section 1.2.1.

canonization process and the canon as textual foundation for the (undivided) church,[2] pertaining especially to the issues of authority, integrity and criterion.

9.1 Authority, integrity, criterion

The biblical texts viewed as Christian canon are held to be authoritative writing, present in the church as a sign[3] – i.e. they only present themselves to the one who is ready to accept them as such, who looks for him- or herself, and actually sees something there of this canonical claim. 'Authority in this sense, properly understood, has nothing to do with blind obedience to commands. Indeed, authority has to do not with obedience but rather with knowledge.'[4] The authority considered here is not something that has been primarily bestowed by the faith community, but is earned. 'It rests on acknowledgment and hence on an act of reason itself which, aware of its own limitations, trusts to the better insight of others.'[5] With respect to the Christ-event of the biblical account, these 'others' are believed to be the more well-informed textual witnesses, the 'apostles' and the 'prophets'. Through their appropriation, the textual foundation that the Bible is for the church is made into living tradition.

By the logic of the canonical text in its 'final' literary form, each textual unit is assigned a specific role to perform within the biblical whole.[6] However, the whole, in light of which the various textual units are understood, is not limited to the text in isolation from its construction as regulative text for the church universal. Being the *church's Scripture*, the canon exhibits textual organization that displays a process of theological interpretation, not only various ecclesial readings, but also, more fundamentally, the ecclesial reception of the text as canonical text.

Just as canonical reading of the biblical texts is analytical of apostolic and catholic faith, so are, *mutatis mutandis*, the canon criteria of apostolicity

---

[2]   See my central thesis, section 1.2.1.
[3]   Cf. the opening section of this study.
[4]   Gadamer, *TM*, 279. Gadamer's argument is applied primarily to the authority that a person has. Regarding the literary, historical and theological accounts of the biblical writings, both text and person (author and reader) are to be reckoned with.
[5]   Ibid.
[6]   Cf. Wall, 'The Significance of a Canonical Perspective of the Church's Scripture', in *The Canon Debate*, (eds) L. M. McDonald and. J. A. Sanders (Peabody, MA: Hendrickson, 2002), 536.

and catholicity analytical of the biblical texts as canonical texts. In fact, this principle of mutuality, entangled in the emerging textuality of these texts, is most important for the texts to be collected in order to form a structured whole in the first place. And, correspondingly, as historical criticism has repeatedly demonstrated, to the extent that the apostolicity and early catholicity of these texts are questioned, so are their unity as a textual whole; a unity also problematized by biblical scholarship for other reasons.[7]

Even these texts themselves constitute a criterion of what is to count as apostolic and catholic, of what is to be read in worship or taught in catechetical instruction. Still, the biblical texts seen as canon are not understood apart from the canonizing process as guided by the specific criteria of apostolicity, catholicity, established usage and the Christian biblical narrativity pattern. That is to say, the texts of the Old and New Testaments, construed as a bipartite canon for the church, are not simply a library of independent books.[8] They also form a single book, Scripture, with its many subdivisions, but still with one central theme: the message of the gospel.[9]

Due to the canonical process, these interdependent writings emerge as an intratextual scriptural matrix. They make up an authoritative collection of largely self-referring and self-interpretive prophetic and apostolic pieces of literature, with a storyline – indispensable for ecclesial identity.[10] In the wording of Robert Wall:

> The trust the church now grants these sacred writings is deeply rooted in this canonical process, not as a knee-jerk response to a precedent set by the primitive church, but in confidence that these same writings would continue to mediate a word from God to subsequent generations of believers.[11]

In the following, I want to keep focusing upon the 'canon-logic' tied to

---

[7] See further, section 9.6.

[8] Taken by themselves, some or all of the writings now contained in the New Testament would not be considered equally authoritative or be read in the same way as now were it not for their inclusion in the canon.

[9] Plantinga, *Two (or More) Kinds of Scripture Scholarship* (Grand Rapids: Paternoster & Zondervan, 2003), 25. Cited in Ch. 1, n. 5.

[10] Cf. Childs, *The New Testament as Canon: An Introduction* (London: SCM, 1984), 14: 'the process of canonical shaping stood in close theological continuity with the original kerygmatic intention of the New Testament writers to use their medium as a means of proclaiming the gospel and not to preserve an archive of historical records.'

[11] Wall, 'The Significance of a Canonical Perspective of the Church's Scripture', 530.

this canonization process, in particular its theological implications.[12] As an integral part of my canon definition, this has by and large been the task set out also in previous chapters: How and to what extent are the Christian Scriptures made to function as canon?

Central to this task is to identify the notion of canon on a fundamental level. In the sections below I shall address the issues of the canon's inherent authority, the transparency of the canonical text and the canon's unifying function in the midst of scriptural diversity. I shall also treat the dynamic involved in the interaction between the canon as criterion, and the criteria determining this canon.

First is a discussion on the canon as a necessary free power against its interpretive communities.

9.2 Canon: A free power against its interpreters

Granted the composite character of the concept of canon, described previously, it belongs to the nature of the canon that it cannot, non-reductionistically, be defined in any final way, other than by its own self-attestation. Nor is this something that its interpretive communities should wish for, if the canon is to remain in its specific function as a free power. In this way it may function as criterion for its interpreters. In other words, due to its emergence as apostolic literature – as Christian *Urliteratur*[13] – the scriptural canon sets itself apart and is present as a free, largely self-referring (and in this sense closed),[14]

---

[12] I am here making rather free use of the term 'canon-logic' and the notion of the logic of canon, as employed by Albert Outler, Brevard Childs and Robert Wall. Cf. Wall, 'The Significance of a Canonical Perspective of the Church's Scripture'.

[13] See section 9.5.3.

[14] This self-referentiality varies within the biblical text, and from writing to writing. Generally, NT Scriptures refer back to OT texts (some three thousand references and allusions can be found in NA[27]), and vice versa, according to the biblical textuality pattern. Regarding the OT, it is understood, more or less, as closed before the NT material is fixed in writing (cf., e.g. Josephus, *Contra Apionem* 1.37–41), and thus referred to as a single corpus, named the prophets, the Scriptures, the law and the prophets or the like. Similarly, and due to the oral–written character of the gospel in the Apostolic period, the Pauline corpus refers back to an institution, namely the apostleship of Paul. In the Petrine and Johannine writings a similar textual pattern can also be demonstrated. The NT Petrine literature, further, refers, e.g. to the Pauline corpus. As shown above, the *nomina sacra* and the codex format, too, help the construal of patterns of self-referentiality, as do, of course, the various liturgical and catechetical uses of the Scriptures. For other possible literary features making up a coherent textuality on the canonical level within the NT corpus, see Trobisch, *The First Edition of the New Testament* (Oxford: Oxford University Press, 2000).

self-regulative and self-interpretive authority and norm.[15] The canon is canon first of all against the church.[16]

Not only is an absolutely closed canon an historical and theological impossibility,[17] its subject matter – the question of God and God's Messiah – calls for continuous careful attention to the integrity and meaning of these texts as canonical texts. Beside this perennial ecclesial function, there are, as well, ever new and varied applications in which the canon is expected to attain new functions. This is so, despite the many forceful metanarratives and absolutified views so closely interconnected with the Christian Scriptures. In fact, this strong expectation for present and future application of the canon, in accord with its various scriptural genres, makes these writings far more influ-ential within their interpretive communities than can be expected for classics generally. This, of course, poses new questions to the problem and possibility of the canon.

To question these past, present and future applications means 'to lay open, to place in the open.'[18] As against the fixity of opinion, questioning potentially makes the 'object' and all its possibilities fluid. The interpretive communities of the canon, therefore, at times find themselves in a state in which what was previously secure and taken for granted, now, by inner and outer questioning, is placed in the open.

To take but one recent example of such hermeneutical situatedness – leading to ambivalence, or even distress – where modes of interpretations clash, or stand against one another: In the fourth volume of the *Scripture and Hermeneutics* series, the co-editor Craig Bartholomew presents the Old Testament narratives as making 'a strong historical truth-claim'. This historical concern of his is far from uncontested among Old Testament scholars. In the wake of the literary turn in biblical studies, another major agenda within recent scholarship has been to view the biblical texts as literature, where the

---

[15] Authority here has to do not so much with obedience but rather with an act of acknowledgment and knowledge – the knowledge, namely, that the biblical witness is superior to the subsequent church in judgement in matters regarding the foundations of faith and practice. See further *TM,* 279.

[16] On the church's responsibilities towards the world in this – that is, of providing a canon also for the world – and in other regards, see Jenson, 'The Church's Responsibility for the World', in *The Two Cities of God: The Church's Responsibility for the Earthly City,* (eds) C. E. Braaten and R. W. Jenson (Grand Rapids: Eerdmans, 1997), 1–10.

[17] However, cf. Metzger, *The Canon of the New Testament,* 275 (quoted in section 9.9); see also sections 9.4, and 1.1 and 1.2.4, n. 61.

[18] Gadamer, *TM,* 367.

Old Testament narratives have been studied primarily without controlling regard for the historical reference of the text. As to this possibility, however, M. Sternberg – though himself a trained literary scholar – directs severe criticism. He writes: 'Were the narrative written or read as fiction, then God would turn from the lord of history into a creature of the imagination, with the most disastrous results.'[19] As the question of God is pivotal for any understanding of Scripture, Sternberg's methodological worry has bearing also on issues pertaining to the canon.[20]

Thus, while the whole theme of canonicity may be concealed by the agendas set for biblical and Bible-related scholarship, the scriptural text manifests features partly nameless, which elude the control of scholarly method.

It is clear that canonical meaning here, or, more specifically, the scholarly opinion on scriptural signification, is a more dynamic and open category than the canon's authoritative function towards the church and the academy (the privileging of biblical writings in biblical and religious studies). It is also clear that, in its function as criterion for ecclesiastical life and teaching, the canon needs to be precisely that which it is set apart as – or rather, sets itself apart as – namely a free textual power.

To the church and its call, there are crucial aspects pertaining to meaning that are not open to unending methodological negotiation, such as the canon's trinitarian (or triadic) narrative quality. The ecclesiastical reading cannot be construed in a non-narrative and non-trinitarian way without, at the same time, reducing this essential canonical function. Thus, the trinitarian structure of church dogma is, on a fundamental level, not a post-biblical, extra-textual doctrinal construal, but an integral part of the literary, ritual and theological basis from which the Scriptures attain their function as canon for church dogmatics.[21] That is to say, there are canonical functions, such as the one just mentioned, that are part of the self-regulating free power that the canon is, being, at the same time, central to ecclesial identity and belonging.

---

[19] Sternberg, *The Poetics of Biblical Narrative: Ideological Literature and the Drama of Reading* (Bloomington: Indiana University Press, 1985), 32; cited in Bartholomew, 'Introduction', in *'Behind the Text: History and Biblical Interpretation'*, vol. 4, (eds) C.S. Evans et al. (Grand Rapids: Zondervan, 2003), 10.
[20] Cf. section 1.3.2.
[21] Cf. Chs 1–8, esp. Chs 3, 7 and 8.

The central function of the canon here comes to the fore, namely its distinctive address, first of all, to the church. This is achieved, not only through the specific textual, ritual and theological qualities of Christian Scripture, but also – most importantly for the canonical address – by means of its being written down – its writtenness. As Karl Barth stresses, 'in unwritten tradition the Church is not addressed; it is engaged in dialogue with itself.' From this it follows that,

> apart from the undeniable vitality of the Church itself[,] there stands confronting it a concrete authority with its own vitality, an authority whose pronouncement is not the Church's dialogue with itself but an address to the Church, and which can have *vis-à-vis* the Church the position of a free power and therefore of a criterion, then obviously in its writtenness as 'Bible' it must be distinguished from and given precedence over the purely spiritual and oral life of ecclesiastical tradition.[22]

Two essential features of a canon for a community are stressed here, namely its function as address and as criterion; that is, as canon, regulating, in this case, ecclesial existence, identity and belonging via this address. This takes place by means of the 'undeniable vitality' of the canon in its primary function – that is, as address, directly to the church, and indirectly to the world.[23]

I have argued that it is only as sign that the biblical writings can be seen as canon for the church, i.e. what is shown in this specific textual construal is only accessible to the readers and listeners who look for themselves and, being addressed,[24] genuinely see something there of this integral whole. When seen otherwise, the texts in question are viewed in some other way. So, when perceived as canon, they are taken as a unified – and for the church universal, most importantly, also as a unifying – whole; normative, first of all, for the church body of Christ believers.[25]

---

[22] Barth, *Church Dogmatics* I/1 (Edinburgh: T&T Clark, 1936–2), 106.

[23] This distinction between direct and indirect canonical address is one among several reasons for critiquing traditional biblical criticism's isagogical treatment of the issue of canon. The academic reception of the church's scriptural canon only takes place by means of ecclesial mediation.

[24] How this comes about, more exactly, falls outside the limits of this study.

[25] Cf. Campenhausen, *Die Entstehung der christlichen Bibel* (Tübingen: Mohr Siebeck, 2003), 3. The classic, broadly understood, concept of canon is – in line also with more recent scholarship – identified by von Campenhausen as the 'Vorstellung der Maßgeblichkeit oder Normativität'.

Still, the powerful effective-history of the canon, not only in the West – as its 'Great Code' – but globally, has deeply affected various cultural and linguistic patterns of thought and practice.[26]

9.3 The 'selflessness' of the canonical text

'What is it that makes the Bible of the Old and New Testaments the Canon?' Karl Barth asks in the first volume of his *Church Dogmatics*. 'Why must the Church's recollection of God's past revelation always have the Bible as its concrete object?'[27] Barth's own postponing, or even avoidance, of an answer may seem surprising to the reader being used to his often extensive theological expositions and elaborations. 'It is no evasion of this question,' he proceeds, 'which we are always right to raise afresh, if in the first instance we reply at once that the Bible constitutes itself the Canon. It is the Canon because it imposed itself upon the Church as such, and continually does so.'[28]

Now, how could this be understood from the horizon of contemporary theology? Early in his *Systematic Theology*,[29] while discussing the character and function of Christian dogma, Wolfhart Pannenberg stresses the fact that among the early church teachers ecclesiastical dogmas were understood to be divine truth. In other words, though formulated by humans and coloured by human institutional interests, they were, none the less, held to be somehow divinely revealed. Even conciliar decrees were understood in this way: the truth of dogmas were not legally established but simply presupposed, since they were held to be revelatory. And, as Pannenberg points out, '[u]p to the beginnings of the modern era both academic and ecclesiastical exposition of scripture made it its task to investigate the authoritative content of Christian doctrine as the revelation of God.'[30]

---

[26] Therefore, a more thorough study on the canon should take into account a wide range of applications in society, such as other canon formations affected by the biblical canon, as well as various cultural, juridical, literary, religious, philosophical and aesthetic expressions indebted to the Christian canon. This task, however, falls outside the limits set for the present work.

[27] Barth, *CD*, I/1, 107.

[28] Ibid.

[29] Pannenberg, *Systematic Theology*, vol. 1 (Grand Rapids: Eerdmans, 1991), 10.

[30] Ibid, 8.

Although Barth does not equate the scriptural witness with revelation,[31] he nevertheless puts forth the canon as integral to Christian church dogmatics: 'When the Church heard this word – and it heard it only in the prophets and apostles and nowhere else – it heard a magisterial and ultimate word which it could not ever again confuse or place on a level with any other word.'[32] Yet, despite being scripturally codified, this word itself is not the central content of revelation, which is the Triune God as known in and through Jesus Christ.[33] Even this finds textual expression in the biblical presentation, which as such is highly authoritative, too: 'Why and in what respect does the biblical witness have authority?' Barth asks. 'Because and in the fact that he [it] claims no authority for himself [itself], that his [its] witness amounts to letting that other itself be its own authority.'[34]

Using Barth's formulation, the reader is here reminded of the 'selflessness', or transparency, of the biblical witness, and the inherent resistance by all church dogma against humanly established *de iure* sanctioning, including as well teaching on the canon. In this regard Barth's sensitivity regarding the revelation of God is worth stressing; to him revelation is clearly theologically defined, standing on its own. The establishment of divine truth does not need any support whatsoever by man or by man-made *de iure* sanctioning. Not least ecclesially concerned thinking on the canon may consider this. Again, the very modest claim made for canonical Scripture in *The Formula of Concord*,[35] in which the individual biblical writings are not even enumerated, is well worth reconsidering also in this respect. However, as we shall see, sometimes the number of books do seem to matter.

---

[31] On canon and revelation, cf., e.g. sections 1.1 and 1.2.1, nn. 28 and 29.
[32] Barth, *CD*, I/1, 108.
[33] As argued above, it appears to be a particular role of the *nomina sacra* in the Christian Bible codices to draw attention to this, or a similar transparency function of the text. See Ch. 3.
[34] Ibid, 112.
[35] Schaff, ed., 'The Formula of Concord', in *The Creeds of Christendom, with a History and Critical Notes*, vol. 3 (New York: Harper & Brothers, 1877 [1576]), 93–180.

9.4 On numbers: Why these texts and not others?

Given a selection of texts, one may wonder why those texts were included, and not others. Furthermore, seeing to the unity of the whole selection, one may also ask if the exact number of texts is significant. Interestingly, when studying the Christian canon formation, we may have noted the great significance that certain numbers – such as 4, 22 and 66 – have had in the selection process.

The continuing privileging of the 27 writings of the New Testament, the 66 or 72 (or some other number) of the Old and New Testaments can be seen as a contingent ecclesial act. Maybe these writings could have been others; nevertheless, as pointed out in the introductory chapter, the present scope, structure and function of the biblical canon is by no way accidental. In fact, when presented in this way, an answer to the posed question may begin to take form, by adding some important distinctions.

First of all, on a basic level, the problem of the canon is not only, or primarily, an issue of enumerating some precise, or imprecise, number of writings, where, for example, the canonicity of Deuteronomy, Isaiah, The Book of Esther, The Gospel of Matthew and The Letter of Jude or 3 John are compared, becoming just a number or equally significant parts, one sixty-sixth, of the whole Bible. Again, stressing this point, canonicity or canonization has not primarily to do with arithmetic, with the aim of reaching a particular number. The narrative and theological concerns involved here seem more important.

However, regarding the textual structure, beside the various liturgical and theological functions of the canon, certain numerical *ad hoc* components do appear to matter. This phenomenon, as pointed out above (Ch. 4), can be seen in Early Judaism, but also within the early Christian movement, for example by the emphasis laid on the numbers 3, 4, 7, 8 (e.g. the eight books of the so called *Praxapostolos*), 14, 22, 24 or 27. The church seems to have continued attaching weight to such numbers, or numerology, when viewing the New Testament as a scriptural corpus: three or four textual corpora are often held to constitute the New as well as the Old Testament. The number 27 (=3×3×3), discussed by Jerome, probably takes its starting point in the New Testament, while the fixation of the Syrian NT of 22 writings most probably can be derived from the number of Jewish Scriptures, made to correspond to the Hebrew alphabet. This all has to do with: 1) relating the two testaments to one another; 2) establishing a New Testament canon; and 3) establishing an entire and circumscribed Bible. The number 2 seems to be important, too, when taking the two main collections of writings into account: the 'Old Testament' and the emerging 'New Testament'. Within each of these, the number 2 figures again: Law and Prophets alongside Gospel and Apostle(s). This bipolar structure of Scripture has been emphasized recently by François Bovon,[36] who points to this structure in several of the early Christian texts: Paul adding his epistles to the oral gospel, the story of Jesus and the story of the witnesses of the Resurrection in Luke. A 'logic' proper to Christianity appears: 'it closely associates the gospel as the foundational event and the gospel as good news. By so doing, it proclaims a historic beginning and claims an indispensable apostolic mediation.'[37] Similarly emphasizing this basic two-part configuration of Christian textuality, the Sunday lectionary readings from the New Testament soon became two, in both the East and the West. In the Western Church, the main lectionary readings on Sundays eventually became two (cf. Ch. 7).

Two Testaments, often two lectionary readings, two major collections within each Testament. Furthermore, the probable 'doubling' of the early Pauline letter corpus to seven churches (the Muratorian fragment), resulting in a 14-letter corpus.[38] In fact, this ordering of the biblical material into a twofold structure, also observable in Marcion in his Gospel and Apostle, sets a limit in principle for the canonical circumscription of the biblical writings. Also, from the early second century on, the church found a mystical significance attached to the number four (2+2; 2×2), particularly as applied to the fourfold Gospel. One gospel, four accounts. And, parallel to this, one Bible, four (alternatively two, six or eight) main text corpora. Twenty-two (XXII) writings in the OT as well as in some early NT collections. And, most signifi-

---

[36] Bovon, 'The Canonical Structure of Gospel and Apostle', in *The Canon Debate*, (eds) L. M. McDonald and J. A. Sanders, (Peabody, MA: Hendrickson, 2002), 516–27.

[37] Ibid., 527.

[38] Theologically, the number 'two' figures as well, e.g. through the two major ways of interpreting Scripture: law and gospel, alongside the early apostolic and sub-apostolic teaching of the Two Ways, the early binitarian structure of the kerygma, and the First and the Second Coming of Christ. For problems involved in the various number of letters included in the early stages of formation of the Pauline Corpus, see Porter, 'When and How was the Pauline Canon Compiled? An Assessment of Theories', in *The Pauline Canon*, ed. Stanley E. Porter (Leiden: Brill, 2004), 95–127.

cantly, $3\times3\times3$ (=27) writings make up the canonical New Testament, and 7×7 (=22+27) or 3×22 (=39+27) books constitute the canonical Scriptures as a whole, as widely received by the churches. Much numerical fascination and speculation! Much ado about nothing?

Of course, numerics cannot be the main point (though, for example, in Pythagorean and Platonic circles numbers were ontologically important).[39] It may rather be seen as encouraging and confirming riddles to play with during days of rest after creation has taken place. Content must be the major principle – or should we think otherwise?

So, why these texts and not others?

9.5 The emergence of the hermeneutical problem involved in the canonizing process

By about the end of the first century there had arisen a body of Christian documents read in public worship, broadly recognized and cited as regulative texts, and used in the context of instruction. In this sense, as Theodor Zahn rightly argued a century ago, there was already a canon of Christian NT Scriptures in existence by AD 80–110 that had arisen spontaneously from the church's inner life, consisting of Gospels and Epistles.[40] This function of the new apostolic literature is extensively testified to by the use made of these writings in the Apostolic Fathers. Also in Justin (ca. AD 150–60) such spontaneous, non-reflective, usage of the literature can be seen. At this moment in the history of the canon, frequent appeal is made to this literature as inherently authoritative. Inter- and intratextual patterns of scriptural interpretation have already become standardized.

However, Adolf von Harnack, in his discussions with Zahn, never accepted this approach towards NT canonicity. According to von Harnack's view – which eventually became the consensus position until only recently – scholars

---

[39] See, e.g. Jay Kennedy's 'The Plato Code', in *The Philosopher's Magazine*, 2010: 51. Cf. also the role of isopsephy in *Barn.* 9, Matt. 1, Rev. 13 and possibly John 20.30. See sections 3.4.1 and 3.4.6.

[40] See, e.g. Gamble, 'The New Testament Canon: Recent Research and the Status Quaestionis', in *The Canon Debate*, (eds) L. M. McDonald and J. A. Sanders (Peabody, MA: Hendrickson, 2002) , 267f.; Barton, *The Spirit and the Letter: Studies in the Biblical Canon* (London: SPCK, 1997), 1ff.; and Swarat, *Alte Kirche und Neues Testament: Theodor Zahn als Patristiker* (Wuppertal and Zürich: Brockhaus, 1991).

are not justified in speaking of an NT canon before the literature in view is put fully on a par with the Jewish Scriptures by the end of the second century.

A third major scholarly position is outlined by A. C. Sundberg, arguing that a canon is at hand only when the definite scope of the included writings can be shown to be catalogued in particular so-called canon lists,[41] irrespective of variations in contemporary regional canons in use.

While the main contours of these three positions are well known to biblical scholarship, the implied hermeneutics involved in each of the three models is only rarely discussed.[42]

According to John Barton, the question of the canon 'bundles together so many questions that apparently conflicting solutions of it seldom in reality share any common ground on which to meet and clash.' His solution is to attempt to take the question apart. His way towards conceptual clarity – pointing out the various interrelated topics inherent in the inquiry – may however lead to a surprising outcome: '[to] find that the question of the canon has disappeared, and that the urn has broken in our hands.'[43]

What Barton is saying is that the question of the canon ultimately turns out to be 'what in German is called a *Scheinfrage*, an illusory question or pseudo-problem. It is not that there are no questions of substance involved in it, but that (as usually understood) it bundles together too many questions.'[44] Or, alternatively, that the historic-critical question of the canon, in the end, turns out to be a 'no-question'. That is to say, there are no good 'answers' to the question, the way it is posed, within the scholarly framework chosen. To me, this often seems to be the case also when the question is raised within various ecclesiastical settings. The question, 'Why these texts and not others?' is only rarely taken seriously.

My own hermeneutical concern is both similar to and different from Barton's. Similar, to the extent that an analysis of the canon, the taking apart, is thought to lead to greater conceptual clarity. The division of this study into four parts is but one example of this common concern. Different, however, to

---

[41] The most well-known example would be the 65-book (or 49-book) canon drawn up by Athanasius in AD 367.

[42] Cf., however, Barton, *The Spirit and the Letter*, 1ff.; and Gamble, 'The New Testament Canon: Recent Research and the Status Quaestionis', 267–94.

[43] Barton, *The Spirit and the Letter*, 2.

[44] Ibid. See citation above.

the extent that my study puts more emphasis on theological argumentation, by emphasizing a unity, as well as unifying theological forces inherent in the canonical process. From the historian's viewpoint – though perhaps this should not be taken too literally – Barton even suggests that the historical problem of the canon may disappear altogether. In my reading, this means that there are reasons to hope for sensible solutions to the historical problem of the canon. In addition, the question of the canon, still rightfully being asked, will also be handed over to theologians and others interested.

As for the ecclesial concern, it seems that reflection on the concept of canon is largely seeking to know the already known. These writings were present in the community – probably without being much reflected on in terms of their writtenness – as regulative for church life. But why? The question did not arise naturally until there were reasons to pose it. However, even from very early on, in the first century, a partly spontaneous, partly deliberate textual structuring appears to be taking place. It seems to me that, as part of a canon formation, some of the early church leaders must have been conscious of several new and possibly even radical moves in the faith communities. A time for reflection on these matters had begun, tied to the inner life of early Christianity. There seems to have been an increased need for understanding – and for better knowing the already known.[45]

A hermeneutical problem was emerging, due largely to the death of major first-generation Christian leaders – James (d. AD 62), Peter and Paul (d. ca. AD 64) – and the loss of the powerful Jewish communal context that had kept things clear by 'absorbing' the various views of individuals and particular groups within the community into itself. Now, the situation for the emergent Christian community was changing in the process of gradual separation from the original apostles and from the synagogue. The church was instead confronting its own new identity alongside alien traditions. Furthermore, it had to face the Jewish tradition which it no longer unquestioningly accepted. Interestingly, as indicated by Gadamer, the hermeneutical problem here only seems to emerge clearly 'when there is no powerful tradition present to absorb one's own attitude into itself and when one is aware of confronting an alien tradition to which he has never belonged or one he no longer unquestioningly

---

[45]   Cf. Gadamer, *Philosophical Hermeneutics* (Berkeley: University of California Press, 1976), 45.

accepts.'[46] In other words, as the nascent church confronted alien Hellenistic and Jewish traditions, especially Jewish traditions it could no longer accept, the hermeneutical problem seems to have emerged with unprecedented force in areas relating to Scripture, interpretation and canon.

9.5.1 Canon and traditionalism

As has been repeatedly pointed out by some of Gadamer's critics, there is a clear danger connected with the apparent uncritical stance he takes towards tradition. When dealing with the notion of biblical canonicity, for example, there is obviously the risk of taking over so-called traditional ecclesial or 'heretical' readings that happen to be bad readings; or, of misunderstanding the particular textual tradition that the canon constitutes. Beside these, there certainly are other risks as well. Even the canon as canon can be misused. The Bible itself may in various ways become an idol, an end in itself for theological, religious and ecclesial purposes. An exteriorly present canon is far from identical with an interiorly motivated canonical reading. It is possible to have a canon, and still not have it. Kierkegaard's famous mirror and letter parables on James 1.22–27 are here worth noticing.[47]

For various reasons readers of canonical Scripture have sometimes felt the need to 'protect' themselves from these texts, for example by historical-critical or theological methodologies, or by having writings excluded from the lectionary readings. Historically, another strategy has been to avoid usage of some, or all, Scriptures intended for catechumens, young persons, women or laity. Furthermore, a multitude of biblical passages are, for various reasons, hardly ever preached or commented on. Some of these are, at least on some level, offensive to such an extent that readers have felt the need to either shun them altogether, or, when that is not possible, to guard themselves against certain readings or texts. In many churches and congregations this issue has showed to be recurrent, e.g. when deciding what texts to include in the readings, or on what texts and themes to expound.

---

[46] Ibid., 46.
[47] Kierkegaard, *For Self-Examination: Recommended for the Times* (Minneapolis: Augsburg, 1940). Cf. Vanhoozer, *Is There a Meaning in This Text? The Bible, the Reader, and the Morality of Literary Knowledge* (Grand Rapids: Zondervan, 1998), 15f.

However, although exclusion or protection are common examples of such ecclesiastical and readerly (defence) mechanisms, the strategy usually chosen by the church, not least in dealing with the Old Testament material, has been to eliminate exegetically those ideas which have not been compatible with Christian dogmatics and moral teaching.[48] Various typological and allegorical as well as historical models of interpretation were therefore used in order to harmonize such 'hard sayings' with Christian teaching.[49] Another common strategy was to make frequent use of a selection of Old Testament sayings, according to early patterns of biblical interpretation as developed in the first and early second century.[50] In all these instances, however, Gadamer notes, 'the dogmatic tradition of the Christian Church remained the unshakable basis of all interpretation.'[51] At an early date, this dogmatic tradition was so intimately identified with canonical Scripture that they could not easily be distinguished. The twofold canon, the Rule (Canon) of Faith and the canon of Scripture were, in effect, often amalgamated. Although distinguishable, they were considered to be two inseparable sides of one and the same textual norm – the 'rule of the gospel' in short form and in long form (see further, Ch. 8). Other such textual strategies, related to the basic 'grammar' of Christian faith, have been treated throughout the book (Chs 1–8).

There is, however, more than one way of relating to canonical texts and readings. There are various ways of both hearing and interpreting these texts, even to the point of undoing or deconstructing the text or message handed on.

So, there is not only the risk of 'defencelessness' towards canonical texts, of being too open to tradition. There is also the risk of being too critical towards, or of not being prepared to hear, these texts on their own terms. After all, as I have already stressed, the act of preserving them and using them can be seen as an act of reason. One of the primary reasons for setting the writings off as canon in the first place was the claim made for these writings: By them we

---

[48] So Gadamer, *Philosophical Hermeneutics*, 46
[49] For an overview of exegetical strategies employed by the early church teachers, see Young, *Biblical Exegesis and the Formation of Christian Culture* (Cambridge: Cambridge University Press, 1997).
[50] On this, see, e.g. Stuhlmacher, *How To Do Biblical Theology* (Princeton Theological Monograph Series 38; Eugene, OR: Pickwick Publications, 1995); and Skarsaune, *The Development of Scriptural Interpretation in the Second and Third Centuries – except Clement and Origen* (Göttingen: Vandenhoeck & Ruprecht, 1996).
[51] Gadamer, *Philosophical Hermeneutics*, 46.

can know better. And, most importantly, the canon, together with a canonical interpretive approach, aspire to solve various difficulties arising when reading Scripture. Violate, offensive and oppressive texts may be 'absorbed' into the Christian communal reading strategies that we may call 'canonical'. Augustine's appeal to the unifying category of *Caritas* (Greek ἀγάπη) in this connection is well known.

9.5.2 Integrity despite diversity

The theme of unity and diversity has been variously addressed throughout our discussion.[52] A most characteristic feature of the canon, beside its character of address, criterion and narrative, is its unity: Scripture as a unified whole. Perhaps the first Christian thinker who emphasized this was Irenaeus (see Ch. 8), but he has had many followers, not only among the church teachers of the Patristic and Middle Ages or the Reformation Period, but also among contemporary hermeneuts, literary critics and theologians. The Patristic scholar Frances Young, in one of her publications, points to this feature of canonicity within an historical context: '[t]he unity of the scriptures is recognised to have been a dogma among the Fathers. The effect of this on exegesis, however, has not previously been discussed.'[53] Presumably this should be taken as saying something of the question of God, the way Christian dogma usually does. And, for both early and later church teachers, the unity of the Scriptures – which implied a specific relation between the Old and the New Testaments – was not only of indirect importance in formulating the church's trinitarian or christological doctrines. For example, the early creeds were shaped in closest possible connection to scriptural ideas and concepts, and so formed a basis for further Christian theologizing.[54]

By means also of their privileged place in worship, ecclesial practice and teaching, these texts form a unity, not only among themselves, but in relation to the community – as an ecumenically authoritative and unifying text and narrative. Therefore, it is not merely various individual stories of Jesus the

---

[52] See above, esp. sections 1.0, 6.6 and Ch. 8.
[53] Young, *Biblical Exegesis and the Formation of Christian Culture*, 7.
[54] Cf. Gadamer, *TM*, 331f.; cited in Ch.1, n. 50; and Kelly, *Early Christian Creeds* (New York: Longman, 3rd rev. edn, 1972).

Messiah that meet the reader and hearer of the New Testament, but, first and foremost, a single Christian narrative.

The narrative unity is indicated in the text in various ways, supra-textually by the *nomina sacra*, intertextually by the multitude of overriding textual combinations between biblical texts on all levels, sub-textually by typical 'apostolic' interpretive patterns of usage of the Old Testament in the New (and vice versa). However, as Paul Minear notes (see section 7.7.9), we should also take into account that the whole gospel is being heard in and with each new Scripture reading before the faith community: 'the audience already knew the course of later events in the story of Jesus'. These stories' context was provided by all the memories of the community, 'up to the time of each successive reading'.[55] This awareness of scriptural sequentiality and canonical context can also be noted on the part of the authors and redactors of the New Testament writings. Much of Brevard Childs's scholarly work has aimed at making this point: Canonization as something inherent on all levels of the coming-into-being of the church's Scriptures.

The notion of canon is used to signify the integrity of the Scriptures and their mediation as a unity to future readers. Canon and canonization thus become part of the basic dogmatic tradition of the Christian church. This is being stressed also within the hermeneutical agenda of Gadamer's *Truth and Method*: Behind the Scripture Principle of the Reformation, i.e. the canonical principle that Scripture functions (or should function) as its own interpreter – *sui ipsius interpres* – lies a postulate 'that is itself based on a dogma, namely that the Bible is itself a unity'.[56] This dogmatically grounded assertion of the Bible's unity (implicit in Protestantism, and, with a different emphasis, explicit in Catholicism) led in the early church to the combination of dogmatic concerns and a developing biblical hermeneutic attached to canonical Scripture.

> In dealing with the Old Testament, for example, Christian theology very quickly faced the problem of eliminating exegetically those ideas which were not

---

[55] Minear, *The Bible and the Historian: Breaking the Silence About God in Biblical Studies* (Nashville: Abingdon, 2002), 91f.

[56] Gadamer, *TM*, 176. See in this connection the remark above by Frances Young. Cf. Karl Barth's definition of the Scripture Principle: 'The church recognises the rule of its proclamation solely in the Word of God and finds the Word of God solely in Holy Scripture', *The Theology of the Reformed Confessions*. Columbia Series in Reformed Theology, trans. and annot. D. L. Guder and J. J. Guder (Louisville, KU: Westminster John Knox, 2002), 41.

compatible with Christian dogmatics and moral teaching. Along with allegorical and typological interpretation, historical considerations also served this end, as Augustine demonstrated, for instance, in his *De Doctrina Christiana*. But in all such cases, the dogmatic tradition of the Christian Church remained the unshakable basis of all interpretation. Historical considerations were unusual and secondary aids to the understanding of Scripture.[57]

However, the textuality of canonical Scripture, built up in this way, according to Gadamer, soon embraced this dogmatic postulate and text hermeneutic into itself. This event marks out the formation of the Christian Bible as the apostolic, ecclesiastically construed and transmitted canon.

Hence, Gadamer can also say of Scripture that it has 'an absolute priority over the doctrine of those who interpret it.'[58] This view of canonical textuality and function is in line with my elaboration of the concept of canon in the previous chapters. The 'unshakable' dogmatic basis of ecclesial identity, thus, is inseparable from the text as canonical text, and vice versa. This is about as close as I come to an understanding of Gadamer's as well as Barth's reflections on this aspect of the canon, as a foundational basis (or postulate) for ecclesial existence.

In Barth's wording, 'the Bible constitutes itself the Canon. It is the Canon because it imposed itself upon the Church as such, and continually does so … the Bible is the Canon just because it is so.'[59] To Barth, this is a postulate, which he believes he is not, for good reason, justified to further theologically elaborate on. Thus, this dogmatically and textually grounded postulate of Scripture's unity is, in the end, axiomatic of Christian faith. That is, it is part of what it is to be a Christian, to embrace belief in the Bible's unity – and to have some personal experience, as well, of biblical canonicity's imposing itself upon the body of Christ believers. In this way the canon (as sign) remains in its function as a free power against its many both powerful and less powerful interpreters.

In Dietrich Bonhoeffer's phrasing:

It is really the biblical text as such that binds the whole Christian community into a unity. It assures us of our being bound together in one family of brothers

---

[57] Gadamer, *Philosophical Hermeneutics*, 46.
[58] Gadamer, *TM*, 331.
[59] Barth, *CD* I/1, 107.

and sisters not only with the Christian community of all past and future ages but with the whole church of the present. As such, the biblical text is of enormous unifying, ecumenical significance.[60]

9.5.3 Canon then, canon now

Canon then, canon now. How do they relate? It is the claim of the present study that the canon of the early as well as the contemporary church belong together and therefore need to be treated alongside each other. They are both being authoritatively addressed by the same apostolic and prophetic texts.

In fact, it belongs to the nature of the Christian tradition to be historical, and so to be in continual dialogue with its foundational sources and documents, becoming in this respect contemporaneous with the present situation. Because '[t]he story of Jesus Christ has to be history, not in all its details, but in its core, if the Christian faith is to continue.'[61] By the canon in its function as instrument for the faith community, the church preserves and actualizes 'the gospel' in its capacity as regulative historical tradition. In this act, however, the Scriptures being preserved attain functions that extend far beyond mere preservation or actualization. Crucial here is the subject matter (*Sache*) – the Word of God, which is believed to continuously address readers and hearers by means of these instruments – being a place 'where the church may reliably expect to encounter God's communicative presence, God's self-attestation.'[62] Indeed, seen in this perspective, '[w]hat speaks to us in Holy Scripture does not rest primarily upon the art of writing, but upon the authority of the one who speaks to us in the Church.'[63]

In the previous chapters, past and present aspects of the canon have been explored, focusing on linguistic and tradition-related, material and textual, performative, and ideational dimensions of biblical canonicity. Due to the canon's past and present function – as classic, liturgical and theological writing – providing textual basis for the faith community, there is potential for present and future application. And, contrariwise, the communal appropriation of

---

[60] Bonhoeffer, *Reflections on the Bible: Human Word and Word of God* (Peabody, MA: Hendrickson, 2004), 31.
[61] Pannenberg, *An Introduction to Systematic Theology*, 5. Cited in Ch. 1, n. 76.
[62] Webster, 'The Dogmatic Location of the Canon', 30. Cited in Ch. 1, n. 29.
[63] Gadamer, *The Relevance of the Beautiful and Other Essays*, 142. Cited in Ch. 1, n. 82.

these writings as canon for today's community has much to gain from research on the rich history and tradition associated with this canon.

Even so, the present community has an advantage in relation to its past. The temporal distance to its own past has the particular potential of solving questions of critique relating, e.g. to the canon. The community of the present has had time to distinguish true and useful prejudices – by which it may understand the tradition(s) pertaining to the canon – from false ones, by which it misunderstands. 'Temporal distance', Gadamer remarks, 'obviously means something other than the extinction of our interest in the object. It lets the true meaning of the object emerge fully. … [Temporal distance] lets local and limited prejudices die away, but allows those that bring about genuine understanding to emerge clearly as such.'[64] Even if not absolutely closed, the idea of a closed canon (still being as if open towards its interpretive communities) may be considered also in view of the following:

> In fact the important thing is to recognize temporal distance as a positive and productive condition enabling understanding. It is not a yawning abyss but is filled with the continuity of custom and tradition, in the light of which everything handed down presents itself to us. Here it is not too much to speak of the genuine productivity of the course of events. Everyone is familiar with the curious impotence of our judgment where temporal distance has not given us sure criteria.[65]

The 'final' shape of the canonical texts expresses something of this understanding more clearly than do earlier forms of the canonical writings. In other words, the category of reception is central when seeking to comprehend these texts as part of a larger textual corpus. Even the old debate between Catholics and Protestants on Scripture and tradition may be highlighted by the role here ascribed to temporal distance. Temporal distance (tradition) may be needed in order to discern the object (Scripture) more clearly. The Reformation as well as the Counter-Reformation, and, later on, the ecumenical movement, can all be conceived within such a hermeneutical frame.

Interestingly, Gadamer categorizes the Christian New Testament as an instance of *Urliteratur*. He points out three characteristics of such *Urliteratur*: 1) as witness of an authentic tradition; 2) as 'eminent text', that is, as

[64] Gadamer, *TM*, 298.
[65] Ibid., 297.

address connected with preaching/hearing; and 3) as sign (see below). Again, temporal distance is needed for the 'final' form of this literature to be viewed in this way.[66]

In particular two features have been applicable to the concept of canon as it developed in the second-century church, namely what Gadamer calls: 1) the retrospective element; and 2) the normative consciousness behind the concept of the classic. Regarding the former element, Gadamer comments: 'What gives birth to the classical norm is an awareness of decline and distance. It is not by accident that the concept of the classical and of classical style emerges in late periods.'[67] The same thought is expressed by scholars on the biblical canon. Adolf von Harnack, e.g. states that '[t]he greater became the distance in time from the Apostolical Age the more sacred became the series of writings that had Catholic character and Apostolic title, *just because of these properties and the distance.*'[68]

Again, as argued above, it is only as sign that the biblical writings can be seen as canon for the church, that is, what is shown in this specific textual 'construal' is only accessible to the one who looks for him- or herself and actually sees something there of this ecclesial portrayal of the whole. When seen otherwise, the texts in question are viewed in some other way. Hence, when perceived as canon, they are taken as a unified – and for the church universal, most importantly, also as a unifying – whole, being normative for the church body of Christ believers.[69]

9.6 Canon as *Scripture*

> Strangely, or not so strangely, the first and last books of the NT present themselves as scripture. ... [I]t attests the existence of the idea of distinctively Christian scriptures before the end of the first century.[70]

---

[66] See Lawrence, 'Gadamer, the Hermeneutic Revolution, and Theology', in *The Cambridge Companion to Gadamer*, ed. R. J. Dostal, (Cambridge: Cambridge University Press, 2002), 190f.

[67] Gadamer, *TM*, 288.

[68] Harnack, *The Origin of the New Testament and the Most Important Consequences of the New Creation* (London: Williams & Norgate, 1925), 23.

[69] So Campenhausen, *Die Entstehung der christlichen Bibel*, 3.

[70] Smith, 'When Did the Gospels Become Scripture?', *JBL* 119 (2000): 15. Cf. Ashton, *Understanding the Fourth Gospel* (Oxford: Oxford University Press, 2nd edn, 2007), 344.

The truth, or the possible truth, of this claim heavily affects the problem of the canon as it has been formulated by the scholarly consensus for more than a century. To discern what is, and what is not, Christian Scripture seems, to some extent, to be an issue addressed already within the NT writings themselves. In fact, it accords well with what we know of their reception in the faith communities, that they were read in worship on a par with the Scriptures from early on.[71] Furthermore, they were accorded a special status, similar to that of Scripture and underlined by the early introduction of *nomina sacra* in both OT and NT texts. This is in line with a tendency in the early second century to draw on the emerging NT much more heavily than on the old Scriptures (see section 3.7). The reason why the new writings on a few occasions could be quoted as Scripture from early on – thereby assuming a status similar to that of the inspired, prophetic writings – was the authority which was recognized in the apostolic tradition focusing on Jesus' words and deeds. In addition, if we choose not to make a sharp distinction between the transmission of the oral and the written gospel tradition, we may find the Jesus logia being already of equal or superior authority with that of Scripture from the beginning. So, when words of Jesus are quoted as Scripture in *2 Clement* (2.4) and *Barnabas* (4.14), this comes as no surprise.[72]

Still, when discussing the scriptural status of the new Christian writings, we need to bear in mind that the earliest Christian writers do not place these in exactly the same literary category as that of the Jewish Scriptures. The influential church writer Justin Martyr, for example, never uses the introductory formula 'as it is said in Scripture' (or equivalents) when quoting from a New Testament writing; and when speaking of Scripture, he always

---

[71] Our earliest direct witness is Justin, but the influence on all Christian discourse affected by the Gospel of Matthew, as indicated by Massaux and Bellinzoni (*The Influence of the Gospel of Saint Matthew on Christian Literature Before Saint Irenaeus* [Macon, GA: Mercer University Press, and Leuven, Belgium: Peeters, 1990–93]) points to both a liturgical and a non-liturgical usage of the writing on a regular basis. Moreover, liturgical usage of emerging NT texts seems to be presupposed already in 2 Pet. 3.16 and appears to be a major reason for writing down Mark and Matthew. On *Barn.* 4.14, see footnote below. See also section 7.5, n. 39.

[72] For *Barn.* 4.14, see Rhodes, *The Epistle of Barnabas and the Deuteronomic Tradition* (WUNT 2/188; Tübingen: Mohr Siebeck, 2004), 153ff; and W.-D. Köhler (*Die Rezeption des Matthäusevangeliums in der Zeit vor Irenäus* [WUNT 2/22; Tübingen: Mohr Siebeck, 1987]), who argues that dependence on Matthew is quite possible for *Barn.* 4.14; 5.8f and 7.9b. Metzger's argument to the contrary is unconvincing: *The Canon of the New Testament*, 57. Cf. also Bokedal, 'Scripture in the Second Century', in *The Sacred Text: Excavating the Texts, Exploring the Interpretations, and Engaging the Theologies of the Christian Scriptures*, (eds) Michael Bird and Michael Pahl (Piscataway, NJ: Gorgias, 2010), 48ff.

refers to the books of the Hebrew Bible.[73] On the other hand, in his account of the public reading in the service of worship in *1 Apol.* 67, 'the Memoirs of the Apostles' (i.e. the Gospels) are mentioned alongside and even prior to 'the writings of the Prophets'. In Justin, the 'writtenness' of 'the Memoirs' is emphasized in his *Apology* as well as in the *Dialogue*.[74] These new authoritative scriptures – the 'Gospels' – which Justin is the first to mention in the plural (*1 Apol.* 66), are present in the communities of faith. However, although these writings already bear the names 'Memoirs' and 'Gospels', we can conclude that it is still quite another thing to explicitly call them 'Scripture'. In consideration of the ongoing dialogue with the synagogue (and not only with Justin's fictive dialogue partner Trypho), and the rather precise meaning of the notion of Scripture in the Jewish setting, we can imagine that it would have been quite odd to speak in public with Jews of the Gospels in the same way as of the Law and the prophetical writings. In other words, it seems to be more a question of terminology and exact reference, rather than the implicit exclusion of Christian writings, when the idiom 'it is said in the Scriptures' is being used. At this early date, the phrase did not yet generally denote the new writings soon to be included in the 'New Testament'. The first Christian writers, who clearly take this final step in the reception of the new Scriptures, are Tatian (AD 170–5) and Irenaeus (ca. AD 180) in their ample treatment of the Gospels as Scripture, fully on a par with the books of the Jewish Scriptures.[75]

Nevertheless, this way of picturing the development is not quite correct for at least two reasons. First, the Christian Scriptures (the Septuagint and the new ecclesial writings) are not, in general, accepted by the Jews as Scripture. Second, the format chosen for the Christian Scriptures towards the end of the second century, the codex rather than the scroll, together with the exchange of the Tetragrammaton for Christian *nomina sacra* imply that we are

---

[73] Skarsaune, *In the Shadow of the Temple: Jewish Influences on Early Christianity* (Downers Grove, IL: InterVarsity, 2002), 280. However, cf. Bellinzoni, in *The Influence of the Gospel of Saint Matthew*, Book 3, Massaux and Bellinzoni, 186: 'Justin … seems to have considered the entire gospel [Matthew] as scripture. He introduced many passages drawn from Mt. with the formula γέ γραπται, and he used this same formula in one passage (*Dial.* 49.5) in which he reported, not a saying of Christ, but a thought of the gospel writer.'

[74] See esp. *1 Apol.* 66 and *Dial.* 98-107, ed. Markovich; cf. also Stanton, 'The Fourfold Gospel', *New Testament Studies* 43 (1997): 330f.

[75] For Irenaeus' approach to the Gospels in this regard, cf. the balanced judgement by Stanton, *Jesus and Gospel* (Cambridge: Cambridge University Press, 2004), 106.

dealing with a modified version, a slightly different conception, of the Jewish Scriptures. The Scriptures of the church were in several respects something partly different from the Scriptures of the synagogue. This is worth having in mind when we study the Christian writings becoming Scripture, if by that we mean Scripture exclusively as it was understood by the synagogue.

So, the question posed by Moody Smith – 'When did the Gospels become Scripture?' – is somewhat ambiguous. What does 'become Scripture' mean? From the above discussion we may still perhaps want to conclude that by 'Scripture' in the Jewish and Christian settings of the first and second centuries more or less the same characteristics are connoted. Nevertheless, as the Christian Scriptures are formed into something distinctly different as compared to the Jewish Bible, the notion of Scripture is somewhat changed. The development of the Christian church into a *tertium genus* against both the synagogue and the gentiles carries with it some new particularly Christian conceptions, such as the understanding of the church as a new 'Israel', as the people of a new covenant with its own authoritative writings.[76] The emergence of a distinctly Christian scriptural corpus needs to be understood against this backdrop.

9.7 In search of ancient canon criteria: Undisputed biblical writings

Studying the earliest history of the New Testament canon is perplexing due to the unexpectedly smooth, natural, apparently undramatic and passive formation of the first Christian s/Scriptures, and their addition to the corpus of Scriptures designed for divine lection. Theodor Zahn concluded from this that there was already a New Testament at hand by the early second century, although this collection of writings was not yet attributed the dogmatic label 'Scripture'. More recently, scholars have followed Zahn to some degree. The question of when the Gospels and other 'NT' writings become Scripture is raised with a new sensitivity and emphasis. A way to start providing a

---

[76] See, e.g. Hvalvik, *The Struggle for Scripture and Covenant: the purpose of the epistle of Barnabas and Jewish-Christian competition in the second century* (Tübingen: Mohr Siebeck, 1996).

response is to refer to this early 'passive' canon formation as related to the category of the apostolic.

By the notion of apostolicity (*1 Clem.* 5; *Ignat. Rom.* 4.3) the church directly or indirectly draws a dividing line between itself at the present and its earliest existence, defined by the apostles and their immediate followers. In this process of differentiation, the distinction between text and commentary is made. Understood in this way, the criterion of apostolicity is crucial.[77] The notion of Scripture, then, merges prophetic and apostolic texts that are revered as especially sacred and authoritative.[78]

However, with regard to some of the undisputed canonical writings that became part of the New Testament, we do not encounter an emphasis on criteria at all; and the criterion of apostolicity is not stressed until later, well into the second century. However, in Irenaeus, Tertullian and, as we will see below, Jerome, apostolicity turns out to be the principal canon criterion; nevertheless, in all of these writers some additional criteria are taken on board as well.

For the earliest period, though, when the Gospels are commonly thought to have been composed, *prima facie*, the notion of apostolicity as a major component is largely absent. The Gospels may have been published as anonymous pieces of literature (Martin Hengel famously disputes this). Even so, we are not in a position to dismiss the tacit influence of this criterion altogether, which becomes clear from even a brief look at the NT literature.[79] The epistles of Paul make up a good example. Although most of his writings can be regarded as occasional documents addressing particular issues specific for the community in question, it is still the case that these letters – though discussing particularities and problems connected to a specific time and place – are means of Paul's apostolic presence among the churches. As the distinction between oral and written communication ought not to be over-emphasized, Paul's apostolic presence and authority is perpetuated, and

---

[77] See, e.g. Cullmann, *Die Tradition und die Festlegung des Kanons durch die Kirche des 2. Jahrhunderts* (Göttingen: Vandenhoeck & Ruprecht, 1970), 99f.

[78] Cf. William Graham's definition of 'canon', cited in Smith, 'When Did the Gospels Become Scripture?', 18.

[79] Cf. esp. some of the literary titles included in the emerging NT indicating apostolic authorship. See also, e.g. Skarsaune, 'Hvilket lys kaster NT's kanonhistorie over teologihistorien i det 1. århundre?', *Religio* 25 (1986): 63–83.

sanctioned, already in 2 Pet. 3.15f., where the Pauline letters seem to be regarded as Scripture.[80] Worth noting in this regard is the apparent intention laid down already by the author and his associates of having his letters read out aloud before the community (1 Thess. 5.27; Col. 4.16). This could imply that they were already meant to be authoritative texts, perhaps somehow along the lines of the Scriptures, from the outset.[81] The authoritative tone of Paul talking as an apostle is noteworthy in this regard. Lee McDonald remarks that this suggests that Paul 'also viewed his writings as authoritative if not prophetic (1 Cor. 5.3; 6.1–6; 7.10–11, 17–20, 40; 11.23-34, Gal. 5.1–4, *passim*).'[82] 'Prophetic' in this connection would then mean 'inspired'.[83] In the early second century, before the time of Marcion's arrival in Rome, two collections of Pauline letters may have been circulating among the faith communities, one 10- and one 13-letter corpus.[84] At this early date, the letters are attaining not only scriptural functions, but also canonical status to the extent that the corpus may be regarded as more or less closed.[85]

Nevertheless, throughout the period when the writings to be eventually included in the NT were composed, some other characteristic features, besides that of apostolic authorship, come to the fore, functioning as forms of internal forces affecting the process of canonization.

First, that the Christian community saw itself as an outgrowth of Judaism and the fulfilment of its Scriptures, has implications for the formation of new, specifically Christian writings. Everywhere in the NT we find references to the Scriptures; in the 27th edition of Nestle-Aland, *Novum Testamentum*

---

[80] On pre-Marcionite Pauline letter corpora, cf. Schmid, *Marcion und sein Apostolos: Rekonstruktion und historische Einordnung der marcionitischen Paulusbriefausgabe* (Berlin and New York: Walter de Gruyter, 1995); and, more recently, Porter 'When and How was the Pauline Canon Compiled?'. For an interesting comment on oral and written communication in Paul, see Bauckham, *For Whom Were Gospels Written?* (Grand Rapids: Eerdmans, 1998), 28f.: 'Paul seems only to have written anything when distance required him to communicate in writing what he would otherwise have spoken orally to one of his churches. It was distance that required writing, whereas orality sufficed for presence'; cf. also Smith, 'When Did the Gospels Become Scripture?', 4f.

[81] So McDonald, 'Indentifying Scripture and Canon in the Early Church: The Criteria Question', in *The Canon Debate*, (eds) L. M. McDonald and J. A. Sanders (Peabody, MA: Hendrickson, 2002), 419, n. 9.

[82] Ibid.

[83] On the inspiration of Scripture from a Jewish viewpoint, see, e.g. Strack and Billerbeck, *Kommentar zum Neuen Testament aus Talmud und Midrasch, I–IV* (München, 1922–8 [reprint 1974–8]).

[84] Schmid, *Marcion und sein Apostolos.*

[85] Both these collections, one containing 10 letters without the Pastorals, addressed to church leaders, and another containing 13, may be considered to be in principle closed. That Hebrews, a disputed writing with unknown author, is (later) added to the collection in the East (already in P[46]) does not change this.

Graece, some 3,000 citations and allusions are listed. This most typical feature of Christian Scripture is missing, for example, in the *Gospel of Thomas.*[86] In stark contrast to the NT writings, Scripture in the *Gospel of Thomas* is neither cited nor presupposed;[87] and there is no recognized scriptural story for which this Gospel could 'present itself as the next chapter'.[88] From this, Moody Smith concludes that the *Gospel of Thomas* was written 'not for biblical religion but, so to speak, for another, new, esoteric religion.'[89]

Smith has observed some crucial features pertaining to the problem of canon in the core writings of the New Testament. Asking whether the New Testament authors intended to write Scripture, and adhering to Richard Bauckham's thesis of a wide circle of Gospel audiences,[90] Smith remarks that the Gospels most probably were intended for a liturgical setting. 'If one asks for what purpose were the Gospels written or what function did they fulfill, one can scarcely exclude public reading in services of worship as a likely possibility.'[91] He further argues that the leap from the authoritative use of the gospel tradition in preaching or catechesis in the 50s AD to the reading of the Gospels in church worship a hundred years later is quite reasonable, despite the fact that we cannot document the earlier stages. In order to prove his case – that the Gospels by their redactors were intended as Scripture – Smith seeks to demonstrate the (incipient) scriptural status of Matthew:

> Matthew begins with a genealogy that sets Jesus in the context … of the Davidic monarchy. … Jesus represents the restoration of that dynasty and therefore of the history of Israel and the history of salvation. Thus Jesus continues the biblical narrative. … [The account of] Jesus' birth is then punctuated by scriptural prophecies, which interestingly enough, are not introduced as scripture – as if scripture were in a different category from this Gospel – but as what was spoken by the prophets.

---

[86] Layton, 'The Gospel according to Thomas', in *The Gnostic Scriptures,* trans. B. Layton (London: SCM, 1987), 380–99.

[87] Saying 66, Smith remarks ('When Did the Gospels Become Scripture?', 14), reflects Psalm 118.22, but does not cite it as Scripture.

[88] Ibid.

[89] Ibid.

[90] Bauckham, 'For Whom Were Gospels Written?' (Grand Rapids: Eerdmans, 1998); cf. Stanton, *The Gospels and Jesus* (Oxford: Oxford University Press, 2nd edn, 2002), 56f.; Bauckham argues that the Gospels are not, as is commonly assumed, occasional documents written to *one* community, but writings addressed to a wider circle of readers.

[91] Smith, 'When Did the Gospels Become Scripture?', 5f., n. 10.

Next in Smith's argument is a reference to the five thematic discourses in Matthew – probably paralleling the five books of Moses – as definitive presentations of Jesus' teaching. The closing Great Commission (28.19f.) attains the function as a salvation-historical apex. [92]

A similar analysis is then made for Luke and the Book of Revelation. Smith's main concern is to present these core writings of the NT as providing a continuation of the scriptural story.

> [T]he early Christian claim that the narrative and prophecies of old are fulfilled and continued in Jesus and the church prefigures, perhaps even demands, the production of more scripture, which will explain how this happened. Such scripture is required to explain this not first of all to outsiders but rather to Christians themselves. It becomes an essential part of their identity and self-understanding.[93]

The NT writings which address the issue of Scripture in this direct way were still, it seems, circulating and received in the faith communities without any discussion as to the criteria of their status as authentic texts. This was rather something that was taken for granted. The continuation of the biblical story, as presented by these scriptures, was and remained the inherent criterion carried by these most crucial writings for Christian identity (especially Matthew, Luke-Acts and Revelation; but also Mark and John). Hence, we are dealing with something which we could call the narrative self-authenticating character of these texts as they were received as Scripture in the Christian communities.

9.8 In search of ancient canon criteria: Disputed biblical writings

Concerning the great majority of the Jewish Scriptures, their reception as canon were never seriously questioned by the church. Some Christian leaders, it is true, were influenced by the Rabbinic discussions as to the status of Ecclesiastes, Song of Songs and Esther.[94] In the famous *Thirty-Ninth*

---

[92] Ibid., 7f.
[93] Ibid., 12.
[94] Leiman, 'Inspiration and Canonicity: Reflections on the Formation of the Biblical Canon', in *Jewish*

Festal Epistle of Athanasius, for example, his Old Testament canon contains only 65 books; Esther is counted among the books valuable for instruction in piety for those 'who have recently joined us', together with Wisdom of Solomon, Wisdom of Sirach, Judith, Tobit, the *Didache* and the *Shepherd* of Hermas (the most popular non-canonical writing before the fourth century).[95]

Those who followed the Jewish Rabbinic practice regarding canonical scope – which included most church leaders up to the fourth century[96] – did not count the disputed so-called Apocryphal writings among the canonical books;[97] i.e. the Hebrew Bible/Old Testament was by many understood as closed, at least in principle (cf. Josephus, *Against Apion* 1.37-41), when the cessation of prophecy was generally believed to have occurred, some time in the late Persian or the early Hellenistic Period.[98] For three centuries, until the Constantinian Era, the principal criterion concerning canonical scope of the Christian Old Testament, thus, was inclusion in the Jewish canon; or rather, the Jewish as well as the Christian canon principle was 'authorship in the canonical period of inspiration'.[99] As Oskar Skarsaune has pointed out, this canon principle would lead to discussions as to which books claiming to stem from this period in fact did so, and could be shown to be authentic. Eventually two effective Old Testament canons emerged in the church, one of the 'learned theologians', who kept to the Jewish canon, and one of the laypeople and many of the clergy, who in addition to the 39 OT books included in their bibles some or all of the Apocrypha.[100]

---

and *Christian Self-Definition*, vol. 2, (eds) E. P. Sanders et al. (Philadelphia: Fortress, 1981), 317, n. 22: 'it was precisely the inspired status of these biblical books that was at stake in the rabbinic discussions.' Ibid., 61: The Rabbis, thus, did not suggest '*new* candidates for inclusion in the biblical canon'. Leiman also underscores that nowhere in Rabbinic literature, in the Apocrypha or in Josephus, is it mentioned that a book was *added* to the biblical canon as it emerged in the second century CE.

[95] Osiek, *The Shepherd of Hermas* (Hermeneia; Minneapolis: Fortress, 1999), 1.

[96] Beckwith, *The Old Testament Canon of the New Testament Church and its Background in Early Judaism* (Grand Rapids: Eerdmans, 1985); cf. my discussion in 8.3.5.

[97] This did not, however, mean that they were not used. On the contrary, some of the Apocryphal writings could be used rather frequently, as in Origen, without being included in the Old Testament canon.

[98] Leiman, 'Inspiration and Canonicity: Reflections on the Formation of the Biblical Canon', 61. Cf. also Beckwith, *The Old Testament Canon of the New Testament Church and its Background in Early Judaism* (Grand Rapids: Eerdmans, 1985); and Skarsaune, 'Loven, Profetene og Skriftene: Jødedommens Bible: kanon og tekst', in *Blant skriftlærde og fariseere: Jødedommen i oldtiden*, ed. H. Kvalbein; Skarsaune, *In the Shadow of the Temple*, 291f.

[99] Ibid., 292.

[100] Ibid.

In the second and third centuries, a similar pattern can be observed for the main part of the emerging New Testament. The canonical status of some 20 of these writings was hardly ever seriously disputed in the early church; Eusebius and Origen therefore counted these among the *homologoumena*, the undisputed writings. As in the case with the Old Testament, Skarsaune proffers an analogous principal criterion of canonicity for the New Testament – that of apostolicity – that sets out to explain this:

> the basic principle behind the New Testament canon is as clear and self-evident as that behind the Old Testament: the normativity of the documents is defined by author and period of authorship, which makes the debate about the extent of the canon basically a debate about 'genuine' or 'fake' attributions. This also means that this debate is probably never closed once and for all.[101]

9.8.1 Jerome on the disputed writings

Now, if we look at the seven commonly disputed writings,[102] the so-called *antilegomena*, of the New Testament, Jerome's (b. ca. AD 346) occasional comments concerning these books are instructive for the criteria discussion. Many of the specific canon criteria usually associated with the Patristic Age, such as apostolicity, orthodoxy, antiquity, inspiration and usage, here naturally come to the fore. When discussing James, 'who is called the brother of the Lord', Jerome comments: 'He wrote a single epistle, which is reckoned among the seven Catholic Epistles, and even this is claimed by some to have been published by someone else under his name, and gradually as time went on to have gained authority' (*De Vir. Ill.* 2).[103] We see here the most common criterion of canonicity at work, that of apostolicity. At this early period, this criterion comes close to what we could call authenticity. A writing is an authentic canonical writing only if written, or on reasonable grounds claimed

---

[101] Ibid., 297.
[102] If by the 'New Testament' – following David Trobisch – we mean the edition of the Christian writings so labeled from the mid- to late second century on, we do not need to consider in this connection writings not included, such as *1* and *2 Clement*, *Barnabas*, the *Shepherd* of Hermas and the *Didache*; or apocryphal (i.e. non-canonical) gospels, which were excluded (if at all considered) from the canon by the mainstream church. For the *Apocalypse of Peter*, see Metzger, *The Canon of the New Testament: Its Origin, Development, and Significance* (Oxford: Clarendon Press, 1987), 184; regarding the Epistle to the Laodiceans, composed perhaps towards the end of the third century, Jerome says that 'it is rejected by everyone' (*De Viris Ill.* 5).
[103] The Fathers of the Church 100:7.

to be written, by an apostle. However, Jerome meets the suspicion towards James in this regard by referring to two other criteria.

First, and most noteworthy, the Letter of James is already 'reckoned among the seven Catholic Epistles'. It is already included in one of the part collections of the literary canon as received by the church. This is the specific implicit and explicit argument used by David Trobisch throughout his *First Edition of the New Testament*.[104] As noted at the outset of the present study, discussions on the biblical canon tend to presuppose a canon which is already there (see section 2.1). James is already seen as part of a sub-collection within the collection of New Testament writings, namely the Catholic Epistles. These are often included within a single codex, which normally embraces Acts as well, the so called *Praxapostolos*.[105] To be included in this codex is one aspect of the final form of the text,[106] and the questioning of James quite naturally affects, somehow, also the other writings of the *Praxapostolos*. This is the way I read the implicit (or explicit?) argument put forth by Jerome. In other words, although it is not the only reason or 'criterion', James is canonical because it is already (received as) canonical. Of course, this type of circular reasoning would not be possible to maintain were it not for the two undisputed corpora of Christian writings, the Gospels and the letters of Paul, providing, by analogy, 'canonical force' even to this third collection of apostolic writings. Furthermore, the core writings within the third collection, Acts, 1 John and 1 Peter, are attributed more or less undisputed authority among the faith communities.

The other criterion applied to James is that of usage: 'and even this is claimed by some to have been published by someone else under his name, and gradually as time went on to have gained authority' (*De Vir. Ill.* 2).[107] In one way or another, this criterion is always present for all the writings eventually to be included in the New Testament. In the words of von Harnack: 'The greater became the distance in time from the Apostolical Age the more sacred

---

[104] Trobisch, *First Edition*.

[105] See Trobisch, *First Edition*, 25–8. For a different treatment of James and the NT canon, see Nienhuis, *Not by Paul Alone: The Formation of the Catholic Epistle Collection and the Christian Canon* (Waco, TX: Baylor University Press, 2007).

[106] The Greek NT codices typically contain Acts + Catholic Epistles (ca. 30 majuscules and 40 minuscules extant) and Acts + Catholic Epistles + Pauline Letters (ca. 8 majuscules and 256 minuscules extant); see Epp ('Issues in the Interrelation of New Testament Textual Criticism and Canon', in *The Canon Debate*, (eds) L. M. McDonald and J. A. Sanders [Peabody, MA: Hendrickson, 2002], 487), who bases his figures on Kurt and Barbara Aland.

[107] The Fathers of the Church 100:7.

became the series of writings that had Catholic character and Apostolic title, *just because of these properties and the distance.*[108] However, as Moody Smith and others have emphasized,[109] Apocryphal writings could for internal and external reasons never have made it into the canon. The implied criterion of usage cannot stand by itself.

Another disputed writing, the Epistle of Jude, is rejected by a great many, Jerome says, because of its reference to the apocryphal *Book of Enoch*; '[n]evertheless, by age and use it has gained authority and is reckoned among the Holy Scriptures' (*De Vir. Ill.* 4).[110] Two criteria, antiquity and usage, are here appealed to.

Dependent apostolicity is a slightly different criterion of authenticity, as compared to that of immediate apostolicity. This is indirectly taken into account when discussing 2 and 3 John. Jerome tells us that they 'are said to be the work of John the elder',[111] for John the apostle was the author of the Epistle that begins, 'What was from the beginning' (*De Vir. Ill.* 9).[112] John the presbyter most probably stood in a direct relationship to the apostolic circle; according to some more recent scholarship, he was the head of the Johannine school.[113] Papias' widely known words, as reported by Eusebius, are illuminating:

> [B]ut if ever anyone came who had followed the elders, I inquired into the words of the elders, what Andrew or Peter or Philip or Thomas or James or John or Matthew, or any other of the Lord's disciples, had said, and what Aristion and *John the elder*, disciples of the Lord's, were saying (*Eccl. Hist.* III, 39.4; my italics).[114]

We are here dealing with the earliest church's understanding of what we may call apostolicity. According to some scholars, John the elder could have been

---

[108] Harnack, *The Origin of the New Testament and the Most Important Consequences of the New Creation*, 23.
[109] Smith, 'When Did the Gospels Become Scripture?'.
[110] The Fathers of the Church 100:11.
[111] The author of 2 and 3 John designates himself the Elder (*presbyteros*).
[112] The (canonical) tradition, which can be traced back to Irenaeus (3 John not referred to), ascribes all the Johannine NT writings, the Fourth Gospel, 1, 2 and 3 John and the Apocalypse, to John the son of Zebedee, which is identified with the Beloved Disciple of the Fourth Gospel (*Adv. Haer.* II, 22.5; III, 1.1; 3.4; 16.5; IV, 20.11).
[113] Hengel, *The Johannine Question* (London: SCM, and Philadelphia: Trinity Press International, 1989); Stuhlmacher, *Biblische Theologie des Neuen Testaments: Band II: Von der Paulusschule bis zur Johannesoffenbarung Der Kanon und seine Auslegung* (Göttingen: Vandenhoeck & Ruprecht, 1999), 203–06.
[114] LCL 153:293; modified.

the founder of 'the Johannine circle'. Indirectly or directly, he was possibly responsible for the redaction of the *Corpus Johanneum*. In a particular way he would then be a representative of authoritative 'apostolic' tradition. For the Patristic Age, the principal canon criterion of apostolicity implied that the writing in question should be authentic, that is written by an apostle (such as Matthew, John or Paul) or a personal follower of an apostle (such as Mark, Luke or John the elder).[115]

The criterion of apostolicity is also at stake when Jerome discusses 2 Peter (*Epist.* 120). In order to solve the difference in style between the two Epistles attributed to Peter, he suggests that the apostle made use of two different amanuenses.

Finally, Hebrews and Revelation, the two remaining disputed books, are discussed by Jerome in a letter from AD 414:

> [T]he epistle which is entitled 'To the Hebrews' is accepted as the apostle Paul's not only by the churches of the east but by all church writers in the Greek language of earlier times, although many judge it to be by Barnabas or by Clement. It is of no great moment who the author is, since it is the work of a churchman and receives recognition day by day in the churches' public reading. If the custom of the Latins does not receive it among the canonical scriptures, neither, by the same liberty, do the churches of the Greeks accept John's Apocalypse. Yet we accept them both, not following the custom of the present time but the precedent of early writers, who generally make free use of testimonies from both works. And this they do, not as they are wont on occasion to quote from apocryphal writings, as indeed they use examples from pagan literature, but treating them as canonical and ecclesiastical works. (*Epist.* 129.3).[116]

---

[115] Stuhlmacher, *Biblische Theologie des Neuen Testaments: Band II: Von der Paulusschule bis zur Johannesoffenbarung Der Kanon und seine Auslegung*, 203: 'Aus den *Johannesbriefen* kann man erschließen, daß der Presbyter eine eigene Schule begründet und Schüler um sich gesammelt hat, wie es vor ihm schon antike Philosophen, jüdische (Weisheits-) Lehrer wie Ben Sira oder auch Paulus (vgl. Apg 19,9) getan hatten'; Skarsaune, *In the Shadow of the Temple*, 295: As for the principal canon criterion to be applied to the Gospels, Skarsaune remarks: 'As time went by, this became the simple criterion of establishing which gospel writings should be regarded authentic and therefore authoritative: those written by apostles (Matthew, John) or personal followers of apostles (Mark, Luke). Modern scholars may think that all four Gospels belong to the last category (Matthew being produced within "the school of Matthew" rather than by the apostle himself, and John coming from "the Johannine circle"), but even so, the fact remains undisputed even in the most critically-minded scholarly circles: the four Gospels in the New Testament are the only such writings produced in the first century A.D. and deriving from the first-through-second generations of disciples'; on dependent canonicity, see further Sundberg, 'Dependent Canonicity in Irenaeus and Tertullian', in *Studia Evangelica* 3, ed. F. L. Cross (Berlin: Akademie-Verlag, 1964), 403–9.

[116] Citation from Bruce, *The Canon of Scripture* (Downers Grove, IL: InterVarsity, 1988), 226f.

Here catholicity is the major criterion for demonstrating the canonicity of Hebrews. The Epistle to the Hebrews, Jerome maintains, is received by the churches of the East as well as by all church writers of the Greek language before his days. The second argument, it seems, is the criterion of usage combined with that of antiquity ('by all Church writers of the Greek language before our days'). If not altogether neglected, the apostolic origin of the Epistle is here placed in the background. Yet, the issue of apostolicity – together with issues regarding the Epistle's teaching – still seems to constitute the root to the letter's disputed status. However, Jerome's reference to a 'churchman' of the earliest ecclesiastical period ('it makes no difference whose it is, since it is from a churchman') perhaps suggests that it qualifies as apostolic, according to the definition presented above. As it turns out, from early on the Epistle to the Hebrews is often part of the Pauline letter corpus (already P[46], ca. AD 200).

The final argument for the canonicity of Hebrews, and in particular also for the Apocalypse, is once again the circular argument, here used with even more emphasis: the book is canonical, because it is (received as) canonical; i.e. the judgement of canonical status for any writing in today's church (Jerome's day) is dependent on the canonical status of the writing in the earliest church: 'we follow by no means the habit of today, but the authority of ancient writers.' In use here is Jerome's early fifth-century argument (AD 414) of antiquity combined with a claim for canonicity. It *is* canonical because it *was and remained* canonical for the ancient church. In the case of the Book of Revelation, we know that it did not become seriously disputed until around the early third century when the Roman presbyter Gaius and Dionysius of Alexandria began questioning its authenticity (see section 4.7), that is, its apostolicity in the strict sense. Such a narrow understanding of apostolicity, however, was, as we have seen, not generally applied to the emerging New Testament.[117] Lurking in the background, however, is the question of authority associated with the apostles and their immediate followers.

---

[117] Later Eusebius adopts the position of Dionysius of Alexandria, concluding that John the elder and not the apostle John wrote the Apocalypse.

9.9 The authority of the new writings

The earliest attestation to a Pauline letter corpus appears to be 2 Pet. 3.15f. So, whether or not considered to be a part of the Scriptures (cf. 2 Pet. 3.16), the Pauline writings were used as an authority by 2 Peter and by some of the early Apostolic Fathers. Ignatius of Antioch, for example, seems to know 1 Corinthians more or less by heart. When we look at the formation of the New Testament with this in mind, we might be struck by a paradox noted by Franz Stuhlhofer:

> The early Church cited the Old Testament as 'Scripture', but to begin with tended to possess it only in a fragmentary form. The New Testament, on the other hand, was widely available and was used much more heavily, but was not yet cited as 'Scripture'.[118]

This soon resulted in the early placing of the new Christian writings alongside the (Jewish) Scriptures. As we have seen above, several factors affected this process. Nevertheless, a rather unexpected element in the NT canonization here comes to the fore. John Barton directs our attention to this phenomenon when discussing 'old and new' in the church:

> For Christians as for Jews and, indeed, for pagans, the idea of Scripture inherently contained the idea of age and venerability. Passivity was the major factor in the reception of certain books as holy, and this depends on attributing a high value to the past. What is old is more reliable than what is new.[119]

In contrast to this general pattern, the authority of the New Testament writings asserted itself by means of quite a different set of criteria. Barton continues:

> The Gospels were received as, in practice, even more important than the Jewish Scriptures *before* they were old enough to have a natural aura of sacred antiquity. Paul's epistles were preserved and collected while Paul was still a comparatively recent memory. Revelation, which despite some doubts in the East was none the less widely accepted as an inspired book from early times, was not a pseudepigraphical ancient prophecy like Enoch or even Daniel, but the record of a vision accorded to a modern prophet. ... This attitude, so unusual in the ancient

---

[118] Stuhlhofer, *Der Gebrauch der Bibel von Jesus bis Euseb: Eine statistische Untersuchung zur Kanonsgeschichte* (Wuppertal: Brockhaus, 1988), 68.
[119] Barton, *The Spirit and the Letter*, 65.

world, presumably has something to do with the early Christian conviction that a new and unprecedented era had arrived with Jesus and the apostolic Church. Newness was no longer a sign of inferiority but a mark of authenticity.'[120]

This thoughtful portrayal of the authoritative elements involved in the canonical process stands out even against such a fit criterion of canonicity as that of 'established usage', which Harry Gamble singles out as 'the most powerful commendation of a writing' in shaping the New Testament canon.[121] It is only later – from the third century on, until the present – that the criterion of 'established usage' naturally becomes a dominating element. In a classic phrasing Bruce Metzger can therefore say:

> [W]hile the New Testament canon should, from a theoretical point of view, be regarded as open in principle for either the addition or the deletion of one or more books, from a practical point of view such a modification can scarcely be contemplated as either possible or desirable. ... The canon by which the Church has lived over the centuries emerged in history, the result of a slow and gradual process. To be sure, in this canon there are documents less firmly attested by external criteria than others. But the several parts have all been cemented together by usage and by general acceptance in the Church, which has recognized, and recognizes, that God has spoken and is speaking to her in and through this body of early Christian literature. As regards this social fact, nothing can be changed.[122]

9.10 Same but different: Relating local canons to the notion of an ideal catholic canon

When we seek to understand biblical canonicity, we soon find that the different local canons in the history of the church do vary in scope. There were from early on local canons that, although varying in scope, happened to be largely identical. These variations, when taken together, may be said to approximate, or reach towards, an ideal and – to a certain degree – abstract notion of canon. We could say that there is a dialectic between the various local canons

---

[120] Ibid., 67.
[121] Gamble, 'The Canon of the New Testament', in *The New Testament and Its Modern Interpreters*, (eds) E. J. Epp and G. W. MacRae (Society of Biblical Literature, 1989), 220.
[122] Metzger, *The Canon of the New Testament*, 275.

in history and the ideal conception of canon that comes to expression in and through these existing canons. The concrete historical expressions of this ideal canon can from one viewpoint be seen as representing the ideal notion of canonicity (cf. section 6.4.4). In practice, this means that the concept of canon, which basically refers to the quality of normativeness, mostly attains the function of a rule or standard within the ecclesiastical context (and sometimes elsewhere). This dialectics between existing historical artefacts (manuscripts) and their corresponding ideal conception also come to expression in the 11 different uses of the word 'canon', introduced in Chapter 2 above, namely: canon *as Scripture, as regional list of Old and New Testament writings, as the book(s) of the Bible, as Rule of Faith, as scriptural intertext, as scriptural metatext, as Old and New Testaments, as the prophetic and apostolic Scriptures, as collection of authoritative writings, as divine lection of Scripture* and *as classic collection of literature.* Another possible, and perhaps less abstract, way of viewing this dialectic between various local canons in history, on the one hand, and an ideal conception of canon, on the other, would be by reference to the notion of unity, which was considered especially important during the Patristic Age.

In fact, if we were to single out one feature only as having the largest impact on the canonical process of the late second century, it would arguably be the endeavour towards unity, including unity in all church doctrine and the teaching of the church as a harmonious whole (cf. section 8.3.1). This strive towards unity naturally also affected the process of canonization prior to the efforts at conformism in the wake of the Constantinian Era.

When applying the word 'canon' to the collection of New Testament writings in the vein of Theodor Zahn, canon *as collection of authoritative writings* implies that the New Testament canon emerged spontaneously and by natural growth. As soon as an apostolic writing is cited by an early Christian writer we have early evidence of its canonicity. Zahn arrives at the conclusion that there was already a Christian canon by the end of the first/early second centuries. In Barton's words:

> [T]here was already, according to Zahn, a collection that we may without anachronism call the New Testament, even though he knew that this term did not itself become current until later. The essential point in Zahn's reconstruction is that the New Testament was a spontaneous creation of the first generations

of Christians, not something forced on the Church by internal or external pressures. As such, it belonged to the earliest period of the Church, as citations and allusions from the Apostolic Fathers onwards made evident.[123]

We know from history that this perspective of canon, despite its strength, also creates a well known problem, namely that of undisputed and disputed canonical writings. The dialectics here immediately presents itself. A canon of Scripture is, or at least ought to be, by its very definition closed, and to imply closedness as a part of its normative function. However, as the canons of various communities vary in shape, the empirical descriptive definition of canon must be the one given by Origen and Eusebius, which includes both undisputed and disputed writings. That is, if we want an ecumenical canon that all would agree on, we would have to exclude all disputed writings, along the lines suggested by Kurt Aland. Apparently, the approach of Origen comes close to the empirical approach that Zahn requests, without strong involvement of theological considerations. Using a thought from the Swedish theologian Anders Nygren, this approach aims at focusing upon the role of the self-evident in the history of the canon.[124] When the church began to reflect on the question of its canon, some 20 or 30 NT, or potential NT, writings already existed in the leading Christian congregations. A couple of decades later Origen made clear that the large bulk of these writings had never been disputed amongst the faith communities. They constituted, so to say, the core canon of Scriptures alongside the Pentateuch, the Prophets and the Psalms. In a famous passage in Eusebius' *Church History*, Origen's view of the New Testament writings in this respect is reviewed:

> [I]n the first of his [*Commentaries*] *on the Gospel according to Matthew*, defending the canon of the Church, he [Origen] gives his testimony that he knows only four Gospels, writing somewhat as follows: '... as having learnt by tradition concerning the four Gospels, which alone are unquestionable in the Church of God under heaven ... And Peter ... has left one acknowledged epistle, and, it may be, a second also; for it is doubted. ... John, who has left behind one Gospel ... wrote also the Apocalypse ... He has left also an epistle of a very few lines, and, it may be, a second and a third; for not all say that

---

[123] Barton, *The Spirit and the Letter*, 3.
[124] Nygren, 'Det självklaras roll i historien', in Nygren, *Tro och vetande: religionsfilosofiska och teologiska essayer* (Helsingfors: Luther-Agricola-sällskapet, 1970).

these are genuine ...' Furthermore, he [Origen] thus discusses the Epistle to the Hebrews, in his *Homilies* upon it: 'That the character of the diction of the epistle entitled To the Hebrews has not the apostle's rudeness in speech, who confessed himself rude in speech, that is, in style, but that the epistle is better Greek in the framing of its diction, will be admitted by everyone who is able to discern differences of style. But again, on the other hand, that the thoughts of the epistle are admirable, and not inferior to the acknowledged writings of the apostle, to this also everyone will consent as true who has given attention to reading the apostle. ... But as for myself, if I were to state my own opinion, I should say that the thoughts are the apostle's, but that the style and composition belong to one who called to mind the apostle's teachings and, as it were, made short notes of what his master said. If any church, therefore, holds this epistle as Paul's, let it be commended for this also. For not without reason have the men of old time handed it down as Paul's. But who wrote the epistle, in truth God knows. Yet the account which has reached us [is twofold], some saying that Clement, who was bishop of the Romans, wrote the epistle, others, that it was Luke, he who wrote the Gospel and the Acts. (*Hist. Eccl.* VI, 25.3-14)[125]

In this summary account of the received NT writings from Origen, the canon criterion *par préférance* – that of apostolicity – is assumed. We also note that in Origen's view, when commenting on 2 Tim. 3.16 (*De principiis*, Preface 8),[126] the apostolic Scriptures are regarded as no less inspired by the Spirit of God than the Old Testament writings. Still, the historical awareness of some diversity demonstrated in the above quote is also part of Origen's analysis. As Eusebius, in the lead of Origen, continues to reflect on the scriptural canon, he, too, chooses as his scholarly method a historical descriptive approach.[127] For Eusebius, what characterizes the reception of a canonical (ἐνδιάθηκος; encovenanted/testament-ed) writing is first of all that it is undisputed with regard to its divine status; and second, that it is generally received and used in the faith communities as well as by Christian authors (see further, sections 2.6 and 6.4.4).[128]

---

[125] LCL 265:74-79.

[126] ANF 4: 241.

[127] Cf. Barton, *The Spirit and the Letter*, 1–5; and Lindblom, *Kanon och apokryfer: Studier till den bibliska kanons historia* (Uppsala: Svenska kyrkans diakonistyrelses bokförlag, 1920), 52–9. See n. 126.

[128] Regarding the so called *antilegomena*, the disputed writings, Johannes Lindblom in his study *Kanon och apokryfer* (p. 53) arrives at the conclusion – *pace* Zahn – that Eusebius places these disputed writings, such as 2 Peter and Revelation, in the same category as the so called false writings (τὰ νό θα). Lindblom argues that the label τὰ νόθα simply is synonymous with τὰ ἀντιλεγόμενα. He,

9.11 Canon criteria: Some final remarks

Criteria of canonicity such as apostolicity, catholicity, orthodoxy and established usage are simultaneously part and parcel of the very concept of canon. Canonical here usually does not mean anything less than apostolic (in the broad sense), catholic and orthodox. That is to say, a writing is canonical if it is regarded as having received some form of apostolic sanction, having been used for a long time in a majority of the communities, and if it is not conflicting with the church's apostolic faith (see further, section 6.4.4).[129]

Three of our earliest accounts of the early shape of the New Testament canon come from Irenaeus, Origen and Eusebius. They all point to apostolicity as the major canon criterion. Accordingly, in his monograph on apostolicity, G. Blum shows that Irenaeus' main argument against the Gnostics is the particular and exclusive relationship between the apostles and the teaching of the church, which he sought to legitimize throughout his *Adversus Haereses*.[130] Still, according to Blum, Irenaeus' concept of apostolicity is primarily of a dogmatic kind. Blum argues that Irenaeus only rarely mentions individual apostles or talks of the 12 apostles as a group. Instead he prefers the collective concept 'the apostles', which from an historical point of view appears to be less precise. As Blum sees it:

> It is not the individual personalities that receive the primary attention in Irenaeus, but the entirety of the apostles. Their significance is located in the unified, normative witness of the revelatory events. It is in this way that Irenaeus' concept of the apostle is primarily dogmatic in character and to a lesser extent historical.[131]

---

too, is careful to underline the historical method employed by Eusebius (*Kanon och apokryfer*, 53): 'It should be noted that Eusebius, in this place in his church history, does not himself primarily wish to make a basic classification of the scriptures held to be sacred, addressed to the leadership of the church. Nor is his major intention to investigate what status the different scriptures had in the congregations at his time. What he wants is to present the results he has reached during the investigation of the ecclesial authors' assessments concerning the biblical scriptures. Eusebius works here as an historian and sets forth the judgments achieved in his reading of the ecclesial literature.' My trans.

[129] For the relation between apostolicity and the Rule of Faith in the early church, see Bokedal, 'The Rule of Faith: Tracing its Origins', *Journal of Theological Interpretation* 7, no. 2 (forthcoming).

[130] Blum, *Tradition und Sukzession: Studien zum Normbegriff des Apostolischen von Paulus bis Irenäus* (Berlin, Hamburg: Lutherisches Verlagshaus, 1963), 163.

[131] Ibid., 164.

Yet, as Blum points out, behind the dogmatic notion of the apostolic there is also 'a clear conception of the historical role of the apostles'.[132]

So, for the church of the first four centuries, the specifically Christian Scriptures had a unique authority because they were considered to be apostolic – in the historical as well as the theological sense, as exemplified by Irenaeus. In most early Fathers the concept of apostolicity is the primary criterion for establishing canonicity. Eusebius' objection to what he considered to be heretical writings – e.g. the 'Gospel of Peter' and the 'Gospel of Thomas' – was that they were not of apostolic origin (apostolic origin is here decided on the basis of usage by earlier church writers and freedom from schismatic bias). As mentioned above, Oskar Skarsaune similarly stresses apostolicity as the one decisive criterion of canonicity.[133] It therefore seems that the early church's reflections on the canon were exclusively discussions on authenticity (apostolicity in the historical sense) and apostolic teaching (orthodoxy).[134]

Contrary to the scholarly consensus, Skarsaune argues that the criterion of apostolicity can be traced back to the first century.[135] According to von Campenhausen, on the other hand, the authority of the canonical Gospels towards the late second century is only secondarily based on apostolic origin and primarily on the authority of Jesus. Accordingly, in the struggle with Marcion, the church created a new criterion, that of apostolicity, based on the picture of the 12 original apostles. Parallel to this development, Campenhausen maintains, 'apostolic' pseudepigrapha were written, such as the Petrine and the Johannine letters, and two of the Gospels were made apostolic by using the apostolic names of Matthew and John.[136] But, as Skarsaune points out, a 12-apostle model and the three-pillar model (James, Peter, John) would make out neither a good anti-Marcionite argument nor a good anti-Gnostic one. Instead, we still have reasons to think that the central criterion of apostolicity

---

[132] Ibid., 163.

[133] So also Flesseman-van Leer, *Tradition and Scripture in the Early Church* (Leiden: Gorcum & Prakke, 1953).

[134] Skarsaune, 'Hvilket lys kaster NT's kanonhistorie over teologihistorien i det 1. Århundre?', 76. For an emphasis on the criterion of orthodoxy as a primary criterion, see De Jonge, 'Introduction: The New Testament Canon', in *The Biblical Canons*, Bibliotheca Ephemeridum Theologicarum Lovaniensium, (eds) J.-M. Auwers and H. J. de Jonge (Leuven: Leuven University Press, 2003), 312–19.

[135] Ibid. Cf. also n. 127 above.

[136] For references to Campenhausen in this regard, see Skarsaune, 'Hvilket lys kaster NT's kanonhistorie over teologihistorien i det 1. århundre?', 65.

goes back, not only to Justin, but all the way into the New Testament.[137] Robert Grant's general description of the early canonical process in the opening lines of his *Historical Introduction to the New Testament* may here be helpful:

> The New Testament canon consists of those books which the Church came to regard as definitive expressions of its faith and life as set forth in the earliest period of its existence. The books were written by apostles or by disciples of the apostles, though the question of authorship is not especially significant; the Church itself was the Church of the apostles.[138]

These books gradually came to be cherished as definitive expressions of the faith. During this process the concept of a Christian scriptural canon is established.

9.12 Linguistic and tradition-related, material–textual, performative and ideational dimensions of the biblical canon

The structure of this study is based on four different aspects of the canon, its formation and significance. These aspects were presented in the Introduction. In this pre-concluding section of the present chapter, focusing especially on the issues of scriptural authority, integrity and criteria, I shall outline some connections between these issues and the above-mentioned aspects of the canon.

The three fields of signification – the material, performantial (performative) and ideational – referred to above, have been used by Jens Loenhoff to develop a semiotic definition of culture.[139] I have used this definition by analogously describing the notion of canon in these terms.[140] In order to emphasize a sociolinguistic setting for the biblical canon within the Christian community, this semiotic definition has proved to be helpful. To recapitulate, by modifying Robert Schreiter's elaboration of Loenhoff's definition of

---

[137] See Skarsaune, 'Hvilket lys kaster NT's kanonhistorie over teologihistorien i det 1. århundre?'.

[138] Grant, *A Historical Introduction to the New Testament* (London: Collins, 1963), 25. Cf., however, Webster's comment in Ch. 1, n. 21.

[139] See section 1.3.3.

[140] Cf. Young, *Virtuoso Theology: The Bible and Interpretation* (Cleveland, OH: The Pilgrim Press, 1993), 58: When discussing the biblical theology of Irenaeus, Young talks of 'canons of interpretation at once drawn from within the texts themselves and also external to them, belonging to a 'common semiotic system' embodied in the "socioloinguistic community"'. Cf. section 2.7.

culture, I proposed the following wording for a semiotic canon definition (see section 1.3.3, corresponding to the outline in four parts, Parts One to Four, of the present study):[141]

1)   The canon is *sanctioned by tradition* – it pertains to linguistic and other tradition(s), and to something durative by establishing a nameless authority and authoritative tradition over time. (Part One, Ch. 2).

2)   The canon is *material* – an artefact embracing symbolizations that become a source of identity; and *textual* – a meaningful and structured whole, the meaning of which transcends the sum of its individual words and sentences. (Part Two, Chs 3–6).

3)   The canon is *performative* – it involves rituals that bind the members of the church together to provide them with a participatory way of embodying and enacting their histories and values. (Part Three, Ch. 7).

4)   The canon is *ideational* by providing systems or frameworks of meaning which serve both to interpret the world (theological perspectives) and to provide guidance for living in the world. This dimension of canon embodies beliefs, values, attitudes and rules for behavior. (Part Four, Chs 8 and 9).

Of these four elements, the first, with its appeal to a nameless authority over time, is perhaps the most mysterious. Due to this dimension of canon, it is virtually impossible to make significant changes to the 27-book corpus making up the New Testament as received by the churches.

The textual–material aspect, on the other hand, is arguably the most noticeable by focusing upon the Bible *as book*, containing a textual whole (with a rather well defined and, in principle, fixed number of writings included), and as a concrete physical entity, including design and material details that single it out as the *Christian* Bible.

However, the performative element also distinctly manifests itself, in church ritual and worship, and elsewhere. By highlighting this element the reader can more easily become aware of the canon as designed to function in an ecclesial setting in general and within a liturgical framework in particular.

---

[141] Schreiter, *The New Catholicity: Theology between the Global and the Local* (Maryknoll, NY: Orbis Books, 1997), 29.

As stressed by Martin Hengel, the Gospels, at least Mark, Matthew and John, were written in the first place for worship – worship in the first-century church onwards.

The fourth element, the ideational aspect, although somewhat more abstract, is none the less indispensable for understanding the emergence and character of the canon. This element particularly singles out the theological, partly non-physical and non-ritual cultural-linguistic aspects of the canon. Canon criteria such as apostolicity, orthodoxy and catholicity belong here as well as the theological framework provided by the Rule of Faith.

The inquiry, accordingly, has not been limited to enumerating the books included in the biblical canon at a particular stage of its history of formation. Numerous such studies, focusing primarily on extrinsic canonical shape, have been made.[142] Rather, the intention has been to investigate the idea and concept of the canon as applied to the biblical writings from the first, second, third and fourth centuries on, by presenting more of a 'thick description',[143] a semiotic analysis, of the Christian notion of canon, involving dialogue between scholars from different disciplines.

This rendering of the canon concept might seem somewhat odd, and there are, of course, definitions of canon reached at more easily. I will therefore end this section by briefly presenting some further support for the proposed working definition.

First, the four elements used in the definition are helpful by focusing on a comprehensive view of canon. If, for example, ideational aspects (such as the category of apostolicity) tend to be emphasized when discussing the reception of the New Testament canon, another important criterion, the regular usage of a writing in the communities, might easily be neglected. Such usage pertains to the performative dimension in the proposed model (e.g. divine lection, private devotion and catechetical instruction). The eventual exclusion of the *Epistle of Barnabas* and *1 Clement* as well as the inclusion of Hebrews can be partly accounted for by emphasizing both these aspects.

Second, the canonical status at times attributed to the *Shepherd* of Hermas

---

[142] For a survey of literature on the NT canon, see Metzger, *The Canon of the New Testament*, 11–36. For the Christian Bible as a whole, see Sanders and McDonald, *The Canon Debate* (Peabody, MA: Hendrickson, 2002); and McDonald, *The Biblical Canon: Its Origin, Transmission, and Authority* (Peabody, MA: Hendrickson, 2007).

[143] The term is borrowed from the cultural anthropologist Clifford Geertz.

in some early communities can be explained largely by referring to the performantial category within the semiotic field. The argument for the *Shepherd* to be non-canonical, however, was justified by drawing on the concept of apostolicity (largely covered by the time-aspect, 'after [their] time', in the Muratorian fragment). Its eventual exclusion is thus commented on by the author of the Muratorian Canon around AD 200:[144]

> But Hermas wrote the *Shepherd* quite lately in our time in the city of Rome, when on the throne of the church of the city of Rome the bishop Pius, his brother, was seated. And therefore it ought indeed to be read, but it cannot be read publicly in the Church to the other people either among the prophets, whose number is complete, or among the apostles, for it is after [their] time.[145]

For the author of this important text, the periods of the prophets as well as the apostles are now past. Thus, the number of writings by their hands to be included in the canon is in principle closed, and the collection of the prophets is held to be 'complete'. (Earlier in the Muratorian fragment this may be the immediate reason for including the *Book of Wisdom* among the 'New Testament' writings.[146]) Again, the *Shepherd* of Hermas was authored in the Post-Apostolic Period, so the main ideational arguments used in the Muratorian fragment for its exclusion from the corpus of biblical writings are that the *Shepherd* is non-apostolic and composed too late.

Third, as regards the Old Testament canon, both ideational and performantial dimensions are involved, as well as physical dimensions of canonicity (e.g. reverence for Torah scrolls).[147] Some of these are inscribed in the scriptural corpora themselves, which are thus also held to be sacred as artefacts. In the synagogue, as in the church, where this material side of the canon has been emphasized, the high reverence for the Scriptures as sacred artefacts

---

[144] On alternative datings, see Schnelle, *Einleitung in das Neue Testament* Göttingen: Vandenhoeck und Ruprecht, 1996); and Hahneman, *The Muratorian Fragment and the Development of the Canon* (Oxford: Clarendon Press, 1992).

[145] Cited from Schneemelcher, 'General Introduction', in *New Testament Apocrypha*, vol. 1: *Gospels and Related Writings*, ed. W. Schneemelcher (Cambridge: James Clarke & Co. Ltd, and Louisville: Westminster John Knox Press, 1991; 2nd edn), 36); modified. Cf. Metzger, *The Canon of the New Testament*, 307.

[146] On the *Book of Wisdom*, see further, section 8.3.5.

[147] For comments on the synagogue in this regard, see Barton, *The Spirit and the Letter*, 106ff.

has played a major role for the transmission (e.g. from the Old to the New Testament) and manifestation of canonical status (cf. Ch. 4).

Fourth, the Rule of Faith (κανὼν τῆς πίστεως), which was used by the early church to designate the sum content of apostolic teaching as set down in Scripture, pre-baptismal confession and apostolic teaching patterns also played a crucial role for the formation and early function of the biblical canon. In the ecclesial discourse of the late second century, the notions of biblical canon and Rule of Faith were mutually interacting. Moreover, both entities were sometimes embraced by the concept of canon as used, e.g. by Irenaeus of Lyons (cf. Ch. 8). My proposed semiotic definition accounts for the dynamic and flexible notion of canon needed to relate the two: the primarily literary–material and the primarily ideational-doctrinal dimensions of canon.

Fifth, the second-century ecclesial concept of canon presupposes a thorough knowledge of the cultural and linguistic setting in which it appeared, the cultural-linguistic matrix of the Christian community.[148] Within this context the concept was used as a form of cultural code in order to define an apostolic–catholic Christian identity or sense of belonging. In this connection the concept could be described as a high-context code that was fixed within the high-context culture of the second-century church. Therefore, to understand what 'canon' meant – and still by and large means to the Christian community – requires 'extensive knowledge of the historical background and ethos of the community' in question.[149] The problem of the context, in other words, must be further elaborated to attain a better understanding of the canon concept. This is especially important in a high-context setting like the one encountered in the (early) church. Thus, my broad semiotic framing is here helpful – with its textual and contextual emphases within the four fields of signification: the linguistic and tradition-related, the material–textual, the ritual and the ideational.

Other ways of describing canonicity may be integrated into this semiotic definition. So, in Chapter 2, what I have named canon *as Scripture, as (regional) list of Old and New Testament writings, as the book(s) of the Bible, as Rule of Faith, as scriptural intertext, as scriptural metatext, as Old and New*

---

[148] I have borrowed the term 'cultural-linguistic' from the theologian George Lindbeck, *The Nature of Doctrine. Religion and Doctrine in a Postliberal Age* (London: SPCK, 1984).

[149] Schreiter, *The New Catholicity,* 37.

Testaments, as prophetic and apostolic Scriptures, as collection of authoritative writings, as divine lection of Scripture and *as classic collection of literature* can be conceptualized within such a shared semiotic framework.

Sixth, some of the physical and textual characteristics of the biblical manuscripts mark them off as *Christian* texts. They cannot therefore be naturally interpreted, e.g. as Jewish Scriptures or by means of hermeneutical rules that do not take into account these Christian textual identity-markers. Two examples of this type of material–textual aspects of canonical Scripture are the codex as book format and the *nomina sacra*, the Christian contractions of the divine and some other sacred names.

Seventh, real historical thinking must take account of its own historicity, thus learning to view the 'historical object' less as an object, which it is not, but as a unity of history and its being appropriated for every new situation, the relationship of 'the reality of history and the reality of historical understanding'.[150] The tradition-related aspect of the semiotic approach used here takes this relationship into account.

9.13 Conclusion

Several conclusions from this book as a whole, including the present chapter, were introduced in the previous section (9.12). A few additional concluding remarks referring to Chapter 9 should, however, be made.

The three themes of scriptural authority, integrity and criterion were treated in the previous sections in order to highlight the logic coherence of the Christian canon.

I sought to show that there is a rationale of the Christian canon and its formation from a number of viewpoints: the concept, the function, the structure, the interpretation, the history, the tradition, the texts and the collection of the canon. These can also be understood and appropriated from the horizon of present communal concerns and interests. For the canon to serve in its function as canon, it must be a free power vis-à-vis its interpreters in order not to be absorbed into the continuously developing ecclesial

---

[150] Gadamer, *TM*, 299.

tradition. Furthermore, the 'selflessness' of the canonical text was emphasized, underscoring the transparency of the canonical texts, in order to indicate the primary subject matter at stake: the Triune Identity and the revelatory acts of the biblical account referred to by these texts.

I also raised the question 'Why these texts and not others?' A few comments followed on some important numbers associated with the process of canon formation, such as the numbers 2, 3, 4, 7, 8, 14, 22 and 27.

Some central hermeneutical issues relating to the canon are significant for the problem of the canon's logical coherence. The following themes were elaborated in the present chapter: canon and traditionalism, integrity despite diversity, and a section titled 'Canon Then, Canon Now'. Here I dealt with the time factor involved in the transmission of canonical texts, being authoritative texts of the past as well as the present.

In the concluding paragraphs of this chapter, I addressed anew the issues of canon criteria and the biblical accounts as scriptural. The pre-concluding section bound together themes discussed in Chapter 1 onwards with issues treated in the present chapter.

Conclusion

10

The Scriptures and the Lord: General Conclusions

We have seen that 'the Scriptures and the Lord' functions as a summary of what lay at the heart of the canon formation process from the earliest years of the Christian movement. This formula, with variations (e.g. 'the Scriptures and the Gospel'), is found in a number of early Christian sources, 'as the remembered words of Jesus were treasured and quoted, taking their place beside the Law and the Prophets' (Metzger). The chapters in the present work unfold this theme. In fact, this formula, variously expressed, links the complex history of a canon, addressing the church, with the present context of reception.

The canon was formed in a process, with its own particular intention, history and direction. Throughout this study I seek to bridge an understanding of the early canon with its future orientation and reception. History and theology, past and present, are considered alongside each other. For the sake of ecclesial continuity and unity, to a large extent the community in which the Christian core canon appeared and the church that now needs to interpret it are the same community – facing the same canon.

Due to their historical dominion, the texts of the canon engage our attention even today. This fascinating 'drama' of text reception involves not only senders, addressees and communities, but, most fundamentally, also the canonical text *as text*, *as Liturgy of the Word* and *as interpreted Scripture*. Being an integral part of the church's proclamation of the gospel, these canonical texts are preserved and actualized by the interpretive communities being addressed.

In this book, my central thesis is:

Integral to the life of the church, in particular the ecclesial practice of procla-
mation and prayer, the formation and continuous usage of the Christian
biblical canon is an act of literary preservation and actualization of the church's
apostolic normative tradition – 'the Scriptures and the Lord', by which the
church is and remains church, appealing to a variety of textual, ritual and
doctrinal materials.

We have good reasons to hold the view that there was, and to some degree still
is, a canonical process relating to the Christian Bible and its reception. That
means that the 'fully' compiled Bible is the outcome of a complex historical
development, which must not be seen as an *ad hoc* development. The early
Christian community's practice of proclamation and prayer, and the canonical
corpus of Scripture as it has been gradually shaped, are simply the same story
expressed in two media (Jenson). This process of canon formation is fundamental for the Bible to be exactly what it is, the Bible. Due to this process there
is, from the outset, a dynamic built into the forming and interpreting of the
Christian Bible (cf. the practice of searching the Scriptures, John 5.39, Acts
17.11 and Romans 9-11).

With a historical point of departure in revelation, centring in the Christ-
event, the direction of the canon is towards the future. The preservation and
actualization of the scriptural canon is an ongoing process and is integral to
the church, in order for it to be church in changing situations.

Such an understanding of the canon formation process calls for revision of
the following three current views of Scripture canonization:

1. The *significance* of canonizing as exclusively an act of cataloguing of a
   definite list of Scriptures, often ascribed to the late fourth century;
2. The *insignificance* frequently associated with the first- and second-century
   concepts of a Christian biblical canon, sometimes referred to as the
   'pre-history' of the canon, by which is meant the historical preparation,
   ca. AD 30–180, or alternatively ca. AD 30–350, of a sudden canon
   formation; and …
3. The *idea* that the act of receiving the Scriptures as canon is just past
   history, while numerous examples of the act of preserving, actualizing,
   rearranging and reinterpreting Scripture as canon may be enlisted in

the midst of ongoing canon debates. First-, second-, fourth-, sixteenth- and twentieth-century acts of canon reception, canonization and decanonization present themselves (e.g. as addressed at church synods dealing with the question of canon), and new ones appear before the contemporary interpreter. Recent discoveries of 'non-canonical' texts and libraries, popular discussions on ideological readings, and on the number of authentic Gospels, may usher in potential attempts at restructuring the canonical texts and their interpretations. Atheological methodology, deconstruction of ideological and less ideological readings of texts, canonization of Old Testament Apocrypha/Deuterocanonical books, and the sudden disappearance of the *nomina sacra* from contemporary Bibles with the craft of book-printing, are all, directly or indirectly, relating to the historical canon formation process.

The complex phenomenon of the Christian canon formation discussed here unquestionably surpasses the new apostolic writings simply taking their place alongside the Law and the Prophets, and being treated as of equal or superior authority to them. Beside 'the Scriptures' there is another authority involved, namely 'the Lord'. With this in view, the early apostolic writings about 'the Lord' attained authoritative functions, similar to that of the Scriptures. Parallel to this process, the Jewish Scriptures were partly reformed and reread in light of the new revelation of 'the Lord'. The canonical process involves the structuring and restructuring of both Jewish and Christian Scriptures. Accordingly, following on the textual, ritual and theological changes involved, 'the Scriptures' are no longer exactly the same as before. The two concepts 'Scripture' and 'Lord', used by the Christians, are 'the same', and yet 'different' when compared to their Jewish past. This 'sameness in difference' is pivotal also for understanding other features (such as liturgical aspects) of Christian communal identity.

In order to grasp the complex phenomenon of the Christian biblical canon, I have divided the present investigation into four major parts, each treating different aspects of the canonical arrangement of the Christian Scriptures. These are: Part One: linguistic and tradition-related aspects (Ch. 2); Part Two: material and textual aspects (Chs 3–6); Part Three: performative aspects (Ch. 7); and Part Four: ideational aspects (Chs 8 and 9) of the canon. Since each chapter contains its own more detailed conclusions (Chs 2–9), I shall here present a brief overview of each chapter and some overall results.

In the introductory chapter, Chapter 1, I maintain that in the formula 'the Scriptures and the Lord' the nucleus of the formation of a specifically Christian Bible encounters the contemporary reader. I argue that the Christian two-testament Bible, being the basic classic text of the Christian community, may be successfully explained, with this formula in view, as a largely self-referring and self-interpretive textual corpus. Seen as a property of Sacred Scripture, the notion of canon and canon formation is a way of organizing and interpreting Scripture, but also a way of actualizing and preserving the (undivided) church's normative textual tradition. This implies a view of canonical Scripture as a theologically defined literary unity. Though the issue of the canon is multifaceted, for the church it still can be put in a simple formula, as for example in Origen (ca. AD 185–254): 'All the Scriptures are one book because all the teaching that has come to us about Christ is recapitulated in one single whole' (*Joa. Comm.* 5.6). In terms of method, the concepts of *Wirkungsgeschichte*, prejudice and the hermeneutical circle as set forth by Hans-Georg Gadamer are central for the study as a whole. Furthermore, the semiotic approach to cultural study developed by Jens Loenhoff and Robert Schreiter motivates the structuring of the book in four parts, each of which treats a central aspect of the canon.

Various dimensions of the canon and its formation can be distinguished. In Chapter 2, I pursue three parallel undertakings. First, I discuss hermeneutical dimensions tied to the canon, examining the possibility of understanding the canonical process as a whole. The organic continuity and 'self-organizing' character of the canon formation process are discussed, as well as the canon as classic literature. Second, I investigate the term and concept of canon etymologically and with respect to early ecclesial usage. Third, I elaborate a set of signifiers for the different dimensions of the concept of canon. These include canon *as Scripture, as regional list of Old and New Testament writings, as the book(s) of the Bible, as Rule of Faith, as scriptural intertext* and *metatext, as the Old and New Testaments, as the prophetic and apostolic Scriptures, as collection of authoritative writings, as divine lection of Scripture* and *as classic collection of literature.* This set of signifiers helps identify the composition of the canon.

In Chapter 3, the triadic system of the *nomina sacra* is explored. The *nomina sacra* were marked out in basically all Greek Christian Bible manuscripts, both OT and NT, until modern times. The most important of these textual, or supra-textual, markers are LORD, GOD, JESUS, CHRIST and SPIRIT, but also CROSS, HUMAN PERSON, FATHER and SON. The *nomina sacra* practice may have implications for the view of the early Christian manuscripts as scriptural, but also for understanding the emergent Rule of Faith and Christian creeds – reflection on the Trinity – for worship as well as for Bible translation. A re-introduction of *nomina sacra* demarcations into modern Bible editions would better reflect this apparently significant textual dimension of the ancient manuscripts, and better integrate biblical text, canon and creed the way the ancient church did it.

Chapter 4 treats the codex format – another textual as well as material aspect of the canon. The indications that the earliest Christianity deliberately exchanged the scroll for this new book format suggests that the oral gospel tradition tied to 'the Lord' could be naturally, and more easily, placed alongside the Scriptures. Apart from being a more accessible book format than the scroll, the codex, as it became more developed, could also play a role in delimiting the number of writings to be included, the Four-Gospel codex and the Pauline Letter corpus making up the best examples. In any case, the main point here is not whether or not the codex format as such can be shown to have had a direct impact on the formation of the Four-Gospel canon (Skeat, Elliott) or the Pauline corpus (Gamble, Richards), but, rather, whether there is a demonstrable mutuality between the church's strong preference for a fourfold Gospel (and a clearly defined *Corpus Paulinum*) and the technology of Gospel production in the church. We can safely conclude that this is the case, and that both ideational (such as Irenaeus' argument for a delimited Four-Gospel canon) and material-textual dimensions (production of Four-Gospel codices) have bearing on the canonical process. From very early on the codex appears to have become a significant Christian symbol. In John Sharpe's words: 'Whether in frescoes, mosaics, or manuscripts, the codex for Christians is a symbol of their faith in that it represents the Word made flesh.'

Oral and written text – our topic in Chapter 5 – are two parallel modes of structuring the gospel. It should be noted that 'oral text' does not refer to freely narrated stories, but to textual tradition, verbatim accounts and kerygmatic summaries that are orally transmitted. Seeing the mutuality between these textual media is important for understanding the canonical process; and also for today's reception of the canonical text and reading. Marcion's role, which, contrary to some previous research, does not seem to be crucial for the formation of the Christian canon, nevertheless appears to have implications for understanding the ecclesial interaction of oral and written discourse.

The notions of text and textuality are further elaborated in Chapter 6. The following textual features pertaining to canonicity are noted: A text stands on its own (pointing forward) and does not primarily refer back to the original speech or speech situation. A text is a meaningful whole, expressing thematic unity through grammar and semantic progression. The literary text such as the biblical accounts is intended as text, i.e. we point to it as something that 'stands written'. This means that a text is what the word literally says: 'a woven texture that holds together'. The heterogeneous scriptural accounts are held together in the Bible as a unified textual whole. They also, directly or indirectly, ecumenically link their many interpretive communities to one another.

The biblical text refers primarily to its own literary presentation as a meaningful whole. However, this focus on the textual whole is also attentive to historical and salvation-historical dimensions of the text. As to the canonical process, a gradual textual shaping is to be noted, an interaction, during decades and centuries, between textual whole and textual parts. The main thesis of this book – 'the Scriptures and the Lord' – and the rubrics 'Old' and 'New Testament' signify such textual wholes.

Scripture's primary home is the worship of the Christian assembly. Without this dimension of worship taken into account, the canonical writings are incomplete. Chapter 7 deals with canon and ritual interaction. The liturgy of the Christian congregation is pivotal for understanding not only the initial canonizing of the new Christian writings, but also today's liturgical contextualization, as well as the textuality of these writings construed as canon for the church. In addition to this, the arrangement of the writings within the biblical corpus and their lectionary selections and readings may affect the canonical structuring.

To the early Christians, the scriptural canon and the Rule of Faith often functioned as two sides of the same norm. The Scriptures could be seen as an expression of the Rule, and vice versa. In Chapter 8, I treat the theme of canonicity as closely related to this *scopus*, that is, the unified sense aimed at by the scriptural whole when read by the church – from early on designated 'the Rule of Faith'. This Rule appears to be influential in the formation of the canon. Together, Scripture and Rule constitute the texture making up the Christian Bible. Irenaeus' second-century perspective is used to highlight some perennial issues related to the church's canon, such as the canonical formula, the canonical shape and the unity of the Scriptures.

Chapter 9 deals with the logical coherence of the Christian canon: canon as an integrated whole, an authority and criterion – as textual foundation for the (undivided) church. Jerome's understanding of the New Testament canon is reviewed with emphasis given to the role of canon criteria. Different aspects of the canonical process as discussed throughout the book are recapitulated. Particular attention is paid to Karl Barth's approach to the question of canon.

Historically and structurally, I would like to summarize the process of the early canonization of Christian Scripture as follows:

- There always was a narrative and meta-narrative framework associated with the Christian Scriptures. As stressed above, this can be summed up in the apostolic formula, the 'Scriptures and the Lord'. Through the perennial process of Bible exegesis and theology, the church has acknowledged the textual traditions of 'the Lord' as its scriptural centre. Likewise (*mutatis mutandis*) 'the Lord' has been scripturally defined. There never was a 'full' Christian Bible without this centre, nor a canonical process. The scriptural centre was always related to the margins, and vice versa. Thus, a textual midpoint also implied circumscription of the Scriptures. This is the reason why new writings could be included. However, new non-canonical writings, traditions and interpretations, on the other hand, could not easily be added, because of the inherent factors of the canonical process – such as the tradition and text, the ritual and theological agenda, which were themselves related to the canonical function of Scripture.

- Structurally, there was always a 'full' Christian Bible consisting of (in historical order): 1) the Scriptures and 'the Lord'; 2) the Scriptures (including early testimony collections) together with the biblical dyadic–triadic system of the *nomina sacra* which marked out a textual centre; the emerging Christian Bible codices containing the *nomina sacra*; 3) collections of Scriptures interpreted in the light of the Rule of Faith; 4) an Old and New Testament consisting of prior collections (e.g. the fourfold Gospel and Pauline letters) alongside the Rule of Faith; and 5) canon lists and whole-Bible manuscripts of the Old and New Testament Scriptures framed by the Scripture-based Rule of Faith (and the emerging creedal formulations of the early church).

Potentially, this early canon and its *Wirkungsgeschichte* has theological implications for the present. As I have sought to demonstrate in this study, one answer to the question of the canon's present and future possibility may well be sought in the present that is being addressed by these classic texts of the past, addressing future generations of readers.

Finally, there are many ways of viewing the biblical writings. There are also a multitude of ways to deconstruct each of these views and texts. To repeat my introductory line, in Origen's view 'all the Scriptures are one book because all the teaching that has come to us about Christ is recapitulated in one single whole'. Here we need to bear in mind that, as canon, in this theological sense, the Scriptures cannot be read like any other book. Rather, as canonical, the biblical texts are held to be authoritative, divinely inspired writing, present in the church as a sign – i.e. they only present themselves to the one who is ready to accept them as such, who looks for him- or herself, and actually sees something there of this integral whole. But also, as sign, the readings of these foundational texts, like all religious speech encountered in Christianity, represent aids to faith (in the broadest sense).

Bibliography

Abramowski, Luise, 'Die "Erinnerungen der Apostel" bei Justin', in *Formula and Context: Studies in Early Christian Thought*, ed. L. Abramowski (Basingstoke and Brookfield, Vermont: Variorum, 1992), XIV, 341–53.

Achtemeier, Paul J., 'Omne Verbum Sonat: The New Testament and the Oral Environment of Late Western Antiquity', *JBL* 109 (1990): 3–27.

—*Inspiration and Authority: Nature and Function of Christian Scripture* (Peabody, MA: Hendrickson, 1999).

Achtemeier, Paul J., Joel B. Green and Marianne Meye Thompson, *The New Testament: Its Literature and Theology* (Grand Rapids, MI and Cambridge: Eerdmans, 2001).

Aichele, George, *Sign, Text, Scripture: Semiotics and the Bible* (Sheffield: Sheffield Academic, 1997).

—*The Control of Biblical Meaning: Canon as Semiotic Mechanism* (Harrisburg, PA: Trinity Press International, 2001).

Aland, Kurt, *The Problem of the New Testament Canon* (London: Mowbray, 1962).

—*Kurzgefasste Liste der griechischen Handschriften des neuen Testaments,* vol. 1: Gesamtübersicht (Berlin: Walter de Gruyter, 1963).

—'Das Problem des neutestamentlichen Kanons', in *Das Neue Testament als Kanon,* ed. E. Käsemann (Göttingen: Vandenhoeck & Ruprecht, 1970), 134–58.

—*Repertorium der Griechischen Christlichen Papyri,* I-2 (Berlin and New York: Walter de Gruyter, 1976).

Aland, Kurt and Barbara Aland, *The Text of the New Testament: An Introduction to the Critical Editions and to the Theory and Practice of Modern Textual Criticism* (Grand Rapids, MI: Eerdmans, 1989).

Albl, Martin C., *'And Scripture Cannot be Broken': The Form and Function of the Early Christian Testimonia Collections* (Leiden: Brill, 1999).

Alexander, Loveday, 'Ancient Book Production and the Circulation of the Gospels', in *The Gospels for All Christians: Rethinking the Gospel Audiences*, ed. R. Bauckham (Grand Rapids, MI: Eerdmans, 1998), 71–105.

Ashton, John, *Understanding the Fourth Gospel* (Oxford: Oxford University Press, 2nd edn, 2007).

Auerbach, Erich, *Mimesis: The Representation of Reality in Western Literature*, trans. Willard R. Trask (Princeton, NJ: Princeton University Press, 1953).

Augustine, *City of God*, trans. Henry Bettenson (London: Penguin, 1972).

Auwers, J.-M. and H. J. de Jonge (eds), *The Biblical Canons*. Bibliotheca Ephemeridum Theologicarum Lovaniensium (Leuven: Leuven University Press, 2003).

Balla, Peter, *Challenges to New Testament Theology: An Attempt to Justify the Enterprise* (Tübingen: Mohr Siebeck, 1997).

—'Challenges to Biblical Theology', in *New Dictionary of Biblical Theology*, (eds) T. D. Alexander and B. S. Rosner (Leicester: InterVarsity, 2000), 20–7.

—'Evidence for an Early Christian Canon (Second and Third Century)', in *The Canon Debate*, (eds) L. M. McDonald and J. A. Sanders (Peabody, MA: Hendrickson, 2002), 372–85.

Barker, Don, 'The Dating of New Testament Papyri', *NTS* 57 (2011): 571–82.

Barnabas, Epistle of, The Ante-Nicene Fathers, vol. 1, (eds) A. Roberts and J. Donaldson (Edinburgh: T&T Clark; Grand Rapids, MI: Eerdmans, reprinted 1994), 133–49.

Barr, James, *Holy Scripture: Canon, Authority, Criticism* (Oxford: Clarendon, 1983).

Barth, Karl, *Church Dogmatics* (abbreviated *CD*) vols. I/1 and I/2 (Edinburgh: T&T Clark, 1936–1962).

—*Die Schrift und die Kirche*, Theologische Studien 22 (Zollikon – Zürich: Evangelischer Verlag, 1947).

—*The Epistle to the Romans*, trans. Edwyn C. Hoskyns (Oxford: Oxford University Press, 1933, 1968).

—*The Göttingen Dogmatics: Instruction in the Christian Religion*, vol. 1 (Grand Rapids, MI: Eerdmans, 1991).

—*The Theology of the Reformed Confessions*. Columbia Series in Reformed Theology, trans. and ann. D. L. Guder and J. J. Guder (Louisville: Westminster John Knox, 2002).

Bartholomew, Craig G., 'Introduction', in *'Behind the Text: History and Biblical Interpretation'*, vol. 4, (eds) C. G. Bartholomew, S. C. Evans, M. Healy (Grand Rapids, MI: Zondervan, 2003), 1–16.

Bartholomew, Craig G., Scott Hahn, Robin Parry, Christopher Seitz, and Al Wolters, (eds), *Canon and Biblical Interpretation*, vol. 7, The Scripture and Hermeneutics Series (Milton Keynes and Waynesboro, GA: Paternoster, 2006).

Barton, John, *Oracles of God: Perceptions of Ancient Prophecy in Israel after the Exile* (London: Darton, Longman and Todd, 1986).

—*Reading the Old Testament: Method in Biblical Study* (London: Darton, Longman and Todd, 1996).

—*The Spirit and the Letter: Studies in the Biblical Canon* (London: SPCK, 1997).

—'Marcion Revisited', in *The Canon Debate*, (eds) L. M. McDonald and J. A. Sanders (Peabody, MA: Hendrickson, 2002), 341–54.

Barton, John and Michael Wolter (eds), *Die Einheit der Schrift und die Vielfalt des Kanons/The Unity of Scripture and the Diversity of the Canon*, Beihefte zur Zeitschrift für die neutestamentliche Wissenschaft und die Kunde der älteren Kirche, vol. 118 (Berlin: Walter de Gruyter, 2003).

Bauckham, Richard, 'Sabbath and Sunday in the Post-Apostolic Church', in *From Sabbath to Lord's Day: A Biblical, Historical and Theological Investigation*, ed. D. A. Carson (Grand Rapids, MI: Zondervan, 1982), 251–98.

—'The Lord's Day', in *From Sabbath to Lord's Day: A Biblical, Historical and Theological Investigation*, ed. D. A. Carson (Grand Rapids, MI: Zondervan, 1982), 221–50.

—'For Whom Were Gospels Written?', in *The Gospels for All Christians: Rethinking the Gospel Audiences*, ed. R. Bauckham (Grand Rapids, MI: Eerdmans, 1998), 9–48.

—*God Crucified: Monotheism and Christology in the New Testament* (Carlisle: Paternoster, 1998).

—*Jesus and the Eyewitnesses: The Gospels as Eyewitness Testimony* (Grand Rapids, MI: Eerdmans, 2006).

—*Jesus and the God of Israel: 'God Crucified' and Other Studies on the New Testament's Christology of Divine Identity* (Colorado Springs: Paternoster, 2008).

Baum, Armin Daniel, 'Papias, der Vorzug der *Viva Vox* und die Evangelienschriften', *New Testament Studies* 44 (1998): 144–51.

Beaton, Richard C., 'How Matthew writes', in *The Written Gospel*, (eds) Markus Bockmuehl and Donald A. Hagner (Cambridge: Cambridge University Press, 2005), 116–34.

Becker, Jürgen, 'Paul and His Churches', in *Christian Beginnings: Word and Community from Jesus to Post-Apostolic Times*, ed. J. Becker (Louisville, KY: Westminster and John Knox, 1993), 132–210.

Beckwith, Roger T., *The Old Testament Canon of the New Testament Church and its Background in Early Judaism* (Grand Rapids, MI: Eerdmans, 1985).

—'The Jewish Background to Christian Worship', in *The Study of Liturgy*, (eds) C. Jones, E. Yarnold, G. Wainwright and P. Bradshaw (London: SPCK, rev. edn 1992), 68–80.

—*Calendar and Chronology, Jewish and Christian: Biblical, Intertestamental and Patristic Studies* (Leiden: Brill, 1996).

Bedodi, Flavio, 'I "nomina sacra" nei papiri greci veterotestamentari precristiani', *Studia Papyrologica* 13 (1974): 89–103.

Beek, A. van de, 'Being Convinced: On the Foundations of the Christian Canon', in *Canonization and Decanonization: Papers Presented to the International Conference of the Leiden Institute for the Study of Religions (LISOR), Held at Leiden 9–10 January 1997*, (eds) A. van der Kooij and K. van der Toorn (Leiden: Brill, 1998), 331–49.

Bell, Catherine, *Ritual Theory, Ritual Practice* (New York: Oxford University Press, 1992).

Benoit, André, *Saint Irénée: Introduction a l'étude de sa théologie* (Paris: Presses universitaires de France, 1960).

Beyer, H. W., 'Kanon', in *Theologisches Wörterbuch zum Neuen Testament*, vol. 3, ed. G. Kittel (Stuttgart: 1937), 600–06.

Beyschlag, Karlmann, *Grundriß der Dogmengeschichte*, vol. 1 (Darmstadt: Wissenschaftliche Buchgesellschaft, 1982).

Birdsall, J. Neville, 'Review of *Les débuts du codex*. Alain Blanchard, ed., 1989', *JTS* 41 (1990): 634–37.

Black, Matthew, 'The Chi-Rho Sign – Christogram and/or Staurogram?', in *Apostolic History and the Gospel: Biblical and Historical Essays Presented to F. F. Bruce on his 60th Birthday*, ed. W. W. Gasque (Exeter: Paternoster, 1970).

Blackman, Edwin Cyril, *Marcion and his Influence* (London: SPCK, 1948).

Blanchard, Alain, ed. *Les débuts du codex*. Bibliologia. Elementa ad librorum studia pertinentia (Turnhout: Brepols, 1989).

Blanchard, Yves-Marie, *Aux sources du canon, le témoignage d'Irénée* (Paris: Les Éditions du Cerf, 1993).

Blowers, Paul M., 'The *Regula Fidei* and the Narrative Character of Early Christian Faith', *Pro Ecclesia* 6 (1997): 199–228.

Blum, Georg Günter, *Tradition und Sukzession: Studien zum Normbegriff des Apostolischen von Paulus bis Irenäus* (Berlin, Hamburg: Lutherisches Verlagshaus, 1963).

Bokedal, Tomas, 'Scripture in the Second Century', in *The Sacred Text: Excavating the Texts, Exploring the Interpretations, and Engaging the Theologies of the Christian Scriptures*, (eds) Michael Bird and Michael Pahl (Piscataway, NJ: Gorgias, 2010), 43–61.

—'Notes on the *Nomina Sacra* and Biblical Interpretation', in *Beyond Biblical Theologies*, (eds) Heinrich Assel, Stefan Beyerle and Christfried Böttrich (WUNT 295; Tübingen: Mohr Siebeck, 2012), 263–95.

—'The Rule of Faith: Tracing Its Origins', *Journal of Theological Interpretation* 7, no. 2 (forthcoming).

Bokser, Ben Zion, *Pharisaic Judaism in Transition* (New York: Bloch Publishing Company, 1935).

Bonhoeffer, Dietrich, *Reflections on the Bible: Human Word and Word of God*, trans. M. Eugene Boring, ed. M. Weber (Peabody, MA: Hendrickson, 2004).

Bovon, François, 'The Canonical Structure of Gospel and Apostle', in *The Canon Debate*, (eds) L. M. McDonald and J. A. Sanders (Peabody, MA: Hendrickson, 2002), 516–27.

Bradshaw, Paul F., *Daily Prayer in the Early Church: A Study of the Origin and Early Development of the Divine Office* (London: SPCK, 1981).

—*The Search for the Origins of Christian Worship: Sources and Methods for the Study of Early Liturgy* (New York: Oxford University Press, 2002).

Breck, John, *Scripture in Tradition: The Bible and its Interpretation in the Orthodox Church* (Crestwood, NY: St. Vladimir's Seminary Press, 2001).

Brinktrine, Joh., 'Der Gottesname "AIA" bei Theodoret von Cyrus', *Biblica* 30 (1949), 520–23.

Brown, Delwin, *Boundaries of Our Habitations: Tradition and Theological Construction* (New York: State University of New York Press, 1994).

Brown, Schuyler, 'Concerning the Origin of the Nomina Sacra', *Studia Papyrologica* (1970), 7–19.

Brox, Norbert, *Kirchengeschichte des Altertums* (Düsseldorf: Patmos Verlag, 1992).

—'Die biblische Hermeneutik des Irenäus', *Zeitschrift für antikes Christentum* vol. 2 (1998), 26–48.

Brox, Norbert, ed., *Irenäus von Lyon: Adversus Haereses, Gegen die Häresien II. Griechisch, Lateinisch, Deutsch*, Fontes Christiani, trans. N. Brox (Freiburg im Breisgau: Herder, 1993).

Bruce, F. F., *The Canon of Scripture* (Downers Grove, IL: InterVarsity, 1988).

Bruns, Gerald L., *Hermeneutics Ancient and Modern* (New Haven and London: Yale University Press, 1992).

Bultmann, Rudolf, 'The Problem of Hermeneutics', in *Essays: Philosophical and Theological*, trans. J. C. G. Greig (New York: Macmillan, 1955).

—*Theology of the New Testament*, vol. 2, trans. Kendrick Grobel (London: SCM, 1955).

Byrskog, Samuel, *Jesus the Only Teacher: Didactic Authority and Transmission in Ancient Israel, Ancient Judaism and the Matthean Community* (Stockholm: Almqvist & Wiksell International, 1994).

—*Story as History – History as Story: The Gospel Tradition in the Context of Ancient Oral History* (WUNT 123; Tübingen: Mohr Siebeck, 2000).

—Review article on Rudolf Bultmann's *The History of the Synoptic Tradition*, *JBL* 122 (2003): 549–55.

Byrskog, Samuel and Werner H. Kelber (eds), *Jesus in Memory: Traditions in Oral and Scribal Perspectives* (Waco, TX: Baylor University Press, 2009).

Calvin, Jean, *Institutes of the Christian Religion,* ed. J. T. McNeill, trans. F. L. Battle (Philadelphia: Westminster, 1960 [1559]).

Campenhausen, Hans von, *The Formation of the Christian Bible*, trans. J. A. Baker (Philadelphia: Fortress, 1972).

—*Die Entstehung der christlichen Bibel* (Tübingen: Mohr Siebeck, 2003).

Carr, Thomas K., *Newman & Gadamer: Toward a Hermeneutics of Religious Knowledge* (Atlanta, GA: Scholars Press, 1996).

Carson, D. A., ed., *From Sabbath to Lord's Day: A Biblical, Historical and Theological Investigation* (Grand Rapids, MI: Zondervan, 1982).

Chapman, Stephen B., 'How the Biblical Canon Began: Working Models and Open Questions', in *Homer, the Bible, and Beyond: Literary and Religious Canons in the Ancient World,* (eds) M. Finkelberg and G. Stroumsa (Leiden: Brill, 2003), 29–51.

Charles, R. H., *The Testaments of the Twelve Patriarchs* (London: Adam and Charles Black, 1908).

Childs, Brevard S., *Introduction to the Old Testament as Scripture* (London: SCM, 1979).

—*The New Testament as Canon: An Introduction* (London: SCM, 1984).

—*Old Testament Theology in a Canonical Context* (Philadelphia: Fortress, 1985).

—*Biblical Theology of the Old and New Testaments* (London: SCM, 1992).

—*Biblical Theology: A Proposal* (Minneapolis: Fortress, 2002).

—*The Church's Guide for Reading Paul: The Canonical Shaping of the Pauline Corpus* (Grand Rapids, MI and Cambridge: Eerdmans, 2008).

Clabeaux, John J., 'Marcion', in *The Anchor Bible Dictionary,* vol. 4, ed. D. N. Freedman (New York: Doubleday, 1992), 514–16.

Clement of Alexandria, *The Stromata or Miscellanies*, The Ante–Nicene Fathers, vols 1 and 2, (eds) A. Roberts and J. Donaldson (Edinburgh: T&T Clark and Grand Rapids, MI: Eerdmans, reprinted 1994), 299–568.

—*Miscellanies [Stromateis], Book VII*, Introduction, translation and notes by F. J. A Hort and J. B. Mayor, Greek and Roman Philosophy, vol. 9, ed. L. Tarán (New York and London: Garland Publishing, 1987).

Cohon, S., *Jewish Theology* (Assen: Royal van Gorcum, Prakke & Prakke, 1971).

Collins, Raymond F., *The Birth of the New Testament* (New York: Crossroad, 1993).

Connolly, R. H. *Didascalia Apostolorum, the Syriac Version translated and accompanied by the Verona Latin Fragments* (Oxford: Oxford University Press, 1929).

Cosgrove, C. H., 'Justin Martyr and the Emerging Christian Canon: Observations on the Purpose and Destination of the Dialogue with Trypho', *Vigiliae Christianae* 36 (1982): 209–32.

Cöster, Henry, *Kyrkans historia och historiens kyrka* (Stockholm/Stehag: Symposion, 1989).

Cross, F. M., *From Epic to Canon: History and Literature in Ancient Israel* (Baltimore and London: Johns Hopkins University Press).

Cullmann, Oscar, 'The Plurality of the Gospels as a Theological Problem in Antiquity: A Study in the History of Dogma', in *The Early Church*, ed. O. Cullmann (London: SCM, 1956), 35–54.

—'Die Tradition und die Festlegung des Kanons durch die Kirche des 2. Jahrhunderts', in *Das Neue Testament als Kanon*, ed. K. Aland (Göttingen: Vandenhoeck & Ruprecht, 1970), 98–108.

Davies, Philip R., *Whose Bible is it Anyway?* (Sheffield: Sheffield Academic, 1995).

Dei Verbum 21 in *Concilio Vaticano II*, B. A. C. (Madrid: La Editorial Catolica, 3rd edn, 1966).

Deines, Roland, 'Writing Scripture in the First Century', *European Journal of Theology* (forthcoming)

Derrida, J., *Of Grammatology* (Baltimore and London: Johns Hopkins University Press, 1976).

—*Deconstruction and Criticism* (London: Routledge and Kegan Paul, 1979).

Denzinger, Henrici, *Enchiridion symbolorum definitionum et declarationum de rebus fidei et morum* (Freiburg im Breisgau: Herder, 1991).

Dinkler, Erich, *Signum Crucis* (Tübingen: Mohr Siebeck, 1967).

Dohmen, Christoph and Manfred Oeming, *Biblischer Kanon warum und wozu? Eine Kanontheologie*, Quaestiones disputatae 137, (eds) H. Fries and R. Schnackenburg (Freiburg: Herder, 1992).

Donaldson, James, ed. *Constitution of the Holy Apostles [Const. Apost.]* The Ante-Nicene Fathers, vol. 7, (eds) A. Roberts and J. Donaldson (Edinburgh: T&T Clark and Grand Rapids, MI: Eerdmans, reprinted 1994), 391–505.

Dostal, Robert J., 'Gadamer: The Man and His Work', in *The Cambridge Companion to Gadamer*, ed. R. J. Dostal (New York: Cambridge University Press, 2002), 1–35.

Dostal, Robert J., ed., *The Cambridge Companion to Gadamer* (New York: Cambridge University Press, 2002).

Driver, G. R., 'Abbreviations in the Massoretic Text', *Textus* 1 (1960): 112–31.

Dunn, James D. G., 'Levels of Canonical Authority', *New Horizons in Biblical Theology* 4 (1982): 13–60.

—*The Living Word* (London: SCM, 1987).

—*The Partings of the Ways: Between Christianity and Judaism and their Significance for the Character of Christianity* (London: SCM, 1991).

—*Jesus Remembered*, Christianity in the Making 1 (Grand Rapids, MI: Eerdmans, 2003).

Eco, Umberto, *A Theory of Semiotics* (Bloomington: Indiana University Press, 1976).

—'Interpretation and History', in *Interpretation and Overinterpretation*, ed. S. Collini (Cambridge: Cambridge University Press, 1992), 23–44.

Edwards, James R., 'A Nomen Sacrum in the Sardis Synagogue', *JBL* 128(4) (2009): 813–21.

Edwards, Mark, *Catholicity and Heresy in the Early Church* (Farnham: Ashgate, 2009).

Ehrman, Bart D. ed., *The Apostolic Fathers*, 2 vols, The Loeb Classical Library 24 and 25 (Cambridge, MA: Harvard University Press, 2003).

Elliott, J. Keith, 'Manuscripts, the Codex and the Canon', *JSNT* 63 (1996).

—'The Early Text of the Catholic Epistles', in *The Early Text of the New Testament*, (eds) Charles E. Hill and Michael J. Kruger (Oxford: Oxford University Press, 2012), 204–24.

Ellis, E. Earle, *The Old Testament in Early Christianity: Canon and Interpretation in the Light of Modern Research* (Grand Rapids, MI: Baker Book House, 1991).

—*Christ and the Future in New Testament History* (NovTSup 97; Leiden: Brill, 2000).

Epp, Eldon Jay, *New Testament Papyrus Manuscripts and Letter Carrying in Greco-Roman Times* (Minneapolis: Fortress, 1991).

—'The Significance of the Papyri for Determining the Nature of the New Testament Text in the Second Century: A Dynamic View of Textual Transmission', in *Studies in the Theory and Method of New Testament Textual Criticism*, vol. 45, (eds) E. J. Epp and G. D. Fee (Grand Rapids, MI: Eerdmans, 1993), 274–97.

—'The Codex and Literacy in Early Christianity and at Oxyrhynchus: Issues Raised by Harry Y. Gamble's *Books and Readers in the Early Church*', *Critical Review of Books in Religion* 11 (1998): 15–37.

—'Issues in the Interrelation of New Testament Textual Criticism and Canon', in *The Canon Debate*, (eds) L. M. McDonald and J. A. Sanders (Peabody, MA: Hendrickson, 2002), 485–515.

Eriksson, Leif, *Auktoritet och nådemedel: Några huvuddrag i Martin Luthers bibelsyn* (Åbo: Studier utgivna av Institutionen för systematisk teologi vid Åbo akademi, nr 25, 1994).

Eusebius, *The Ecclesiastical History [Hist. Eccl.]*, vol. 1. trans. Kirsopp Lake, Loeb Classical Library 153 (Cambridge, MA: Harvard University Press, 1926).

—*The Ecclesiastical History [Hist. Eccl.]*, vol. 2. trans. J. E. L. Oulton, Loeb Classical Library 265 (Cambridge, MA: Harvard University Press and London: Heinemann, 1932, reprinted 1942).

Farley, Edward and Peter C. Hodgson, 'Scripture and Tradition', in *Christian Theology: An Introduction to Its Traditions and Tasks*, (eds) P. C. Hodgson and R. H. King (Philadelphia: Fortress, 1985), 61–87.

Fernhout, Rein, *Canonical Texts: Bearers of Absolute Authority: Bible, Koran, Veda, Tipitaka: A Phenomenological Study*, trans. Henry Jansen and Lucy Jansen-Hofland (Amsterdam: Rodopi, 1994).

Finkelberg, Margalit and Guy G. Stroumsa, 'Introduction: Before the Western Canon', in *Homer, the Bible, and Beyond: Literary and Religious Canons in the Ancient World*, (eds) M. Finkelberg and G. G. Stroumsa (Leiden: Brill, 2003), 1–8.

Finkelberg, Margalit and Guy G. Stroumsa (eds), *Homer, the Bible, and Beyond: Literary and Religious Canons in the Ancient World* (Leiden: Brill, 2003).

Finnegan, Ruth, *Oral Poetry: Its Nature, Significance and Social Context* (Cambridge: Cambridge University Press, 1977).

Fisch, Thomas, ed., *Liturgy and Tradition: Theological Reflections of Alexander Schmeemann* (Crestwood, New York: St. Vladimir's Seminary Press, 1990).

Flesseman-van Leer, Ellen, *Tradition and Scripture in the Early Church* (Leiden: Gorcum & Prakke, 1953).

Foucault, Michel, 'Nietzsche, Freud, Marx', *Cahiers de Royaumont philosophie* 6 (1967): 183–200.

Ford, David F., *Self and Salvation: Being Transformed* (Cambridge: Cambridge University, 1999).

Frank, Isidor, *Der Sinn der Kanonbildung* (Freiburg: Herder, 1971).

Frei, Hans. *The Identity of Jesus Christ* (Philadelphia, Fortress, 1975).

—'The "Literal Reading" of Biblical Narrative in the Christian Tradition: Does It Stretch or Will It Break?', in *The Bible and the Narrative Tradition*, ed. F. McConnell (New York: Oxford University Press, 1986), 36–77.

Frye, Northrop, 'The Double Mirror', *Bulletin of the American Academy of Arts and Sciences* 35 (1981): 32–41.

—*The Great Code. The Bible and Literature* (New York and London: Harcourt Brace Jovanovich, 1981).

Gadamer, Hans-Georg, 'Zur Problematik des Selbstverständnisses: Ein hermeneutischer Beitrag zur Frage der "Entmythologisierung"', in *Gesammelte Werke, Vol. 2: Hermeneutik II* (Tübingen: Mohr Siebeck, 1961), 121–32.

—*Philosophical Hermeneutics.* trans. David E. Linge (Berkeley: University of California, 1976).

—'Text und Interpretation', *Gesammelte Werke*, vol. 2 (Tübingen: Mohr Siebeck, 1993 [1983]), 330–60.

—'Der "eminente" Text und seine Wahrheit', in *Gesammelte Werke*, vol. 8 (Tübingen: Mohr Siebeck, 1986), 286–95.

—*The Relevance of the Beautiful and Other Essays*, trans. Nicholas Walker (New York: Cambridge University Press, 1986).

—*Truth and Method* (abbreviated *TM*), trans. Joel Weinsheimer and Donald Marshall (New York: Continuum, 1989).

—*Wahrheit und Methode: Grundzüge einer philosophischen Hermeneutik* (abbreviated *WM*), Gesammelte Werke, vol. 1 (Tübingen: Mohr Siebeck, 6th edn, 1990 [1960])

—*The Beginning of Philosophy*, translated by Rod Coltman (New York: Continuum, 1998).

—*Gadamer in Conversation: Reflections and Commentary*, trans. and ed. R. E. Palmer (New Haven: Yale University Press, 2001).

Gamble, Harry Y., 'The Canon of the New Testament', in *The New Testament and Its Modern Interpreters*, (eds) E. J. Epp and G. W. MacRae (Society of Biblical Literature, 1989), 201–43.

—*The New Testament Canon: Its Making and Meaning* (Philadelphia: Fortress, 1985).

—'The Pauline Corpus and the Early Christian Book', in *Paul and the Legacies of Paul*, ed. W. S. Babcock (Dallas: Southern Methodist University Press, 1990), 265–80.

—'Canon: New Testament', in *Anchor Bible Dictionary*, vol. 1, ed. D. N. Freedman (New York: Doubleday, 1992), 852–61.

—*Books and Readers in the Early Church: a History of Early Christian Texts* (New Haven: Yale University Press, 1995).

—'The New Testament Canon: Recent Research and the Status Quaestionis', in *The Canon Debate*, (eds) L. M. McDonald and J. A. Sanders (Peabody, MA: Hendrickson, 2002), 267–94.

Geertz, Clifford, *The Interpretation of Cultures* (New York: Basic Books, 1973).

Gerhardsson, Birger, *Memory and Manuscript: Oral Tradition and Written Transmission in Rabbinic Judaism and Early Christianity* (Lund: C. W. K. Gleerup and Copenhagen: Ejnar Munksgaard, 1961).

—'Oral Tradition (New Testament)', in *A Dictionary of Biblical Interpretation*, (eds) R. J. Coggins and J. L. Houlden (London: 1990), 500.

—*The Reliability of the Gospel Tradition* (Peabody, MA: Hendrickson, 2001).

—'The Secret of the Transmission of the Unwritten Jesus Tradition', *NTS* 51(1) (2005): 1–18.

Goldingay, John, *Models for Scripture* (Grand Rapids, MI: Eerdmans and Carlisle: Paternoster, 1994).

Graham, W. A., *Beyond the Written Word: Oral Aspects of Scripture in the History of Religion* (Cambridge: Cambridge University Press, 1987).

Grant, Robert M., *A Historical Introduction to the New Testament* (London: Collins, 1963).

—*Heresy and Criticism: The Search for Authenticity in Early Christian Literature* (Louisville, KY: Westminster and John Knox, 1993).

Gregory, Andrew F. and Christopher M. Tuckett, (eds), *The Reception of the New Testament in the Apostolic Fathers* (Oxford: Oxford University Press, 2005).

Grenholm, Christina, *The Old Testament, Christianity and Pluralism*, Beiträge zur Geschichte der biblischen Exegese 33 (Tübingen: Mohr Siebeck, 1996).

Grondin, Jean, *Hans-Georg Gadamer: A Biography*, trans. J. Weinsheimer (New Haven and London: Yale University Press, 2003).

Gunton, Colin E., *Father, Son & Holy Spirit: Toward a Fully Trinitarian Theology* (London: T&T Clark, 2003).

Haelst, Joseph van, *Catalogue des papyrus littéraires juifs et chrétiens* (Paris: Publications de la Sorbonne, 1976).

—'Les origines du codex', in *Les débuts du codex*, vol. 9, ed. A. Blanchard (Turnhout: Brepols, 1989), 13–35.

Hägglund, Bengt, 'Die Bedeutung der "regula fidei" als Grundlage theologischer Aussagen', *Studia Theologica* 12 (1958): 1–44.

—'Autorität und Tradition', *Studia Theologica* 27 (1973): 1–24.

—'Katholizität und Bekenntnis', in *Kirche – Sakrament – Amt: Deutsch-Skandinavische Theologentagung vom 25. – 28. August 1974 in Ratzeburg. Texte und Gottesdienste*, ed. U. Asendorf (Hamburg: Verlag Herbert Renner, 1976), 1–14.

—*Chemnitz – Gerhard – Arndt – Rudbeckius: Aufsätze zum Studium der altlutherischen Theologie*, Texte und Studien zum Protestantismus des 16. bis 18. Jahrhunderts (TSP), vol. 1 (Waltrop: Verlag Hartmut Spenner, 2003).

—*Sanningens regel: Regula Veritatis: Trosregeln och den kristna traditionens struktur* (Skellefteå: Artos & Norma bokförlag, 2003).

Hagner, Donald A., *The Use of the Old and New Testaments in Clement of Rome* (Leiden: Brill, 1973).

Hagner, Donald A. and Stephen E. Young, 'The Historical-Critical Method and the Gospel of Matthew', in *Methods for Matthew*, ed. M. A. Powell, Methods in Biblical Interpretation (Cambridge: Cambridge University Press, 2009), 11–43.

Hahneman, Geoffrey Mark, *The Muratorian Fragment and the Development of the Canon* (Oxford: Clarendon, 1992).

Haines-Eitzen, Kim, *Guardians of Letters: Literacy, Power, and the Transmitters of Early Christian Literature* (Oxford: Oxford, 2000).

Hallonsten, Gösta, 'Kommentar – ett katolskt perspektiv', in ... *att i allt bekänna Kristus*, (eds) G. Hallonsten and P. E. Persson (Stockholm: Verbum, 2000), 105–20.

Halversen, John, 'Oral and Written Gospel: A Critique of Werner Kelber', *NTS* 40 (1994): 180–95.

Hamel, Christopher de, *The Book. A History of the Bible* (London: Phaidon, 2001).

Haran, Menahem, 'Problems of the Canonization of Scripture', in *The Canon and Masorah of the Hebrew Bible. An Introductory Reader*, ed. S. L. Leiman (New York: KTAV, 1974).

Harnack, Adolf von, *Das Neue Testament um das Jahr 200: Theodor Zahn's Geschichte des Neutestamentlichen Kanos (erster Band, erste Hälfte) geprüft* (Freiburg: Mohr Siebeck, 1889).

—*Lehrbuch der Dogmengeschichte*, vol. 1 (Tübingen: Mohr Siebeck, 1909).

—*Marcion: Das Evangelium vom fremden Gott: Eine Monographie zur Geschichte der Grundlegung der katholischen Kirche* (Leipzig: J. C. Hinrichs'sche Buchhandlung, 1921).

—*Marcion: das Evangelium vom fremden Gott; eine Monographie zur Geschichte der Grundlegung der katholischen Kirche. Neue Studien zu Marcion* (Darmstadt: Wissenschaftliche Buchgesellschaft, 2nd edn, 1924).

—*The Origin of the New Testament and the Most Important Consequences of the New Creation*, trans. J. R. Wilkinson (London: Williams & Norgate, 1925).

—'Das Alte Testament in den paulinischen Briefen und in den Paulinischen Gemeinden,' *SBA* (Phil.-hist. Kl.) (1928): 124–41.

Harris, J. Rendel, *Testimonies*, 2 vols. (Cambridge: Cambridge University Press, 1916–20).

Harris, William V., *Ancient Literacy* (Cambridge, MA and London: Harvard University Press, 1989).

Hays, Richard B., *Echoes of Scripture in the Letters of Paul* (New Haven and London: Yale University Press, 1989).

—*The Moral Vision of the New Testament: A Contemporary Introduction to New Testament Ethics* (San Francisco: HarperCollins, 1996).

—'Can the Gospels Teach Us How To Read the Old Testament', *Pro Ecclesia* 11 (2002): 402–18.

Hays, Richard B., Stefan Alkier and Leroy A. Huizenga (eds), *Reading the Bible Intertextually* (Waco, TX: Baylor University Press, 2009).

Head, Peter M., 'Is P[4], P[64] and P[67] the Oldest Manuscript of the Four Gospels? A Response to T. C. Skeat', *NTS* 51 (2005): 450–57.

Heath, Jane, '*Nomina Sacra* and Sacra Memoria Before the Monastic Age', *JTS* 61, no. 2 (2010): 516–49.

Hengel, Martin, *Die Evangelienüberschriften: vorgetragen am 18. Oktober 1981* (Heidelberg: Carl Winter Universitätsverlag, 1984).

Hengel, Martin, *The Johannine Question* (London: SCM and Philadelphia: Trinity Press International, 1989).

Hengel, Martin, *The Four Gospels and the One Gospel of Jesus Christ* (London: SCM, 2000).

—*Between Jesus and Paul: Studies in the Earliest History of Christianity* (Eugene, OR: Wipf and Stock, 2003 [1983]).

—'Eye-witness memory and the writing of the Gospels', in *The Written Gospel*, (eds) Markus Bockmuehl and Donald A. Hagner (Cambridge: Cambridge University Press, 2005), 70–96.

—*Die vier Evangelien und das eine Evangelium von Jesus Christtus: Studien zu ihrer Sammlung und Entstehung* (WUNT 224; Tübingen: Mohr Siebeck, 2008).

Hengel, Martin and Roland Deines, 'Die Septuaginta als 'christliche Schriftensammlung' und das Problem ihres Kanons', in *Verbindliches Zeugnis 1: Kanon – Schrift – Tradition*, (eds) W. Pannenberg and T. Schneider (Freiburg im Breisgau: Herder and Göttingen: Vandenhoeck & Ruprecht, 1992), 34–127.

Hengel, Martin and Anna Maria Schwemer, *Paul between Damascus and Antioch: The Unknown Years* (Louisville: Westminster John Knox, 1997).

Hennings, Ralph, 'Der Briefwechsel zwischen Augustinus und Hieronymus und ihr Streit um den Kanon des Alten Testaments und die Auslegung von Gal. 2,11–14' in *Suppl. Vigiliae Christinae (formerly Philosophia Patrum): Texts and Studies of Early Christian Life and Language,* vol. XXI, (eds) J. den Boeft, B. D. Ehrman, J. van Oort, D. T. Runia, C. Scholten and J. C. M. van Winden (Leiden: Brill, 1994).

Hill, Charles E., *Who Chose the Gospels? Probing the Great Gospel Conspiracy* (Oxford: Oxford University Press, 2010).

—'The Four Gospel Canon in the Second Century', paper presented at the SBL, San Francisco, SBL Consultation on the Cross, Resurrection, and Diversity in Earliest Christianity (2011). Available online at http://austingrad.edu/images/SBL/Four%20Gospel%20Canon%20.pdf (accessed 2 September 2012).

Hill, Edmund, ed., trans., 'Teaching Christianity', *The Works of Saint Augustine* I/11 (New York: New City Press, 1996).

Hoffmann, R. J., *Marcion: On the Restitution of Christianity* (Chico, CA: AARAS, 1984).

Hofius, Otfried, 'Das apostolische Christuszeugnis und das Alte Testament. Thesen zur Biblischen Theologie', in *Eine Bibel – zwei Testamente: Positionen Biblischer*

Theologie, (eds) C. Dohmen and T. Söding (Paderborn: UTB für Wissenschaft, 1995), 195–208.

Hoh, J., *Die Lehre des hl. Irenäus über das Neue Testament* (Münster i. W.: Verlag der Aschendorffschen Verlagsbuchhandlung, 1919).

Holmes, Michael W., *The Apostolic Fathers: Greek Texts with English Translations* (Grand Rapids, MI: Baker, 3rd edn, 2007).

—'The Biblical Canon', in *The Oxford Handbook of Early Christian Studies*, (eds) Susan Ashbrook Harvey and David G. Hunter (Oxford: Oxford University Press, 2008), 406–26.

—'Text and Transmission in the Second Century', in *The Reliability of the New Testament: Bart D. Ehrman & Daniel B. Wallace in Dialogue*, ed. Robert B. Stewart (Minneapolis: Fortress, 2011), 61–79.

Holmgren, Fredrick C., *The Old Testament and the Significance of Jesus: Embracing Change – Maintaining Christian Identity: The Emerging Center in Biblical Scholarship* (Grand Rapids, MI: Eerdmans, 1999).

Horbury, William, *Jews and Christians: In Contact and Controversy* (Edinburgh: T&T Clark, 1998).

Horsley, G. H. R., 'Classical Manuscripts in Australia and New Zealand and the Early History of the Codex', *Antichthon: Journal of the Australian Society for Classical Studies* 27 (1995): 60–85.

Horst, Pieter W. van der, 'Was the Synagogue a Place of Sabbath Worship before 70 CE?', *Jews, Christians, and Polytheists in the Ancient Synagogue: Cultural Interaction during the Greco-Roman Period*, ed. Steven Fine (London: Routledge, 1999), 18–43.

Howard, George, 'The Tetragram and the New Testament', *JBL* 96 (1977): 63–83.

Hubert, Henri, and Marcel Mauss, *Sacrifice: Its Nature and Function*, trans. W. D. Hall (Chicago: University of Chicago Press, 1981 [1898]).

Hurtado, Larry W., 'Christ-Devotion in the First Two Centuries: Reflections and a Proposal', *Toronto Journal of Theology* 12 (1996): 17–33.

—*One God, One Lord: Early Christian Devotion and Ancient Jewish Monotheism* (Edinburgh: T&T Clark, 1998).

—'The Origin of the Nomina Sacra: A Proposal', *JBL* 117 (1998): 655–73.

—*At the Origins of Christian Worship: The Context and Character of Earliest Christian Devotion* (Grand Rapids, MI: Eerdmans, 1999).

—'The Earliest Evidence of an Emerging Christian Material and Visual Culture: The Codex, the *Nomina Sacra* and the Staurogram', in *Text and Artifact in the Religions of Mediterranean Antiquity*, Studies in Christianity and Judaism/Études sur le christianisme et le judaïsme; vol. 9, (eds) S. G. Wilson and M. Desjardins (Waterloo, ON: Wilfrid Laurier University Press, 2000), 271–88.

—'Religious Experience and Religious Innovation in the New Testament', *JR* 80 (2000): 183–205.

—*Lord Jesus Christ: Devotion to Jesus in Earliest Christianity* (Grand Rapids, MI: Eerdmans, 2003).

—*The Earliest Christian Artifacts: Manuscripts and Christian Origins* (Grand Rapids, MI: Eerdmans, 2006).

—'The New Testament in the Second Century: Text, Collections, Canon', in *Transmission and Reception: New Testament Text-Critical and Exegetical Studies*, (eds) J. W. Childers and D. C. Parker (Piscataway, NJ: Gorgias, 2006), 3–27.

—'Early Christian Manuscripts as Artifacts', in *Jewish and Christian Scripture as Artifact and Canon*, (eds) Craig A. Evans and H. Daniel Zacharias, Studies in Scripture in Early Judaism and Christianity 13, ed. Craig A. Evans (London and New York: T&T Clark, 2009), 66–81.

—*God in New Testament Theology* (Nashville: Abingdon, 2010).

Hvalvik, Reidar, 'Barnabas 9.7-9 and the Author's Supposed Use of Gematria', NTS 33 (1987): 276–82.

—*The Struggle for Scripture and Covenant: the purpose of the epistle of Barnabas and Jewish-Christian competition in the second century* (Tübingen: Mohr Siebeck, 1996).

Irenaeus, *Proof of the Apostoloc Preaching [Epideixis]*, translated and annotated by J. P. Smith, Ancient Christian Writers, No. 16 (New York: Newman Press, 1952).

—*Irenæus against heresies [Adversus haereses]*, The Ante–Nicene Fathers, vol. 1, (eds) A. Roberts and J. Donaldson (Edinburgh: T&T Clark and Grand Rapids, MI: Eerdmans, reprinted 1994), 309–567.

Jankowski, Stanislaw, 'I "nomina sacra" nei papiri dei LXX (secoli II e III d. C.)', *Studia Papyrologica* 16 (1977): 81–116.

Janowski, Bernd, 'Der eine Gott der beiden Testamente: Grundfragen einer Biblischen Theologie', *Zeitschrift für Theologie und Kirche* 95 (1998): 1–36.

Jaschke, Hans-Jochen, 'Irenäus von Lyon', *TRE,* Vol. 16 (1987), 258–68 .

Jasper, David, *Readings in the Canon of Scripture: Written for our Learning* (New York: St. Martin's and Macmillan, 1995).

—*A Short Introduction to Hermeneutics* (Louisville, KY: Westminster and John Knox, 2004).

Jauss, Hans Robert, *Die Theorie der Rezeption – Rückschau auf ihre unerkannte Vorgeschichte* (Konstanz: Universitätsverlag Konstanz GMBH, 1987).

Jeanrond, Werner G., *Text and Interpretation as Categories of Theological Thinking*. trans. Thomas J. Wilson (Dublin: Gill and Macmillan, 1988).

—*Theological Hermeneutics: Development and Significance* (London: SCM, 1994 [1991]).

—*Call and Response: The Challenge of Christian Life* (Dublin: Gill & Macmillan, 1995).

—'Text: II Religionsphilosophisch/III. Fundamentaltheologisch', *Religion in Geschichte und Gegenwart*, 4th edn, vol. 8 (2005), 198.

—'Text/Textuality', in Kevin J. Vanhoozer (ed.), *Dictionary for Theological Interpretation of the Bible* (London: SPCK and Grand Rapids, MI: Baker, 2005), 782–84.

Jenson, Robert W., 'Hermeneutics and the Life of the Church', in *Reclaiming the Bible for the Church*, (eds) C. E. Braaten and R. W. Jenson (Grand Rapids, MI: Eerdmans, 1995), 89–105.

—*Systematic Theology*, vol. 1: *The Triune God* (New York: Oxford University Press, 1997).

—'The Church's Responsibility for the World', in *The Two Cities of God: The Church's Responsibility for the Earthly City*, (eds) C. E. Braaten and R. W. Jenson (Grand Rapids, MI: Eerdmans, 1997), 1–10.

—*Systematic Theology*, vol. 2: *The Works of God* (New York and Oxford: Oxford University Press, 1999).

—'The Religious Power of Scripture', *Scottish Journal of Theology* 52 (1999): 89–105.

Jerome, St., *On Illustrious Men*, The Fathers of the Church. A New Translation, trans. Thomas P. Halton (Washington, DC: The Catholic University of America, 1999).

Johansson, Torbjörn, *Reformationens huvudfrågor och arvet från Augustinus. En studie i Martin Chemnitz' Augustinusreception* (Göteborg: Församlingsförlaget, 1999).

Johnson, Luke Timothy, *Religious Experience in Earliest Christianity: A Missing Dimension in New Testament Studies* (Minneapolis: Fortress, 1998).

Johnson, William A., *Bookrolls and Scribes in Oxhyrhynchus* (Toronto: University of Toronto, 2004).

Jonge, H. J. de, 'Introduction: The New Testament Canon', in *The Biblical Canons*, Bibliotheca Ephemeridum Theologicarum Lovaniensium, (eds) J.-M. Auwers and H. J. de Jonge (Leuven: Leuven University Press, 2003), 209–19.

Jonge, M. de, ed., *The Testament of the Twelve Patriarchs*, vol. 1.2, Pseudepigrapha Veteris Testamenti Graece, (eds) A. M. Denis and M. de Jonge (Leiden: Brill, 1978).

Jonge, M. de, trans. 'The Testaments of the Twelve Patriarchs, in *The Apocryphal Old Testament*, ed. H. F. D. Sparks (Oxford, Clarendon Press, 1984).

Jongkind, Dirk, *Scribal Habits of Codex Sinaiticus* (Piscataway, NJ: Gorgias, 2007).

Josipovici, Gabriel, *The Book of God: A Response to the Bible* (New Haven: Yale University Press, 1988).

Jowett, Benjamin, 'On the Interpretation of Scripture', *The Interpretation of Scripture and Other Essays* (London: Routledge, 1860).

Jülicher, Adolf, *Einleitung in das Neue Testament* (Tübingen: Mohr Siebeck, 1931).

Jungmann, Josef A., *Missarum Sollemnia: Eine Genetische Erklärung der römischen Messe,* vol. 1 (Wien: Herder, 2 Aufl., 1949 [1948]).

—*The Early Liturgy: To the Time of Gregory the Great* (Notre Dame, IN: University of Notre Dame Press, 1959).

Just, Arthur A., *The Ongoing Feast: Table Fellowship and Eschatology at Emmaus* (Pueblo, Collegeville, MN: Liturgical Press, 1993).

Käsemann, Ernst, 'The Canon of the New Testament and the Unity of the Church', in *Essays on New Testament Themes* (London: SCM, 1968), 95–107.

Käsemann, Ernst, ed., *Das Neue Testament als Kanon* (Göttingen: Vandenhoeck & Ruprecht, 1970).

Katz, Peter, 'The Early Christians' Use of Codices Instead of Rolls', *JTS* 46 (1945): 63–5.

Kautzsch, E., ed., *Die Apokryphen und Pseudepigraphen des Alten Testaments* (Tübingen: Mohr Siebeck, 1900).

Kee, H. C., 'Testament of the Twelve Patriarchs: A New Translation and Introduction', in *The Old Testament Pseudepigrapha: Apocalyptic Literature and Testaments*, ed. J. H. Charlesworth (New York: Doubleday, 1983).

Kelber, Werner H., *The Oral and the Written Gospel: The Hermeneutics of Speaking and Writing in the Synoptic Tradition, Mark, Paul, and Q* (Bloomington and Indianapolis: Indiana University Press, 1983, New Introduction 1997).

Kelhoffer, James A., '"How Soon a Book" Revisited: ΕΥΑΓΓΕΛΙΟΝ as a Reference to 'Gospel' Materials in the First Half of the Second Century'. *ZNW* 95 (2004): 1–34.

Kelly, J. N. D., *The Pastoral Epistles* (Peabody, MA: Hendrickson, 1960).

—*Early Christian Creeds* (New York: Longman, 3rd rev. edn, 1972).

Kelsey, David H., *Proving Doctrine: The Uses of Scripture in Modern Theology* (Harrisburg, PA: Trinity Press International, 1999).

Kennedy, G. A., *A History of Rhetoric II: The Art of Rhetoric in the Roman World 300 BC – AD 300* (New York: Princeton, 1972).

—'Classical and Christian Source Criticism', in *The Relationships among the Gospels: An Interdisciplinary Dialogue*, vol. 5, ed. W. O. Walker (San Antonio:, 1978), 125–55.

Kennedy, Jay, 'The Plato Code', *The Philosopher's Magazine*, 51 (2010).

Kenyon, F. G., 'Nomina Sacra in the Chester Beatty Papyri', *Aegyptus* (1933): 5–10.

Kereszty, Roch, 'The Unity of the Church in the Theology of Irenaeus', *The Second Century* 4 (1984): 202–18.

Kermode, Frank, 'The Argument about Canons', in *The Bible and the Narrative Tradition*, ed. F. McConnell (New York: Oxford University Press, 1986), 78–96.

Kierkegaard, Søren, *For Self-Examination: Recommended for the Times*. trans. Edna Hong and Howard Hong (Minneapolis: Augsburg, 1940).

Knox, John, *Marcion and the New Testament: An Essay in the Early History of the Canon* (Chicago: The University of Chicago Press, 1942).

Koester, Helmut, *Introduction to the New Testament* (Philadelphia: Fortress and Berlin: Walter de Gruyter, 1984).

—'From the Kerygma-Gospel to Written Gospels', *NTS* 35 (1989): 361–81.

—*Ancient Christian Gospels: Their History and Development* (London: SCM and Philadelphia: Trinity Press International, 1990).

Köhler, W.-D., *Die Rezeption des Matthäusevangeliums in der Zeit vor Irenäus* (WUNT 2/22; Tübingen: Mohr Siebeck, 1987).

Kooij, A. van der and K. van der Toorn (eds), *Canonization and Decanonization*. Studies in the History of Religions (Leiden: Brill, 1998).

Kort, Wesley A., *'Take, Read': Scripture, Textuality, and Cultural Practice* (Pennsylvania: The Pennsylvania State University Press, 1996).

Kraft, Robert A., 'The Codex and Canon Consciousness', in *The Canon Debate*, (eds) L. M. McDonald and J. A. Sanders (Peabody, MA: Hendrickson, 2002), 229–33.

—'The "Textual Mechanics" of Early Jewish LXX/OG Papyri and Fragments', in *The Bible as Book: The Transmission of the Greek Text*, (eds) S. McKendrick and O. O'Sullivan (London: British Library, 2003), 51–72.

Kunze, Johannes, *Glaubensregel, Heilige Schrift und Taufbekenntnis: Untersuchungen über die dogmatische Autorität, ihr Werden und ihre Geschichte, vornehmlich in der alten Kirche* (Leipzig: Dörffling & Franke, 1899).

Laato, Antti, *Monotheism, the Trinity and Mysticism: A Semiotic Approach to Jewish-Cristian Encounter* (Frankfurt am Main: Peter Lang: Europäischer Verlag der Wissenschaften, 1999).

Lake, Kirsopp, *The Apostolic Fathers*, 2 vols, The Loeb Classical Library (London: William Heinemann, 1945).

Laird, Benjamin, 'Early Titles of the Letters of the Pauline Corpus' (paper presented at the annual Graduate Conference for Biblical and Early Christian Studies. St Andrews, Scotland, June 8 2012).

Lamb, J. A., 'The Place of the Bible in the Liturgy', *The Cambridge History of the*

Bible, (eds) P. R. Ackroyd and C. F. Evans (Cambridge: Cambridge University Press, 1970).

Lampe, Peter, *Die stadtrömischen Christen in den ersten beiden Jahrhunderten: Untersuchungen zur Sozialgeschichte* (Tübingen: Mohr Siebeck, 1989).

Lathrop, Gordon W., *Holy Things: A Liturgical Theology* (Minneapolis: Fortress, 1993).

Lawrence, Fred, 'Gadamer, the Hermeneutic Revolution, and Theology', in *The Cambridge Companion to Gadamer,* ed. R. J. Dostal (New York: Cambridge Univeristy Press, 2002), 167–200.

Layton, Bentley, ed., 'The Gospel according to Thomas', in *The Gnostic Scriptures,* trans. B. Layton (London: SCM, 1987) 380–99.

Leiman, Sid Z., 'Inspiration and Canonicity: Reflections on the Formation of the Biblical Canon' in *Jewish and Christian Self-Definition,* vol. 2, (eds) E. P. Sanders, A. I. Baumgarten and A. Mendelson (Philadelphia: Fortress, 1981).

Lemcio, Eugene E., 'The Unifying Kerygma of the New Testament', *JSNT* 33 (1988): 3–17.

—'The Unifying Kerygma of the New Testament (II)', *JSNT* 38 (1990): 3–11.

—*The Past of Jesus in the Gospels* (SNTS MS 68; Cambridge, Cambridge University Press, 1991).

Lemcio, Eugene and Robert W. Wall, *The New Testament as Canon: A Reader in Canonical Criticism* (Sheffield: Sheffield Academic, 1992).

Lessing, Gotthold, *Lessing's Theological Writings,* trans. Henry Chadwick (Stanford: Stanford University Press, 1956).

Levine, Lee I., *The Ancient Synagogue: The First Thousand Years* (New Haven and London: Yale University Press, 2000).

Lieberman, Saul, *Hellenism in Jewish Palestine: Studies in the Literary Transmission Beliefs and Manners of Palestine in the I Century B.C.E. – IV Century C.E* (New York: The Jewish Theological Seminary of America, 1950).

Lietzmann, H., 'Wie wurden die Bücher des Neuen Testaments Heilige Schrift?' in *Kleine Schriften,* ed. H. Lietzmann, TU 68; ed. K. Aland, vol. 2 (Berlin: Akademie, 1958), 15–98.

Lieu, J. ''The Parting of the Ways': Theological Construct or Historical Reality' *JSNT* 56 (1994): 101–19.

Lindbeck, George, *The Nature of Doctrine. Religion and Doctrine in a Postliberal Age* (London: SPCK, 1984).

—'Scripture, Consensus, and Community', in *Biblical Interpretation in Crisis: The Ratzinger Conference on Bible and Church,* Encounter Series, vol. 9, ed. R. J. Neuhaus (Grand Rapids, MI: Eerdmans, 1989), 74–101.

Lindblom, Johannes, *Kanon och apokryfer: Studier till den bibliska kanons historia* (Uppsala: Svenska kyrkans diakonistyrelses bokförlag, 1920).

Lindemann, A., *Paulus im ältesten Christentum: Das Bild des Apostels und die Rezeption der paulinischen Theologie in der frühchristlichen Literatur bis Marcion*, Beiträge zur Historischen Theologie 58, ed. J. Wallman (Tübingen: Mohr Siebeck, 1979).

—'Der Apostel Paulus im 2. Jahrhundert', in *The New Testament in Early Christianity/ La réception des écrits néotestamentaires dans le christianisme primitif*, LXXXVI, ed. J.-M. Sevrin (Leuven: Leuven University Press, 1989).

Loenhoff, Jens, *Interkulturelle Verständigung. Zum Problem grenzüberschreitender Kommunikation* (Leske and Budrich: Oplade, 1992).

Loughlin, Gerald, 'The Basis and Authority of Doctrine', in *The Cambridge Companion to Christian Doctrine*, ed. C. E. Gunton (Cambridge: Cambridge University Press, 1997), 41–64.

Marcovich, Miroslav, ed., *Iustini Martyris Apologiae pro Christianis [1 Apol]*, Patristische Texte und Studien 38 (Berlin and New York: Walter de Gruyter, 1994).

—*Iustini Martyris Dialogus cum Tryphone*, Patristische Texte und Studien 47 (Berlin and New York: Walter de Gruyter, 1994).

Margolis, Joseph, *Interpretation Radical but Not Unruly: The New Puzzle of the Arts and History* (Berkeley: University of California, 1995).

Marxen, Willi, *Introduction to the New Testament* (Philadelphia: Fortress, 1968).

Mason, Steve, 'Josephus and His Twenty-Two Book Canon', in *The Canon Debate*, (eds) L. M. McDonald and J. A. Sanders (Peabody, MA: Hendrickson, 2002), 110–27.

Massaux, Édouard, ed. and with an introduction and addenda by A. J. Bellinzoni, *The Influence of the Gospel of Saint Matthew on Christian Literature Before Saint Irenaeus*. trans. Norman J. Belval and Suzanne Hecht (Macon, GA: Mercer University Press, and Leuven: Peeters, 1990–93).

Mathison, Keith A., *The Shape of Sola Scriptura* (Moscow, ID: Canon Press, 2001).

McDonald, Lee Martin, *The Formation of the Christian Biblical Canon* (Peabody, MA: Hendrickson, 1995).

—'Indentifying Scripture and Canon in the Early Church: The Criteria Question', in *The Canon Debate*, (eds) L. M. McDonald and J. A. Sanders (Peabody, MA: Hendrickson, 2002), 416–39.

—*The Biblical Canon: Its Origin, Transmission, and Authority* (Peabody, MA: Hendrickson, 2007).

—*Forgotten Scriptures: The Selection and Rejection of Early Religious Writings* (Louisvilly, KY: Alban Books, Westminster John Knox Press, 2009).

McGiffert, Arthur C., *The Apostles' Creed. Its Origin, its Purpose, and its Historical Interpretation. A Lecture, with Critical Notes* (Edinburgh, 1902).

McHugh, John, 'In Him was Life', in *Jews and Christians: The Parting of the Ways* A.D. *70 to 135*, vol. 66, ed. J. D. G. Dunn (Tübingen: Mohr Siebeck, 1989).

McIver, Robert K., *Memory, Jesus, and the Synoptic Gospels* (Atlanta, GA: Society of Biblical Literature, 2011).

McNamee, Kathleen, *Abbreviations in Greek Literary Papyri and Ostraca*, Bulletin of the American Society of Papyrologists, Supplements 3 (1981).

Melanchthon, Philip, *Loci Communes*, trans. J. A. O Preus (St. Louis, MO: Concordia Publishing House, 1992 [1543]).

Mendels, Doron, *The Media Revolution of Early Christianity: An Essay on Eusebius's Ecclesiastical History* (Grand Rapids, MI: Eerdmans, 1999).

Merk, Otto and Michael Wolter (eds), 'Papyrus Yalensis 1 als ältest bekannter christlicher Genesistext: Zur Frühgeschichte des Kreuz-Symbols', in *Im Zeichen des Kreuzes: Aufsätze von Erich Dinkler* (Berlin and New York: Walter de Gruyter, 1992), 341–45.

—*Im Zeichen des Kreuzes: Aufsätze von Erich Dinkler*. Beihefte zur Zeitschrift für die neutestamentliche Wissenschaft und die Kunde der älteren Kirche, vol. 61, ed. Erich Gräßer (Berlin and New York: Walter de Gruyter, 1992).

Metzger, Bruce M. 'Greek Lectionaries and a Critical Edition of the Greek New Testament', in *Die alten Übersetzungen des Neuen Testaments, die Kirchenväterzitate und Lektionare: der gegenwärtige Stand ihrer Erforschung und ihre Bedeutung für die griechische Textgeschichte*, Arbeiten zur Neutestamentlichen Textforschung, vol 5, K. Aland, ed. (Berlin: Walter de Gruyter, 1972), 479–97.

—*Manuscripts of the Greek Bible: An Introduction to Greek Palaeography* (New York and Oxford: Oxford University Press, 1981).

—*The Canon of the New Testament: Its Origin, Development, and Significance* (Oxford: Clarendon Press, 1987).

Metzger, Bruce M. and Bart D. Ehrman, *The Text of the New Testament: Its Transmission, Corruption, and Restoration* (New York and Oxford: Oxford University Press, 4th edn, 2005).

Meyer, Ben F., *Reality and Illusion in New Testament Scholarship: A Primer in Critical Realist Hermeneutics* (Collegeville, MN: A Michael Glazier Book, The Liturgical Press, 1994).

Millard, A., *Reading and Writing in the Time of Jesus* (BS 69; Sheffield: Sheffield Academic, 2000).

Minear, Paul S., *The Bible and the Historian: Breaking the Silence About God in Biblical Studies* (Nashville: Abingdon, 2002).

Moberly, R. W. L., *The Bible, Theology, and Faith: A Study of Abraham and Jesus* (Cambridge: Cambridge University Press, 2000).

Moltmann, Jürgen, *The Theology of Hope* (London: SCM, 1967).

Morgan, Don F., *Between Text and Community: The 'Writings' in Canonical Interpretation* (Minneapolis: Fortress, 1990).

Morgan, Robert and John Barton, *Biblical Interpretation* (New York: Oxford University Press, 1988).

Moule, C. F. D., *The Birth of the New Testament* (London: Adam & Charles Black, 1966).

Munck, Johannes, 'Presbyters and Disciples of the Lord in Papias', *HTR* 52 (1959), 223–43.

Murphy, Tim, 'Elements of a semiotic Theory of Religion', *Method & Theory in the Study of Religion* 15 (2003): 48–67.

Murphy-O'Connor, Jerome, *Paul the Letter-Writer: His World, His Options, His Skills* (Collegeville, MN: Michael Glazier and The Liturgical Press, 1995).

Müller, Mogens, 'The Hidden Context: Some Observations to the Concept of the New Covenant in the New Testament', in *Texts and Contexts: Biblical Texts in Their Textual and Situational Contexts*, (eds) T. Fornberg and D. Hellholm (Oslo/Copenhagen/Stockholm/Boston: Scandinavian University Press, 1995), 649–58.

—*The First Bible of the Church: A Plea for the Septuagint* (Sheffield: Sheffield Academic, 1996).

Mutschler, Bernhard, *Irenäus als johannischer Theologe: Studien zur Schriftauslegung bei Irenäus von Lyon* (Studien und Texte zu Antike und Christentum 21; Tübingen: Mohr Siebeck, 2004).

Nachmanson, Ernst, 'Die schriftliche Kontraktion auf den griechischen Inschriften', *Eranos* 10 (1910): 101–41.

Nardoni, Enrique, 'Origen's Concept of Biblical Inspiration', *The Second Century* 4 (1984): 9–23.

Nestle–Aland, Novum Testamentum Graece, 27th edn (NA[27]), (eds) Barbara Aland, Kurt Aland and Johannes Karavidopoulos (Stuttgart: Deutsche Bibelgesellschaft, 1994).

Neusner, Jacob and Bruce D. Chilton, *Revelation: The Torah and the Bible* (Valley Forge, PA: Trinity Press International, 1995).

Newman, Carey C., James R. Davila and Gladys S. Lewis (eds), *The Jewish Roots of Christological Monotheism: Papers from the St. Andrews Conference on the Historical Origins of the Worship of Jesus* (Leiden: Brill, 1999).

Nienhuis, David R., *Not by Paul Alone: The Formation of the Catholic Epistle Collection and the Christian Canon* (Waco, TX: Baylor University Press, 2007).

Noble, Paul R., *The Canonical Approach: A Critical Reconstruction of the Hermeneutics of Brevard S. Childs* (Leiden: Brill, 1995).

Nygren, Anders, 'Det självklaras roll i historien', in *Tro och vetande: religionsfilosofiska och teologiska essayer* (Helsingfors: Luther-Agricola-sällskapet, 1970), 92–101.

Öberg, Ingemar, *Bibelsyn och bibeltolkning hos Martin Luther* (Skellefteå: Artos and Norma bokförlag, 2002).

O'Callaghan, Jose, *Nomina Sacra in Papyrus Graecis Saeculi III Neotestamentariis* (Rome: Biblical Institute Press, 1970).

—"Nominum sacrorum' elenchus in Graecis Novi Testamenti papyris a saeculo IV usque ad VIII', *Studia Papyrologica* 10 (1971): 99–122.

O'Connor, M., 'How the Text is Heard: The Biblical Theology of Brevard Childs', *Religious Studies Review* 21 (1995): 91–6.

O'Reilly, Jennifer, 'Gospel Harmony and the Names of Christ: Insular Images of a Patristic Theme', in *The Bible as Book: The Manuscript Tradition*, (eds) J. L. Sharpe III and K. van Kampen (London: The British Library & Oak Knoll Press in association with The Scriptorium: Center for Christian Antiquities, 1998), 73–88.

Ohlig, Karl-Heinz, *Die theologische Begründung des neutestamentlichen Kanons in der alten Kirche* (Düsseldorf: Patmos, 1972).

Ohme, Heinz, *Kanon ekklesiastikos* (Berlin: Walter de Gruyter), 1998.

Olsson, Birger, ed., *Kristna tolkningar av Gamla testamentet* (Stockholm: Verbum, 1997).

Oppel, Herbert, 'Κανών. Zur Bedeutungsgeschichte des Wortes und seiner lateinischen Entsprechungen (regula-norma)', in *Philologus: Zeitschrift für das klassische Altertum, Supplementband 30*, Heft 4, (eds) A. Rehm and J. Stroux (Leipzig: Dieterich'sche Verlagsbuchhandlung, 1937).

Origen, *Commentaire sur Saint Jean [Joa. Comm.]*, Texte Grec avant-propos, traduction et notes par C. Blanc, Sources Chrétiennes 120 (Paris: Les Éditions du Cerf, 1966).

—*De Principiis [On First Principles]*, The Ante–Nicene Fathers, vol. 4, (eds) A. Roberts and J. Donaldson, (Edinburgh: T&T Clark and Grand Rapids, MI: Eerdmans, reprinted 1994), 239–384.

Osborn, Eric F., *Justin Martyr* (Tübingen: Mohr Siebeck, 1973).

—'Reason and the rule of faith in the second century AD', in *The Making of Orthodoxy: Essays in Honour of Henry Chadwick*, ed. R. Williams (Cambridge: Cambridge University Press, 1989), 40–61.

—*Irenaeus of Lyons* (Cambridge: Cambridge University Press, 2001).

—*Clement of Alexandria* (Cambridge: Cambridge University Press, 2005).

Osiek, Carolyn, *The Shepherd of Hermas* (Hermeneia; Minneapolis: Fortress, 1999).

Paap, A. H. R. E., *Nomina sacra in the Greek Papyri of the First Five Centuries A.D.: The Sources and Some Deductions* (Leiden: Brill, 1959).

Palmer, Richard E., *Hermeneutics, Interpretation Theory in Schleiermacher, Dilthey, Heidegger, and Gadamer* (Evanston: Northwestern University Press, 1969).

Pannenberg, Wolfhart, *Revelation as History*, trans. D. Granskou (New York: Macmillan, 1968).

—*An Introduction to Systematic Theology* (Edinburgh: T&T Clark, 1991).

—*Systematic Theology,* vol. 1, trans. Geoffrey W. Bromiley (Grand Rapids, MI: Eerdmans, 1991).

Pannenberg, Wolfhart and Theodor Schneider, (eds), *Verbindliches Zeugnis 1: Kanon - Schrift- Tradition*. Dialog der Kirchen (Freiburg im Breisgau: Herder, and Göttingen: Vandenhoeck & Ruprecht, 1992).

Parker, D. C., *Codex Bezae: An Early Christian Manuscript and Its Text* (Cambridge: Cambridge University Press, 1992).

—*An Introduction to the New Testament Manuscripts and their Texts* (Cambridge: Cambridge University Press, 2008).

Pedersen, E. Th., *Luther som skriftfortolker I. En studie i Luthers skriftsyn, hermeneutik og exegese* (Copenhagen: Nyt Nordisk Forlag, 1959).

Peirce, Charles S., *The Collected Papers of Charles Sanders Peirce* (Cambridge, MA: Harvard University Press, 1934–36).

Philo, *The Works of Philo,* trans. C. D. Yonge (Peabody, MA: Hendrickson, 1993).

Pietersma, Albert, 'Kyrios or Tetragram: A Renewed Quest for the Original LXX', in *De Septuaginta: Studies in honour of John William Wevers on his sixty-fifth birthday*, (eds) A. Pietersma and C. Cox (Mississauga, ON: Benben Publishers, 1984), 85–101.

Plantinga, Alvin, 'Two (or More) Kinds of Scripture Scholarship', in *'Behind the Text': History and Biblical Interpretation*, 4, (eds) Craig Bartholomew, C. Stephen Evans, Mary Healy, Murray Rae (Grand Rapids, MI: Paternoster & Zondervan, 2003), 19–57.

Porter, Stanley E., 'When and How was the Pauline Canon Compiled? An Assessment of Theories', in *The Pauline Canon*, ed. Stanley E. Porter (Leiden: Brill, 2004), 95–127.

—'Paul and the Process of Canonization', in *Exploring the Origins of the Bible*, (eds) Craig A. Evans and Emanuel Tov (Grand Rapids, MI: Baker, 2008), 173–202.

Porter, Stanley E., ed., *Hearing the Old Testament in the New Testament* (Grand Rapids, MI and Cambridge: Eerdmans, 2006).

Prigent, Pierre, *Justin et l'Ancien Testament* (Paris: Librairie Lecoffre, 1964).

Räisänen, Heikki, *Beyond New Testament Theology: a Story and a Programme* (London: SCM, 2nd edn, 2000).

Ratzinger, Joseph, in *Das zweite Vatikanische Konzil,* vol. 2, (eds) Heinrich Suso Brechter, Herman Häring, Karl Rahner, Joseph Ratzinger (Freiburg im Breisgau: Herder, 1968).

Reijners, G. Q., *The Terminology of the Holy Cross in Early Christian Literature: As Based upon Old Testament Typology* (Nijmegen–Utrecht: Dekker & Van de Vegt N.V., 1965).

Resnick, Irven M., 'The Codex in Early Jewish and Christian Communities', *The Journal of Religious History* 17 (1992): 1–17.

Richards, E. Randolph, *The Secretary in the Letters of Paul* (WUNT 2/42; Tübingen: Mohr Siebeck, 1991).

—*Paul and First-Century Letter Writing: Secretaries, Composition and Collection* (Downers Grove, IL: InterVarsity, 2004).

Riesner, Rainer, *Jesus als Lehrer: Eine Untersuchung zum Ursprung der Evangelien-Überlieferung* (Tübingen: Mohr Siebeck, 3rd edn, 1988).

—'Jesus as Preacher and Teacher', in *Jesus and the Oral Gospel Tradition*, ed. Henry Wansbrough (London and New York: T&T Clark, 1991), 185–210.

Rhodes, J. N., *The Epistle of Barnabas and the Deuteronomic Tradition* (WUNT 2/188; Tübingen: Mohr Siebeck, 2004)

Roberts, Alexander and James Donaldson, *The Ante–Nicene Fathers: The Writings of the Fathers down to A.D. 325* (Edinburgh: T&T Clark and Grand Rapids, MI: Eerdmans, 1993 [1885]).

Roberts, C. H., 'The Codex', *Proceedings of the British Academy* 40 (1954): 169–204.

—'Books in the Graeco-Roman World and in the New Testament', in *The Cambridge History of the Bible*, vol. 1: *From the Beginnings to Jerome*, (eds) P. R. Ackroyd and C. F. Evans (Cambridge: Cambridge University Press, 1970), 48–66.

—*Manuscript, Society and Belief in Early Christian Egypt* (Oxford: Oxford University Press, 1979).

Roberts, Colin H. and T. C. Skeat, *The Birth of the Codex* (London: Oxford University Press, 1983).

Rordorf, Willy, *Sabbat und Sonntag in der Alten Kirche: Geschichte des Ruhe- und Gottesdiensttages im ältesten Christentum*, Traditio Christiana 2 (Zürich: Zwingli-Verlag, 1972).

—'La Bible dans l'enseignement et la liturgie des premières communautés chrétiennes', in *Bible de tous les temps,* vol. 1: *Le monde grec ancien et la Bible*, ed. C. Mondésert (Paris: Beauchesne Éditeur, 1984), 69–94.

Royse, James R., 'The Early Text of Paul (and Hebrews)', in *The Early Text of the New Testament*, (eds) Charles E. Hill and Michael J. Kruger (Oxford: Oxford University Press, 2012), 175–203.

Rudberg, Gunnar, *Neutestamentlicher Text und Nomina sacra* (Uppsala: A.-B. Akademiska Bokhandeln, 1915).

Sanders, E. P., *Jewish Law from Jesus to the Mishnah* (London: SCM and Philadelphia: Trinity Press International, 1990).

Sanders, James A., *Canon and Community: A Guide to Canonical Criticism* (Philadelphia: Fortress, 1984).

—'Canon: Hebrew Bible', in *Anchor Bible Dictionary*, vol. 1, ed. D. N. Freedman (New York: Doubleday, 1992), 837–52.

Sanders, James A. and Lee Martin McDonald (eds), *The Canon Debate* (Peabody, MA: Hendrickson, 2002).

Scalise, Charles J., *From Scripture to Theology: A Canonical Journey into Hermeneutics* (Downers Grove, IL: InterVarsity, 1996).

Schaff, Philip, ed., 'The Augsburg Confession', in *The Creeds of Christendom, with a History and Critical Notes*, vol. 3 (New York: Harper & Brothers, 1877 [1530]), 3–73.

—'The Formula of Concord', in *The Creeds of Christendom, with a History and Critical Notes*, vol. 3 (New York: Harper & Brothers, 1877 [1576]), 93–180.

Schleiermacher, Friedrich, *The Christian Faith* (Edinburgh: T&T Clark, 1999 [1830]).

Schmid, Ulrich, *Marcion und sein Apostolos: Rekonstruktion und historische Einordnung der marcionitischen Paulusbriefausgabe* (Berlin and New York: Walter de Gruyter, 1995).

Schmidt, Daryl D., 'The Greek New Testament as a Codex', in *The Canon Debate*, (eds) L. M. McDonald and J. A. Sanders (Peabody, MA: Hendrickson, 2002), 469–84.

Schmithals, Walter, 'Die Bedeutung der Evangelien in der Theologiegeschichte bis zur Kanonbildung', in *The Four Gospels*, vol. 1, (eds) F. Van Segbroeck, C.M. Tuckett, G. Van Belle and J. Verheyden (Leuven: Leuven University Press, 1992), 129–57.

Schneemelcher, Wilhelm, 'Bibel III: Die Entstehung des Kanons des Neuen Testaments und der christlichen Bibel', *Theologische Realenzyklopädie*, 6, (eds) G. Krause and G. Müller (Berlin and New York: Walter de Gruyter, 1980), 22–48.

—'General Introduction', in *New Testament Apocrypha*, vol. 1: *Gospels and Related Writings*, ed. W. Schneemelcher (Cambridge: James Clarke & Co. Ltd, and Louisville: Westminster John Knox Press, 1991; 2nd edn), 9–76.

Schnelle, Udo, *Einleitung in das Neue Testament* (Göttingen: Vandenhoeck und
    Ruprecht, 1996).

Schrage, Wolfgang, *Unterwegs zur Einheit und Einzigkeit Gottes: Zum
    'Monotheismus' des Paulus und seiner alttestamentlich-frühjüdischen
    Tradition*, Biblisch-Theologische Studien 48 (Neukirchen–Vluyn: Neukirchener,
    2002).

Schreiter, Robert J., *Constructing Local Theologies* (Maryknoll, NY: Orbis, 1985).

—*The New Catholicity: Theology between the Global and the Local* (Maryknoll, NY:
    Orbis, 1997).

Schröter, Jens, 'Jesus and the Canon': The Early Jesus Traditions in the Context of the
    Origins of the New Testament Canon, in *Performing the Gospel: Orality, Memory,
    and Mark*, (eds) Jonathan A. Draper, John Miles Foley and Richard A. Horsley
    (Minneapolis: Fortress, 2006), 104–22.

Schubert, Erika Dinkler-von, 'CTAYPOC: Vom 'Wort vom Kreuz' (1 Kor 1,18) zum
    Kreuz-Symbol', in *Byzantine East, Latin West: Art-Historical Studies in Honor of
    Kurt Weitzmann*, (eds) C. Moss and K. Kiefer (Princeton, NJ: Department of Art
    and Archaeology, Princeton University Press, 1995).

Schubert, Paul, 'Editing a Papyrus', in *The Oxford Handbook of Papyrology*, ed. Roger
    Bagnall (Oxford and New York: Oxford University Press, 2009).

Seeberg, D. Alfred, *Der Katechismus der Urchristenheit* (Leipzig: A. Deichert'sche
    Verlagsbuchhandlung Nachf. [Georg Böhme], 1903).

Sharpe, John, 'Some Representations of the Book and Book-Making, from the
    Earliest Codex Forms to Jost Amman', in *The Bible as Book: The Manuscript
    Tradition*, (eds) J. L. Sharpe III and K. van Kampen (London: The British Library
    and Oak Knoll Press in association with The Scriptorium: Center for Christian
    Antiquities, 1998), 197f.

Shin, Daniel, 'Some Light from Origen: Scripture as Sacrament', *Worship* 73 (1999):
    399–425.

Sirat, Colette, 'Le livre hébreu dans les premiers siècles de notre ère: le témoignage
    des textes', in *Les débuts du codex: Actes de la journée d'étude organisée à Paris les 3
    et 4 juillet 1985 publiés par A. Blanchard*, 9, ed. A. Blanchard (Turnhout: Brepols,
    1989), 115–24.

Skarsaune, Oskar, 'Loven, Profetene og Skriftene: Jødedommens Bible: kanon og
    tekst', in *Blant skriftlærde og fariseere: Jødedommen i oldtiden*, ed. H. Kvalbein
    (Oslo: Verbum, 1984), 157–227.

—'Hvilket lys kaster NT's kanonhistorie over teologihistorien i det 1. århundre?',
    Religio 25 (1986): 63–83.

—*The Proof from Prophecy: A Study in Justin Martyr's Proof-Text Tradition: Text-Type, Provenance, Theological Profile* (Leiden: Brill, 1987).

—'Den første kristne bibel: Et blad av kodeksens historie', in *Det levende Ordet: Festskrift til professor dr. theol Age Holter*, ed. I. Asheim (Oslo, 1989), 29–43.

—'From Books to Testimonies: Remarks on the Transmission of the Old Testament in the Early Church', *Immanuel* 24/25 (1990): 207–19.

—'Kodeks og kanon: om brug og avgrensning av de gammeltestamentlige skrifter i oldkirken', in *Text and Theology: Studies in Honour of Professor dr. theol. Magne Sæbø Presented on the Occasion of His 65th Birthday*, ed. A. Tångberg (Oslo: Verbum, 1994), 237–75.

—'The Development of Scriptural Interpretation in the Second and Third Centuries – except Clement and Origen', in *Hebrew Bible/Old Testament: The History of Its Interpretation*, vol. 1, ed. M. Sæbø (Göttingen: Vandenhoeck & Ruprecht, 1996), 373–442.

—*Troens ord: De tre oldkirkelige bekjennelsene* (Oslo: Luther Forlag, 1997).

—*In the Shadow of the Temple: Jewish Influences on Early Christianity* (Downers Grove, IL: InterVarsity, 2002).

Skeat, T. C., 'Early Christian Book-Production: Papyri and Manuscripts', in *The Cambridge History of the Bible*, vol. 2, *The West from the Fathers to the Reformation*, ed. G. W. H. Lampe (Cambridge, Cambridge University Press, 1969), 54–79, 512–13.

—'Irenaeus and the Four-Gospel Canon', *Novum Testamentum* 34 (1992): 194–9.

—'The Origin of the Christian Codex', *Zeitschrift für Papyrologie und Epigraphik* 102 (1994): 263–68.

—'The Oldest Manuscript of the Four Gospels?', *NTS* 43 (1997): 1–34.

Smith, D. Moody, 'When Did the Gospels Become Scripture?', *JBL* 119 (2000): 3–20.

—*The Fourth Gospel in Four Dimensions: Judaism and Jesus, the Gospels and Scripture* (Columbia, SC: University of South Carolina, 2008).

Sparks, H. F. D., ed., *The Apocryphal Old Testament* (Oxford: Clarendon Press, 1984).

Stanton, Graham N., 'The Fourfold Gospel', *NTS* 43 (1997): 317–46.

—*The Gospels and Jesus* (Oxford: Oxford University Press, 2nd edn, 2002).

—*Jesus and Gospel* (Cambridge: Cambridge University Press, 2004).

Stendahl, Krister, *Meningar* (Älvsjö: Verbum, 1986), English original: *Meanings, The Bible as Document and as Guide* (Philadelphia: Fortress, 1984).

Sternberg, Meir, *The Poetics of Biblical Narrative: Ideological Literature and the Drama of Reading* (Bloomington: Indiana University Press, 1985).

Strecker, Georg, 'Schriftlichkeit oder Mündlichkeit der synoptischen Tradition?

Anmerkungen zur Formgeschichtlichen Problematik', in *The Four Gospels*, vol. 1, (eds) F. Van Segbroeck, C.M. Tuckett, G. Van Belle and J. Verheyden (Leuven: Leuven University Press, 1992), 159–72.

Striker, G., 'κριτήριον τῆς ἀληθείας', *NAWG.PH* 2 (1974), 51–110.

Stringer, Martin, 'Text, Context and Performance: Hermeneutics and the Study of Worship', *Scottish Journal of Theology* 52 (2000): 365–79.

Studer, Basil, *Trinity and Incarnation: The Faith of the Early Church* (Edinburgh: T&T Clark, 1993).

Stuhlhofer, Franz, *Der Gebrauch der Bibel von Jesus bis Euseb: Eine statistische Untersuchung zur Kanonsgeschichte* (Wuppertal: R. Brockhaus Verlag, 1988).

Stuhlmacher, Peter, *Wie treibt man Biblische Theologie?* (Neukirchen–Vluyn: Neukirchener, 1995). English translation: *How To Do Biblical Theology*, Princeton Theological Monograph Series, 38 (Eugene, OR: Pickwick Publications, 1995).

—*Biblische Theologie des Neuen Testaments: Von der Paulusschule bis zur Johannesoffenbarung Der Kanon und seine Auslegung* vol. 2 (Göttingen: Vandenhoeck & Ruprecht, 1999).

Sundberg, A. C., 'Dependent Canonicity in Irenaeus and Tertullian', in *Studia Evangelica* 3, ed. F. L. Cross (Berlin: Akademie-Verlag, 1964,) 403–9.

—*The Old Testament of the Early Church* (Cambridge, MA: Harvard University Press, 1964).

—'Towards a Revised History of the New Testament Canon', in *Studia Evangelica*, 4, ed. F. L. Cross (Berlin: Akademie-Verlag, 1968), 452–61.

Swanson, Reuben, ed., *New Testament Greek Manuscripts: Variant Readings Arranged in Horizontal Lines Against Codex Vaticanus. 1 Corinthians* (Wheaton, IL: Tyndale House Publishers, and Pasadena, CA: William Carey International University Press, 2003).

Swarat, Uwe, *Alte Kirche und Neues Testament: Theodor Zahn als Patristiker* (Wuppertal and Zürich: R. Brockhaus Verlag, 1991).

Talley, Thomas J., *The Origins of the Liturgical Year* (New York, Pueblo, Collegeville, MN: The Liturgical Press, 1986; 2nd emended edn, 1991).

Taylor, Miriam S., *Anti-Judaism and Early Christian Identity: A Critique of the Scholarly Consensus* (Leiden and New York, Köln: Brill, 1995).

Tertullian, *Against Praxeas [Adversus Praxean]*, The Ante–Nicene Fathers, vol. 3, (eds) A. Roberts and J. Donaldson (Edinburgh: T&T Clark and Grand Rapids, MI: Eerdmans, reprinted 1994), 598–627.

—*An Answer to the Jews [Adversus Iudaeos]*, trans. S. Thelwall, The Ante–Nicene Fathers, vol. 3, (eds) A. Roberts and J. Donaldson (Edinburgh: T&T Clark and Grand Rapids, MI: Eerdmans, reprinted 1994), 151–73.

—*On Fasting [De leiunio]*, trans. S. Thelwall, The Ante-Nicene Fathers, vol. 4, (eds) A. Roberts and J. Donaldson (Edinburgh: T&T Clark and Grand Rapids, MI: Eerdmans, reprinted 1994), 102–14.

—*On the Apparel of Women [De cultu feminarum]*, trans. S. Thelwall, The Ante-Nicene Fathers, vol. 4, (eds) A. Roberts and J. Donaldson (Edinburgh: T&T Clark and Grand Rapids, MI: Eerdmans, reprinted 1994), 14–25

—*The Five Books Against Marcion [Adversus Marcionem]*, The Ante-Nicene Fathers, vol. 3, (eds) A. Roberts and J. Donaldson (Edinburgh: T&T Clark and Grand Rapids, MI: Eerdmans, reprinted 1994), 271–474.

—*The Prescription Against Heretics [De praescriptione haereticorum]*, The Ante-Nicene Fathers, vol. 3, (eds) A. Roberts and J. Donaldson (Edinburgh: T&T Clark and Grand Rapids, MI: Eerdmans, reprinted 1994), 243–65.

The Bible and Culture Collective, ed., *The Postmodern Bible* (New Haven: Yale University Press, 1995).

Theissen, Gerd, *A Theory of Primitive Christian Religion* (London: SCM, 1999).

—*The New Testament: History, Literature, Religion* (London: T&T Clark, 2003).

Theron, Daniel J., *Evidence of Tradition* (Grand Rapids, MI: Baker Book House, 1957).

Thiselton, Anthony C., *The Two Horizons: New Testament Hermeneutics and Philosophical Description with Special Reference to Heidegger, Bultmann, Gadamer, and Wittgenstein* (Grand Rapids, MI: Eerdmans, 1980).

—*Language Liturgy and Meaning* (Bramcote, Nottingham: Grove Books, 1986).

—*New Horizons in Hermeneutics: The Theory and Practice of Transforming Biblical Reading* (Grand Rapids, MI: Zondervan, 1992).

Thomassen, Einar, ed. *Canon and Canonicity: The Formation and Use of Scripture* (Copenhagen: Museum Tusculanum Press, 2010).

Thompson, John L., *Writing the Wrongs: Women of the Old Testament among Biblical Commentators from Philo through the Reformation* (Oxford: Oxford University Press, 2001).

Thompson, Michael B., 'The Holy Internet: Communication Between Churches in the First Christian Generation', in *The Gospels for All Christians: Rethinking the Gospel Audiences*, ed. R. Bauckham (Grand Rapids, MI: Eerdmans, 1998), 49–70.

Todorov, Tzvetan, *Symbolik och tolkning,* trans. M. Rosengren (Stockholm/Stehag: Symposion, 1989), French original: *Symbolisme et interprétation* (Paris: Editions du Seuils, 1978).

Tov, Emanuel, *Textual Criticism of the Hebrew Bible* (Minneapolis: Fortress, 3rd rev. ed, 2012).

Tracy, David, 'Writing', in *Critical Terms for Religious Studies*, ed. M. C. Taylor (Chicago: University of Chicago Press, 1998), 383–93.

Traube, Ludwig, *Nomina sacra: Versuch einer Geschichte der christlichen Kürzung* (München: C. H. Beck'sche Verlagsbuchhandlung, 1907).

Treu, Kurt, 'Die Bedeutung des Griechischen für die Juden im römischen Reich', *Kairos* 15 (1973): 123–44.

Tripp, D. H., 'The Letter of Pliny', in *The Study of Liturgy*, (eds) Cheslyn Jones, Edward Yarnold, Geoffrey Wainwright and Paul Bradshaw (London: SPCK, 1992), 80–1.

Trobisch, David, *Die Entstehung der Paulusbriefsammlung: Studien zu den Anfängen christlicher Publizistik* (Göttingen: Vandenhoeck & Ruprecht, 1989).

—*Die Endredaktion des Neuen Testaments: Eine Untersuchung zur Entstehung der christlichen Bibel* (Freiburg: Universitätsverlag Freiburg Schweiz and Göttingen: Vandenhoeck & Ruprecht, 1996), English translation: *The First Edition of the New Testament* (Oxford: Oxford University Press, 2000).

Troyer, Kristin De, 'The Pronunciation of the Names of God', in *Gott Nennen*, (eds) I. U. Dalferth and P. Stoellger, Religion in Philosophy and Theology 35 (Tübingen: Mohr Siebeck, 2008), 143–72.

Tuckett, C. M., "'Nomina sacra': Yes or No?', in *The Biblical Canons*, Bibliotheca Ephemeridum Theologicarum Lovaniensium, (eds) J.-M. Auwers and H. J. de Jonge (Leuven: Leuven University Press, 2003), 431–58.

Turner, C. H., 'The *Nomina Sacra* in Early Latin Christian MSS.', *Studi e Testi* 40 (1924): 62–74.

Turner, Eric G., *The Typology of the Early Codex* (Philadelphia: University of Pennsylvania Press, 1977).

Ulrich, Eugene, 'The Notion and Definition of Canon', in *The Canon Debate*, (eds) L. M. McDonald and J. A. Sanders (Peabody, MA: Hendrickson, 2002), 21–35.

Unnik, W. C. van, 'Notes on the Nature of Clemens Alexandrinus' *Canon Ecclesiasticus*', in *Sparsa Collecta: The Collected Essays of W. C. van Unnik*, vol. 3, ed. W. C. van Unnik (Leiden: Brill, 1961), 40–9.

—Ἡ καινὴ διαθήκη - a Problem in the early History of the Canon', in *Sparsa Collecta: The Collected Essays of W. C. van Unnik*, vol. 1, ed. W. C. van Unnik (Leiden: Brill, 1961), 157–71.

Vanhoozer, Kevin J., *Is There a Meaning in This Text? The Bible, the Reader, and the Morality of Literary Knowledge* (Grand Rapids, MI: Zondervan, 1998).

—*First Theology: God, Scriptures & Hermeneutics* (Downers Grove, IL: InterVarsity and Apollos, 2002).

Vaticana, Libreria Editrice, *Catechism of the Catholic Church* (London: Geoffrey Chapman, 1994).

Verheyden, Joseph, 'The Canon Muratori: A Matter of Dispute', in *The Biblical Canons*, (eds) J.-M. Auwers and H. J. de Jonge, Bibliotheca Ephemeridum Theologicarum Lovaniensium (Leuven: Leuven University Press, 2003), 487–556

Via, Dan O., *What Is New Testament Theology?* (Minneapolis: Fortress, 2002).

Wainwright, Geoffrey, *Doxology: The Praise of God in Worship, Doctrine and Life* (London: Epworth, 1982 [1980]).

Wall, Robert W., 'Reading the Bible from within Our Traditions', in *Between Two Horizons: Spanning New Testament Studies and Systematic Theology*, (eds) J. B. Green and M. Turner (Grand Rapids, MI: Eerdmans, 2000), 88–107.

—'The Significance of a Canonical Perspective of the Church's Scripture', in *The Canon Debate*, (eds) L. M. McDonald and J. A. Sanders (Peabody, MA: Hendrickson, 2002), 528–40.

Walser, Georg, *The Greek of the Ancient Synagogue: An Investigation on the Greek of the Septuagint, Pseudepigrapha and the New Testament* (Stockholm: Almqvist & Wiksell International, 2001).

Warnke, Georgia, *Gadamer: Hermeneutics, Tradition, and Reason* (Stanford: Stanford University Press, 1987).

Warren, Bill, 'The Transmission of the Remembered Jesus: Insights from Textual Criticism', in *Memories of Jesus: A Critical Appraisal of James D. G. Dunn's Jesus Remembered*, (eds) Robert B. Stewart and Gary R. Habermas (Nashville: B&H Publishing Group, 2010), 159–72.

Wasserman, Tommy, 'The Early Text of Matthew', in *The Early Text of the New Testament*, (eds) Charles E. Hill and Michael J. Kruger (Oxford: Oxford University Press, 2012), 83–107.

Watson, Francis, *Text, Church, and World* (Edinburgh: T&T Clark, 1994).

—*Text and Truth: Redefining Biblical Theology* (Edinburgh: T&T Clark and Grand Rapids, MI: Eerdmans, 1998).

—'The Bible', in *The Cambridge Companion to Karl Barth*, ed. J. Webster (Cambridge: Cambridge University Press, 2000), 57–71.

—*Paul and the Hermeneutics of Faith* (London: T&T Clark, 2004).

Watson, Francis, ed., *The Open Text* (London: SCM, 1993).

Webster, John, 'The Dogmatic Location of the Canon', *Neue Zeitschrift für systematische Theologie und Religionsphilosophie* 43 (2001): 17–43.

—*Holy Scripture: A Dogmatic Sketch* (Cambridge: Cambridge University Press, 2003).

Weiss, Johannes, *Das Urchristentum* (Göttingen: Vandenhoeck & Ruprecht, 1917).

Weitzmann, Kurt, *Illustrations in Roll and Codex* (Princeton, NJ: Princeton University Press, 1970).

Weitzmann, Kurt, ed. *Age of Spirituality: Late Antique and Early Christian Art, Third to Seventh Century* (New York: The Metropolitan Museum of Art, published in association with Princeton University Press, 1979).

Westcott, Brooke Foss, *A General Survey of the History of the Canon of the New Testament* (London and New York: Macmillan, 1896).

Westra, Liuwe H., *The Apostles' Creed: Origin, History, and Some Early Commentaries* (Turnhout: Brepols, 2002).

Wicker, James E., 'Pre-Constantinian *Nomina Sacra* in a Mosaic and Church Graffiti', *Southwestern Journal of Theology* 52:1 (2009): 52–72.

Wilken, Robert L., 'The Jews and Christian Apologetics After Theodosius I *Cunctos Populos*', *HTR* 73 (1980): 451–71.

—*John Chrysostom and the Jews: Rhetoric and Reality in the Late 4th Century* (Berkeley and Los Angeles: University of California, 1983).

—'In novissimis diebus. Biblical Promises, Jewish Hopes and Early Christian Exegesis', *Journal of Early Christian Studies* 1 (1993): 1–19.

Williams, A. Lukyn, 'The Tetragrammaton – Jahweh, Name or Surrogate?', *ZAW* 54 (1936): 262–69.

Wilson, R. S., *Marcion: A Study of a Second Century Heretic* (London: Clarke, 1933).

Wolterstorff, Nicholas, *Divine discourse: philosophical reflections on the claim that God speaks* (New York: Cambridge University Press, 1995).

Wrede, William, 'The Tasks and Methods of "New Testament Theology"' in Robert Morgan, *The Nature of New Testament Theology. The Contribution of William Wrede and Adolf Schlatter*, SBT Second Series 25 (London: 1973 [1897]), 68–116.

Wright, G. Ernest, *God Who Acts: Biblical Theology as Recital* (London: SCM, 1952).

Wright, N. T., *The New Testament and the People of God,* vol. 1 (Minneapolis: Fortress, 1992).

Young, Frances M., *Virtuoso Theology: The Bible and Interpretation* (Cleveland, OH: The Pilgrim Press, 1993).

—*Biblical Exegesis and the Formation of Christian Culture* (Cambridge: Cambridge University Press, 1997).

Zahn, Theodor, *Geschichte des Neutestamentlichen Kanons,* vol. 1 (Erlangen: Verlag von Andreas Deichert, 1888).

—*Einige Bemerkungen zu Adolf Harnack's Prüfung der Geschichte des neutestamentlichen Kanons (Erster Band. Erste Hälfte.)* (Erlangen and Leipzig: A. Deichert'sche Verlagshandlung Nachf. [Georg Böhme], 1889).

—*Geschichte des Neutestamentlichen Kanons,* vol. 2 (Erlangen and Leipzig: A. Deichert'sche Verlagsbuchh. Nachf. [Georg Böhme], 1890).

—*Den blivende betydning af den nytestamentlige kanon for Kirken* (Kristiania:

Steen'ske bogtrykkeri og forlag [Th. Steen], 1899). German original: *Die bleibende Bedeutung des neutestamentlichen Kanons für die Kirche: Vortrag auf der luterischen Pastoralkonferenz zu Leipzig am 2. Juni 1898* (Leipzig: A. Deichert'sche Verlagsbuchhandlung Nachf. [Georg Böhme], 1898).

—*Athanasius und der Bibelkanon.* Sonderabdruck aus der Universität Erlangen zur Feier des achtzigsten Geburtstages Sr. königlichen Hoheit des Prinzregenten Luitpold von Bayern (Erlangen and Leipzig: A. Deichert'sche Verlagsbuchhandlung Nachf. [Georg Böhme], 1901).

—*Grundriss der Geschichte des Neutestamentlichen Kanons: Eine Ergänzung zu der Einleitung in das Neue Testament* (Leipzig: A. Deichert'sche Verlagsbuchh. Nachf. [Georg Böhme], 1901).

Zenger, Erich, *Einleitung in das Alte Testament, Studienbücher Theologie*, vol. 1,1 (Stuttgart: Kohlhammer, 6th edn, 2006).

Index of Modern Authors

Index of Names and Subjects

Index of Ancient, Medieval and Early Modern Sources